T0387147

THE INFORMATION SOCIETY

THE INFORMATION SOCIETY

Critical Concepts in Sociology

Edited by
Robin Mansell

Volume II
Knowledge, Economics and Organization

Routledge
Taylor & Francis Group

LONDON AND NEW YORK

First published 2009
by Routledge
2 Park Square, Milton Park, Abingdon, Oxon, OX14 4RN, UK

Simultaneously published in the USA and Canada
by Routledge
270 Madison Avenue, New York, NY 10016

Routledge is an imprint of the Taylor & Francis Group, an informa business

Typeset in 10/12pt Times NR MT by Graphicraft Limited, Hong Kong
Printed and bound in Great Britain by
the MPG Books Group

British Library Cataloguing in Publication Data
A catalogue record for this book is available from the British Library

Library of Congress Cataloging in Publication Data
The information society : critical concepts in sociology / edited by Robin Mansell.
p. cm. — (Critical concepts in sociology)
Includes bibliographical references and index.
ISBN 978-0-415-44308-1 (set, hardback) — ISBN 978-0-415-44309-8 (volume 1, hardback)
— ISBN 978-0-415-44310-4 (volume 2, hardback) — ISBN 978-0-415-44311-1 (volume 3,
hardback) — ISBN 978-0-415-44312-8 (volume 4, hardback)   1. Information
society. I. Mansell, Robin.
HM851.I5324 2009
303.48′33—dc22
2008042128

ISBN 10: 0-415-44308-3 (Set)
ISBN 10: 0-415-44310-5 (Volume II)

ISBN 13: 978-0-415-44308-1 (Set)
ISBN 13: 978-0-415-44310-4 (Volume II)

Publisher's Note

References within each chapter are as they appear in the original
complete work.

CONTENTS

CONTENTS

CONTENTS

ACKNOWLEDGEMENTS

The publishers would like to thank the following for permission to reprint their material:

Elsevier for permission to reprint Carlota Perez (1983). Structural Change and Assimilation of New Technologies in the Economic and Social Systems. *Futures*, 15(5): 357–375.

The American Economic Association and Paul A. David for permission to reprint Paul A. David (1990). The Dynamo and the Computer: An Historical Perspective on the Modern Productivity Paradox. *The American Economic Review*, 80(2): 355–361.

Elsevier for permission to reprint Christopher Freeman and Luc Soete (1990). Fast Structural Change and Slow Productivity Change: Some Paradoxes in the Economics of Information Technology. *Structural Change and Economic Dynamics*, 1(2): 225–242.

The Association for Evolutionary Economics for permission to reprint William H. Melody (1987). Information: An Emerging Dimension of Institutional Analysis. *Journal of Economic Issues*, XXI(3): 1313–1339. © 1987, the Association for Evolutionary Economics.

Taylor & Francis for permission to reprint Hernan Galperin (2004). Beyond Interests, Ideas, and Technology: An Institutional Approach to Communication and Information Policy. *The Information Society*, 20(3): 159–168.

Greenwood Publishing Group for permission to reprint Dallas W. Smythe (1981). Communications: Blindspot of Economics. In William H. Melody, Liora Salter and Paul Heyer (eds), *Culture, Communication and Dependency: The Tradition of H. A. Innis* (pp. 111–125). Norwood, NJ: Ablex.

Oxford University Press for permission to reprint Robin Cowan, Paul A. David, and Dominique Foray (2000). The Explicit Economics of Knowledge Codification and Tacitness. *Industrial and Corporate Change*, 9(2): 211–253.

Oxford University Press for permission to reprint W. Edward Steinmueller (2000). Will New Information and Communication Technologies Improve the 'Codification' of Knowledge? *Industrial and Corporate Change*, 9(2): 361–376.

Blackwell Publishing for permission to reprint Magnus Bergquist and Jan Ljungberg (2001). The Power of Gifts: Organizing Social Relationships in Open Source Communities. *Information Systems Journal*, 11(3–4): 305–320.

The American Economic Association, Josh Lerner and Jean Tirole for permission to reprint Josh Lerner and Jean Tirole (2005). The Economics of Technology Sharing: Open Source and Beyond. *Journal of Economic Perspectives*, 19(2): 99–120.

MIS Quarterly for permission to reprint Brian Fitzgerald (2006). The Transformation of Open Source Software. *MIS Quarterly*, 30(3): 587–598. Copyright © 2006 by the Regents of the University of Minnesota.

Sage Publications for permission to reprint Patricia Arriaga (1985). Toward a Critique of the Information Economy. *Media, Culture and Society*, 7(3): 271–296.

Elsevier for permission to reprint Ernest J. Wilson III (1998). Inventing the Global Information Future. *Futures*, 30(1): 23–42.

Sage Publications for permission to reprint Lishan Adam and Frances Wood (1999). An Investigation of the Impact of Information and Communication Technologies in Sub-Saharan Africa. *Journal of Information Science*, 25(4): 307–318.

Elsevier for permission to reprint Eszter Hargittai (1999). Weaving the Western Web: Explaining Differences in Internet Connectivity among OECD Countries. *Telecommunications Policy*, 23(10/11): 701–718.

Sage Publications for permission to reprint Robin Mansell (2002). From Digital Divides to Digital Entitlements in Knowledge Societies. *Current Sociology*, 50(3): 407–426.

Mark Warschauer for permission to reprint Mark Warschauer (2002). Reconceptualizing the Digital Divide. *First Monday* 7(7).

Elsevier for permission to reprint J. J. Britz, Peter. J. Lor, I. E. M. Coetzee and B. C. Bester (2006). Africa as a Knowledge Society: A Reality Check. *International Information & Library Review*, 38(1): 25–40.

Elsevier for permission to reprint Jan A. G. M. van Dijk (2006). Digital Divide Research, Achievements and Shortcomings. *Poetics*, 34(4–5): 221–235.

Sage Publications for permission to reprint Rob Kling (1991). Computerization and Social Transformations. *Science, Technology & Human Values*, 16(3): 342–367.

Harvard Business Publishing for permission to reprint Shoshana Zuboff (1982). New Worlds of Computer-Mediated Work. *Harvard Business Review*, 60(5): 142–152.

INFORMS and Wanda J. Orlikowski for permission to reprint Wanda J. Orlikowski (2000). Using Technology and Constituting Structures: A Practice Lens for Studying Technology in Organizations. *Organization Science*, 11(4): 404–428.

Sage Publications for permission to reprint Michael Brocklehurst (2001). Power, Identity and New Technology Homework: Implications for 'New Forms' of Organizing. *Organization Studies*, 22(3): 445–466.

Disclaimer

The publishers have made every effort to contact authors/copyright holders of works reprinted in *The Information Society (Critical Concepts in Sociology)*. This has not been possible in every case, however, and we would welcome correspondence from those individuals/companies whom we have been unable to trace.

INTRODUCTION TO VOLUME II

Robin Mansell

> Knowledge has been at the heart of economic growth and the gradual rise in levels of social well-being since time immemorial. The ability to invent and innovate, that is to create new knowledge and new ideas that are then embodied in products, processes and organizations, has always served to fuel development.
>
> (David and Foray 2003: 20)

Knowledge and economics

In this volume the focus is on the relationships between knowledge and the economy and organization that are interwoven with conceptions of 'the Information Society' and related ideas such as 'the Knowledge Society'. The papers in part 3 centre on economic perspectives and are followed by papers focusing on new open network models of organization, works on the digital divide and, lastly, papers representing research on organizational change.

Economists have concluded that knowledge creation is an important driver of the economy, typically making little distinction between information and knowledge. From this perspective, it is a very short step from the Information Society to the Knowledge Society, the terminology most often used in the papers in this volume. Of course, ideas about knowledge are not the exclusive preserve of economic analysis and there have been many efforts in the policy arena to identify the implications of the labels 'knowledge society' and 'knowledge economy'. For example, UNESCO's definition emphasizes capabilities and the variety and especially the plurality of societies: 'Knowledge societies are about capabilities to identify, produce, transform, disseminate and use information to build and apply knowledge for human development' (2005: 5). This contrasts with the OECD's (1996) definition of a knowledge-based economy as one that is very strongly dependent on production, distribution and use of knowledge as embodied in human beings and in *technology*. These labels and the terms 'network economy' and 'network society' are not entirely interchangeable. However, those who use the 'knowledge' terminology are likely to highlight features that are dependent on digital information and the cognitive processes and learning that are necessary to transform information into useable knowledge.

The economist's emphasis on the knowledge-based economy reflects an interest in intangible sources of economic value. As Paul A. David and Dominique Foray indicate:

> The crux of the issue lies in the accelerating (and unprecedented) speed at which knowledge is created, accumulated and, most probably, depreciates in terms of economic relevance and value. This trend has reflected, *inter alia*, an intensified pace of scientific and technological progress. . . . Knowledge-based activities emerge when people, supported by information and communication technologies, interact in concerted efforts to co-produce (i.e. create and exchange) new knowledge.
>
> (David and Foray 2003: 20, 27)

The problem of information

Developments in information societies pose interesting questions for market analysis. This is because, from an economic vantage point, information has peculiar characteristics compared to tangible goods. Information is intangible, non-rivalrous (one can give it to someone else and still possess it) and non-excludable (it cannot be taken back once it has been given and receivers can pass it on without giving it up). It is difficult, therefore, to analyse market dynamics where information plays a significant role because conventional economic models are not designed to take account of these features of information. In particular, once information is produced it requires considerable effort to prevent its being passed on to others, while information and communication technologies (ICT) make the costs of information reproduction negligible, creating a paradox over how to finance its initial (first copy) production costs. Although George Stigler was quick to realize this, he suggested that mainstream economics has been reluctant to challenge the uncertainties that the growing dependence on information creates for economies:

> One should hardly have to tell academicians that information is a valuable resource: Knowledge *is* power. And yet it occupies a slum dwelling in the town of economics. Mostly it is ignored: the best technology is assumed to be known; the relationship of commodities to consumer preferences is a datum. And one of the information-processing industries, advertising, is treated with a hostility that economists normally reserve for tariffs and monopolists.
>
> (Stigler 1961: 213)

Stigler was mainly concerned with information and the determination of prices in markets.[1] Another economist who specialized in the study of the economics of information, Donald Lamberton (1986, 1971), identified further issues, including those relating to Information Society debates. He warned that an overemphasis on information processing technologies could lead to a situation in which much information is processed but little knowledge creation or learning occurs. This might be the outcome if too little attention is given to human capital and to the importance of different kinds of knowledge. As the Internet has become the site of growing volumes of commercial activity, the argument that information is an 'experience good', that is, that the ability to make choices about information depends on the experience of the person choosing, was discussed and popularized in the economics and management literatures, notably by Carl Shapiro and Hal Varian (1999) in their book *Information Rules.*

Productivity paradox

Economists seek to understand what factors lead to increases in productivity, that is, the possibility of producing more with constant capital and labour inputs. Increasing productivity is sufficient for economic growth, a central goal (or bias) of capitalist societies. Together with those offering optimistic views of the Information Society, economists have sought to attribute increasing productivity to technological innovation, especially in ICTs. Because these technologies can be employed in many different contexts to improve productivity, Timothy Bresnahan and Manuel Trajtenberg (1995) coined the term General Purpose Technologies (GPT), which has been taken up by others (e.g. Helpman 1998; Lipsey *et al.* 2005), to explore processes of growth and development. Bresnahan and Trajtenberg argued that, 'most GPTs play the role of "enabling technologies", opening up new opportunities rather than offering complete, final solutions' (1995: 84). Other economists have extended the use of the GPT terminology to identify earlier technologies with a pervasive effect such as the steam engine and electricity. David (1990), for example, suggested that there might be similarities in productivity growth between the eras of electrification and computerization.

The implications for firms, industries, national economies and the global economy of the convergence of digital information and communication technologies and their application to create global networks and new means of economic and social interaction are still being worked out. Pronounced differences in the economic performance of different countries cannot be explained fully by their levels of investment in new digital technologies. For example, the implications of investment in these technologies for changes in productivity are not straightforward. Robert Solow challenged his colleagues by declaring 'you can see the computer age everywhere but in the productivity statistics' (1987: 36), prompting contributions from economists such as Moses Abramovitz and Paul A. David (1996), Robert Gordon (2004), Dale Jorgenson and Kevin Stiroh (2000) about the sources of productivity improvement. Other economists, such as Erik Brynjolffson and Lorin Hitt (Brynjolffson and Hitt 2003) in the United States and Nick Bloom and John Van Reenen (2007) in Britain, are conducting enterprise-level studies of productivity to account for aggregate patterns of productivity change and to identify the contribution of specific business processes to performance.

Much of this research is quantitative, but there is a strand of research in this area which adopts a multi-method approach, bringing together micro- and macro-level empirical analysis. In Europe this is represented, for example, by the work of Christopher Freeman and others, including Luc Soete (Freeman *et al.* 1982; Freeman 1988; Freeman and Soete 1990, 1997), and of Carlota Perez (1983), which was influential in debates about knowledge economies and the way technological innovations lead to shifts in technological 'style' or in 'techno-economic paradigm' (Perez 1985). The work of these authors explained how changes in micro-electronics technologies could have destabilizing effects on the economy, and led to research on how technological change influences productivity and economic growth. They argued that as a new technology spreads, a new 'common sense' takes hold which begins to pervade all aspects of individual and institutional endeavour. Change is disruptive, resulting in the obsolescence of skills and qualifications, the dislocation of people, and wealth creation for some and not for others, and therefore needs a policy response.

Institutional dynamics

Looking at information societies from a perspective that combines insights from economics and political theory reveals more of the features of institutional dynamics. For instance, Dallas Smythe (1977, 1981) was concerned with inequality and what he thought was a 'blindspot' in Western Marxist analysis, that is, the failure of scholars to understand that the commodification of information relies upon the willingness of audiences (users) to market goods and services to themselves for the benefit of advertisers and information producers. Smythe's approach sparked a debate (Murdock 1978) which is relevant today as online marketing comes increasingly to depend on audiences or users who are willing to co-produce information and to click through advertising-supported content.

Other work related to information societies and their institutional dynamics includes William Melody's (1985, 1991) research on oligopolistic competition and the behaviour of transnational corporations in the information economy and his particular interests in the mechanisms of unequal exchange and human capital formation. Others working in this tradition include Hernan Galperin (2004), who analysed the strategic interests and incentives that motivate individuals within policy-making institutions to influence outcomes in the information and communication marketplace. My work has also addressed the strategic interests of those shaping policy institutions and those active in the private sector (Mansell 1997). Antonelli *et al.* (2000), more centrally within economics rather than political economy, provide an account of the relationship between knowledge production and ICT, also signalling the importance of the co-production of knowledge and its need for sophisticated human capabilities.

The knowledge economy is said by many to depend on content creation, but this may not be the main consideration as the knowledge-based economy expands, at least in terms of economic growth. Andrew Odlyzko (2001) argues, for example, that 'content is not king' and that the real driver of the economy will be communication services. This raises questions about whether Web 2.0 developments, which rely on the co-production of content and information, will support online business models organized around the willingness of the majority of users to produce. In a broader context, content industries, or what are often called the 'creative industries', have been examined from an institutional perspective by Andy Pratt (1997) and Paschal Preston and Aphra Kerr (2001).[2]

Knowledge codification

Information cannot be transformed into useful knowledge without a process of learning. In the economics literature there is debate about whether the possibility of codifying knowledge using advanced digital technologies means that learning can now occur more easily, assuming the learner has the appropriate literacy and access to knowledge repositories. Some argue that tacitness (knowing more than one can say) still matters and that a rapid expansion, on a global basis, of the opportunities for learning will not occur, at least not in a way that enhances the opportunities for the poor.

The issue here is whether digital technologies can be used to represent knowledge as information, that is, to store and reproduce information in a way that will enable more people to gain knowledge without the benefit of interaction with others who are already knowledgeable. This is examined by Edward Steinmueller (2000) and by Robin Cowan *et al.* (2000), who argue that methods for such 'knowledge codification' exist and can be extended, while Björn Johnson *et al.* (2002) are more sceptical that digital codification of information will make a substantial difference to learning and, ultimately, to knowledge creation and wealth-creating opportunities for the poor.

Open networking

Discussion about the potential of the knowledge economy to facilitate new opportunities for learning and knowledge accumulation is also found in the literature on the benefits of open networks and information sharing. Magnus Berguist and Jan Ljungberg (2001) surveyed the literature, attempting to explain individuals' collaboration in open source software development projects, while Josh Lerner and Jean Tirole (2005) advanced a specific economic theory of such individual collaboration, and Brian Fitzgerald (2006) reflected on these activities from the software engineering perspective.

Others, including David Lancashire (2001), Stefan Koch and Georg Schneider (2002), Erik von Hippel (2001) and von Hippel and Georg von Krogh (2003), have done extensive work on processes of innovation and learning in these open software projects. They examine the new models of innovation and the extent to which altruism and other factors support the sustainability of open network models. And a focus on the potential benefits of the distributed organization of work within these settings and for innovative activity and new sources of wealth creation is present in the work of Jean-Michel Dalle and Paul A. David (2007) and David and Francesco Rullani (2008).

Inequality and the digital divide

Notwithstanding the opportunities created by the spread of digital technologies, the increasingly global reach of the Internet and mobile telecommunication networks and open collaborative models for innovation and learning, there is concern that these developments also give rise to new sources of inequality. Many authors argue that the digital divide terminology emphasizes arbitrary dualisms (information haves and have-nots). It is argued that it is the structural dynamics and power relations in a given society that influence the terms on which people may be able to participate in their information societies. Mark Warschauer's (2002, 2004) work has been influential in calling for an analytical framework that focuses on social inclusion rather than on arbitrary divides. Jan van Dijk's (2005) and Pippa Norris's (2001) work highlights the need for comparative research and studies to address the shortcomings of digital divide research: for example van Dijk's claim of 'its lack of theory, conceptual definition, interdisciplinary approach, qualitative research and longitudinal research' (2006: 1).

Contributors to research on the digital divide include those who argue that eventually the new technologies and applications will 'trickle down' to reach even the poorest users (Compaine 2001) and those who claim that poverty will prevent effective access and participation in the absence of market intervention. Others argue that the design, cost and application of new technologies must be tailored to specific needs and choices (Couldry 2003). Patricia Arriaga's early work criticizing the idea of the Information Society is a strong statement, consistent with Couldry's viewpoint:

> it cannot be assumed that the effect on capital accumulation of 'informatization' policies and programmes – that is, the massive introduction and utilization of information goods and services in

all spheres of social life – would be the same for every social formation regardless of any other economic, political and social determinants. . . . The information society is not the clean, antiseptic and apolitical society we have been told it is, where democracy and freedom will rule. Capitalism is still the name of the game and profitability its main drive.

(Arriaga 1985: 294)

Ernest Wilson (2004) demonstrates how difficult it is to address the sources of exclusion for those located in areas with severe structural and institutional constraints. A comprehensive review of these constraints is provided by William Drake and Wilson (2008), who also provide insight into the policy measures that may encourage greater equity in, access to and use of global networks. Eszter Hargittai's (2003, 2004) work illustrates empirical research on the way the spread of the Internet varies in the industrialized countries, pointing to factors that may explain this. This work is very instructive, because it should sensitize those who envisage a rather globally homogeneous Information Society to the fact that developments in the wealthy countries have been quite heterogeneous – thus, this should also be expected for developing countries.

A major shortcoming of research in this area is the comparatively small amount of work on the poorest countries. Lishan Adam and Francis Wood (1999), Johannes Britz *et al.* (2006) and Leo Van Audenhove *et al.* (1999; Van Audenhove 2003) go some way to redressing this.[3] Many of the policy measures aimed at addressing divides are influenced by neo-liberal assumptions about markets and regulation, an issue discussed by Jairo Lugo and Tony Sampson (2008) in their comments on 'other pathways' to overcome exclusion. My own research (Mansell 1997, 2001, 2002, 2006; Mansell and Wehn 1998) also highlights the inappropriate transfer of assumptions about information societies and the uses of technologies in developing country contexts.

Widespread organizational change

Early studies on innovations in data processing leading to the automation of public services were conducted in the United States, for example by Kenneth Kraemer *et al.* (1980), who suggested that the introduction of information systems might lead to both centralized and decentralized systems, with contradictory implications for policy and practice. Rob Kling's (1991) work was influential in encouraging a focus on the social and cultural implications of the information systems used within public and private sector organizations, as was Robert Galliers's (1991) work on strategic planning. In taking issue with technology-driven approaches, Galliers argued that 'if one takes a socio-technical perspective on information systems (i.e. a more holistic stance), it can be argued that information systems are as much concerned with human activity and organisation as they are with technology – if not more so' (1991: 60).

A socio-technical approach was central to Claudio Ciborra's (1992, 2002) analyses of information systems and his suggestion that 'tinkering' best characterizes the design and implementation of these systems. He underlined the need to understand the phenomenological experience of interaction with technology.[4] Research in this tradition focuses on the situated character of information systems implementation and on processes of negotiation and meaning creation within communities. Wanda Orlikowski (1992, 2002) adapted Anthony Giddens's structuration theory in her analysis of how new practices are developed. This work was complemented by Susan Leigh Star and Karen Ruhleder's (1996) research on the infrastructure (technological and organizational), which provides insights into the reasons for success and failure in the development of information systems.

The implications of new ICT systems in the light of associated organizational changes in the workplace have been extensively investigated by Shoshana Zuboff (1988, 2004), and also by Michael Brocklehurst (2001) through his research on homeworking, which highlights the reproduction of power relations.

Conclusion

This volume of Master Works on *The Information Society* focuses on the economic features of information and factors that contribute to a growing emphasis on the dynamics of knowledge-based economies – accentuating the role of markets and highlighting that information is a peculiar resource. The knowledge-based society perspective of the Information Society also underlines the way that organizations are becoming more dependent on information to operate. The problems created by inequalities in capabilities to design, access and use new ICT – often described as the result of a digital divide – are illustrated here, as is research on the power relations articulated within organizations when these technologies are introduced.

The papers selected for this volume, focusing for the most part on economic issues, treat markets as institutions embedded in specific political, social and cultural contexts. This work points to the variety and uncertainty accompanying the evolution of today's information societies, as does the work of mainstream economists who tackle the peculiarities of information markets. The difference lies in the former's openness to the idea that the situated aspects of ICT systems within organizations require detailed empirical analysis if they are to be understood. It is clear from the works collected in this volume that there are no inevitable consequences associated with the evolution of information societies. However, there are dominant models and visions that require empirical assessment.

Notes

1 In 2001 George A. Akerlof, University of California Berkeley, A. Michael Spence, Stanford University, and Joseph E. Stiglitz, Colombia University in the United States, were awarded the Sveriges Riksbank Prize in Economic Sciences in Memory of Alfred Nobel, for their work on the economics of information, specifically on markets with asymmetric information.
2 Healy (2002) provides a survey of the literature on digital technology and cultural goods, while Deuze (2006, 2008) examines digital culture in terms of participation and the experience of work.
3 Initiatives to map the developments in information and communication technologies in sub-Saharan Africa and Asia include Research ICT Africa, at http://www.researchictafrica.net/, and LIRNE*Asia's* initiative at http://www.asianict.lirneasia.org/about.php. See also Banerjee and Logan (2008).
4 Lave and Wenger (1991), Wenger (1998) and Brown and Duguid (2000) offer accounts of how communities and networks of practice evolve and sustain themselves. These have been applied in analyses of how network technologies and information applications are used by social actors.

References

Abramovitz, M. and David, P. A. (1996). 'Technological Change and the Rise of Intangible Investments: The US Economy's Growth-path in the Twentieth Century'. In D. Foray and B.-Å. Lundvall (eds), *Employment and Growth in the Knowledge-based Economy* (pp. 35–60). Paris: OECD.

Adam, L. and Wood, F. (1999). 'An Investigation of the Impact of Information and Communication Technologies in Sub-Saharan Africa'. *Journal of Information Science*, 25(4): 307–18.

Antonelli, C., Geuna, A. and Steinmueller, W. E. (2000). 'Information and Communication Technologies and the Production, Distribution and Use of Knowledge'. *International Journal of Technology Management*, 20(1–2): 72–94.

Arriaga, P. (1985). 'Toward a Critique of the Information Society'. *Media, Culture and Society*, 7(3): 271–96.

Banerjee, I. and Logan, S. (eds) (2008). *Asian Communication Handbook 2008*. Singapore: AMIC and Wee Kim Wee School of Communication and Information, Nanyang Technological University.

Berguist, M. and Ljungberg, J. (2001). 'The Power of Gifts: Organizing Social Relationships in Open Source Communities'. *Information Systems Journal*, 11: 305–20.

Bloom, N. and Van Reenen, J. (2007). 'Measuring and Explaining Management Practices across Firms and Nations'. *Quarterly Journal of Economics*, 122(4): 1,351–408.

Bresnahan, T. F. and Trajtenberg, M. (1995). *General Purpose Technologies 'Engines of Growth?'* NBER Working Paper Series, WP4148, Cambridge, MA: National Bureau of Economic Research: n.p.

Britz, J. J., Lor, P. J., Coetzee, I. E. M. and Bester, B. C. (2006). 'Africa as a Knowledge Society: A Reality Check'. *International Information & Library Review*, 38(1): 25–40.

Brocklehurst, M. (2001). 'Power, Identity and New Technology Homework: Implications for "New Forms" of Organizing'. *Organization Studies*, 22(3): 445–66.

Brown, J. S. and Duguid, P. (2000). *The Social Life of Information*. Cambridge, MA: Harvard Business School Press.

Brynjolfsson, E. and Hitt, L. M. (2003). *Computing Productivity: Firm-Level Evidence*. Cambridge, MA: MIT.

Ciborra, C. U. (1992). 'From Thinking to Thinkering: The Grassroots of IT and Strategy'. *The Information Society*, 8(4): 297–309.

—— (2002). *The Labyrinths of Information: Challenging the Wisdom of Systems*. Oxford: Oxford University Press.

Compaine, B. M. (ed.) (2001). *The Digital Divide: Facing a Crisis or Creating a Myth?* Cambridge, MA: MIT Press.

Couldry, N. (2003). 'Digital Divide or Discursive Design? On the Emerging Ethics of Information Space'. *Ethics and Information Technology*, 5(2): 89–97.

Cowan, R., David, P. A. and Foray, D. (2000). 'The Explicit Economics of Knowledge Codification and Tacitness'. *Industrial and Corporate Change*, 9(2): 211–54.

Dalle, J.-M. and David, P. A. (2007). 'Simulating Code Growth in Libre (Open Source) Mode'. In E. Brousseau and N. Curien (eds), *Internet and Digital Economics: Principles, Methods and Applications* (pp. 391–422). Cambridge: Cambridge University Press.

David, P. A. (1990). 'The Dynamo and the Computer: An Historical Perspective on the Modern Productivity Paradox'. *American Economic Review*, 80(2): 355–61.

—— and Foray, D. (2003). 'Economic Fundamentals of the Knowledge Society'. *Policy Futures in Education*, 1(1): 20–49.

—— and Rullani, F. (2008). 'Dynamics of Innovation in an "Open Source" Collaboration Environment: Lurking, Laboring, and Launching FLOSS Projects on SourceForge'. *Industrial and Corporate Change*, 17(4): 647–710.

Deuze, M. (2006). 'Participation, Remediation, Bricolage: Considering Principal Components of a Digital Culture'. *Information Society*, 22(2): 63–75.

—— (2008). *Media Work*. Cambridge: Polity Press.

Drake, W. J. and Wilson, E. J. (eds) (2008). *Governing Global Electronic Networks*. Cambridge, MA: MIT Press.

Fitzgerald, B. (2006). 'The Transformation of Open Source Software'. *MIS Quarterly*, 30(3): 587–98.

Freeman, C. (1988). 'Information Technology and the New Economic Paradigm'. In H. Schutte (ed.), *Strategic Issues in Information Technology: International Implications for Decision Makers* (pp. 159–75). Berkshire: Pergamon Infotech.

—— Clarke, J. and Soete, L. (1982). *Unemployment and Technical Innovation: A Study of Long Waves and Economic Development*. Westport, CT: Greenwood Press.

—— and Soete, L. (1990). 'Fast Structural Change and Slow Productivity Change: Some Paradoxes in the Economics of Information Technology'. *Structural Change and Economic Dynamics*, 1(2): 225–42.

—— and Soete, L. (1997). *The Economics of Industrial Innovation*, third edition. London: Pinter (A Cassel Imprint).

Galliers, R. D. (1991). 'Strategic Information Systems Planning: Myths, Reality and Guidelines for Successful Implementation'. *European Journal of Information Systems*, 1(1): 55–64.

Galperin, H. (2004). *New TV, Old Politics: The Political Economy of Digital Television in the United States and Britain*. Cambridge: Cambridge University Press.

Gordon, R. J. (2004). 'Five Puzzles in the Behavior of Productivity, Investment, and Innovation'. In A. Lopez-Claros and X. Sala-i-Martin (eds), *The Global Competitiveness Report 2003–04* (pp. 117–35). New York and Oxford: Oxford University Press.

Hargittai, E. (2003). 'The Digital Divide and What to Do with It'. In D. C. Jones (ed.), *The New Economy* (pp. 822–38). San Diego, CA: Academy Press.

—— (2004). 'Internet Access and Use in Context'. *New Media & Society*, 6(1): 137–44.

Healy, K. (2002). 'Survey Article. Digital Technology and Cultural Goods'. *Journal of Political Philosophy*, 10(4): 478.

Helpman, E. (ed.) (1998). *General Purpose Technologies and Economic Growth.* Cambridge, MA: MIT Press.

Johnson, B., Lorenz, E. and Lundvall, B.-Å. (2002). 'Why All this Fuss about Codified and Tacit Knowledge?' *Industrial and Corporate Change*, 11(2): 245–62.

Jorgenson, D. W. and Stiroh, K. J. (2000). 'Raising the Speed Limit: US Economic Growth in the Information Age'. *Brookings Papers on Economic Activity*, 31(1): 125–211.

Kling, R. (1991). 'Computerization and Social Transformations'. *Science, Technology and Human Values*, 16(3): 342–67.

Koch, S. and Schneider, G. (2002). 'Effort, Coordination and Co-operation in an Open Source Software Project'. *Information Systems Journal*, 12(1): 27–42.

Kraemer, K. L., Dutton, W. H. and Northrop, A. (1980). 'Management Control, the Automated Budget and Information Handling'. *Information Privacy*, 2(1): 7–16.

Lamberton, D. M. (1986). 'Information, Economic Analysis and Public Policy'. *Prometheus*, 4(1): 214–19.

—— (ed.) (1971). *The Economics of Information and Knowledge.* Harmondsworth: Penguin.

Lancashire, D. (2001). 'Code, Culture and Clash: The Fading Altruism of Open Source Development'. *First Monday*, 6(12): n.p.

Lave, J. and Wenger, E. (1991). *Situated Learning: Legitimate Peripheral Participation.* New York: Cambridge University Press.

Lerner, J. and Tirole, J. (2005). 'The Economics of Technology Sharing: Open Source and Beyond'. *Journal of Economic Perspectives*, 19(2): 99–120.

Lipsey, R. G., Carlaw, K. I. and Bekar, C. T. (2005). *Economic Transformations: General Purpose Technologies and Long-term Economic Growth.* Oxford: Oxford University Press.

Lugo, J. and Sampson, T. (2008). 'E-Informality in Venezuela: The "Other Path" of Technology'. *Bulletin of Latin American Research*, 27(1): 102–18.

Mansell, R. (1997). 'Strategies for Maintaining Market Power in the Face of Rapidly Changing Technologies'. *Journal of Economic Issues*, XXXI(4): 969–89.

—— (2001). 'Digital Opportunities and the Missing Link for Developing Countries'. *Oxford Review of Economic Policy*, 17(2): 282–95.

—— (2002). 'From Digital Divides to Digital Entitlements in Knowledge Societies'. *Current Sociology*, 50(3): 407–26.

—— (2006). 'Ambiguous Connections: Entitlements and Responsibilities of Global Networking'. *Journal of International Development*, 18(4): 1–13.

—— and Wehn, U. (eds) (1998). *Knowledge Societies: Information Technology for Sustainable Development*. Oxford: Published for the United Nations Commission on Science and Technology for Development by Oxford University Press.

Melody, W. H. (1985). 'The Information Society – Implications for Economic Institutions and Market Theory'. *Journal of Economic Issues*, 19(2): 523–39.

—— (1991). 'The Information Society: The Transnational Economic Context and its Implications'. In G. Sussman and J. A. Lent (eds), *Transnational Communications: Wiring the Third World* (pp. 27–41). London: Sage.

Murdock, G. (1978). ' "Blindspot about Western Marxism". A reply to Dallas Smythe'. *Canadian Journal of Political and Social Theory*, 2(2): 109–19.

Norris, P. (2001). *Digital Divide: Civic Engagement, Information Poverty and the Internet Worldwide*. Cambridge: Cambridge University Press.

Odlyzko, A. M. (2001). 'Content Is Not King'. *First Monday*, 6(2): n.p.

Organization for Economic Cooperation and Development (OECD) (1996). *The Knowledge-based Economy*. Paris: OECD GD(96)102.

Orlikowski, W. J. (1992). 'The Duality of Technology – Rethinking the Concept of Technology in Organizations'. *Organization Science*, 3(3): 398–427.

—— (2002). 'Knowing in Practice: Enacting a Collective Capability in Distributed Organizing'. *Organization Science*, 13(3): 249–73.

Perez, C. (1983). Structural Change and Assimilation of New Technologies in the Economic and Social-Systems'. *Futures*, 15(5): 357–75.

—— (1985). 'Microelectronics, Long Waves and World Structural-Change – New Perspectives for Developing-Countries'. *World Development*, 13(3): 441–63.

Pratt, A. C. (1997). 'Production Values: From Cultural Industries to the Governance of Culture'. *Environment and Planning A*, 29(11): 1,911–17.

Preston, P. and Kerr, A. (2001). 'Digital Media, Nation-states and Local Cultures: The Case of Multimedia "Content" Production'. *Media, Culture & Society*, 23(1): 109–31.

Shapiro, C. and Varian, H. R. (1999). *Information Rules: A Strategic Guide to the Network Economy*. Cambridge, MA: Harvard Business Press.

Smythe, D. W. (1977). 'Communications: Blindspot of Western Marxism'. *Canadian Journal of Political and Social Theory*, 1(3): 1–27.

—— (1981). *Dependency Road: Communications, Capitalism, Consciousness and Canada*. Norwood, NJ: Ablex.

Solow, R. M. (1987). 'We'd Better Watch Out'. *New York Review of Books, New York Times*, 12 July: 36.

Star, S. L. and Ruhleder, K. (1996). 'Steps Towards an Ecology of Infrastructure: Design and Access to Large Information Spaces'. *Information Systems Research*, 7(1): 111–34.

Steinmueller, W. E. (2000). 'Will New Information and Communication Technologies Improve the "Codification" of Knowledge?' *Industrial and Corporate Change*, 9(2): 361.

Stigler, G. J. (1961). 'The Economics of Information'. *Journal of Political Economy*, 69(3): 213–25.

United Nations Educational, Scientific and Cultural Organization (UNESCO) (2005). *Towards Knowledge Societies: UNESCO World Report*. Paris: UNESCO Publishing.

Van Audenhove, L. (2003). *Towards an Integrated Information Society Policy in South Africa: An Overview of Political Rhetoric and Policy Initiatives 1994–2000*. Johannesburg: HSRC Press.

—— Burgelman, J. C., Nulens, G. and Cammaerts, B. (1999). 'Information Society Policy in the Developing World: A Critical Assessment'. *Third World Quarterly*, 20(2): 387–404.

van Dijk, J. A. G. M. (2005). *The Deepening Divide: Inequality in the Information Society*. London: Sage.

—— (2006). 'Digital Divide Research, Achievements and Shortcomings'. *Poetics*, 34(4–5): 221–35.

von Hippel, E. (2001). 'Innovation by User Communities: Learning from Open-source Software'. *MIT Sloan Management Review*, 42(4): 82–6.

von Hippel, E. and von Krogh, G. (2003). 'Open Source Software and the "Private–Collective" Innovation Model: Issues for Organization Science'. *Organization Science*, 14(2): 209–23.

Warschauer, M. (2002). 'Reconceptualizing the Digital Divide'. *First Monday*, 7(7): n.p.

—— (2004). *Technology and Social Inclusion: Rethinking the Digital Divide*. Cambridge, MA: MIT Press.

Wenger, E. (1998). *Communities of Practice: Learning, Meaning, and Identity*. New York: Cambridge University Press.

Wilson, E. J. (2004). *The Information Revolution and Developing Countries*. Cambridge, MA: MIT Press.

Zuboff, S. (1988). *In the Age of the Smart Machine: The Future of Work and Power*. New York: Basic Books.

—— (2004). 'Managing the Informated Organization'. In F. Webster (ed.), *The Information Society Reader* (pp. 313–26). London: Routledge.

Part 3

KNOWLEDGE AND ECONOMICS

24

STRUCTURAL CHANGE AND ASSIMILATION OF NEW TECHNOLOGIES IN THE ECONOMIC AND SOCIAL SYSTEMS

Carlota Perez

Source: *Futures* 15(5) (1983): 357–75.

Through generating a set of hypotheses about the interrelationship between diffusion of new technologies and economic development, the author seeks to identify the causal mechanisms of the depressions in the trough of the Kondratiev long wave. A model of the capitalist economy and an analysis of its structural patterns and processes are proposed, and from an examination of the technoeconomic and socioinstitutional characteristics of the fourth Kondratiev, some institutional requirements for the next upswing are elaborated.

A set of hypotheses about the interrelationship between the diffusion of new technologies and economic development is presented in this article. With it we attempt to approach the causal mechanisms of the widespread depressions experienced every five or six decades by the economic system, corresponding to the troughs of the long waves, statistically identified by Nikolai Kondratiev[1] in the 1920s. In so doing, we hope to provide a framework with which to meet Nathan Rosenberg's challenge to specify "the conditions which would need to be fulfilled in order for technological innovation to generate long cycles in economic growth . . ."[2]. We also hope to open new lines of research leading to possible counter-long-cyclical policies.

We start from a somewhat Schumpeterian view of the role of innovation in provoking the cyclical behaviour of the capitalist economy. But, departing at least partially from his view, we postulate that Kondratiev's long waves are not a strictly economic phenomenon, but rather the manifestation, measurable in economic terms, of the harmonious or disharmonious behaviour of the total socioeconomic and institutional system (on the national and international levels).

A structural crisis (ie the depression in a long wave), as distinct from an economic recession, would be the visible syndrome of a breakdown in the complementarity between the dynamics of the economic subsystem and the related dynamics of the socio-institutional framework. It is, in the same movement, the painful and conflict-ridden process through which a dynamic harmony is reestablished among the different spheres of the total system.

The resulting complementary trends represent what we might call a 'mode of development' understood as a general pattern of growth, based on a set of accepted social and institutional mechanisms, national and international, influencing the operation and evolution of factor and other markets.

What provides the direction and shape of the movement are successive technological styles—or, if you prefer, successive quantum jumps in the general best-practice frontier-based on a constellation of interrelated innovations both strictly technical and organizational, the diffusion of which is propelled by the profit motive.

So for us the long waves represent distinct successive modes of development, responding to distinct successive technological styles. However, although we identify modes of development as stretching from trough to trough of each Kondratiev, we propose that technological styles evolve roughly from the peak of one long wave to the peak of the next. This is the crucial point on which medium- and long-term forecasting could be based. We claim that the crisis is brought about by the introduction of a new technological style when—and because—the previous one approaches the limits of its potentialities. Its initial diffusion, up to a certain critical level, both provokes the crisis of the old mode and sets the guidelines for the next mode of development, during which the new style will display its full potential.

Kondratiev'[3] had certainly mentioned that during the downswing, together with other characteristic phenomena, there was "an especially large number of important discoveries and inventions in the technique of production . . . which, however, are usually applied on a large scale only at the beginning of the next long upswing".

However, Kondratiev emphasized that this and other recurring relationships did nothing more than further confirm the existence of the long waves. He strongly emphasized that he did not "by any means hold that they contain the explanation".

Thus, as far as the causation mechanism is concerned, Kondratiev does not make any explicit commitment to the role of innovation (at least, not in the article we are analysing). He attempts to demonstrate the existence of long waves, he denies the possibility that they may be due to random factors, and advances his opinion that their causes are "Inherent in the essence of the capitalistic economy".

For Schumpeter[4], who does set out to build a theory of the causation mechanism, innovation is the single root cause of the cyclical behaviour of the capitalist economy. For him there is no essential difference between short, medium and long cycles, except the relative importance and weight of the specific innovation or cluster of innovations provoking them. Notably, the Kondratiev long waves would be carried by a series of interrelated innovations. Each of them would consist of an 'industrial revolution' and the absorption of its effects.

In spite of the complexity of Schumpeter's total model and of his constant reference to the historical context, for him the systemic process unfolds *within* the economic sphere conceived as a self-regulating organism which provokes its own disturbances (innovations) and absorbs its impacts by constantly striving towards new higher equilibria. As for the rest of society, it suffers and profits from this recurrent process of 'creative destruction', it is slowly and profoundly transformed; it is sometimes an obstacle, at other times a stimulus, but it is mainly an environment. Social conditions and the institutional framework are conditioning and conditioned by economic evolution, but they do not form a total structure with the economic system. They are therefore excluded from the causation mechanism for cyclical behaviour.

This is, in our opinion, the reason why even though Schumpeter's theory is generally associated with the explanation of crises or great depressions, he in fact gives a much better account of the shorter cycles and recessions than of the deeper long-cycle depressions.

Even his language is revealing of this uneasy spot in his model. He speaks of prosperity and recession when referring to the juglar intermediate cycles, but he uses the term 'abnormal liquidation' to name the path from recession towards the trough of a long wave and 'recovery' or 'revival' for the beginning of a long upswing. In fact, his model does not really provide a 'natural' exit from a depression—so much so that, despite his strongly inimical attitude towards outside intervention in the self-regulating economic system, he reluctantly admits that "the case for government action in depression, especially of government action of certain types, remains, independently of humanitarian considerations, incomparably stronger than it is in recession".[5]

Strictly speaking, if the system worked as Schumpeter says, deep depressions would be abnormal phenomena and their historical regularity indeed puzzling. Bypassing the problem by invoking the idea of an 'industrial revolution' is in conflict with the identification of the market as the absorption mechanism. Presumably, although the innovations do come in clusters, they are not absolutely synchronic in their introduction, and the market should be able to gradually absorb them through short or medium wave-like movements.

Thus Schumpeter does lay the foundations for a theory of the cyclical nature of the capitalist economy but *not* of long waves.

Model of the capitalist system

We propose that the capitalist system be seen as a single very complex structure, the subsystems of which have different rates of change. For the sake of simplicity we can assume two main subsystems: on the one hand a technoeconomic, and on the other a social and institutional, the first having a much faster rate of response than the second. The long waves would be successive phases in the evolution of the total system or, as we have termed them, successive modes of development. The root cause of the dynamics of the system would be the profit motive as generator of innovations in the productive sphere, understood in the broadest sense as a way of increasing productivity and expected profits from new investment.

Each mode of development would be shaped in response to a specific technological style understood as a kind of paradigm for the most efficient organization of production, ie the main form and direction along which productivity growth takes place within and across firms, industries and countries. The particular historical form of such a paradigm would evolve out of certain key technological developments, which result in a substantial change in the relative cost structure facing industry and which, at the same time, open a wide range of new opportunities for taking advantage of this particular evolution. In essence we assume a strong feedback interaction between the economic, social and institutional spheres which generates a dynamic complementarity centred around a technological style as roughly defined above. The upswing of the Kondratiev wave would be sustained and stimulated by the harmonious evolution of such complementarity up to the point where the underlying technological style approaches the limits of its potential for increasing productivity and profits.

To surmount this barrier, through trial and error, a new technological style emerges in the productive sphere to which the prevailing social and institutional framework is no longer suited. The new dynamics introduced in the system produce greater and greater disruption in the previously ex- pected evolution of most markets, gradually transforming the social fabric and rendering the institutional mechanisms—which have a high degree of natural inertia, strengthened by the confidence of previous successes—more and more obsolete and counterproductive. This process would be visible as the downswing of the Kondratiev wave, eventually leading to a crisis of the whole system.

The structural crisis thus brought about is, then, not only a process of 'creative destruction' or 'abnormal liquidation' in the economic sphere, but also in the socio-institutional. In fact, the crisis forces the restructuring of the socio-institutional framework with innovations along lines that are complementary to the newly attained technological style or best-practice frontier. The final form the structure will take, from the wide range of the possible, and the timespan within which the transformation is effected to permit a new expansionary phase will, however, ultimately depend on the interests, actions, lucidity and relative strength of the social forces at play.

This rough summary of the form in which we see the evolution of the system should serve to hint at the way in which we envisage predictability to be possible at a time when the usual extrapolations seem powerless. If the characteristics of the new technological style (which is already in place) can be identified, and the trends created by its diffusion—both in the economic and extraeconomic spheres—can be disentangled from those belonging to the waning style, then the general lines of transformation can be prefigured and serve as criteria for purposive action. We return briefly to this point in the concluding section of this paper. Let us now proceed to give a more precise definition of the elements of the model we have sketched.

Model elements

'Technological styles'

We have been speaking of 'technological styles'. Others may prefer to call them 'technoeconomic paradigms' or 'patterns'. It is not easy to find the ideal term with which to convey the features of the phenomenon we are trying to describe. By 'technological style' we mean a kind of 'ideal type' of productive organization or best technological 'common sense' which develops as a response to what are perceived as the stable dynamics of the relative cost structure for a given period of capitalist development.

As long as the expected pattern of evolution of the relative costs of various types of material inputs, various types of equipment and different segments of labour skills follows the expected trends, managers and engineers will apply what becomes the 'technical common sense' to make incremental improvements along the natural trajectories of the technologies in place, or radical technological changes in those branches of production of goods or services which have not yet achieved the 'ideal type' of productive organization.

Thus, for a given period, with a given set of expected trends in the relative cost structure, more and more branches of the economy will tend to apply the prevailing technological style, understood as the most rational and efficient way of taking advantage of the general cost structure. The establishment of such a style or paradigm is grounded on the introduction of a cluster or constellation of interrelated innovations, both technical and managerial, which lead to the attainment of a general level of total factor or physical productivity clearly superior to what was 'normal' with the previous technological style.

This quantum jump in productivity can be seen as a technological revolution, which is made possible by the appearance in the general cost structure of a particular input that we could call the 'key factor', fulfilling the following conditions:

- Clearly perceived low—and descending—relative cost;
- Unlimited supply for all practical purposes;
- Potential all-pervasiveness;
- A capacity to reduce the costs of capital, labour and products as well as to change them qualitatively.

The conjunction of all these characteristics in a particular type of input, which, from a technical point of view, was probably available long before, occurs as a response to a persistent demand for technologies capable of surmounting the limits of the technological trajectories based on the use of the prevailing (or previous) 'key factor'.[6] However, once this conjunction of characteristics crystallizes and the evolution of the relative cost structure is modified in a manner generally perceived as long-term, engineering and investment behaviour tends to shift towards new technological paths. We then witness not only the establishment of a new 'best productive common sense' which strives to get maximum advantage of the new key factor, across wide families of related or apparently unrelated technologies, but also a sustained bias in favour of its intensive use, both in radical and in subsequent incremental innovations.

As we mentioned above, the appearance of the new 'key factor' and the technological style that takes shape around its characteristics are phenomena that occur near the peak and during the downswing of the *previous* Kondratiev. The transformations they generate in the productive sphere through their gradual diffusion will demand complementary innovations in the social and institutional spheres in order to give way to a new long wave upswing.

We suggest the role of key factor was played by low-cost and steam-powered transportation in the second Kondratiev; by low-cost steel for the third; low-cost energy, in the form of oil and energy-intensive materials, for the fourth; and is now being played by low-cost microelectronics on the way towards the fifth upswing.

As examples of what constitutes a technological style one might turn to the most recent and best known, which would be those shaped by low-cost energy between the third and fourth Kondratiev and, as we propose, by low-cost microelectronics between the fourth and fifth. The first would be the extension of the continuous flow concept of the chemical industry to the mass production of discrete identical units made with energy-intensive materials (the prototype of which was Henry Ford's assembly line), complemented on the organizational level by a sharp separation of management and administration from production, bringing Taylor's ideas of 'scientific management' to their ultimate consequences. The second, taking advantage of the characteristics of microelectronics, could perhaps be the flexible batch production network where all activities (managerial, administrative, productive, etc) are integrated in a total information-intensive system to turn out information intensive products or services.

Investment patterns

This brings us to another element of the model, namely the contention that the emergence of a new technological style is accompanied by a general shift in investment patterns from the areas that were best adapted to the old style towards those most amenable to the new paradigm. This shift would result in a change in the relative importance of the different branches and in the specific intersectoral relationships. In concrete terms we think that it is possible to distinguish for each technological style—and therefore for each Kondratiev upswing—a specific network of interbranch relationships which describes the main characteristics of the distribution of production between branches and between large and small firms in relation to their weight in the gross product.

Essentially there would be three main types of branches determining the shape and rhythm of economic growth for the period.

A. The *carrier branches* which are those that make intensive use of the key factor, are the best adapted to the 'ideal' organization of production, induce a great variety of investment opportunities up- and downstream (among them, and most important, great infrastructural investment of specific kinds) and, therefore, become the vectors of the technological style, having great influence in the general rhythm of economic growth.

B. The *'motive branches'*, which are responsible for the production of the key factors and other inputs directly associated with them and have, therefore, the role of maintaining and deepening their relative cost advantage. Thus, while the motive branches create the conditions for the development of the technological style, the growth of their own market depends on the rhythm of generalization of the style across industries.

C. The *'induced branches'*, whose development is both a consequence of and complementary to the growth of the carrier branches, only multiply in bandwagon fashion once the necessary social and institutional innovations, together with the appropriate infrastructural investment, have opened the way for the upswing and the generalization of the new technological style. They often use precisely the types of labour displaced by the carrier branches, which is why the initial technical unemployment effect provoked by diffusion in the downswing can be countered during the upswing.

Of course, there are many other branches which produce necessary goods under older, less productive, technological styles or with 'odd' highly specific technologies which are never generalizable—or at least not yet. Some of the first are able to get on the bandwagon of the prevailing style through technological innovations, the general tendency indeed being to try to achieve as much as possible in that direction. But the main argument is that the complementary growth of the carrier and motive branches is the engine that moves the economy and that those branches will tend to be increasingly concentrated in the hands of the largest firms for the period.

Upswing characteristics

In summary, we suggest that the upswing of a Kondratiev long wave begins when a harmonic complementarity has been achieved, through adequate social and institutional innovations, between the 'technoeconomic paradigm', which emerged and developed in the previous Kondratiev peak and downswing, and the socio-institutional climate. This unleashes the swarming process and generates the wave of infrastructural investment that induces the attainment of full growth potential, through accelerated diffusion and ultimate generalization of the paradigm. It is a period of bandwagon effects, when one after another all productive units—and even social activities of all kinds—tend to apply what is then generally considered as the 'optimal or ideal form of productive organization'. A particular form of growth stabilizes; a particular way of life takes shape for the different segments of the population; a set of international investment production and trade patterns evolves; (utterly) refined statistical models of the economy can be made-and *can work;* economic science can develop with relative confidence with *ceteris paribus* assumptions; the trajectories of a large cluster of technologies become 'common sense' and seem to belong to the 'nature of things'; state policies, be they laissez jaire or Keynesian or whatever, are seen more as objects of refinement than of radical change because their effectiveness seems to have been 'demonstrated'.

Now, if we remember that the technological style that is then in the process of generalization throughout the system had been introduced during the previous wave, shifting investment of large firms into those branches that have now become the 'carrier' and 'motive' branches, or allowing the appearance of new firms that quickly reach high growth, we can reasonably assume that it is in these branches that the first symptoms of exhaustion of the technological trajectories will be felt.

Presumably then, these would be the most likely to start searching within the large universe of the technologically feasible, though perhaps not yet the economically profitable, for new products and new processes that are either labour- or materials- or capital-saving, or seem to offer potential growth prospects. Some of these may result in outright fiascos, others would be the early prototypes of a possible future technological style, placing a strong demand and possibly high investment in developing the cost-cutting possibilities of the possible future key factor.

Presumably also, since the limits to a particular technological trajectory tend to translate for the firm into a reduction of the rate of profit or—a similar phenomenon—in a decrease in the expected rate of return from further investment along the same lines, the search for new profit opportunities might not be directed at investment in risky technological innovations but rather towards mergers and acquisitions or less orthodox speculative activities in whatever is found suitable in the particular period. From the mid-1960s to the early 1970s there were waves of mergers as well as of speculation with money and raw materials; there was persistent recourses to refined manipulation such as 'transfer pricing' and 'leads and lags' in international payments, as well as to developments such as 'tax havens' and other non-productive disruptive practices.

Here a brief reference to Mensch's[7] approach to the theory of long waves should be made. For him investments in alternative types of capital goods are made as a result of "systematic downgrading in operative value" of existing fixed capital in plant and equipment. We fully agree with this contention but part company with him, following Freeman, Clark and Soete[8], when it comes to the difference between process innovations and product innovation. Whereas Mensch holds that basic innovations are made in the depths of a downturn, we would contend that the main process innovations (together, we would add, with those associated with the key factor and the main new organizational paradigm) could well have been made during the later part of the upswing and the beginning of the downswing. So, by the time depression arrives, the new generation of equipment and the organizational pattern that accompanies it, is already in the market, and what occurs is the application of this equipment mainly to product innovations. It is then vital to distinguish between the initial diffusion of a technological style which is made with 'idle' capital in a period of prosperity (and can be as primitive and costly and risky as Rosenberg[9] suggests) and the further diffusion of a tested technological style which is the most natural investment choice in a period of depression, if and when new investment is to be made in those conditions.

Thus our contention is that once the initial successful crystallization of the main elements of the new set of technologies has taken place, the peak of the Kondratiev is produced, as the conjunction of the attainment of the old best productive frontier by most of the economy (including the laggards) and a certain degree of diffusion of the new paradigm—within the old mould.

Thus, the peak of the long cycle is a kind of economic frenzy of a relatively short duration, but appearing as the promise of everlasting upward progress, while the old branches are still joining the bandwagon and new products and processes associated with the emerging technological style produce one big success story after another. This situation creates unwarranted expectations as to the health of the system and its unlimited opportunities, and it also tends to give undue confidence in the institutional mechanisms, reinforcing their rigidity and inertia. It is in the midst of such high growth that the seeds of the contraction are sown.

Downswing characteristics

The descent of the Kondratiev wave sees the exhaustion of the new product and process investment opportunities associated with the prevailing technological style at the same time as the exhaustion of the technological trajectory of the carrier branches (even as their output may continue to grow with inflationary trends). These events affect the motive branches, whose capacity to continue maintaining the relative cost advantage of the key factors is reduced, not only for similar technical reasons but also by the very fact that their main sources of market growth are contracting.

At the same time, those segments of business whose growth potential had seemed unhampered and those of labour, whose job and earnings prospects had been more or less 'guaranteed' during the upswing, are the hardest hit (a shift which might, by the way, hint at why they tend to support 'strong' solutions to return to 'order').

As the various disequilibria manifest themselves in the various markets (labour, inputs, money, equipment) as a result both of the contraction in the old dynamics and of the unexpected market trends generated by the new investment patterns, more and more pressure is put on the state to find new means of stimulating and 'managing' the economy. The Keynes and the Schumpeters offer radically new theories and the Roosevelts and the Hiders establish radically new economic and political management mechanisms, while many others just offer to apply sternly more of the same old successful recipes.

The downswing is then a period of experimentation at all organizational levels of society, characterized by the proliferation of reassessments, proposed solutions and trial-and-error behaviour stimulated by the increasing gravity of the crisis. All this occurs in the face of the weight of tradition, of established ideas, of vested interests and other inertial forces which actively oppose the required transformations.

For the working population it is generally a period of great suffering, as it is they, together with the weaker countries on the international level, who tend to carry the burden of the reaccommodation of the system. Meanwhile, on the economic level, the firms that are able relatively to escape the crisis

26

are those linked to the production or use of the new key factor, which becomes more and more visible in the relative cost structure. It is towards these areas that new investment tends to go, intensifying the disruptive effects of the new technological style and sending signals in all directions for the adequate social and institutional changes required.

Patterns and processes of transformation

We have defined a technological style as a kind of paradigm for the most effective organization of production, and have also suggested that this generates a particular pattern of interbranch relationships related also to the distribution of production between large and smaller firms. We now want to add that each technological style generates a typical pattern of transformation in the occupational structure, and a set of distinct trends in the spatial distribution of production on the international and national scales[10].

We concentrate below on the way the occupational structure is affected by the paradigm shift and its diffusion. For ease of presentation we make use of the specific example of the 'assembly line' technological style which in our view shaped the fourth Kondratiev upswing.

The chain of relationships important for our purposes is represented in Figure 1. First, we briefly discuss what is meant by each of the elements and relationships indicated.

The profit motive should encounter no difficulty when presented as the propelling force and the organizing principle of the capitalist system. In this particular chain of events, however, it has been singled out as the criterion for choosing a particular type of equipment and a specific form of organization of production taking into account the existing pattern of available technology, opportunities, and especially of relative factor costs, including the evolution of the key factor we defined before and of the various skill segments of the labour force.

While the profit motive is the propeller, the technological style is the steering mechanism. In the chain of relationships now under analysis, we

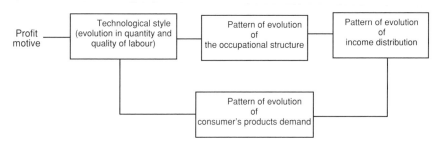

Figure 1 Chain of relationships.

focus on its optimal paradigm for the usage of labour both in quantity and quality, ie on the 'ideal skill mix' in relation to the total mass of wages and salaries.

Taylorism—seeds of the Fourth Kondratiev

As an illustration, we look at the historical moment at which the seeds of the recently prevailing paradigm were sown—when Frederick Winslow Taylor transformed the productive organization at the Bethlehem Steel yards at the turn of the 20th century. This event can be considered as the invention and first introduction of that particular social *and* institutional innovation *within* the productive sphere.

Occupational structure

According to Taylor's description[11], over 500 labourers worked at different tasks in the yard, in gangs of anywhere up to about 75 men, each group under a foreman. Management merely indicated to the foremen what was to be done and trusted the experience of both foremen and workers (who often used their own tools) to do the job in their own way. Three years later there were only 140 labourers in the yard, each accomplishing the work previously done by three or four men but now with standardized, carefully designed company tools, and following strict standardized procedures determined by time and motion studies[12]. A planning room carefully prepared the following day's work for each individual worker and coordinated all movements in the yard. It was staffed with engineers, time and motion men, draughtsmen, a clerical staff, a telephone and messenger system, etc. The single group-foremen had been substituted by a set of functional overseers who coordinated, trained, timed and measured work and in general acted as the agents of the planning department.

The new organization, despite the new planning and toolroom expenses, despite the much higher salaries of the new white-collar staff, and even though the wages of the remaining labourers had been increased by 60%, more than halved the cost of handling a ton of metal, from 7.2 cents/ton to 3.3 cents/ton[13]. And the new scientific management techniques yielded equivalent cost-cutting results when applied to everything from bricklaying to ball-bearing quality inspection and to machine-shop work.

Although Taylorism is only the seed out of which continuous massproduction evolved as a fully fledged technological style, even in its earliest form, it serves the purpose of our present analysis. It is not difficult to imagine how, with such results, the profit motive would propel the application of scientific management techniques. Then, as one firm after another reduces the usual size of its work force in relation to output and transforms its composition, new trends can be expected to become gradually visible in the total occupational structure. The truly magnified effect historically occurred of course with the diffusion of Ford's assembly-line style, combined with the internal combustion engine and low-cost oil. But let us follow the logic of Taylor's innovation for the sake of simplicity.

The diffusion and generalization of a technological style implies a transformation in the occupational profile of the working population along certain main trends. It is a dynamic and not a static pattern. It can best be understood as a set of different growth rates for different categories, resulting from the prevailing direction of changes in the organization of production. This type of transformation has, of course, many important social and labour market implications, which are not pursued in this paper.

Following our illustration through, the growth of a new layer of white-collar workers between managers and foremen, and the reduction of the number of manual labourers required for a given output, introduce a new pattern of evolution in the occupational structure. Initially, the old trends are not eliminated, for much of the growth in the aggregate takes place along traditional lines. The new trends appear simply as counter-trends, curbing and transforming the lines of the old pattern. Yet each business cycle serves to filter out the old and strengthen and accelerate the application of the new style and the visibility of its consequences on the occupational structure of employment (and of unemployment!).

Income distribution

But this change in occupational structure is accompanied by corresponding trends in income distribution. In Taylor's first experiment the salary mass was more than halved while the workforce was cut to less than a third. However, the main change was in the distribution of the globally reduced labour costs. From a three-layer structure of managers, clerks and foremen, and labourers, translating into about one high and one medium salary for every 70 to 80 lowwage labourers, the new organization implied a complex hierarchy of salaries. The ranks of the 'middle-income' groups began to swell. Just as the salary mass was being cut and being redistributed within the enterprises, the income mass in the form of wages and salaries was being redistributed in society at large (and many were getting nothing at all).

Product demand

Again, the evolution in the income distribution translates into changes in the pattern of product demand. In our illustration, the new income distribution makes headway in a market sharply divided into luxury and staple goods (food, clothing and rent). The traditional middle class—the small proprietors and the educated few—consume from (and often cater to) both markets. Now gradually the staple markets begin to shrink relatively and a new middle-range demand pattern emerges and tends to grow.

But how does this affect the diffusion of the technological style as indicated in the diagram? At first, we can assume that the new middle layer of salaried workers grows slowly and joins the ranks of the traditional middle class in market behaviour. After all, people choose what to buy from what is available. But the particular evolution of market potential and market stagnation does not go unnoticed by producers. However faulty the information at hand may be, under the conditions we have been following, it is unlikely that an entrepreneur would launch a new investment to cater to a dwindling market such as cotton textiles, for instance. Instead, he might apply the new potential for productivity increase to turning a luxury good into one accessible to the growing middle layer, which is what Ford set out to do with his Model-T, and many others after him.

Transformation process

Thus, the diffusion of a new form of organization of production requiring a new skill profile, translates into changes in income distribution which, in turn, affect the pattern of demand, signalling to producers the general characteristics of the new types of products which would both cater to the growing markets and be capable of being produced with the new technological style through which the process becomes a gradually accelerating feedback loop. This constant propagation increases the disruptive effects in the downswing and the harmony in the upswing.

Thus, the introduction of the assembly line as the optimum extension of 'scientific management' contained the crystallization of a change of paradigm for the manufacturing of discrete products along the continuous-flow concept of the chemical industries. It also implied a change in occupational structure, which tended to make blue-collar labour more homogeneous and ultimately led to a restructuring of the skill-based trade unions to the branch-based labour unions, while it created a pattern of growth of white-collar labour in an increasing hierarchy. It eventually led to a transformation in the product structure, where mass-produced energy-consuming durable consumer goods made with energy-intensive materials would be gradually introduced into the sprawling suburban homes, which the automobile itself and the expansion of the road network, together with the increase in 'middle-range' incomes made possible.

As Landes[14] so well expressed it, "The motor car industry was beginning to play ... (by the end of the interwar period) a role analogous to that of the railroad in the mid-nineteenth century: it was a huge consumer of semi-finished and finished intermediate products ... and components...; it had an insatiable appetite for fuel and other petroleum products; it required a small army of mechanics and service men to keep it going; and it gave a powerful impetus to investments in social and overhead capital (roads, bridges, tunnels). At the same time, it posed new technical problems in metallurgy, organic chemicals, and electrical engineering, eliciting solutions that had important consequences for other industries as well".

Thus, there was an accelerated process of diffusion in the main carrier branch, spurred by and spurring the oil industry, already run by a few giants, and rapidly finding lower-cost sources in Mexico, then Venezuela and South-East Asia (although the radical cost-cutting was to be made possible by the 'freeflowing' light oil from the Arabian Peninsula in the 1930s). From a peak average of $2.00/bbl in the war and afterwar period (1915–20), the price of oil decreased to an average $1.35/bbl in the 1926–30 period and to $0.83/bbl in the postcrash years (1931–35). The average price of electricity in the USA, on the other hand, had fallen 41% by 1928 with respect to 1902 (or 31% in constant terms).

Mass production technological style

We thus suggest that in the 1910s and 1920s, the technological style that shaped the fourth Kondratiev mode of development with its carrier and motive branches and its typical skill profile was already emerging and diffusing.

Both massive oil production and assembly-line technology were US-based, and the fastest rates of growth in electricity production and in radio and car sales took place in the USA. The greater weight of the old style and the divided markets of Europe seemed to inhibit the achievement of the full potential for mass production of identical units inherent in the new style. The USA had all the conditions for proceeding unhampered to become the world centre of the new mode of development[15].

But to make the transition from a system based on the growth of steel, capital goods, heavy electrical equipment, great engineering works (canals, bridges, dams, tunnels) and heavy chemistry, mainly geared towards big spenders, such as other capitalists or governments, into a mass production system catering to consumers and the massive defence markets, radical demand management and income redistribution innovations had to be made of which the directly economic role of the state is perhaps the most important.

The big upswing of the world economy after the second world war was then a period in which there was a good 'match' between the requirements of a mass production technological style, based on the almost universal availability of cheap oil, and the social and institutional framework within which this technological style could flourish. But this good 'match' was only achieved after a period of deep depression and social turmoil in the 1930s and after a major world war. During the 1930s, it was by no means clear how to achieve a set of appropriate institutional and social responses. As already indicated, the solutions which were then advocated and applied varied across a wide range from fascism to the New Deal and Communism[16]. It was only after the second world war that gradually a mode of development crystallized in the leading industrial countries, which did create the necessary harmonization of institutional framework with technological style.

Socio-institutional structures

Among the main institutional changes which promoted this good 'match' were, on the national level, the major expansion of the role of the state in economic life. The Keynesian policies which, in one form or another, were adopted by most countries led to various demand management mechanisms both directly through infrastructural, defence and public service spending, and indirectly through income redistribution by means of taxation, interest rate management and massive government employment. More indirect but equally essential for demand management was the elaborate public statistics apparatus, which served both public policy and private investment and market forecasting.

Another important socio-institutional change was the rapid expansion of massive secondary and higher education to provide the enormous increase in requirements of 'white-collar', technical and clerical employees, together with the expansion of the various national forms of public health systems. Both were also great sources of employment and hence of income redistribution.

On the more directly economic level innovations such as large-scale consumer credit methods, and the expansion of publicity, the mass communications industry and the various forms of planned obsolescence, further increased the means of orienting the use of disposable income into intensive consumption of the various goods typical of the mass-production style (and later also of those which became the forerunners of the style to come).

The institutional acceptance of the labour unions as legal representatives of the workers (especially in the carrier branches) both fostered the growth of disposable income and stimulated the application of labour-saving incremental innovations, within old plants or in new investment, along the trajectory of the technological style. In general, the evolution of non-union labour wages tended somewhat to follow the trends set by union labour. Thus, one could consider it as an indirect form of demand management.

At the level of the firm, a new 'ideal type' of organization for giant firms emerged with horizontal integration and a complex managerial system which allowed reaching optimum plant size under a much larger optimum size of firm. Its workings were thoroughly described by Peter Drucker[17] in *The Concept of the Corporation*, based on his study of General Motors. Accompanying this organization was the in-house R and D laboratory, which earlier had only developed as a necessary feature of such science-based industries as chemistry and electricity, but could now serve the controlled and sophisticated forms of competition which came to characterize oligopolies.

This particular development was a crucial element of the 'militaryindustrial complex' which, following the prototype of the Manhattan Project which produced the A-bomb, brought state, scientific, technological and industrial efforts to focus on pre-defined goals, eliciting a flurry of innovation requirements for new materials and processes which could later spin-off from military to civilian uses, once their primitive more costly stages of development had been borne by defence contracts.

On the international level, the Bretton Woods Agreement established a solid basis for the regulation of intercountry trade and investment (recognizing the hegemony of the USA in the new arrangement) and the Marshall Plan stimulated general international growth of investment and markets. Decolonization broke the empire-based barriers on investment and trade and allowed the energy- and materials-producing motive branches from different developed countries to establish more flexible competition arrangements to use the low-cost sources available in the developing countries. At the same time, the massive market growth needs of the technological style provoked an increasing number of 'common market' type agreements, as well as the 'local subsidiary' response of the carrier branches to the developing countries' tariff barrier policies. However, most international institutions and especially the UN organization were more of a facilitating nature than actually 'managing' economic growth, when compared to the main national institutions.

This impressionistic and incomplete list of the social and institutional innovations of the fourth Kondratiev mode of development, can be also considered—if our hypothesis about long waves is an acceptable approximation to the way the process evolves—as a list of obsolete mechanisms as regards the effective institutions required to unleash the upswing of the fifth Kondratiev based on microelectronics.

Institutional requirements for the next upswing

According to the foregoing hypotheses, the social sciences would today have a tremendous job of disentangling the new trends generated by the already established technological style, with its family of interrelated technologies and more or less visible trajectories, from what are in fact either waning trends, due to the exhaustion of the old paradigm, or temporary responses, which will disappear once the transition is effected. In a sense, during the upswing we are dealing with statistical distributions where the 'mode' tends to coincide with the 'mean', but in downswings and crises we deal with bimodal distributions where the 'mean' aggregate *means* very little. Again, during the upswing qualitative factors can be relatively ignored in quantitative measurement, whereas interdisciplinarity and qualitative case study type research is indispensable during downswings.

In particular the precise detection of the characteristics of the new paradigm is essential to point to the institutional solutions which, at the same time as they open the way for the generalization of the new paradigm, find the appropriate solutions to make the lot of those who would have been its inevitable victims less painful or even better.

This is not to say there is a one-to-one correspondence between the general characteristics of the technological style and those of the adequate socioinstitutional framework. We have already emphasized that there can be a wide range of scenarios, all valid as far as making high rates of growth possible, but vastly different as to their social consequences, as indeed was visible in the previous trough in the 1930s. Furthermore, the direction in which the technological trajectory of the new style will be exploited is not predetermined either, except in the general range of its possibilities. With these warnings in mind, one can nevertheless point out some basic elements, stemming from the essential features of the new technological potential and which are likely to characterize whatever valid alternatives are applied.

One of these elements stems from the fact that the new style seems to have a strong transnational dimension, based on the provision of the unprecedented data-management capabilities and telecommunications infrastructure for the efficient management of giant, complex, flexible, transnational conglomerates, which allow maximizing long-term profits and optimizing factor use on a planetary scale. So, national 'solutions' of the kind we grew accustomed to in the waning Kondratiev, seem ill adapted to manage an economy based on the new paradigm.

Another element pointing towards the need for a supranational framework is the enormous potential increase in plant scale for certain types of products. The radical productivity increases possible with computer-aided design and manufacturing, numerical control and distributed intelligence in the erstwhile less productive 'craft' technologies for the batch manufacture of capital goods, allow enormous increases in plant scale, where size of plant is not necessarily equivalent to size of market for one product but for a large, changing family of products. And these possible increases can, in that and other branches, involve the integration into one continuous process of various intermediate products, together with the final flexible output, increasing the scaling-up potential. In the production of services, especially information and telecommunications, it is even more evident that the larger the market and the wider the coverage, the lower the unit cost and the larger the stimulus for the flourishing of the multiple investment opportunities that take advantage of the availability of these decreasing cost services.

The particular potential for flexible product mix and relatively quick changes in product design would allow the application of rapid obsolescence practices in capital goods (and software) for the office and for the production of goods and services. So, whereas mass production markets grew on the basis of personal income and defence expenditures, flexible capital goods production with constant upgrading of technology and software, would thrive with the proliferation of small- and medium-sized producers in developed and developing countries.

Again, since the technological style favours information-intensive products and services for both producers and consumers, the opening of an everincreasing range of 'bandwagon' application opportunities might depend on the growth of a massive world telecommunications infrastructure[18].

Thus, the new potential for giant firms and very large-scale production in certain key areas, coupled with the opportunities for 'induced' decentralized production in other branches, indicate that national markets are a hindrance to full deployment. Thus, in one form or another, supranational management mechanisms seem necessary, among which some kind of international income redistribution system would appear as the basis for the appropriate, sustained market growth.

In recent years proposals have been heard for international Keynesianism, worldwide 'Marshall Plans', a new international economic order, industrial redeployment and other sorts of supranational arrangements. Yet most governments, especially in developed countries, still seem to place hope on nationally bound mechanisms.

As far as social organizations are concerned, there are two particularly worthy of note: the ecological movement and OPEC. The new technological style is fundamentally materials-saving. We consider only a few of its characteristics. It allows unprecedented downsizing of most products, reduces waste, permits production to closer tolerances, controls energy use, eliminates many moving parts, opens the possibility of closed-loop no-waste systems, etc. At the same time, in an indirect way, its full deployment would tend to fulfil many needs with services rather than products, and substitute much physical transportation with telecommunications while drastically diminishing paper consumption. Hence many demands of the ecological movement, which are in fact a rejection of the materials-intensive, energy-intensive waning style, can be met with a further diffusion of the applications of microelectronics. At the same time, the high cost of energy and materials should do nothing but stimulate investment in such applications. Thus the ecological movement can, at least in part, be seen as one of the forces contributing to the replacement of the 'old' style. Equally, OPEC, far from being the culprit of the crisis, might in fact be the prototype for a social organization of raw materials producers which, in a double role analogous to that of labour unions in the fourth Kondratiev, would serve as a stimulus for furthering the new technology along its trajectory and as an indirect income redistribution mechanism.

Concerning the occupational structure, the new technology seems to produce a centrifugal distribution with rapid growth of the highly qualified top of the scale and of the rapidly trained material or information feeders, panel watchers, button pushers, etc. This is in strong contrast with the rapid growth of the middle range in the previously prevalent technological style. Consequently, if states are efficiently to solve the technical unemployment problem, the focus would have to be placed on the middle strata, both for recycling and for creating conditions for the growth of the appropriate small and medium firms (organized perhaps by the displaced middle managers), capable of generating employment for qualified workers and markets for the office and production equipment producers.

Overall though, a very salient characteristic of the new technological system is its capacity to cope with variety, diversity and dispersion at all levels, as opposed to the prevailing need for 'massification', homogenization, and agglomeration typical of the paradigm about to be replaced. This might mean that the range of valid scenarios is particularly wide and furthermore, that these might be capable of accommodating an even wider range of social choice and institutional arrangements at the micro level.

Whether these are some of the correct conclusions or not, only further research and practical experimentation can tell. Under present conditions, optimism is on very shaky grounds but, if our hypotheses seem plausible, then it can only be grounded on the capacity to accept change and to innovate boldly on the social and institutional spheres and, we contend, on a planetary scale.

Notes

1 N. D. Kondratiev, "The long waves in economic life", *Review of Economic Statistics*, *17*, Nov 1935, pages 105–115.
2 N. Rosenberg and C. R. Frischtak, *Technological Innovation and Long Waves* (Stanford University, Mimeo, January 1983), page 3.
3 Kondratiev, op *cit*, ref 1.
4 J. S. Schumpeter, Business Cycles: A Theoretical, Historical and Statistical Analysis of the Capitalist Process, Vol I (McGraw-Hill, New York, 1939), page 223.
5 Ibid, page 155.
6 The actual combination of 'accidental' and 'purposive' events leading to this particular development are not discussed here. Suffice it to note that the relative autonomy of science leads to a universe of the technologically feasible which is, at any time, much greater than the economically profitable.
7 G. Mensch, Ch. Continho, K. Kaasch, "Changing capital values and the propensity to innovate", *Futures*, *13* (4), August 1981, page 283.
8 C. Freeman, J. Clark, L. Soete, Unemployment and Technical Innovation: A Study of Long Waves and Economic Development (Frances Pinter, London, 1982).
9 Rosenberg and Frischtak, op *cit*, ref 2, pages 10–11.
10 We believe that each new technological style, being based on a shift in the general relative cost structure, provokes a corresponding change in the pattern of international relative cost advantages. However, this point is not pursued further in this paper.

11 F. W. Taylor, The Principles of Scientific Management (Norton, NY, 1967).

12 We might note in passing that 'standardization' was a key concept in the prevailing paradigm of the third Kondratiev within which this very influential organizational innovation was born.

13 Again, we might note that we had suggested low-cost steel as the key factor in the third Kondratiev, so any cost-cutting improvements in the motive branch producing it contributed to the upswing.

14 D. S. Landes, *The Unbound Prometheus* (Cambridge University Press, 1972), page 442.

15 This heavy early commitment and the consequent full adaptation to that particular technological style might help explain why today a country like Japan finds it easier to embrace the new style and make the institutional changes required, than the USA.

16 As far as the mass production technological style that subtends these widely differing institutional and social arrangements there are no discernible differences, which serves to illustrate the vastly diverging range of alternatives opening before society at each critical phase.

17 P. F. Drucker, *Concept of the Corporation* (Mentor, NY, 1972).

18 This sort of two-tier arrangement can be seen as somewhat analogous to the third Kondratiev, when large producers hardly ever catered directly to consumers but rather, using the low-cost steel of the motive branches, concentrated their growth in large infrastructural works, heavy chemistry and equipment goods in the civil, mechanical and electrical engineering carrier branches, while electricity, small motors and power tools allowed deconcentrated production for consumer and other smaller-scale markets.

25

THE DYNAMO
AND THE COMPUTER

An historical perspective on the modern productivity paradox

Paul A. David *

Source: *The American Economic Review* 80(2) (1990): 355–61.

Many observers of recent trends in the industrialized economies of the West have been perplexed by the conjecture of rapid technological innovation with disappointingly slow gains in measured productivity. A generation of economists who were brought up to identify increases in total factor productivity indexes with "technical progress" has found it quite paradoxical for the growth accountants' residual measure of "the advance of knowledge" to have vanished at the very same time that a wave of major innovations was appearing — in microelectronics, in communications technologies based on lasers and fiber optics, in composite materials, and in biotechnology. Disappointments with "the computer revolution" and the newly dawned "information age" in this regard have been keenly felt. Indeed, the notion that there is something anomalous about the prevailing state of affairs has drawn much of its appeal from the apparent failure of the wave of innovations based on the microprocessor and the memory chip to elicit a surge of growth in productivity from the sectors of the U.S. economy that recently have been investing so heavily in electronic data processing equipment (see, for example, Stephen Roach, 1987, 1988; Martin Baily and Robert Gordon, 1988). This latter aspect of the so-called "productivity paradox" attained popular currency in the succinct formulation attributed to Robert Solow: "We see the computers everywhere but in the productivity statistics."

If, however, we are prepared to approach the matter from the perspective afforded by the economic history of the large technical systems characteristic of network industries, and to keep in mind a time-scale appropriate for thinking about transitions from established technological regimes to their respective successor regimes, many features of the so-called productivity paradox will be found to be neither so unprecedented nor so puzzling as they might otherwise appear.

I

My aim here simply is to convince modern economic analysts (whether perplexed by the productivity slowdown, or not) of the immediate relevance of historical studies that trace the evolution of techno-economic regimes formed around general purpose engines.[1] The latter, typically, are key functional components embodied in hardware that can be applied as elements or modular units of the engineering designs developed for a wide variety of specific operations or processes. Accordingly, they are found ubiquitously distributed throughout such systems when the latter have attained their mature, fully elaborated state. James Watt's (separate condenser) steam engine design springs to mind readily as an example of an innovation that fulfilled this technological role in the first industrial revolution. My particular line of argument will be better served, however, by directing notice to the parallel between the modern computer and another general purpose engine, one that figured prominently in what sometimes is called the "second Industrial Revolution" — namely, the electric dynamo. (But, see also Herbert Simon, 1986.)

Although the analogy between information technology and electrical technology would have many limitations if taken very literally, it proves illuminating nonetheless. Computer and dynamo each form the nodal elements of physically distributed (transmission) networks. Both occupy key positions in a web of strongly complementary technical relationships that give rise to "network externality effects" of various kinds, and so make issues of compatibility standardization important for business strategy and public policy (see my 1987 paper and my paper with Julie Bunn, 1988). In both instances, we can recognize the emergence of an extended trajectory of incremental technical improvements, the gradual and protracted process of diffusion into widespread use, and the confluence with other streams of technological innovation, all of which are interdependent features of the dynamic process through which a general purpose engine acquires a broad domain of specific applications (see Timothy Bresnahan and Manuel Trajtenberg, 1989). Moreover, each of the principal empirical phenomena that make up modern perceptions of a productivity paradox had its striking historical precedent in the conditions that obtained a little less than a century ago in the industrialized West, including the pronounced slowdown in industrial and aggregate productivity growth experienced during the 1890–1913 era by the two leading industrial countries, Britain and the United States (see my 1989 paper, pp. 12–15, for details). In 1900, contemporary observers well might have remarked that the electric dynamos were to be seen "everywhere but in the productivity statistics!"

II

At the turn of the century, farsighted engineers already had envisaged profound transformations that electrification would bring to factories, stores, and homes. But the materialization of such visions hardly was imminent. In 1899 in the United States, electric lighting was being used in a mere 3 percent of all residences (and in only 8 percent of urban dwelling units); the horsepower capacity of all (primary and secondary) electric motors installed in manufacturing establishments in the country represented less than 5 percent of factory mechanical drive. It would take another two decades, roughly speaking, for these aggregate measures of the extent of electrification to attain the 50 percent diffusion level (see my 1989 paper, Table 3, for estimates and sources). It may be remarked that, in 1900, an observer of the progress of the "Electrical Age" stood as far distant in time from the introduction of the carbon filament incandescent lamp by Edison, and Swann (1879), and of the Edison central generating station in New York and London (1881), as today we stand from comparable "breakthrough" events in the computer revolution: the introduction of the 1043 byte memory chip (1969) and the silicon microprocessor (1970) by Intel. Although the pace of the computer's diffusion in the business and public sectors of the industrialized societies during the past two decades has been faster than that recorded for the dynamo during its comparable early phase of adoption, it has been estimated that only 10 percent of the world's 50 million business enterprises today are using computers, and only 2 percent of the world's business information has been digitized (see Peter Lewis, 1989).

The history of electrification after 1900 (see I. C. R. Byatt, 1979; Thomas Hughes, 1983; Ryoshin Minami, 1987) lends considerable plausibility to the "regime transition thesis" of Christopher Freeman and Carlotta Perez (1990). They suggest that productivity growth has been sluggish, and very well might remain so because the emergence and elaboration of a new techno-economic regime based on computer and communications innovations (supplanting the mature, ossified Fordist regime of mass production) will, more than likely, be a protracted and historically contingent affair.

Certainly, the transformation of industrial processes by the new electric power technology was a long-delayed and far from automatic business. It did not acquire real momentum in the United States until after 1914–17, when regulated regional utility rates for electricity were lowered substantially in relationship to the general price level (see my 1989 paper: Table 4, Fig. 14), and central station generating capacity came to predominate over generating capacity in *isolated* industrial plants. Furthermore, factory electrification did not reach full fruition in its technical development nor have an impact on productivity growth in manufacturing before the early 1920s. At that time only slightly more than half of factory mechanical drive capacity had been electrified. (On the significance for derived productivity growth of attaining 50 percent diffusion, see my 1989 paper, Appendix A.) This was four decades after the first central power station opened for business.

The proximate source of the delay in the exploitation of the productivity improvement potential incipient in the dynamo revolution was, in large part, the slow pace of factory electrification. The latter, in turn, was attributable to the unprofitability of replacing still serviceable manufacturing plants embodying production technologies adapted to the old regime of mechanical power derived from water and steam. Thus, it was the American industries that were enjoying the most rapid expansion in the early twentieth century (tobacco, fabricated metals, transportation equipment, and electrical machinery itself) that afforded greatest immediate scope for the construction of new, electrified plants along the lines recommended by progressive industrial engineers (see Richard DuBoff, 1979, p. 142; and Minami, pp. 138–41). More widespread opportunities to embody best-practice manufacturing applications of electric power awaited the further physical depreciation of durable factory structures, the locational obsolescence of older-vintage industrial plants sited in urban core areas, and, ultimately, the development of a general fixed capital formation boom in the expansionary macroeconomic climate of the 1920s.

The persistence of durable industrial facilities embodying older power generation and transmission equipment had further consequences that are worth noticing. During the phase of the U.S. factory electrification movement extending from the mid-1890s to the eve of the 1920s, the "group drive" system of power transmission remained in vogue (see Duboff, p. 144; Warren Devine, 1983, pp. 351, 354). With this system (in which electric motors turned separate shafting sections, so that each motor would drive related groups of machines), the retrofitting of steam- or water-powered plants typically entailed adding primary electric motors to the original stock of equipment. While factory owners rationally could ignore the sunk costs of the existing power transmission apparatus, and simply calculate whether the benefits in the form of reduced power requirements and improved machine speed control justified the marginal capital expenditures required to install the group drive system, productivity accountants would have to reckon that the original belt and shaft equipment (and the primary engines that powered them) remained in place as available capacity. The effect would be to raise the capital-output ratio in manufacturing, which militated against rapid gains in total factor productivity (TFP) — especially if the energy input savings and the quality improvements from better machine control were left out of the productivity calculation.

This sort of overlaying of one technical system upon a preexisting stratum is not unusual during historical transitions from one technological paradigm to the next. Examples can be cited from the experience of the steam revolution (G. N. von Tunzelmann, 1978, pp. 142–43, 172–73). Indeed, the same phenomenon has been remarked upon recently in the case of the computer's application in numerous data processing and recording functions, where old paper-based procedures are being retained alongside the new, microelectronic-based methods — sometimes to the detriment of each system's performance (see, for example, Baily and Gordon, pp. 401–02).

Finally, it would be a mistake to suppose that large potential gains from factory electrification were obtainable from the beginning of the century onward, just because there were farsighted electrical engineers who at the time were able to envisage many sources of cost savings that would result from exploiting the flexibility of a power transmission system based on electric wires, and the efficiency of replacing the system of shafting and belts with the so-called "unit drive" system. In the latter arrangement, individual electric motors were used to run machines of all sizes (see Devine, pp. 362ff). The advantages of the unit drive for factory design turned out to extend well beyond the savings in inputs of fuel derived from eliminating the need to keep all the line shafts turning, and the greater energy efficiency achieved by reducing friction losses in transmission. Factory structures could be radically redesigned once the need for bracing (to support the heavy shafting and belt-housings for the transmission apparatus that typically was mounted overhead) had been dispensed with. This afforded 1) savings in fixed capital through lighter factory construction, and 2) further capital savings from the shift to building single-story factories, whereas formerly the aim of reducing power losses in turning very long line shafts had dictated the erection of more costly multistory structures. Single-story, linear factory layouts, in turn, permitted 3) closer attention to optimizing materials handling, and flexible reconfiguration of machine placement and handling equipment to accommodate subsequent changes in product and process designs within the new structures. Related to this, 4) the modularity of the unit drive system and the flexibility of wiring curtailed losses of production incurred during maintenance, rearrangement of production lines, and plant retrofitting; the entire power system no longer had to be shut down in order to make changes in one department or section of the mill.

Although all this was clear enough in principle, the relevant point is that its implementation on a wide scale required working out the details in the context of many kinds of new industrial facilities, in many different locales, thereby building up a cadre of experienced factory architects and electrical engineers familiar with the new approach to manufacturing. The decentralized sort of learning process that this entailed was dependent upon the volume of demand for new industrial facilities at sites that favored reliance upon purchased electricity for power. It was, moreover, inherently uncertain and slow to gain momentum, owing in part to the structure of the industry responsible for supplying the capital that embodied the new, evolving technology. For, the business of constructing factories and shops remained extremely unconcentrated, and was characterized by a high rate of turnover of firms and skilled personnel. Difficulties in internalizing and appropriating the benefits of the technical knowledge acquired in such circumstances are likely to slow experience-based learning. A theoretical analysis of an interdependent dynamic process involving diffusion and incremental innovations based upon learning-by-doing (see my paper with Trond Olsen, 1986) demonstrates that where the capital goods embodying the new technology are competitively supplied, and there are significant knowledge spillovers among the firms in the supplying industry, the resulting pace of technology adoption will be slower than is socially optimal.

III

The preceding review of the sources of "diffusion lags" bears directly on the relationship between the timing of movements in industrial productivity, and the applications found for electric power within the industrial sector. A somewhat different class of considerations also holds part of the explanation for the sluggish growth of productivity in the United States prior to the 1920s. These have to do more with the deficiencies of the conventional productivity measures, which are especially problematic in treating the new kinds of products and process applications that tend to be found for an emergent general purpose technology during the initial phases of its development. Here, too, the story of the dynamo revolution holds noteworthy precedents for some of the problems frequently mentioned today in connection with the suspected impact of the computer (see, Baily-Gordon; and Gordon-Baily, 1989): 1) unmeasured quality changes associated with the introduction of novel commodities; and 2) the particular bias of the new technology toward expanding production of categories of goods and services that previously were not being recorded in the national income accounts.

In the case of the dynamo, initial commercial applications during the 1890–1914 era were concentrated in the fields of lighting equipment and urban transit systems. Notice that qualitative characteristics such as brightness, ease of maintenance, and fire safety were especially important attributes of incandescent lighting for stores and factories, as well as for homes — the early electric lighting systems having been designed to be closely competitive with illuminating gas on a cost basis. Likewise, the contributions to the improvement in economic welfare in the form of faster trip speeds and shorter passenger waiting times afforded by electric streetcars, and later by subways (not to mention the greater residential amenities enjoyed by urban workers who were enabled to commute to the central business district from more salubrious residential neighborhoods), all remained largely uncaptured by the conventional indexes of real product and productivity.

Measurement biases of this kind persisted in the later period of factory electrification, most notably in regard to some of the indirect benefits of implementing the "unit drive" system. One of these was the improvement in machine control achieved by eliminating the problem of belt slippage and installing variable speed d.c. motors. This yielded better quality, more standardized output without commensurately increased costs (see Devine, pp. 363ff). Factory designs adapted to the unit drive system also brought improvements in working conditions and safety. Lighter, cleaner workshops were made possible by the introduction of skylights, where formerly overhead transmission apparatus had been mounted; and also by the elimination of the myriad strands of rotating belting that previously swirled dust and grease through the factory atmosphere, and, where unenclosed within safety screening, threatened to maim or kill workers who became caught up in them.

These more qualitative indirect benefits, however, came as part of a package containing other gains that, as has been seen, took the form of more readily quantifiable resource savings. Consequently, a significantly positive cross-section association can be found between the rise in the industry's TFP growth rate (adjusted for purchased energy inputs) during the 1920s, vis-à-vis the 1910s, and the proportionate increase of its installed secondary electric motor capacity between 1919 and 1929. Making use of this cross-section relationship, approximately half of the 5 percentage point acceleration recorded in the aggregate TFP growth rate of the U.S. manufacturing sector during 1919–29 (compared with 1909–19) is accounted for statistically simply by the growth in manufacturing secondary electric motor capacity during that decade (see my 1989 paper, Table 5, and pp. 26–27).

But, even that did not exhaust the full productivity ramifications of the dynamo revolution in the industrial sector during the 1920s. An important source of measured productivity gains during this era has been found to be the capital-saving effects of the technological and organizational innovations that underlay the growth of continuous process manufacturing, and the spread of continuous shift-work, most notably in the petroleum products, paper, and chemical industries (see John Lorant, 1966, chs. 3, 4, 5). Although these developments did not involve the replacement of shafts by wires, they were bound up indirectly with the new technological regime build up around the dynamo. Advances in automatic process control engineering were dependent upon use of electrical instrumentation and electro-mechanical relays. More fundamentally, electrification was a key complementary element in the foregoing innovations because pulp- and paper-making, chemical production, and petroleum refining (like the primary metals, and the stone, clay and glass industries where there were similar movements towards electrical instrumentation for process control, and greater intensity in the utilization of fixed facilities) were the branches of manufacture that made particularly heavy use of electricity for process heat.

IV

Closer study of some economic history of technology, and familiarity with the story of the dynamo revolution in particular, should help us avoid both the pitfall of undue sanguinity and the pitfall of unrealistic impatience into which current discussions of the productivity paradox seem to plunge all too frequently. Some closing words of caution are warranted, however, to guard against the dangers of embracing the historical analogy too literally.

Computers are not dynamos. The nature of man-machine interactions and the technical problems of designing efficient interfaces for humans and computers are enormously more subtle and complex than those that arose in the implementation of electric lighting and power technology. Moreover, information as an economic commodity is not like electric current. It has special attributes (lack of superadditivity and negligible marginal costs of transfer) that make direct measurement of its production and allocation very difficult and reliance upon conventional market processes very problematic. Information is different, too, in that it can give rise to "overload," a special form of congestion effect arising from inhibitions on the exercise of the option of free disposal usually presumed to characterize standard economic commodities. Negligible costs of distribution are one cause of "overload"; information transmitters are encouraged to be indiscriminate in broadcasting their output. At the user end, free disposal may be an unjustified assumption in the economic analysis of information systems, because our cultural inheritance assigns high value to (previously scarce) information, predisposing us to try screening whatever becomes available. Yet, screening is costly; while it can contribute to a risk-averse information recipient's personal welfare, the growing duplicative allocation of human resources to coping with information overload may displace activities producing commodities that are better recorded by the national income accounts.

In defense of the historical analogy drawn here, the information structures of firms (i.e., the type of data they collect and generate, the way they distribute and process it for interpretation) may be seen as direct counterparts of the physical layouts and materials flow patterns of production and transportation systems. In one sense they are, for they constitute a form of sunk costs, and the variable cost of utilizing such a structure does not rise significantly as they age. Unlike those conventional structures and equipment stocks, however, information structures per se do not automatically undergo significant physical depreciation. Although they may become economically obsolete and be scrapped on that account, one cannot depend on the mere passage of time to create occasions to radically redesign a firm's information structures and operating modes. Consequently, there is likely to be a strong inertial component in the evolution of information-intensive production organizations.

But, even these cautionary qualifications serve only to further reinforce one of the main thrusts of the dynamo analogy. They suggest the existence of special difficulties in the commercialization of novel (information) technologies that need to be overcome before the mass of information-users can benefit in their roles as producers, and do so in ways reflected by our traditional, market-oriented indicators of productivity.

Notes

* Discussions with Paul Rhode were particularly helpful early in the research. I am grateful for comments from Steve Broadberry, Jonathan Cave, Nick Crafts, among the participants in the Economic History Summer Workshop held at Warwick University, July 10–28, 1989; from Timothy Taylor; and from Shane Greenstein, Avner Greif, Edward Steinmueller, and other participants in the Technology and Productivity Workshop at Stanford, October 1989.

1 This paper draws upon material developed in a longer work — my 1989 paper.

References

Baily, Martin N. and Gordon, Robert J., "The Productivity Slowdown, Measurement Issues, and the Explosion of Computer Power," *Brookings Papers on Economic Activity*, 2:1988, 347–420.

Bresnahan, Timothy F. and Trajtenberg, Manuel, "General Purpose Technologies and Aggregate Growth," Working Paper, Department of Economics, Stanford University, January 1989.

Byatt, I. C. R., *The British Electrical Industry 1875–1914: The Economic Returns to a New Technology*, Oxford: Clarendon Press, 1979.

David, Paul A., "Computer and Dynamo: The Modern Productivity Paradox in a Not-Too-Distant Mirror," Center for Economic Policy Research, No. 172, Stanford University, July 1989.

——, "Some New Standards for the Economics of Standardization in the Information Age," in P. Dasgupta and P. L. Stoneman, eds., *Economic Policy and Technological Performance*, London: Cambridge University Press, 1987, ch. 7.

—— **and Bunn, Julie A.,** "The Economics of Gateway Technologies and the Evolution of Network Industries: Lessons from Electricity Supply History," *Information Economics and Policy*, Spring 1988, *4*, 165–202.

—— **and Olsen, Trond E.,** "Equilibrium Dynamics of Diffusion when Incremental Technological Innovations are Foreseen," *Ricerche Economiche*, October–December, 1986, *40*, 738–70.

Devine, Warren, Jr., "From Shafts to Wires: Historical Perspective on Electrification," *Journal of Economic History*, June 1983, *43*, 347–72.

DuBoff, Richard, *Electrical Power in American Manufacturing 1889–1958*, New York: Arno Press, 1979.

Freeman, Christopher, and Perez, Carlotta, "The Diffusion of Technical Innovations and Changes of Techno-economic Paradigm," in F. Arcangeli *et al.*, eds., *The Diffusion of New Technologies*, Vol. 3: *Technology Diffusion and Economic Growth:*

International and National Policy Perspectives, New York: Oxford University Press, forthcoming 1990.

Gordon, Robert J. and Baily, Martin, N., "Measurement Issues and the Productivity Slowdown in Five Major Industrial Countries," OECD, Directorate of Science, Technology and Industry, Paris, June 1989.

Hughes, Thomas P., *Networks of Power: Electrification in Western Society, 1880–1930*, Johns Hopkins University Press, 1983.

Lewis, Peter H., "The Executive Computer: Can There Be Too Much Power?," *New York Times*, December 31, 1989, p. 9.

Lorant, John H., *The Role of Capital-Improving Innovations in American Manufacturing during the 1920's*, New York: Arno Press, 1966.

Minami, Ryoshin, *Power Revolution in the Industrialization of Japan: 1885–1940*, Tokyo: Kinokuniya Co., 1987.

Roach, Stephen S., "America's Technology Dilemma: A Profile of the Information Economy," *Special Economic Study — Morgan Stanley*, New York, September 22, 1987.

——, "White Collar Productivity: A Glimmer of Hope?," *Special Economic Study — Morgan Stanley*, New York, September 16, 1988.

Simon, Herbert A., "The Steam Engine and the Computer: What Makes Technology Revolutionary?," *EDUCOM Bulletin*, Spring 1986, *22*, 2–5.

von Tunzelmann, G. N., *Steam Power and British Industrialization to 1860*, Oxford: Clarendon Press, 1978.

26

FAST STRUCTURAL CHANGE AND SLOW PRODUCTIVITY CHANGE

Some paradoxes in the economics of information technology

Christopher Freeman and Luc Soete[1]

Source: *Structural Change and Economic Dynamics* 1(2) (1990): 225–42.

Introduction

This paper sets out some of the apparent contradictions between fast structural change as a result of the emergence and introduction over the last decade of 'new' powerful information technologies and the continuous slow productivity growth with which most OECD countries appear to be confronted. That apparent productivity paradox has been the subject of an increasing number of studies and analyses following Solow's remark that computers could be seen everywhere except in the productivity statistics.[2]

In this paper we do not intend to review the by now extensive literature[3] on this subject, but sketch out some of our own arguments (Freeman and Soete, 1987a; OECD, 1988) based on the importance of the structural change features associated with the realization of the productivity **potential** of new information technologies.

To do so we first discuss briefly the nature and characteristics of technological change in information technology. We argue that the latter can indeed be identified as a pervasive, generic technology with often dramatic potentials for productivity gains with respect to all production factors. In Section 2 we then discuss at greater length some of the employment and macro-economic structural change implications. Finally, in Section 3, the more micro-economic, organizational implications are discussed.

1. New information technologies:
a pervasive new technology system

When considering which technologies are having the most significant impact on OECD economies and are likely to continue to do so in the near future, possibly at an even larger scale, there is probably widespread agreement that new 'Information' technologies are at the core of the debate. These technologies, often referred to as 'Information Technology' (IT) comprise the combination of a large number of technical and organizational innovations in electronic computers, software engineering, control systems, integrated circuits, and telecommunications, which have made it possible to collect, generate, analyse, and diffuse large quantities of information at minimal cost.

Despite the sometimes dramatic breakthroughs in other areas of technological change, such as biotechnology or new materials, the impact of these changes is generally assumed not to have affected (yet) most economies to the same extent and to be unlikely to do so in the near future.

The widespread recognition and singling out of IT as being at the centre of the present rapid rate of technological change in most OECD countries is not surprising. As Flamm observes:

> the price of information processing and computing power . . . has fallen at a roughly continuous rate of some 25 per cent per year in nominal terms, almost thirty per cent per year in real terms, over the last three decades. By way of contrast, the commodity price most affected by technical progress during the first industrial revolution—cotton cloth—fell at a rate of roughly 3.4 per cent per year, a full order of magnitude more slowly, during the late eighteenth and early nineteenth centuries.
>
> (Flamm, 1987)

It is this dramatic decline in information costs which is at the core of the pervasive and all-encompassing impact of IT. The continuous fall in these costs has led to the further opening up of areas of application, far beyond those initially considered to be the most likely to be impacted. Thus whereas the discussion in the 1950s and early 1960s was primarily in terms of 'automation', 'advanced mechanization' in Einzig's (1957) words, whereby the focus was on new process technologies reducing in the first instance man-hours per unit of output and leading to dedicated mass and flow production systems, the discussion today is in terms of the application and 'process' impact of IT in service activities such as office 'automation', material and capital-saving processes such as inventory control, as well as the creation of new products or the opening up of new areas of 'trade'.

As one of us argued at greater length at the OECD's 25th Anniversary symposium (Freeman, 1986), it is preferable to talk about 'information technology' rather than 'automation' because it reflects more accurately the convergence in the late 1970s and 1980s of computer technology with related developments in telecommunications. This combination is extremely powerful, both in terms of the economic and of the technical advantages, and it means that the actual and potential applications of the new technology go far beyond those which were customarily considered in the 1950s debates on automation. A second reason for preferring the concept of 'information technology' rather than automation is fundamental to the consideration of the employment issue. 'Automation' tends to carry with it the connotation of an exclusive concern with *process* innovation. Although labour-saving technical change is most certainly one of the major economic advantages of the new technology, this aspect has been greatly over-emphasized at the expense of other equally important characteristics. Thus, information technology has already demonstrated very great advantages in material-saving, energy-saving, and capital-saving applications as, for example, in the reduction of the number of mechanical and electronic components in a wide range of engineering products from cash registers to machine tools, or in the reduction of stocks of components, materials, work-in-progress, and finished products, through far more efficient systems of inventory control and better communications with suppliers and distributors alike. More fundamentally, the emphasis on labour-saving process automation technology tends to overshadow the development of new *products* and of new *services* associated with the new technology.

Before discussing some of these 'potential' implications on the basis of some of the stylized features of these new 'information technologies', we turn to a brief historical review of the emergence and growth of electrical and electronics technology and the structural changes brought about in most OECD countries.

1.2. The historical setting: from 'electricals' to 'micro-electronics'

Apart from the chemical industry, the electrical industry has undoubtedly been one of the most important industrial 'carriers' of technological advance in the twentieth century. It grew out of a cluster of electro-mechanical innovations, following the discovery and industrial exploitation of electricity at the end of the nineteenth century. Technical developments in electrical power-generating equipment, engines, basic active and passive components (thermionic valves, cathode-ray tubes, resistors, capacitors, etc.) and industrial components (such as transducers, actuators, controls) brought about the development of a cluster of industries producing capital equipment for the generation of electricity, the transformation of electricity into motion, the control of industrial processes and, later on, even the transmission of information and new consumer durables (such as radios and television sets).

Within these clusters of electro-mechanical technologies, it is fair to say that technical change proceeded at a relatively high rate and that new products and applications emerged almost continuously. Closely related to this rapid rate of technical change, and essential to the growth of the electrical industry, demand growth was stimulated by five main factors:

(i)   the substitution of electricity for steam-power as a source of industrial energy;
(ii)   the increasing mechanization of processes of production, increasing electricity requirements per unit of output and, consequently, the demand for electrical capital equipment;
(iii) the development of an electricity grid for domestic use;
(iv)   the introduction of new electrical consumer goods (such as lamps, radios, refrigerators, and washing machines); and
(v)   the development of a telecommunications network.

Considering the overall growth pattern and development of industrialized countries this century, especially since the First World War, the electrical industry has clearly been essential to their internal adjustments and dynamics. Quite high rates of growth were made possible by the relative consistency between patterns of change in the 'technological system', the productive (economic) structure, and social relations. The appearance and growth of electrical technologies, like other technical changes, increased labour productivity through the modernization of production, also led to the creation of a wide span of new commodities. On the 'macro-social' level electrical technologies proved vital to the establishment of 'Taylorism' and 'Fordism' in production processes. The wage basket (and more generally the consumer basket) underwent dramatic change, with electricity-based commodities (radios, TVs, washing machines, refrigerators, telephones, etc.) becoming major demand items, while real wages showed a long-term upward trend. It could be argued that one industrial counterpart of the 'Keynesian era' was technical progress in the electrical industries (another being automobiles).

Economically speaking, the 'virtuous circle' between expansion of demand and improvements in production can be described as technical progress roughly matching relatively high rates of growth of labour productivity with income elasticities of demand for the corresponding products well above one. Internationally, the spread of best practice techniques of production and US patterns of consumption throughout the OECD countries allowed the rapid growth of international trade both in electrical equipment and in electrical consumer durables. The 'foreign trade multiplier' associated with such rapidly growing trade flows permitted and/or enhanced high domestic growth rates.

However, the structure and dynamism of the electrical industry were to be affected most radically by the emergence of a completely new technological system based on electronics. Electronics is, of course, a form of electrical system (all electrical systems derive from flows of electrons in the form of an electrical current). To the extent that electronic circuits handle much smaller currents than traditional electric currents and incorporate 'active' components that are capable of modifying the flow of electricity, electronics has a quite distinct technological boundary.

Since the invention of the computer and the transistor in the 1940s, radical and rapid technological developments have produced a wide variety of new devices based first upon semiconductor technology replacing the thermionic valve and secondly upon the digital processing of information. Just as traditional electro-mechanical technologies were founded upon the scientific discoveries of classical physics in electricity, electronics arose largely out of the scientific development of quantum physics, particularly the analysis of solid state atomic properties.

The progress in semiconductor technology has been characterized by Dosi (1984) as corresponding to a 'natural' trajectory of technological advance. This trajectory of technical progress was characterized by the miniaturization of electronic components, decreasing costs per component, faster processing of electrical signals and enhanced reliability, plus a few ancillary dimensions such as electrical noise immunity, frequency range, and heat dispersion. It is widely accepted that these semiconductor developments were at the heart of the rapid rate of technological change in electronics revolution; they affected not only every subsector of the electrical industry but indeed the whole spectrum of manufacturing industries. Three semiconductor innovations were fundamental: the solid state amplifying transistor (1948) which could increasingly be substituted for the thermionic valve, thus instantly reducing the size and energy consumption per active electronic component; the integrated circuit (1960–1) which facilitated the manufacture of large numbers (up to several thousands) of components on a single chip; and the microprocessor (1971) which constituted an integrated circuit of such complexity that it could embody a complete processing unit (i.e. a miniaturized but complete computer).

User sectors were affected by this *micro*electronics 'revolution' in three ways. First, the amount of information which could be processed was vastly increased while the time required was reduced. This not only implied straightforward quantitative improvements but also facilitated such new operations as the handling in real time of complex sets of information which had been technically and/or economically infeasible with previous technologies. Secondly, it brought about a drastic cut in the cost per unit (bit) of processed information. Thirdly, and following on from the previous two points, the economic incentive to adopt increased significantly and so did the number of adopters.

These characteristics contributed to the elevation of microelectronics to a 'pervasive' technology, affecting practically all sectors of the economy. As Freeman *et al.* (1982) observe:

It is indeed difficult to think of an industry or occupation which will not be affected by microelectronics. The former Conservative Party spokesman on technology, Ian Lloyd, could think of only a few; among them were the makers of top hats, handloom weavers in the Outer Hebrides and psychoanalysts. He may well have been wrong about at least two of these.

(Freeman *et al.*, 1982, 119)

1.3. From 'microelectronics' to 'IT'

These dramatic cost-cutting and scaling-down functions of electronics have led many to regard the speed of technical change in microelectronics as 'revolutionary'. Following Freeman (1986), the most important characteristics of present-day information technologies could be summarized as follows:

(i) A continuing very high rate of technical change in the cluster of electronics-related industries themselves, as well as in a wide range of applications. Underlying this process is the continuing dramatic improvement in large-scale integration of electronic circuits, and the continuing fall in costs which this permits. The revolutionary developments in integrated circuits have their parallel in *communication* technology, where fibre optics have made possible similar drastic improvements in costs and performance. The convergence of these technological advances means that the capability for communicating, processing, and storing information is still improving very rapidly and is becoming even cheaper. This leads to the development of new types of data banks and information services and has profound consequences for the *integration* and *control* of productive activities. The capability which IT confers to integrate design, manufacture, procurement, sales, administration, and technical service in any enterprise means that the tendency is towards computer-integrated manufacturing systems and all-electronic office systems, but it is very unlikely that this implies either an 'unmanned' factory or a 'paperless' office. Rather is it more likely that there will be a wide variety of 'configurations' of machines and equipment.

(ii) The capability which IT confers to improve the *quality* of products, processes, and services. On-line monitoring and control of quality of output has already led to dramatic improvements in industries as diverse as colour television and passenger cars. It leads to capital-saving, labour-saving, materials-saving, and energy-saving improvements in production processes since it reduces the numbers of rejects and wasted components both for intermediate and final output.

(iii) The capability which IT confers to link up networks of component and material suppliers with assembly-type firms (as in the automobile industry) or with service firms (as in the hotel and catering industries). An equally important function which IT can perform is with respect to linkages between procedures, wholesalers, and retailers. In both cases it is the combination and convergence of communications with computer technology which permits savings in inventories at all levels in the system, especially in work-in-progress, and a more rapid and sensitive response to daily changes in consumer demand (as, for example, IKEA in the furniture industry or Benetton in the clothing industry). Furthermore, the new flexibility and speed of communication systems and their links with data banks creates the possibility for a wider variety of new 'Value-Added Networks' (VANS) and new types of information service.

(iv)   Much greater flexibility in rapid model changes and design changes. Some analysts have referred to this phenomenon as 'economies of scope' replacing to some extent 'economies of scale'. Whereas previous assembly line and flow production systems were relatively inflexible and based on the continuous replication of vast numbers of standardized, homogeneous products, the new flexibility conferred by IT permits more rapid changes of tooling and dies, so that small production runs become economic and the prospects for small and medium-sized firms are greatly changed, reducing the barriers to entry and permitting major changes in industrial structure.

(v)   A reduction in electro-mechanical components and in various stages of component transformation as a result of the redesign of products and processes. This leads to substantial savings of materials and energy, as well as to a process of structural change which involves the loss of jobs in some sectors of metals and metal goods and an increase in jobs in some sectors of the electronics component industry, electronic products, and producer services.

(vi)   As a result of the changes outlined above and in particular as a result of the continuing high rate of technical change in the microelectronics and computer industries themselves, a strong tendency towards a more rapid rate of product and process change and more intense technological competition. In turn, this strengthens the demand for new skills and services in design, development, software engineering, and microelectronics products generally, affecting both in-house skill and employment profiles and the growth of new services, information flows, and supplies of equipment. The more rapid rate of product and process change is itself facilitated and stimulated by the diffusion of computer-aided design systems.

(vii)   All of this means that IT is not only affecting the structure of the economy in terms of new industries and services but is also affecting profoundly the internal structure and management of all enterprises and the relationships between them.

Although almost everyone would accept most aspects of this description of the actual and potential impact of IT, there is still much doubt about the structural and macro-economic implications of information technology. For example, it is often said that the output and employment of the IT sector amounts to less than 10 per cent of manufacturing production even in the leading countries. How then can it be so important? But more importantly, and as indicated above with respect to the so-called Solow-paradox, there is at least until now little evidence of any 'dramatic' productivity gain either at the macro or individual firm level. In the following two sections we go somewhat deeper into these arguments. In the next section we turn first to the employment and productivity implications of the diffusion of this new technology.

2. Information technology, employment, and productivity

A great deal has been written on this issue since the employment–technology relationship first began to be systematically examined about 200 years ago. This is neither the place for an examination of the various schools of thought that have emerged, nor for an exhaustive summary of the more recent literature in this area, which is considerable (see, for example, Freeman and Soete, 1985 and 1987a, de Wit, 1989). Rather, we take three major conclusions emerging from this literature as the point of departure.

First, over the long term, technological progress is one of the main, if not the main, driving forces behind rising levels of growth and efficiency, employment, standards of living, and social welfare. Secondly, a satisfactory analysis of employment impacts must consider the macro-system as a whole: loss of jobs from one firm, industry, or region may be compensated or more than compensated by new jobs elsewhere in the system. Movement of jobs across national frontiers is one special aspect of this redistribution process. Finally, the process of employment 'compensation' is neither automatic nor instantaneous and, unless ameliorated, it can be painful for society.

There is actually a wider area of agreement than is sometimes assumed between 'neo-Schumpeterians', who put the main emphasis on structural change, and those who put the main emphasis on compensation mechanisms. All economists accept that there are substantial time-lags and institutional rigidities affecting the adjustment process, and (at least since Ricardo) that the adjustment of employment to new technologies and new patterns of investment is a complex process, which does not necessarily or immediately tend towards a full employment dynamic equilibrium. The difference lies primarily in the relative emphasis on factor price mechanisms on the one hand and the pattern of technical, structural, and institutional change on the other. We argue that the diffusion of major new technologies represents a shift to new production functions rather than an equilibrating movement of factor substitution based on relative factor prices. Moreover, we have stressed that it is the drastic fall in the costs of the storage, process-ing, and transmission of information which is the most dynamic influence rather than the relative prices of traditional factor inputs. This means that although the new technologies are potentially both labour-saving and capital-saving their employment impact cannot be precisely foreseen.

We shall argue in this section, however, that if the productivity gains, both in capital and labour productivity, are clearly apparent, this offers a favourable prospect for a wave of employment generating new investment, based on the provision of a range of new products and services, as well as on the more efficient production of old ones. As Keynes (1930) recognized in his *Treatise on Money*, the Schumpeterian explanation of major invest-ment booms is still the most convincing and this offers the best hope of attaining high levels of employment and sustained non-inflationary growth. The issues currently in the forefront reflect the two-edged sword nature of the new technologies. At one end of the spectrum there is the *fear* of new technologies unleashing rising levels of unemployment. Associated with this are related concerns about changing composition of employment, leaving a segment of the labour force which is poorly equipped with new skills either disenfranchised or condemned to low-wage, unstable work. The other end of the spectrum emphasizes *hope*; it sees rapid diffusion of new technologies as the principal way out of the unsatisfactory pace of job generation that has been experienced in Europe since the early 1970s.

Cutting across these polar views one central concern relates to the speed and difficulties of adjustment. For some observers, the process of adjust-ment to technological change, although not instantaneous, nevertheless does not pose any more serious challenges than do adjustments need arising from other changes such as a shift in trade patterns. For others as for us, the slow and painful pace of adjustment is the main issue. New technologies have changed the rules of the game, we would argue, and require fundamental changes in societal attitudes and institutions, without which the fear of rising unemployment levels is real and the hope of a major stimulus to jobs mere wishful thinking.

We have argued in the previous section that information technology is so pervasive and has so many new features that it has indeed 'changed the rules of the game' throughout the system. It is the latest hurricane in Schumpeter's successive 'creative gales of destruction'. Whereas incremental innovations do not give rise to major problems of structural adjustment, the introduc-tion of a radically new technology system gives rise to many such problems. It does so because it requires a redesign and new configuration of the capital stock, a new skill profile in the labour force, new management structures and work organization, a new pattern of industrial relations, and a new pattern of institutional regulation at national and international levels—for example, in relation to the global telecommunications network or traded information services.

In this section we shall argue that it is precisely this break with past methods of organizing design, production, distribution, and marketing which leads to problems of structural adjustment and in some cases to a slow-down in productivity growth. Furthermore, we shall argue that the employment-generating potential of the diffusion of the new technologies can only be fully unleashed as the organizational and institutional problems associated with any such wave of technical change are satisfactorily resolved. We discuss first of all the productivity 'paradox' and then turn to the issue of organizational, institutional, and social change.

The main conclusions are that the new technologies can make a major contribution to employment generation if—and this is a big if—the macro policy stance is appropriate, and consistent micro-structural policies and steps are undertaken, by government, various social groups, and society at large, to realize the employment potential inherent in these technologies. It is concluded that not adopting new technologies would be detrimental to job growth, especially when a region or nation lags behind while others forge ahead. Hence, the screening of new technologies and their speedy diffusion become key areas of policy concern.

Historically, productivity growth has played the major role in raising income and employment levels. A significant part of productivity growth, in turn, comes from technological progress. Hence technological progress is a key element determining long-term job growth and social progress. The importance of technological progress then depends on three factors: first, the degree of the productivity augmentation potential; secondly, the degree of its diffusion in the economy; finally, whether the potential is actually realized in practice. As to the first issue, we have already considered the nature of the new technologies currently being experienced and how pervasive they potentially are. This section focuses on the importance of the productivity potential, the role technological change plays in generating this potential, and how the potential gets translated into employment levels. It also discusses some aspects of the diffusion rate, particularly in relation to the cross-sector diffusion of pervasive technologies.

Why is it that aggregate productivity growth rates have declined since at least the early 1970s at the same time as OECD economies are widely believed to be in the midst of a major wave of technological change? Among the major possible explanations we shall briefly consider:

(i)   Lags in the diffusion of productivity gains based on technological progress from the 'leading edge' (sometimes 'high tech' industries) to the rest of the economy.

(ii)   Lags in the translation of *potential* productivity gains into *actual* productivity gains arising from organizational, social, and institutional factors.

(iii) The possibility that the *real* productivity gains are underestimated because of the inability of a present measurement system to record

some of the *quality* improvement associated with information technology and biotechnology. This might be especially true in the service
sector where the output measurement problem has been a source of
concern for a long time.

(iv) Disequilibria associated with the uneven pattern of technical change
and the varied institutional response at national level may lead to a
slow-down in world economic growth, which feeds back in adverse
effects on productivity.

It should be noted first that in the sectors in which new technologies
have diffused significantly, productivity growth has indeed been higher than
for the rest of industry. A recent EEC study separates the sectors covering
electrical equipment and electronics, information technology, automated
office equipment and precision instruments, and chemicals and pharmaceuticals from other industries (EEC, 1985). These sectors could be used
as a rough proxy for the high-tech sector (various problems encountered in
defining the high-tech sector are treated later in the article). Measured over
the period 1973–81, total factor productivity for this high-tech sector was
significantly higher than for the manufacturing sector as a whole (Table 1),
particularly in the leading industrial countries.

One of the difficulties in assessing the effects of technical change in
various sectors of industry lies in the classification systems. Thus, although
the category of 'high-tech' industries often used to separate R and D-
intensive industries gives a very rough approximation of those areas most
affected by the wave of technical change, it conceals many anomalies. Thus,
for example, the aggregation of 'electrical equipment' with 'electronics' can
be particularly misleading. Whilst the electronic industries are undoubtedly
the leading edge of the new wave of information technology, 'electrical

Table 1 Total Factor Productivity 1973/1981–3 (Average annual growth rate).

	Total manufacturing	*High-tech sector (1)*
Belgium	2.6	2.6
Germany	1.5	2.7
France	2.0	2.4
Italy	1.7	3.8
Netherlands	1.5	0.9
UK	0.1	1.7
Europe—6	1.4	2.6
USA	0.2	1.2
Japan	2.9	8.1

Note: High-tech (strong demand sector): electrical equipment and electronics; information
technology, automated office equipment and precision instruments; and chemicals and
pharmaceuticals.
Source: EEC (1985).

equipment' includes some sectors which are manufacturing traditional electro-mechanical products with a contrasting pattern of employment trends, productivity trends, investment, R and D, and output growth. A statistical 'average' of these two sectors does not therefore convey the true picture of what has been happening in the electronics industry itself. Similar considerations apply, for example, to the divergent trends between various sectors of the chemical industry.

Particular interest therefore attaches to those measurements of productivity trends which separate the *electronic* industries from the other manufacturing sectors. Based on post-war evidence but limited to the UK, Fig. 1 brings together the growth rates in labour and capital productivity in eighteen industrial sectors for which 'official' capital stock estimates are available. Growth in labour productivity is represented on the vertical axis and growth in capital productivity on the horizontal axis. What is particularly striking here is that the electronic industries are the *only* ones to show a growth in capital productivity, as well as a high rate of increase in labour productivity.

Whilst total factor productivity has continued to increase in most OECD countries, although at a slower rate than in the 1960s, capital productivity has been declining in most sectors in many countries. The fact that the computer industry in particular runs counter to this trend is of some interest. It offers the hope that as computerized capital equipment diffuses through the rest of the economy, it may be possible to realize much greater gains in both labour and capital productivity. This hope rests on the fact that the IT industries are the main users of their own technology (Fig. 2) and therefore may to some extent foreshadow the shape of things to come.

This raises the whole question of the diffusion process across sectors of the economy. With a pervasive technology, such as IT, this is one of the main problems of structural adjustment. It is hardly surprising that the computer industry itself is able to make the most effective use of its own technology, or that the electronic components and instrument industries are close behind. They have after all been accumulating know-how about both hardware and software for several decades. They have a pool of skilled labour and competent management which is thoroughly familiar with the problems. They have also been investing heavily in R and D, in software and in new capital (Fig. 2).

Nor is it really surprising that manufacturing and service industries which have little previous experience with this radically new technology should experience innumerable difficulties and 'snarl-ups' as they attempt to use it. They frequently lack the necessary skills as well as the management competence. It is no longer a question of an incremental improvement in an established trajectory with which they were familiar but of a break with the past. In his book on *The Advent of the Automatic Factory*, written in 1952, John Diebold showed astonishing foresight about these problems. Whilst

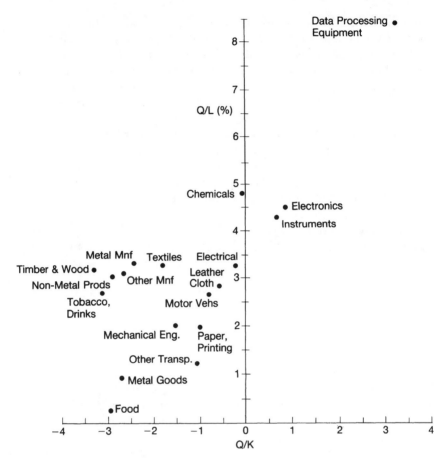

Figure 1 Post-war growth in labour (*Q/L*) and capital productivity in the UK manufacturing sectors (1918–84 by SIC sector). *Q*, net output; *L*, employees in employment; *K*, official SCO capital stock estimates. All figures are average annual growth rates. Level of disaggregation is the highest one available in terms of Capital stock estimates, except for electronics, which has been estimated on the basis of Soete and Dosi (1983). All sectors have been normalized to their 1980 SIC definition.

Source: Soete (1987).

others were predicting mass unemployment and de-skilling because of computerized automation, Diebold pointed to the *new* skills that would be required, especially in design and maintenance, on an enormous scale. He also pointed out that computerization involved the *redesign* of the whole range of *products* as well as *processes.* This would not be possible without changes in *structures* of most firms to facilitate the flow of information between R and D, design, production, and marketing. This in turn would require changes in the structure of management to facilitate *horizontal*

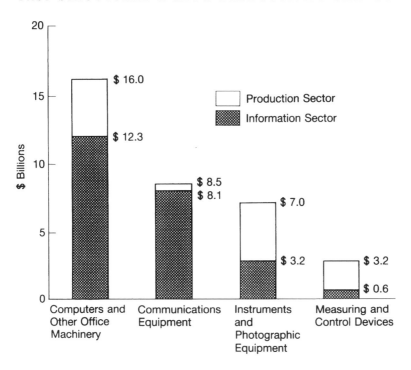

Figure 2 Uses of high-tech equipment. (Allocation of private domestic final shipments in *1982*).
Source: Roach (1986).

movement of people and information. The simple availability of computer hardware was only the most elementary first step and the whole process would be a matter of decades not years.

Events have proved Diebold completely right. It is only in the 1970s and 1980s that computerized automation in the form of FMS, CIM, CAD, etc., has really taken off (Fig. 3) and it has a very long way to go. This applies *a fortiori* to computerization in the service sector. In this complex diffusion process it is necessary to adapt computer technology (especially software) and telecommunication technology to the *specific* needs of each sector and each enterprise. All managers of information systems and of software consultancy firms would confirm that this is far from Lockett (1987) in his study of information technology innovations in a large multinational company, who pointed out that an intense dialogue between the provider and the user was an essential condition of the successful implementation of IT innovations. An experimental 'R and D' approach was necessary.

These findings broadly confirm the earlier findings of innovation research in the 1960s and 1970s (Rothwell, 1984)—that the understanding of user

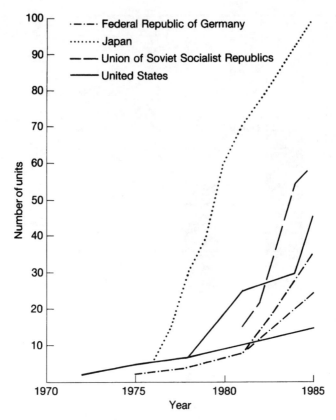

Figure 3 Growth of FMS in the Federal Republic of Germany, Japan, the USSR, and the United States (Units). ·—·—· Federal Republic of Germany; ········ Japan; —— Union of Soviet Socialist Republics; —— United States.

Note: The two curves for the United States apply to a wider and a stricter definition, respectively, of FMS. For the Federal Republic of Germany, an interval estimate is given for the number of FMS installed at the end of 1984.

Source: Ayres (1987).

needs was the most important condition for successful innovations. However, in the case of information technology this requirement of 'user-friendliness' is exceptionally important and attended by special problems. In the first place, the user often finds great difficulty in conceptualizing and specifying the precise nature of the requirement. Secondly, the provider rarely has the possibility of understanding this requirement immediately from the outside. Thirdly, the technology itself is still extremely fluid. Finally, the introduction of IT frequently brings with it the need for reorganization of management itself and/or production systems. It is to this last issue that we turn now.

3. By way of conclusion: organizational and social factors in moving from potential to actual productivity gains

An historical analogy with the diffusion of electric power may be useful here. The key technical innovations were made between the 1860s and 1880s. With the establishment of effective generating and transmission systems in the 1880s and 1890s (which also involved a wave of social, legal, and organizational innovations) the emphasis shifted to diffusion of applications of electric power throughout the economy both in industry and households. In this phase, although technical innovations continued at a high rate and big improvements were made in the available hardware, the key problem was the organizational change in firms, change in skills, factory layout, and in attitude of engineers, managers, and workers. Warren Devine (1983) has described this change in words which might also be applied to the diffusion of computerized automation.

> Replacing a steam engine with one or more electric motors, leaving the power distribution system unchanged, appears to have been the usual juxtaposition of a new technology upon the framework of an old one. . . . Shaft and belt power distribution systems were in place and manufacturers were familiar with their problems. Turning line shafts with motors was an improvement that required modifying only the front end of the system. . . . As long as the electric motors were simply used in place of steam engines to turn long line shafts, the shortcomings of mechanical power distribution systems remained.

It was not until after 1900 that manufacturers generally began to realize that the indirect benefits of using unit electric drives were far greater than the direct energy saving benefits. Unit drive gave far greater flexibility in factory layout, as machines were no longer placed in line with shafts, making possible big capital savings in floor space. For example, the US Government Printing Office was able to add forty presses in the same floor space. Unit drive meant that trolleys and overhead cranes could be used on a large scale, unobstructed by shafts, countershafts, and belts. Portable power tools increased even further the flexibility and adaptability of production systems. Factories could be made much cleaner and lighter, which was very important in industries such as textiles and printing, both for working conditions and for product quality and process efficiency. Production capacity could be expanded much more easily. The full expansionary benefits of electric power on the economy depended, therefore, not only on a few key innovations in the 1880s, but on the development of a new paradigm or production and design philosophy. This involved the redesign of machine tools and much other production equipment. It also involved the relocation of many plants and industries, based on the new freedom conferred by electric power transmission and local generating capacity.

The analogy between electrification and computerization is a useful one because it illustrates the long time scales involved in any type of technical change which affects a very broad range of goods and services, where many products and processes have to be redesigned to realize the full potential of the new technology. Perez (1987) has pointed out that the dominant technologies of a particular period actually become an integrated web since they are developed together to take advantage of a specific range of new technical and economic opportunities, whether related to electricity and cheap abundant steel, or to electronic computers, cheap integrated circuits, and universal cheap telecommunications. As the techno-economic paradigm crystallizes and develops, the interrelated advantages become more and more apparent and the logic of the new system comes to seem self-evident. A flow of new technical and organizational innovations helps to resolve the main problem and bottlenecks. But in the early stages there are great difficulties and risks in adopting the new equipment because it is not yet an integrated system, and adoption involves a piecemeal trial-and-error process of learning by doing and using.

These considerations mean that it would be quite unreasonable to expect sudden increases in productivity in sectors far removed from the new technology. Such increases could be expected to emerge only after a fairly long process of familiarization, of developing customized equipment, new skills, and new management attitudes and structures. Here we stress primarily the cross-sectoral aspect of the diffusion process, the learning by doing and by interacting (Lundvall, 1988) and the time-lags involved in moving from the *potential* productivity gains of a radical new technology system to their *actual* realization.

The case of Japan is a particularly interesting one in this context. Japanese industry and the Japanese government were quick to realize the importance of cross-sectoral diffusion of information technology (Freeman, 1986). It was apparently in Japan that the expression 'mechatronics' was coined and a law on the fusion of mechanical and electronic technologies was passed as early as 1971. This gave incentives and encouragement to the applications of IT in mechanical engineering and other metal-working industries. Kodama (1985) attributes much of the extraordinary Japanese success in robotics, machine tools FMS, and other sectors to this 'fusion' approach to new technology and has illustrated it from Japanese R and D statistics, which permit the identification of this cross-industry development. This approach has apparently also been important in service industries and in construction, accounting in part for the exceptional performance of the Japanese financial services and the growing world-wide competitive challenge of the construction industry. It is reported that large 'intelligent' buildings now under construction in Tokyo have an electronic 'content' as high as 30 per cent. We are long familiar with the fact that the electronic content of a fighter aircraft or a battleship may be as high as 50–75 per cent, or in the case of machining systems 25–50 per cent, but the notion of the 'electronic content' of 'smart' buildings or financial systems is still somewhat unfamiliar. This illustrates very nicely the whole point about cross-sector diffusion.

Success stories are of course not confined to Japan. Although that country does appear to have been particularly successful, there are many examples from the United States and Europe. Some of the Nordic countries offer interesting cases. The Finnish forest industry is one such case, where user–producer collaboration has led to successful applications of process control instrumentation. The Swedish engineering industries have matched Japan in the production and use of robotics. The relative success of both the Nordic model in the implementation of IT and of the Japanese model suggest that there is no unique national or cultural peculiarity about this type of technical change, although of course national cultures do affect the nature and speed of institutional response to new technological opportunities. This point is confirmed by the experience of Japanese companies operating in the USA and in Europe. Productivity gains have been made in overseas plants which are similar to those in Japan. What is particularly striking is that these are sometimes achieved almost entirely by the introduction of Japanese management techniques, working practices, and organizations rather than by new hardware, as, for example, in the GM/Toyota collaboration.

There are, however, interesting counter-examples. Prais (1986) reports the case of a Japanese subsidiary operating in the UK which experienced much lower productivity levels in its UK plant than in Japan, although the technology and the hardware were identical. The problem was the lack of skills in electronic maintenance work. This illustrates the main point which we have tried to emphasize in this discussion of productivity slow-down: the translation of *potential* to *actual* productivity gains depends on a complex social process of adjustment involving training, re-skilling, combining new with old technologies, the development of new management and organizational structures, new patterns of work-force collaboration, and other social changes. The availability of new hardware and new fixed investment is of course an essential factor but it is only a first step, and should often actually be *preceded* by an intense process of training and reorganization to get the best results. Although they are very different in some respects, the Japanese and Nordic 'models' have in common an intense process of work-force involvement and consultation, together with extensive training and re-training.

There are various possible explanations why the more recent technological advances in information technology have not made the impact on productivity growth many had expected. In line with some of the recent arguments advanced by David (1989), we have stressed here the importance of the many structural changes including institutional and social changes required for the full realization of the productivity gains associated with the application of new information technologies.

Notes

1 We are grateful to an anonymous referee for critical comments.
2 Made in his book review of Cohen and Lysman, *Manufacturing Matters.*
3 For more detail we refer the reader to our own contributions to the OECD Conference on this subject held in June 1989, the Proceedings of which will be published shortly. (Freeman, 1989 and Soete *et al.*, 1989).

References

AYRES, R. V. (1987). 'Future Trends in Factory Automation', IIASA Working Paper WP 87-2, Luxemburg.

BARRAS, R. (1986). 'Towards a Theory of Innovation in Services', *Research Policy,* **15,** no. 4, 161–73 (August).

BRUNETTA, R. (1987). 'Contribution to the Experts' Groups on Social Aspects of New Technologies' (mimeo).

DAVID, P. (1989). 'Computer and Dynamo: The Modern Productivity Paradox in a Not Too-Distant Mirror'. OECD Conference on the Productivity Paradox, EEC (1985). *Euroeconomy,* no. 25 (September).

DIEBOLD, J. (1952). *Automation: The Advent of the Automatic Factory.* New York, Van Nostrand.

DOSI, G. (1984). *Technical Change and Industrial Transformation.* London, Macmillan.

DUNGAN, P. and YOUNGER, A. (1985). 'New Technology and Unemployment: A simulation of Macro-economic Impacts and Responses', *Journal of Policy Modelling,* 595–619.

EEC (1985), *Euroeconomy,* no. 25 (September).

EINZIG, P. (1957). *Economic Consequences of Automation,* Seeker and Warburg, London, 1957.

FLAMM, K. (1987). *Targetting the Computer.* Washington, DC. The Brookings Institute.

FREEMAN, C., CLARK, J., and SOETE, L. (1982). *Unemployment and Technical Innovation, A Study of Long Waves and Economic Development.* London, Francis Pinter.

—— (1986). 'The Challenge of New Technologies'. OECD 25th Anniversary Symposium, Paris.

—— (1989). 'The Nature of Innovation and the Evolution of the Production System', paper presented at the OECD Conference on 'Science, Technology and Economic Growth', June 5–9, Paris.

—— and SOETE, L. (1985). 'Information, Technology and Employment. An Assessment', Brussels, IBM—Europe.

—— and SOETE, L. (Eds.) (1987a). *Technical Change and Full Employment.* Basil Blackwell, London.

—— —— (1987b). 'Factor Substitution and Technical Change', in C. Freeman and L. Soete (eds.), *Technical Change and Full Employment.* Basil Blackwell, Oxford.

KATSOULACOS, Y. (1986). *The Employment Effect of Technical Change: A Theoretical Study on New Technology and the Labour Market.* Brighton, Wheatsheaf Books Ltd.

KEYNES, J. M. (1930). 'A Treatise on Money', vol. 2, London, Macmillan.

KODAMA, F. (1985). 'Mechatronics Technology as Japanese Innovation: A Study of Technological Fusion'. Graduate School for Policy Science, Soitama University, Tokyo.

LEONARD, J. (1986). 'Technological Change and the extent of Frictional and Structural Unemployment'. National Academy of Sciences Panel on Technological Change and Employment (June).

LOCKETT, M. (1987). 'The Factors Behind Successful IT Innovations', Oxford, Templeton College (mimeo).

LUNDVALL (1988). 'Innovation as an Interactive Process: User-Producer Relations', in Dosi *et al., Technical Change and Economic Theory*, London, Pinter Publishers.

MADISON, A. (1987). 'Growth and Slowdown in Advanced Capitalist Economies: Techniques of Quantitative Assessment', *Journal of Economic Literature*, 639–98 (June).

NELSON, R. (1981). 'Research on Productivity Growth and Productivity Differences Dead Ends and New Departures', *Journal of Economic Literature* (September).

—— and WINTER, S. (1982). *An Evolutionary Theory of Economic Change.* Cambridge, Harvard University Press.

OECD (1984). *Employment Outlook.* Paris.

—— (1985). 'Employment and Technology'. Manpower and Social Affairs Committee MAS(86)6.

—— (1986). 'The Supply Side in the OECD's Macro-economic Model', *OECD, Economic Studies*, no. 6, 75–131.

—— (1987*a*). 'Total Factor Productivity: Some Causes and Implications for Its Slowdown'. Working Party No. 1 of the Economic Policy Committee, CPE/WP1(87)4.

—— (1987*b*). *Employment Outlook.* Paris.

—— (1987*c*). 'Technological Change and the Job Turnover Process: Some Preliminary Explorations with the Job Turnover Database'. Experts' Meeting on Technology and the Job Turnover Process, 28–29 September, Paris.

—— (1987*d*). 'Technical Change and Employment: Macro Effects, Joint ESD/SME INTERLINK Simulations'. Prepared for the Meeting of a Group of Experts on the Social Aspects of New Technologies.

—— (1988). 'New Technologies in the 1990s, A Socio-economic Strategy'. Paris.

PASINETTI, L. (1981). *Structural Change and Economic Growth: A Theoretical Essay on the Dynamics of the Wealth of Nations.* Cambridge, Cambridge University Press.

PEREZ, C. (1985). 'Micro-electronics, Long Waves and World Structural Change: New Perspectives of Developing Countries', *World Development*, **13**, no. 3, 441–63.

PEREZ, C. (1987). 'The New Technologies: An Integrated View', SPRV, University of Sussex, Brighton, English Translation; originally in *La Rercera revolucion Industrial.* Ed. C. Ominami, Buenos Aires, Argentina.

PRAIS, S. J. (1986). *Educating for Productivity: Comparison of Japanese and French Schooling and Vocational Preparation.* London, National Institute of Economic and Social Research.

67

RADA, J. F. (1986). 'Information Technology and Services', in O. Giavini (ed.), *The Emerging Service Economy*. Oxford, Pergamon Press.

ROACH, S. (1986). Macro realities of the information economy. In: R. Landau and N. Rosenberg (eds) *The Positive Sum Strategy; Harnessing Technology for Economic Growth*. Washington NAS, National Academy Press, Washington.

ROTHWELL, C. (1984). 'Company Employment Policies and New Technology in Manufacturing and Service Sectors', in Warner, M. *Microprocessors Manpower and Society: A Comparative, Cross-National Approach*, Aldershot: Gower.

—— (1987). 'The Newly Emerging Information Technology Sector', in C. Freeman and L. Soete (eds.), *Technical Change and Full Employment*. Basil Blackwell, Oxford.

—— and DOSI, G. (1983). *Technology and Employment in the Electronics Industry*, London, Pinter Publishers.

—— VERSPAGEN, B., PAVITT, K., and PATEL, P. (1989). 'Recent Comparative Trends in Technology Indicators in the OECD area' Workshop OECD, International Seminar on Science, Technology and Economic Growth, June 5–8.

STONEMAN, P. (1983). *The Economic Analysis of Technological Change*. Oxford, University Press.

WIT, de, R. (1989). On the Modelling of Employment and Technological Change, MERIT Research Memorandum 89–030.

27

INFORMATION

An emerging dimension of institutional analysis

William H. Melody

Source: *Journal of Economic Issues* XXI(3) (1987): 1313–39.

The functioning of society depends upon information and its effective communication among society's members. Information, and the means for its communication, have a fundamental and pervasive influence upon all institutions. The economic characteristics of information and communication systems affect the nature of the information that is generated and the conditions under which it is used and interpreted.

In the broadest sense, the social, cultural, political and economic institutions in any society are defined according to the characteristics of the shared information within those institutions. In the narrower economic sense, perhaps the most important resource determining the economic efficiency of any economy, industry, production process, or household is information and its effective communication. The characteristics of information define the state of knowledge that underlies all social and economic processes. They provide the foundation upon which explanations of social reality are structured.

Information is as central to the study of the functioning of economic systems as is air to the study of the functioning of the human body. Yet throughout the history of economic thought, information has received relatively little direct attention. Like air, information generally is assumed to be absolutely essential, but nevertheless pervasive, costless, and seldom worthy of special attention. If, in some circumstances, information is artificially restricted, economists of all stripes generally conclude that this is undesirable. It is assumed, sometimes naively, that expanded information cannot help but improve the efficiency of any economic system.

In neoclassical theory, the fundamental assumption of "perfect information" or "perfect knowledge" typically is noted so that the analysis can proceed quickly to the important economic issues.[1] Institutional economists do not assume away the information issues, and on occasion draw attention to information deficiencies as part of explanations of economic problems. But even they only rarely have looked more deeply into the significance of information structures in society for the evolution of economic and social institutions. It is apparent that the structure of economic and political institutions in society creates serious information problems. Yet very little is known about the relations between information structures and other institutional characteristics, or how changing information structures affect the rise and fall of particular institutions.

It is indeed ironic that a profession that devotes itself to the pursuit of knowledge about the economic system has paid so little attention to the significance of information as a crucial factor affecting the performance and direction of change within the system. This article examines the conceptof information within the context of the institutionalists' perspective. It illustrates the role that information has played in the work of selected leading institutionalists and argues that greater attention to the role of information offers promising possibilities for enriching the study of economic institutions. It also examines how new information and communication technologies are being applied in a manner that is likely to fundamentally alter the existing structure of economic institutions and to stimulate the development of a wide variety of "information markets" in a new rapidly growing sector of the economy.

In the economics literature the terms "information" and "knowledge" tend to be used interchangeably. To many people the term "knowledge" implies the notion of truth, or at least a higher level of intelligence or expertise. Such usage is not intended here. The terms will be treated essentially as synonyms meaning "to be aware," that is, to be informed. "Knowledge" sometimes denotes an aggregation of a range of different types of information, as in "the stock of knowledge," thus permitting information to be examined as having both a stock and a flow dimension. Communication adds an important spatial dimension to information and often introduces fundamental changes in the structure of information flows and the quality of the information communicated.

Information and institutions

An institution, as succinctly described by Walton Hamilton "connotes a way of thought or action of some prevalence and permanence, which is embedded in the habits of a group or the custom of a people" [Hamilton 1968, p. 84]. Its dynamic character is vividly captured by Wesley Mitchell: "as ways of working shift, they will engender new habits of thinking, which will crystallize into new institutions, which will form the cultural setting for further cumulative changes in ways of working, world without end" [Mitchell 1936, p. 310].

70

Institutions reflect the patterns of interaction between and among individuals, acting within or between groups, or through formal organizations. Patterns of interaction may be determined by custom, law, organizational role or some other guideline for behavior. It is the patterns of interaction that maintain an institution, and changes in patterns of interaction bring about changes in institutions. The essence of this interaction is the communication of information.

Both the definition and structure of all institutions are significantly influenced by the state of information. Institutions are created from the development of a desire to share information, thereby cultivating patterns of interaction, that is, communication or information exchange. Institutions become structured in particular ways to achieve desired internal and external information flows. The institutional structure changes when, for whatever reason, the information flows change. Institutions die when the incentive or the ability to maintain the information flows and communication links ceases. Institutions can be described according to their informational characteristics, and one way to study institutional change would be to focus directly upon an institution's changing information structure.

Equally significant for economic analysis is the fact that institutions also generate information for the external environment that is employed by other institutions and individuals for decision making. For any particular institutional structure in society, there will be an associated information structure that will influence how that society functions. Some institutional structures will provide conditions and incentives conducive to the creation and diffusion of more information than others. The structure and quality of information is likely to change as a result of changes in institutional structure. If institutional change is desired, it may be necessary to change the information structure as a prerequisite to, or as an essential aspect of effective institutional change.

The importance of information flows and communication patterns to the establishment and maintenance of particular institutions has been well understood by policy makers since earliest times. Trade routes and communication links were deliberately designed to maintain centres of power and to overcome international comparative disadvantages. Britain still benefits substantially from its historically established communication links with its former colonies, long after the empire's formal demise. Universal telephone service was adopted as a policy objective in the Communications Act of 1934 to encourage economic and social interaction within the United States and to promote nationhood. The mandate of the Canadian Broadcasting Corporation includes a requirement to promote national unity. The European Economic Community is attempting to foster a new European identity by promoting increased communication and information exchange (including trade) among its member countries, in an attempt to ward off growing economic and cultural penetration of Europe, primarily by the United States.

Those factors that influence information and communication structures are central to the study of all institutions, and sometimes are controlling with respect to economic institutions.

The dimensions of information

For purposes of economic analysis, information can be viewed from a number of different perspectives. One is as an overall enviromental condition, that is, the general descriptive information that provides the institutional background for economic decisions, such as news about political and social developments, the state of war and peace in the world, the crime rate, general employment levels in the economy, et cetera. Although such information is not tied directly to most individual decisions on economic matters, this background information provides assurance that the general institutional environment is reasonably stable. It provides the confidence for individuals to go ahead with decisions that will be made using other more direct and detailed information, and narrower and more precise decision criteria that are applicable only in a reasonably stable institutional environment.

The total body of this type of information provides a certain protection that minimizes the risk of short-term disaster. It is essentially a public good. It represents the broad information structures upon which the economy builds. It is a type of information "commons." The size and structure of the information commons may vary substantially among societies and among groups and sectors within societies. In developed countries, the information commons tends to be much more extensive than in developing countries. The characteristics of the information commons, including the type and structure of the information generated, and the terms and conditions for access to it are matters of fundamental importance to the study of institutional change. A change in the size and structure of the information commons may be an essential component of plans designed to promote desired changes in the institutional structure of society.

Many decisions require only instrumental, ephemeral information of no lasting decisional significance—for example, the price of strawberries in the local market today. Although any particular piece or bit of such information is relevant and applicable only to a single, specific short-run decision, it may be necessary to establish a communication system by which such information can be supplied on a continuing basis, as through stock quotation or press wire services, television and radio stations, the telephone network. The structure of the communication system established, in turn will cultivate particular patterns of interaction—that is, institutionalized behavior. In this instance the structure of the communication system established for supplying the information may influence the essential character of the institutional interactions more than the information itself.

Some information is of more lasting value and is stored in the memories of people, in books, on film, on computer tapes and in other ways. From a societal standpoint the accumulation of information represents the total stock of knowledge. It is increased as a result of improvements in science and technology, developments in the arts and letters, an improved understanding of the workings of society, and in other ways. From this perspective, technology can be represented as a particular application of stored information in the total stock of knowledge. New technical artifacts simply represent the physical embodiment of a particular set of information drawn from the state of knowledge. Considerable research is directed toward creating new information that will add to society's stock of knowledge. The accumulation of science and technological information in particular is seen as a stepping-stone to the accumulation of capital and economic growth. Most education and training involves an attempt to diffuse portions of the existing stock of knowledge throughout society.

The most significant application of the concept of information is with respect to the long-run accumulation and diffusion of knowledge in society. Its direct connection to the economic problem of the long-run accumulation of capital is through the concept of technology. If capital accumulation is stimulated by the application of new technologies, then the accumulation of information is at the heart of the capital accumulation process. In like manner, information is directly connected to the economic concern for the long-run diffusion of wealth and income. The diffusion of knowledge through education and training is not just a type of analysis where the information diffusion happens to run parallel to the diffusion of wealth. The diffusion of knowledge is an essential component of the process of diffusing wealth and promoting economic development.

It is of course necessary to note that not all information contributes to the stock of knowledge. But neither does all investment contribute to the stock of capital. There are crucial structural and qualitative aspects of both concepts that require careful consideration.

The concept of information also provides a common ground for relating economic issues to the social, political, and cultural aspects of institutions. Information is often a component of social, political, and cultural analysis, and where it is not, a manageable extension of the analysis often can capture it. The major difficulty that has persisted has been in linking up economic concepts with those of the other social sciences. The concept of information not only can enrich more narrowly based economic analysis, but also can provide a link to the other social sciences.

Information in the evolution of economic thinking

It is not possible to provide here a comprehensive review of the treatment of "information" in the history of economic thought. However an overview of selected landmark and illustrative applications will provide an appropriate historical context for addressing current issues.

Adam Smith, Karl Marx, and the classical school of economists were primarily concerned about the long-run accumulation of capital in a dynamic economic system and its implications for society. Although the concept of information was seldom used as a focal point for their analyses, the implications of information and communication systems upon economic institutions and economic growth were recognized frequently. In his classic explanation of how the division of labor is limited by the extent of the market, Smith noted the influence of the communication system as a crucial factor in determining the extent of the market, and thereby the division of labor: "As by means of water-carriage a more extensive market is opened to every sort of industry than water-land carriage alone can afford it, so it is upon the sea coast, and along the banks of navigable rivers, that industry of every kind naturally begins to subdivide and improve itself."[2]

In Smith's analysis of economic development he recognized that the diffusion of knowledge through the learning process was the cornerstone of development. The development of particular skills was essential to the division of labor. This information process would stimulate an increase in the productive powers of labor and the accumulation of capital.

Marx made frequent reference to the role of communication systems in the evolution of capitalism. In *Grundrisse*, he stated:

> the more production comes to rest on exchange value, hence on exchange, the more important do the physical conditions of exchange—the means of communication and transport—become for the costs of circulation. Capital by its nature drives beyond every spatial barrier. Thus the creation of the physical condition of exchange—of the means of communication and transport—the annihilation of space by time—becomes an extraordinary necessity for it.[3]

Marx frequently drew attention to the fact that improvements in the means of communication facilitate competition among workers in different localities and turn local competition into national. He argued that the opportunities created by the development of transport and communication facilities tended to drive capitalism in the direction of ever more remote markets until a world market is reached. He even foreshadowed the development of markets in information itself:

> Institutions emerge whereby each individual can acquire information about the activity of all others and attempt to adjust his own accordingly, e.g., lists of current prices, rates of exchange, interconnections between those active in commerce through the

mails, telegraphs, etc. (the means of communication of course grow at the same time). This means that, although the total supply and demand are independent of the actions of each individual, everyone attempts to inform himself about them, and this knowledge then reacts back in practice on the total supply and demand.[4]

In contrast, the neoclassical school, in attempting to tighten up its analytical apparatus, established the assumption of "perfect information" or "perfect knowledge" in neoclassical theory, thereby restricting their frame of reference to static analysis, freezing technological options and the state of knowledge. The fundamental dynamic issues of the long-term accumulation of capital and economic growth over time, and under conditions of changing information, technology, and institutions were simply excluded from consideration.

It should be noted that there have been attempts to break out of the straitjacket of neoclassical theory by relaxing its most suffocating assumption of perfect information, while still retaining its basic analytical structure. For example, there has been a recognition that neoclassical theory depends crucially on the characteristics of the structure of property rights that have been assumed [Demsetz 1967]. Efficient markets must be supported by an efficient system of property rights. Unfortunately the usual solution is to assume a perfect market in tradeable property rights. In addition, Kenneth Arrow, Kenneth Boulding, Friedrich von Hayek, Fritz Machlup, Jacob Marschak, George Shackle, Herbert Simon, Jack Hirshleifer, Donald Lamberton and others have exposed further weaknesses and limitations of neoclassical theory arising from its assumption of perfect information. These critiques, coming primarily from neoclassical economists, have painted neoclassical theory further and further into the corner as a unique theory, so abstracted from reality as to be of little, if any relevance.[5] Nevertheless, the neoclassical school continues to perform more and more elegant intellectual pirouettes in its attempts at theoretical restoration of the perfect information assumption.

Institutional economists and most Keynesians have carried on in the tradition of Smith, Marx and the classical economists. They too examine the long-term development of the economy within analytical frameworks where issues of information and communication in the economy are recognized as significant aspects of the institutional structure. Imperfect information forms an integral part of Keynesian analysis. For example, Keynes's explanation of wage rigidity rested primarily on the fact that labor would rely on information of wage-rate experience (that is, historical information) in negotiations for future wage-rates, not on perfect information about future labor markets. Keynesian analysis often considers the deficient, real world information that decision makers actually rely on as an important factor in the analysis. Similarly, business cycle theorists from all schools of economic thought have recognized the crucial influence of lagged information on current decisions as a determinant of the course of economic development.

In addressing the long-term dynamics of capitalism, Joseph Schumpeter focused upon the "creative destruction" of technological change as a primary force bringing about change in economic, social, and political institutions. He spawned a growing field of research directed to explaining innovation and diffusion processes in the evolution of the economy, in which the diffusion of information plays a significant role, for example, through patents. This has led to the study of science and technology policies that might promote the accumulation of new knowledge that will stimulate the invention and innovation of new technologies.[6] Although this line of research is not often associated with institutional economics, it is operating within the same theoretical framework.

For the most part, institutional economists have tended to treat information and communication in much the same manner as the classical economists and the Keynesians. Where and when it has been revealed as a significant factor in the analysis it has been recognized and incorporated. Veblen, for example, emphasized that consumer preferences were learned and conditioned by the information environment, and that the conditions of supply were primarily determined by the institutional implications of technical change. He rejected the fundamental assumptions in neoclassical theory with respect to information as applied to both demand and supply in establishing his overall analytical framework for institutional economic analysis. Within this general overall analytical framework, the accumulated and shared information within the institutional structure of society becomes a major determinant of the conditions of demand and supply.

John R. Commons extended the analysis to encompass institutional reform through government regulation, that is, "collective action in restraint, liberation, and expansion of individual action [Commons 1934, p. 73]. But effective regulation requires information with respect to the potential implications of various reform possibilities and standards of regulation. Although Commons was directly involved in the design of many social reforms, and painstakingly gathered substantial empirical information as a basis for those reforms, he did not really focus directly upon the state of information as a key factor in his institutional analysis. Nevertheless, it must be observed that many of the social reforms arising from Commons's research had the effect of expanding the information available to less powerful groups in society, thereby improving their negotiating power.

For most of the current generation of institutionalists, the structure of information in society is not a major issue directing their research, although information deficiencies do arise reasonably frequently as part of explanations for inequalities in society. For a few, information has become more central. For example, Philip A. Klein has concluded that concentrated corporate wealth and power corrupts the flow of information to the general public. This prevents the real "emergent values" of the majority from arising and a "higher efficiency" level in the economy from being achieved. Klein's institutional reform centers on the information structure in society so that the nation's decisionmaking is more informed and more sensitive to the real values of the majority of consumers [Klein 1985].[7]

Harold A. Innis

Harold A. Innis was one of the few economists to attempt a full integration of evolutionary economics and information and communication into a social science based institutional analysis.[8] His early work in the 1920s on the economic history of Canada showed how the westward expansion of Canada was influenced by an extension of the transport and communication system to meet political and economic objectives [Innis 1923]. His next work showed how the economic development of Canada was influenced by the demand for furs in Europe, Canada's unique geographical characteristics, and the drive of technology to exploit the fur resource [Innis 1956].

He then turned to the implications of the development of mechanized communication, beginning with printing, publishing, and mass communication via radio. He showed how the enourmous expansion of a commercially based printing press, and an emphasis on freedom of the press, had tended to support institutional changes such as the growth of monopolies, the entrenchment of biased viewpoints and the extension of compulsory education. He argued that these developments tended to intensify nationalism, constrain freedom of speech, and resist the power of thought. The press and radio broadcasts to the world, he argued, do not address the individual or facilitate dialogue.

Finally Innis broadened his scope of inquiry to a study of the history of communication in the development of civilizations. He focused particularly on the role communication systems have played in extending the power of "empires." He argued that in any society the media of communication greatly influences the forms of social organization and thereby the patterns of individual association. New competing communication media alter the forms of social organization, create new patterns of association, develop new forms of knowledge, and often shift the centers of power.

In his books *Empire and Communications* and *The Bias of Communication* Innis observed that any medium of communication is "biased" in its tendency to permit control over extended periods of time or over extended geographical space [Innis 1964; 1972]. He argued that communication and information systems used in ancient civilizations such as parchment, clay, and stone were durable and difficult to transport. These characteristics are conducive to control over time, but not over space. These systems are time-biased. Paper is light, less durable, and easily transportable with reasonable speed. It is spatially biased; it permitted administration over great distances, and therefore, the geographical extension of empires.

In cultural terms, time-biased media are associated with traditional societies that emphasize custom, continuity, community, the historical, the sacred, and the moral. They are characterized by stable, hierarchical social orders that tend to stifle individualism as a dynamic for change, but permit individualism in the rich expressiveness of language and the range of human emotion. Time-biased communication systems are found in societies with rich oral traditions or with sophisticated writing technologies where access is limited to a privileged few.

Space-biased communication and information systems, for example, the modern media of print, telephone, radio and television, have an orientation toward the present and the future, the expansion of empires, an increase in political authority, the creation of secular institutions and the growth of science and technical knowledge. They are characterized by the establishment of systems of information exchange and mass communication that are extremely efficient, but which cannot convey the richness, diversity, and elasticity of the oral tradition.

Innis concluded that the particular technology of communication and information systems, depending upon their bias, tended to confer monopolies of authority and knowledge either on religion, through sacred order and moral law, or on the state, through the technical order and civil law. An overemphasis, or monopoly of either time- or space-biased modes of communication was the principle dynamic of the rise and fall of empires. Such a bias toward either time or space produced instability in society. A stable society was possible only with the development of mechanisms that preserved a balance between the time and space orientations.

Innis was unique among his contemporaries in recognizing the high degree of interdependence between economic institutions and communication and information systems. He noted that communication patterns and information flows are central to economic development. He argued that communication technologies are the building blocks for most other technologies in the economic system. At the same time he recognized that economic incentives and market forces have powerful influences on communication patterns and information flows, which cannot be ignored in any realistic analysis of communication and economic development [Melody, Salter and Heyer 1981, Chap. 1].

In recent years there have been only a few economists working directly at the intersection of economics and communication and information institutions. Leaders among these include Herbert I. Schiller and Dallas W. Smythe. Schiller has documented many of the evolutionary changes in social institutions that are beginning to unfold as the new information and communication technologies are introduced and has examined the relations between changing information and communication institutions and economic and political developments [Schiller 1981]. Smythe, a pioneer in the exploration of the economics of communication, has drawn particular attention to the role of the mass media in creating and conditioning consumer preferences and in molding public opinion and has examined its significance for economic theory of all kinds.[9] Smythe also has examined the implications of U.S. domination of the information and communication environment in Canada for Canadian economic dependency, Canadian collective consciousness, and the development of economic policy that contains desired "cultural screens" [Smythe 1981].

Information and markets

The concept of information in institutional analysis is not discrete, standing alone or alongside the economic concepts. Rather it is an integral part of most economic concepts used by institutionalists. Information is an important dimension of other concepts, including such key concepts as "technology," "consumer preference," and, as has been shown above, the fundamental concept of "institution." Economists ignore the information dimension of these concepts at their peril, as it may be crucial for the effective application of the more familiar economic concepts.

This can be illustrated by reference to one of the most important concepts in economic analysis, that is, the "market." Throughout history, the notion of the market has preoccupied economists. Different schools of economic thought conceive of market relations differently, but a concern for the nature of market relations and their implications always has rested at the very heart of economics.

The general definition of a market is the provision of exchange opportunities between buyers and sellers. Without exchanges, or transactions, there is no market. The rate of exchange is the market price, which is determined by the conditions of supply and demand. Certain aspects of the market can be examined as an abstract exercise in logic by assuming that the only matter of significance is a single exchange price at a moment in time, and then varying the number of buyers and sellers—and quantities supplied and demanded—under conditions where each has perfect information and is maximizing short-run profit. This grossly oversimplified analysis, typical of neoclassical theory, tells us something about the nature of market exchanges, but it also leaves out a lot. It focuses on a few surface characteristics of markets and a method of calculation, ignoring the institutional foundation of the market and many important structural aspects of markets, all of which are essential to preparing the ground for the ultimate market exchanges.

An exchange can only take place if there is a commodity, or service, to be traded. Trade requires ownership, that is, enforceable property rights in the commodity being traded. The specific characteristics of property rights in tradeable commodities have varied significantly over the last several centuries and do so today among different countries, and even among localities within countries. The notion of property rights, as C. B. MacPherson has demonstrated, embodies a large collection of specific rights that define the terms and conditions for the use and exchange for property [MacPherson 1978]. It is a dynamic concept subject to ongoing change, as current debates in many countries relating to changes in patent and copyright laws demonstrate. The vast majority of goods and services that are exchanged do not carry with them total freedom for the owner of the property to do with it whatever he or she pleases. Zoning regulations, product safety standards, and cultural norms illustrate some of the constraints on the terms and conditions of trade.

This is an area where the work of Commons is so instructive. Examining more deeply the concept of the market exchange, Commons enriched it by treating it as a social relation rather than a statistical artifact. He defined the social relation as a "transaction," rather than a simple exchange, thereby capturing a sense of the real world participants in the exchange as something more than abstract entities. The participants were "going concerns," engaged in the exchange of ownership rights in accordance with a set of "working rules." The working rules specified a system of rights and obligations for citizens in their transactions with others. Much of Commons's research was directed to gathering detailed information about the nature and determinants of "transactions." Then economic problems could be addressed by taking legal or other steps to change the underlying structure of rights and obligations embodied in working rules and ownership. Commons was working at the institutional foundation of markets rather than focusing on surface manifestations.

Commons's analysis may have been enriched if he had paid more attention to the information dimension of his concepts, because differences in the informational aspect of the neoclassical concept of "exchange" and Commons's concept of "transaction" are significant. The information associated with a market "exchange" in neoclassical theory is essentially limited to price information. That is the key, if not the only factor governing the exchange. The market "transaction" involves much more information that is not readily available, and therefore not recognized by the concept of exchange. Although Ayres is certainly right in criticizing the "obsession of our science with price theory," one of the difficulties of digging deeper into the institutional foundations of economic concepts is that the information aspects tend to become more significant, but also often more difficult to assess [Ayres 1944].

The historic debate in economics between the relative merits of the market versus central planning as the best mechanism for allocating resources most efficiently in society hinges upon the role attributed to information and communication. Hayek's seminal 1945 article, "The Use of Knowledge

80

in Society," cogently presented the case for the superiority of the market. He stated:

> The various ways in which the knowledge on which people base their plans is communicated to them is the crucial problem for any theory explaining the economic process. And the problem of what is the best way of utilizing knowledge initially dispersed among all the people is at least one of the main problems of economic policy—or of designing an efficient economic system.[10]
>
> [Hayek 1945, p. 520]

The system that is most efficient, argued Hayek, depends "mainly on the question under which of them we can expect that fuller use will be made of the existing knowledge" [Hayek 1945, p. 521]. The knowledge that is needed is the overwhelmingly massive amount of detailed unorganized information with respect to the particular circumstances of individual buyers and sellers. Such information cannot hope to be captured in time, if at all, to facilitate coordinated central planning. The beauty of the price system is that it is a mechanism for capturing and communicating all this detailed unorganized information that reflects the myriad of individual buyer and seller, day-to-day decisions under continuously changing circumstances.

Economists cannot disregard the "unavoidable imperfection of man's knowledge and the consequent need for a process by which knowledge is constantly communicated and acquired" [Hayek 1945, p. 530]. Argued Hayek, "To assume all the knowledge to be given to a single mind in the same manner in which we assume it to be given to us as the explaining economists is to assume the problem away and to disregard everything that is important and significant in the real world" [Hayek 1945, p. 530].

Most neoclassical economists marvelled at the triumph of the market, but rejected Hayek's advice. Having accepted the fact of real world information deficiencies to shoot down the central planning option as horribly imperfect, most neoclassical economists have fled from the challenge of examining information deficiencies in real world market systems, preferring to maintain the idealistic perfect information assumption. This of course begs the real issue that Hayek raised. To the best of my knowledge, there has been no serious testing of Hayek's information hypothesis, either by neoclassical or institutional economists, although the work of Machlup can be seen as offering potentially relevant insights on this issue [Machlup 1980–1984].

Hayek assumed perfect knowledge on the part of individual buyers and sellers with respect to their own individual alternatives, preferences, circumstances, and ability to maximize their own best interests. He relaxed the perfect knowledge assumption only with respect to the knowledge that individual buyers and sellers would have about the behavior of all other buyers and sellers or about the complex set of market interrelations in the economy. But he also assumed that individual supply and demand would be unaffected by developments about which the individual sellers and buyers had no information. Thus, he assumed that individual demand was independently determined, and not influenced by the demand of others or any other external events.

The problem Hayek addressed then was how to use this known "perfect information" that individuals had about their own circumstances most efficiently to allocate resources in the economy. But the advantage Hayek claims for the market only applies to a condition of perfectly competitive markets. When markets are imperfect, individuals do not have sufficient information to know what will best serve their own interests. Boulding makes the point well.

> It is one thing to look at a price tag and to know that any amount can be bought or sold at this price. It is quite another thing to discover a demand function, which is a set of *possible* prices and *possible* quantities, only one of which is given in present experience. Thus making what seems like a simple extension of the model from perfect markets to imperfect markets actually involves us in an information problem of first magnitude. We move from a situation where the information required for the making of a rational decision is a simple number such as a price, given by simple observation, to a situation where the information required is a set of functional relationships which are *not* given by simple observation, because what needs to be known is not what *is* but what *might be*. Of course, what needs to be known for a rational decision is always what "might be." In the case of perfect competition, however, the happy situation prevails that what might be can be deduced immediately from what is at the moment. In the case of imperfect competition this is not so. In one case we are driving a straight road and can easily project our present direction for miles ahead; in the second case we are driving a twisting mountain track where we cannot see more than a few feet round the bend, and where the position of the moment tells us very little about where we might be next week.
>
> [Boulding 1960, underscoring in the original]

Moreover, even if the prices in imperfect markets did capture the perfect knowledge by individual buyers and sellers with respect to their individual circumstances, those market prices would not bring about an efficient allocation of resources. Under monopoly conditions, for example, this information would simply result in a monopoly price. In imperfect markets, a requirement for an optimal allocation of resources would be that prices not be set on the basis of this limited set of perfect knowledge by individual buyers and sellers.

In addition, Hayek's assumption about independent atomistic decisionmaking based on individual preferences made in a vacuum, and uninfluenced by other individuals, institutions, and developments in the economy, is necessary to keep his market alternative from being defeated by the same information complexity problem that he attributes to central planning. In addition, Hayek does not address the issue of coordinating non-price information, a common function for social insitutions; nor does he entertain the possibility that in some circumstances collective decisions may yield better results for all individuals than the sum of individual decisions. Moreover, since information does not conform to the classical properties of privately supplied commodities, it is likely to be underproduced relative to what would obtain if it were a perfect private good [Arrow 1962; Samuelson 1954]. Further, many types of information take on the characteristics of public goods.

Hayek clearly has not demonstrated the superiority of the market as the most efficient system for allocating resources. He has drawn attention to one aspect of the problem that has highlighted an advantage of coordination of certain types of information through market prices. But his real contribution has been to focus debate in this long-standing economic controversy upon the role and characteristics of information in the institutional structure, a crucial aspect of the issue that far too often is neglected. It is disappointing that the debate on this important information issue has not been sharpened significantly since Hayek's article. An efficient allocation of resources in society will require an institutional structure that contains elements of both planning and markets. It is important that the structure be designed to reflect the comparative advantage of each in the areas to which they are applied. On the basis of the present state of knowledge, economists can offer precious few guidelines on this fundamental policy issue.

More recently, O. E. Williamson has used an updated version of the Hayek analysis to argue the opposite case. He has introduced the concept of "transaction costs" to neoclassical theory in recognition of the fact that in imperfect markets involving complex technologies, the costs of negotiation may become significant. Although Williamson claims that his concept of transaction costs is drawn from Commons, and that his analysis represents the "new institutional economics," the concept does nothing more than recognize that market transactions are not free (a traditional assumption of neoclassical theory). Institutional issues are not even addressed.

According to Williamson, transaction costs are driven up by bounded rationality, opportunism and asset specificity, that is, inadequate information, a failure of communication, and a high degree of uncertainty. Because market transactions are too complex and costly it is more efficient to integrate vertically and horizontally, thereby avoiding the market and the necessity for settling on a price. By avoiding the market, large conglomerate corporations will be in a better position to plan and to supply their products more efficiently. Apparently large-scale planning is now superior to the market in coordinating economic activity. Williamson does not attempt any empirical tests of his theory; nor does he discuss the relative merits of public versus private planning. His case rests upon assumptions about the information and communication characteristics of the market transaction in a technologically advanced economy. The information and communication aspects of this issue definitely need attention from institutional economists.

Some characteristics of information in the information economy

Some authors believe that society is moving beyond industrial capitalism to an information-based economy.[11] In fact, detailed investigation certainly would show that societies have always been information-based. The oral traditions of the most primitive tribes were rich in information. The changes of recent years have been primarily in the market characteristics of information. First, the technology of generating, processing, and transmitting information at drastically reduced unit costs has provided quantum leaps in the capacity to supply information. Second, in the real economic markets— if not the economic theories—it has been discovered that many kinds of information heretofore not provided through formal market systems, have high exchange market values. It is now profitable to search for many new kinds of information that, in times past, were not sought because it was not profitable. Information that previously was outside the market and not included as economic activity has now been drawn into the market.[12]

The rapid rise of information markets is made possible by the interaction of advances in computer and telecommunication technologies. Advances in the computer industry have pushed back the intensive limit of the market by reducing the costs of generating more and more kinds of data. Advances in telecommunication have pushed back the extensive geographical limit to encompass global markets. However, it is important to distinguish the economic implications of the new technology facility systems that provide the infrastructure within which information is generated and processed, and over which it travels, and the information services themselves—the content that is provided over the facility systems.

In the narrow economic sense, the facility systems of computers, satellites, fibre-optic cables, terminals, and so forth, are no different, as a production process, than any other production or manufacturing process. What renders the facility systems important is that the information services must be provided over them. Therefore, the efficiency of the facility system is a significant factor influencing the efficiency of the information services provided over them. A nation with an efficient facility system may have major advantages in the competition for global information markets that will cut across most information services.

Information as an economic resource

The stock of knowledge in society, the skills and education of the populace, the detailed factual information relating to such things as science and technology, the working of production processes, the interrelationships among the different sectors of the economy, represent a primary resource. The value of this stock of knowledge to society depends upon how pervasively it is spread throughout that society and upon the institutions for maintaining, replenishing and expanding the stock of knowledge, that is, its educational and training system and research generating new knowledge. Economic benefits come in the form of improved decisionmaking throughout the economy.

Once information has been generated, the cost of replicating it is very much lower than the cost of generating it in the initial instance. The consumption of information by one user does not destroy it, as occurs with almost all other resources and products. The information remains to be consumed by others, the only additional costs being those associated with bringing the same information and additional consumers of it together under conditions where it can be consumed, that is, learned. And once a given level of penetration is reached, a multiplier effect comes into play with many types of information, as the information is spread throughout society outside the formal processes of learning and training. Hence, although the costs of adding to the stock of knowledge may be very great, there are generally very significant economies in diffusing that information throughout society, and to other societies, if the incentive exists to do so. The implications of this economic characteristic of relatively low-cost replication of information can be extremely beneficial under some circumstances, such as the spreading of knowledge, but it creates special problems and difficulties under other circumstances.

Much of the information that has become important as a resource input to industrial and commercial production processes is specialized information sought to provide "inside" knowledge of the behavior of purchasers of a firm's products, suppliers of a firm's other resources, competitors, government regulators, and the like. In essence, in imperfect economic markets, this inside information for private consumption strengthens the negotiation and marketing position of the organizations that have access to it. Such information may or may not be costly to obtain, but its economic value clearly lies in its scarcity—in the monopoly of information. Once such information becomes generally known to all interested parties, its economic value dissipates drastically.

Specialized information services for the private consumption of a restricted clientele are springing up daily. They range from special research studies of the details of international markets for a group of transnational corporations to confidential assessments of the negotiating strength of a specific customer, competitor, labor union, or government regulatory agency for a specific negotiation. Because of the low cost of replication of such information —usually the cost of using the nearest copying machine—and the relative ease of information theft, which does not require the physical removal of the information, the value of such information can be extremely tenuous without extreme security. The same economies of information replication that can facilitate the spreading of knowledge throughout society can lead to the rapid destruction of the economic value of many kinds of specialized knowledge.

Information as final consumer product

The characteristics of information as a final consumer product vary depending upon what kind of information is desired, by what users and for what purposes. Perhaps the greatest potential expansion of the information market now underway is for specialized data that can: (1) facilitate decisionmaking, for example, shopping selections; (2) permit greater efficiency in the performance of certain activities, for example, banking; and (3) provide new forms of entertainment, for example, video games. The combination of specialized data banks, computer programs and advanced telecommunication systems make possible individual access through the market to specialized information for private consumption. The economic incentive for the act of promotion and expansion of such systems is very great, given the drastically reduced unit costs of adding subscribers to systems already established.

The new technologies also make possible the creation of specialized data banks of detailed personal information about individuals for selected users like credit bureaus or government agencies. In many instances, the market value of this information is greater if access to the information is restricted. This has raised concern that the new market conditions for information make it both profitable and efficient for invasions of personal privacy.

Many governments already have taken steps to attempt to restrain the march of information markets into the details of people's personal lives and to regulate the conditions of access to certain kinds of data banks, such as, credit, medical, and tax files. The pursuit, sale and use of information in accordance with the incentives of the marketplace apparently is not going to be unrestricted. In the Commons tradition, a change in the working rules of social interaction will modify the institutional nature of these transactions.

The mass entertainment market, most pervasively illustrated by television, takes on somewhat different characteristics. The economies of information replication are very substantial. The costs of copying program information already created is nominal, and the cost of serving larger audiences rather than smaller ones is minimal. With satellites, the additional cost of transmission to more locations is reduced to the cost of the receiving terminals. With the new telecommunication technology, the economies of replicating existing information have become enormous. In addition, the market value of mass entertainment information is not based on restricting access to this information, but in promoting it. Those restrictions that do exist from time to time are tools to maximize profit through discriminatory pricing, rather than attempts to restrict the scope of the market.

News, as a particular form of public or mass information, has very similar economic characteristics to mass entertainment. The major differences are the time sensitivity of the economic value of most news and the fact that most news is sold as an intermediate product by news agencies to distributors such as newspapers and television stations. Finally, we should recognize those unique information markets where purchasers pay to have selective information sent to influence third parties, that is, advertising. This, of course, introduces a special problem of the quality of the information because frequently the market incentive is to supply misleading information.

Some implications for industrial structure and market development

Information markets can be classified into two general categories: (a) those in which maximum market value is achieved by the maximum dispersion of the information; and (b) those in which maximum market value is achieved by restricting information to specialized users who value its scarcity and seek a monopoly of specific information. The former is represented primarily by information provided to the public for mass consumption and is best illustrated by entertainment television; the latter is represented by the generation of specialized information that provides a valuable knowledge differential relative to adversarial interests, and is illustrated by confidential assessments of the strengths and weaknesses of negotiating adversaries.

The maximum dispersion category is characterized by extremely low costs of information replication. With increasing costs for generating original information and reduced costs of replicating it from previous already low levels, the economic incentives to expand the market for existing information to a global basis are increased. In application, this means, for example, that the economic incentive to dump old U.S. television programs in greater quantities and in more countries is increased. The differential cost to other countries of choosing to produce original material at home instead of purchasing U.S. network reruns, is increasing significantly.

The second category, markets based on creating a monopoly of certain information, is less influenced by the low costs of information replication, although buyers with similar interests may economize by sharing in certain information purchases. Rather, information generation becomes a focal point for competing interests attempting to obtain a competitive advantage. As such, it imposes a cost on all competitive and adversarial interests if they hope to maintain their relative positions in the market. An opportunity is provided to buy an information advantage. A barrier to entry is created for those who cannot afford to compete at the information game. Since most major market transactions in international commerce ultimately boil down to bilateral monopoly, or oligopoly negotiations, the new information possibilities have the potential for significantly affecting the results of such negotiations. Transaction costs of the Williamson variety may simply be a manifestation of the tendency of oligopoly markets to create artificial barriers to entry that appear in the form of increased transaction costs.

The production characteristics of relatively high costs of establishing most data services and relatively low costs of extending the market for services already created provide a powerful force toward centralization of control and monopoly. Thus, competitive forces in many information markets are likely to be rather weak. This, in turn, can be expected to raise important issues of government policy with respect to information monopolies.

As a commodity, information can be extremely tenuous. The quality of information may vary substantially. And quality control may be impossible. It is certainly impossible to know in advance whether information you are receiving is truthful and accurate. If you knew, you would not be buying the information. And for many types of information, it will be impossible to assess the quality of it even after the fact. The risks of carelessly assembled, false, misleading and biased information are increased because of the inherent characteristics of information as a marketable commodity.

The extension of the market to encompass information as a commodity also opens a market in its shadow for misinformation. The more valuable formal information becomes to decision-makers, the more devastating misinformation can be. If demands for positive information to enhance a firm or government agency's relative position can be met through the market, then the same objective could be achieved by purchasing misinformation and having it sent directly to an adversary.

Public policy issues

The successful development of information markets for the benefit of all sectors of society will require major adaptations by both private and public institutions. If markets in tradeable information are going to work efficiently and equitably, they must be developed upon a foundation of public information that provides the education and training necessary for citizens to function effectively as workers, managers, consumers and responsible citizens. Determining the appropriate adaptations, both by the public and the private sectors, to the new information and communication environment is a crucial task to which institutional analysis can contribute significantly.

Many individuals and organizations can benefit substantially from the rapid expansion of the information and communication sector, but at least some are likely to be disadvantaged, in both relative and absolute terms, especially if traditional public and social services are displaced, downgraded or made more expensive. To illustrate, a considerable portion of the information now accessible through public libraries is subject to commoditization and sale in private markets, where it would be accessible only through telecommunication-based information services. In recent years, many libraries have expanded access to a variety of bibliographic databases. But they have cut back their physical holdings of government reports and statistics, general research reports and studies, periodicals, and even books. This has facilitated research projects with the funding support to pay for computer searches and acquisition of the desired material. But most academic researchers, students, and the lay public can rarely afford to use computer searches, and are increasingly frustrated by the more limited access to hardcopy resources.

The telephone system is being upgraded to the technical standards of an integrated services digital network (ISDN) that is more efficient for the plethora of new information services required by sophisticated high volume users. But it may be significantly more expensive for small volume users and users with only local telephone service requirements. This could make it more difficult to extend basic telephone service coverage to a larger proportion of the population [Melody 1986].

The characteristics of information markets create special problems associated with the technological transfer of computer and telecommunication technologies to developing countries. The market incentives are to sell new technology facility systems in developing countries to establish the infrastructure for both the domestic and international communication of information services. Given the established base of information in the technologically advanced countries, and their lead in establishing new information services, the information flows are predictable. Final consumer information, such as television programs (often accompanied by advertising), is likely to dominate the flow from developed to developing countries. Specialized information markets that create value as a result of the monopoly of information is likely to generate a dominant flow of information about developing countries to developed countries and transnational corporations. Indeed these trends have already been documented.[13] These conditions in the information market will facilitate the penetration of developing country markets for the full range of economic goods and services by those organizations that have access to the specialized information. Of course, it may place developing country firms and agencies at an increased competitive disadvantage in their own countries because of an information deficiency about conditions there.

A major challenge for public policy will be to find methods to ensure that developments in the information and communication sector do not exacerbate class divisions in society and that its benefits are spread across all classes. This will require new conceptions and operational definitions of the "public interest" and of public services, new interpretations of the requirements of social policy, and the design of new institutional structures for its effective implementation.

Conclusion

The concept of information has been central both to economic problems and to economic theory of all kinds. In most circumstances, information issues have not been formally recognized because they are embedded as an integral part of more familiar economic concepts. But, as has been demonstrated above, the solution to many classic economic debates rests on the analysis, or assumptions, with respect to the information aspects of the problem.

The rapid improvements in information and communication technologies that are now being implemented throughout the world portend fundamental changes in society's economic, political, social, and cultural institutions. The growing importance of mechanized information and communication, and of the global markets that they permit, will force economists of all schools of thought to examine more carefully the information dimensions of their theories.

For institutional economists, conditions could not be better. Dynamic institutional change is forcing the concerns of public policy to pay more attention to those issues that institutionalists study. In the evolving institutional structure of society, opportunities are appearing for institutionalists to develop their research so as to inform public policy decisions. Now they have an opportunity to do more than just interpret the world. In the Commons tradition, they can participate in changing it!

Notes

1 George J. Stigler has observed:

> One should hardly have to tell academicians that information is a valuable resource: knowledge *is* power. And yet it occupies a slum dwelling in the town of economics. Mostly it is ignored: the best technology is assumed to be known; the relationship of commodities to consumer preferences is a datum. And one of the information producing industries, advertising, is treated with a hostility that economists normally reserve for tariffs or monopolists
>
> [Stigler 1968, p. 171]

2 Smith [1977], quoted in G. J. Stigler, *Selections from The Wealth of Nations* (New York: Appleton-Century-Crofts, 1959), p. 15.
3 Marx [1977], quoted in Yves de la Haye, *Marx and Engels on the Means of Communication.* (New York: International General, 1979), p. 125.
4 Ibid., pp. 102–3.
5 See Lamberton [1984]; also Lamberton [1971].
6 See Nelson and Winter [1982] and Freeman [1982].
7 See also Gruchy [1986, at pp. 813 and following].

8 See Melody, Salter, and Heyer [1981].
9 Dallas W. Smythe, "Communications: Blind Spot of Economics," in Melody, Salter, and Heyer [1981].
10 See also Arrow [1974].
11 See for example: Bell [1973] and Porat [1978].
12 See Melody [1985].
13 See for example: Pipe [1979a] and Pipe [1979b].

References

Arrow, K. J. 1962. "Economic Welfare and the Allocation of Resources for Invention." In *National Bureau of Economic Research: the Rate and Direction of Inventive Activity: Economic and Social Factors*, pp. 609–25. Princeton University Press.

———. 1974. "Limited Knowledge and Economic Analysis," *American Economic Review* 64 (March): 1–10.

Ayres, C. E. 1944. *The Theory of Economic Progress: A Study of the Fundamentals of Economic Development and Cultural Change.* Michigan: New Issues Press, Western Michigan University.

Bell, Daniel. 1973. *The Coming of Post-Industrial Society: A Venture in Social Forecasting.* New York: Basic Books.

Boulding, K. E. 1960. "The Present Position of the Theory of the Firm." In *Linear Programming and the Theory of the Firm.* Ed. K. E. Boulding and W. A. Spivey, pp. 1–17. New York: Macmillan.

———. 1966. "The Economics of Knowledge and the Knowledge of Economics," *American Economic Review* 56 (May): 1–13.

Commons, John R. 1934. *Institutional Economics: Its Place in Political Economy.* Madison: University of Wisconsin Press.

Demsetz, H. 1967. "Toward a Theory of Property Rights," *American Economic Review* 57 (May): 347–59.

Dorfman, J. 1934. *Thorstein Veblen and His America.* New York: Viking.

Freeman, C., ed. 1982. *The Economics of Industrial Innovation.* London: Frances Pinter.

Gruchy, Allan G. "The Cremona Foundation and the St. Mary's College Conference on Institutional Economics." *Journal of Economic Issues* 20 (September 1986): 805–23.

Hamilton, Walton H. 1968. "Institution." In *International Encyclopedia of Social Sciences*, Vol. 3. New York: MacMillan.

Hayek, F. A. von. 1945. "The Use of Knowledge in Society," *American Economic Review* 35 (September): 519–30.

Innis, Harold A. 1923. *A History of the Canadian Pacific Railway.* Toronto: Toronto University Press.

———. 1956. *The Fur Trade in Canada.* Toronto: University of Toronto Press [1930].

———. 1964. *The Bias of Communication.* Toronto: University of Toronto Press [1952].

———. 1972. *Empire and Communications.* Revised by Mary Q. Innis. Toronto: University of Toronto Press [1950].

———. 1973. "The Work of Thorstein Veblen." In *Essays in Canadian Economic History.* Ed. Mary Q. Innis, pp. 17–26. Toronto: University of Toronto Press [1929].

Jussawalla, M. and Lamberton, D. M., eds. 1982. *Communication Economics and Development.* New York: Pergamon Press.

Klein, P. A. 1985. "A Reappraisal of Institutionalism—its Critics and Adherents." Statement presented to the Conference on Institutional Economics, June.

Koopmans, T. C. 1957. *Three Essays on the State of Economic Science.* New York: McGraw-Hill.

Lamberton, Donald M. 1984. "The Emergence of Information Economics." In *Communication and Information Economics.* Ed. Meheroo Jussawalla and Helen Ebenfield, pp. 7–22. New York: North Holland.

——, ed. 1971. *Economics of Information and Knowledge.* Middlesex: Penguin.

Machlup, F. 1980–1984. *Knowledge: Its Creation, Distribution, and Economic Significance.* Princeton, N.J.: Princeton University Press.

Macpherson, C. B., ed. 1978. *Property: Mainstream and Critical Positions.* Toronto: University of Toronto Press.

Marx, Karl. 1977. *Grundrisse: Foundations of the Critique of Political Economy.* London: Penguin Books [1939–1941].

Melody, William H. 1985. "The Information Society: Implications for Economic Institutions and Market Theory." *Journal of Economic Issues* 19 (June): 523–39.

Melody, William H., L. Salter, and P. Heyer. 1981. *Culture, Communication, and Dependency: The Tradition of H. A. Innis.* Norwood, N.J.: Ablex.

——. 1986. "Telecommunication: Policy Directions for the Technology and Information Services." *Oxford Surveys in Information Technology*, Vol. 3, Middleton, K., and M. Jussawalla. 1981. *Economics of Communication: An Annotated Bibliography with Abstracts.* New York: Pergamon Press.

Mitchell, Wesley C. 1964. *What Veblen Taught: Selected Writings of Thorstein Veblen.* New York: Sentry Press Reprints of Economics Classics [1936].

Nelson, R. R. and S. Winter. 1982. *An Evolutionary Theory of Economic Change.* Cambridge, Mass: MIT Press.

Newman, Geoffrey. 1976. "An Institutional Perspective on Information." *International Social Science Journal* 28: 466–92.

Pipe, G. Russell. 1979a. "National Policies, International Debates." *Journal of Communication* 29 (Summer): 114–23.

——. 1979b. "Transnational Information Flows." *Intermedia* 7.

Porat, M. U. 1971. *The Information Economy.* Washington: Office of Telecommunications, U.S. Department of Commerce.

——. 1978. "Global Implications of Information Society." *Journal of Communication* 28 (Winter): 70–80.

Samuelson, P. A. 1954. "The Pure Theory of Public Expenditure." *Review of Economics and Statistics* 36 (November): 387–89.

Schiller, Herbert I. 1981. *Who Knows: Information in the Age of the Fortune 500.* Norwood, N. J.: Ablex, 1981.

Schumpeter, Joseph A. 1954. *A History of Economic Analysis.* Ed. Elizabeth Boody Schumpeter. New York: Oxford University Press.

Smith, Adam. 1977. *An Inquiry into the Nature and Causes of the Wealth of Nations.* 5th ed. New York: Modern Library.

Smythe, Dallas W. 1981. *Dependency Road: Communications, Capitalism, Consciousness and Canada.* Norwood, N.J.: Ablex.

Stigler, George J. 1968. *The Organization of Industry.* Homewood, Ill.: Irwin.

Veblen, T. 1919. "The Place of Science in Modern Civilization." In *The Place of Science in Modern Civilization.* New York: Viking.

28

BEYOND INTERESTS, IDEAS, AND TECHNOLOGY

An institutional approach to communication and information policy

Hernan Galperin

Source: *The information Society* 20(3) (2004): 159–68.

This article examines the theoretical assumptions generally used in communication and information policy studies, and suggests that more attention to the institutional determinants of public policies is needed. The first part discusses three altern- ative theoretical approaches: the interest-group approach, the ideological approach, and the technology-centered approach. The second part outlines the conceptual tools of the new institutionalism approach and discusses its application for the study of regime change in telecoms and media. The third part presents an abbreviated example of such application to the case of U.S. spectrum policies and the licensing of digital broad- casting. The conclusion suggests new directions for research aimed at broadening the set of social actors participating in the global governance of new technologies.

Over the past decades, communication and information policy research has generated an impressive amount of knowledge about the wide range of public policy issues that have accompanied the emergence of the informa- tion economy. From spectrum licensing to interconnection, access, privacy, standards, intellectual property rights, and ownership, scholars have dis- sected every major policy issue of the day. However, much less attention has been paid to the dynamics of the policymaking process itself. In other words, we know quite a lot about the intricacies of each policy question (though we might not agree on the policy prescriptions that follow) but relatively little about the underlying forces shaping actual policy outcomes. As argued in this article, this has often precluded scholars and public interest advocates from participating more effectively in substantive policy debates alongside industry stakeholders, regulators, and legislators, particularly as the locus of policy debate shifts toward nontraditional rulemaking bodies.

The field of communication and information policy studies comprises a wide range of theoretical approaches borrowed from a number of preexisting disciplines, in particular economics, political science, law, and sociology. Throughout these disciplines we find different theoretical assumptions about how public policies are formed and embedded into legislation and government initiatives. These assumptions, though not always explicitly articulated, are critical for they provide the analytical link between policy inputs (i.e., collective demands and preferences regarding a particular issue) and outputs (i.e., the actual policies adopted). This article discusses the assumptions generally used in the field of communication and information policy studies and suggests that the field would benefit—in terms of both academic progress and policy impact—from greater attention to the institutional setting within which policy actors operate.

The article begins with a taxonomy of theoretical approaches that have traditionally informed communication and information policy research. Three main approaches are identified: the interest-group approach, the ideological approach, and the technology-centered approach. I suggest that these approaches often overlook long-term institutional factors that shape the way in which regulators and legislators react to policy demands and translate those demands into government action. Drawing on the new institutionalism approach, I then suggest that closer attention to state actors and structures is needed, as well as to the links between societal preferences and actual policy outcomes. In turn, I illustrate this conceptual framework by examining the case of spectrum allocation policies in the introduction of digital broadcasting services in the United States. The conclusion suggests new directions for communication and information policy research that informs the current debate on how best to govern new communication technologies that extend beyond traditional policymaking institutions.

A taxonomy of theoretical approaches

Gourevitch correctly asserts that in order to explain public policies scholars must "have some way of accounting for the connection between policy and choice—between what could be done and the various factors that shape what decision makers actually choose to do" (1986, p. 54). In other words, we must somehow link politics and policies. With a few notable exceptions (e.g., Mosco, 1988; Horwitz, 1989; Dutton, 1992; Mueller, 1995), the determinants of government action remain remarkably undertheorized in the field of communication and information policy studies. Nonetheless, it is common to find analytical assumptions about the dynamics of policymaking that explain why governments make certain choices and not others. Within the vast universe of communication and information policy studies these theoretical assumptions vary widely. For simplicity, I focus here on the large body of work that has attempted to explain the dramatic changes in the regulation of communication and information industries in both developed and developing nations since the 1980s. By focusing on that subset of the field I necessarily ignore many nuances, as well as a sizable body of literature published prior to those changes.[1] Such focus is nonetheless necessary to provide a useful mapping of the intellectual field that outlines dominant approaches and reveals research gaps.

The interest-group approach

For every major policy issue in the media, telecom, and information technology industries there are competing groups and organizations advocating different courses of action. These range from well-funded trade associations to small think tanks and informal advocacy networks. Their battle in different policy arenas—legislatures, regulatory agencies, the courts, and often the media—is the most visible aspect of the contested regulatory changes associated with the rise of the information economy. The interest-group approach stresses this push and pull between competing stakeholders. The basic unit of analysis is a social aggregation called the interest group, whose preferences are typically determined by its long-term economic interests. Because policies affect the distribution of resources among market actors, it is logical that these actors attempt to influence policy outcomes in a variety of ways. As Olson (1971) and others have shown, the higher and more concentrated are the stakes, the more a group will seek to organize and participate in the policy process to promote its cause. It is thus not surprising to observe the mushrooming of trade groups and advocacy organizations dedicated to communication and information policy in the past decades.

In this approach, policy outcomes are typically explicated by the organization and the resources available to interest groups and their support coalitions. In other words, policy outcomes are a function of the power that each interest group is able to amass and wield in support of its preferred outcome. Such power can be measured in a number of ways: the amount of campaign contributions to political candidates, the ability to provide votes, the resources available for lobbying regulators and influencing public opinion, the sheer wealth of the organization and/or its members, etc. As a general rule, the more powerful is the interest group, the more likely it is that government policies will reflect its preferences (Posner, 1974; Becker, 1983). As the preferences and/or the distribution of resources among these groups vary over time, so do the relevant regulatory regimes. For example, the breakup of AT&T has been often explained as a result of changes in the preferences of large telecom users and the emergence of new market entrants, which together successfully organized to challenge the monopoly regime (e.g., Brock, 1994). The weakening of the labor unions has often been cited as a decisive factor behind telecom and media reforms in Europe (e.g., Thatcher, 1999).

There is much variety within the interest-group approach. Pluralists regard elected officials and bureaucrats as rather neutral brokers of compromises between competing stakeholders (e.g., Krasnow & Longley, 1978), while neo-Marxists (e.g., Schiller, 1982) tend to think of them as systematically captured by the most powerful ones. What these scholars have in common is a focus on the balance of power between interest groups as the key explanatory variable of regulatory action. Because state actors are weak, acting only reactively to regulatory demands from self-interested actors, the translation of preferences into policies is generally not problematized. The underlying logic of interest group analysis is often circular: Regulation reflects the interests of the most powerful stakeholders, and the evidence that these are in fact the most powerful stakeholders is that government rules protect and serve their interests.

Most varieties of the interest group approach see a rather small margin for public interest advocacy. For the pluralist, the key problem is one of collective action. The benefits of policies that supply collective goods are typically diffused among users and would-be market entrants, while the costs are highly concentrated among incumbents (Stigler, 1971). These will therefore have greater incentives to organize and influence policy—the fewer are the beneficiaries, the easier it is to amass resources and coordinate actions against public interest reforms. Regulatory politics will thus tend to favor concentrated interests at the expense of the public interest (e.g., Geller, 1998). Neo-Marxists are, generally speaking, equally pessimistic: Elected officials and bureaucrats tend to be biased toward the most powerful economic groups, either because they share ideological prescriptions or because their interests are aligned with those of large corporations. Government policies, in the long run, will tend to protect the large firms upon which the state depends for investment, employment, and taxation (Garnham, 1990; Murdock & Golding, 1999).

Identifying the economic interests at play and the distributional effects of alternative courses of action is important to understand government action. Nonetheless, the determinants of public policies are too often inferred from a post facto analysis of winners and losers, when in fact several empirical studies have proved that such analysis is often misleading. For example, Vogel (1996) has convincingly shown that the liberalization of entry in the British telecommunications industry did not occur as a result of pressure from large users or potential market entrants (who ultimately benefited from the introduction of competition to British Telecom), but rather emerged from a militant Conservative cabinet determined to reduce the power of the labor unions and overhaul the industrial structure of the "old Britain." As

96

Hall (1997) and others have argued, the main analytical problem of the interest group approach stems from its conceptualization of political power. Such power is not an inherent property of social actors, but rather a relational variable—a function of certain institutional arrangements that make policymakers more receptive to certain demands and ideas than others. In short, identifying winners and losers is not enough to make causal assertions about the determinants of public policies. While communication and information policy scholars often equate favorable outcomes with interest group power, more rigorous attention to the links between competing social demands and government action is needed.

The ideological approach

Ideas play a powerful role in shaping communication and information policies. They permeate policymaking not only because they define how political actors interpret the issues at stake but also because they alleviate uncertainties and help define "acceptable" courses of action (North, 1990). This is particularly important when the likely effects of alternative policy choices are largely unknown, which is often the case in the regulation of rapidly evolving technologies (e.g., Will unlicensed bands lead to spectrum congestion? Will open access rules inhibit infrastructure investments?). In contexts of high informational uncertainty, prior beliefs about the nature of the policy problem, acceptable courses of action, and the most effective policy instruments become critical (Goldstein & Keohane, 1993). Thus, ideological paradigms often provide the basic cognitive template through which decision makers interpret complex problems and assess the validity of alternative policies.

Paradigm shifts have often been linked to policy changes in information and communication industries. According to Derthick and Quirk (1985), the American bureaucratic tradition of recruiting "inners and outers" provided a fertile ground for the dissemination of the academic critique of regulation among regulatory agencies in the late 1970s and early 1980s, which set the stage for the reforms later adopted in telecommunications and other sectors. Others have suggested that the international diffusion of the information economy paradigm helped galvanize support for privatization and liberalization in communication infrastructure sectors (Dutton, 1992; Mosco, 1998). Likewise, scholars have attributed the liberalization of the European media sector to a fundamental ideological shift in the policy goals associated with broadcasting: Once conceived as a reservoir for public debate and national culture, the Euro bureaucrats now considered television as a critical component of the European information economy (e.g., Burgelman, 1997).

Ideology has a natural importance in explaining policy choices. After all, what are these choices but ideas translated into government action? Ideological paradigms, however, do not emerge ex nihilo, nor do they diffuse automatically. There must be vehicles for the creation and transmission of ideas. Several organizations perform this function, among them universities, think tanks, trade groups, companies, government agencies, advocacy groups, and so on. For any policy issue at stake there is no lack of competing paradigms to choose from. The problem is to explicate why policymakers embrace certain ideas and not others. This directs our attention to the operating procedures that routinely filter information into the policymaking process, among them the recruiting practices of government agencies, the personal networks that might exist between regulators and stakeholders, the established practices for information seeking, and so on (Hall, 1986). In other words, the task is to understand the patterns by which certain policy prescriptions are formed, disseminated, and validated within a context of incomplete information and competing interpretations about the issue at stake and the desirable course of action.

The technological approach

Technological change has played a central role in reshaping information and communication industries in the past decades. It is thus not unusual to find interpretations of technology as the critical determinant of public policies in telecommunications and media (e.g., Mulgan, 1991). Such interpretations were popularized by a large body of "grayliterature" (i.e., publications issued by government agencies, trade organizations, research centers, professional associations, etc.) that brought attention to the significance of the changes taking place (e.g., EC, 1993; OECD, 1997). While this perspective has seeped into academia, scholars have generally taken a more nuanced approach to the role of technology in driving policy change. An influential body of research stems from the seminal work of Ithiel de Sola Pool (1983). Pool argued that each new advance in communications technology disturbs the established industry arrangements, challenging economic privileges as well as the existing legal apparatus. New technologies—in his words, "technologies of freedom"—compel policy reforms as governments and firms seek to adapt business practices and policy instruments to the new technological environment. Pool correctly notes, however, that such adaptation can take many forms:

> The characteristics of media shape what is done with them, so one anticipates that these technologies of freedom will overwhelm all attempts to control them. Technology, however, shapes the structure of the battle, but not every outcome. While the printing press was without doubt the foundation of modern democracy, the response to the flood of publishing that it brought forth has been censorship as often as press freedom.
>
> (1983, p. 251)

Pool's work has nonetheless been often used to advance the idea that new technologies make most existing regulatory controls in telecoms and media obsolete. In this approach, innovations in information processing linked with advances in transmission technologies have created exogenous pressure on the regimes that sustained telecom monopolies and sheltered broadcasters from competition. In response, governments have been forced to liberalize entry, relax controls on pricing and technical standards, and take a back seat on matters of content. The argument rests on three main propositions. First, technological change has raised the cost of regulation relative to its benefits (Huber, 1997). Second, digital convergence has undermined the industry equilibrium based on clear demarcations between types of services (OFTEL, 1995). Third, serious enforcement problems have emerged as governments struggle to impose national laws on increasingly global networks (Johnson & Post, 1996).

It is beyond dispute that technological innovation is a major factor shaping communication and information technology policy. But the intermediating factors between new technologies and changes in the regulatory environment must be spelled out in the analysis. Because new technologies have altered the basic parameters of the information and communication industries (relative prices, industry boundaries, entry and exit barriers, etc.), political and market actors have sought to adapt the rules of the game to their benefit—either to preserve the established regime (as in the example discussed later) or to challenge it. But the outcome of such battles has varied widely, dictated more by a political than a technological logic. For example, it is well established that government responses to innovations in telecommunications have been quite different among developed as well as developing countries (Levy & Spiller, 1996; Petrazzini & Krishnaswamy, 1998).

While new technologies enable some choices and preclude others, policy outcomes ultimately depend on the interaction between the attributes of innovations and the permeability of existing regimes for change (Zysman, 1994; Benkler, 1998). The variety in national approaches to every major issue in communication and information policy, from local loop unbundling to digital copyright law, amply demonstrates that technology alone cannot explain the course of policy. This type of reasoning has been more often used to justify than to explain policy changes. The fact remains that institutions and social actors are key mediators between technological innovation and policy reforms, which ultimately makes the outcome more unpredictable than many would like to think, or preach.

Institutions, incentives and policy choices

The taxonomy of theoretical approaches just presented is neither exhaustive nor exclusive. There are certainly other ways to explore the determinants of information and communication policies, and one often finds studies that

—either implicitly or explicitly—span more than one approach. The mapping nonetheless reveals major gaps in our understanding of why policymakers embrace certain paradigms and favor certain interests over others. Two important points have emerged from this review. First, policymakers often make choices that are not reducible to the preferences of powerful interest groups. Of course, political autonomy varies widely for different policy bodies as well as across nations. For example, British ministers typically have at their disposal an array of instruments to enact regulatory reforms that American policymakers can only dream of (Weaver & Rockman, 1993). Still, it remains analytically important to consider the preferences of different government actors—however constrained they might be—as separate from those of other stakeholders.

Second, the state is not simply an open arena where interest groups wage rent-seeking battles. The organization of the political system, the operating procedures of regulatory agencies, the opportunities for judicial reviews—these and other arrangements are significant because they often determine whose voices are heard in the policy process and whose are silenced, which groups sit at the bargaining table and which do not, or whose proposals are deemed acceptable and whose are not. Therefore, in order to understand why certain stakeholders are consistently favored over others, why certain governments are capable of passing reforms and others are not, or why diffused interests are represented in some cases and not others, it is necessary to examine the institutional fabric that underlies the making of information and communication policies.

Such is the starting point for the conceptual framework generally known as new institutionalism. The label refers to a broad range of studies bound together by their emphasis on institutional factors to explain policy and economic outcomes (Krasner, 1989; North, 1993; Cowhey & McCubbins, 1995). The term "new" is intended to acknowledge the roots of this approach in the works of classic political economists such as Max Weber, Thorstein Veblen, and Karl Polanyi, who first conceptualized the relation between legal institutions, economic performance, and social interactions (Stinchcombe, 1997). The new institutionalism approach nonetheless differs from earlier institutional analysis in a number of ways. First, it takes a broader view of institutions, looking not only at formal political structures but also at informal arrangements such as routine organizational procedures and accepted behavioral norms (March & Olsen, 1984). Second, current institutional analysis avoids the grand theorizing characteristic of earlier social thinking, focusing instead on middle-range studies that connect specific economic and policy outcomes with particular institutional patterns at the regional, national, or even local level.

Institutional analysis focuses attention on state actors and structures to explain public policies. It underscores how both formal and informal arrangements shape political interactions and influence the outcome of government action. In general terms, institutions refer to, as North explains, the "composite of rules, informal constraints (norms of behavior and conventions) and their enforcement characteristics. Together they define the humanly devised constraints that shape human interaction. They are the rules of the game and therefore define the way the game is played" (1990, p. 364). Hall (1992) further distinguishes three layers. At the more general level lie the basic organizational arrangements associated with the state (e.g., a democratic political system) and the economy (e.g., market capitalism). This the level at which classical political economists and contemporary neo-Marxist work.

Second follows the more specific organizational arrangements of the modern state, such as regime type (e.g., parliamentary vs. presidential systems), the organization of interest groups, the electoral system, and the regulatory design. There is a growing body of work that demonstrates the analytical strength of these variables to explain communication and information policies, particularly in comparative perspective. For example, Noll and Rosenbluth (1995) find that the differences in telecommunications reforms adopted in Japan and the United States can be traced back to their distinct political arrangements: In Japan, centralized decision making and a single legislative body elected in multimember districts stacked the deck in favor of piecemeal deregulation to protect large domestic equipment manufacturers, while the American system of federal government, separation of powers, and legalized rulemaking created less opportunities for managing market entry and exit, thus favoring more rapid liberalization.

At the lowest level of generalization are the standard procedures and operational routines of bureaucratic agencies. These include both formal rules (e.g., mandatory consultation procedures) and informal patterns of behavior (e.g., standard recruiting practices). These variables have also proved fertile for policy analysis. For example, Noll (1986) suggests that the complex, evidence-based procedure for rulemaking and the adjudication of disputes that the FCC must follow, while minimizing bureaucratic discretion, also tends to benefit stakeholders with significant informational and organizational resources. This tends to inhibit new technology adoption because the agency is often reluctant to endorse technologies that well-organized incumbents are likely to challenge in the courts or Congress.

An institutional approach does not ignore ideological factors or interest-group pressure as important determinants of policy outcomes. It nonetheless suggests that a complex web of institutions mediates between these and government officials, filtering ideas and pressure in specific ways. As noted, policymakers make choices within an institutional structure that defines the information available to them, the policy instruments at hand, the way interest groups are organized, the costs and rewards associated with alternative courses of actions, and the legacy of past policies. This structure not only determines the capabilities and constraints of those who *make* policy but also of those who try to *influence* policy. Thus the choice of institutional design affects the ability of different interests to influence outcomes. As we discuss in the conclusion, this has been at the core of debates about the emerging governance regime for the global Internet.

Another strength of institutional analysis is the internalization of so-called path-dependency effects. These result when long-term commitments made by individuals or firms constrain future policy trajectories (Krasner, 1989; North, 1993). Because these commitments often represent sunk costs, market actors tend to resist policies that significantly alter the established rules of the game, thus facilitating policy choices consistent with the existing institutional regime and inhibiting those deflecting from it. Changes are possible at the margin, but major shifts require the mobilization of considerable political resources, and often side payments to compensate losses incurred by individuals or organizations. These conceptual tools, borrowed from the work of economic historians (e.g., David, 1986; Arthur, 1989), have been increasingly applied to understand the evolution of policy in communication and information industries, where sunk costs in infrastructure, research and development (R&D), and so forth can be substantial. For example, Cherry and Bauer (2002) argue that the peculiar historical path of telecom reforms in the United States made tariff rebalancing more difficult than in the European Union (EU) because the breakup of AT&T created intense regulatory conflict between the regional Bell operating companies (RBOCs) and long-distance operators. Similarly, Benkler (1998) finds that spectrum management policies in the United States solidified a model of infrastructure development dependent on large investments by a handful of licensees, which over time has inhibited alternative models based on unlicensed spectrum bands and small-scale operators.

The new institutionalism approach thus provides a solid conceptual foundation to examine the determinants of communication and information policies, and is particularly useful for international comparisons and the study of long-term policy patterns. It fills significant theoretical gaps in the field by redirecting attention to the institutional context within which public policies emerge. The following section provides an abbreviated example of such approach. It examines long-term trends in spectrum licensing policies in the United States, with particular attention to the licensing of digital terrestrial broadcasting in the mid-1990s, and discusses alternative explanations for the observed bias in favor of incumbent local broadcasters. A more exhaustive elaboration of the argument can be found in Galperin (2004).

The determinants of U.S. spectrum policies, or why broadcasters always get what they want

The broadcast spectrum band comprises 67 channels spanning 402 MHz in the VHF and UHF bands. These valuables frequencies are home to

1,700-plus full-power stations across 210 local markets, an average of only about 8 stations per market.[2] There are two main reasons for this under-utilization: first, technical rules that provide for wide separation between stations to prevent interference (so-called "guard bands"), and second, the fact that many small local markets cannot support more than a few stations. Until the 1980s there was little pressure to address this situation because demand for spectrum grew slowly, and technological innovations made possible the utilization of previously unusable frequencies as well as the more intensive use of existing ones. While tensions occasionally surfaced, increased spectrum supply minimized conflict.

Since then, however, demand has soared as a result of the exponential growth of mobile telephony and other wireless communication services. Pressure to revise the existing allocation of spectrum rights began to mount as analysts warned of a severe frequency drought. Digital broadcasting, on the other hand, promised to bring some relief to the spectrum crunch. The new technology made possible better utilization of radio frequencies by allowing several stations to be transmitted within a standard broadcast channel (6 MHz), and by allowing licensees to broadcast much closer to each other, thereby reducing the need for large vacant intervals between stations. Digital broadcasting thus invited sweeping reforms in the allocation of broadcast spectrum. Yet a series of policy choices made by the Federal Communications Commission (FCC) since the late 1980s and ratified by Congress in 1996 left the existing spectrum regime almost intact.

The original plan for the introduction of digital broadcasting grew out of political maneuvering by incumbent local stations to deter spectrum sharing with new wireless services. In 1985, a number of parties petitioned the FCC to relax restrictions on the sharing of UHF channels by land mobile operators. The coalition was led by Motorola, which manufactured the two-way radios used by public safety organizations and commercial delivery companies. Since the early 1970s, land mobile and analog TV had been sharing a small portion of the UHF spectrum (channels 14–20). The coalition demanded that the sharing agreement be extended to other unused UHF channels and that interference-prevention rules be relaxed. Broadcasters vehemently opposed the proposal and persuaded the FCC that such reallocation would obstruct the upgrading of existing services to high-definition TV (HDTV). This sparked a chain of events that led to the formulation of a government plan to upgrade the entire broadcast TV infrastructure from analog to digital.

The plan was conceived in the late 1980s by an FCC advisory committee (the Advisory Committee on Advanced Television Service) largely controlled by incumbent broadcasters. Not surprisingly, it called for limiting the allocation of digital TV licenses to local incumbents, each of which would receive a second 6-MHz channel to launch digital services. After a transition period (initially 15 years, later reduced to 10), analog transmissions would cease and the channels would be returned to the government for reallocation to new services. In the most crowded markets, some low-power broadcasters would have to be displaced to make room for new digital allotments to full-power incumbents. Ironically, the American public would end up with less choices than in analog TV.

As the process unfolded, a broad alliance of interest groups, political entrepreneurs, academics, and public interest advocates coalesced against the plan. The context resembled the 1967–1975 period, when an heterodox political coalition challenged the existing license renewal process (Horwitz, 1989). The new coalition was also heterodox: It included free-market academics and taxpayer groups demanding that the new licenses be auctioned, media access advocates pressing for better opportunities for community and noncommercial TV, and wireless operators seeking cheaper access to the airwaves. Key allies were found in the White House, in Congress, and even within the FCC.[3] For the first time, having broadcasters pay for spectrum was being seriously debated in Congress and elsewhere.

Broadcast trade groups led by the National Association of Broadcasters (NAB) mounted a formidable lobbying campaign in support of the original licensing plan. Local stations across the nation ran spots prepared by the NAB claiming that spectrum auctions threatened free local TV and urged viewers to mobilize against the "TV Tax." The context presaged an uphill battle for broadcasters. Both parties agreed on the need to balance the federal budget, and the billions of dollars raised by the PCS license auctions in early 1995 created strong incentives for considering alternative licensing schemes, including auctions. The demand for spectrum continued to soar, and the White House as well as several senior FCC staff members clearly favored a plan that could make more frequencies immediately available for other users. Moreover, the elite press was unabashedly critical of the plan for its largesse with broadcasters, a largesse estimated to be worth somewhere between $11 and $70 billion.

The issue came to a climax in early 1996, when Congress prepared for a final vote on the new Telecom Act. Ultimately, the bill that passed met broadcasters' key demands: The FCC would dole out digital TV licenses to existing licensees exclusively, with few strings attached.[4] Combined with a number of other favorable provisions (a rise in ownership caps, the extension in the duration of broadcast licenses, and reduced scrutiny for license renewals), there was hardly more than broadcasters could have bargained for. A year later, Congress introduced an equipment penetration safeguard that effectively extended the deadline for the return of analog channels well beyond the original 10-year period.

Let us now consider how each of the theoretical approaches discussed earlier sheds light on this outcome. To some, the answer is evident: The Congressional majority yielded to the lobbying campaign organized by the powerful broadcast interests. But the question of why this lobbying effort was more effective than that of the coalition that opposed the plan remains open. After all, the coalition also included large corporations such as mobile telephony operators and many of the information technology industry heavyweights. In terms of their degree of organization and the resources available for political action, these stakeholders can hardly be considered less "powerful" than local broadcasters (unless power is measured by successful influence on policy outcomes, which as noted before is a circular argument). The interest-group approach thus tells us little about why broadcasters were able to block reforms. The ideological approach seems equally unsatisfactory. In fact, if anything, there was growing consensus among academics and the policy elite that the transition to digital demanded serious spectrum management reforms (e.g., Pepper & Levy, 1999; Sunstein, 2000). The technology approach is also of little explanatory value: As a matter of fact, most other nations have introduced a digital multiplexing scheme whereby incumbents broadcasters are expected to share capacity with new entrants (Galperin, 2002).

Let us turn now to the examination of the institutional arrangements within which U.S. spectrum policies are formulated. Consider the American electoral system. The system is based on single-member districts elected in most cases by plurality of votes, creating strong incentives for congressional representatives to develop a personal vote (Cain *et al.*, 1984; Cox & McCubbins, 2001). In other words, the fortunes of individual congressional members are tied less to the party's national performance than to each one's ability to raise campaign funds and deliver benefits to constituencies within their districts. The system is also unique for its lax rules on political advertising and the lack of mandatory free airtime for political candidates (Norris, 2000). Cultivating friendly relations with local broadcasters is therefore crucial for nurturing a personal vote. These relations are based on what Hazlett and Spitzer (2000) have described as a quid pro quo between legislators and broadcasters: Valuable spectrum rights are traded for "good" political behavior.

Therefore, in rejecting auctions and endorsing the licensing plan, legislators were not simply reacting to pressure from a powerful interest group. They were also self-interestedly defending a convenient arrangement that tends to favor incumbent reelection, since incumbents are typically better funded and attract more coverage than challengers (Snider, 2001). With general elections only months away, the Congressional majority acted conservatively against alternative licensing plans which carried high political risks in the present but uncertain future rewards. The original licensing plan was an attempt to reinvent spectrum scarcity when the new technology in fact challenged it, and thus extend the existing quid pro quo between legislators and local broadcasters into the digital TV era.

In historical perspective, the fact that U.S. spectrum policies have consistently benefited incumbent broadcasters (at the expense of other well-organized and well-financed interest groups) reflects not only the "power" of the NAB and other broadcast trade groups but more critically the organization of the American electoral system which tends to create shared preferences between local licensees and incumbent legislators. While the FCC has in recent times often challenged this arrangement, legislators have a variety of instruments at their disposal to secure agency compliance, including—as in the preceding example—direct legislation.[5] It is interesting to note that in other nations different political arrangements have favored different licensing schemes for digital TV. In Britain, for example, a prohibition on political advertising on TV and strict rules about editorializing and report-ing create less opportunities for bargains between broadcasters and elected officials, since there is less at stake to begin with. Not surprisingly, the licensing of digital broadcasting has been accompanied by drastic reforms in the allocation of spectrum rights.

Conclusion

The new institutionalism has much to offer to communication and information policy scholars at a time when the governance regime for new technologies is growing in complexity. Today, the rules created and enforced by traditional regulatory bodies on a national scale are now only part of a multilayered regime that includes international treaties, voluntary self-regulation, and semipublic cooperative arrangements under the umbrella of a vast collection of organizations (Marsden, 2000; Drake, 2001). This opens a fertile new territory for institutional analysis, for it provides the conceptual tools to investigate the implications of different institutional designs for the global governance of new information and communication technologies. There is a growing body of literature exploring how different choices in the operating procedures of nontraditional policymaking arenas such as ICANN and IETF affects the ability of different interests to influence outcomes (e.g., Froomkin, 2000; Mueller, 2002; Price, 2002). While the implications of different policymaking arrangements at the national level are rather well understood, we are only now starting to grasp those of a more fluid, ad hoc, non-sovereignty-based process of regulating global networks. For example, what would be the result of increased ITU oversight of the Internet as demanded by many developing nations in the World Summit on the Information Society? In this sense, institutional analysis can product-ively inform these ongoing debates.

An important component of this research agenda will be to map out the changing balance of power resulting from this transformation in the global communication order. As noted, an important contribution of insti-tutional analysis has been to reveal the structural barriers faced by public interest groups in communication and information policymaking at the national level, among them lack of bureaucratic transparency (particularly in developing nations), complex rulemaking processes, and lengthy consultation and appeal procedures, all of which militates against representation of diffused interests. Generally speaking, traditional rulemaking bodies, at both the national and international level, were not designed to accommodate participation by nontraditional political actors (e.g., NGOs). As new policymaking arenas emerge and old ones are reconfigured, an institutional perspective could similarly contribute to detect new mechanisms of exclusion, and hence could inform the creation of arrangements that enable broader participation by new actors in the governance of global communications.

Notes

1 In particular, this ignores the seminal work of Harold Innis, Dallas Smythe, Herbert Schiller, and several others.
2 According to the most recent data produced by the FCC Media Bureau (September 2003).
3 In fact, FCC Chairman Reed Hundt proved to be one of the more staunch critics of the digital TV licensing plan (see Hundt, 2000).
4 In return, local incumbents agreed to the formation of an ad hoc Presidential committee to advise the government on the public interest obligations to be imposed on digital broadcasters. After fifteen months of deliberations, the committee produced a rather toothless report that is yet to translate into any substantive rules (Taylor & Ornstein, 2002).
5 For a discussion see McCubbins and Schwartz (1984).

References

Arthur, Brian. 1989. Competing technologies, increasing returns, and lock-in by historical events. *Economic Journal* 99:116–131.

Becker, Gary. 1983. A theory of competition among pressure groups for political influence. *Quarterly Journal of Economics* 98(3):371–400.

Benkler, Yochai. 1998. Communications infrastructure regulation and the distribution of control over content. *Telecommunications Policy* 22(3):183–196.

Brock, Gerald W. 1994. *Telecommunication policy for the information age: From monopoly to competition.* Cambridge, MA: Harvard University Press.

Burgelman, Jean-Claude. 1997. Issues and assumptions in communications policy and research in Western Europe: A critical analysis. In *International media research: A critical survey*, eds. J. Corner, P. Schlesinger, and R. Silverstone, pp. 123–153. New York: Routledge.

Cain, Bruce E., Ferejohn, John A., and Fiorina, Morris P. 1984. The constituency service basis of the personal vote for U.S. representatives and British members of parliament. *American Political Science Review* 78(1):110–125.

Cherry, Barbara A., and Bauer, Johannes M. 2002. Institutional arrangements and price rebalancing: Empirical evidence from the United States and Europe. *Information Economics and Policy* 14:495–517.

Cowhey, Peter F., and McCubbins, Matthew D., eds. 1995. *Structure and policy in Japan and the United States.* New York: Cambridge University Press.

Cox, Gary W., and McCubbins, Mathew D. 2001. The institutional determinants of economic policy outcomes. In *Presidents, parliaments, and policy*, eds. S. Haggard and M. D. McCubbins, pp. 21–63. New York: Cambridge University Press.

David, Paul A. 1986. *Narrow windows, blind giants, and angry orphans: The dynamics of systems rivalries and dilemmas of technology policy.* CEPR Working Paper 10. Stanford, CA: CEPR.

Derthick, Martha, and Quirk, Paul J. 1985. *The politics of deregulation.* Washington, DC: Brookings Institution.

Drake, William. 2001. Communications. In *Managing global issues: Lessons learned*, eds. P. J. Simmons and C. de Jonge Oudrat, pp. 25–74. Washington, DC: Carnegie Endowment for International Peace.

Dutton, William. 1992. The ecology of games shaping telecommunications policy. *Communication Theory* 2(4):303–328.

European Commission. 1993. *White paper on growth, competitiveness, and employment: The challenges and ways forward into the 21st century.* COM(93) 700 final. <http://europa.eu.int/en/record/white/c93700/contents.html>

Froomkin, Michael. 2000. Semi-private international rulemaking: Lessons learned from the WIPO domain name process. In *Regulating the global information society*, ed. C. T. Marsden, pp. 211–232. New York: Routledge.

Galperin, Hernan. 2002. Can the U.S. transition to digital TV be fixed?: Some lessons from the European Union case. *Telecommunications Policy* 26(1–2):3–15.

Galperin, Hernan. 2004. *New TV, old politics: The transition to digital TV in the U.S. and Britain.* New York: Cambridge University Press.

Garnham, Nicholas. 1990. *Capitalism and communication: Global culture and the economics of information.* London: Sage.

Geller, Henry. 1998. Public interest regulation in the digital TV era. *Cardozo Arts & Entertainment Law Journal* 16(2–3):341–368.

Goldstein, Judith L., and Keohane, Robert O. 1993. Idea and foreign policy. An analytical framework. In *Ideas and foreign policy: Beliefs, institutions, and political change*, eds. J. L. Goldstein and R. O. Kehoane, pp. 3–30. Ithaca, NY: Cornell University Press.

Gourevitch, Peter. 1986. *Politics in hard times: Comparative responses to international economic crises.* Ithaca, NY: Cornell University Press.

Hall, Peter A. 1986. *Governing the economy: The politics of state intervention in Britain and France.* New York: Oxford University Press.

Hall, Peter A. 1992. The movement from Keynesianism to monetarism: Institutional analysis and British economic policy in the 1970's. In *Structuring politics: Historical institutionalism in comparative analysis*, eds. S. Steinmo, K. Thelen, and F. Longstreth, pp. 90–113. New York: Cambridge University Press.

Hall, Peter A. 1997. The role of interests, institutions, and ideas in the comparative political economy of the industrialized nations. In *Comparative politics: Rationality, culture, and structure*, eds. M. I. Lichbach and A. S. Zuckerman, pp. 174–207. New York: Cambridge University Press.

Hazlett, Thomas W., and Spitzer, Matthew L. 2000. Digital television and the quid pro quo. *Business and Politics* 2(2):115–159.

Horwitz, Robert B. 1989. *The irony of regulatory reform: The deregulation of American telecommunications.* New York: Oxford University Press.

Huber, Peter. 1997. *Law and disorder in cyberspace: Abolish the FCC and let common law rule the telecosm.* New York: Oxford University Press.

Hundt, Reed E. 2000. *You say you want a revolution: A story of information age politics.* New Haven, CT: Yale University Press.

Johnson, David R., and Post, David. 1996. Law and borders—The rise of law in cyberspace. *Stanford Law Review* 48:1367–1402.

Krasner, Stephen D. 1989. Sovereignty: An institutional perspective. In *The elusive state: International and comparative perspectives*, ed. J. A. Caporaso, pp. 69–96. New York: Sage.

Krasnow, Erwin G., and Longley, Lawrence D. 1978. *The politics of broadcast regulation.* New York: St. Martin's Press.

Levy, Brian, and Spiller, Pablo T., eds. 1996. *Regulations, institutions, and commitment.* New York: Cambridge University Press.

March, James G., and Olsen, Johan P. 1984. The new institutionalism: Organizational factors in political life. *American Political Science Review* 78:734–749.

Marsden, Chris T. 2000. Introduction: Information and communications technologies, globalisation, and regulation. In *Regulating the global information society*, ed. C. T. Marsden, pp. 1–40. New York: Routledge.

McCubbins, Mathew D., and Schwartz, Thomas. 1984. Congressional oversight overlooked: Police patrols versus fire alarms. *American Journal of Political Science* 28(1):165–179.

Mosco, Vincent. 1988. Toward a theory of the state and telecommunications policy. *Journal of Communication* 38(1):107–124.

Mosco, Vincent. 1998. Myth-ing links: Power and community on the information highway. *The Information Society* 14(1):57–62.

Mueller, Milton. 1995. Why communications policy is passing "mass communication" by: Political economy as the missing link. *Critical Studies in Mass Communication* 12(4):457–472.

Mueller, Milton. 2002. *Ruling the root: Internet governance and the taming of cyberspace.* Cambridge, MA: MIT Press.

Mulgan, Geoff J. 1991. *Communication and control: Networks and the new economies of communication.* New York: Guilford.

Murdock, Graham, and Golding, Peter. 1999. Common markets: Corporate ambitions and communication trends in the UK and Europe. *Journal of Media Economics* 12(2):117–132.

Noll, Roger G. 1986. The political and institutional context of communication policy. In *Marketplace for telecommunications: Regulation and deregulation in industrialized democracies*, ed. M. S. Snow, pp. 42–65. New York: Longman.

Noll, Roger G., and Rosenbluth, Frances M. 1995. Telecommunications policy: structure, process, outcomes. In *Structure and policy in Japan and the United States*, eds. P. F. Cowhey and M. M. McCubbins, pp. 119–165. New York: Cambridge University Press.

Norris, Pippa. 2000. *A virtuous circle: Political communications in postindustrial societies.* New York: Cambridge University Press.

North, Douglass C. 1990. *Institutions, institutional change, and economic performance.* New York: Cambridge University Press.

North, Douglass C. 1993. Toward a theory of institutional change. In *Political economy: Institutions, competition, and representation*, eds. W. Barnett, M. Hinich, and N. Schofield, pp. 61–69. New York: Cambridge University Press.

Office of Telecommunications. 1995. *Beyond the telephone, the television, and the PC.* London: OFTEL.

Olson, Mancur. 1971. *The logic of collective action: Public goods and the theory of groups.* Cambridge, MA: Harvard University Press.

Organization for Economic Cooperation and Development. 1997. *Global information infrastructure–global information society: Policy requirements.* Paris: OECD.

Pepper, Robert, and Levy, Jonathan. 1999. Convergence: Public benefits and policy challenges. In *Convergence in European digital TV regulation*, eds. C. T. Marsden and S. Verhulst, pp. 21–36. London: Blackstone Press.

Petrazzini, Ben, and Krishnaswamy, Girija. 1998. Socioeconomic implications of telecommunications liberalization: India in the international context. *The Information Society* 14(1):3–18.

Pool, Ithiel de Sola. 1983. *Technologies of freedom.* Cambridge, MA: Harvard University Press.

Posner, Richard. 1974. Theories of economic regulation. *Bell Journal of Economics and Management Science* 5(2):335–358.

Price, Monroe. 2002. *Media and sovereignty: The global information revolution and its challenge to state power.* Cambridge, MA: MIT Press.

Schiller, Dan. 1982. *Telematics and government.* Norwood, NJ: Ablex.

Snider, James H. 2001. The paradox of news bias: How local broadcasters influence information policy. In *Politics, discourse, and American society: New agendas*, eds. R. P. Hart and B. H. Sparrow, pp. 111–128. New York: Rowman & Littlefield.

Stigler, George. 1971. The theory of economic regulation. *Bell Journal of Economics and Management Science* 2(1):1–21.

Stinchcombe, Arthur. 1997. On the virtues of the old institutionalism. *Annual Review of Sociology* 23:1–18.

Sunstein, Cass R. 2000. Television and the public interest. *California Law Review* 88:499–564.

Taylor, Paul, and Ornstein, Norman. 2002. *A broadcast spectrum fee for campaign finance reform.* New America Foundation Spectrum Series Working Paper 4, June. <www.newamerica.net>

Thatcher, Mark. 1999. *The politics of telecommunications: National institutions, convergence, and change in Britain and France.* New York: Oxford University Press.

Vogel, Steven K. 1996. *Freer markets, more rules: Regulatory reform in advanced industrial countries.* Ithaca, NY: Cornell University Press.

Weaver, Kent R., and Rockman, Bert A., eds. 1993. *Do institutions matter?: Government capabilities in the United States and abroad.* Washington, DC: Brookings Institution.

Zysman, John. 1994. How institutions create historically rooted trajectories of growth. *Industrial and Corporate Change* 3:243–283.

29

THE KNOWLEDGE-BASED ECONOMY

A Sisyphus model[1]

Don Lamberton

Source: *Prometheus* 15(1) (1997): 73–81.

Abstract

The current fashionable emphasis on the knowledge-based economy is missing the real significance of the dichotomy between tacit and codified knowledge. A continuing input of tacit knowledge is essential to sustained innovation and growth. Without this, the modern thrust towards codification based on IT can lead to an economy with plenty of processing capacity but no new knowledge to process.

My objective in this paper is a very limited one, i.e. to suggest that the current fashionable emphasis on the knowledge-based economy is missing the real significance of the dichotomy between tacit and codified knowledge. Had I been able to follow Michael Kirby's dictum that a good paper should try to make only one point, that is the point I should have striven for—although I should have reserved the right to make that point in several ways.

It may help if we avoid the wasted words and hours that can so easily be devoted to purely semantic issues—to the different meanings of information and knowledge. If we can be broadminded enough to extend our thinking from economics (whatever that is) to the study of information-processing, why should we not take in knowledge-structures as well? After all, it has been said that "as a rule, information is designed to effect or affect knowledge".[2] So let us reject the claim that "the narrow focus is science and the wide lens is speculation".[3] There is also a very practical reason to adopt this stance. As Arrow remarked, "information is a descriptive term for an economically interesting category of goods which has not hitherto been accorded much attention by economic theorists".[4] Attention has shifted in the quarter of a century since he wrote those words but not enough to invalidate his assessment.

Who/what is Sisyphus? Sisyphus was a legendary king of Corinth. It was his punishment in Hades to roll a heavy rock up a hill. As he neared the top, the rock was subjected to some exogenous force and rolled down again. The process went on endlessly.

Let me sketch the content of this paper. First, I shall look to the dichotomy between tacit and codified knowledge, as reflected in the work of some recent contributors: Nelson and Winter, Eliasson and Abramovitz and David and then, turning the clock back, as discussed by one of the pioneers, scientist philosopher Michael Polanyi.[5] Then I shall examine some recent versions of the knowledge-based economy: Eliasson, Abramovitz and David and the recent study of the Australian case commissioned by ASTEC and CSIRO.[6]

Next, I shall suggest as a starting point a simple model in which there are two kinds of knowledge, tacit and codified. Finally, I enter a plea for a taxonomy of information based on a characteristics approach as a possible means of building more complex models which might depict successfully the role of knowledge in the processes of economic growth.

Tacit and codified knowledge

Nelson and Winter start from Polyani's observation: "We know more than we can tell". They assign a "central place" to "knowledge that cannot be articulated". They reason from cases like the skills of swimming, driving and landing a plane to the case of the researcher attempting to model human psychological processes. In each, they say, "language is an imperfect tool for conveying the information they need". They sense ambivalence on the part of both learner and researcher: "Both hope that words will smooth their individual paths to achievement; both know that there is no distinction in the achievement if the path is *too smooth*" [Italics added].

They try to identify the determinants of the degree of tacitness: "much operational knowledge remains tacit because it cannot be articulated fast enough, because it is impossible to articulate all that is necessary to a successful performance, and because language cannot simultaneously serve to describe relationships and characterize the things related".

Difficulties begin to arise when the skills change to those of the businessman —and here Nelson and Winter are on common ground with some of the old debates. They contrast orthodoxy which stresses choice and deliberation with their own approach which emphasizes "the *automaticity* of skillful behavior and the suppression of choice that this involves". We might note that others have levelled just this indictment against orthodoxy, e.g. "Conventional economics is not about choice, but about acting according to necessity".[7]

The Nelson and Winter approach goes on to make a valuable contribution through the concept of organizational routine—as organizational memory, a truce among organization members, and as a target. It does not seem to me, however, that they succeed in so broadening the tacit part of the information activities that it could deal with what they admit is "fundamental ambiguity" shrouding the set of innovation alternatives.

They wish to emphasize the evolutionary aspect:

> Real search processes take place in specific historical contexts, and their outcomes clearly depend in part on what those contexts contain in the way of problem solutions that are available to be "found". What there is to be found consists in large part of the fruits, by-products, and residues of information-processing activities elsewhere in the society. The flow of general social history thus impinges directly on the firm through its search activities, and searching at t is not the same thing as searching at $T > t$.[8]

The general social history, especially of the firm and the members of that organization, can open the way for real innovation, for the crossing of many different kinds of borders, for the solution that comes before the problem. These activities involve tacit knowledge; and that tacit knowledge can be viewed as either used as such, perhaps secretly; or, more probably, used as an input to organizational routines that in effect require that the tacit knowledge is converted to codified knowledge.

So I was led to look elsewhere. Gunnar Eliasson[9] likewise builds on the Polanyi contribution. For him, "information . . . [means] coded and communicable knowledge, that can be articulated and understood if the requisite receiver competence exists". So here a new element seems to be introduced—competence in information-handling.

Of course, competence in some general sense had been widely assumed in conventional theory and much effort has gone, especially on the part of management experts, into persuading business and governments that it can be identified and created in return for an appropriate consultancy fee.

Eliasson argues that communicating knowledge is more than a matter of transaction costs.

> There are various ways of demonstrating the existence of tacit knowledge beyond the notion of prohibitive costs to communicate. If individuals in teams or organizations exhibit sufficient heterogeneity in competence or talent there will always be significant knowledge

that cannot be communicated due to lacking receiver competence
... It is "tacit" to those who don't understand.[10]

So here tacitness seems to come about simply as a consequence of specialization; and it can emerge also because there is learning-by-doing with a
variety of learning experiences.[11] It still does not address the possibility of
new knowledge. So I suggest that there are two problems here for economics;
first, it is unsatisfactory to assume that all knowledge is codifiable; and,
second, even when tacitness is introduced into the analysis, we have to be
careful about the source of the tacitness.

Another comprehensive exploration of these matters is contained in the
report of an OECD conference in 1994.[12] Foray and Lundvall note several
propositions: first, the production and distribution of knowledge has special characteristics which are not compatible with mainstream economic
theory; second, knowledge plays an important role in the economy; third,
the importance of that role may have been increasing; fourth, investment
in knowledge and capabilities is characterized by increasing returns; fifth,
there has been a proliferation of new disciplines and sub-disciplines, e.g.
economics of intellectual property rights, standardization and information
technology.

They then argue that fundamental principles of economic analysis are not
easily applied to knowledge activities; that there have been major changes in
the mode of production and distribution of knowledge—"a new dynamic
between the formation of tacit versus codified knowledge"; and that "the
most pertinent political issues of the present era", e.g. globalization, underdevelopment and environmental sustainability, "[c]annot be understood and
tackled adequately without a rethinking of economics, where the focus is
on knowledge and learning".

Abramovitz and David contributed the opening paper to this OECD
collection. In their first paragraph, they concede critical roles for tacit
knowledge but then focus attention on codified knowledge and "the impetus
imparted to investment in intangible, knowledge-intensive forms of wealth".
As befits the computer age, the codified component is compact and standardized and easily transmitted, stored and reproduced, and, more contentiously,
transferable "over long distances and across organisational boundaries at
low cost".

While they concede further that the growth of codified knowledge is not
all there is to the story of the rise in intangible investments, their failure to
deal explicitly with *tacit* knowledge means that the contribution of that
component cannot be acknowledged fully. I shall return to this later.

Now consider the pioneer's views:

The declared aim of modern science is to establish a strictly
detached, objective knowledge. Any falling short of this ideal is

accepted only as a temporary imperfection, which we must aim at eliminating. But suppose that tacit thought forms an indispensable part of all knowledge, then the ideal of eliminating all persona] elements of knowledge would, in effect, aim at the destruction of all knowledge. The ideal of exact science would turnout to be fundamentally misleading and possibly a source of devastating fallacies.[13]

This does, of course, point to a self-contradiction in the advice I have been in the habit of giving to STEP and other research students: "Find a good problem. Ask a question". Polanyi's comment follows Plato: if you know what you are looking for, there is no problem; if you do not know what you are looking for, you cannot expect to find anything. A solution lies in the role of tacit knowledge of "as yet undisclosed, perhaps as yet unthinkable, consequences". Perhaps this links with Don Aitkin's comments about serendipity, although I personally think the role of tacit knowledge is far removed from accidental discovery.[14]

So we are left, according to Foray and Lundvall, with skills, shared beliefs and modes of interpretation (which I suggest may or may not be able to be articulated). I read of late that "facilitated monitoring" is being recommended by consultants as a way of maintaining skills and passing them from one generation to the next.

The knowledge-based economy

The difficulties in the way of implementing the tacit *vs* codified dichotomy are considerable. There is a well-established effort to gather information relating to an information sector and this stands in contrast to analytical efforts that see both tacit and codified knowledge activities as integral parts of all economic activity. One approach that hints at what we now seek dates back to the 1970s OECD work which sought to distinguish routine information activities from non-routine.[15] These same difficulties surface again in the more recent knowledge-based studies.

In the works cited earlier, Eliasson provides tables of labour use but these are in effect rearrangements of the information sector categories: New Knowledge Creation is the old Information Producers; Economic Coordination takes the place of Information Processors and Information Infrastructure; Knowledge and Information Transfer corresponds to Information Distributors.

Creation of New Knowledge breaks down into R&D and Design. But we are no closer to a separation of tacit from codified. R&D work and expenditure clearly takes in routine activities: maintaining the scientific enterprise, printing and publishing, updating observation records, and, dare we say it, meeting at conferences and seminars. Recent discussions about the effectiveness of R&D subsidies would seem to have accepted what many knew already that marketing and much else could be included if the incentive were great enough.

Abramovitz and David analyze investment in intangibles, primarily in education but also R&D and health, safety and mobility. But surely much of what is captured in these categories is well and truly codified.

A similar but more extreme treatment seems to emerge in the ASTEC/ CSIRO study of Australia and the knowledge economy. As Engelbrecht observes this study (over) emphasizes R&D: "R&D is only one of the many growth factors. The role and importance of human capital in the growth process, and its formation through various forms of education and learning, is not even explored. Neither is the role of organisational capital and competencies, or issues concerning national and international knowledge spillovers. The national system of innovation is reduced to the R&D system.[16]

So I suggest we are not getting much help from the knowledge-based economy fashion with the empirical work. To date it has been very largely a renaming of the information sector initiative.

A model of the knowledge process

I suggested earlier that we can begin with a two categories of knowledge model: tacit and codified. Keynes was content to assume that information/ knowledge was part of all investment outlay—he hazarded a guess that it was about 5%. Perhaps we can as a start recognize the importance of tacit knowledge in a similar fashion—say, 10% of information outlays.

The process can be envisaged as one in which the tacit knowledge producing activity initiates an innovation process. Successive phases would be the creation of tacit knowledge, its application and conversion in part to codified form, in parallel with maintenance of a stock of tacit knowledge. Production, application and maintenance of both kinds of knowledge each require their supporting organizational capital. Modelling must avoid the linear thinking habits of scientists and science policy writers; there is much scope for feed-back loops.

Central to this process is the conversion of tacit to codified. This has been much affected by information technology developments.[17] It may well be that this brings a form of lock-in. Kenneth Boulding confessed, thirty years ago, to being worried about one aspect of these developments:

> The very power of the computer to simulate complex systems by very high-speed arithmetic may prevent search for those simplified formulations which are the essence of progress in theory. I have an uneasy feeling, for instance, that if the computer had been around at the time of Copernicus, nobody would have ever bothered with him, because the computers could have handled the Ptolemaic epicycles with perfect ease.[18]

116

I suggest that tacit knowledge may suffer the same neglect as those "simplified formulations". This points to a weak link in what is now being called the spiral process.[19]

A second weak link involves the crossing of boundaries, especially organizational ones. Much writing assumes that once knowledge is codified, the available information technology effects transfer. The reality would seem to be that codification, because it is not a purely technical matter but involves human and organizational capabilities, runs up against limits of affordability.[20] As a consequence, codification may be achieved only locally rather than extend more widely to regions and internationally. It is much more likely that the paths will be determined by preexisting networks which are part of organizational capital. And all this may be modified depending on how important are elements of secrecy and the erosion of private property rights in information. Arrow has drawn attention to the erosion of the informational advantage that is often the primary value possessed by the firm and to the possibly significant impact on the future development of firms.[21]

A taxonomy of information

Modelling of the knowledge process can begin with the tacit and codified dichotomy and proceed along the lines I have suggested. However, a wider view is called for if the notions of the knowledge-based economy and the new growth theory initiative are to be fused together. Here, I suggest that the major task to be tackled is the development of a taxonomy of information.[22] If, as sector studies have suggested, information-handling activities of all kinds together constitute the major claim on resources, the present statistical coverage of those activities must be judged completely inadequate by comparison with the richness of detail available for agricultural and manufacturing activities. Data problems with respect to some major activities are growing. For example, deregulation/privatization is reducing significantly the data available for the key telecommunications industry, the justification being protection of commercial interests.

I know there are serious conceptual and measurement problems but surely the statistical agencies can do better than at present. A first step would be to make a start with developments that have assumed some importance: computers, videos, VCRs, ATMx, etc. To do this runs the risk of recording the items of technology hardware and telling little about their use or about information activities in general. To illustrate, in the case of telephones, we are given statistics of sets and lines. An attempt can be made to ascertain the pattern of calls, their duration and purpose, e.g. different demand elasticities have been found for domestic calls that are work-related as opposed to those concerned with family matters or entertainment.[23]

Potentially important dichotomies have emerged. In addition to tacit/codified, consumption *vs* investment, private *vs* social are applicable. There is a need to identify characteristics that are economically significant. Weerahandi *et al.* of Bell Communication Research developed a framework for forecasting demand and new services using the characteristics approach.[24] Unfortunately, they focussed on the characteristics of the technology rather than of information. Examples of needed dimensions are the frequency of observation, the static or dynamic nature of the information, the degree of accuracy required, the promptness with which it must be made available, the complementary information needed, and the universality of its distribution.

Pieces, batches or flows?

I find it interesting that Arrow in his seminal 1962 paper formulated his influential propositions relating to divisibility and appropriability with respect to "a given piece of information" or "a given body of information".[25] Some time later Machlup, writing about optimum utilization of knowledge, tried to simplify matters by dealing with "some particular, specific batches of knowledge", although his view was that [k]nowledge is not a pile of homogeneous material, but a complex structure of heterogeneous thoughts, each available at zero marginal cost but usable only together with resources available only at positive, and often very high cost".[26]

Now both these authors recognized the flow nature of information. In fact, Arrow was later to define the firm as "an incompletely connected network of information flows" and Machlup always made much of the distinction between stocks and flows. But just as Arrow, as he developed his ideas about the economics of information, was led to question Jevons' slogan, "bygones are forever bygones", I should like to question some aspects of his 1962 paper.[27]

If pieces of information are not identical items in a pile but rather complement, or serve as substitutes for, each other—if they fit together in a developing "structure of heterogeneous thoughts", e.g. complementarity between tacit and codified knowledge, does this modify the reasoning about divisibility and appropriability?

A piece of information may be useless without the needed complements and those complements may be dated. In a sense, the flow may be divided into dated pieces but the prize goes to whoever secures all the pieces in the sequence. Perhaps the "building on the shoulders of giants" points to this line of thought. Perhaps data registration rights are a good practical illustration: denial of access to data submitted to secure registration of, for example, a chemical compound, can, when the patent terminates, be a formidable barrier to entry by a generic producer.

When we move away from the well-defined piece of information, divisibility takes on a different meaning. We can even imagine situations in which a buyer may be willing to buy the same piece of information twice! We should

118

therefore ask whether this modifies the standard conclusion about the creation of pervasive economies of scale. Similarly, appropriability is transformed. Strategic considerations enter and a technological leader may well be able to create unassailable informational barriers to entry.

Perhaps these ideas follow on from some of the perceptive comments we can find in discussion of decision processes. A. G. Hart long ago commented on decisions "taken in the consciousness that they are part of a developing chain",[28] and more recently Stiglitz pleaded for modelling of the economy "in which information is continuously being collected and processed and in which decisions, based on that information, are continuously being made".[29]

Tacit knowledge plays a major role in this shift of focus. Such knowledge is central to the "structure of heterogenous thoughts" and we need to find a place for it in our analysis.

Similarly, we need to find policy ways to foster the role of tacit knowledge. This means looking for the weak points in the process: the initiation of the creation of tacit knowledge, the converting of tacit into codified knowledge, and the maintenance of the stock of tacit knowledge. The danger is that IT carry the day and the knowledge-based economy find that it has plenty of processing capacity but no new knowledge to process. I am reminded of Norbert Weiner's comment about his colleagues' aspirations to extend to social sciences the method of the natural sciences:

> From believing this necessary, they come to believe it possible. In this ... they show an excessive optimism, and a misunderstanding of the nature of all scientific achievement.[30]

The dangerous belief now is that all important knowledge can be codified. I am inclined to the view that it is neither necessary nor possible. The reality is much closer to the labour of Sisyphus.

Notes and references

1 Support from the Telstra Fund for Social and Policy Research in Telecommunications is gratefully acknowledged.
2 F. Machlup & Una Mansfield, 'Cultural Diversity in Studies of Information', in: F. Machlup & U. Mansfield (Eds.), *The Study of Information: Interdisciplinary Messages* (New York, Wiley, 1983), p. 9.
3 *Ibid.*
4 K. J. Arrow, *Collected Papers of Kenneth J. Arrow: Volume 4, The Economics of Information* (Oxford, Blackwell, 1984), p. 138.
5 R. R. Nelson & S. G. Winter, *An Evolutionary Theory of Economic Change* (Cambridge, MA, Harvard University Press, 1982); G. Eliasson *et al.*, *The Knowledge Based Information Economy* (Stockholm, Industrial Institute for Economic and Social Research, 1990); G. Eliason, *Firm Objectives, Controls and Organization: The Use of Information and the Transfer of Knowledge within the Firm* (Dordrecht, Kluwer Academic Publishers, 1996); M. Abramovitz & P. A.

David, 'Technological Change and the Rise of Intangible Investments: The US Economy's Growth-path in the Twentieth Century', in: OECD Documents, *Employment and Growth in the Knowledge-based Economy* (Paris, OECD, 1996); P. J. Sheehan *et al.*, *Australia and the Knowledge Economy: An Assessment of Enhanced Economic Growth Through Science and Technology* (Melbourne, Centre for Strategic Economic Studies, 1995); Michael Polanyi, *The Tacit Dimension* (London, Routledge & Regan Paul, 1967).

6 Eliasson *et al.*, *op. cit.*, Ref. 5; Eliasson, *op. cit.*, Ref. 5; Abramovitz & David, *op. cit.*, Ref. 5; Sheehan *et al.*, *op. cit.*, Ref. 5.

7 G. L. S. Shackle, *Decision, Order and Time in Human Affairs* (Cambridge, Cambridge University Press, 1969), 2nd Edn., p. 272.

8 Nelson & Winter, *op. cit.*, Ref. 5, p. 172.

9 Eliasson *et al.*, *op. cit.*, Ref. 5.

10 *Ibid.*, p. 17.

11 Eliasson, *op. cit.*, Ref. 5, p. 16.

12 OECD, *op. cit.*, Ref. 5.

13 *Ibid.*, p. 20.

14 He adds: "In fact, had anyone sought money from us [the ARGC] on the argument that he or she would do some research in the hope that an accidental discovery would arise, we should have thought them barmy" ('The Australian Research Grants Committee: An Account of the Way Things Were', *Prometheus*, *14*, 2, December 1996, p. 189). Note, however, that the medieval Latin *invenire* meant accidental discovery while *ars* meant technological knowhow.

15 OECD, *Information Activities, Electronics and Telecommunications Technologies, Volume 1* (Paris, OECD, 1981), Table I.3, p. 30.

16 H-J. Engelbrecht, 'Review of Australia and the Knowledge Economy', *Prometheus*, *14*, 2, December 1996, p. 266.

17 See, for example, Masu Uekusa, 'The Effect of Innovations in Information Technology on Corporate and Industrial Organization in Japan', in: Takashi Shiraishi & Shigeto Tsuru (Eds), *Economic Institutions in a Dynamic Society: Search for a New Frontier* (London, Macmillan, 1989), pp. 162–183; Geert Duysters, *The Dynamics of Technical Innovation: The Evolution and Development of Information Technology* (Cheltenham, UK, Edward Elgar, 1996).

18 K. E. Boulding, 'The Economics of Knowledge and the Knowledge of Economies', *American Economic Review*, LVI. 2, pp. 1–13, 1966, reprinted in D. M. Lamberton (Ed.), *Economics of Information and Knowledge* (Harmondsworth, UK, Penguin Books, 1971), p. 32.

19 See Foray & Lundvall, OECD Documents, *op. cit.*, Ref. 5.

20 See, for example, Pavel Pelikan, 'Language as a Limiting Factor for Centralization', *American Economic Review*, *59*, 4, 1969, pp. 625–631; Eric Brousseau, 'EDI and Inter-firm Relationships: Towards a Standardization of Coordination Processes?', *Information Economics and Policy*, 6(3–4), 1994, pp. 319–347.

21 K. J. Arrow, 'Methodological Individualism and Social Knowledge', *American Economic Review*, *84*(2), 1994, pp. 1–9.

22 D. M. Lamberton, 'Introduction: "Threatened Wreckage", or New Paradigm?', in: D. M. Lamberton (Ed.), *The Economics of Communication and Information* (Cheltenham, UK, Edward Elgar, 1996), pp. xiii–xxviii; *Information Economics: Research Strategies*, University of Strathclyde Department of Management Science Working Paper 96/11; 'A Taxonomy of Information', in: A. Mayere (Ed.), *Economic de l'information* (Paris, Hanrattan, forthcoming).

23 L. D. Taylor, *Telecommunications Demand in Theory and Practice* (Dordrecht, Kluwer Academic Publishers, 1994), p. 262.

24 S. Weerahandi, R. S. Hisiger & V. Chien, 'A Framework for Forecasting Demand and New Services and Their Cross Effects on Existing Services', *Information Economics and Policy*, 6, 2, 1994, pp. 143–162.

25 K. J. Arrow, 'Economic Welfare and the Allocation of Resources for Invention', in: National Bureau of Economic Research. *The Rate and Direction of Inventive Activity: Economic and Social Factors*, reprinted in D. M. Lamberton Ed., *The Economics of Communication and Information* (Cheltenham, UK, Edward Elgar, 1996), pp. 227–243.

26 F. Machlup, 'Optimum Utilization of Knowledge', *Knowledge, Information, and Decisions: Society*, 20, 1, 1982, pp. 8–10.

27 D. M. Lamberton, 'Innovation and Intellectual Property', in: M. Dodgson & R. Rothwell (Eds.), *The Handbook of Industrial Innovation* (Cheltenham, UK, Edward Elgar, 1994), pp. 304–306.

28 A. G. Hart, as quoted in D. M. Lamberton, 'Information and Profit', in: C. F. Carter & J. L. Ford (Eds), *Uncertainty and Expectations in Economics: Essays in Honour of G. L. S. Shackle* (Oxford, Blackwell, 1972), p. 208.

29 J. E. Stiglitz, 'Information and Economic Analysis: A Perspective, *Economic Journal*, Supplement to Vol. 95, 1985, p. 23.

30 Quoted by Murray Eden, 'Cybernetics: Closing the Loop', in: Machlup & Mansfield, *op. cit.*, Ref. 2, pp. 469–470.

30

COMMUNICATIONS

Blindspot of economics*

Dallas W. Smythe

Source: William H. Melody, Liora Salter and Paul Heyer (eds) (1981) *Culture, Communication and Dependency: The Tradition of H. A. Innis*, Norwood, NJ: Ablex, pp. 111–25.

The mass media of communications (principally television, radio, and the press) were a systemic invention of capitalism, developed since the last quarter of the nineteenth century. They were innovated to aid in the mass marketing of consumer goods and services produced by giant oligopolistic corporations using science both in managing production and marketing. Their principal product is audiences, which are sold to advertisers. Thereafter "audience-power" is exercised by the population mass-marketing consumer goods and services to themselves at no further cost to producing firms.

The mass media first appeared in the United Slates and England in the 1890s. Since World War II they have been the leading formation among the transnational corporations which have substituted cultural imperialism around the world in the interest of the capitalist core for earlier formal empire. That giant corporations manage demand has been observed by a few institutional and Marxist economists, although not by the dominant neoclassical economists. But the role of the market for audiences, produced by mass media and bought by advertisers, has been totally ignored. Economists have omitted to take account of a building block in economic reality which is crucially important to the functioning on monopoly (or corporate) capitalism.

Not surprisingly, the distance from recognition of the reality of mass communications in economic life differs according to the methodological/ideological stance of economists. In general, neoclassical theorists ignore the existence of mass communications, advertising, the conditions and ultimate consequences of the production and consumption of audience-power, and the fact of demand management by what is coming to he recognized as Consciousness Industry (the cluster of institutions most directly concerned in the design of consumer goods and services, their packaging, audience production, advertising, and marketing). Keynesians, despite their focus on aggregate demand management in the economy using tax, public expenditure, interest rate and money supply policies, have paid scarce attention to the implications of mass communication. A few institutional economists, for example, Galbraith[1] and Boulding,[2] do recognize the existence of the mass media, the reality of demand management by giant corporations through advertising, market research, product and package design, but stop short of recognizing the audience commodity. Marxist economists, like their bourgeois contemporaries, either ignore mass communications, demand management, and the audience commodity (such as Lenin) or they recognize mass communications and demand management but fail to see the significance of the market for audiences and audience-power (Baran & Sweezy[3]). Harold Innis also did not address the significance of mass communication in either his economic or his communication writings.

Neoclassical economics

Advertising is the unexplored frontier which has been an embarrassment to economic theorists since Alfred Marshall noticed it and naively distinguished between "combative" and "constructive" advertising.[4] At that point economic theory leapt into a psychological conception of advertising, one of manipulation, influence, persuasion, and so on, and stopped viewing it as an economic process. E. H. Chamberlin's comments to the effect that the objective is to establish "control of the buyer's consciousness" have been acquiesced in ever since by economic theorists.[5]

The "ostrich head in the sand" effect that economic theory exhibits regarding mass communications and advertising is traceable methodologically to its essentially idealistic perspective which substitutes for institutional analysis of oliogopolistic reality the projection of competitive models that now correspond to nothing significant in the real world. What do advertisers buy? Stigler defines "selling media" as the object purchased with advertising expenditures.[6] In fact, of course, the object purchased is *audiences produced* by "selling media." Kaldor defines the function of advertising as ". . . undoubtedly the provision of information concerning the prices and qualities of goods and services available in the markets."[7] The list of supposed objects of advertising expenditures could be extended lengthily and would yield a variety of idealistic, subjective entities: information, messages, images, meaning, manipulation, education. The consequence is that economic theorists get diverted from real products and real markets in which advertisers deal—audience-power and audience-markets—into innumerable cul-de-sacs. For example, Kaldor, regarding advertising "information" as the object of the exercise, treats *it* as a commodity, produced under joint-supply conditions with the product being advertised, and thus finds himself with a market for "advertising service" between advertising producers and advertising "buyers," for whom its price is always zero.[8] His logic is inescapable, given his wrong conception of the advertising process: The buyer of advertised goods is being subsidized by the advertiser by getting the advertisements at no price. What a bonus for the consumer, who of course is assumed to have sufficient information to exercise his/her consumer "sovereignty"! It is some kind of indoor sport for economic theorists and we find, inter alia, Lester G. Telser elaborating a model of "Supply and Demand for Advertising Messages"[9] untroubled by the fact that in the real world there is no such market but there is a market in which advertisers buy audiences produced by the communications mass media which somehow escapes his attention.

An amazing metaphysical tour de force of similar character is that of Stigler and Becker, concerning theory of taste.[10] Neoclassical economic theory eschewed applying marginal theory to phenomena outside the markets in which firms seek profits ("externalities" if they took the form of constraints on market behavior). Stigler and Becker violate this self-imposed restraint by projecting "a generalized calculus of utility-maximizing behavior" into nonmarket phenomena, specifically a taste for musical appreciation, for addictive commodities, and for fashion (including the role of advertising). They invent a subsequent generation of "commodities," which are produced by consumers who ". . . maximize a utility function of objects of choice, called commodities, that they produce with market goods, their own time, their skills, training, and other human capital and other inputs."[11] Thus the factors used by the consumer to produce the commodity (for self consumption, presumably) "music appreciation" include music lessons, attendance at musical performances, time spent on both, and so on. The "commodity" produced by addictions is "euphoria"; that from styled products bought in the real market for real prices, "social distinction." Economic concepts such as capital, investment, division of labor, price are all applied in this purely subjective fantasy without the quotation marks that might warn readers they were being used metaphorically and without rigor. Thus in one paragraph the terms "human capital conducive to music appreciation," "music capital," and "music human capital" slither around, undefined.[12] The authors take seriously Galbraith's charge that corporate capitalism manages demand through advertising and creates desires among consumers. Predictably, given the authors' ideological presuppositions, they argue "it is neither necessary nor useful to attribute to advertising the function of changing tastes."[13] By a definitional sleight-of-hand concerning the information content of advertising, and by integrating end-product advertising expenditures in the real world with their imaginary market in second-generation "commodities" produced by consumers for their own consumption, they use their marginal utility formulas to refute Galbraith. Lo and behold, the by-gone days when people did produce a substantial portion of their own consumption goods, such as baking meat pies, have been reproduced, only now the purchased ingredients are frozen foods and microwave ovens, and the "commodity" produced and consumed in the home is not edible food, but the "social distinction" resulting from popping the frozen meat pie into the microwave oven for a minute and then whisking it onto the damask-covered table for the happy family to greet ecstatically—just as in the television commercials.

Harvey Leibenstein in *Beyond Economic Man*[14] has been seen by many as offering significant improvements over the neoclassical marginalists. Arguing that the latter, with their idée fixe about allocative efficiency, have a useless tool, he analyzes what he calls "X-efficiency" by which he refers to all manner of motivational devices available to management which significantly affect the firm's profit performance. In several chapters he attempts to provide an "atomistic theory of consumers' behavior." Here he departs from the neoclassical assumption of consumer rationality by introducing what he calls "the snob effect," "the Veblen effect" (conspicuous consumption), and game theory as applied to intrahousehold allocation of spendable income. It is understandable that such innovations would cheer up academic economists, even if the cultural lag is remarkable. (Snobbery has been a conspicuous feature of capitalism, since the thirteenth century[15] and Veblen's Theory of the Leisure Class appeared some eighty years ago, game theory about thirty-five years ago.) Such anecdotal excursions lend a tinge of realism to the economists' indoor game. The fact remains, however, that Leibenstein does not recognize the role of demand management by monopoly corporations by means, inter alia, of advertising to get audience members to do their marketing for them, unpaid. Although he divides utility in unconventional ways (empathy utility, nonfunctional utility, and frustration utility), he never seems to escape the basic and naive notion that utility as a pleasure–pain calculus is the psychological footing of neoclassical economics. Moreover, in pursuit of his X-efficiency factor, he completely ignores the role of imagination and motivation in what we now call Consciousness Industry even from the standpoint of profits-for-the-firm. That the role of Consciousness Industry may produce fatal contradictions for the monopoly capitalist system is a systemic X factor which any exercise such as his, based on the capitalist firm as solidly as any neoclassical economist, could not be expected to envisage. I refer here merely to the tendency of capitalist industry to generate ever more trivial product and style changes which contribute, for example, to the present evidence of rigidity in the face of the energy crisis in the capitalist core. More dramatic contradictions abound in the real world.

Apart from the stultified area of neoclassical marginal theory proper, it should be noted that efforts have been made to apply conventional theory to advertising on several overlapping fronts.[16] Joseph Bain and others have analyzed its relation to the growth of monopoly with an eye to the problems faced by the Antitrust Division and Federal Trade Commission in the United States, while Kaldor, Else, and Taplin considered similar and related issues in Britain. Two economists have tried to synthesize a long list of studies, which apply traditional microtheory with statistical techniques to advertising.[17][18] Because the methods used failed to cope with the material historical processes by which monopoly capital achieved hegemony, their books are inconclusive except negatively. For example, Schmalensee concludes, "There is no evidence to suggest that advertising outlays have permitted some firms to create barriers to entry. . . . So far it, along with many other problems involving advertising's effects, has not been solved."[19]

Economists increasingly since the early 1960s have shown interest in developing theories of taste and buying behavior, joining in the interest of major firms in market research. For example, the authors of two short articles in 1978 cautiously recognize some of the large volume of evidence from psychology and sociology concerning consumer behavior while seeming to glance fearfully over their shoulders at the dogma of marginal theory.[20] A third, T. A. Marschak, reveals the deep contradiction between the conservative tradition of marginal neoclassicism and reality, boldly asserting that the former ". . . risks turning Economic Man into a complex monster of calculated schizophrenia. . . ."[21] In the "long-forbidden territory" of tastes in real life, Marschak identifies (but does not analyze) three relevant issues: (1) nonrenewable resource exhaustion and consumer taste; (2) the relation of advertising, education, and the mass media to taste formation; and (3) disenchantment with purchased goods as the measure of welfare. None of these exercises in economic theory involve recognition of demand management by monopoly capitalism, and the role of the mass media in producing the marketing agent for it (the audience). Among bourgeois economists that leaves institutional economists to be considered.

Institutional analysis

As noted above, Galbraith, prominent among institutional economists, comes close to confronting the audience market but stops short at the traditional psychological curtain drawn by Chamberlin. He realistically identifies the dependence of corporate capitalism on the regular creation of wants through advertising, model changes, and so on. He properly criticizes the fixation on durable goods production, inherited from the classical economists, and at the root of the theory of F. H. Knight and his disciples. He also summarizes the rationale with which economists conceal their blindness to the audience commodity:

> The theory of consumer demand, as it is now widely accepted—is based on two broad propositions. . . . The first is that the urgency of wants does not diminish appreciably as more of them are satisfied,

126

or ... to the extent that this happens it is not demonstrable and not a matter of any interest to economists or for economic policy. When man has satisfied his physical needs, then psychologically grounded desires take over. These can never be satisfied, or in any case no progress can be proved. ... The second proposition is that wants originate in the personality of the consumer or in any case that they are *given data* for the economist. The latter's task is merely to seek their satisfaction. He has no need to enquire how these wants are formed.[22]

In his later *The New Industrial State,* he sharpens the analysis of demand management, applying it both to the civilian and to the military sectors. He emphasizes the essential function that advertising and related activities perform in creating demand for commodities in particular and in general, including the practice of going into debt to buy them: "Advertising and salesmanship—the management of consumer demand—are vital for the planning in the industrial system. At the same time, the wants so created insure the services of the worker."[23] Indeed, he carries the argument to the brink of discovery of the audience market:

The present disposition of conventional economic theory to write off annual outlays of tens of billions of dollars of advertising and similar sales costs by the industrial system as without purpose or consequence is, to say the least, drastic. No other legal economic activity is subject to similar rejection. The discovery that sales and advertising expenditures have an organic role in the system will not, accordingly, seem wholly implausible.[24]

He then draws back from the prospect of analyzing the "organic role" of the most essential market for the existence of modern monopoly capitalism: the audience. As will be argued below, the audience is now the unnoticed form which stands in contradiction to the domination by commodities in the capitalist core area. It just might be the organic agent that may act to transfer the system at its core. Short of this eventuality, analysis of its role could serve many needs of industry, government, and education.

Marxist economics

Have Marxist economists carried the theoretical analysis of monopoly capitalism any further than Galbraith? Marxists from Marx until about 1920, including Lenin, could hardly be expected to recognize and deal with the demand management function of advertising and mass communication on behalf of monopoly capitalism, the characteristics of which had not yet developed.[25] Accordingly, it is not surprising that those Marxists held a manipulative, idealist theory of communications. For Marx, "ideology" was considered to act as a sort of invisible glue that holds together the capitalist system. This subjective substance, divorced from concrete historical materiality, is similar to such concepts as "ether"; that is, the proof of its existence is found to be the necessity for it to exist so that certain other phenomena may be explained. It was thus an idealist, *pre*scientific rather than a nonscientific explanation. For Marxists after about 1920, the concrete material basis existed on which ideology could be approached scientifically, and the mass media of communications were central to that approach. The first question that historical materialists should ask about mass communication systems is what economic function for capital do they serve, attempting to understand their role in the reproduction of capitalist relations of production. What is surprising, given the methodological commitment of Marxists to historical material realism, is to find that Marxists writing since about 1920 hold a subjective and superficial view of the commodity produced by the mass media of communications under monopoly capitalism. For them, as for bourgeois economists, it is manipulation, information, images, and so on. This is conspicuously true for the Frankfurt School. It is also true for those who take a more or less Marxist view of communications (Nordenstreng, Enzensberger, Hamelink, Schiller, Murdock, Golding, and myself until recently). I am therefore suggesting that the literature of Marxism is conspicuously lacking in materialist analysis of *how* "Consciousness Industry" uses advertising and other mass media content to produce and reproduce a certain ideology. *Why* Marxists have had a blindspot about the relation of mass media, audiences, advertisers, the labor theory of value and ideology to each other it is not my present task to determine.[26]

Baran and Sweezy in *Monopoly Capital* recognize the demand management practices of monopoly capitalist corporations, but they, like Galbraith, draw back from the brink of recognizing the reality of the audiences as the principal product of the mass media, produced to sell to advertisers.

Exploring the blindspot

Even a little analysis permits us to raise questions that may open up that blindspot for exploration:

1. What do advertisers buy with their advertising expenditures? As hard-nosed businessmen they are not paying for advertising for nothing, nor from altruism. I suggest that what they buy are the services of audiences with predictable specifications, who will pay attention in predictable numbers and at particular times to particular means of communication (television, radio, newspapers, magazines, billboards, and third-class mail).[27] As collectivities these audiences are commodities. As commodities, they are dealt with in markets by producers and buyers (the latter being advertisers). Such markets establish prices in the familiar mode of monopoly capitalism.

128

Both these markets and the audience commodities traded in are specialized. The audience commodities bear specifications known in the business as "the demographics." The specifications for the audience commodities include age, sex, income level, family composition, urban or rural location, ethnic character, ownership of home, automobile, credit card status, social class, and, in the case of hobby and fan magazines, a dedication to photography, model electric trains, sports cars, philately, do-it-yourself crafts, foreign travel, kinky sex, and so on.

2. Are audiences homogenous? By no means, although all of them have the common features of being produced by mass media and priced and sold in oligopolistic markets to advertisers for whom they perform services which earn their keep, that is, keep advertisers advertising because the expenditure is productive from the advertisers' standpoint. Audiences produced for sale to advertisers fall into two groups: those produced in connection with marketing consumers' goods and those for producers' goods. The latter are typically produced by trade or business media (magazines, newspapers, or direct mail). The buyers of producers' goods are typically institutions (government in the case of the "Military Sales Effort" or private corporations) which presumably buy on specifications of objective qualities. Moreover, this latter type of advertising is a relatively small part of the total. For these reasons the following analysis will disregard this category of audience.

Strategically the most important class of audiences are produced for advertisers marketing consumers' goods. Again, these audiences fall into two classes. The first of these are for producers of what Julian L. Simin calls Homogenous Package Goods (HPG), which have certain common features: "(1) Slight or no objective physical difference between the brands; (2) Low unit cost; (3) Short time period between repeated purchases; (4) Large total dollar volume for each product industry; (5) Except for liquor, heavy use of television as an advertising medium; and (6) Large proportions of sales spent for advertising."[28] In the HPG category are soft drinks, gum, candy, soaps, cleaners, waxes, and other household cleaning products, tobacco products, beer, wine, liquor, gasoline, patent drugs, perfumes, cosmetics, deodorants, razor blades and other personal toiletry articles, as well as fast foods and restaurants. The second subclass of audiences for consumers' goods is that for durable consumer goods. Here are automobiles, snowmobiles, clothes, boats, shoes, hobby equipment (e.g., cameras, sports equipment, household tools), electric household appliances, and the like. Although objective qualitative characteristics are ascertainable, annual style changes dominate them. It is the consumer goods advertisers whose audiences are produced by the mass media to generate the "demand" that can increase GNP.

3. How are advertisers assured that they are getting what they pay for when they buy audiences? A subindustry sector of the Consciousness Industry checks to determine. The socioeconomic characteristics of the

delivered audience readership *and* its size are the business of A. C. Nielsen and a host of competitors who specialize in rapid assessment of the delivered audience commodity. The behavior of the members of the audience product under the impact of advertising and the "editorial" content is the object of market research by a large number of independent market research agencies as well as by similar staffs located in advertising agencies, in the advertising corporation and in media enterprises.

4. What institutions produce the commodity which advertisers buy with their advertising expenditures? The owners of television and radio stations and networks, newspapers, magazines and enterprises which specialize in providing billboard and third class advertising are the principal producers. This array of producers is interlocked in many ways with advertising agencies, talent agencies, package program producers, film producers, news "services" (e.g., AP, UPI, Reuters, CP), "syndicators" of news "columns," writers' agents, book publishers, and motion picture producers and distributors. Last, but by no means least, in the array of institutions that produce the audience commodity is the family. The most important *resource* employed in producing the audience commodity are the individuals and families in the nations that permit advertising.

5. What is the purpose of the so-called entertainment, information, and educational material content? As well as the advertising material in the mass media, the "programs" themselves are advertisements. The content between the formal advertising material is a lure or inducement (or gift, bribe, or free lunch) to recruit potential members into the audience and to maintain their loyal attention to the advertisments. The analogy of such material to the free lunch in the old-time saloon, suggested by A. J. Liebling,[29] is appropriate: The free lunch consists of material to whet the prospective audience member's appetites and thus: (1) attract and keep them attending to the program, newspaper, or magazine; and (2) cultivate a mood conducive to favorable reaction to the explicit and implicit messages from the advertiser. In the policy of the mass media, the characteristics of the free lunch must always be subordinated to those of the formal advertisements, because the purpose of the mass media is to produce audiences to sell to the advertisers. Therefore a "program" that is more arousing than the adjacent advertisements will not survive, and it could only survive the preliminary screening because of faulty judgment on part of the media management. The cost per unit of time or space of producing an explicit advertisement is many times the cost per unit of time or space of producing the free lunch (in a ratio of 8 or 10 to 1 in television), which is a rough index of the relative attention paid to the qualities of the two. There is of course, a market for the free lunch, and this market spans not only the totally advertiser-dependent media (television and radio) but also cinema, magazines, newspapers, and book industries. A particular commodity in the free lunch market (*Roots*, for example) will appear in more than one of these media, sometimes simultaneously (as with the book and film *China Syndrome*) and often subsequently in other media, in each case being edited appropriately to fit the buyers' needs.

Under monopoly capitalism television-radio programs are provided "free" and newspapers and "consumer" magazines at prices that perhaps cover delivery (but not production) costs. In the case of newspapers and some magazines, some readers typically buy the media product *because* they want the advertisements rather than the free lunch. Such is the case with classified advertisements and display advertising of products and prices by local merchants in newspapers. Likewise, product information in advertisements in certain magazines (e.g., hobby magazines) may be the object of purchase by the consumer.

Of course, to call the traditional "news" content of the newspaper a free lunch does not denigrate the role of the mass media in daily setting an agenda for everyone's attention or of the prime significance of that role. On the contrary, it emphasizes an essential aspect of *how* some items get on the agenda, and with what priority, and how other agenda items are left off.

6. What is the nature of the service performed for the advertiser by the members of the purchased audiences? In economic terms, the audience commodity is a nondurable producers' good which is bought and used in the marketing of the advertiser's product. The work audience members perform for the advertiser to whom they have been sold is to learn to buy goods and to spend their income accordingly. Sometimes it is to buy any of the class of goods (for example, an aircraft manufacturer is selling air transport in general, or the dairy industry, all brands of milk), but most often it is a particular "brand" of consumer goods. In short, they work to create the demand for advertised goods that is the purpose of the monopoly capitalist advertisers. While doing this, audience members are simultaneously reproducing their own labor power. In this regard, it is appropriate to avoid the trap of manipulation explanation by noting that if such labor power is, in fact, loyally attached to the monopoly capitalist system, this would be welcome to the advertisers whose existence depends on the maintenance of that system. In reproducing their labor power, workers respond to other realistic conditions that may on occasion surprise and disappoint the advertisers. It seems, however, that when workers under monopoly capitalist conditions serve advertisers to complete the production process of consumer goods by performing the ultimate marketing service for them, these workers are making decisive material decisions that will affect how they will produce and reproduce their labor power. As the Chinese emphasized during the Cultural Revolution, if people are spending their time catering to their individual interests and sensitivities, they cannot be using the *same* time to overthrow capitalist influence and to build socialism.

7. How does demand management by monopoly capitalism by means of advertising relate to the labor theory of value, to "leisure" and to "free time"?

As Bill Livant puts it, the power of the concept of surplus value ". . . rests wholly on the way Marx solved the great value problem of classical political economy, by *splitting the notion of labor in two*, into labor in productive use and labor power (the capacity to labor)."[30] Labor in productive use in the production of commodities-in-general was Marx's concern in the three volumes of *Capital*, except for Volume 1, Chapter 6 and scattered passages in the *Grundrisse*. It is clear from these passages that Marx assumed that labor power is produced by the laborer and by his or her immediate family *under the conditions* of handicraft production. In a word, labor power was "home-made" in the absence of dominant brand-name commodities, mass advertising and the mass media (which had not yet been invented by monopoly capitalism). In Marx's period and in his analysis, the principal aspect of capitalist production was the alienation of workers from the means of producing commodities-in-general. Now the principal aspect of capitalist production has become the alienation of workers from the means of producing and reproducing themselves. The prevailing western Marxist view today still holds the incorrect assumption that the laborer is an independent commodity producer of labor power which is his to sell. As Livant states it:

> What often escapes attention is that just because the laborer sells it (his or her labor power) does not mean that he or she produces it. We are misled by fixating on the true fact that a human must eat and sleep into thinking that therefore the seller of labour power must also be the producer. Again the error of two combines into one.[31]

In the original blindspot article I contended that work time included all but sleeping time. In the capitalist core area I now believe work time for most people is twenty-four hours a day. George Allen, famous professional football coach in the United States, may be closer to the mark than most economists, though typically conservative, when he tells his players, "Nobody should work all the time. Leisure time is the five or six hours you sleep at night. You can combine two good things at once, sleep and leisure."[32]

It should be clear that for at least several generations labor power in advanced monopoly capitalist countries has been produced primarily by institutions *other* than the individual and his/her family. The mass media of communications and advertising play a large and probably dominant role through the process of consumption (by guiding the making of the shopping list) as well as through the ideological teaching that permeates both the advertising and ostensibly nonadvertising material with which they produce the audience commodity.[33] When cosmetic counters in department stores display "Boxed Ego" (Vancouver, December, 1975), the dialectical relation of the material and consciousness aspects of the production of labor power should be evident.

132

If between 1850 and 1960 the average worker gained seven hours per week of apparent "nonwork" time, how much time does he now spend as part the audience product of the mass media—time sold to the advertisers?[34] David Blank, economist for the Columbia Broadcasting System, in 1970 found that the average person watched television twenty-three hours per week on an annual basis, listened to the radio for eighteen hours per week and read newspapers and magazines seven hours per week.[35] If we look at the audience product in terms of families rather than individuals, we find that in 1973 advertisers in the United States purchased television audiences for an average of a little more than forty-three hours per home per week.[36] By industry usage, this lumps together specialized audience commodities sold independently as "housewives," "children," and "families." In the "prime time" evening hours (7:00 P.M. to 11:00 P.M.), the television audience commodity consisted of a daily average of 83.8 million people in the United States, with an average of two persons viewing per home. Women were a significantly larger proportion of this prime time audience than men (forty-two per cent as against thirty-two per cent, while children were sixteen per cent and teenagers, ten per cent).

We do not know even approximately how the worker's exposure to the mass media articulates with the other components in his/her use of time when not at the job front. It is relatively easy to determine how much radio listening and newspaper and magazine reading takes place while traveling to and from work. But much television and radio programing is attended to incidentally while people engage in other activities such as performing household chores, visiting with friends, reading, and now even while attending spectator sports.[37]

Audience members bear directly a heavy cost in dollars for the privilege of being in the audience and getting their daily work assignments from the advertisers. In Canada in 1975 the annual cost to audience members of providing their own broadcast receivers (and paying for cable television) consistent of depreciation, interest on investment, maintenance and electric power, amounted to slightly more than $1.8 billion, while the over-the-airbroadcasters (Canadian Broadcasting Corporation plus private broadcasters) and cable television operators' costs were about $631 million —a ratio of about three to one.

Constrained by the ideology of monopoly capitalism, the bourgeois notion of free time and leisure is only available to those who have no disposable income (and for whom it is, of course, a bitter mockery) and to those who are so rich that, as Linder says, for them, "the ultimate luxury is to be liberated from the hardships of having to do one's own buying."[38] For everyone else, "free time" and "leisure" belong only in the monopoly capitalist lexicon alongside "free world," "free enterprise," "free elections," "free speech," and "free flow of information."

What has happened to the time workers spend off-the-job is that enormous pressures on this time have been imposed by all consumer goods and service branches of monopoly capitalism. Individual, familial, and other associative needs must be dealt with, but in a real context of products and advertising which, taken together, make the task of the individual and family basically one of *coping* while being constantly on the verge of being overwhelmed by these pressures. In this context, the work of the audience members which advertisers find productive for them is one of learning the cues used when the audience member makes up his/her mental shopping list and spends his/her income.

8. Does the audience commodity perform an essential economic function? Baran and Sweezy state that "advertising constitutes as much an integral part of the system as the giant corporation itself"[39] and that "advertising has turned into an indispensable tool for a large sector of corporate business."[40] In this they go as far as Galbraith who said ". . . the marginal utility of present aggregate output, ex-advertising and salesmanship is zero."[41] When the president of the Revlon corporation says: "We manufacture lipsticks. But we sell hope," he is referring to the creation of products initially posited by it as objects in the form of a need felt by the consumers—similarly with Contac-C, the proprietary cold remedy, which so disturbed Baran and Sweezy.[42] The denial of the productivity of advertising is unnecessary and diversionary: a cul-de-sac derived from the premonopoly-capitalist state of development, a dutiful but unsuccessful and inappropriate attempt at reconciliation with *Capital*.

9. Why have economists been indifferent to the historical process by which advertising, brand-name merchandise, and the mass media of communications have developed in monopoly capitalism over the past century? Why do they continue to regard the press, television, and radio media as having the prime function of producing news, entertainment and editorial opinion and not audiences for sale to advertisers? My original "blindspot" paper offered a preliminary analysis of the dynamics of the process by which Consciousness Industry developed through the merger movement and created the mass media to produce audience power.

Conclusion

The mass media institutions in monopoly capitalism developed the equipment, workers, and organization to produce audiences for the purposes of the system between about 1875 and 1950. The prime purpose of the mass media complex is to produce people in audiences who work at learning the theory and practice of consumership for civilian goods and who support (with taxes and votes) the military demand management system. The second principal purpose is to produce audiences whose theory and practice confirms the ideology of monopoly capitalism (possessive individualism in an authoritarian political system). The third principal purpose is to produce public opinion supportive of the strategic and tactical policies of the state (e.g., presidential candidates, support of Indochinese military adventures, space race, detente with the Soviet Union, rapprochement with China, and ethnic and youth dissent). Necessarily in the monopoly capitalist system, the fourth purpose of the mass media complex is to operate itself so profitably as to ensure unrivaled respect for its economic importance in the system. It has been quite successful in achieving all four purposes.

If we recognize the reality of monopoly capitalism buying audiences to complete the mass marketing of mass produced consumer goods and services, we have begun to grapple with the contradiction between capital and labor in the period of monopoly capitalism when most people work *all the time*; not only when at the job front where they are paid for working but also in every other mode for which they are not paid.

It appears that in seeming to perfect its system for managing demand through producing and consuming audiences for the purpose of marketing its products, monopoly capital has produced its principal antagonist: people commodified in audience markets who are consciously seeking noncommodified group relations. A symptom is a downward trend in television viewing in 1977 and 1979 in the United States after thirty years of rising viewing.[43] It has long been noticed that all traditional social institutions (family, church, labor union, political party, and so on) have been stripped of much of their traditional purpose by the impact of mass produced communications. The mysticism attached to technique has incorrectly assumed that the medium basically defines the audience. As an historical analysis of the rise of the mass media will show, the opposite has been true: the availability and actions of the audience is the basic feature in the definition of the medium, singly and collectively. By placing the contradiction between advertisers/media on the one hand and audiences on the other on the level of social relations, we are on solid ground and can repudiate the mysticism of the "technological" trap by which audiences are tied to hardware, software, and technique (as in Innis, McLuhan, and others).

Notes

* An earlier essay exposed the blindspot of western Marxist scholars to the reality of communications. Here the analysis is generalized to encompass all branches of the contemporary economic theory. The argument here builds on that in "Communications: Blindspot of Western Marxism." *Canadian Journal of Political and Social Theory*, Vol. 1, No. 3, Fall, 1977, pp. 1–27.

1 Galbraith, J. K. *The New Industrial State*. Boston: Houghton Mifflin, 1967.
2 Boulding, K. *Econoimc Analysis*. New York: Harper, 1955.
3 Baran, P. A., and Sweezy, P. M. *Monopoly Capital*. New York: Monthly Review Press, 1966.
4 Marshall, Alfred. *Industry and Trade*. London: Macmillan, 1922.

5 Chamberlin, E. H. *The Theory of Monopolistic Competition.* Cambridge, Mass.: 1931, pp. 119, 133–134.
6 Stigler, G. J. *The Theory of Price.* New York: Macmillan, 1961.
7 Kaldor, N. "The Economic Aspects of Advertising." *Review of Economic Studies*, Vol. 18, 1950, p. 1.
8 The buyer of advertised goods is charged no price for the advertising. *Sup. cit.*, p. 2.
9 Tesler, Lester G. "Supply and Demand for Advertising Messages." *American Economic Review*, May, 1966, pp. 457–466.
10 Stigler, George J., and Becker, Gary S. "DeGustibus non est Disputandum." *American Economic Review*, Vol. 67, No. 2, March, 1977, pp. 76–90.
11 *Ibid.*, p. 77.
12 *Ibid.*, p. 78.
13 *Ibid.*, p. 84.
14 Leibeutein, Harvey. *Beyond Economic Man.* Cambridge, Mass.: Harvard University Press, 1976.
15 See, for example, Martines, Lauro. *Power and Imagination: City States in Renaissance Italy.* New York: Knopf, 1979, p. 85.
16 See Doyle, Peter. "Economic Aspect of Advertising: A Survey." *Economic Journal* Vol. 78. 1968, pp. 570–602.
17 Simon, Julian L. *Issues in the Economics of Advertising.* Urbana: University of Illinois Press, 1970.
18 Schmalensee, R. *The Economics of Advertising.* Amsterdam/London: North–Holland Publishing Company, 1972.
19 *Ibid.*, p. 244.
20 Pollack, Robert A. "Endogenous Tastes in Demand and Welfare Analysis" Pessemier, Edgar A. "Stochastic Properties of Changing Preferences." *American Economic Review*, May, 1978 pp. 374–379; 379–385.
21 Marschak, T. A. "On the Study of Taste Changing Policies." *American Economic Review*, May, 1978, pp. 386–391.
22 Galbraith, J. K. *The Affluent Society.* Boston: Houghton–Mifflin, 1958, pp. 143–144. Emphasis added.
23 Galbraith, J. K. *The New Industrial State, sup. cit.*, p. 273.
24 *Ibid.*, p. 205.
25 Lenin had a manipulative theory of the mass media and admitted naivete in this respect. "What was the fate of the decree establishing a state monopoly of private advertising issued in the first weeks of the Soviet government? . . . It is amusing to think how naive we were . . . The enemy, i.e., the capitalist class retaliated to this decree of the state power by completely repudiating that state power." "Report on the New Economic Policy," Seventh Moscow Gubernia Conference of the Russian Communist Party, October 21, 1921, in *Lenin About the Press.* Prague: International Organization of Journalists, 1972, p. 203. Lenin's *Imperialism* is devoid of recognition of the relation of advertising to monopoly capitalism and imperialism.
26 The analysis here presented originally aimed to stimulate debate among Marxists over this issue. Following publication of the original "Blindspot" article, the *Canadian Journal of Political and Social Theory* published "Blindspots about Marxism: A Reply to Dallas Smythe" by Graham Murdock and my "Rejoinder to Graham Murdock" (Vol. 2, No. 2, 1978, pp. 109–119, and 120–127) and "The Audience Commodity: On the 'Blindspot' Debate," by Bill Livant (Vol. 3, No. 1, 1979, pp. 91–106).

27 It is argued by one of my critics that a better term for what advertisers buy would be "attention." At our present naive stage concerning the matter, it does *seem* as if attention is indeed what is bought. But where people are paid for working on the job, should Marxists say that what the employer buys is "labor power" or "the manual dexterity and attention necessary for tending machines?" Where I refer to audiences as being produced, purchased, and used, let it be understood that I mean "audience-power," however it may turn out upon further realistic analysis to be exercised.

28 Simon, Julian L. *Sup. Cit.*, p. 271.

29 Liebling, A. *The Press*. New York: Ballantine, 1961.

30 Livant, William. "Notes on the Development of the Production of Labour Power." 22 March, 1975 (dittoed).

31 Livant, William. "More on the Production of Damaged Labour Power." 1 April, 1975 (dittoed).

32 Quoted in Terkel, Louis. *Working*. New York: Pantheon, 1974, p. 389.

33 For the present purposes I ignore the ancillary and interactive processes which contribute to the production of labor power involving also the educational institutions, the churches, labor unions, and a host of voluntary associations (for example, YMCA, Girl Scouts).

34 In the "Blindspot" paper I contrasted the hours of work at the job front and the condition of reproducing labor power (including so-called leisure time between 1850 and 1960).

35 Blank, David M. "Pleasurable Pursuits—The Changing Structure of Leisure-time Spectator Activities." National Association of Business Economists, Annual Meeting, September, 1970 (dittoed).

36 *Broadcasting Yearbook*, 1974, p. 69.

37 For many years patrons at professional baseball and football games have been listening to portable radios broadcasting the same game. By the mid-1970s patrons at professional football games were beginning to watch the same game on portable television sets for the "instant replays."

38 Linder, Staffen B. *The Harried Leisure Class*. New York: Columbia University Press, 1970, p. 123.

39 Baran, P. A., and Sweezy, P. M. *sup. cit.*, p. 122.

40 *Ibid.*, p. 119.

41 Galbraith, J. K. *The Affluent Society, sup. cit.*, p. 160.

42 Referring to a reported $13 million advertising budget, which produced $16 million in drug store sales, expressed in wholesale prices, they say: "Allowing for a handsome profit margin, which of course is added to selling as well as production cost, it seems clear that the cost of production can hardly be more than a minute proportion of even the wholesale price." Baran, P. A., and Sweezy, P. M., *sup. cit.*, p. 119.

43 *Time*, 12 March, 1979, p. 57.

31

THE EXPLICIT ECONOMICS
OF KNOWLEDGE CODIFICATION
AND TACITNESS

Robin Cowan, Paul A. David and Dominique Foray

Source: *Industrial and Corporate Change* 9(2) (2000): 211–53.

This paper attempts a greater precision and clarity of understanding concerning the nature and economic significance of
knowledge and its variegated forms by presenting 'the skeptical
economist's guide to "tacit knowledge'". It critically reconsiders
the ways in which the concepts of tacitness and codification
have come to be employed by economists and develops a more
coherent re-conceptualization of these aspects of knowledge
production and distribution activities. It seeks also to show
that a proposed alternative framework for the study of knowledge codification activities offers a more useful guide for
further research directed to informing public policies for science,
technological innovation and long-run economic growth.

1. Introduction: what's all this fuss over
tacit knowledge about?

With increasing frequency these days references appear in the economics
literature to 'tacit knowledge'. More often than not the meaning of this term
itself is something that remains literally tacit—which is to say, those who
employ it are *silent* as to its definition. Something is suggested nevertheless
by the common practice of juxtaposing mention of tacit knowledge and
references to 'codified knowledge'. What is all this about? Why has this distinction been made and what significance does it have for economists?

Polanyi (1958, 1967) introduced the term into modern circulation, by
pointing to the existence of 'the tacit dimension of knowledge', a form or
component of human knowledge distinct from, but complementary to, the
knowledge explicit in *conscious* cognitive processes. Polanyi illustrated this
conceptualization by reference to a fact of common perception: we all are
often aware of certain objects without being focused on them. This, he

maintained, did not make them the less important, as they form the context that renders focused perception possible, understandable and fruitful. Reference to the findings of Gestalt psychology in regard to other perceptual phenomena formed another important aspect of Polanyi's conceptualization of tacit knowledge: people appear to be perceptually (and/or intellectually) aware of some objects and things about the world only as *entities*—as illustrated by the identification of a particular human face or voice.[1] Knowledge of this kind consists of *holistic* understandings, and thus is not completely amenable to purely reductionist analyses.

Subsequently, the term 'tacit knowledge' has come to be more widely applied to forms of personal knowledge that remain 'UN-codified' and do not belong in the category of 'information', which itself is thought of as an ideal-type good having peculiar economic features that differentiate it from other, conventional economic commodities.[2] One may observe the growing practice among economists of juxtaposing 'tacit' and 'codified' knowledge, which casually applies the former term as a label for the entire (residual) category of knowledge that cannot be seen to be conveyed by means of codified, symbolic representations, i.e. transmitted as 'information'. In this process of inflating the usage of the term, the emphasis upon context and contextual understanding that was present in psychological references to the 'tacit dimension' of human knowledge has been largely discarded. Tacit knowledge thus has come to signify an absolute type, namely: 'not codified knowledge'. Among economists it is used more and more in this way, without explicit definition, and therefore without further explication of the conditions that might underlie 'tacitness' or the resort to codification of knowledge.

But, more than having become merely another overly vague bit of fashionable economic jargon, 'tacit knowledge' now is an increasingly 'loaded' buzzword, freighted with both methodological implications for microeconomic theory in general, and policy significance for the economics of science and technology, innovation, and economic growth. Indeed, references to 'tacitness' have become a platform used by some economists to launch fresh attacks upon national policies of public subsidization for R&D activities, and equally by other economists to construct novel rationales for governmental funding of science and engineering research and training programs.

The first-order result of all this would seem to have been the creation of a considerable amount of semantic and taxonomic confusion. In and of itself, this might be both expected and tolerable as a transient phase in any novel conceptual development. Unfortunately, one cannot afford to be so sanguine, because those very same confusions are being exploited to advance economic policy conclusions that claim to be grounded upon propositions that are well established (if only recently recognized in economics) about the existence of different kinds of knowledge pertinent to scientific, technological

139

and organizational innovation. In our view, however, such claims in many instances are neither analytically nor empirically warranted.

This essay responds to a felt need for greater precision and clarity of understanding concerning the nature and economic significance of knowledge and its variegated forms, by presenting what might be described as 'the skeptical economist's guide to "tacit knowledge"'. Our skepticism, however, does not extend to questioning the seriousness of the array of issues that economists and others have been discussing under the general rubric of tacit knowledge, which truly are important and deserving of careful consideration. Furthermore, we acknowledge that some of the now-classic contributions to the economics of scientific and technological innovation, when regarded from an epistemological perspective, appear unwarrantedly simplistic in their handling of some subtle questions concerning 'knowledge' and 'information', and the relationship between the two.

Our immediate purposes in this paper are to critically reconsider the ways in which the concepts of tacitness and codification have come to be employed by economists, and to develop a more coherent re-conceptualization of these aspects of knowledge production and distribution activities. We seek to show, further, that a proposed alternative framework for the study of knowledge codification activities—perhaps because it rests upon explicit microeconomic foundations—offers a more useful guide for further research directed to informing public policies for science, technological innovation and long-run economic growth.

The following section elaborates on our contention that the terminology and meaning of 'tacitness' in the economics literature, having drifted far from its original epistemological and psychological moorings, has become unproductively amorphous; indeed, that it now obscures more than it clarifies. Among the matters that thereby have been hidden are some serious analytical and empirical flaws in the newly emerging critique of the old economics of R&D. By the same token, we also can identify equally serious flaws in the novel rationale that has recently been developed for continuing public support of R&D activities, based upon the alleged inherent tacitness of technological knowledge.

An explicit re-examination of some fundamental conceptual underpinnings in this area is therefore in order. Although this requires that we re-open questions which readers coming to the topic from economics may feel are settled well enough for their purposes, a persuasive case can be made for doing so; and setting it forth in section 3, we seek to show that a new taxonomic framework would prove helpful in clearing away a number of the conceptual confusions that presently are impeding the progress of research in this area. Such a framework is proposed in section 4, providing a topography of 'knowledge transaction activities', the salient features of which are discussed in section 5. A number of advantages afforded by the novel conceptual structure (those that are discernible *a priori*) are indicated in section 6. But, as the proof of any pudding of this kind is to be found only in the eating, we proceed to put it to practical use in section 7, where we consider the economic costs and benefits of codification activities in different knowledge environments, thereby exposing the main endogenous determinants of the dynamic path of the boundary between what is and is not codified in the existing state of knowledge. Section 8 concludes with some brief comments indicating the implied directions for theoretical and empirical work needed to further explore this promising vein in the economics of knowledge.

2. How the tacit dimension found a wonderful new career, in economics

To motivate this undertaking we begin with a closer look at the intellectual background of the increasing frequency with which the notion of tacit knowledge currently is entering economic policy discussions. It is fair to say that economists have not had much preparation to deal with the recent debates that are emerging in their midst over the nature of knowledge and the significance of its tacit dimension. This is understandable, because the popular social science career of this concept began elsewhere . . . long ago, and in a far distant discipline.

Must economists now prepare themselves to become ever more deeply involved in discussions of the nature of knowledge, and begin to care about the various categories into which other disciplines claim knowledge should be sorted? Is this not something better left for epistemologists and others of similar philosophical inclination? Although one might be tempted to answer the latter in the affirmative, it is now too late to ignore the very meaning of something that a large and growing number economists and other social scientists seem bent upon discussing. It seems helpful, therefore, to approach the subject with some background awareness of the historical path by which 'tacitness' made its way from the philosophical writings of Polanyi (1958, 1967) into widespread currency in the economic journals.

2.1 The roots in the sociology of scientific knowledge, and cognitive science

The pioneering role was taken by those who called themselves 'sociologists of scientific knowledge' (SSK), thereby distinguishing their purpose and approach from that of the then mainstream Mertonian school in the sociology of science. Proponents of the SSK program were more interested in the role of social forces (under which both economic and political interests were subsumed) in shaping the cognitive aspects of scientific work. The traditional approach in the sociology of knowledge had, by contrast, tended to focus attention upon the role of macro-institutional settings, reward structures and the like, in mobilizing resources for the pursuit of scientific knowledge and organizing the conduct of research. By and large, it had thereby eschewed direct engagement with the epistemological issues that occupied philosophers of science, and so it appeared to accept if not endorse the latter's formal accounts of 'the scientific method' as the 'disinterested confrontation of logically derived propositions (theory) with empirical evidence (fact)'.

That picture, however, did not appear to square with the one found by some SSK-inspired students of contemporary scientific practice. They observed that some kinds of knowledge deployed in scientific inquiry—most notably that relating to the assembly and operation of experimental apparatus and instrumentation, and the interpretation of the data which these generated—were not communicated as hypotheses or codified propositions, or by any means resembling the formalized modes of discourse with which philosophy of science traditionally had been preoccupied. Rather, working scientists appeared to be more occupied with 'craft knowledge', and much of what seemed crucial to their research efforts was not being transmitted among them in the form of any explicit, fully codified statements.

Collins's (1974) notably influential study in this vein examined the early construction of the TEA laser in a number of laboratories, and reported that none of the research teams which succeeded in building a working laser had done so without the participation of someone from another laboratory where a device of this type already had been put into operation. For Collins, '[t]he major point is that the transmission of skills is not done through the medium of written words'. Subsequent contributors to the sociology of scientific and technological knowledge have read this and other, kindred observations as showing that 'the diffusion of knowledge could not be reduced to the mere transmission of information' (Callon, 1995).

A contrast thus was posed between the 'algorithmic model' of knowledge production, which is concerned exclusively with the generation of consistent propositions and the transmission of explicit declarative statements, on the one hand, and the so-called 'enculturation model' of scientific activities on the other. This distinction was invoked primarily by philosophers and sociologists who sought to challenge the idea that science, and specifically the modern scientific method, was a source of 'privileged' statements. The putative privilege in question derived from the implication that scientific statements could be stripped from the social contexts in which they had been formed and in which they had acquired meaning, and consequently could be promulgated as part of an authoritatively universal, 'codified' body of knowledge about the physical world. Challengers of that view leaned heavily on the seeming importance of tacit knowledge in the actual conduct of scientific activities.

At this juncture in the narrative a few remarks should be entered about the distinction observed here between 'information' and 'knowledge', terms that we shall continue to avoid using interchangeably. We find it useful to operationally define an item of information as a message containing structured data, the receipt of which causes some action by the recipient agent—without implying that the nature of that action is determined solely and uniquely by the message itself. Instead, it is the cognitive context afforded by the receiver that imparts meaning(s) to the information-message, and from the meaning(s) follow the specific nature of the induced action(s). The term 'knowledge' is simply the label affixed to the state of the agent's entire cognitive context.[3]

The algorithmic model to which reference has been made above, strictly interpreted, implies the absence of any meaningful distinction between information and knowledge. Under this approach all the cognitive and behavioral capabilities of whatever human or non-human agent is being described must have been reduced to 'code', that is, to structured data and the necessary instructions for its processing. Only in that way could a purely algorithmic actor generate further data and/or instructions for future actions—whether those were physical actions, or simply the processing, classification, storage, retrieval and transmission of information. It is possible, therefore, to say that what an (algorithmic) economic agent 'knows' is nothing more nor less than 'information'.

To stop there, of course, would be to ignore, *inter alia*, the manifest differences between intelligent human agents and computers. Humans create new categories for the classification of information, and learn to assign meanings to (sensory) data inputs without the assistance of programmed instructions of which they are consciously aware. Not surprisingly, then, the term 'knowledge' is applied in ordinary language when referring to human capacities that appear to be accessed without the intermediation of any formal code. In other words, humans (and other living creatures) 'know things' that they have not acquired as 'information' and which, not having been reduced to symbolic representations (code), are held in forms that are not readily available for communication to others—at least not explicitly as 'information-bearing' messages. At the same time, however, it is no less important to notice that the capacities of humans to 'decode', interpret, assimilate and find novel applications for particular items of information entail the use of still other items of information. These latter equally are part (and may well form the critical part) of the 'cognitive context' within which the recipient of a given message assigns to it 'meaning(s)'. Moreover, there is nothing in this observation that would imply a lack of awareness on the part of the individual concerned about the pertinent 'information context', or any inability to transmit it to others.

2.2 From evolutionary economics to management strategy and technology policy

For some considerable time, economists took little if any interest in the question of separating the notion of knowledge from their idea of information, and scarcely noticed the sequel distinction that other disciplines had drawn between the algorithmic and enculturation models of learning and associated behaviors. But things have moved on from that stage, and in several directions. A parallel and related course of development also has been evident in the management studies literature, from the early formulations such as that provided by Winter (1987), to the recent wave of books on 'knowledge management', as exemplified by Leonard-Barton (1995), Nonaka and Keuchi (1995) and Davenport and Prusak (1998).

Thus, the importance of tacit knowledge as a strategy asset is acknowledged today by students of rational management practices on the one hand,[4] and at the same time is cited as being crucial by critics of the 'algorithmic' approach of modern economic analysis of all aspects of human behavior. In its latter manifestations, the concept of the inextricable tacitness of human knowledge forms the basis of arguments brought not only against the residue of behaviorist psychology which remains embedded in the neoclassical formulation of microeconomic analysis, but against virtually every construction of rational decision processes as the foundation for modeling and explaining the actions of individual human agents.

Whether the emergence of these disparate intellectual developments can be said to constitute scientific 'advance', however, remains another matter. Quite clearly, the challenge being brought against algorithmic representations of knowledge generation and acquisition goes much deeper than arguments for 'bounded' rationality following the work of Newell and Simon (1972); and it has been argued in far more sweepingly general terms by critics of the whole artificial intelligence (AI) program such as Hofstader (1979) and, more recently, Penrose (1989, 1997). In those quarters, tacit knowledge has come to stand for the aspects of human intelligence that cannot be mimicked by *any* (computer) algorithm.

It may be remarked that were the latter rather nihilistic arguments against the quest for AI to be read as statements conditional on the presently available and *foreseeable* states of technology, rather than as absolute assertions of impossibility, this would leave room for the boundary between tacit knowledge and knowledge of other kinds to be other than inextricably fixed. Instead, what was tacit, and correspondingly what was not, would be subject to some future readjustments by improvements in the performance of computer hardware and software—because increasing processing speeds, reduced access times, expanded storage and more efficient algorithm designs permitted the faithful reproduction of an increasing range of human capabilities.[5] The resolution of debates over the mutability of this boundary would carry many implications for economics, but, as will be seen, the way in which the idea of tacitness has come to be used opens the possibility that still other, non-technological conditions also are influential in determining what knowledge is codified and what is not.

One may locate the seedbed of the modern flowering of economic discussions of tacit knowledge in the early attention that was directed to Polanyi's writings by Nelson and Winter's (1982) widely noticed critique of neoclassical analysis and initiation of a program of research in evolutionary economics.[6] Their discussion of the parallels between individual human skills and organizational capacities (Nelson and Winter, 1982, ch. 4) gave particular prominence to the concept of tacit knowledge, and expanded upon its significance for economists concerned with the internal workings of the firm.[7] Those passages remain as perceptive and stimulating, and as fresh and balanced today as when they first appeared, almost two decades ago, and it is a pity that a larger proportion of the economists who now talk about tacit knowledge and its implications do not appear to have acquainted themselves with this 'local source'.[8]

What Nelson and Winter (1982) say about the nature and significance of tacitness in knowledge conveys not just one sharply defined concept, but a nexus of meanings, each carrying somewhat distinctive implications. Their first reference to the term (1982, p. 73), for example, offers only a parenthetical clarification: 'The knowledge that underlies skillful performance is in large measure tacit knowledge, *in the sense that* the performer is not fully aware of the details of the performance and finds it difficult or impossible to articulate a full account of those details' (emphasis added).

Yet, as is made clear shortly following this statement, Nelson and Winter accept Polanyi's (1967) account of such situations as being contextual, rather than absolute: 'the aim of a skillful performance' may 'be achieved by the observance of a set of rules which are not known as such to the person following them'. Reference then is made to Polanyi's earlier philosophical work, *Personal Knowledge* (1958, p. 49), where an example is presented of a swimmer keeping himself buoyant by regulating respiration, yet remaining unconscious of doing so. In this case the operant rule ('never empty your lungs fully') plainly is one that is articulable, could be known to another person, and so might be transmitted verbally by a swimming instructor— were the latter aware of the principle of buoyancy. In other words, Nelson and Winter (1982, p. 77) do not insist, any more than did Polanyi, that tacitness implied 'inarticulability', even though the inarticulability of some (personal) knowledge logically implied that the latter would remain tacit.

On the question of 'awareness', Nelson and Winter (1982, p. 78) recognize that the skillful performer may have 'subsidiary awareness' of the rules that are being followed, while being 'focally aware' of some other—most probably novel—facet of the task in which she is engaged. This reinforces an appreciation of the contextual boundaries within which knowledge will be tacit, rather than explicitly recognized and articulated. Yet, if one can describe behavior in terms of 'rule conformity', then it is clear that the underlying knowledge is *codifiable*—and indeed may have previously been codified.

Most significant still, for what we shall say about the more recent strain of the literature on tacitness, is Nelson and Winter's (1982, p. 78) acknowledgement that this quality *is not inherent in the knowledge*. They write: 'The same knowledge, apparently, is more tacit for some people than for others. Incentives, too, clearly matter: when circumstances place a great premium on effective articulation, remarkable things can sometimes be accomplished'. In amplification of this point, they offer the example of an expert pilot giving successful verbal instruction via radio to a complete novice as to how to land an airplane—even though the 'expert' had never had occasion previously to make explicit what was entailed in his successful performance of a landing. Indeed, their section on 'Skills and Tacit Knowledge' concludes by emphasizing that

> ... costs matter. Whether a particular bit of knowledge is in *principle* articulable or necessarily tacit is not the relevant question in most behavioral situations. Rather, the question is whether the costs ... are sufficiently high so that the knowledge *in fact* remains tacit.
>
> (p. 80)

This important set of observations deserved much more attention and elaboration than it has been accorded by the subsequent literature, and we have sought (in section 7, below) to begin the work of rectifying this oversight.

It is unfortunate that these more complicated aspects of the concept had been all but forgotten, were they ever widely grasped when 'tacitness' made its debut on the economic policy stage. Among the most notable of the uses to which the idea of tacit knowledge is being put on the more mundane levels at which most economists operate, and certainly the uses that have the greatest impact in economic policy circles, has been the qualification—and in some instances the outright rejection—of the practical policy conclusions drawn from the classic information-theoretic analysis of the economics of R&D activities.

Following the seminal work of Arrow (1955, 1962) and Nelson (1959), an entire generation of economists treated scientific and technological knowledge as 'information'. To that degree, they reasoned, the knowledge generated by research activities possessed certain generic properties of public goods. Much of the case for government subsidization of science and engineering research, and for innovative activity more generally, came to be grounded on the proposition that *qua* information, such knowledge could not be optimally produced or distributed through the workings of competitive markets.

Nowadays we are more and more frequently instructed otherwise. In the newer understanding of science and technology as being pursuits inextricably involved with tacit knowledge, it is claimed that the old public policy rationales are exploded; the essential understandings are said to be the portion of knowledge that remains uncodified, and so deprived of the public goods properties that would result in informational spillovers and market failure. Thus, as this argument concludes, the traditional economic case for subsidizing science and research in general collapses, as there is little or no basis for a presumption of market failure. Similar arguments are advanced in the context of policy debates over the role of intellectual property rights in providing incentive for innovation: the claim is that the information presented (in codified form) in a patent is insufficient to allow others to actually make use of the patented invention, and it is the correlative 'tacit knowledge' that resides with the innovator that provides the real source of private, rent-appropriating (monopoly) power.[9]

But, at the same time, tacit knowledge is invoked by defenders of government subsidization of science as part of a strategic innovation policy. A standard argument against public subsidy to science is that foreigners engaging in applied, commercially oriented R&D would free-ride (since information is a public good and travels freely) by exploiting the basic knowledge discoveries that *our* researchers vie to codify for disclosure in the scientific journals and similar archival publications. To this, the proponents of a strategic role for tacit knowledge reply, nations and regions, like individual enterprises undertaking R&D investments, can count on the benefits of 'sticky data'—to use von Hippel's (1993) arresting term. Knowledge does not travel freely, a condition that rests largely on the importance of tacit knowledge residing only in the heads of the scientists and engineers engaged in its production. Codified knowledge may have low marginal costs of transmission and is thus slippery and hard to contain, but that is largely irrelevant if what one needs is its 'sticky', tacit counterpart.[10]

The inherent 'stickiness' of certain kinds of knowledge, consequently, enables business (or other) entities to protect their ability to appropriate the benefits derivable from their research investments fully, by controlling access to the repositories of uncodified knowledge. For this, minimal recourse is required to the protection of intellectual property in the form of patents and copyrights; a mixture of trade secrecy law and labor law (master–servant relations) governing the behavior of current and former employees may be enough. Thus, curious though it may seem, the tacit dimension of scientific and technological knowledge has found a new career for itself in science and technology policy debates: it is beginning to supplant its now dubious companion, 'codified knowledge', as the core of a new rationale for government research funding intended to build national and regional 'competitiveness' through innovation.

According to this application of the argument, even though the essential tacit knowledge concerning how to exploit what has been invented might be less than perfectly 'sticky', what this implies is that its economic benefits are only available to be captured locally. In other, more formal, terms, it is asserted that the marginal costs of knowledge transmission rise very rapidly with 'distance' from the context in which such knowledge was generated. Research by-products in the form of technological knowledge—being concerned with how best to get instrumentation involving chemical, mechanical, electrical and optical processes to work—are seen as inherently more strongly tacit in nature. That is held to be particularly beneficial for would-be commercial developers who are able to situate closer to the locus of such discoveries (see e.g. Pavitt, 1987; Nelson, 1992; Patel and Pavitt, 1995).

A broad policy implication following from this is that for an economy to have a strong, innovative manufacturing sector, it is necessary also to have correspondingly strong applied and basic research activities situated in close proximity to the production operations themselves. The new innovation strategy perspective that has now formed around the concept of tacitness in the business management literature is illustrated by the following passage (Kay, 1999, p. 13):

> Since 'knowledge that'—the characteristic discoveries of natural science— is easily transmitted, one solution [to the problem of creating 'knowledge-based competitive advantages'] is to continually innovate and stay one step ahead. And that kind of innovative capacity depends on knowledge that isn't 'knowledge that', but 'knowledge how'—i.e. Tacit knowledge. Tacit knowledge can take many forms, but it cannot be written down. It is unique to an organization—and therefore cannot be copied . . . The benefits of such tacit knowledge arise only through a culture of trust and knowledge-sharing within an organization . . .

Such considerations apply not only to scientific and engineering know-how, but also, and perhaps more strongly, to marketing, and internal management knowledge pertaining to business organizations, all of which have strongly contextual elements that make them 'natural' contributors to what von Hippel (1994) refers to as 'sticky information'.

Thus, a notion that took its origins in the psychology of visual perception and human motor skills has been wonderfully transmuted, first from an efficient mode of mental storage of knowledge into a putative epistemological category (having to do with the nature of the knowledge itself), from there into a phenomenon of inarticulable inter-organizational relationships and finally to one of the keys to corporate, and perhaps also national, competitive advantage!

A corollary of arguments in the latter vein is that the case for granting public subsidies and tax concessions to private companies that invest in R&D would seem to be much weakened, were it not for the difficulties caused these firms by the circulation of their research personnel.[11] Scientific and engineering staff are able to carry critical tacit knowledge off to potential rival firms that offer them better terms of employment, including equity ownership in 'start ups' of their own. In the logic of this approach, recognition of the criticality of tacit knowledge argues for further strengthening of trade secrecy protections, to block those 'leakages' and altogether eliminate the market failure rationale for governmental support of the performance of R&D by the private sector.[12] That leaves the way open for those who wish to mount an essentially 'techno-mercantilist' argument for R&D subsidies, grounded on the idea that the country can benefit from job-creation, etc., if its firms win the race to be first to launch new products in international markets. It is, in effect, a new strategic trade policy argument, grounded on the claim that tacit knowledge permits national appropriation of the direct and indirect benefits of monopolizing international product niches by being 'first to invest'.

We see a need to put the economics of tacit and codified knowledge on analytically firmer and terminologically more precise foundations than those upon which most of the recent literature presently rests. The foregoing account of the wonderful career that has thrust 'the tacit dimension' into the science and technology policy limelight serves, at least, to identify a number of issues that are of sufficient importance to warrant much more careful consideration. The notion that the economic case for public support of science and engineering should now be based upon the inherently tacit and 'craft' nature of research activities certainly is rather paradoxical. Taken at face value, it would suggest that intellectual property protection is unjustified, since, in the 'natural' state of things, there are no 'externalities' of new knowledge. By implication, the patent system's exchange of monopoly of use for 'disclosure' allows the patentee to retain the tacit knowledge without which the information contained in the patent really is useless.

But, before rushing to discard everything we know about the economics of R&D, scientific skepticism instructs us to pause and ask whether the epistemological foundations of these new propositions really are all that solid. We should therefore question whether the economic functioning and attributes of tacit and codified knowledge are well understood by those who would invoke those matters in the context of current innovation policy debates.

3. Codification and tacitness reconsidered

It will be easiest for us to start not with concept of tacit knowledge but at the opposite and seemingly less problematic end of the field, so to speak, by asking what is to be understood by the term 'codified knowledge'. Its obvious reference is to *codes*, or to standards—whether of notation or of rules, either of which may be promulgated by authority or may acquire 'authority' through frequency of usage and common consent, i.e. by *de facto* acceptance.

Knowledge that is recorded in some codebook serves *inter alia* as a storage depository, as a reference point and possibly as an authority. But information written in a code can only perform those functions when people are able to interpret the code; and, in the case of the latter two functions, to give it more or less mutually consistent interpretations. Successfully reading the code in this last sense may involve prior acquisition of considerable specialized knowledge (quite possibly including knowledge not written down anywhere). As a rule, there is no reason to presuppose that all people in the world possess the knowledge needed to interpret the codes properly. This means that what is codified for one person or group may be tacit for another and an utterly impenetrable mystery for a third. Thus *context*—temporal, spatial, cultural and social—becomes an important consideration in any discussion of codified knowledge.

In what follows, we make extensive use of the notion of a codebook. We use 'codebook' both to refer to what might be considered a dictionary that agents use to understand written documents and to apply it also to cover the documents themselves. This implies several things regarding codification and codebooks. First, codifying a piece of knowledge adds content to the code-book. Second, codifying a piece of knowledge draws upon the pre-existing contents of the codebook. This creates a self-referential situation, which can be particularly severe when the knowledge activity takes place in a new sphere or discipline. Initially, there is no codebook, either in the sense of a book of documents or in the sense of a dictionary. Thus initial codification activity involves creating the specialized dictionary. Models must be developed, as must the vocabulary with which to express those models. When models and a language have been developed, documents can be written. Clearly, early in the life of a discipline or technology, standardization of the language (and of the models) will be an important part of the collective activity of codification. When this 'dictionary' aspect of the code-book becomes large enough to stabilize the 'language', the 'document' aspect can grow rapidly [for a further discussion of this issue see Cowan and Foray (1997)]. But new documents will inevitably introduce new concepts, notation and terminology, so that 'stabilization' must not be interpreted to imply a complete cessation of dictionary-building.

The meaning of 'codification' intersects with the recent literature on economic growth. Much of modern endogenous growth theory rests on the notion that there exists a 'world stock of knowledge' and, perhaps, also a 'national knowledge-base' that has stock-like characteristics. This is true particularly of those models in which R&D is seen as both drawing upon and adding to 'a knowledge stock' which enters as an input into production processes for other goods. How ought we to characterize this, or indeed any related conceptualization of a world stock of knowledge? Implicit in this literature is that this stock is codified, since part or all of it is assumed to be freely accessible by all economic agents in the system under analysis. Unpacking this idea only partially suffices to reveal some serious logical difficulties with any attempt to objectify 'a social stock of knowledge', let alone with the way that the new growth theory has sought to employ the concept of an aggregate knowledge stock.[13]

The 'new growth theory' literature falls squarely within the tradition emphasizing the public-goods nature of knowledge. So, one may surmise that the world stock of knowledge surely has to be the union of private stocks of codified knowledge: anything codified for someone is thereby part of the world knowledge stock. Such reasoning, however, may involve a fallacy of composition or of aggregation. One might reasonably have thought that the phrase 'world knowledge stock' refers to the stock available to the entire world. But if the contextual aspect of knowledge and codification (on which, see *supra*) is to be taken seriously, the world stock of codified knowledge might better be defined as the *intersection* of individuals' sets of codified knowledge—that being the portion that is 'shared' in the sense of being both known and commonly accessible. It then follows that the world stock of knowledge, being the intersection of private stocks, whether codified or tacit, is going to be very small.[14]

The foregoing suggests that there is a problem in principle with those models in the 'new growth theory' which have been constructed around (the formalized representation of) a universal stock of technological knowledge to which all agents might contribute and from which all agents can draw costlessly. That, however, is hardly the end of the difficulties arising from the primacy accorded to the accumulation of 'a knowledge stock' in the recent literature on endogenous economic growth. The peculiarities of knowledge as an economic commodity, namely, the heterogeneous nature of ideas and their infinite expansibility, have been cast in the paradigm 'new economic growth' models as the fundamental non-convexity, responsible for increasing returns to investment in this intangible form of capital. Heterogeneity implies the need for a metric in which the constituent parts can be rendered commensurable, but given the especially problematic nature of competitive market valuations of knowledge, the economic aggregation problem is particularly vexatious in this case.

Furthermore, the extent to which the infinite expansibility of knowledge actually is exploited therefore becomes a critical matter in defining the relevant stock—even though in most formulations of new growth theory this matter has been glossed over. Critics of these models' relevance have quite properly pointed out that much technologically relevant knowledge is not codified, and therefore has substantial marginal costs of reproduction and reapplication; they maintain that inasmuch as this so-called 'tacit knowledge' possesses the properties of normal commodities, its role in the process of growth approaches that of conventional tangible capital.[15] If it is strictly complementary with the codified part of the knowledge stock, then the structure of the models implies that either R&D activity or some concomitant process must cause the two parts of the aggregate stock to grow *pari passu*. Alternatively, the growth of the effective size of the codified knowledge stock would be constrained by whatever governs the expansion of its tacit component. Pursuing these points further is not within the scope of this paper, however; we wish merely to stress once again, and from a different perspective, that the nature of knowledge, its codification or tacitness, lurks only just beneath the surface of important ideas about modern economic growth.

Leaving to one side, then, the problematic issue of defining and quantifying the world stocks of either codified knowledge or tacit knowledge, we can now turn to a fundamental empirical question regarding tacit knowledge. Below, we address explicitly whether some situations, described as rife with tacit knowledge, really are so, but for the moment we can make an important point without entering into that issue.

Some activities seem to involve knowledge that is unvoiced—activities which clearly involve knowledge but which refer only seldomly to texts; or, put another way, which clearly involve considerable knowledge beyond the texts that are referred to in the normal course of the activity.[16] Thus we can ask why is some knowledge silent, or unvoiced? There are two possible explanations: the knowledge is unarticulable or, being capable of articulation, it remains unvoiced for some other reason.

Why would some knowledge remain unarticulable? The standard economist's answer is simply that this is equivalent to asking why there are 'shortages', to which one must reply 'there are no shortages' when there are markets. So, the economist says, knowledge is not articulated because, relative to the state of demand, the cost and supply price is too high. Articulation, being social communication, presupposes some degree of codification, but if it costs too much actually to codify, this piece of knowledge may remain partly or wholly uncodified. Without making any disparaging remarks about this view, we can simply point out that there is some knowledge for which we do not even know how to begin the process of codification, which means that the price calculation could hardly be undertaken in the first place. Recognition of this state of affairs generates consensus on the uncodifiable nature of the knowledge in question. We raise this to emphasize the important point in what follows that the category of the unarticulable (which may be coextensive with the uncodifiable) can safely be put to one side. That, of course, supposes there is still a lot left to discuss.

It is worth taking note of the two distinctions we have just drawn, and the degree to which they define coextensive sets of knowledge. Knowledge that is unarticulable is also uncodifiable, and vice versa: if it is (not) possible to articulate a thought so that it may be expressed in terms that another can understand, then it is (not) possible to codify it. This is the source of the statement above that articulation presupposes codifiability. It is not the case, though, that codifiability necessitates codification; a paper may be thought out fully, yet need not actually be written out. Operationally, the codifiability of knowledge (like the articulable nature of a thought) cannot be ascertained independently from the actions of codification and articulation. But, when we consider the question of the status of knowledge with reference to multiple contexts, the preceding strictly logical relations (implied by a single, universal context) are not exhaustive categories. Thus we see the possible emergence of an additional category: codified (sometime, somewhere) but not articulated (now, here).[17] This observation implies that care needs to be taken in jumping from the *observed* absence of codified knowledge in a specified context to the conclusion that only some non-codifiable (i.e. tacit) knowledge is available or employed.

It is within the realm of the codifiable or articulable-yet-uncodified that conventional price and cost considerations come into play in an interesting way, for within that region there is room for agents to reach decisions about the activity of codification based upon its costs and benefits. We shall discuss the factors entering into the determination of that knowledge-status more fully below.

4. A proposed topography for knowledge activities

We now proceed to examine a new knowledge topography, from which it will soon be evident that the realm of 'the tacit' can be greatly constricted, to good effect. The new topography we propose is meant to be consulted in thinking about where various knowledge transactions or activities take place, rather than where knowledge of different sorts may be said to reside. We should emphasize that as economists, and not epistemologists, we are substantively more interested in the former than in the latter.

By knowledge activities we refer to two kinds of activities: the generation and use of 'intellectual (abstract) knowledge'; and the generation and use of 'practical knowledge', which is mainly knowledge about technologies, artifacts (how to use this tool or this car, or how to improve their performances) and organizations.

Given that definition, we need to clarify the distinction between knowledge embodied in an artifact and codified knowledge about an artifact. The distinction between embodied and disembodied knowledge is a nice way for economists to capture features of intersectoral flows (of technologies), particularly in an input–output framework. Therefore, the fact that knowledge is embodied in a machine tool is not to be conflated with the codification problem. Knowledge about the production and the use of artifacts, however, falls within our set of issues about codification: does the use of this new tool require the permanent reference to a set of codified instructions or not? We can put this point in a slightly different way. From the perspective of a producer, any artifact, from a hammer to a computer, embodies considerable knowledge. The artifact often is an exemplar of that knowledge, and can sometimes be thought of as a 'container' or 'storage vessel' for it, as well as the means through which the knowledge may be marketed. From the point of view of the user, however, this is not necessarily the case. While any user will admit that the producer needed a variety of kinds of knowledge to produce the artifact, this is of little practical interest. The knowledge of interest to the purchaser of a hammer or a PC, whether codified or not—and indeed that often is the issue—is how to use the artifact, rather than the knowledge that was called upon for its design and fabrication. Of course, the latter may bear upon the former.

Part of the reason for this interpretation of what is to be located in our topography is simply that discussions about 'where knowledge resides' are difficult to conduct without falling into, or attempting to avoid, statements about the relative sizes of the stocks of tacit and codified knowledge, and their growth rates. By and large, pseudo-quantitative discussions of that sort rarely turn out to be very useful; indeed, possibly worse than unhelpful, they can be quite misleading. Although there is no scarcity of casual assertions made regarding the tendency toward increasing (relative) codification, the issue of the relative sizes of the constituent elements of the world stocks of scientific and technological knowledge resists formal quantitative treatment. That is to say, we really cannot hope to derive either theoretical propositions or empirical measures regarding whether or not the relative size of the codified portion must be secularly increasing or decreasing, or alternatively, whether there is a tendency to a steady state. The fundamental obstacle is the vagueness regarding the units in which 'knowledge' is to be measured.

To begin, we shall consider a topological tree structure in which distinctions are drawn at four main levels. A tripartite branching on the uppermost level breaks the knowledge transaction terrain into three zones: articulated (and therefore codified), unarticulated and unarticulable. Setting the third category aside as not very interesting for the *social* sciences, we are left with the major dichotomy shown in Figure 1:

(a) *Articulated (and thus codified).* Here knowledge is recorded and referred to by 'the group', which is to say, 'in a socio-temporal context'. Hence we can surmise that a codebook exists, and is referred to in the usual or standard course of knowledge-making and -using activities.

(b) *Unarticulated.* Here we refer to knowledge that is not invoked explicitly in the typical course of knowledge activities. Again, the concept of a context or group is important.

In case (a) a codebook clearly exists, since this is implicit in knowledge being or having been codified. In case (b) two possible sub-cases can be considered. In one, knowledge is tacit in the normal sense—it has not been recorded either in word or artifact, so no codebook exists. In the other, knowledge may have been recorded, so a codebook exists, but this book may not be referred to by members of the group—or, if it is, references are so rare as to be indiscernible to an outside observer. Thus, at the next level,

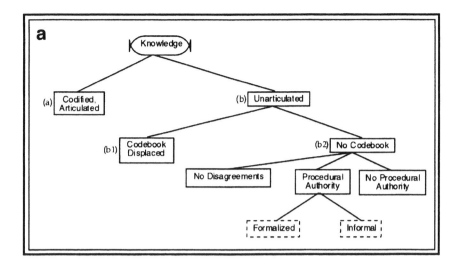

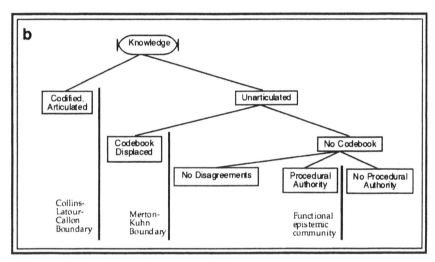

Figure 1 (a) A tree structure for codified and uncodified knowledge. (b) Boundaries in the knowledge space.

'unarticulated' splits into two branches: (b.1) in the situation indicated to the left, a source or reference manual does exist but it is out of sight, so we say the situation is that of a *displaced codebook*; and (b.2) to the right lie those circumstances in which there truly is no codebook, but in which it would be technically possible to produce one.

(b.1)   When a codebook exists, we still may refer to the situation in which knowledge is unarticulated because within the group context the codebook is *not manifest*; it is not explicitly consulted, nor in evidence, and an outside observer therefore would have no direct indication of its existence. The contents of the codebook in such situations have been so thoroughly internalized, or absorbed by the members of the group, that it functions as an implicit source of authority. To the outside observer, this group *appears* to be using a large amount of tacit knowledge in its normal operations.[18]

A 'displaced codebook' implies that a codified body of common knowledge is present, but not manifestly so. Technical terms figure in descriptive discussion but go undefined because their meaning is evident to all concerned; fundamental relationships among variables are also not reiterated in conversations and messages exchanged among members of the group or epistemic community.[19] In short, we have just described a typical state of affairs in what Kuhn (1962) referred to as 'normal science'; it is one where the knowledge base from which the researchers are working is highly codified but, paradoxically, its existence and contents are matters left tacit among the group unless some dispute or memory problem arises. We may analogously describe 'normal technology' as the state in which knowledge about artifacts is highly codified but the codebook is not manifest.

Identification of the zone in which knowledge is codified but the existence of codification is not manifest is an extremely important result. But it poses a very difficult empirical problem (or perhaps a problem of observation). This point is crucial in understanding the economic problem raised by the management of knowledge in various situations: when the codebook is displaced and knowledge is highly codified, new needs for knowledge transfer or storage (or knowledge transactions generally) can be fulfilled at a rather low cost (the cost of making the existing codebook manifest), whereas when there is no codebook at all, the cost will be very high (the cost of producing a codebook, which includes costs of developing the languages and the necessary models).

This suggests that it would be useful to reconsider closely the many recent empirical studies that arrive at the conclusion that the key explanation for the observed phenomenon is the importance of tacit knowledge. That perhaps is true, but it is quite difficult to document convincingly; most of such studies fail to prove that what is observed is the effect of 'true tacitness', rather than highly codified knowledge without explicit reference to the codebook. By definition, a codebook that is not manifest will be equally not observed in that context, so it is likely that simple proxies for 'tacitness' (such as whether communication of knowledge takes place verbally in face-to-face transactions rather than by exchanges of texts) will be misleading in many instances. Differentiating among the various possible situations certainly requires deep and careful case studies.

(b.2)   When there is no codebook, we again have a basic two-way division, turning on the existence or non-existence of disputes. There may be no disagreements. Here there is stabilized uncodified knowledge, collective memory, convention and so on. This is a very common situation with regard to procedures and structures within organizations. The IMF, for example, has nowhere written that there in only one prescription for all the monetary and financial ills of the world's developing and transition economies; but, its advisers, in dispensing 'identikit' loan conditions, evidently behaved as if such a 'code' had been promulgated. Such uncodified-but-stable bodies of knowledge and practice, in which the particular epistemic community's members silently concur, will often find use as a test for admission to the group or a signal of group membership to outside agents.

Where there are disagreements and no codebook is available to resolve them within the group, it is possible that there exist some rules or principles for dispute resolution. Elsewhere, such 'procedural authority' may be missing. This is the chosen terrain of individual 'seers', such as business management gurus like Tom Peters, and others who supply a form of 'personal knowledge about organizational performance'. Equivalently, in terms of the outward characteristics of the situation, this also might describe the world of 'new age' religions—in contradistinction to structured ecclesiastical organizations that refer to sacred texts.

There is, however, another possibility, which creates a three-fold branch from node b.2: it may be the case that when disagreements arise there is some procedural authority to arbitrate among the contending parties. Recall that the situation here, by construction, is one in which the relevant knowledge is not codified, and different members of the organization/group have distinct bodies of tacit knowledge. When these sources of differences among their respective cognitive contexts lead to conflict about how to advance the group's enterprise or endeavor, the group cannot function without some way of deciding how to proceed—whether or not this has been explicitly described and recorded. Clearly, once such a procedure is formalized (codified), we have a recurrence of a distinction paralleling the one drawn at the top of the tree in Figure 1, between codified and 'unarticulated'. But this new bifurcation occurs at a meta-level of *procedures* for generating and distributing knowledge, rather than over the contents of knowledge itself. We can, in principle, distinguish among different types of groups by using the latter meta-level codified–tacit boundary. So the whole taxonomic apparatus may be unpacked once again in discussing varieties of 'constitutional' rules for knowledge-building activities. But that would carry us too far from our present purposes.

5. Boundaries in the re-mapped knowledge space and their significance

Across the space described by the foregoing taxonomic structure it is possible to define (at least) three interesting boundaries. The 'Collins–

Latour–Callon' boundary would separate articulated codified knowledge from all the rest—assigning observational situations in which there was a displaced codebook to the same realm as that in which learning and transmission of scientific knowledge, and *praxis*, were proceeding in the absence of codification. The line labeled 'the Merton–Kuhn boundary' puts codified and codebook-displaced situations together on its left side, and would focus primary attention there—as it constituted the distinctive regions occupied by modern science. That would leave all the rest to general psychological and sociological inquiries about 'enculturation processes' involved in human knowledge acquisition.

Our branching structure recognizes that it is possible, nonetheless, for *epistemic communities* to exist and function in the zone to the right of the Merton–Kuhn boundary. Such communities, which may be small working groups, comprise knowledge-creating agents who are engaged on a mutually recognized subset of questions, and who (at the very least) accept some commonly understood procedural authority as essential to the success of their collective activities. The line labeled the 'functional epistemic community boundary' separates them from the region immediately to their right in the topography. Beyond that border lies the zone populated by personal (and organizational) gurus of one shape or another, including the 'new age' cult leaders in whom procedural and personal authority over the conduct of group affairs are fused.

As is clear from the foregoing discussion, there are two quite distinct aspects of knowledge that are pertinent in the codified–tacit discussions, although they are often left unidentified. On the one hand, knowledge might or might not be presented or stored in a text. This is the notion associated with codification. On the other hand, there is the degree to which knowledge appears explicitly in standard activities. Here, we can think of knowledge as being *manifest* or not. Figure 2 elaborates these two properties in a tableau. For this purpose we have used a 3 × 3 matrix, in which one axis represents the extent of codification: codified, partially codified, and uncodified; the other axis represents the extent to which the knowledge is manifest, or commonly referred to in knowledge endeavors: manifest, alluded to, and latent. These divisions that are indicated along the vertical and horizontal axes are patently arbitrary, for mixtures in the ordinary human knowledge activities form a continuum, rather than a set of discrete boxes.

To make clearer the meaning of Figure 2, it may be useful to look specifically at the four extreme cases: the corners north-west, south-west, north-east and south-east. Both the codified–manifest case (the north-west corner) and the uncodified–latent case (the south-east corner) describe situations which are easily comprehensible because the criteria fit together naturally. The codified–latent case (the north-east) was described as a situation in which the codebook is displaced while knowledge is not tacit. Finally the uncodified–manifest case (south-west) describes situations in which agents start to make

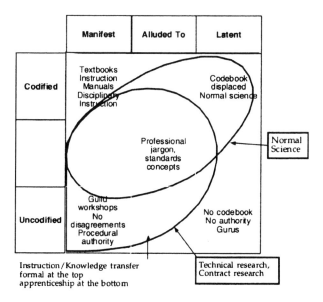

Figure 2 Classification of knowledge and knowledge generation activity on two axes.

their discoveries, inventions and new ideas manifest (in order to diffuse them) but still cannot use a full and stabilized codebook to do so; and even 'writing' a book with which to make this new knowledge manifest does not necessarily imply codification. It is possible that the vocabulary or symbolic representation employed is highly idiosyncratic, that there are many ambiguities, and so on. This implies that while certain aspects of codification may be present (in knowledge storage and recall, for example), other important aspects (such as an agreed vocabulary of expression) can be missing.

The overly sharp coordinates nevertheless give us a tableau which can be used heuristically in distinguishing major regions of the states-space within which knowledge-groups can be working at a given moments in their history. Instruction or deliberate knowledge transfer is thus roughly situated in the tableau's 'manifest' column, spilling over somewhat into the 'alluded to' column. Formal instruction comes near the top ('codified'), whereas apprenticeship lies near the bottom ('uncodified') of the array. The world of normal science inquiries extends across the ellipse-shaped region that is oriented along the minor diagonal (southwest–northeast axis) of the array, leaving out the north-west and south-west corners. In the former of the two excluded regions codified knowledge is most plainly manifested for purposes of didactic instruction, in which reference is made to textbooks, grammars and dictionaries, manuals, reference standards, and the like. In contrast, most craft apprenticeship training, and even some computer-based tutorial programs, occupy the lower portion of the 'soft-trapezoidal' region covering the left side of the array in Figure 2: a mixture of both codified and uncodified procedural routines are made manifest, through the use of manuals as well as practical demonstrations, whereas other bodies of codified knowledge may simply be alluded to in the course of instruction.[20]

The boundaries of the world of engineering and applied R&D also extend upwards from the south-west corner in which closed, proprietary research groups function on the basis of the uncodified skills (experience-based expertise) of the team members, and their shared and manifest references to procedures that previously were found to be successful. But, if we are to accept the descriptions provided for us by articulate academic engineers, those boundaries are more tightly drawn than the ones within which science-groups operate; in particular they do not reach as far upwards into the area where there is a large body of latent but nevertheless highly codified knowledge under-girding research and discovery (see, e.g., Vincenti, 1990; Ferguson, 1992).

6. On the value of this re-mapping

What value can be claimed for the topography of knowledge activities that we have just presented? Evidently it serves to increase the precision and to allow greater nuance in the distinctions made among types of knowledge-getting and transferring pursuits. But, in addition, and of greater usefulness for purposes of economic analysis, it will be seen to permit a more fruitful examination of the influence of external, economic conditions upon the codification and manifestation of knowledge as information. A number of the specific benefits derived from looking at the world in this way warrant closer examination, and to these we now turn.

6.1 On the topography itself

Figures 1 and 2 clean up a confusion concerning the putative tacitness of the working knowledge of scientists in situations that we have here been able to characterize by applying the 'displaced codebook' rubric. A number of studies, including some widely cited in the literature, seem to have placed undue reliance upon an overly casual observational test, identifying situations where no codebook was manifestly present as instances showing the crucial role of 'tacit knowledge', pure and simple (see e.g. Collins, 1974; Latour and Woolgar, 1979; Latour, 1987; Traweek, 1988). It now should be seen that this fails to allow for the possibility that explicit references to codified sources of 'authority' may be supplanted by the formation of 'common knowledge' regarding the subscription of the epistemic community to that displaced but nonetheless 'authoritative' body of information.

The location of the Collins–Latour–Callon boundary in Figure 1, and its relationship to the regeneration of knowledge in tacit form, signifies that this latter process—involving the mental 'repackaging' of formal algorithms and other codified materials for more efficient retrieval and frequent applications, including those involved in the recombinant creation of new knowledge—rests upon the pre-existing establishment of a well-articulated body of codified, disciplinary tools.[21]

Economists' recent concerns with the economics of knowledge tend to lie in the 'no disagreements' (uncodified, manifest) box in Figure 2. We are talking here about the literature that views reliance upon 'sticky data' or 'local jargons' as methods of appropriating returns from knowledge. This is the region of the map in which knowledge-building gives rise to the 'quasi' aspect of the description of knowledge assets as quasi-public goods. The immediate implication is that to determine the degree to which some particular pieces of knowledge are indeed only quasi-public goods calls for a contextual examination of both the completeness of the codification and the extent of manifestation.

The argument has recently been advanced, by Gibbons *et al.* (1996), that an emergent late twentieth century trend was the rise of a new regime of knowledge production, so-called Mode 2. This has been contrasted with the antecedent dominant organizational features of scientific inquiry, associated with Mode 1: in particular, the new regime is described as being more reliant upon tacit knowledge, and transdisciplinary—as opposed to the importance accorded by Mode 1 to the publication of codified material in areas of disciplinary specialization as the legitimate basis of collegiate reputational status, selection decisions in personnel recruitment, and the structuring of criteria for evaluating and rewarding professional performance. Doubts have been raised about the alleged novelty and self-sufficiency of Mode 2 as a successor that will displace the antecedent, highly institutionalized system of research and innovation (see e.g. David *et al.*, 1999, and references therein). But the main point to be noted in the present context is that such coherence and functionality as groups working in Mode 2 have been able to obtain would appear to rest upon their development of procedural authority to which the fluid membership subscribes.

6.2 On interactions with external phenomena

How do changes in information and communications technologies impinge upon the distribution of knowledge production and distribution activities within the re-mapped space described by our topography? The first and most obvious thing to notice is the endogeneity of the boundaries (which we discuss more fully in the next section). In the new taxonomy there are two interesting distinctions: knowledge activities may use and produce codified or uncodified knowledge, or they may use and produce knowledge that is either manifest or latent. We should re-state here that 'boundary' is not being used in reference to the distribution of the world knowledge stock, but instead to the prevailing locus of the activities of knowledge agents in a specific cognitive, temporal and social milieu. Nevertheless, it is most likely to be true that the situation of a group's knowledge stock will be intimately related to, and possibly even coterminous with, the location of its knowledge production activities.

Organizational goals affect the manifest–latent boundary. Activities that couple teaching with research, for example, will be pushed towards the more fully 'manifest' region of the state space. This consideration will be important in studies of the economics of science, and of the institutional organization of academic research activities more generally.[22]

The positioning of the endogenously determined boundary separating the codified from the uncodified states of knowledge activities will be governed by the following three sets of forces, which we examine at greater length below. For the present it is sufficient simply to note that these include: (i) costs and benefits of the activity of codification; (ii) the costs and benefits of the use of the codified knowledge (data compression, transmission, storage, retrieval, management, etc.); and (iii) feedbacks that arise because of the way codified knowledge is used to generate further codified knowledge.

A given discipline's age (or the stage of development reached in the life cycle of a particular area of specialization) affects both of the boundaries. The evolution of a discipline, a technological domain (or of a research group or a community of practitioners) may now be described as a movement in the two-dimensional plane of the tableau in Figure 2. Let us illustrate this by taking a lead from Kuhn (1962) and begin, early in the life cycle of a research program, with activities centered in the south-east corner of the array: a disparate collection of individual researchers and small teams, working without any commonly accepted procedural authority, generating knowledge that remains highly idiosyncratic and uncodified, and having only a very restricted scope for transmission of its findings beyond the confines of the immediate work-group(s). Subsequently, if and when these investigations have begun bearing fruit, work in the field coalesces around a more compact set of questions and the locus of its knowledge activities shifts westward, as agents make their discoveries and inventions manifest either in physical artifacts, conference presentations and published papers. This is where the codification process begins. But even though scholarly texts may be produced, because the concepts involved and language in which these reports are couched have not yet been thoroughly standardized, codification must still be considered very incomplete. Thenceforward, the emerging discipline's course follows a northerly track, spreading towards the north-east as disputes arise from inconsistencies in description and interpretation, and conflicts emerge over the specifics of the way the language is to be standardized. As these debates are resolved and closure on a widening range of issues is achieved, the characteristic activities migrate eastward in the space of Figure 2, landing up in the region where most of the actual research activity is carried on within the 'latent–codified' and 'manifest–partially codified' domains that typify normal science.

7. The economic determinants of codification

The preceding exposition focused first upon the conceptual distinctions separating types of knowledge activities and then upon the locations of knowledge activities in the space thus delineated. In any topographic discussion there is a temptation to treat boundaries between regions as having been imposed from outside the system that is under examination. In a sense this is proper, in that structures are often in principle distinct from the activities that make them. But inasmuch as we are dealing here with knowledge, and the latter is seen today to be so central to the process of economic growth, a treatment of the subject would be more useful were it to deal with the genesis of our structural boundaries and the forces that determine their positions in different areas of knowledge formation. This becomes all the more relevant inasmuch as the main concern here is not primarily taxonomic; we are less interested in delineating the nature and varieties of human knowledge than in being able to explain and predict the changes taking place in the character of economically significant knowledge activities.

Another way of highlighting this issue is to return briefly to the previous discussion of the critique of the implicit assumptions of new growth theory in regard to the composition of the knowledge stock. Both sides in this incipient debate over the economic role of the tacit dimension have tended to accept a view of the 'composition of knowledge by type' (i.e. the codified–tacit mix) as being determined exogenously, outside the sphere of economics—and, therefore, as a matter that may be left to the epistemologists, cognitive scientists and students of human psychologists. But, in focusing upon those extra-economic conditions bearing upon the supply side of knowledge production and distribution activities, that implicit approach ignores the influence of the range of considerations that impinge upon the *demand* for codified versus uncodified knowledge. Some of these factors involve institutional arrangements affecting the structure of relative rewards for codification activities, whereas others have to do with the state of available technologies affecting the costs of rendering knowledge in codified form and the storage, retrieval and transmission of information. In the remainder of this section, therefore, we make a start towards a more systematic economic analysis of the matter.

7.1 The endogeneity of the tacitness–codification boundary

Any individual or group of agents makes decisions about what kind of knowledge activity to pursue and how it will be carried on. Should the output be codified or remain uncodified? Are the inputs to be made manifest or latent in the production process? For an economist, there is a simple one-line answer: the choices will depend on the perceived costs and benefits. The implication is that where knowledge activities are located (the extent to which agents codify their knowledge for example) will depend on economic considerations, and that the boundaries may move in response to changes that are external to the knowledge system *per se*. The significance of this requires some further discussion, if only because it represents a novel (if obvious) departure from the usual way in which the problem of tacitness has been framed.

In analyzing the economics of this choice, we need—even more so than above—to consider only knowledge which is codifiable. Several different situations can arise: knowledge can be in a state of true tacitness but codifiable; the codebook can exist or not; and it can be displaced or not. Each situation generates its own cost–benefit structures, which we will address through the concept of the knowledge activity environment.

The endogeneity of the tacit–codified boundary (or the Merton–Kuhn boundary in Figure 1a) refers to the fact that the agents pursuing a knowledge activity have a choice regarding whether or not to codify the knowledge they use and produce. In practice, the extent to which both 'new' and 'old' knowledge becomes codified in a particular environment is determined by the structure of the prevailing costs and benefits of doing so. Many factors —such as the high cost of codifying a certain type of knowledge, to take the simplest example—can decrease the incentives to go further, by lowering the private marginal rate of return on codification investments. A low rate of return may in turn result in the existence of a large community of people possessing tacit knowledge. In other words, there will be a market for the workers whose functions include the storage and transfers of the knowledge from firm to firm. Of course, the presence of a thick labor market as a medium through which knowledge can be accessed further reduces incentives to codify, provided that the heterogeneity, perishability and autonomy of these organic knowledge repositories does not give rise to offsetting costs. (See the discussion of policy issues in section 2, above.)

A self-reinforcing, positive feedback process of that kind can generate multiple equilibria. If, for example, there are high returns to codification, more knowledge will be codified. This will decrease the value of alternative (thick labor market) means of maintaining and distributing (tacit) knowledge. As the market for labor to perform that function shrinks, the relative value of codification would tend to increase further. Thus there are two possible equilibria: one with significant resources devoted to codification and a resulting high incentive to codify; and one with few resources so devoted, a thick, active market for skilled labor as the mechanism for storing and disseminating knowledge, and thus low incentives to codify. This conclusion rests on there being substitutability in the production process between the types of knowledge transferred by these two mechanisms.

This focus on endogenous limitations indicates that costs and benefits and the resulting incentive structures are pivotal in shaping the dynamics of codification. Emphasizing the role of the incentive structures by no means implies that the codification of new forms of knowledge is an instantaneous process: moving the boundaries between codified and tacit parts of the stock of knowledge is a matter of long-term technological and institutional evolution, involving changes in incentive structures, and in costs and benefits.

7.2 Costs, benefits and the knowledge environment

In order to understand the sources and magnitudes of costs and benefits, it is necessary to put them in the context of the knowledge environment. A first and straightforward point is that the incentives will depend to a very great extent on the possibility of proceeding to codification on the basis of preexisting codebooks [languages, models and techniques, in the terminology of Cowan and Foray (1997)].

When the language and the model already exist, the fixed costs, those born to generate the now standard models and languages, have already been sunk: languages and models have been developed by past work, and are known by codifiers and users. Such a situation describes both cases in which codebooks are manifest and those in which codebooks are displaced. The idea here is that some existing body of well-developed, stable, codified knowledge, often one that is displaced, contains the necessary concepts and relations with which to codify the knowledge in question. The only cost then is the variable one. On the other hand, if codebooks do not exist, or are incomplete or ambiguous, costs of codification entail more than simply the variable costs. Further, before a language has been standardized and is stable, linguistic ambiguity implies that codes which appear to represent codified knowledge can change their meanings as the language is developed and refined, and as vocabulary expands and changes. It is thus useful to differentiate between contexts of stability and contexts of change.

7.3 Costs and benefits in a stable context

In a stable context—when there is a community of agents who have made the necessary initial investments to develop a language and to maintain efficient procedures of language acquisition for new entrants—the transfer of messages can be assimilated to transfer of knowledge, and storing messages means recording knowledge.

On the benefits side, the efficiency gains from codification will be greater in very large systems that must coordinate the complementary activities of many agents. We identify five classes among such situations: (i) systems involving many agents and many locations; (ii) systems strongly based on recombination and reuse, and which take advantage of the cumulativeness of existing knowledge (rather than on independent innovation); (iii) systems that require recourse to detailed memory; (iv) systems which need particular kinds of description of what (and how) the agents do; and (v) systems characterized by an intensive usage of information technologies. We take these up for further discussion *ad seriatim*.

First, codification will provide high benefits in stable systems characterized by specific requirements of knowledge transfer and communication. Such needs may arise from a tendency towards delocalization and externalization, or from the development of cooperative research, entailing a spatial distribution with activity at many places. This first effect can be appreciated without any ambiguity, for example, in science. It operates, however, within a given 'clique' or network—that is, a community which shares common codes and codebooks (whether or not the latter are manifestly present to hand) and such tacit knowledge as is used in interpreting messages exchanged among the members.

Second, in (stable) systems of innovation where advances and novelties mainly proceed from recombination, reuse and cumulativeness, benefits of codification are important. Gibbs (1994, 1997) claims that the very limited progress in the productivity of software engineering is due to an excessive dependence on craft-like skills (in contrast, for example, with chemical engineering). The schema that Gibbs has in mind is that once an algorithm is written as a piece of code, it can be used in many applications—at least in principle. The practical difficulty in doing so arises in part because of a lack of standardization both in the way code is written and the way algorithms are employed. This lack of technological rationalization impedes the full realization of the opportunities provided by the reuse and recombination model.

Third, codification holds out great benefits for systems that require extensive memory and retrieval capacities (e.g. firms and organizations that have extended product or process development cycles or high rates of personnel turnover, and institutions confronted by a major technological bifurcation). In those settings, under-investment in codification increases the day-to-day costs of locating frequently applied knowledge; and, where there are critical bodies of knowledge that are not kept in more-or-less continuous use, inadequate codification and archiving heightens the risks of 'accidental uninvention'. For example, according to Mackenzie and Spinardi (1995), in the nuclear weapons design process specific local and uncodified knowledge was so important that there was a constant appreciable risk that critical elements of the knowledge base would be lost simply through the turnover of scientists and engineers—a risk of technological retrogression, or at best of costly reconstruction of the organization's previous capabilities (competencies).

The same argument is readily extended to apply in situations where knowledge has been thoroughly codified in the form of algorithms, or operating instructions, but the text of the 'source code' for these—or an understanding of the language in which it was recorded—has ceased to be readily decipherable, or has simply been misplaced or destroyed. The result is a paradoxical one: the technology in which the knowledge has been embedded may continue to work, as is the case when the computer implements the machine-language version of its instructions. But, as has been found to be the case with some major pieces of 'legacy software', the human agents, being no longer able to read or write the source code, are unable to emend or elaborate those machine-language encoded instructions. Nor can they locate and correct defects in the original source code, defects whose existence has become painfully evident. It is possible that even beyond the range of such algorithmic technologies, cultural inventions and culturally transmitted skills important for activities upon which social welfare depends—such as those involved in dispute resolution—may become lost because 'the market' for agents possessing tacit knowledge of that kind is undermined by the competition of more fully codified (legal) procedures.

Fourth, systems that require accurate descriptions of what agents are doing (either to meet quality standards constraints, to patent innovations or to enter into contractual relations with a partner) would greatly benefit from codification. Here we can also include systems confronted with inefficient market transactions, where the traditional mechanisms of legal warranty, insurance, reputation and test are not efficient means to mitigate the effects of information asymmetry in regard to product and service quality (Gunby, 1996). If, however, it is feasible to record production practices, some of the asymmetry can be removed, as the buyer given this information is in a better position to judge the prospective quality of the output. The widely diffused procedural certification standards belonging to the ISO 9000 series were based upon what was, in essence, a linguistic innovation aimed at facilitating codification of quality assurance practices.

Fifth, and last but not least, a sort of cross-situation deals with the lack of productivity gains from the use of information technology (IT), due to incomplete codification. Fully taking advantage of the potential productivity gains of IT typically demands not only the adoption of the technology but also organizational change (see e.g. David, 1991, 1994, 2000; Cowan, 1995, and references therein). But a firm undergoing organizational change does not want to lose functionality in the process. The firm must develop jointly the new technology and organizational structures that will reproduce old functions and create new ones (see David, 1991, 1994). It is obvious that if too much of the old functionality resides in tacit knowledge, or depends heavily on it, this task will be extremely difficult. When the presence of tacit knowledge operates as a bottleneck, impeding the full realization of productivity potential, the firm can expect great benefits from codification (Baumol *et al.*, 1989). This, indeed, may be a critical role played by management consultants, to whom earlier reference was made.

In all these cases, where important operations of transfer, recombination, description, memorization and adaptation of existing knowledge (to IT) are required, it would be very costly and inefficient to keep this knowledge tacit. Thus, there can be under-investment in codification, coexisting with 'excess of tacitness'. Given the nature, degree and pace of recent technical change, it is likely that the current equilibrium involves an allocation of resources devoted to knowledge generation and transmission under conditions of incomplete codification and deliberate under-documentation.

Nonetheless, private resources continue to be poured into the production of differentiated 'information' that is idiosyncratically coded, whether deliberately or inadvertently, because such practices support the producers' intentions to capture private 'information rents'. Such practices also occur within business corporations (and other bureaucracies) where the internal reward mechanisms have failed to align the interests of individuals (possessing specialized knowledge) with those of the larger organizational entity. There, as in the cases where there are social inefficiencies due to the persistence in an uncodified state of knowledge that could be made more widely available in codified form for use by competing business entities, the design of incentive mechanisms is likely to prove more effective than the provision of less costly codification technologies, or the imposition and enforcement of formal disclosure requirements, in eliciting a collectively beneficial change in strategic behaviors.

Many other, rather more subtle issues are involved in considering the means through which firms and other entities can manage a process of codification where a large portion of the critical knowledge base required for functioning of the organization (its so-called 'core competencies') has not been articulated. Quite often one hears of businesses which (in times of stress) apply for help from some external management consultant, who will try to identify what things the troubled firm really 'knows how' to do well. A large body of modern management literature has been spun around that conceptualization of the consultant's role, so it may be reassuring to notice this implication of our topographic structure: collective procedural knowledge may remain unarticulated even though, at some cost, it is perfectly (or at least workably) 'codifiable'.

A more interesting issue for the skeptical economist to ponder in that connection is simply why is it that the organization—having somehow acquired and successfully deployed its 'core capabilities' without needing to make them explicit—should suddenly require, or find it profitable to employ, the costly services of outside management consultants to break the spell of 'tacitness'. In most of the specific cases discussed in the literature of professional business management that question is not posed explicitly. But, there is a suggestion that the organization, perhaps through the attrition of key personnel, may have 'forgotten' what it once understood tacitly and was therefore able to act upon collectively. Another possibility is that the operating environment of the firm might have been radically altered, without prompting a timely revision of the collective awareness of the mismatch created between the opportunities now facing the enterprise and its capabilities for exploiting them. The presumption, therefore, is that it will take too long, or be too risky, to go through a tacit, trial-and-error learning process. Bringing explicit analysis to bear—and so codifying the organization's understanding of itself and its new situation—then is deemed to prove either more expedient or less costly, or both, than continuing to operate in tacit mode (see Cobenhagen, 1998).

7.4 Costs and benefits in the context of change

While many knowledge activities take place in a relatively stable context, some particular domains or sectors are characterized by knowledge environments exhibiting ongoing rapid transformations.

Models and languages are fluid, and the community of agents conversant with the models and languages is itself changing. The fluidity of the language implies that there is uncertainty about what the messages actually mean, because there is uncertainty, and perhaps change, with regard to the vocabulary in which they are written. Even when scientific papers express new discoveries, or re-examine old results in some 'natural' language, much jargon specific to the subject matter remains; 'terms of art' are employed whose meanings are lost on outsiders; and, in formal modeling, definitions of variables specific to the model may remain in flux as the model itself is modified and reconciled with observational data. In an important sense, the progress of research involves—and requires—the stabilization of meanings, which is part of the social process through which the stabilization of beliefs about the reliability of knowledge comes about.

To the extent that codification is taking place under those conditions, the benefits deriving from it have substantial 'spillover' elements, as they contribute largely to the modeling and language development parts of the exercise. There may be competition among different basic models, and so among the basic tenets and vocabulary of the language. Until this competition is resolved, the community of potential knowledge generators and users will have difficulty communicating, and the value of knowledge codification that arises from dissemination will be reduced. Thus the codification process in this environment generates some immediate value, which derives both from worth of the content of the messages that agents can transmit and interpret with less effort and expense, and from the value to the agent of storage and retrieval of his own knowledge. However, it has greater value as an investment good: a contribution to the resolution of the competition among variant languages and models.

It is in the context of change that we expect to find situations of 'excess codification'. That is to say, the accumulation of successive generation of codes can prevent the development of radically new knowledge, simply because explicating and understanding it would require entirely new codes. As argued by Arrow (1974, p. 56), codification entails organizational rigidity and uniformity while increasing communication and transaction efficiency:

> the need for codes mutually understandable within an organization imposes a uniformity requirement on the behavior of participants. They are specialized in the information capable of being transmitted by the codes, so that they learn more in the direction of their activity and become less efficient in acquiring and transmitting information not easily fitted into the code.

It is clear, therefore, that codification can have unfortunate consequences for creativity and radical changes. Like a larger category of coordination mechanisms to which technical interoperability standards belong, codified knowledge can be a potent 'carrier of history'—encapsulating influences of essentially transient and possibly extraneous natures that were present in the circumstances prevailing when particular codes took shape. Having that power, it can become a source of 'lock in' to obsolete conceptual schemes, and to technological and organizational systems that are built around those.[23]

The second problem we have thus identified deals with 'excess inertia'. There are high fixed costs to be borne in the process of codification, especially when the cognitive environment is changing. Roughly put, costs of learning and developing languages in which new codes are being written will be incurred during the period when the knowledge environment is in flux, whereas benefits will accrue (from some of those investment) during a subsequent period of stabilization and widespread dissemination of the information. During a period of change, infrastructure is developed, languages and models are built, learned and standardized, and a community of agents with shared tacit knowledge grows. All of these investments contribute to a reduction in the fluidity of the knowledge environment, and conduce to hastening the enjoyment of the increasing returns from more widespread application that are permitted by the stabilization of organizational and technological knowledge. As a network of users of the knowledge expands, learning costs continue to decline and coordination externalities are likely to grow more significant as a source of social benefits.

If developing new languages and models allocates the fixed cost to one generation while many future generations benefit from the new infrastructure to codify knowledge, there is an intergenerational externality problem which can result in a lack of adequate private (or social) incentives for allocating resources to the development of more powerful codes and systematizing those that already exist. Solutions that would help mitigate this kind of time inconsistency problem entail the development of relevant markets (which may significantly increase the benefits even for the first generation of developers), or the creation of infinitely lived institutions that do not discount the future so strongly. Alternatively, society may rely upon the cultivation of altruistic preferences for the welfare of coming generations, to whom a greater stock of useable knowledge can be bequeathed (see Konrad and Thum, 1993).

8. Conclusions and the direction of further work

This paper has looked intensively and critically at one of the several dimensions David and Foray (1995) identified in their schematic description of the space in which 'knowledge-products' were distributed.[24] Our focus has been maintained on the most problematic and, for many economists, the most esoteric of the three axes defining that space: the dimension along which codification appeared at one extremum and tacitness occupied the other. This has permitted some further unpacking of the economic determinants of codification decisions, and the resources committed thereto, and has revealed that the term tacit is being used so loosely in the current economics of science and technology literature that important distinctions, such as the one separating that which is uncodified in a particular context and that which will not (likely) be codified at all, are blurred or entirely lost.

Also lost from view in too many treatments now appearing in the economics literature dealing with tacit knowledge and experience-based learning (learning 'by doing' and 'by using') is the important difference between procedural knowledge (know-how) and declarative propositions (know-what and know-why) about things in the world. Although the subject of tacit procedural knowledge, and its regeneration in the process of working with previously codified routines, has been highlighted by Cowan and Foray (1997) and touched upon at several places here, the nature of the technological constraints and the role of economic factors affecting the scope for codification in 'cycles of learning and knowledge transformation' are topics that deserve and are likely to repay more thorough exploration.

In drawing out the important distinction between knowledge that is codifiable (in the sense of articulable) and that which actually is codified, and in focusing analytical attention upon the endogenous boundary between what is and what is not codified at a particular point in time, it has not been possible to adequately discuss some quite important 'conditioning' influences. Most notably, this essay has had to leave for future treatment the ways in which the nature of the intellectual property rights regime and the disclosure conventions of various epistemic communities affects private strategies concerning the degree of completeness with which new knowledge becomes codified.

Those interactions, as much as the effects of changes in information technology, will have to be studied much more thoroughly before economists can justly claim to have created a suitable knowledge base upon which to anchor specific policy guidelines for future public (and private) investments in the codification of scientific and technological knowledge.

Acknowledgements

This article originated in a report prepared under the EC TSER Programme's TIPIK Project (Technology and Infrastructure Policy in the Knowledge-Based Economy—The Impact of the Tendency Towards Codification of Knowledge). That draft was presented for discussion by the 3rd TIPIK Workshop, held at BETA, University of Louis Pasteur, in Strasbourg, April 2–4, 1999, where it elicited many helpful comments and suggestions from our colleagues. We acknowledge the contributions of the TIPIK teams lead by Patrick Cohendet, Franco Malerba and Frieder Meyer-Kramer to improving both the substance and the exposition of our arguments, even though it has not been possible for us to do justice to all of their good ideas in the present paper. We are grateful also to Keith Pavitt for his probing critique of an earlier draft, and to W. Edward Steinmueller and an anonymous referee for their editorial questions and recommendations.

Notes

1 Polyani (1967, pp. 4–6): 'I shall reconsider human knowledge by starting from the fact that we can know more than we can tell . . . Gestalt psychology has demonstrated that we may know a physiognomy by intergrating our awareness of its particulars without being able to identify these particulars . . .'

2 Most significant, from the economist's viewpoint, is the absence of super-additivity and the negligible marginal costs of transmitting information. These properties and their implications are discussed more fully in the following text, but the canonical references are Nelson (1959) and Arrow (1962).

3 From the foregoing it should be evident that we do not find it helpful to conflate 'what humans learn in order to assimilate, digest and use information' with the concept of 'tacit knowledge', and thereby to arrive at the glib but empty formalization: 'information = codified knowledge' and 'knowledge' = 'tacit knowledge' + 'information'. The definitions offered in the text make explicit the distinctive usage of the terms *data*, *information* and *knowledge* in Dasgupta and David (1994), David and Foray (1995) and Cowan and Foray (1997). As we point out below, when knowledge is defined in this way, i.e. as an attribute of individual agents, some delicate conceptual issues arise when one tries to be precise in extending the notion by speaking of 'social knowledge' as the attribute of some collectivity of agents.

4 The definition of 'knowledge' given in the text (above) is broadly consonant with, albeit rather more spare than the way the term is being used in this literature, as may be seen by the following 'working definition' offered by Davenport and Prusak (1998, p. 5): 'Knowledge is a fluid mix of framed experience, values, contextual information, and expert insight that provides a framework for evaluating and incorporating new experience and information. It originates and is applied in the minds of knowers.'

5 Balconi (1998) explores the effects of changes in the modern technology of steel product manufacturing upon the boundary between the codified and the tacit elements of the knowledge deemed relevant for production operations and worker training. The relevance here is simply that this boundary is mutable under the influence of technological changes other than those in the domain information technology narrowly construed.

6 For the subsequent elaboration of a more thorough-going rejection of microeconomic optimization, in the evolutionary models of Schumpeterian competition, see e.g. Dosi (1988), Dosi et al. (1988) and Dosi and Egidi (1991). Evolutionary modeling in economics now spans a wide range of practice in regard to how 'bounded' the bounded rationality of agents is assumed to be. Anderson (1994) discusses this and other issues in the algorithmic representation of the general class of 'Nelson–Winter type' models.

7 Skinner (1994, p. 11) points out that the use made of Polanyi's concept by Nelson and Winter (1982) emphasized what cognitive scientists refer to as the 'granularity' of the efficient mode of mental storage for learned skills and procedures ('routines'), rather than for the storage of declarative statements. Skinner suggests that, in developing the former theme, Nelson and Winter were influenced strongly by the previous work in cognitive science and AI, e.g. by Newell and Simon's (1972) formulation of a production system model of information processing for 'learning,' and the idea of learned routines being holistically stored for recall (as 'scripts')—a concept due to Shank (1988), who was a leading figure in cognitive science and AI fields on the faculty of Yale University during the 1970s and 1980s (as were Nelson and Winter).

8 Had things been otherwise, it seems only reasonable to suppose that we would have been spared at least the more serious confusions and unwarranted generalizations that have become commonplace in the literature.

9 For further discussion see Arundel and Kabla (1999). The force of such claims would seem restricted largely to the case of process patents rather than product patents. Arundel (1996, 1997) reports that the CIS survey of EU firms found that 18–20% of respondent companies in the size range above 199 employees regarded process patents as a 'very important or crucial' source of competitive advantage, whereas in the case of product patents the corresponding figure was in the 30–40% range.

10 In subsequent work, von Hippel (1994) generalizes the idea of stickiness so that it covers all situations in which there is an appreciable cost of transferring information, relevant for innovative activities. In principle, at least, von Hippel's use of the notion of 'stickiness' makes no distinction between transfer costs consisting of pure rents imposed by the owners of intellectual property rights, on the one hand, and real social resource costs such as those entailed in physically transporting an expert for the purpose of demonstrating the proper use of a novel product or process in a distant location.

11 We can observe that the more things change the more they stay the same. We have moved from the view that the problem to be solved arises from the fact that a firm's *knowledge* is easily appropriated by other firms. Acknowledging the importance of tacit knowledge, and thus that the initial problem may not be so severe, we face a 'new problem' stemming from the fact that a firm's *knowledge workers* are easily appropriated by other firms. In both cases the general issue remains, however—fluidity of knowledge or information (whether transmitted through codified knowledge or labor mobility) is good for the economy but may be bad for the individual firm that bears the costs of enlightening its competitors.

12 See, for example, Kealey (1996) on industrial secrecy as the suitable 'remedy' for the problem of informational spillovers from research, and the critique of that position in David (1997).

13 See Machlup (1980, pp. 167–169) for a discussion of 'the phenomenological theory of knowledge' developed by Schutz and Luckmann (1973, chs 3–4). The latter arrive at a concept described by Machlup as: 'the fully objectivated [*sic*] knowledge of society, a social stock of knowledge which in some sense is the result of a socialization of knowledge [through individual interactions involving private stocks of subjective but inter-subjectively valid knowledge] and contains at the same time more *and* less than the sum of the private stocks of subjective knowledge. . . . This most ingenious phenomenological theory of the stock of knowledge in society is not equipped to deal with . . . the problem of assessing the size of the stock and its growth.'

14 It is clear that the availability of two operators—union and intersection—when combined with two types of knowledge—tacit and codified—leads to a situation in which 'the world stock of knowledge' is going to take some further defining.

15 This view could be challenged on the grounds that knowledge held secretly by individuals is not distingushable from labor (tangible human capital) as a productivity input, but, unlike tangible physical capital, the existence of undisclosed knowledge assets cannot be ascertained. Machlup (1980, p. 175), in the sole passage devoted to the significance of tacit knowledge, adopts the latter position and argues that: 'Generation of socially new knowledge is another non-operational concept as long as generation is not complemented by dissemination. . . . Only if [an individual] shares his knowledge with others can one recognize that new knowledge has been created. Generation of knowledge without dissemination is socially worthless as well as unascertainable. Although "tacit knowledge" cannot be counted in any sort of inventory, its creation may still be a part of the production of knowledge if the activities that generate it have a measureable cost.'

16 We note that activities involving 'unvoiced knowledge' are often assumed to involve thereby tacit knowledge. We argue below that this is too hasty.

17 In understanding these distinctions it is important to remember that we are discussing knowledge activities, and the kinds of knowledge used in them. Thus we can observe activities in which the knowledge has been codified at some point in history but is not articulated in current endeavors.

18 Here we may remark that the ability to function effectively, possibly more effectively with the codebook out of sight (e.g. to pass closed-book exams), often is one criterion for entry, or part of the initiation into the group. Not being truly an initiated 'insider' is generally found to be a considerable impediment to fully understanding the transactions taking place among the members of any social group, let alone for would-be ethnographers of 'laboratory life'.

19 This often infuriates outsiders, who complain vociferously about excessive jargon in the writings and speeches of physicists, sociologists, economists, psychologists and . . .

20 A number of interesting examples are presented in Balconi's (1998) study of worker training programs in the modern steel-making industry, showing that what formerly could justifiably be described as 'rules of the art' have been transformed into codified knowledge of a generic sort, as well as explicit operating procedures for the plant in question. According to Balconi (pp. 73–74), an overly sharp distinction has been drawn by Bell and Pavitt (1993) when they contrast the nature of the 'learning within firms' that is necessary to augment the content of the formal education and training conducted by institutions outside industry.

In the cases she discusses, 'the aim of training [provided within the industry] is to transmit know-how by teaching know-why (the explanations of the causes of the physical transformations carried out [in the plant]), and know-what (codified operation practices)'.

21 Further, in much the same vein, it is quite possible that practiced experimental researchers, having developed and codified procedures involving a sequence of discrete steps, may be observed discussing and executing the routine in a holistic manner—even to the point of finding it difficult to immediately articulate every discrete constituent step of the process. The latter is a situation found quite commonly when experienced computer programmers are asked to explain and document the strings of code that they have just typed. The phenomenon would seem to have more to do with the efficient 'granularity' for mental *storage and recall* of knowledge, than with the nature of the knowledge itself, or the manner in which it was initially acquired.

22 A recent exemplification of the application of the approach formalized here is available in Geuna's (1999) studies of the economics of university funding for research in science and engineering, and how different funding structures affect the types of activity within the modern European university system.

23 The argument follows that developed by David (1994) regarding the sources of path-dependence in the evolution of organizations and institutions, without reiterating the important respects in which those social entities differ from technological constructs.

24 The other two dimensions of that space are the continuum between secrecy and full disclosure, and the spectrum of asset ownship status ranging from legally enforced private property rights to pure public goods. See David and Foray (1995, 1996) for further explication.

References

Anderson, E. S. (1994), *Evolutionary Economics: Post-Schumpeterian Contributions*. Pinter: London.

Arrow, K. J. (1955), 'Economic Aspects of Military Research and Development,' RAND Corporation Memorandum D-3142, August 30.

Arrow, K. J. (1962), 'Economic Welfare and the Allocation of Resources to Inventive Activity,' in R. Nelson (ed.), *The Rate and Direction of Technical Change*. National Bureau of Economic Research: New York.

Arrow, K. J. (1974), *The Limits of Organization*. Norton: New York.

Arundel, A. (1996), 'Enterprise Strategies and Barriers to Innovation: Preliminary Descriptive Results for the CIS Subjective Questions,' paper prepared for EIMS, DGXIII, Luxembourg, May.

Arundel, A. (1997), 'Enterprise Strategies and Barriers to Innovation,' in A. Arundel and R. Garrelfs (eds), *Innovation Measurement and Policies*, pp. 101–108. European Commission, EIMS publication 50.

Arundel, A. and I. Kabla (1998), 'What Percentage of Innovations are Patented? Empirical Estimates for European Firms,' *Research Policy*, **27**, 127–141.

Balconi, M. (1998), 'Technology, Codification of Knowledge and Firm Competences,' *Revue Internationale de Systémique*, **12**, 63–82.

Baumol, W., S. Batley Blackman and E. Wolff (1989), *Productivity and American Leadership: The Long View*. MIT Press: Cambridge.

Bell, M. and K. Pavitt (1993), 'Technological Accumulation and Industrial Growth: Contrasts between Developed and Developing Countries,' *Industrial and Corporate Change*, **2**, 157–201.

Callon, M. (1995), 'Four Models of the Dynamics of Science,' in S. Jasanoff (ed.), *Handbook of Science and Technology Studies*, pp. 29–63. Sage: Thousand Oaks, CA.

Cobenhagen, J. (1999), 'Managing Innovation at the Company Level: A Study on Non-sector-specific Success Factors,' PhD dissertation (to be defended), Maastricht University.

Collins, H. M. (1974), 'The TEA Set: Tacit Knowledge in Scientific Networks,' *Science Studies*, **4**, 165–186.

Cowan, R. and D. Foray (1997), 'The Economics of Codification and the Diffusion of Knowledge,' *Industrial and Corporate Change*, **6**, 595–622.

Cowan, R. (1995), 'The Informatization of Government as an Economic Opportunity,' *STI Review*, **16**.

Dasgupta, P. and P. A. David (1994), 'Towards a New Economics of Science,' *Research Policy*, **23**, 487–521.

Davenport, T. H. and L. Prusak (1998), *Working Knowledge: How Organizations Manage What they Know*. Harvard Business School Press: Boston, MA.

David, P. A. (1991), 'General Purpose Engines, Investment and Productivity,' in E. Deiaco, E. Hornell and G. Vickery (eds), *Technology and Investment*, pp. 141–154. London: Pinter Publishing.

David, P. A. (1994), 'Why are Institutions the "Carriers of History"?: Path Dependence and the Evolution of Conventions, Organizations and Institutions,' *Economic Dynamics and Structural Change*, **5**, 205–220.

David, P. A. (1997), 'From Market Magic to Calypso Science Policy: A Review of T. Kealey's *Economic Laws of Scientific Research*,' *Research Policy*, **26**, 229–255.

David, P. A. (2000), 'Understanding Digital Technology's Evolution and the Path of Measured Productivity Growth: Present and Future in the Mirror of the Past,' in E. Brynolfsson and B. Kahin (eds), *Understanding the Digital Economy*. MIT Press: Cambridge, MA (forthcoming).

David, P. A. and D. Foray (1995), 'Accessing and Expanding the Science and Technology Knowledge Base,' *STI*, **16**, 13–68.

David, P. A. and D. Foray (1996), 'Information Distribution and the Growth of Economically Valuable Knowledge: a Rationale for Technological Infrastructure Policies,' in M. Teubal *et al.* (eds), *Technological Infrastructure Policy: an International Perspective*, pp. 87–116. Kluwer Academic Publishers: Dordrecht.

David, P. A., D. Foray and W. E. Steinmueller (1999), 'The Research Network and the New Economics of Science: from Metaphors to Organizational Behavior,' in A. Gambardella and F. Malerba (eds), *The Organization of Inventive Activity in Europe*, pp. 303–342. Cambridge: Cambridge University Press.

Dosi, G. (1988), 'Sources, Procedures and Microeconomic Effects of Innovation,' *Journal of Economic Literature*, **26**, 1120–1171.

Dosi, G. and M. Egidi (1991), 'Substantive and Procedural Uncertainty,' *Journal of Evolutionary Economics*, 1, 145–168.

Dosi, G., C. Freeman, R. Nelson, G. Silverberg and L. Soete (eds) (1988), *Technical Change and Economic Theory*. Pinter: London.

Ferguson, E. S. (1992), *Engineering and the Mind's Eye*. MIT Press: Cambridge, MA.

Geuna, A. (1999), *Resource Allocation and Knowledge Production: Studies in the Economics of University Research*. E. Elgar: Cheltenham.

Gibbons, M., C. Limoges, H. Nowotny, S. Schwartzman, P. Scott and M. Trow (1996), *The New Production of Knowledge*. Sage: London.

Gibbs, W. W. (1994), 'The Crisis in Software,' *Scientific American*, **241**, 261–267.

Gibbs, W. W. (1997), 'Taking Computers to Task,' *Scientific American*, **277**, 282–289.

Gunby, P. (1996), 'Explaining Adoption Patterns of Process Standards,' PhD Dissertation, Department of Economics, The University of Western Ontario.

Hofstader, D. (1979), *Gödel, Escher, Bach: An Eternal Golden Braid*. Basic Books: New York.

Kay, J. (1999), 'Money from Knowledge,' *Science and Public Affairs*, April, 12–13.

Kealey, T. (1996), *Economic Laws of Scientific Research*. Macmillan: London.

Konrad, K. and M. Thum (1993), 'Fundamental Standards and Time Consistency,' *Kyklos*, **46**, 607–632.

Kuhn, T. (1962), *The Structure of Scientific Revolutions*. University of Chicago Press: Chicago, IL.

Latour, B. (1987), *Science in Action: How to Follow Scientists and Engineers Through Society*. Harvard University Press: Cambridge, MA.

Latour, B. and S. Woolgar (1979), *Laboratory Life: The Construction of Scientific Facts*. Princeton University Press: Princeton, NJ.

Leonard-Barton, D. (1995), *Well-springs of Knowledge*. Harvard Business School Press: Boston, MA.

Machlup, Fritz (1980), *Knowledge: Its Creation, Distribution and Economic Significance. Vol. I. Knowledge and Knowledge Production*. Princeton University Press: Princeton, NJ.

Mackenzie, D. and G. Spinardi (1995), 'Tacit Knowledge, Weapons Design and the Uninvention of Nuclear Weapons,' *American Journal of Sociology*, **101**.

Nelson, R. R. (1959), 'The Simple Economics of Basic Scientific Research,' *Journal of Political Economy*, **67**, 323–348.

Nelson, R. R. (1992), 'What Is "Commercial" and What is "Public" about Technology and What Should Be?,' in N. Rosenberg, R. Landau and D. Mowery (eds), *Technology and the Wealth of Nations*, ch. 3, pp. 57–72. Stanford University Press: Stanford, CA.

Nelson, R. R. and S. Winter (1982), *An Evolutionary Theory of Economic Change*. Harvard University Press: Cambridge, MA.

Newell, A. and H. A. Simon (1972), *Human Problem Solving*. Prentice-Hall: Englewood Cliffs, NJ.

Nonaka, I. and H. Keuchi (1995), *The Knowledge Creating Company*. Oxford University Press: New York.

Patel, P. and K. Pavitt (1995), 'Patterns of Technological Activities: Their Measurement and Interpretations,' in P. Stoneman (ed.), *Handbook of the Economics of Innovation and Technical Change*, pp. 14–51. Blackwell: Oxford.

Pavitt, K. (1987), 'The Objectives of Technology Policy,' *Science and Public Policy*, **14**, 182–188.

Penrose, R. (ed.) (1997), *The Large, the Small and the Human Mind*. Cambridge University Press: Cambridge. Penrose, R. and M. Gardner (1989), *The Emperor's New Mind: Concerning Computers, Minds, and the Laws of Physics*. Oxford University Press: Oxford.

Polanyi, M. (1967), *The Tacit Dimension*. Doubleday: New York.

Polanyi, M. (1958), *Personal Knowledge: Towards a Post-critical Philosophy*. Routledge & Kegan Paul: London.

Schutz, A. and T. Luckmann (1973), *The Structures of the Life-world* [translated by R. M. Zaner and A. T. Engelhardt Jr]. Northwestern University Press: Evanston, IL.

Shank, R. (1998), 'What is AI, Anyway?,' in D. Partridge and Y. Wilks (eds), *The Foundations of Artificial Intelligence: A Sourcebook*. Cambridge University Press: New York, pp. 3–13.

Skinner, R. E. (1994), 'Making Tacit Knowledge Explicit,' Working Paper, Stanford Knowledge Systems Laboratory, Stanford University.

Traweek, S. (1988), *Beam Times and Life Times: The World of High Energy Physicists*. Harvard University Press: Cambridge, MA.

Vincenti, W. G. (1990), *What Engineers Know and When They Know It: Analytical Studies in Aeronautical History*. The Johns Hopkins University Press: Baltimore, MD.

von Hippel, E. (1993), 'Trading in Trade Secrets,' *Harvard Business Review*, February/March, 59–64.

von Hippel, Eric (1994), '"Sticky Information" and the Locus of Problem Solving: Implications for Innovation,' *Management Science*, 40, 429–439.

Winter, S. G. (1987), 'Knowledge and Competence as Strategic Assets,' in D. J. Teece (ed.), *The Competitive Challenge*, ch. 8, pp. 159–184. Ballinger: Cambridge, MA.

32

WILL NEW INFORMATION AND COMMUNICATION TECHNOLOGIES IMPROVE THE 'CODIFICATION' OF KNOWLEDGE?

W. Edward Steinmueller

Source: *Industrial and Corporate Change* 9(2) (2000): 361–76.

New software technologies for personal productivity, research documentation and workgroup applications are analysed as instances of knowledge 'codification'. The analysis reveals that the social processes governing disclosure and cooperation in codification processes are as necessary as technological capabilities for some of the most promising applications. The conclusions suggest that research should focus on the nature and processes of 'epistemic' communities (collective efforts organized to pursue common goals that are governed by procedural authority) to better understand how codification works.

1. Introduction

Information and communication technologies (ICTs) most often are defined in terms of their capacities to acquire, store, process and transmit information. It is generally known that the information processing and distribution capabilities of these technologies are improving dramatically over time. In what sense might these technologies enhance our capabilities to store and reproduce knowledge? If information is, in practical terms, the same as knowledge, an individual or organization can reproduce knowledge by sending it as information using these technologies. If knowledge is distinct from information, we have to question whether it is possible to find a means of reproducing it through information exchange. These two possibilities represent the crux of the contemporary debate about the 'codification' of knowledge. Under what circumstances is it possible to reproduce knowledge by exchanging information and under what circumstance is it not possible?

If there are circumstances when it is possible to reproduce knowledge by exchange of information, then we may refer to the informational representation of that knowledge as a 'code' and the process of making the representation can be designated as 'codification'. 'Knowledge codification' only recently has become a term of art for those interested in the economics of technology (see Cowan and Foray, 1997). The term has been used for two different types of purposes. The first is to challenge viewpoints that assign a primal importance to 'tacit' knowledge as a determinant of organizational behaviour; that is, knowledge that cannot be adequately articulated for the purpose of exchange or is not so articulated because of the costs of doing so [see Cowan *et al.* (2000) for an illustration of this approach]. The second is to call attention to the variety of techniques and to the scale of investments that are being devoted to the processes of codification. The aims of these techniques and investments include the creation of individual and organizational memory, the reproduction of successful practices across organizational units, and the reconstruction of knowledge exploration and discovery. Focusing on the techniques and investments allows us to be agnostic about the extent and nature of the complementary activities involving 'tacit' knowledge that are needed to achieve specific aims.[1] This paper addresses the second type of purpose and has the aim of achieving a preliminary assessment of the role of 'new' information and communication technologies in intraorganizational contexts, including the use by individuals of such technologies for remembering, reproducing or reconstituting knowledge. The new ICTs examined in this paper involve the use of Internet-related technologies, advanced simulation and modelling techniques, and other recently devised technologies used in the codification process. The focus on the most recent information and communication technologies is chosen for reasons of length and because of the availability of empirical and theoretical examinations of the roles of earlier technologies (see e.g. Strassman, 1990; Simon, 1996).

2. ICTs and knowledge codification: the case of the aid to individual memory

Whatever the other purposes it serves, codified knowledge is produced with the object of being decodified. The context and intended 'recipient' of the 'decodified' knowledge makes a great deal of difference to the costs and feasibility of the initial codification. It is useful therefore to begin the assessment of the role of ICTs in codification by considering what should be the simplest case: knowledge codification by an individual for his or her own use.[2] In particular, let us consider the recording of information by an individual for the purpose of reconstituting current knowledge at a later point in time when they have 'forgotten' what they now know. Such aids to memory as diaries, letter files, manuscripts and laboratory notebooks are not new inventions.

ICTs allow the storage of these memory aids as electronic files. In principle, an individual with access to a mainframe computer system might have begun accumulating such files in the 1950s using IBM or competing tape drives to record data entered on punched cards. This would, however, have been a markedly inferior method for creating aids to memory since the cost and effort to encode this information would far exceed those of even the most expensive stenographic and secretarial services. The practical use of mass storage technology as a viable alternative to traditional encoding methods required substantial advances in not only the storage technology but also the means for entering such data into storage.[3] These were to occur over a prolonged period through the evolution of time-shared access to stand-alone personal computers, which served to bring data entry closer to the desktop and to the day-to-day activities of individuals.[4] By the mid-1980s, one might actually plan a forward-looking strategy for codification of personal memory aids using ICTs in preference to other means. Even today, however, limitations in data entry methods and models for organizing information in computer systems are, for most individuals, far inferior to the more traditional methods of knowledge codification for the purposes of constructing memory aids.

Nonetheless, a process of change is underway by which certain individuals are increasingly likely to use ICTs for purposes similar to those served by traditional methods of recording individual memory aids. For professionals whose work requires substantial written output, the availability of notes on ideas as well as the complete text of prior works provides an incentive to incur the costs of codification. Making this investment allows one to build a stock of intermediate inputs for the creation of new written products and in the process may stimulate the recovery of the knowledge utilized to create the original information. The legal and accountancy professions clearly have substantial incentives to utilize ICTs in this way due to the recurrence of problems for which a related solution is available in previous written text. Correspondingly, as individual communications are increasingly conducted through networked ICTs, the flow of messages created initially for the purpose of communication may be stored for later reference. This substitute for letter files can be organized in ways that allow the recall of information that will prompt the reconstruction of knowledge, particularly if the communication was originally devised as a means of encoding shared or individual knowledge (e.g. emails to oneself). Finally, many professions intensively utilize ICTs to produce specialized informational outputs, such as engineering models and drawings (considered in more detail below), architectural diagrams, programming code, and technical documentation. There are clearly substantial advantages in capturing informational outputs and 'notes' designed to prompt the recall of knowledge relevant for interpreting past work.

All of these examples are confronted by three basic problems that can be illustrated for the case of written expressions, a case where the problem of representation has already been solved. The first is that of organization. Collecting information into storage units (e.g. files) and the organization of information within these storage units is neither natural nor obvious. Even if the individual has a highly structured approach to written expression and can recollect contextual knowledge from previous written expression (the representation problem), the organization of these written expressions involves a substantial 'overhead' cost in manipulating the ICT system.

The costs of information organization are reinforced by a second problem, the rate of technological change in software and systems used to store written expression. The average life of a personal computer system is around three years and that of the software used to encode information is somewhat less. Changes in software and hardware systems (which are not always simultaneous) impose further costs of 'converting' that information which is to be maintained. Unlike paper files, which usually decay gradually and gracefully, most computer files become indecipherable as time progresses, not through physical decay of stored information, but because the software used to access the stored information is replaced.[5] In the language of the codification discussion, 'codebooks' are regularly 'misplaced', requiring reconstruction or the devising of 'converters'.

Third, although paper files may burn, be flooded or be consumed by various organic agents, computer systems are subject to catastrophic failure. Information can only be reliably stored to the extent that it is duplicated on a reliable 'back-up' medium, adding further overhead costs to this form of memory. The spread, as well as the fear, of computer viruses that may destroy codebooks has exacerbated these problems and costs.

The costs of electronic storage of aids to memory are clearly substantial even if we assume the problem of representation is solved. In addition, however, the problem of representation is substantial. Individuals record information in a multiplicity of ways—sketches, outlines, texts, audio recordings, copies of documents, and so forth. Each of these methods of recording information can provide a method for codifying knowledge. At present, available technologies provide electronic substitutes for each of these methods of recording information. Each requires mastery of a different set of skills, as well as the recapitulation of the information organization and preservation problems described above. None of the available methods appears to be substantially more efficient in inputting information, or representing or preserving knowledge, than traditional media preserves.

Moreover, ICT innovation has not been remarkable in providing new tools for data input. There are two main exceptions. The first is capabilities to record video interactions that have become available in advanced office environments as a by-product of conference room or desktop videoconferencing. The second, and only nascent, possibility is that of voice interaction. At present, voice recognition is just entering the mass market as an alternative to the keyboard, and voice interaction is increasingly a part of the telephony environment.

Both of these are potentially revolutionary developments in the means for codifying information, although each pushes at the limits of available technology. The value of video communication lies in its ability to capture the wide range of evocative expression that is possible with human facial expression and body language (gesture), and which substantially augments written text. Audio communication with voice recognition combines a number of cognitive clues in the timbre and cadence of the voice, with the use of the recognized words as means for search and filtering information. Asking one's computer (which has recorded and codified through transcription all of one's telephone conversations) to recall and replay the instances and context of a particular phrase uttered over the past month would provide a new memory aid. It is likely to be far more useful precisely because the process of information capture has been greatly augmented. Nuances of verbal expression are likely to elicit more complex and complete recall processes of knowledge than confronting a memo with the same phrase.

The purpose of introducing these speculative examples is to provide some contrast to the problems encountered in using current systems to perform one of the simplest of knowledge codification processes, the creation of individual memory aids. Similar examples may be constructed for many other 'personal productivity' tools that rely upon information storage for the generation of benefits. The problem in receiving the benefits arises from the costs of current cumbersome processes of data capture and reliable maintenance of information storage which largely or entirely offset the potential benefits from electronic processing of stored data. In short, computer mediation of simple communications with oneself does not yet appear to offer substantial net benefits. A somewhat different picture emerges when we consider how ICT may support individual tasks that involve interpersonal communication (the subject of the next section) or computation (the subject of the penultimate section).

3. ICTs and knowledge codification: the case of aiding group memory

In the previous section, the discussion of individual uses of ICTs for the purposes of creating aids to memory included examples of communication processes drawn from email and telephone conversations. More generally, communication within groups of individuals pursuing similar goals with shared values and operating with a procedural authority (epistemic communities) presents problems of collective recall either of group exchange or individual expression. Here, unlike the case of the individual, the responsibility for memory is undetermined and is often problematic. Individuals are supposed to remember their own creations, or be able to employ an assistant to aid in the process. A group may or may not agree that one of its members will serve this function, which may require the intervention of a procedural authority to resolve the assignment. Even if it is agreed or resolved that one or more individuals will be responsible for the group's memory, the account of that subset may be, from time to time, discordant with other members of the group. This suggests further intervention by procedural authority. For example, formal organizational procedures for the codification of group process such as Robert's Rules of Order provide means to review and amend the 'minutes' of meetings that purport to represent collective deliberations.

The theoretical value of ICTs in augmenting group memory is their ability to record multiple dialogues as a record of the multiplicity of ways in which individuals within an epistemic community may interact in pursuit of common purposes. Many of these interactions may be otherwise unavailable to individuals in the group. Recording them in the form of electronically mediated communication provides a way to expand the participation of a particular individual in group processes without necessarily re-engaging each of the individuals to recapitulate their discussion for the benefit of new members. It is often contended that one of the sources of organizational ineffectiveness is that the costs of interpersonal interaction increase exponentially with the addition of more individuals to a group. There is, in other words, a negative externality of creating acceptable social cohesion within a group as it adds additional members.[6] To the extent that electronically mediated communications allow face-to-face interactions to be more focused, either on specific substantive issues or on building *esprit de corps*, gains are likely to flow from the group use of ICTs as a way of augmenting group memory and information exchange, and mitigating the collective costs of expanding the group.

The availability of collective memory within an epistemic community also allows reduction in the costs of 'remembering' solutions to problems that have been previously discovered and documented. This permits a reduction in the effort devoted to reinvention. For such gains to be realized, the codification of solutions need not be complete.[7] Instead, the purpose of the collective memory is to 'signal' the availability of the previous work and a solution to a problem that might arise again within the community. The gains from this process are both collective and individual, and therefore are incentive-compatible with efforts to contribute to the group memory project. Note that it is important for the group to have some degree of trust and mutual regard for such a system to work, otherwise individuals will not regard the 'solutions' or 'ideas' of others to be worth the time it takes to become aware of and evaluate them in a new context.

When the process of collective memory is extended further to the division of labour through the compartmentalization of efforts, even greater gains are possible if the interfaces among subgroup efforts can be appropriately defined. A common strategy for the solution of knowledge creation problems is to divide them into parts, represented either by competing possible advances or by components that can be combined into an articulated whole. In both cases, the ability to share preliminary results and conjectures, and to discover the rate at which individual groups are progressing, has important implications for the productivity of the collective effort.

Here the problem of incentive compatibility may inveigh against a satisfactory outcome. In addition to the issue previously identified of discordance between individual and group views (here, the individual's own views versus the group's views) of events, there is the additional problem that the recording of interim work can expose ineptitude, mistakes or sloth to common view, i.e. conflicting views of performance. In a system that is used for both monitoring and collective problem solving, it can be expected that individual contributions to the collective memory will reflect self-interest, i.e. a greater level of distortion than simple disagreements over the account of decisions and problem solving activities. Thus, it is important that appropriate social norms, such as clear separation of monitoring from information sharing, are introduced as part of the management of such collective memory systems.

4. ICTs and knowledge codification: social memory

As we move outside the boundary of an epistemic community a wide range of voluntary and exchange-based social groupings appear as possibilities for the use of ICTs as social memory devices. We also enter a domain in which 'off-line' social mechanisms are unavailable for guiding the process of knowledge codification. Unlike the epistemic community, where individuals are able to resolve the problems of shared meaning in a multiplicity of ways, broader social efforts to codify knowledge for the purpose of reproduction face substantial problems in creating a shared 'cultural context'. There are distinct positive benefits and problems with the construction of 'social memory'.

Positive features of social efforts to codify knowledge include the variety that is available through networked connections of individuals distant in space and asynchronous in time. The problem of variety is that selection methods must be devised to sort between productive and unproductive social groupings. Examination of 'virtual communities' suggests that they use a variety of methods to establish these filtering mechanisms. It is possible, for example (Mansell *et al.*, 1998), for the community to establish means by which individuals may accumulate 'reputation' within the community and thereby privilege their contributions relative to those of others. Means for doing this include the ability to cross-reference or cite the contributions of others and to select those contributions that have achieved a high level of either type of reference. Allowing 'open' virtual communities to create 'closed' subgroups serves a similar purpose in which those with the highest mutual regard and interaction are able to interact more intensely and openly than they might be willing to do in the 'open' environment.[8] Both of these possibilities indicate the possibilities for 'open' virtual communities to evolve toward 'epistemic' communities.

A second positive feature of broader social efforts to codify knowledge is the possibility of specialization. By bringing together individuals who might otherwise have enormous difficulty identifying one another through ordinary social mechanisms, the Internet is accelerating the rate at which specialization in some forms of knowledge creation and distribution is possible. There are, of course, problems of appropriability in such ICT-mediated social networks. The reward mechanisms for contributions to the codification effort have to be incentive-compatible with the level of individual effort. This may, however, occur in a variety of ways. Individual contributions may represent incomplete disclosure of their possible contributions and thus serve as an advertising signal of further contribution to be negotiated under appropriate terms.[9] Individuals may be compensated by the 'reputation' they gain from their contributions that allows them then to trade with other individuals.[10] Individuals may receive non-pecuniary benefits from being recognized and appreciated for their contributions. The specific motive for contributions is likely to affect their content.

Disadvantages of social knowledge codification processes include the problems of filtering that are only partially resolved through the mechanisms described above. It is also necessary to address the problems of developing appropriate business models allowing voluntary associations to be transformed into associations based upon exchange. Without such a transformation, many useful knowledge codification efforts that are based upon voluntary effort are likely to be plagued by opportunism and the exhaustion of the good will of the more productive members which can only, at present, be compensated through the sorts of 'currency' described above. A further disadvantage of the social process of codification arises in cases where contention within groups results in 'gridlock' and the inability to adopt a common set of 'procedural rules' for governing collective efforts. Instances of such gridlock are widely apparent in open forums such as those in UseNet, the largest of the newsgroups devoted to specialized discussion topics where it has proven difficult to define boundaries for 'acceptable contributions'. All of these disadvantages serve to transform 'open' social groupings into epistemic communities. This transformation results in some loss of variety and specialization due to arbitrary principles of inclusion and exclusion in the formation of epistemic communities.

The positive and negative mechanisms described above are clearly at work in the development of virtual communities in the inter-networked environment and represent relatively recent applications of ICT to social processes of knowledge codification. Of particular note is the interaction between variety and specialization. Previous efforts to codify knowledge depended upon means for individuals with common interests to 'find' one another in order to establish 'epistemic' communities. The search process has been greatly augmented by the availability of automated cataloguing methods that provide inexpensive means to identify already established communities or isolated individuals with highly specialized interests.

From an economic viewpoint, the principal issues are therefore the effectiveness of social processes for codifying knowledge and the construction and maintenance of the epistemic communities that engage in these processes. These communities allow both knowledge communication and codification to proceed where previously they had either not occurred or suffered from a lack of variety and interest. A means to empirically measure and characterize these developments is urgently needed.

In all three domains that we have just examined, ICTs are playing a major role in augmenting individual and social processes that support knowledge codification with effects that are likely to be very significant for both the variety and complexity of available codified knowledge. The benefits of creating individual aids to memory appear, at least at present, to be more modest than the potential for the use of ICTs in epistemic or 'open' virtual communities. This observation may help to explain a part of the 'productivity paradox', the apparent absence of discernible productivity effects from substantial investments in computer equipment during the period 1970–1990 (Roach, 1987; Strassman, 1990; Sichel, 1997; David and Steinmueller, 2000). The second half of this period was the period of the 'personal computer' (PC) revolution and its possibly mislabelled 'personal productivity' tools. Only during the 1990s have the substantial use of networked PCs and the broader uses of the Internet in business become a major event. If the conjectures of this paper regarding the specific value of knowledge codification in a social context versus the individual context are correct, measurable productivity gains during the 1990s should be discernible and these should also be linked to the extent and nature of networked computer use.

5. Specialized languages, simulation and other forms of symbolic communication

The use of ICTs extends beyond the representation of 'natural language' exchanges to symbolic communication and database representations where a broader case may be developed for the value of ICTs in the knowledge codification process.

The communication of 'symbolic' texts is the most straightforward example of the forms of symbolic communication that are improved through the use of ICTs. In their most direct applications, e.g. scientific publication, the availability of tools for transmitting symbolic codes such as mathematical notation are of great assistance in stimulating communication that might otherwise involve publication delays, cumbersome production methods and idiosyncratic notational conventions. Easing these frictions is, of course, of value and may justify the recording of symbolic information in electronic formats. Further gains are available from the richer system of cross-referencing made available by hypertext links that permit the documentation of terminology, the identification and immediate availability of related work, and so on. Even larger gains from symbolic communication, however, occur in the communication of working models and observational data.

In communicating a working model of a scientific or technical phenomenon, the scientist or technologist is revealing a far richer stock of information about the underlying assumptions and structure of thought than can be communicated in a paper summarizing results. The same principle applies when analysis of a dataset is accompanied by the actual data used to reach the conclusions. In both cases, the recipients of the symbolic communication are able not only to trace and reproduce the work of the original contributor, but also to use the model or data in support of their own assumptions and analysis. The 'generative' quality of such communication more closely mimics features of knowledge that are distinct from information as well as supporting variety and specialization in the development of alternative interpretations and conclusions about scientific and technical phenomena.

Many, perhaps most, laboratory results cannot yet be accurately conveyed as 'working models', while a larger share of observational data can be communicated in this way. The extent to which progress is being made in simulation techniques and the construction of virtual models of physical systems is controversial.[11] Nonetheless, there are areas of significant technological importance such as electronics where there exist widely used symbolic systems for representations of designs and specifications.[12] There is no reason to believe that the existing varieties of virtual models of physical systems have reached limits that prohibit further advance. On the contrary, it is widely believed within the scientific and technological community that such approaches are worthy of substantial further investment.[13]

In communicating observational data there are additional problems of 'free riding' where research groups may wish to retain their observational data for further interpretation and study to be assured that they have exhausted the results they are capable of discovering (Cassier and Foray, 1999). Such 'retention', of course, will threaten to be indefinite without positive incentives to disclose the data and suggest changes in funding practices to arbitrate between individual and social incentives.[14] At the same time, it is important to institute incentive-compatible mechanisms for individuals to disclose their observational data so that credit may be received for their efforts, which contributes to their future efforts.

Symbolic communication offers important advantages for each of the domains previously considered. At the individual level, an aid to memory expressed in the form of a symbolic communication (the most common of which is the spreadsheet) is likely to offer a more effective means of recapitulating the structure of thought, and therefore the knowledge employed, in constructing a model. Similar principles are at work in workgroup communication, within both epistemic and more 'open' social communities, with the additional feature that the working models and observational data may be based upon collective effort and division of labour. Developments in this area are often described by the term 'computer supported collaboration' and are facilitated by the class of software products called 'groupware'.

The aim of 'groupware' has been to facilitate a common electronic format for the recording of information within collective endeavours and to facilitate the 'markup' by individual suggestion, criticism, elaboration and so forth. Various proprietary standards for such formats have been introduced and large user communities have adopted some of these standards, such as Lotus Notes. Since the development of the World Wide Web (WWW), however, there has been a massive expansion in the variety of formats in which information can be exchanged. The number and variety of tools available for developing WWW browser-compatible content are expanding the range of content that can be readily exchanged over the public Internet or in private implementations of Internet technology to create Intranets (internal to the organization) or Extranets (inter-organizational networks). These 'content technologies' present a new set of problems for computer-supported collaboration in the form of increasing information congestion and filtering problems that arise from 'empowering' individuals and groups to become information 'publishers'. In effect, these technologies greatly augment message 'issuing' capabilities without addressing the problems of information location or the collaborative features of information exchange.

Similar problems are apparent in the proliferation of data 'derived' from business operations such as sales transactions, production control data entry and logistical information. The ubiquity of information processing systems assures a growing tsunami of databases that can be 'warehoused' in the hopes that techniques such as 'data mining' will provide useful techniques for discovering patterns of commercial value. These activities have supported the rapid growth in software and systems companies in recent years that claim commercially useful knowledge can be derived from these information resources.

These examples suggest a broader conceptualization of the 'codification' process when symbolic information is involved. Large observational databases (scientific and commercial), 'working models' and simulations, and large-scale computer-supported collaboration share the feature that automated tools are necessary for managing the user's cognitive processes. Incurring the costs of mastering these tools is a necessary prerequisite to using these types of symbolic information. In effect, mastering new languages becomes a requirement for using these information resources, and it is only through these new languages that effective knowledge 'decoding' or knowledge discovery can proceed.

These issues heighten the problems with our existing conceptualizations of the nexus between information and knowledge. From the traditional economic viewpoint, it should be apparent that the enumeration of an informational 'state space' is becoming increasingly infeasible, defeating attempts to rationally order relevant decisions. The recent contributions to the 'new economics of knowledge' fare little better in a world where codebooks and languages are proliferating at an accelerating pace, being 'misplaced' through the process of technological change, and are constructed with varying degrees of effectiveness for particular user communities.[15]

These issues strongly suggest the value of empirical work to discover the heuristics that individuals and groups are using to manage the growing complexity of the information flux associated with knowledge codification. A practical understanding of these heuristics may permit the 're-normalization' of knowledge codification activities as a foundation for more effective positive and normative theories.

6. Conclusion: some notes on empirical investigation of knowledge codification

The foregoing discussion has identified some of the conceptual and empirical issues involved in assessing current debates about the codifiability of knowledge by examining specific instances of practice. A central conclusion of this investigation is that individual cognition and social organization are likely to be as significant in the process of knowledge codification as technological issues.

At the cognitive level of the individual, there is the need for considerably more exchange between the cognitive disciplines, the ethnography and sociology of computer use, and business and economic approaches to decision and choice problems. Although this paper concludes from 'first principles' reasoning that existing individual 'productivity tools' have a modest value compared with the tools developed to facilitate the group process, systematic empirical assessment is needed.

The creation of epistemic communities appears to be a key element in resolving the problems of incentive compatibility in the investment in knowledge codification processes. Therefore, these epistemic communities should receive a high priority in selecting the unit of analysis for the empirical examination of technological advances in codification methods.

The effectiveness of epistemic communities in knowledge codification is likely to vary considerably, and this suggests that the sample of such communities chosen for examination should be carefully considered to avoid problems of incomparability and the indefinite proliferation of 'unlike' case studies. Several of the key features for establishing comparability include:

- the existence of mechanisms for conferring reputational or other rewards to contributors to the codification process
- the separation of monitoring from the communication process to avoid situations where exchanges are shared mythologies
- the selection of epistemic communities using the same tools for comparable but distinct codification processes to facilitate the discovery of variation in the heuristics employed in different contexts

The static efficiency of knowledge codification tools provides a useful starting point for analysis. The more interesting set of issues, however, lies in the dynamics of social networks and the coevolution of codification methodologies and social organization. These issues are of particular instrumental importance in the examination of scientific and technological networks where achieving dynamic efficiencies in codification processes (learning and mutual social adaptation) may help to explain differences in competitive performance.

In adopting a relatively simplistic view of the problems of codification, this paper has bypassed several important questions. We have not assessed the issues involved in bridging or merging communities that have developed distinct 'languages' for codification. There are clearly trade-offs between the advantages of variety and specialization in the development of codification techniques and languages and the subsequent costs of making the resulting codebooks more universal. This paper has also bypassed the issue of the size and extensibility of social communities sharing common approaches to knowledge codification. Authors such as Callon (1994) have persuasively argued that knowledge-creating communities are sharply delimited by the problems of achieving interpersonal interaction and the transfer of the tacit knowledge necessary to participate in research processes. The applicability of this argument to scientific research communities needs to be more thoroughly tested and its pertinence for technological 'communities of practice' needs to be assessed.

Finally, this paper has confined attention to issues of knowledge that are related to physical artefacts generally and scientific and technical knowledge in particular. The codification of other forms of knowledge related to the discriminatory powers of judgement or the creative faculties should also be assessed. More persuasive theories about these types of knowledge and the specific role of ICTs in facilitating their codification require a stronger empirical foundation.

Acknowledgements

The author is grateful to the European Commission for funding the research underlying this paper through the Targeted Socio-economic Research Programme, TIPIK (Technology and Infrastructure Policy in the Knowledge-based Economy—The Impact of the Tendency Toward Codification of Knowledge) Project. The author would also like to thank TIPIK's project coordinator, Patrick Cohendet, and project officer, Ronan O'Brien, for their contributions to the substance and environment of the research. The author benefited from the comments of the anonymous referee, other members of the TIPIK project consortium and, especially, Patrick Cohendet, Paul A. David and Patrick Llerena, who provided particularly useful comments. The usual disclaimers as to the result apply.

Notes

1 This agnosticism is useful in making it unnecessary to analyse the adequacy of 'codification' for capturing cognitive frameworks and understandings, and allows the simplification of this paper's discussion. See Steinmueller (1998) for a more detailed examination of the cognitive issues involved in the codification debate.

2 By focusing on the individual we can assume a degree of continuity in the cognitive process. While the way that we comprehend information over time changes, it may be argued that the variability in individual cognition over time is smaller than that between individuals.

3 To illustrate that memory capacity was not the issue, consider that the dominant tape storage system by the early 1960s could record 17 million characters per tape, or about 5000 pages of text (Bashe *et al.*, 1986, p. 230).

4 For a history of these developments and the related software see Steinmueller (1996).

5 Some mitigation of this problem is available for users who store information in formats designed to be transferable across applications or that 'stick' with a particular software company which offers access to files created by earlier software versions.

6 This is a highly instrumental viewpoint which discounts the value that individuals may receive by such interactions in favour of the view that it is possible to separate (at least at the margin) activities that have the 'purpose' of building social cohesion from the collective performance of other tasks.

7 It may well fall into the regions described by Cowan *et al.* (2000) as following the model of the 'displaced codebook' or procedural authority.

8 Jeong (1999) found that collaborative activities in the 'open source' software community responsible for LINUX involve a mixture of publicly disclosed messages and interpersonal 'chat' messages that are not explicitly archived.

9 The early development of the 'shareware' market may be an instance of such a process in action in which individuals were able to signal their computer programming ability.

10 A pernicious example of this mechanism is 'pirate clubs', epistemic communities based on the violation of copyrights on software, music or multimedia products in which 'reputation' is dependent upon the value of contributions.

11 For example, Arora and Gambardella (1994) and Nightingale (1997) reach different conclusions about the same sorts of scientific research processes.

12 SPICE (Simulation Program Integrated Circuit Emphasis) and other circuit simulation models and symbolic languages for the description of integrated circuit fabrication that allow the reproduction of highly sophisticated working electronic systems and devices are examples of such systems.
13 Antonelli *et al.* (2000) raise the issue of whether public investment in standards for symbolic communication of simulations and other virtual models is warranted to reduce inefficiencies and to prevent larger organizations from achieving undue benefits from the 'integration' of such models.
14 This issue was examined in David and Steinmueller (1991) for the case of economic research.
15 See Cowan *et al.* (2000) for a further explanation of this terminology.

References

Antonelli, C., A. Geuna and W. E. Steinmueller (2000), 'Information and Communication Technologies and the Production, Distribution and Use of Knowledge', *International Journal of Technology Management* (forthcoming).

Arora, A. and A. Gambardella (1994), 'The Changing Technology of Technological Change: General and Abstract Knowledge and the Division of Innovative Labour,' *Research Policy*, 23, 523–532.

Bashe, C. J., L. R. Johnson, J. H. Palmer and E. W. Pugh (1986), *IBM's Early Computers*. MIT Press: Cambridge, MA.

Callon, M. (1994), 'Is Science a Public Good?,' *Science Technology and Human Values*, 19, 395–425.

Cassier, M. and D. Foray (1999), 'The Sharing of Knowledge in Collective, Spontaneous or Collusive Forms of Invention,' Working Paper no. 1, COLLINE TSER Project, IMRI, University of Paris Dauphine, April.

Cowan, R. and D. Foray (1997), 'The Economics of Codification and the Diffusion of Knowledge,' *Industrial and Corporate Change*, 6, 595–622.

Cowan, R., P. A. David and D. Foray (2000), 'The Explicit Economics of Knowledge Codification and Tacitness,' *Industrial and Corporate Change*, 9 (forthcoming).

David, P. A. and W. E. Steinmueller (1991), 'The Impact of Information Technology upon Economic Science,' *Prometheus*, 9, 35–61.

David, P. A. and W. E. Steinmueller (eds) (2000), *Productivity and the Information Technology Revolution*. Harwood Academic Publishers: London.

Jeong, B. S. (1999), 'Analysis of the LINUX System, a New Entrant in the Operating Systems Market: Technological Innovations and Business Models,' unpubished MSc dissertation, 1999.

Mansell, R., I. Schenk and W. E. Steinmueller (1998), 'Trusting on the Net: A Report on Virtual Communities, Intelligent Agents, and Trusted Third Parties,' prepared for NCR Knowledge Laboratory, December.

Nightingale, P. (1997), 'Knowledge and Technical Change: Computer Simulations and the Changing Innovation Process,' unpublished DPhil thesis, SPRU, University of Sussex, May.

Roach, S. S. (1987), 'America's Technology Dilemma: A Profile of the Information Economy,' Special Economic Study–Morgan Stanley, New York, September 22.

Sichel, D. E. (1997), *The Computer Revolution: An Economic Perspective*. Brookings Institution Press: Washington, DC.

Simon, H. A. (1996), *The Sciences of the Artificial*, 3rd edn. MIT Press: Cambridge, MA.

Steinmueller, W. E. (1996), 'The U.S. Software Industry: An Analysis and Interpretative History,' in D. C. Mowery (ed.), *The International Software Industry*. Oxford University Press: Oxford, pp. 15–52.

Steinmueller, W. E. (1998), 'Does Information and Communication Technology Facilitate "Codification" of Knowledge?' TIPIK TSER Programme Working Paper, SPRU, University of Sussex, November.

Strassman, P. A. (1990), *The Business Value of Computers*. Information Economics Press: New Canaan, CT.

Part 4

OPEN NETWORKS

33

THE POWER OF GIFTS

Organizing social relationships in open source communities

Magnus Bergquist and Jan Ljungberg

Source: *Information Systems Journal* 11(3–4) (2001): 305–20.

Abstract

In writings on the open source software development model, it is often argued that it is successful as a result of the gift economy that embraces activities in online communities. However, the theoretical foundations for this argument are seldom discussed and empirically tested. Starting with the 'classic' theories of gift giving, we discuss how they need to be developed in order to explain gift-giving practices in digital domains. In this paper, we argue that the gift economy is important, not only because it creates openness, but also because it organizes relationships between people in a certain way. Open source software development relies on gift giving as a way of getting new ideas and prototypes out into circulation. This also implies that the giver gets power from giving away. This power is used as a way of guaranteeing the quality of the code. We relate this practice to how gifts, in the form of new scientific knowledge, are given to the research community, and how this is done through peer review processes.

Introduction

In writings on open source software, it is often argued that software development is founded on gift relationships, in which pieces of code are shared in the form of gifts to the community of open source developers. Raymond (1999a), for instance, examines the open source hacker milieu as a difference between exchange cultures and gift cultures. Gift cultures differ from exchange cultures in that the latter are characterized by scarcity and the former by abundance. In gift cultures, Raymond argues, social status is determined 'not by what you control but by what you give away' (Raymond, 1999a: 99).

Vaguely referring to the classic work by Mauss (1950/1999), Raymond catches some fundamental and important aspects of the cultural logic of gift-giving and sharing practices that are vital for the success of open source software development. However, he does not really dig into the theoretical foundations that lead to these conclusions. In this paper, we seek to develop Raymond's arguments by relating them to the work of Mauss and his followers.

However, the role of gift economy in modern society is not well researched, and a barrier to this seems to be a tendency to see them as archaic customs (Cheal, 1988). Where the analysis of Marcel Mauss of gift giving in 'prim- itive' cultures is based on the giving of material objects, the understanding of gift giving in open source communities has to be understood as a form of gift giving in a digital world interconnected via global networks.

As a consequence of the understanding of these differences, three themes are going to be discussed:

1   Living in a society dominated by commodity transactions, open source activists have to be socialized into the culture of gift economy. We use some examples to show how the basic norms and values are taught to newcomers (so called 'newbies').
2   Gift giving is, according to Mauss and others, a way of creating and maintaining relationships of power between groups and individuals. Open source gift giving transforms these relationships to interdependencies based on the idea of reputation.
3   Producing good code is important to open source developers. Making the source code open for inspection by peers is regarded as a guarantee of the high quality of source code. Practices have evolved to assure that the best code produced is integrated into the software distributions. Classic theories of gift economies do not clarify how gifts can be treated as parts of quality assessment processes. Here, we will relate open source gift giving to another kind of gift economy – the academic society – and suggest a theoretical framework for how gift giving and peer review systems relate to one another.

The paper is organized in the following way. First, we discuss methodolo- gical implications concerning the different data used in the study. A brief overview of open source actors and stakeholders is then given, followed by a more theoretical discussion about gift economy, where we discuss how this theory needs to be developed in order to capture the intricacies of gift giving in digital domains. Two cases are then presented to highlight different dimensions in gift-giving practices. These examples are followed by a discussion in which we relate open source gift giving to theories of peer

198

review in the academic society. This also adds a new dimension to classic theories on gift giving.

Method

The empirical data have been collected over a period of 2 years in different domains, such as various kinds of web pages, discussions lists and from publications about open source communities and activities.

The empirical data are of two kinds. One is based on texts dealing with the philosophy and ideology of the open source movement, for instance Raymond's (1999b) writings about open source software and why it has become successful. These texts provide important contributions on the open source phenomenon but, at the same time, they have become icons in the community and should rather be read as descriptions of the public image that the community presents to the surrounding world. Raymond's texts and other documents published on community centres, such as http:// www.opensource.org, have also been influential in discussions and debates about the future of open source activities that can be found in discussions lists.

In order to grasp the more dynamic everyday life among open source developers, we have regularly scanned news groups and discussion lists of various sorts. Here, dimensions other than the ones found on 'official pages' (such as http://www.opensource.org) can be found. The official pages are characterized by homogeneity and harmony: the open source community seems to be a gathering without social dynamics and conflicts. In discussion lists and comments, a more agitated representation is found. It is important not to consider this image as more 'real' than the formal and official representation of the movement. They exist alongside and shape the discourse of what the community is about.

The method used can be associated with what Hine (2000) describes as virtual ethnography. Examples are used in the text to illustrate and highlight different claims made by actors who relate themselves to open source software development. We are interested in the cultural logic (values, norms) behind different positions and activities undertaken by actors. For example, when we discuss the habit of flaming developers, we are not interested in the flaming *per se*, but why certain activities give rise to this action.

Open source – actors and stakeholders

We will describe briefly the different roles that may occur in open source projects (for overviews of open source, see Raymond, 1999b; Feller & Fitzgerald, 2000; Ljungberg, 2000) Typically, open source projects start with a single programmer solving a small problem affecting his own work. For example, the origin of WWW was the work by Tim Berners-Lee to help high-energy physicists share their work. Another example is Larry Wall, who wrote the script language Perl to solve some problems in systems administration (O'Reilly, 1999). When open source solutions turns out to be significant and attract attention from others, a plethora of different roles arises. Often, people play several roles, e.g. as both developer and user.

The owner of an open source project is the person (or group) who started the project and has the exclusive right, recognized by the community at large, to redistribute modified versions of the software. According to Raymond (1999b), there are basically three ways to acquire ownership of an open source project: to found it; to have it handed over by the former owner; or to volunteer to take over a dying project in which the former owner has lost interest. As the owner attracts contributors, i.e. people that discover the software and want to contribute to its development, he becomes more of a coordinator or project leader.

Often, a group of core developers write most of the code concerning new functionality, review submitted code and make most of the decisions about releases (Mockus et al., 2000). This could be of a more formal nature as in the Apache core development group, where frequent contributors might be nominated as new members to the group and approved by anonymous voting by the group members. In the Apache case, the core group accounted for more than 80% of the contributions (Mockus et al., 2000), and the Orbiten free software survey showed that 10% of the contributors accounted for 72% of the total code base (Ghosh & Prakash, 2000). This means that almost all the new functionality is implemented and maintained by a small group of core developers.

Defect repair involves a much wider development community, an order of magnitude larger than the core group. Problem reporters are an even wider group. Mockus et al. (2000) showed that, in the Apache project, the role of system tester is almost reserved for the wide community of Apache users.

User support is a more mundane task not so much linked to reputation or other motivational factors affecting the will to contribute. This task seems to be performed mainly by some product users voluntarily providing answers to the questions of other users (Lakhani & von Hippel, 2000).

Today, there are a huge number of users of open source software, most of them not actively contributing to its development. Also, large organizations have become users. By using the software, these actors can, however, still be seen as important contributors. Creating a critical mass of users is import-ant both for the usability of a system or software and for the construction of a symbolic attraction surrounding open source development style.

Commercial businesses tied to open source projects provide additional resources for developing the free components of the software but, even more importantly, it helps to promote the open source packages and drive them into the mainstream (Osterhout, 1999). Companies make money out of open source software by distributing the open source software, by adding value to the open source software by additional proprietary products or by relating to open source software in different ways, such as bundling it with their own products (O'Reilly, 1998).

Gift economy

The open source community is organized around a large stock of devoted hackers who are both producers and users. As there is often no monetary compensation to be expected for efforts conducted, the will to contribute to the community has to be explained in terms other than being based on a more traditional cost–benefit rationality. Raymond (1999a) proposed the idea of open source being a gift culture. Gift cultures are based on gift economies, in which social relations are not regulated by the possession or exchange of money or commodities. Gift cultures are characterized by the creation and maintenance of social relationships based on the economy of gift exchange.

But the idea of gift cultures is a puzzling one. What is it exactly that is given away and why?

The gift-giving relations could be of different kinds, ranging from the gratuitous gift at one extreme to the exploitative relationship at the other (Sahlins, 1972; Godbout, 1998; Godelier, 1999). The classic analysis of the social and cultural context of gift giving is Mauss' *The Gift* (1950/1990). He sees a gift as the transaction of objects coordinated by a system of rules. The rules are in fact symbolic translations of the social structure in a society or a group of members. Mauss does not provide us with a romantic view of gift giving. On the contrary, he argues that giving a gift brings forth a demand for returning a gift, either another object or, in a more symbolic fashion, forces of power connected to the objects. Gift giving therefore creates social interdependencies and becomes a web upon which social structure is organized. To give away something is to express an advantageous position in relation to the recipient.

Mauss frames the general idea surrounding the practice of giving gifts as a culturally defined and socially determining activity in societies. We will come back to this discussion and also take it a bit further by a more close analysis of power relations involved in gift giving in the open source community. But first it is important to distinguish the general idea of gifts and the habit of giving gifts in the 'primitive' societies described by Mauss and the highly technological and, to some extent, virtual societies in which the open source community is located.

Rheingold (1994) often ascribed to the notion of understanding the virtual community custom of giving away pointers, texts, advice or, as is common in open source communities, source code as a special 'gift economy' that is inherent in a more general 'gift culture'. Rheingold describes this as 'a marriage of altruism and self-interest' (Rheingold, 1994: 58).

He also separates two kinds of information-sharing practices. The first can be found among people who are interested in new cultural phenomena that have led them to explore different virtual worlds. They share information about almost everything. But sharing can also mean emotional support. The second consists of professionals who rely on having information constantly at their disposal. This kind of giving away is based on a hunger for intellectual companionship, initially found most commonly among professionals who work more or less on their own, e.g. journalists (see Millen, 2000), freelance artists and designers, programmers, etc. (Rheingold, 1994). Besides a need for social stimulation, they have a shared and immediate demand for accessing relevant information that could not be locally stored or achieved to the extent that is required. By creating a network of contacts, the chances of getting to relevant information sources increases dramatically. At the same time, social relationships are continually developed, creating a kind of social contract in the particular community that arises around a certain type of professional activity. Others, some of them networking only for social reasons, have followed these early adopters.

But the importance of common interests and the Internet as a medium for gift giving is not enough to explain the kind of gift culture that encompasses different online communities such as the open source movement. Kollock (1999) adds to this the character of digital information as an explanation for the intensive sharing of work, social experiences and other forms of knowledge between members of the community. He focuses on the possibility of producing 'an infinite number of perfect copies of a piece of information, whether that be a computer program, a multimedia presentation, or the archives of a long email discussion' (Kollock, 1999: 223). The contributor can give away an infinite number of copies of a document or software without losing it or diminishing its value (which is the case with material objects). The Internet also provides an easy way to distribute large amounts of information. The cost of providing one person with some information is not a greater expense than providing 10 million people with the same information, no matter where in the world the consignees are. And, from the receivers' point of view, the transaction cost of downloading a document is almost the same irrespective of where in the world it is originally posted.

With this in mind, Mauss' discussion of gifts can be seen differently. His argument about the social character of gifts is based on how gifts are perceived and handled in a world of material objects. The scarcity of material objects and the costs associated with transactions are important for how the value of gifts and the giving of gifts are socially constructed. Information and executable software in combination with the Internet radically transforms the context in which we should understand this relation. But, is then the social character of gifts disappearing when anyone can give anything to anybody with a transaction cost close to zero? The answer to this is no, but this does not mean that gifts are used and experienced the same way in virtual communities as in the kind of societies Mauss described.

Two tendencies can be spotted. The almost total reduction of scarcity problems concerning the dissemination of information has increased the consciousness in the community of the presence of other forms of scarcity. This has lead to the development of different practices aimed at decreasing time cycles of innovation and development and scarcities inherent in the organization of cooperation and coordination. Further, the community is primarily a loosely coupled network of individuals with no organizational forces in terms of economy or management that can force other individuals to behave in a certain way. Mauss argues that gifts express, but also create, power relations between people. One of the norms of gift giving is the rule that gifts be accepted. Therefore, the receiver becomes subordinate to the giver. In the open source community, this can be the fact. But the opposite is also important. Refusing to accept a gift can, in some situations, be a way of showing superiority.

In the previous text, we discussed how we should understand theories of gift giving when applying them in digital domains. We will now focus on the practice of gift giving by presenting two cases in the form of excerpts from news group discussions. First, we illustrate how the idea of gift giving is implemented in the community in the form of socialization processes, in which newcomers, so called 'newbies', are taught the rules of the gift economy by more experienced members. We will then relate this to how practising power is linked to gift giving.

Learning the art of gift giving: the newbie case

Newsgroups, frequently asked questions (FAQs) and digests are ways to condense time by making series of questions and answers, mistakes and successes available in a concentrated form. They are easy to access world wide and also cheap.

But, in order to make these tools for information distribution and know-ledge sharing the flexible and manageable channels they are intended to be, it is important to socialize new members of the community into a set of norms and behaviours for a certain kind of communication and cooperation practice. A culture of sharing has evolved, which constitutes the community netiquette. The following example is drawn from a Usenet Linux News Group called *alt.Linux* showing how the basic principles in the culture of sharing are established and made sense of. A question is posted by Darren who is going to install a Linux distribution on his computer and wants some advice from the community on which distribution to choose:

A Linux Newbie

Umm hello, before I get to my point, I'd like to say that I'm pretty new to newsgroups in general and much newer to the Linux community, so please forgive any mistakes I make and, if I offend, point it out to me and I will be more than happy to say that I am sorry.

Now, with that out of the way, I'd like to ask anyone who feels like giving an opinion on what distribution of Linux I should get. I am a first-time user of Linux but I have used Windows since windows95 and I have done work in DOS (I am proficient in DOS but hardly fluent). I am currently considering using Linux because I hate having to reboot my P2450 10 times a day just to get Direct X to work properly. To this end, I have set aside a little under 4 gigs of hard drive space for Linux. I am currently considering Red Hat, Caladra, or SuSE. Any opinions? Comments? Reasons to have me committed? Now if you are going to reply to this (hey it could happen), can I convince anyone to send me an E-mail directly as opposed to just posting to the group? Outlook Express 5 is pretty damn flighty and I don't want to risk losing a valuable opinion. If you would prefer replying to the group that is fine; I am just stating a lose preference. Also, as I am completely new to Linux, I was wondering if anyone could recommend a good book on it? Maybe on Linux in general and the packages I mentioned before? Good lordy this is a long post; I hope no-one flames me . . . Thank you for your time and I hope I haven't earned your malice.

Sincerely, Darren

It is obvious that Darren is familiar with some of the basic rules for socializing in newsgroups, even if he says that he is new to newsgroups in general and the Linux community in particular. He knows that there are certain rules for communicating and that different communities have different rules. He also knows that postings should be kept short and concentrated in order to create a current flow of questions and answers. He articulates a fear of having exceeded an invisible prescription for this specific community and that he is running the risk of being punished the usual way: being flamed (getting hundreds of angry mails from upset 'listeners') in a rude and arrogant way. The strategy used is to approach the community in a humble and respectful way, trying not to upset anyone, even if he breaks some of the rules. He 'pretends' that he does not even expect an answer from the community but, if he does, he wants to make sure that the information (which he presupposes is very valuable) is not lost because of technical errors.

The term 'newbie' is used widely to describe both others and oneself as a dilettante. It is used here in a self-stereotyping way to play down the odds that the community would look upon Darren as a self-sufficient person.

But, having stated his relation and attitude towards the community, Darren attempts to establish a relationship with the potential listeners by telling them something about his personal situation. This is achieved by describing what kind of hardware and software he is using and by stating the problems running the present system, tools and applications.

The strategy is to establish a sense of loyalty towards the community. By 'talking technology', he tries to make himself accountable as fairly knowledgeable when it comes to handling computers in general. The will to abandon the existing platform in favour of a Linux distribution is a kind of a symbolic token given to the community in order to get something valuable back. But this has to be done in a reasonably smooth way. The decision to change platform is not based on blind idealism, but because of bad experiences with the existing equipment. Instead of naïvely celebrating the community and its members, Darren appeals to a certain kind of rationality that, he seems to expect, is addressing a set of community-relevant values.

Instead of reading the posting 'as is', we can understand it as a way to become an insider and thereby gaining access to the knowledge and experience that resides in the community. The answers threaded in the discussion also confirm that some members of the community have accepted Darren as an earnest enquirer and that he has acted in an appropriate way. Twenty minutes after the question is posted, 'Leonard' posts a message that contains not only the information sought after by Darren, but also an additional netiquette handbook appropriate to community standards, pinpointing the rules that the members of the community relate to when networking in newsgroups:

Re: A Linux Newbie
Well Darren, I think you did ok . . .
You didn't post in HTML
You didn't cross-post
You didn't post a binary you weren't a jerk and were generally polite . . .
I'm going to assume you took the time to catch up with the newsgroup before posting to make sure your question hasn't been answered so all proper nettiqite (sp.?) has been obeyed. How nice.
. . . I used Redhat Linux 5.2 when I got started. If I was starting today I would buy the 6.0 or more likely the Mandrake as it is the same stuff for 1/3 the price . . . and I hear it's easier to install.
The learning curve is mighty steep at first, but it gets better and you'll wonder why you waited so long.
As far as books, I found 'Mastering Linux' to be basic, outdated and at times inaccurate . . . and it was far too reliant on the X interface. I actually found the 'Linux for Dummies' book had exactly the same information in much less space, and therefore was

much more helpful (despite the title and the stigma attached to it) and dealt more with the command line. I'm looking for a good intermediate book now. . . .
Good luck
Leonard

As we can see, humility is a strategy to get acceptance from the community, and this is also what the more seniors encourage. In order not to get flamed, inexperienced users often headline their question 'newbie' followed by a topic that is developed further in the message. The norms and values of the community are internalized through these kind of narrative practices.

Network information is important. Being accepted by the community means getting answers to proposed questions. But more important from the point of view of socialization is the interchange of information as a way of creating mutual alliances. Instead of seeing the situation as a kind of information retrieval' situation in which one person receives a piece of information from another, we should understand it as a mutual interchange where one gift is given for another. The newbie gets important information about a subject, or information about how to get further into the community, but also pays back by being willing to mould himself or herself according to community norms and values. 'Looking good' on a Discussions List, with respect to community values and rules of behaviour, can open up doors to further networks of information and contacts with relevant people. But it also means that a certain kind of power relationship is made explicit by some and internalized by others. As a result, newbies are socialized into the specific norms of the community.

The newbie status has, however, developed as a project of its own. An important site for developing, discussing, formalizing and branding the status of newbies is Linuxnewbie.org, a portal created with the explicit aim of being a space where new but generally inexperienced Linux users can meet, get information, pose questions and socialize. Norms are not accepted without protest, and countermovements are being developed.

Power in a gift economy

One easily gets the impression that the sharing of gifts in online communities creates a very friendly and altruistic atmosphere. And indeed it does, to some extent. But it does not mean that social stratification and struggles over power cease to exist. When giving is easy and gifts become non-reducible, dependencies are reshaped and transformed to new kinds of relationships. Gifts are often not given to anyone in particular. They are made public (on web pages) and thereby made available to anyone who cares to make use of them. An application or some information does not really become a gift until someone finds it and makes use of it. If a giver manages to get attention, people will turn the things offered into gifts, which means that a relationship is created between the giver and the user. As gifts do not imply a monetary compensation, virtual community gift giving is managed through acknowledgement: the giver is 'paid' by the community by receiving a certain amount of fame and respect.

As discussed above, giving digital gifts does not remove the inter-dependencies between givers and receivers. But social relationships and obligations between the parties involved in the exchange are restructured based on the character of digital information and the Internet as a social world. In this section, we will discuss this process of social restructuring.

The difference between gift giving and commodity transactions is that the giving of gifts should not involve explicit bargaining. In bargaining, no obligation exists after the exchange is accomplished. Where commodities are exchangeable, gifts are unique. A commodity that is purchased, and then given as a present, is transformed from a product to an obligation. By giving away, the giver shows superiority and the receiver becomes dependent. There is an obligation to repay the gift in the future. As Mauss argued, a gift can be a way of showing social status. The giving of artefacts creates asymmetrical social relationships, especially if the gift can never be refunded and the giver knows it. Cheal (1988) therefore talks about gift giving as based on a moral economy.

On the Internet, however, the receiver is often unknown to the giver (Kollock, 1999). Gifts are placed on various homepages and ftp sites, and anybody can download a piece of information or an executable file and use it for various purposes. But this only counts for the Internet in general. The interesting question is in which social context gift giving on the Internet gets its social meaning. The focus for the production of meaning in the gift economy on the Internet is the various kinds of communities in which people share some understanding of the context they are involved in. They are not unknown to each other, which does not mean that they have to be personally acquainted. The open source community has also become a major player in the development of norms and behaviours related to gift economy as a result of this being something officially dealt with in the community. In these communities, the value of the gifts is dependent on the amount of attention the giver gets from the receivers that choose to make use of the gift.

Rather than taking place in a world of objects or artefacts, gift giving in online communities takes place in a world of information. There is no obliga-tion to pay back but, for the ordinary end-user, there is a moral obligation to pay back in the form of having some solidarity to the community by praising the software, the project owners and/or the major contributors.

There are differences between the meaning and use of gifts in purely social communities and the more product-oriented communities such as the open source. In social MUDs, there are 'only' social relationships to 'deal' with. In some ways, open source gifts look more like traditional commodities and can be used as both a product and a gift for creating and maintaining relationships. For the end-users that do not want to participate in the community, the difference is not so great. Internet technology makes exchange open. Anybody can get hold of the products. It must work this way when the idea is to spread the products in order to make it possible for as many as possible to take part in the development process and add some of their expertise to the ongoing project.

Becoming an owner of a project that becomes successful gives the right to decide who should be entitled to give back and who should not. The more attention an open source project owner gets from the members of the community, the more status and reputation he achieves. And the more a project gets attention, the more users would like to contribute to it and become a part of the project and, as a result of this, get some of the attention (Raymond, 1999a). It is important to note that our use of the concept attention differs considerably from the way it is commonly used in the context of attention economy, e.g. as attention span of an individual (Goldhaber, 1997) or 'focused mental engagement' (Davenport & Beck, 2001: 20). In this paper, attention relates to the logic of how social capital and reputation are formed and gained. Attention in the context of open source is not about being bold and loud, but about being recognized or 'seen' as a good programmer and contributor to the community. The right sort of attention then creates status and reputation. The power structure, compared with gift giving in a world of artefacts, is therefore restructured according to the logic of how reputation is formed in the community.

How then do people who are, or try to be, active in the community relate to this circumstance? In the online magazine *Freshmeat*, an editorial argues for the importance of giving gifts and thereby helping the community to develop high-quality software for the benefit of mankind. The article is followed by 15 comments from readers in which values and norms in the open source gift culture are discussed in relation to how new kinds of power structures are established on the Internet. It is worth noticing that the discussion of power is a reaction to the editor's rather ideal formulation of why hackers should contribute unselfishly to different software development projects.

The discussions reveal that some of the developers/users experience power relationships that are expressed as 'an elitism of the inner circle' and exercised as the right to hinder a person in contributing to the common good. It is argued that the openness of the open source movement is overstated. Practices such as flaming are not only used to exclude people who overrule the core values of the community. In the newsgroup example below, the author of the posting claims that it is also used to exercise power over those who want to contribute to the community by delivering code to different projects:

Giving Back
siberian – April 01st 1999, 21:31 EST
More than once I have had the urge to begin contributing to the
community. I have written code, documented it and gained author-
ization for its release. But at the last minute I always hesitate and
then stop. Why? I think I fear the fangs of the community. At this
point, everywhere I turn, it's a big flamefest and getting quite
tiresome. Its gotten to the point where it seems one has to be some
sort of Jedi Master level coder to contribute. On more then a few
mailing lists, I have seen contributors flamed for their contributions!
Flaming someone for GIVING something away. Its incredible.

On the one hand, there is a message of openness, not only when it comes
to source code, but also that openness is a fundamental feature of open
source as an organizational entity. And indeed there is openness, in the
sense that everything that is shared among the community members is on
display on web pages and discussion lists. But, on the other hand, does the
honouring of the successful projects and the heroes behind them create
boundaries of in-groups and out-groups? There are the ones who are part of
projects, in terms of being accepted as code providers, and there are the
ones who want in but are rejected by the project owners or flamed by other
members of the community.

Another commentator offers some advice on the discussion list. The
creation of power relations is recognized but located in a certain social context in the community:

Flaming
Charles P. Wright – April 02nd 1999, 02:56 EST
You really don't turn into some sort of lightning rod for flaming
if you release your software. That is really only people who put
themselves in high positions (esr, rms) who are subject to that. If
you start your own project you should feel safe from that kind of
crap. And if you get a less than polite email every once and a while
you can just delete it. Knowing people like your project and having
dozens of people contribute code is a real ego boost, not to mention
you get better software than you had yesterday because of it!

Some people, it is argued, place themselves in high positions ('esr' and
'rms' stand for Eric S. Raymond and Richard M. Stallman, who are two
of the most influential people in the community). The strategy proposed in
the posting above is to ignore people in high positions and people who flame
for no reason. The advice is that, if a person is afraid of flaming, it is more
'safe' to start a project of your own than to deliver code to an existing
project.

If the project is not successful, no one will notice it. If it is a hit, a lot of people will try to join and contribute. However, there is a contradiction in this statement. If everybody starts projects of their own rather than helping others with existing projects, no collaboration will occur. Another and perhaps more important topic is how a person should relate to flaming, and what flaming really is about.

Virtual collaboration puts high demands on people having trust in one another. Giving away the best piece of code a person has produced demands strong social ties between the giver and the receiver. The receiver has to present himself and act in a trustworthy way, otherwise the giver will not give away his code. At the same time, the demands for high-quality source code give the project owner the moral right to judge whether a contribution has high enough quality to be considered as part of the final distribution. It becomes important for the receiver to make himself trustworthy in the eyes of the givers. Virtual collaboration and gift giving must thus be based on trust in order to make criticism regarded as something that can contribute to the overall quality of the products:

> Please code!
> *jimduchek* – April 01st 1999, 22:54 EST
> Don't let that stuff put you off! Don't _ever_ listen to anything from anyone you don't respect. The only way to have your code get really good is peer review. If they flame it, they flame it. So what? I've never seen this happen myself, though. Ignore the flames and listen to the REAL comments on your code. As a developer myself, I rarely use patches exactly as they come from user/developers, but I do use almost all of them in some form or another. _NEVER_ write something and don't submit it, it goes against the whole philosophy of free software. Even if it sucks, you'll likely get at least one mail that says 'Your code won't work for us for this reason, and this reason, and this reason.' you just learn from that and keep going. And if not, it gets used, and you get a big ego boost! Ignore the script kiddies, they don't matter a damn bit.

The advice presented is to develop an ability not to listen to critique from someone one does not respect. Filter the flames from good critique, ignore the flames and listen to the good comments.

A problem with the openness of the Internet and the open source community is that anybody can comment even if they are not really serious about the matter in question. One must have the ability to be indulgent towards weirdoes, overlook 'script kiddie' critique, shrug one's shoulders and move on. Good critique should be taken into account, because it is dangerous to ignore critique, as good development is dependent on peer review processes. One has to fight against the 'reinventing-the-wheel' syndrome that seems to be lurking in the virtual bushes. The two strategies proposed are 'trust', if the critique is good, and 'ignorance', if not serious. Talking about a certain kind of critique as 'flaming' creates a mental distance that becomes a resource for the individual in this highly exposed environment:

Nobody has the right. . . .
Angler – May 23rd 1999, 18:41 EST
There are always rude people around. Of course they'll take their sweet time out to flame newbies, or act snobbish. But they seem to be mostly outweighed by the people who are nice, helpful, and patient. One rude email does not a group attitude make. But they are the most vociferous, and the ones we tend to remember with bile. But it's unfair to generalize. I think though that just saying that no one has the right to criticize your software is a dangerous path. Criticism can be constructive – that is, administered with the minimum amount of flame (i.e. none). And you won't learn as quickly if you can't take criticism.
The other kind of criticism – flaming – you can just ignore. But even some rude emails have valid, if stretched, points.
As for newbies getting flamed . . . I believe it happens. But then, such things always happen. There are always jerks in any community, but I don't think it's as prevalent for Linux as some of us believe through rotten experience. If you don't believe me, join a LUG.

If a development process is to produce quality software in a compressed time frame, there must be a hard critique. The problem is who has the right to decide over others. The critique against those who feel that their attempts to give to the community have been ignored is brought back to the fundamental principles of the community. The only reason to deny or refuse a contribution is the ambition to maintain and develop the good quality of open source software development, which is also the core argument for spending time developing such software:

tight code
thi – May 29th 1999, 21:00 EST
flaming newbies happens so newbies can learn how to flame, the essence of improvement is managed change. when the newbie learns to apply the flame to the code and not to their ego, the code is reduced and enhanced. cruft is vaporized, bloat melted, misdesigns highlighted. the remaining skeleton is tight code, on which users drape their cpu cycles to their own needs.
flames by newbies should be culled for the good parts and the rest ignored. this is similar to how one should treat code from newbies.

211

thus the only difference between newbie and non-newbie is completeness.

completeness is rarely well-defined, unfortunately.

This also becomes a way of socializing members. Supporting the norms surrounding the culture of gift giving and freedom of getting in and out of the community and, at the same time, making actors conform to a certain elitism is a tricky business, where different ideologies and individual standards for behaviour occur in sometimes agitated discussions. Being a project owner of a development project that gets noticed is often met with respect. But this esteem is always questioned by the celebration of 'the culture of individuality' and the weak imperative necessities in the form of social ties between contributors and owners.

Gift giving as peer review

As we have seen, it is important in the open source community regularly to return to a basic theme that concerns the question why gift giving is important in order to support open source software development. Values and norms surrounding quality assurance and the sharing of knowledge become a key theme in understanding the open source community's cultural foundations. Here, we argue, academic research has much resemblance to the gift economy, in the sense of non-altruistic gift transactions.

For instance, both Raymond (1999a) and Bezroukov (1999) have noticed the similarities between the open source communities and research communities in academia. If we view open source from the theoretical perspective of peer review, we could gain a more in-depth understanding of both the quality aspect of open source software development and how power relations are socially organized.

In the academy, you give away your knowledge, not because you are altruistic, but because that is the way of career progression within the academic field. You give away knowledge and information in return for status and reputation. The acceptance of a gift by a community implies recognition of the status of the donor and the existence of certain reciprocal rights. Scientific contributions are gifts, as authors normally do not receive royalties or other payments for the publication of results in a journal. Manuscripts for which scientific authors do get paid as textbooks and popular writings are certainly held in much lower esteem (Hagstrom, 1982).

By sharing knowledge and being open about results and methods, the results can be justified and replicated. Others can give contributions by responding or by continuing on the published work, pushing the scientific frontier. By writing and publishing papers and by being referred to by others, you not only share your knowledge, but also become visible in the academic community. The reputation is secured by the rule that one can use knowledge produced by somebody else, but it must always be clear from whom the idea originates. The more other researchers quote your publications, the more your reputation will grow. In scientific communities, it is a mortal sin to use somebody else's knowledge without acknowledging the person who came up with the original idea. Thus, the failure to recognize previous work of others may give rise to strong antagonisms and intense controversy.

The principles for handling the contributions to the scientific community, peer review, were developed through the establishment of a referee system in the first scientific journals in seventeenth- and eighteenth-century Europe (Ziman, 1968; Chubin & Hackett, 1990). It is by now a fairly established academic designation for marking the scientific quality of a piece of work, for assigning a candidate to a position or for approving or rejecting a research proposal. All established researchers are more or less involved in peer review processes, as reviewers of others' articles, project proposals or CVs or by being reviewed themselves.

The peer review system makes it possible to judge whether contributions are good enough to enter the field. Among many contributions, the best ones are chosen. When people make selections, they try to be reasonable in their selections. But what seems reasonable for one person is not always reasonable for another. There are no objective criteria for what counts as 'relevant', 'interesting' or 'new' research. Peer review is thus a social mechanism, through which a discipline's experts or the core members of a community maintain control over new knowledge entering the field (Merton & Zuckerman, 1973; Chubin & Hackett, 1990). Peer review can thus be seen as a way of organizing power relationships within a given community or in relation to other fields of activity.

The open source communities are driven by similar norms. You write a piece of software and provide it to the community. Your contribution is peer reviewed by the owners of a software development project and, if it is good enough, you get your credits in the open source gift economy. A good idea is usable in further research but also gives the owner credits. There is an interesting relationship between how usable an idea is and how much attention it can get. In the academic society, a good theory seem to be more tradable than a partial analysis. Theories can potentially be of general benefit to large parts of the research community. There seem to be a similar relationship concerning the rules governing how ideas are valued in the open source movement. A generally applicable service such as Linus Torvald's Linux operating system becomes, like a theory in the academic society, a general base for others to act upon. This makes Linux famous and Torvalds a respected member of the community. Writing a driver for an application is similar to, let us say, an empirical study in which a theory is used.

Conclusion

In this paper, we have discussed the relationship between the habit of giving gifts and the organization of social relationships between members in the open source community.

It seems to be true that the Internet and the increasing use and importance of digital information have changed the way social relationships are created and maintained in virtual environments compared with those face-to-face settings once studied by anthropologists such as Marcel Mauss, for instance. Understanding gift-giving practices also calls for an understanding of the fundamental social principles on the Internet as a context for human activities. Gifts become valuable when everybody wants to be part of giving them.

Giving away ideas and source code is the base for different kinds of activities in the open source community, which also becomes fundamental for the creation of culture. Values and norms are organized around a giving and/or getting axis. However, this does not mean that people are unable to execute power or make a career, which presupposes some kind of hierarchy. The hierarchy in this virtual environment is a matter of giving or receiving more or less attention. As we have seen, the giver–receiver relationship also changes over time and must be understood as a dynamic process with no fixed dependencies.

Finally, we have discussed gifts and reputation in relation to theories on peer review in order to understand the developers' ambition to guard the quality of the code produced. Producing high-quality source code is the key motivator for members when understanding the open source community as a social actor. The system of giving credits to those that the community thinks deserve it is therefore accepted and even favoured among the community members. One could understand this culture as a kind of amalgamation of collectivism and individualism: giving to the community is what makes the individual a hero in the eyes of others. Heroes are important influences but also powerful leaders. Their presence is important as a way of converging different values and goals in this heterogeneous context, focusing it on common goals, but also legitimizing the asymmetries in power relationships.

References

Bezroukov, N. (1999) Open source software development as a special type of academic research (critique of vulgar Raymondism). *First Monday*, **4** (10). [http://firstmonday.org/issues/issue4_10/bezroukov/index.html].

Cheal, D. (1988) *The Gift Economy*. Routledge, London.

Chubin, D. E. & Hackett, E. J. (1990) *Peerless Science. Peer Review and US Science Policy*. State University of New York Press, Albany.

Davenport, T. H. & Beck, J. C. (2001) *The Attention Economy*. Harvard Business School Press, Boston, MA.

Feller, J. & Fitzgerald, B. (2001) A framework analysis of the open source software development paradigm. In: *Proceedings of the International Conference on Information Systems (ICIS)*, Brisbane, December 2000.

Godbout, J. T. (1998) *The World of the Gift*. McGill-Queen's University Press, London.

Godelier, M. (1999) *The Enigma of the Gift*. Polity Press, Cambridge.

Ghosh, R. & Prakash, V. V. (2000) The Orbiten free software survey. *First Monday*, **7**. [http://www.firstmonday.org/issues/issue5_7/ghosh/index.html].

Goldhaber, M. H. (1997) The attention economy and the Net. *First Monday*, **2**, [www.firstmonday.dk/issues/issues2-4/goldhaber].

Hagstrom, W. (1982) Gift giving as an organizing principle in science. In: *Science in Context*, Barnes, B. & Edge, D. (eds). The Open University Press, Stony Stratford.

Hine, C. (2000) *Virtual Ethnography*. Sage Publications, London.

Kollock, P. (1999) The economies of online cooperation. In: *Communities in Cyberspace*, Smith, M. & Kollock, P. (eds). Routledge, London.

Lakhani, K. & von Hippel, E. (2000) *How Open Source Software Works: 'Free' User-to-User Assistance*. Working Paper 4117. MIT Sloan School of Management, Boston, MA.

Ljungberg, J. (2000) Open source movements as a model for organising. *European Journal of Information Systems*, **9** (4).

Mauss, M. (1950/1999) *The Gift. The Form and Reason for Exchange in Archaic Societies*. Routledge, London.

Merton, R. K. & Zuckerman, H. (1973) Institutionalized patterns of evaluation in science. In: *The Sociology of Science*. Storer, N. W. (ed.). The University of Chicago Press, Chicago.

Millen, D. (2000) Community portals and collective goods: conversation archives as an information resource. In: *Proceedings of HICSS33*.

Mockus, A., Fielding, R. & Hersleb, J. (2000) A case study of open source software development: the Apache server. In: *Proceedings of the International Conference on Software Engineering (ICSE) 2000*. Limerick, Ireland.

O'Reilly, T. (1998) *The Open Source Revolution. Release 1.0, Esther Dyson's Monthly Report*. [www.edventure.com/release1/1198.html (22 August 1999)].

O'Reilly, T. (1999) Lessons from open source development. *Communications of the ACM*, **42** (4), 33–37.

Osterhout, J. (1999) Free software needs profit. *Communications of the ACM*, **42** (4), 38–39.

Raymond, E. S. (1999a) Homesteading the Noosphere. In: *The Cathedral and the Bazaar: Musings on Linux and Open Source by an Accidental Revolutionary*, Raymond, E. S. O'Reilly and Associates, Sebastopol, CA. [www.tuxedo.org/~esr/writings/homesteading/homesteading.html].

Raymond, E. S. (1999b) *The Cathedral and the Bazaar: Musings on Linux and Open Source by an Accidental Revolutionary*. O'Reilly and Associates, Sebastopol, CA.

Rheingold, H. (1994) *Virtual Community*. Minerva, London.

Sahlins, M. (1972) *Stone Age Economics*. Aldine-Atherton, Chicago.

Ziman, J. M. (1968) *Public Knowledge. An Essay Concerning the Social Dimension of Science*. Cambridge University Press, Cambridge.

34

THE ECONOMICS OF
TECHNOLOGY SHARING

Open source and beyond*

Josh Lerner and Jean Tirole

Source: *Journal of Economic Perspectives* 19(2) (2005): 99–120.

The open source process of production and innovation seems very unlike what most economists expect. Private firms usually pay their workers, direct and manage their efforts, and control the output and intellectual property thus created. In an open source project, however, a body of original material is made publicly available for others to use, under certain conditions. In many cases, anyone who makes use of the material must agree to make all enhancements to the original material available under these same conditions. This rule distinguishes open source production from, say, material in the public domain and "shareware." Many of the contributors to open source projects are unpaid. Indeed, contributions are made under licenses that often restrict the ability of contributors to make money on their own contributions. Open source projects are often loosely structured, with contributors free to pursue whatever area they feel most interesting. Despite these unusual features, recent years have seen a rise of major corporate investments into open source projects; for instance, IBM is reported to have spent over $1 billion in 2001 alone on such projects.[1]

The most prominent example of open source production is software, which involves developers at many different locations and organizations sharing code to develop and refine computer programs. The importance of open source software can be illustrated by considering a few examples. The market for server software, which is used by the computers that make web pages available to users through the Internet, has been dominated by the open source Apache project since the inception of systematic tracking by Netcraft in 1995. As of March 2004, more than two-thirds of servers employed this or other open source products, rather than commercial alternatives from

Microsoft, Sun and other firms. The open source operating system called Linux accounts for 23 percent of the operating systems of all servers; moreover, Linux has rapidly outstripped Microsoft's Windows program as the operating system most frequently embedded into products ranging from mobile phones to video recording devices.[2] Open source software is dominant in a number of other areas as well; for example, PERL and PHP are the dominant scripting languages.

Open source software seems poised for rapid growth in the future. A recent survey of chief information officers suggests that Linux will play an increasingly important role as the operating system for web servers. Linux also has plenty of room to grow in the market for desktop operating systems; at the end of 2003, only 1.4 percent of the queries to Google came from machines running Linux, although that share was rising.[3] The dissemination of open source databases remains in its infancy, but these are projected to become by 2006 significant challengers to commercial systems sold by firms such as IBM and Oracle.[4] As of March 2004, the website SourceForge.net, which provides free services to open source software developers, listed over 78,000 open source projects.

The article reviews the intriguing and rapidly growing phenomenon of open source production. After describing briefly the origins of open source software, we examine the incentives and roles of the various actors in the open source process. We end by highlighting how exploring open source can help us understand other economic problems, as well as considering the prospects of the open source model spreading to other industries and the parallels between open source and academia.

A brief history of open source software

Software development has a tradition of sharing and cooperation. But in recent years, both the scale and formalization of the activity have expanded dramatically with the widespread diffusion of the Internet. We will highlight three distinct eras of cooperative software development.[5]

During the first era, the 1960s and 1970s, many of the key features of computer operating systems and the Internet were developed in academic settings such as Berkeley and MIT, as well as in central corporate research facilities where researchers had a great deal of autonomy, such as Bell Labs and Xerox's Palo Alto Research Center. Software can be transmitted in either "source code" or "object (or binary) code." Source code is the code using languages such as Basic, C and Java. Object, or binary, code is the sequence of 0s and 1s that directly communicates with the computer, but which is difficult for programmers to interpret or modify. Most commercial software vendors today provide users only with object or binary code; when the source code is made available to other firms by commercial developers, it is typically licensed under very restrictive conditions. However, in this first era, the sharing by programmers in different organizations of the source code for computer operating systems and for widely used transmission protocols was commonplace. These cooperative software development projects were undertaken on a highly informal basis. Typically, no efforts to delineate property rights or to restrict reuse of the software were made. This informality proved to be problematic in the early 1980s, when AT&T began enforcing its (purported) intellectual property rights related to the operating system software UNIX, to which many academics and corporate researchers at other firms had made contributions.

In response to the threats of litigation over UNIX, efforts to formalize the ground rules behind the cooperative software development process emerged, which ushered in the second era. The critical institution during this period was the Free Software Foundation, begun by Richard Stallman of the MIT Artificial Intelligence Laboratory in 1983. The foundation sought to develop and disseminate a wide variety of software without cost. The Free Software Foundation introduced a formal licensing procedure, called a General Public License, for a computer operating system called GNU. (The name GNU is a recursive acronym which stands for "GNU's Not UNIX.") In keeping with the philosophy of the organization that this software should be free to use, free to modify and free to redistribute, the license aimed to preclude the assertion of copyright or patent rights concerning cooperatively developed software. Also, in exchange for being able to modify and distribute the GNU software, software developers had to agree to a) make the source code freely available (or at a nominal cost) to whomever the program is distributed; and b) insist that others who use the source code agree to do likewise. Furthermore, all enhancements to the code—and even in many cases code that intermingled the cooperatively developed software with that developed separately—had to be licensed on the same terms. This kind of license is sometimes called "copyleft," because if copyright seeks to keep intellectual property private, copyleft seeks to keep intellectual property free and available. These contractual terms are distinct from "shareware," where the binary files, but not the underlying source code, are made freely available, possibly for a trial period only. The terms are also distinct from public domain software, where no restrictions are placed on subsequent users of the source code: those who add to material in the public domain do not commit to put the new product in the public domain. Some projects, such as the Berkeley Software Distribution (BSD) effort, took alternative approaches during the 1980s. The BSD license also allows anyone to copy freely and modify the source code, but it is much less constraining than the General Public License: anyone can modify the program and redistribute it for a fee without making the source code freely available as long as they acknowledge the original source.

The widespread diffusion of Internet access in the early 1990s led to the third era, which saw a dramatic acceleration of open source activity.

The volume of contributions and diversity of contributors expanded sharply, and numerous new open source projects emerged, most notably Linux, an operating system related to UNIX, developed by Linus Torvalds in 1991. Another innovation during this period was the proliferation of alternative approaches to licensing cooperatively developed software. In 1997, a number of individuals involved in cooperative software development adopted the "Open Source Definition." These guidelines took an ecumenical approach to licenses: for instance, they did not require that proprietary code compiled with the open source software become open source software as well.

The actors' strategies in open source

The key actors in an open source product are the individual contributors and for-profit companies. Both sets of actors respond to the legal incentives embodied in open source production. We will take up the individual contributors, for-profit firms and legal incentives in turn.

What motivates open source contributors?

The decision to contribute without pay to freely available software may seem mysterious to economists. However, the standard framework of labor economics can be adapted to capture activity in the open source environment (Lerner and Tirole, 2002).

The unpaid programmer working on an open source software development project faces a variety of benefits and costs. The programmer incurs an opportunity cost of time, which can manifest itself in different ways. For example, a programmer who works as an independent on open source projects forgoes the monetary compensation that could otherwise be earned by working for a commercial firm or a university. For a programmer with a commercial company, university or research lab affiliation, the opportunity cost of working on open source software comes from not focusing on other tasks. For example, the academic's research output may sag and the student's progress toward a degree slow down.

Several short- or long-run benefits may counter these costs. First, open source programmers may improve rather than reduce their performance in paid work. This outcome is particularly relevant for system administrators looking for specific solutions for their company. Second, the programmer may find intrinsic pleasure if choosing a "cool" open source is more fun than a routine task set by an employer. Third, in the long run, open source contributions may lead to future job offers, shares in commercial open source-based companies, or future access to the venture capital market, and last (but not least) ego gratification from peer recognition. Of course, different programmers may put different values on monetary or personal payoffs and on short-term or long-term payoffs.

Economic theory suggests that long-term incentives for working on an open source project are stronger under three conditions: 1) the more visible the performance to the relevant audience (peers, labor market and venture capital community); 2) the higher the impact of effort on performance; and 3) the more informative the performance about talent (for example, Holmström, 1999).[6] The first condition gives rise to what economists call "strategic complementarities." To have an "audience," programmers will want to work on software projects that will attract a large number of other programmers. This argument suggests the possibility of multiple equilibria. The same project may attract few programmers because programmers expect that other programmers will not be interested; or it may flourish as programmers (rationally) have faith in the project.

To compare programmers' incentives in the open source and proprietary settings, we need to examine how the features of the two environments shape incentives. From the standpoint of the individual, commercial projects typically offer better current compensation than open source projects, because employers are willing to offer salaries to software programmers in the expectation that they will capture a return from a proprietary project. Yet even commercial firms that compensate programmers may want their employees to work on open source projects. Besides the strategic reasons described below, we already noted that the impossibility of appropriating one's contribution to an open source project can be offset if the activity brings private benefits like the ability to fix bugs and customize the product to one's own ends for the programmer. (Commercial software vendors—like Microsoft in its shared source initiative—have sometimes tried to emulate this benefit by opening their code to selected users under a confidentiality arrangement.) Also, open source code may already be familiar to programmers: because it is freely available to all, it can be used in schools and universities for learning purposes, thus creating an "alumni effect." (Again, commercial software vendors are trying to emulate this benefit through university licenses to, say, Windows code.)

When we consider the delayed rewards of working on an open source project, the ability to signal a high level of competence may be stronger in the open source mode for three reasons. First, in an open source project, outsiders can see the contribution of each individual, whether that component "worked," whether the task was hard, if the problem was addressed in a clever way, whether the code can be useful for other programming tasks in the future, and so forth. Second, the open source programmer takes full responsibility for the success of a subproject, with little interference from a superior, which generates information about ability to follow through with a task. Finally, since many elements of the source code are shared across open source projects, more of the knowledge they have accumulated can be transferred to new environments, which makes programmers more valuable to future employers.

These incentives are likely to be stronger and the project more successful if there is an effective leader. While the leader of an open source project has no formal authority—that is, he cannot direct any one to do anything—the leadership often has considerable "real authority," in the terminology of Aghion and Tirole (1997). Leaders play a key role in formulating the initial agenda, setting goals as the project evolves and resolving disputes that might lead to the splintering or outright cessation of the project.

The empirical evidence is largely consistent with the belief that individual contributors to open source projects do benefit directly. The sole econometric study we are aware of, by Hann, Roberts, Slaughter and Fielding (2004), examines contributors to the Apache project, drawing on a wide variety of project records. The authors complement these data with a survey on employment, which yield useable data for multiple years for 147 contributors to the project. The authors then estimate a series of regressions, in which they use the logarithm of earnings in a given year as the dependent variable, and information on the respondents' background, work experience and contributions to and current position in the Apache project in the previous year as independent variables. While in a number of projects such as Linux there is an undisputed central leader, in Apache and many other projects a series of committees at different levels resolves open issues. As a result, there are five observable levels of recognition or rank within the Apache Software Foundation (ASF), which runs the project: in order of increasing status, the titles are developer, committer, project management committee member, ASF member and ASF board member. Advancement is made in recognition of an individual's commitment and contributions to an Apache project. To control for unobserved individual characteristics, individual fixed effects are employed. The results suggest that the sheer volume of contributions to the Apache project have little impact on salary. But individuals who attain high rank in the Apache organization enjoy wages that are 14 to 29 percent higher, whether or not their work directly involves the Apache program. The results appear to be robust to controls for the possible alternative explanations: for instance, the authors address the possibility that Apache promotions may be driven by commercial success by using lags of the key independent variables.

Academics have also attempted to understand motivations of those who work on open source projects through surveys. Given the inherent subjectivity of these assessments and the self-serving biases in reporting, the low response rates that many of these surveys have obtained, and the sensitivity of some of these questions, it is perhaps not surprising that self-reported motivations vary considerably across studies. For instance, Haruvy, Wu and Chakravarty (2003) find that commercial objectives—particularly, the promise of higher future earnings—are an important driver of contributions to open source projects. However, Lakhani and von Hippel (2003) suggest that the overwhelming driver of open source contributors is the need to solve their own specific programming needs, while a Boston Consulting Group (2003) survey implies that intellectual curiosity is the most important determinant.

How do commercial firms work and compete with open source?

Commercial companies may interact with an open source project in a number of ways. While improvements in the open source software are not appropriable, commercial companies can benefit if they also offer expertise in some proprietary segment of the market that is complementary to the open source program. Also, firms may temporarily encourage their programmers to participate in open source projects to learn about the strengths and weaknesses of this development approach. For-profit firms may compete directly with open source providers in the same market. Finally, commercial companies may interface with the open source world because it generates good public relations with programmers and customers.

A for-profit firm that seeks to provide services and products that are complementary to the open source product, but are not supplied efficiently by the open source community, can be referred to as "living symbiotically." IBM, which has made open source software into a major focus for its consulting business, exemplifies this approach. A commercial company in this situation will want to have extensive knowledge about the open source movement, and may even want to encourage and subsidize open source contributions, both of which may cause it to allocate some programmers to the open source project. Because firms do not capture all the benefits of the investments in the open source project, however, the free-rider problem often discussed in the economics of innovation should apply here as well. Subsidies by commercial companies for open source projects should remain somewhat limited.

The *code release* strategy arises when companies release some existing proprietary code and then create a governance structure for the resulting open source development process. For example, IBM released half-a-million lines of its Cloudscape program, a simple database that resides inside a software application instead of as a full-fledged database program, to the Apache Software Foundation. Hewlett-Packard released its Spectrum Object Model-Linker to the open source community to help the Linux community write software to connect Linux with Hewlett Packard's RISC computer architecture. This strategy is to give away the razor (the released code) to sell more razor blades (the related consulting services that IBM and Hewlett Packard hope to provide).[7]

When can it be advantageous for a commercial company to release proprietary code under an open source license? In general, it will make sense if the increase in profit in the proprietary complementary segment offsets any profit that would have been made in the primary segment, had it not been converted to open source. Thus, the temptation to go open source is particularly strong when the product is lagging behind the leader and making few profits, but the firm sees a possibility that if the released code becomes the center of an open source project and is utilized more widely, the profitability of the complementary segment will increase. (An example may be Netscape's 1998 decision to make "Mozilla," a portion of its browser source code, freely available.) If network effects and switching costs are very strong, the second-best commercial package might have a tiny market share. In these cases, the cost to corporations of releasing code may be very small. Moreover, such a strategy may reassure potential users that the released software will never be withdrawn—and thus that the user will always be able to maintain the product itself.

This motivation can also depend on the evolution of vertical relationships between small and large firms in the software industry in commercial software environments, a subject that would reward further study. Indeed, many small developers are uncomfortable doing business with leading software firms. They fear that the commercial platform owner has an incentive to introduce substitutes in the developers' segment to force prices down in that segment and to raise the demand for licenses to the broad software platform (Farrell and Katz, 2000). By contrast, when a large firm makes its platform available on an open source basis through (say) a General Public License-style license, the small firm need no longer fear being squeezed in this way.

Numerous challenges appear, though, when a for-profit firm seeks to become the center of an open source development project. Leadership by a commercial entity may not internalize enough of the objectives of the open source community. In particular, a corporation may not be able to make a credible commitment to keeping all source code in the public domain and to highlighting important contributions adequately. These difficulties help to explain why Hewlett-Packard released its code through Collab.Net, a venture by leading open source programmers, which organizes open source projects for corporations who wish to open up part of their software. In effect, Collab.Net offers a kind of certification that the firm is committed to the open source project. (The Apache Software Foundation plays a similar role in Cloudscape case mentioned above.) In a theoretical model, Dessein (2002) shows that a principal with formal control rights over an agent's activity in general gains by delegating control rights to an intermediary with preferences or incentives that are intermediate between the principal's and the agent's. The partial alignment of the intermediary's preferences with the agent's fosters trust and boosts the agent's initiative, ultimately offsetting the partial loss of control for the principal. In the case of Collab.Net, the congruence with the open source developers is obtained through the employment of visible open source developers and the involvement of O'Reilly, a technical book publisher with strong ties to the open source community.

While the relative merits of open source and proprietary software are discussed in a number of contributions, direct competition between the two paradigms has received little attention. An exception is Gaudeul (2004), who builds a duopoly model with one open source and one proprietary software project.[8] In his model, open source software has both costs and benefits relative to proprietary software. Open source software suffers from some lack of coordination: the same code may be written twice or not at all. Another cost of open source software in Gaudeul's model is that its designers, the developers, may not bother developing interfaces that appeal to unsophisticated users. By contrast, the profit-maximizing proprietary software firm in his model is keener to develop such an interface. However, the proprietary model must pay its developers and, despite good project coordination, may choose to develop a limited set of features. In this model, the proprietary software is sold to users at a positive price that excludes some possible users. In equilibrium, the open source software, if it survives, is used either by low-demand or low-income consumers, who cannot afford buying the proprietary software, or by developers who like the potentially larger set of features and do not care about the missing or insufficient user interface. Furthermore, the presence of open source software raises welfare, at least if it does not discourage the development of proprietary software with a good interface.

How does the legal system affect open source?

Open source software is shaped by the legal rules under which it operates. In each case, the product originator gives users the right to employ the copyrighted code through a license. But the licenses differ tremendously in the extent to which they enable licensors and contributors to profit from the code that is contributed.

In Lerner and Tirole (2005), we explore what drives firms to choose particular licenses. We begin with a model of license choice. We suppose that an entity, either an individual or a firm, is deciding a) whether to make some software available under an open source license; and b) if so, what type of license to employ. We depict the interactions between the licensor and the community of programmers. The programmers' benefits from working on the project may depend on the choice of license. The licensor must assess how its choice of license, together with project characteristics—such as the environment, the nature of the project and the intended audience—impacts the project's likely success.

The model suggests that permissive licenses such as the Berkeley Software Distribution model, where users retain the ability to use the code as they see fit, will be more common in cases where projects have strong appeal to the community of open source contributors—for instance, when contributors stand to benefit considerably from signaling incentives or when the licensors are well-trusted. Conversely, restrictive licenses such as the General Public License will be commonplace when such appeals are more fragile. Examples of cases where we would expect a restrictive license are projects geared for end users who are unlikely to appreciate the coding, such as computer games, or those sponsored by corporations, who potential contributors might fear would "hijack" the project and use the code for commercial ends.

One of the most visible of the disputes over licensing was the Mozilla case alluded to above. This effort initially encountered severe difficulties because of the license choice. Netscape initially proposed the "Netscape Public License," which would have allowed Netscape to take pieces of the open source code and turn them back into a proprietary project again (Hamerly, Paquin and Walton, 1999). Ultimately, the firm announced the "Mozilla Public License," under which Netscape cannot regain proprietary rights to modifications of the code: in fact, the terms of the final license are even stricter than those of the General Public License.

In Lerner and Tirole (2005), we also present an empirical analysis of the prevalence of different types of open source licenses. The analysis employs nearly 40,000 open source projects in the SourceForge database. Since all of the projects in this database are open source, we focus on whether the license requires that when modified versions of the program are distributed, the source code must be made generally available and/or whether the license restricts modified versions of the program from mingling their source code with other software that does not employ such a license. We term such licenses "restrictive." We find that restrictive licenses are more common for applications geared toward end-users and system administrators—like desktop tools and games. However, restrictive licenses are significantly less common for those applications aimed toward software developers. Restrictive licenses are also less common for projects operating in commercial environments or that run on proprietary operating systems. Projects whose natural language is not English, whose community appeal may be presumed to be much smaller, are more likely to employ restrictive licenses. Projects with less restrictive licenses tend to attract more contributors.

Further issues about open source

This section will highlight three other particularly interesting and challenging areas about open source projects: the quality of their output; whether open source projects should be encouraged by public policy; and how open source projects may be affected by software patents.

What is the relative quality of open source software?

One of the most contentious issues in the literature has been the relative virtues of the open source and proprietary development process. Advocates of open source software have long claimed that the open source development process leads to superior software (for example, Raymond, 1999). A number of studies have sought to explore these claims, but consensus remains elusive.

Kuan (2001) was the first to offer a formal model of some of the advantages of open source software for users. She focused on the consumer's choice between employing "off-the-shelf" commercial software and adapting open source code to the consumer's own use. While the proprietary software can (and indeed must) be used "as is," open source code can be enhanced in quality through the user's efforts. Such refinements, however, require effort, with more effort leading to higher quality code. If consumers differ in type, commercial companies may either offer different quality levels of programs, or else may offer a single product to all users. She shows that under certain circumstances, some consumers will prefer the open source option and invest in producing software that is of superior quality to commercial alternatives. The paper tests this model by comparing dates at which program errors or "bugs" were reported and fixed in three open source programs—Apache, FreeBSD and Gnome—with three commercial projects matched by subject matter and age. For two of the three pairs that she examines, the rate at which bugs are fixed is significantly faster in the open source project, and there is little difference in the third case.

Bessen (2002), in a related paper, emphasizes another dimension along which open source software may have an advantage: the ability of heterogeneous users to customize it to meet their own particular needs. Proprietary software manufacturers cannot anticipate all manifestations of consumer demand, and thus cannot offer every conceivable variation that consumers might desire. Again, consumers face a "make versus buy" choice, where the complexity and idiosyncrasy of the project, as well as the cost of modifications, will drive the choice. While Bessen does not test this model, he cites Franke and von Hippel's (2003) finding that one-fifth of Apache users adapted security features to meet their particular needs as consistent with his model.

While these two authors attribute the superiority of open source projects to the ability of end-users to adapt an initial code base, Johnson (2004) focuses on a different rationale: that open source programs are developed through a superior process that may avoid pathologies that affect commercial projects. In particular, he argues that workers in commercial firms may collude not to report programming errors of fellow employees, lest their own reputation and future earnings be damaged. He hypothesizes that because programmers do not receive wages in open source projects, they will have fewer incentives to engage in such collusion. (Note, though, that the ego gratification and career incentives may also motivate collusion.) It may be argued that the large number of potential eyeballs in open source software makes collusion difficult to sustain. Johnson argues that reduced collusion will lead to open source projects undergoing more peer review and having higher quality.[9]

Another issue that may differentiate proprietary and open source software is security. Open source advocates have argued that when source code is open and freely visible, programmers can readily identify security flaws and other problems: as Eric Raymond (1999) has argued, "to many eyes, all bugs are shallow." Proponents of proprietary software, on the other hand, argue that the openness of the source code allows malicious hackers to figure out its weaknesses. Anderson (2002) argues that under certain plausible assumptions, the openness of the system should have no impact on its security. Making bugs harder for hackers to find by keeping the source code hidden will also mean that software companies have a more difficult time identifying errors through "beta" testing, where lead users experiment with the product, also without access to the underlying source code. (While software firms will also do internal testing by employees with access to the source code, the effort devoted to these "alpha" tests is usually many times smaller than that in later-stage tests.) Thus, he concludes, "other things being equal, we expect that open and closed systems will exhibit similar growth in reliability and in security assurance." However, Anderson does not attempt to assess this claim empirically. Any such effort is difficult because hackers may attack a software program for reasons unrelated to the intrinsic security of the program; for instance, some hackers may derive more gratification from an attack on a leading public company, even though hackers have targeted both commercial and open source programs at various occasions.[10]

Open source and commercial software could be compared as well along numerous other dimensions. For instance, we argue in our 2002 work that it is likely that the incentive structure for open source programmers will lead to poorer documentation and user interfaces in these projects. These claims, and numerous others in the literature, deserve careful scrutiny.

What are appropriate public policies toward open source?

Government commissions and agencies have proposed—and in some cases implemented—a variety of measures to encourage open source developers. For example, in the United States, the President's Information Technology Advisory Committee (2000) recommended direct federal subsidies for open source projects to advance high-end computing, and a report from the European Commission (2001) also discussed support for open developers and standards. Many European governments have policies to encourage the use and purchase of open source software for government use ("Microsoft at the Power Point," 2003). Governments may even mandate the development of localized open source projects, as has occurred in China (Open Source Development Labs, 2004).

Economists have sought to understand the consequences of a vibrant open source sector for social welfare. Perhaps not surprisingly, definitive or sweeping answers have been difficult to come by; instead, the policy conclusions focus on specific instruments in specific contexts. We will first discuss two papers that consider the impact of open source on social welfare more generally and then discuss a number of works that address public policies.

Most analyses have suggested that government support for open source projects is likely to have an ambiguous effect on social welfare. For example, Johnson (2002) presents a model where programmers decide whether to devote effort to a project, in which their contributions become a public good once they are developed. Users thus face a decision whether to enhance an existing open source program or to wait in the hope that another programmer will undertake the development process. Johnson then compares this process to a stylized depiction of the development of proprietary software in a corporate setting. Open source projects have the advantage of being able to access the entire pool of developer talent, not just employees in a single firm. Given the larger talent pool, they can aggregate and exploit more private information. But because of the free riding problem, some potentially valuable projects will not be developed under an open source system. Johnson concludes that a comparison of the social welfare consequences of these two systems is ambiguous.

Casadesus-Masanell and Ghemawat (2003) depict competition between an open source operating system available at no cost and a proprietary commercial product. The crucial feature of their model is on the demand side: the larger the market share of a given operating system, the more valuable that system to users. This effect could be due to better learning about the program's features (if users contribute comments and suggestions to improve the product) or to the presence of complementary software developed by other firms. In this setting, the presence of an open source operating system leads the commercial firm to set lower prices, which in turn means that the overall use of operating systems is higher. However, the value of the commercial system for users is lower: for instance, the presence of a competing product may lead third-party developers to develop fewer complementary products for the commercial operating system. Thus, the presence of open source projects may either make society better or worse off. This model also suggests that in some cases, the proprietary operating system may be able to drive the market share of the open source alternative to zero, and also that the parameter ranges where this will occur need not correspond to those where such an action is socially desirable.

Schmidt and Schnitzer (2002) highlight similarly that open source software has social costs and benefits. Building on a line of economic reasoning that extends back to Arrow (1962) and even earlier, they highlight two countervailing effects. From a static point of view, free or nearly free open source will insure greater social welfare, as virtually any potential user will be able to access software. But from a dynamic perspective, with so few profits to be gleaned, developers may lack incentives to introduce new products. While career concerns and other incentives may motivate developers to identify bugs in open source programs and undertake certain modest adaptations to meet their own needs, they are unlikely to be sufficient to encourage major breakthroughs. The authors argue that while open source programs will enhance social welfare in some settings, this outcome will be far from universal. They caution against subsidies that may lead to an undesirably high level of open source activity.

Saint-Paul (2003) reaches an even bleaker conclusion about the open source phenomenon. He employs a Romer-style endogenous growth model, in which both commercial firms and "philanthropists"—individuals who are willing to give their contributions away for free—innovate. He shows that the free contributions will lead to economic growth, but also reduce the profits, and hence the incentives to innovate, among commercial firms. Unless the proprietary sector is quite profitable, then the second effect will dominate, and innovation and growth be harmed by the presence of open source software. He argues that the negative effect is likely to be even stronger than his model shows, because he neglects, for instance, the possibility that philanthropic products do not meet users' needs as well as commercial products (though see the previous section for a counter-argument) and can also divert programming talent that could have been devoted to commercial products.

In a more informal piece, Shapiro and Varian (2004) suggest another consideration that formal models have not so far discussed: the impact on human capital and entrepreneurship. They suggest that an open system will facilitate learning by students as to how to program and will provide opportunities for third-party developers to introduce complementary products. They argue that all else being equal, these considerations should lead public policymakers in nations that seek to encourage the development of their software industries to boost the development of open source activity.

How will software patents affect open source?

Software patents will interact with open source activity.[11] This issue is clearly a timely one, in light of the litigation launched by the SCO Group, which holds to (at least partial) rights to UNIX (acquired from Novell, who in turn had purchased them from AT&T). Beginning in 2003, the firm initiated a series of lawsuits against, among others, AutoZone, DaimlerChrysler, IBM and Novell, alleging that they were violating SCO's intellectual property by contributing to or using Linux.[12] The allegedly detrimental impact of software patents on open source was also a frequently invoked reason for opposing software patents in the September 2003 debate in the European Parliament on this question.[13]

Software patents create the possibility of holding up software producers. In the case of commercial software, individuals and companies that do not produce software themselves (like hardware manufacturers and software users), but hold a software patent, can try to obtain royalty payments from major software vendors. Large software vendors are less likely to engage in such behaviors against each other, as they have accumulated patent portfolios that they can use for retaliatory purposes against other vendors that would try to hold them up.

Open source software is vulnerable in a different way. After all, the code is free of charge and the contributors hardly solvent for the most part, so attempting to collect royalties is not a powerful incentive. However, firms with software patents may seek damages from large corporate and noncorporate users and firms that service open source software, as SCO is doing, or commercial competitors with software patents may sue open source software to enjoin further utilization of the code. It remains to be seen whether the open source movement will itself enter into defensive patenting, as large commercial vendors already do, or at least make a more concerted effort to forestall patenting by others by aggressively publishing. One intriguing new initiative is the Red Hat Assurance Plan, in which the Linux distributor is offering partial protection against intellectual property litigation.[14]

Another interesting area of study concerns the consequences of users paying royalties for an open source program that also included some commercially patented material. Such royalty demands might trigger "sweetheart" deals between firms, the splitting of open source projects into different branches (often termed "forking") and the privatization of blocks of code. The General Public License seeks to address these problems—and to discourage patent filings by firms working with open source projects—by prohibiting the incorporation of code that is encumbered by patent rights. As section 7 of the license states, "[I]f a patent license would not permit royalty-free redistribution of the Program by all those who receive copies directly or indirectly through you, then the only way you could satisfy both it and this License would be to refrain entirely from distribution of the Program." Many other types of open source licenses, however, do not address this issue.[15]

Another, less prominent, question relates to the impact of patents on the dynamics of information sharing and collaboration among open source contributors. To what extent will the ability of programmers to protect their discoveries with strong patent rights reduce their incentives to participate in open source projects?

To date, very little systematic analysis has examined the implications of patents for open source. However, a broader literature has scrutinized the impact of patenting on the generation and diffusion of scientific knowledge more generally. Since 1980, a series of reforms in the United States and elsewhere have greatly augmented the ability of academic institutions, government laboratories and nonprofit institutions to patent their discoveries, even if governments originally funded the research. This literature has sought to understand the pervasiveness and consequences of the "anticommons" problem (Heller and Eisenberg, 1998): the concern that the patenting of scientific knowledge will lead to lower research productivity, and hence eventually to reduced economic growth. Much of the discussion of these questions to date has featured broad assertions and anecdotal examples (as in Bok, 2003). It is clear from these studies that institutions and researchers have responded to the increased incentives to commercialize products by engaging in more patenting and commercialization activities (for instance, Jaffe and Lerner, 2001; Lach and Schankerman, 2003). Whether these commercial activities have detrimental effects on research and social welfare is much more ambiguous.[16] Given this initial and somewhat contradictory evidence, our ability to draw conclusions for consequences of formal intellectual property rights for open source software is quite limited.

A broader research agenda

The open source process poses numerous interesting issues that extend well beyond the software industry. In this section, we'll highlight three of these. The first issue is the extent to which the open source model can move beyond software into other industries. Second, we'll discuss the way in which firms can accomplish many of the key goals of open source while employing other arrangements. Finally, we'll explore the parallels between open source software and academic research.

Can open source work beyond software?

An interesting question is whether the open source model can be transposed to other industries. Could automobile components be developed in an open source mode, with General Motors and Toyota performing an assembler function similar to that of Red Hat for Linux? Many industries involve forms of cooperation between commercial entities in the form of for-profit or not-for-profit joint ventures. Others exhibit user-driven innovation or open science cultures. Thus, a number of ingredients of open source software are not specific to the software industry. Yet no other industry has yet produced anything quite like open source development.

Although some aspects of open source software collaboration (such as electronic information exchange across the world) could easily be duplicated, other aspects would be harder to emulate. Consider, for example, the case of biotechnology. It may be impossible to break up large projects into small manageable and independent modules, and there may not be sufficient sophisticated users who can customize the molecules to their own needs. The tasks that are involved in making the product available to the end user involve larger expenditures than simply providing consumer support and friendlier user interfaces as in software. The costs of designing, testing and seeking regulatory approval for a new drug are enormous.

More generally, in many industries, the development of individual components requires large-scale teamwork and substantial capital costs, as opposed to (for some software programs) individual contributions and no capital investment (besides the computer the programmer already has). Another obstacle is that in mass-market industries, users are numerous and rather unsophisticated, and so deliver little peer recognition and ego gratification. These characteristics suggests that the open source model may not easily be transposed to other industries, but further investigation is warranted.

Can firms realize the benefits of open source in other ways?

Corporations may emulate some of the benefits attached to open source production either by getting involved in open source themselves or by adopting institutional arrangements that deliver some of these benefits. First, using open source technology encourages users that they will not be "held up" by a future price increase after adopting a technology and that they will always be able to tailor their technology to their own particular needs. Second, open source avoids the problem of a "patent thicket" when multiple firms have overlapping intellectual property rights and at least one party attempts to extract a high fee for its particular contribution. Third, a firm might make a technology open source as a way of trying to certify a technological standard, in which case firms may contribute software to open source to benefit from the endorsement of such a standard, as the Hewlett Packard case discussed above illustrates.

Firms can also address these problems in non-open-source ways, such as patent pools, standard-setting organizations and self-imposed commitments. In a patent pool, firms blend their patents with those of other firms. These pools allow users to access a number of firms' patents simultaneously, thereby avoiding the "patent thicket." In many cases, the pooling agreements also specify the pricing schedule in the agreement that establishes the pool, assuring that no party attempts to extract very high fees or to increase its fees after users are locked in. To be certain, patent pools raise a risk that they can be used to hinder entry, but these concerns can in part be addressed through a careful design of the pool (Lerner and Tirole, 2004a; Lerner, Strojwas and Tirole, 2003).

Standard-setting organizations offer an alternative path for the certification of new technologies. Often firms can choose between standard-setting organizations, and they can seek an endorsement for an emerging technology from an independent and prestigious organization or use a more complacent one (Lerner and Tirole, 2004b). These bodies also help address the other concerns, frequently asking contributors of the key technologies to commit to license the technology on "reasonable and non-discriminatory" terms or to make various other concessions.

Self-imposed commitments can serve much the same role. For instance, firms can commit to license technologies at a given price schedule, or they can commit to provide sufficient information so that users can tailor the technology. An example of the latter is Microsoft's Shared Source Initiative, through the firm shares source code with customers, partners and governments. One open question about many of these self-imposed programs is the extent to which the commitments can be enforced if the firm subsequently changes its design.[17]

Open source production may seem like a unique and idiosyncratic realm. However, many of the issues are seen elsewhere in high-technology industries: when and how to share technology, how to set common standards, and how to combine freely available and commercial components arise both in the open source and the commercial realm. Open source projects and traditional firms can borrow from each other innovative approaches to the underlying problems.

Open source and academia

Open source and academia have many parallels. The most obvious parallel relates to motivation. As in open source, the direct financial returns from writing academic articles are typically nonexistent, but career concerns and the desire for peer recognition provide powerful inducements.

Other similar dynamics are also at work. Consider, for instance, the discussion of motivation for programmers when choosing to which open source project they should contribute. As we highlight above, a critical goal is the selection of a project that is likely to continue to be successful, so that the programmers' contributions are widely recognized, yet which at the same time has interesting and challenging programming challenges to be addressed. These criteria should be familiar to anyone who has advised a doctoral student on the choice of a thesis topic!

However, there are also some substantial differences between the two realms. Here, we will highlight two areas where academic economists could learn from the open source realm. The first of these relates to the incentives to create public goods. Open source contributors often create substantial bodies of code, which are made widely available when completed. Far too often in academic economics, however, we do not see similar dissemination.[18] For instance, an author—after creating a unique dataset for a project—may simply save this information on a personal computer hard disk, rather than making it publicly available. Similarly, while there are some examples of efforts to create shared resources that can be widely used by the economics community—the NBER Patent Citations Database created by Bronwyn Hall, Adam Jaffe and Manuel Trajtenberg is a recent important example—far too often these efforts are neglected because the returns to the project leaders are low. Why it is not commonplace to see economists frequently seeking to establish their reputation by creating original, widely accessible datasets is an interesting question. (Akin to open source, we might anticipate that this strategy might be especially effective for those at smaller and less centrally located institutions.) One explanation might be that data collection is often inspired by what analyses one wants to perform, so it is harder to separate data collection and analysis. In any case, the design of mechanisms that successfully encourage such investments is an important challenge for academic economists.

A second area relates to access to published work. Contributors to open source projects seem to be powerfully spurred by the provisions of these licenses. The assurance that contributions—and subsequent contributions that build on it—will remain publicly accessible incentivizes programmers to write code. By way of contrast, in academic economics, it is standard to assign the copyright to one's work to a commercial publisher. In other areas of academia, this approach is under increasing attack. For instance, recent years have seen the rise of "open access" journals such as the *Public Library of Science*, which make all articles freely accessible and distributable. In response to this challenge, a number of established science journals, such as the *Proceedings of the National Academies of Sciences*, have not only begun providing free access to older issues, but even allowing authors to opt to have their articles immediately publicly accessible with the payment of an additional fee.[19] It is an interesting question as to whether open access will have the same appeal for the economics community.

Final thoughts

This paper has reviewed our understanding of the growing open source movement. We have highlighted how many aspects of open source software appear initially puzzling to an economist. Our ability to answer confidently many of the issues raised here questions is likely to increase as the open source movement itself grows and evolves.

At the same time, it is heartening to us how much of open source activities can be understood within existing economic frameworks, despite the presence of claims to the contrary. The labor and industrial organization literatures provide lenses through which the structure of open source projects, the role of contributors and the movement's ongoing evolution can be viewed.

Notes

* We thank the National Science Foundation and Harvard Business School's Division of Research for financial support. The Institut D'Economie Industrielle receives research grants from a number of corporate sponsors, including France

Telecom and the Microsoft Corporation. We thank Christophe Bisiere, Jacques Cremer, Alexandre Gaudeul, Justin Johnson, Hal Varian and the editors for helpful comments.

1 See <http://news.com.com/2100-1001-825723.html> (accessed March 21, 2004).
2 On web server software and Apache, see <http://news.netcraft.com/archives/web_server_survey.html> (accessed March 21, 2004). On the use of Linux in web server operating systems, see <http://www.pcworld.com/news/article/0,aid, 112840,00.asp> (accessed March 31, 2004). On the use of Linux for embedded software, see <http://www.linuxdevices.com/articles/AT8693703925.html> (accessed March 21, 2004).
3 For the survey of chief information officers, see <http://www.morganstanley.com/institutional/techresearch/pdfs/ciosurvey1203.pdf> (accessed March, 21, 2004). On Linux software used for Google searches, see <http://www.internetnews.com/dev-news/article.php/3302941> (accessed March 31, 2004).
4 The challenge is expected to be led by MySQL, which received a $16 million financing from the venture capital organizations Accel and Benchmark in 2003. MySQL provides its program for free under an open source license and for a substantial fee under a commercial license. See <http://www.informationweek.com/story/showArticle.jhtml?articleID = 18312009> (accessed August 8, 2004).
5 This history is highly abbreviated. See Lerner and Tirole (2002) and the sources cited therein for a longer account.
6 For a discussion as to how firms might otherwise have superior information about employees and how this might deter job offers from outsiders—a problem that open source programming can address—see Greenwald (1986) and Waldman (1984).
7 For more details, see <http://www.infoworld.com/article/04/08/03/HNclouscape_1.html> (accessed August 3, 2004), <http://www.collab.net/customers/cdp_solutions_at_work.html> (accessed March 31, 2004) and the associated links.
8 See also the discussion below of Casadesus-Masanell and Ghemawat (2003).
9 Also in this paper, Johnson (2004) suggests that individuals in commercial software companies may be reluctant to report programming problems to superiors, because the firm's management may be unable to commit not to demand that they then address these issues. In open source projects, programmers can never be compelled to work on fixing a bug that they identify. He predicts that while the speed of the bug fixing process may be slower in open source projects, more problems will ultimately be identified.
10 For a discussion of a hacker attack on Apache, see <http://thewhir.com/marketwatch/hac062102.cfm> (accessed March 31, 2004).
11 In this section, we will avoid discussing the highly contentious and unsettled question of the economic impact of software patents more generally: for more on this topic, see, for instance, Bessen and Hunt (2003), Caillaud (2003), Graham and Mowery (2003) and Hahn and Wallsten (2003).
12 Patent concerns have also slowed the adoption of Linux in the public sector: see, for instance, <http://www.informationweek.com/story/showArticle.jhtml?articleID=26806464> (accessed August 25, 2004) for a discussion of the impact of these concerns on the city of Munich's open source effort.
13 See, for instance, <http://news.zdnet.co.uk/business/legal/0,39020651,39116053,00.htm> (accessed March 26, 2004).
14 For a discussion, see <http://www.redhat.com/about/presscenter/2004/press_blackduck.html> (accessed August 24, 2004). One challenge is that the extent and dispersion of the patent holdings that may impact open source projects: the insurer Open Source Risk Management estimates that there are 283 patents that

might be used in claims against the Linux kernel alone. See <http://www.eweek.com/article2/0,1759,1631336,00.asp> (accessed August 24, 2004).

15 A related danger is that programs will inadvertently infringe patents. Programmers may lack the incentives and skills needed to check whether their contribution infringes awards. As an effort to limit this problem, beginning in May 2004, Linux contributors were required to attest that they have the right to make that contribution. For a discussion, see <http://www.computerworld.com/softwaretopics/os/linux/story/0,10801,93395,00.html> (accessed August 8, 2004).

16 For instance, Thursby and Thursby's (2003) study of six major research universities suggests that while the probability that a faculty member will indicate to his university's technology transfer office that he has made a new discovery has increased ten-fold over the past decade, research productivity in basic research journals has remained constant. On the other hand, Murray and Stern (2003) have shown that papers published in the journal *Nature Biotechnology* are somewhat less likely to be cited in other articles once the corresponding patent application issues. They find that the papers with corresponding patents are initially more heavily cited than those without, but then their citation rate declines more sharply over time.

17 This is also a question for other commitments as well. For one illustration in a standard setting context, see *Rambus Inc. v. Infineon Techs. A*G, 318 F.3d 1081 (Fed. Cir. 2003).

18 Data archiving policies, such as the *American Economic Review*'s, seek to address this problem, but are more the exception than the rule.

19 See, for instance, <http://www.plos.org/about/openaccess.html> and <http://www.pnas.org/cgi/content/full/101/23/8509> (accessed August 10, 2004).

References

Aghion, Philippe and Jean Tirole. 1997. "Formal and Real Authority in Organizations." *Journal of Political Economy.* 105:1, pp. 1–29.

Anderson, Ross. 2002. "Security in Open versus Closed Systems—The Dance of Boltzman, Coase and Moore." Unpublished working paper, Cambridge University.

Arrow, Kenneth J. 1962. "Economic Welfare and the Allocation of Resources for Invention," in *The Rate and Direction of Inventive Activity: Economic and Social Factors.* Richard R. Nelson, ed. Princeton, N.J.: Princeton University Press, pp. 609–26.

Bessen, James. 2002. "Open Source Software: Free Provision of Complex Public Goods." Unpublished working paper, Research on Innovation.

Bessen, James and Robert M. Hunt. 2003. "An Empirical Look at Software Patents." Working Paper 03–17, Federal Reserve Bank of Philadelphia.

Bok, Derek. 2003. *Universities in the Marketplace: The Commercialization of Higher Education.* Princeton, N.J.: Princeton University Press.

Boston Consulting Group. 2003. *Boston Consulting Group/OSDN Hacker Survey.* Boston: Boston Consulting Group.

Caillaud, Bernard. 2003. "La Propriété Intellectuelle sur les Logiciels." *Propriété Intellectuelle.* Conseil D'Analyse Economique, Rapport 41, pp. 113–71.

Casadesus-Masanell, Ramon and Pankaj Ghemawat. 2003. "Dynamic Mixed Duopoly: A Model Motivated by Linux vs. Windows." Strategy Unit Working Paper 04-012, Graduate School of Business Administration, Harvard University.

Dessein, Wouter. 2002. "Authority and Communication in Organizations." *Review of Economic Studies.* 69:4, pp. 811–38.

European Commission, Interchange of Data between Administrations. 2001. "Study into the Use of Open Source Software in the Public Sector." June; Available at <http://europa.eu.int/ISPO/ida/jsps/index.jsp?fuseAction=showDocument&documentID=333&parent=chapter&preChapterID=0-17-134>.

Farrell, Joseph and Michael L. Katz. 2000. "Innovation, Rent Extraction, and Integration in Systems Markets." *Journal of Industrial Economics.* 48:4, pp. 413–32.

Franke, Nikolaus and Eric von Hippel. 2003. "Satisfying Heterogeneous User Needs via Innovation Tool Kits: The Case of Apache Security Software." *Research Policy.* 32:7, pp. 1199–215.

Gaudeul, Alexandre. 2004. "Competition between Open-Source and Proprietary Software: The $(L^A)T_EX$ case Study." Unpublished working paper, Universities of Toulouse and Southampton.

Graham, Stuart and David C. Mowery. 2003. "Intellectual Property Protection in the Software Industry," in *Patents in the Knowledge-Based Economy: Proceedings of the Science, Technology and Economic Policy Board.* Wesley Cohen and Steven Merrill, eds. Washington, National Academies Press.

Greenwald, Bruce C. 1986. "Adverse Selection in the Labour Market." *Review of Economic Studies.* 53:3, pp. 325–47.

Hahn, Robert W. and Scott J. Wallsten. 2003. "A Review of Bessen and Hunt's Analysis of Software Patents." Unpublished working paper, American Enterprise Institute-Brookings Joint Center for Regulatory Studies.

Hammerly, Jim, Tom Paquin and Susan Walton. 1999. "Freeing the Source: The Story of Mozilla," in *Open Sources: Voices from the Open Source Revolution.* Chris DiBona, Sam Ockman, and Mark Stone, eds. Cambridge, Massachusetts: O'Reilly, pp. 197–206.

Hann, Il-Horn, Jeff Roberts, Sandra Slaughter and Roy Fielding. 2004. "An Empirical Analysis of Economic Returns to Open Source Participation." Unpublished working paper, Carnegie-Mellon University.

Haruvy, Ernan E., Fang Wu and Sujoy Chakravarty. 2003. "Incentives for Developers' Contributions and Product Performance Metrics in Open Source Development: An Empirical Investigation." Unpublished working paper, University of Texas at Dallas.

Heller, Michael and Rebecca Eisenberg. 1998. "Can Patents Deter Innovation? The Anticommons in Biomedical Research." *Science.* 280: 5364, pp. 698–701.

Holmström, Bengt. 1999. "Managerial Incentive Problems: A Dynamic Perspective." *Review of Economic Studies.* 66:1, pp. 169–82.

Jaffe, Adam B. and Josh Lerner. 2001. "Reinventing Public R&D: Patent Law and Technology Transfer from Federal Laboratories." *Rand Journal of Economics.* Spring, 32, pp. 167–98.

Johnson, Justin P. 2002. "Open Source Software: Private Provision of a Public Good." *Journal of Economics and Management Strategy.* 11:4, pp. 637–62.

Johnson, Justin P. 2004. "Collaboration, Peer Review and Open Source Software." Unpublished working paper, Cornell University.

Kuan, Jennifer. 2001. "Open Source Software as Consumer Integration into Production." Unpublished working paper, Stanford University.

Lach, Saul and Mark Schankerman. 2003. "Incentives and Invention in Universities." Discussion Paper No. 3916, Centre for Economic Policy Research.

Lakhani, Karim and Eric von Hippel. 2003. "How Open Source Software Works: 'Free' User-to-User Assistance." *Research Policy.* 32:6, pp. 923–43.

Lerner, Josh and Jean Tirole. 2002. "Some Simple Economics of Open Source." *Journal of Industrial Economics.* 52:2, pp. 197–234.

Lerner, Josh and Jean Tirole. 2004a. "Efficient Patent Pools." *American Economic Review.* 94:3, pp. 691–711.

Lerner, Josh and Jean Tirole. 2004b. "A Model of Forum Shopping, with Special Reference to Standard Setting Organizations." NBER Working Paper No. 10664.

Lerner, Josh and Jean Tirole. 2005. "The Scope of Open Source Licensing." *Journal of Law, Economics, and Organization.* 21, forthcoming.

Lerner, Josh, Marcin Strojwas and Jean Tirole. 2003. "Cooperative Marketing Agreements between Competitors: Evidence from Patent Pools." NBER Working Paper No. 9680.

"Microsoft at the Power Point." 2003. *Economist.* September 11.

Murray, Fiona and Scott Stern. 2003. "Do Formal Intellectual Property Rights Hinder the Flow of Scientific Knowledge? Evidence from Patent-Paper Pairs." Unpublished working paper, Massachusetts Institute of Technology and Northwestern University.

Open Source Development Labs. 2004. "OSDL Announces First Chinese Member." January 30; Available at <http://www.osdl.org/newsroom/press_releases/2004/2004_01_30_ beaverton.html>.

President's Information Technology Advisory Committee, Panel on Open Source Software for High End Computing. 2000. "Developing Open Source Software to Advance High End Computing." October; Available at <http://www.hpcc.gov/pubs/pitac/pres-oss-11sep00.pdf>

Raymond, Eric. 1999. *The Cathedral and the Bazaar: Musings on Linux and Open Source by an Accidental Revolutionary.* Cambridge: O'Reilly.

Saint-Paul, Gilles. 2003. "Growth Effects of Non-Proprietary Innovation." *Journal of the European Economic Association: Papers and Proceedings.* 1:2–3, pp. 429–39.

Schmidt, Klaus and Monika Schnitzer. 2003. "Public Subsidies for Open Source? Some Economic Policy Issues of the Software Market." Discussion Paper No. 3793, Centre for Economic Policy Research.

Shapiro, Carl and Hal R. Varian. 2004. "Linux Adoption in the Public Sector." Unpublished working paper, University of California.

Thursby, Jerry and Marie Thursby. 2003. "Has Licensing Changed Academic Research? Issues of Productivity, Faculty Incentives, and Public Policy." Unpublished working paper, Emory University and Georgia Institute of Technology.

Waldman, Michael. 1984. "Job Assignments, Signaling, and Efficiency." *Rand Journal of Economics.* 15:2, pp. 255–67.

35

THE TRANSFORMATION OF OPEN SOURCE SOFTWARE

Brian Fitzgerald

Source: *MIS Quarterly* 30(3) (2006): 587–98.

Abstract

A frequent characterization of open source software is the some-what outdated, mythical one of a collective of supremely talented software hackers freely volunteering their services to produce uniformly high-quality software. I contend that the open source software phenomenon has metamorphosed into a more mainstream and commercially viable form, which I label as OSS 2.0. I illustrate this transformation using a framework of process and product factors, and discuss how the bazaar metaphor, which up to now has been associated with the open source development process, has actually shifted to become a metaphor better suited to the OSS 2.0 product delivery and support process. Overall the OSS 2.0 phenomenon is signific-antly different from its free software antecedent. Its emergence accentuates the fundamental alteration of the basic ground rules in the software landscape, signifying the end of the proprietary-driven model that has prevailed for the past 20 years or so. Thus, a clear understanding of the characteristics of the emergent OSS 2.0 phenomenon is required to address key challenges for research and practice.

Introduction

Just a few years ago, it would have seemed preposterous to suggest that the might of the proprietary software industry, as exemplified by Microsoft, could be threatened by the largely volunteer open source software move-ment. This movement, however, has altered the basic nature of the software industry. On the supply side, fundamental changes have occurred to the development process, reward mechanisms, distribution of development work, and business models that govern how profit can be achieved. On the demand side, the alternatives traditionally available to organizations for software acquisition—buy or build—have been supplemented with another credible alternative—namely, open source. Indeed, a type of Moore's Law effect seems to be taking place as the amount of open source software available increases dramatically every 12 months or so. A range of issues arises also in relation to the altered nature of software support, the need for new models for total cost of ownership (TCO) of software, and perceptions of exposure to the possibility of intellectual property (IP) infringement.

Radical movements often mature to be accommodated into the mainstream. French Impressionist art in the 19th century is a good example. I contend that the open source phenomenon has undergone a significant transformation from its free software origins to a more mainstream, commercially viable form—OSS 2.0, as I term it.[1] This accommodation with the mainstream ensures that the emergent OSS 2.0 phenomenon will continue to thrive as a significant force in the future software landscape. Indeed, it is a harbinger of an end to the current dominance of a proprietary, closed source software model. I illustrate how the quintessential proprietary software company, Microsoft, can appear to satisfy the definition of an open source company, while a quintessential open source company, Red Hat, can appear to resemble a proprietary software company. I identify how OSS 2.0 can accommodate these apparent transformations through achieving a balance between a commercial profit value-for-money proposition while still adhering to acceptable open source community values.

Compounding the fact that the open source phenomenon represents a radical change in the software landscape, it is often mistakenly and paradoxically characterized as a collective of supremely talented developers who volunteer their services to develop very high-quality software by means of a revolutionary new approach. This characterization is a myth as almost every aspect of it can be questioned (Fitzgerald 2005; Michlmayr *et al.* 2005; Rusovan *et al.* 2005; Schach *et al.* 2002). One effect of this outdated characterization is that research to date has focused *inward* on the phenomenon, studying the motivations of individual developers to contribute to OSS projects, or investigating the characteristics of specific OSS products and projects. Such research has been facilitated by the availability of a vast amount of data on mailing lists and portals such as Sourceforge. In the case of the latter, however, it is important to bear in mind that only a small percentage of the 100,000 or so projects are stable and mature.

While some disagreement exists between the free and open source software community as to the definitions of free software versus open source software (www.fsf.org/philosophy/free-software-for-freedom.html), I will not dwell on that here. I first propose a framework to characterize the initial free and open source software (FOSS) phenomenon. While the shift to OSS 2.0 may seem incremental, I use this framework to illustrate the deep nature of the transformation. I also identify key challenges for research and practice that arise as a result of the emergence of OSS 2.0.

Characterizing FOSS

Tushman and Andersen (1986) propose a framework for technological transformation based on two sets of technological factors—namely, process and product. I propose a similar framework to characterize the initial FOSS phenomenon (Table 1, which also presents a characterization of OSS 2.0, discussed in the next section).

FOSS development process

In conventional software development, the development life cycle in its most generic form comprises four broad phases: planning, analysis, design, and implementation. In FOSS development, these stages tended to be configured differently. The first three phases of planning, analysis, and design are concatenated and performed typically by a single developer or small core group. The planning phase is probably best summarized by Raymond's (1999) phrase of a single developer perceiving "an itch worth scratching." This leads to construction of an initial prototype. Given the ideal that a large number of globally distributed developers of different levels of ability and domain expertise should be able to contribute subsequently, the requirements analysis phase was largely superseded. Requirements were taken as generally understood and not needing interaction among developers and end-users. In this regard, FOSS developers were invariably users of the software being developed. This model is perhaps best suited to infrastructure software in horizontal domains. Design decisions also tended to be made in advance before the larger pool of developers starts to contribute. Systems are highly modularized to allow distribution of work and reduce the learning curve for new developers to participate (they can focus on particular subsystems without needing to consider the system in its totality).

In the FOSS development life cycle, the implementation phase consists of several subphases (Feller and Fitzgerald 2002):

- Code: writing code and submitting to the FOSS community for review
- Review: a strength of FOSS is the independent, prompt peer review
- Pre-commit test: the negative implications of breaking the build ensure that contributions are tested carefully before being committed
- Development release: code contributions may be included in the development release within a short time of having been submitted—this rapid implementation being a significant motivator for developers
- Parallel debugging: the so-called Linus' Law ("given enough eyeballs, every bug is shallow") as the large number of potential debuggers on different platforms and system configurations ensures bugs are found and fixed quickly.

Table 1 Characterizing FOSS and OSS 2.0.

Process	FOSS	OSS 2.0

Development Life Cycle	• Planning—"an itch worth scratching"
	• Analysis—part of conventional agreed-upon knowledge in software development
	• Design—firmly based on principles of modularity to accomplish separation of concerns
	• Implementation
	  • Code
	  • Review
	  • Pre-commit test
	  • Development release
	  • Parallel Debugging
	  • Production Release
	(often the planning, analysis, and design phases are done by one person/core group who serve as "a tail-light to follow" in the bazaar)
		• Planning—purposive strategies by major players trying to gain competitive advantage
		  Analysis and design—more complex in spread to vertical domains where business requirements not universally understood
		• Implementation subphases as with FOSS, but the overall development process becomes *less* bazaar-like
		• Increasingly, developers being paid to work on open source

Product Domains	• Horizontal infrastructure (operating systems, utilities, compilers, DBMS, web and print servers)	• More visible IS applications in vertical domains

Primary Business Strategies	• Value-added service-enabling
	• Loss-leader/market-creating
		• Value-added service enabling
		  • Bootstrapping
		  Market-creating
		  • Loss-leader
		  • Dual product/licensing
		  • Cost reduction
		  • Accessorizing
		• Leveraging community development
		• Leveraging the open source brand

Product Support	• Fairly haphazard—much reliance on e-mail lists/bulletin boards, or on support provided by specialized software firms	• Customers willing to pay for a professional, whole-product approach
Licensing	• GPL, LGPL, Artistic License, BSD, and emergence of commercially oriented MPL • Viral term used in relation to licenses	• Plethora of licenses (85 to date validated by OSI or FSF) • Reciprocal term used in relation to licenses

- Production release: a relatively stable, debugged production version of the system is released

The management of this process varies a great deal. Different projects have varying degrees of formalism as to how decisions are made, but the principle of "having a tail-light to follow" (Bezroukov 1999) captures the spirit well. Often, the initial project founder or small core group make the key decisions in accordance with the process outlined in the life cycle above.

FOSS product domains

Due to the globally distributed nature of the development community (most members never meet face-to-face), FOSS products have tended to be infrastructural systems in horizontal domains. Their requirements are part of the general taken-for-granted wisdom of the software development community. Thus, the most successful FOSS products—the Linux operating system, the Apache web server, the Mozilla browser, the GNU C compiler, the Perl scripting language, and MySQL database management system—are all examples of horizontal infrastructure software.

Primary FOSS business strategies

Several FOSS business strategies have been proposed (Hecker 2000; Raymond 1999). Two have been most significant—namely, value-added service-enabling and loss-leader/market-creating.

An early example of the value-added service-enabling model was Cygnus Solutions, which integrated a suite of GNU tools and sold support services and other complementary software products. Red Hat is probably the most well-known proponent of this strategy. Effectively, Red Hat simplifies the task facing end-users in deploying an overall open source solution, such as Linux, that requires complex configuration of different components.

In the loss-leader/market-creating model, the open source product is distributed for free, but with the end goal of enlarging the market for alternative, closed source products and services. For example, the open source Sendmail product enlarges the subsequent market for Sendmail Pro, a product with extra functionality that is distributed for a fee.

FOSS product support

The nature of product support in FOSS has been haphazard and bazaar-like and is different from the proprietary model. Requests for support and solutions are commonly sent to forums such as bulletin boards and mailing lists. In some cases, support may be purchased from a competent third-party provider. For example, Linux support is available from HP or IBM, or a specialized (often local) software firm may offer support and consultancy services. While many organizations are reluctant to rely on bulletin boards for support, they may be equally reluctant to purchase consultancy support to deploy a solution effectively (Fitzgerald and Kenny 2003).

FOSS licensing

Ironically, given the perceptions that FOSS is collectivist and anti-intellectual property, the success of the open source model is due largely to the use of licensing, albeit in a form that counters the normal restrictive sense. Property rights are vested in the author through copyright, with liberal rights granted to others under license. In the FOSS era, the principal licenses have been the GNU Public License (GPL), the Lesser GPL (LGPL), the Artistic License, and the Berkeley System Distribution (BSD). This era also saw the emergence of the commercially oriented Mozilla Public License (MPL), which has been quite influential.

The earliest open source license, the GPL, was created in the mid 1980s to distribute the GNU project software. Most open source software to date has been distributed under the GPL, Linux being one high-profile example. The GPL subverts the traditional concept of restricted access through copyright by ensuring complete, unrestricted access to all open source software and any derivatives. These must also be licensed under the same terms, referred to as "copyleft—all rights reversed." This latter guarantee of the same rights to subsequent users caused such licenses to be termed *viral*.

The GPL is controversial, because it requires that all applications that contain GPL software are also released under a GPL license. A modified version, the Lesser GPL (LGPL) was created when this proved impractical. The LGPL differs from the GPL in two main ways. First, it is intended for use with software libraries (it was initially known as the Library GPL). Second, the software may be linked with proprietary code, which is precluded by the GPL.

Another early license that achieved fairly widespread use is the BSD license, which imposes few restrictions. Its main requirement is the retention and acknowledgment of previous contributors' work.

The FOSS era also saw the creation of the commercially oriented Mozilla Public License (MPL) by Netscape. The MPL was significant because it focused on the conversion of a commercial software product to open source. This process raised significant challenges. It rendered the GPL problematic, because each licensor whose software was incorporated into the Netscape browser would have had to use the same open source license. Netscape was also concerned that an academic-style license would not guarantee that developers would contribute back to the community. It created a new license, the MPL, to address these specific concerns.

Characterizing OSS 2.0

The term *open source* was coined in 1998 to place the phenomenon on a more business-friendly footing than that associated with the ambiguous *free software*. The latter led to the common misperception that individuals or organizations could not make money with free software. The open source initiative succeeded spectacularly well, and the emergent OSS 2.0 has a very strong commercial orientation. Table 1 summarizes how OSS2.0 differs from its FOSS antecedent.

OSS 2.0 development process

The largely voluntary nature of FOSS led to a vacuum in relation to strategic planning (competing with Microsoft on the desktop being one example of a questionable strategy). In the OSS 2.0 development life cycle, in contrast, strategic planning moves to the fore. The haphazard principle of individual developers perceiving "an itch worth scratching" is superseded by corporate firms considering how best to gain competitive advantage from open source. For example, Red Hat has published an architecture roadmap that details its plans to move open source up the software stack toward middleware and management tools. Other proprietary companies have also seen the strategic potential of open source to alter the competitive forces at play in their industry, perhaps to grow market share or undermine competition. For example, IBM is a strong supporter of Linux, because it erodes the profitability of the operating system market and adversely affects competitors like Sun and Microsoft.

Analysis and design

As already discussed, FOSS products were targeted primarily at horizontal infrastructure where requirements and design issues were largely part of the established wisdom, thus facilitating a global developer base. Most business software, however, exists in vertical domains where effective requirements analysis poses real problems. Students and developers without any experience in the application area lack the necessary knowledge to derive the accurate requirements that are a precursor to successful development. In OSS 2.0, therefore, the analysis and design phases have become more deliberate. In many cases, based on the earlier phase of strategic planning, paid developers will be assigned to work on open source products in vertical domains.

Given the increasingly commercial nature of OSS 2.0, more rigorous project management is required to achieve a professional product. As a consequence, a shift is occurring whereby the management of the development process is becoming *less* bazaar-like. This outcome is already evident in the formalized meetings for a number of popular open source products (for example, the

Apache conferences in the United States and Europe, the regular Zope/ Plone development project meetings, and the GNOME annual project conferences) (German 2003). These meetings bring together developers to coordinate and plan further development. The legal incorporation of several open source projects ostensibly reduces the risk of litigation for individual developers (O'Mahony 2005), while allowing these projects to accept donations, perhaps to implement requested functionality.

OSS 2.0 product domains

Interestingly, in the highly competitive software world, several open source products have nudged out proprietary alternatives to emerge as "category killers"—that is, products of sufficiently high quality and popularity that they obviate the need for development of competitive products. Also, OSS 2.0 is moving from deployment as back-office, invisible infrastructure to front-office, highly visible deployment of IS applications in vertical domains. An example is the Beaumont Hospital case study (Fitzgerald and Kenny 2003), where a number of in-house developed applications are being made available on an open source basis to other healthcare agencies. In the context of open source, this development is significant. To date, it has often been assumed that open source products will not affect many vertical domains, because developers will not perceive an "itch worth scratching" there. If, however, organizations in these areas subscribe to the open source philosophy and contribute specialist expertise to open source projects, the model will spread to more vertical applications.

OSS 2.0 business strategies

The FOSS era had two overarching "families" of revenue models—value-added service-enabling and loss-leader market-creating. These models are still applicable in OSS 2.0, but they are further nuanced. Other strategies have also emerged, including leveraging community software development and leveraging the open source brand. Moreover, companies may not stick solely to one of these models and may employ pragmatic hybrids instead.

Value-added service-enabling in OSS 2.0

Building a lucrative service and support business on top of open source was discussed earlier. Companies like Red Hat and Novell have realized large revenues through annual subscriptions. This bootstrapping model is taken to a higher level in OSS 2.0, where open source products are treated as a platform—somewhat similar to a highway or a telecommunications infrastructure. A company bootstraps its own value-added specialty on top of this infrastructure. Small software companies can become part of an

246

ecosystem offering consultancy, service, and support of open source products. One example would be to purchase a single support license from MySQL and sell local support to a number of customers. Roughly 90 percent of customer support requests are probably easily dealt with directly, and the 10 percent of complicated issues could be passed to MySQL for resolution, and then the solution passed back to the local customers.

High-profile organizations like Amazon, Google, and Salesforce.com take advantage of the reliability and low cost of open source to create a platform on which they can offer value-added services in their own business domains. For the most part, the use of open source is invisible to their customers. These companies also customize open source products to suit their internal needs. Moreover, because they are not redistributing software, they are not faced with any problems of noncompliance with the GPL.

Market creation strategies in OSS 2.0

The other FOSS era business strategy discussed above is the loss-leader market-creating strategy. In OSS 2.0, the emphasis is firmly focused on market creation through a loss-leader approach and involves products with dual licensing, cost reduction, and accessorizing.

Integrated development environments (IDEs) have illustrated this approach. Traditionally, IDEs were expensive proprietary applications, which were especially lucrative if they attracted a large license-paying user base. When IBM chose to move its Eclipse IDE to open source, the decision seemed surprising because the source code was valued at $40 million. IBM has had massive compensations, however. It substantially increased its popularity as a development platform and expanded the market for its complementary products. Several other companies have now also moved their proprietary IDEs to open source, including Sun with NetBeans and BEA with Beehive.

Several examples of dual product/licensing exist. MySQL provides a high-profile example of such a strategy. Millions of free copies of MySQL have been downloaded. Of these, about one customer in every thousand has purchased a commercial license from MySQL. This proportion seems small, but it amounts to thousands of fee-paying customers. Other dual-product strategies include Red Hat with Fedora and Enterprise Linux, Sun with StarOffice and OpenOffice, and Iona Technology with Celtix and Artix.

Companies can also leverage the commodification effect that has occurred with open source. They take advantage of open source in terms of its low cost, reliability, and portability across platforms. For example, Oracle can reduce the overall cost of database implementation for its customers, and IBM can reduce the overall cost of servers. In the area of embedded systems, open source is fast becoming dominant. Here, companies are concerned with open standards, stability, high performance, small footprint, and the ability to run on generic hardware. A vibrant, responsive development community exists and is willing to port to other platforms and write extra utilities.

Several companies leverage open source as a base upon which they offer products other than software. For example, HP promotes open source in areas that facilitate the deployment of its hardware, while the O'Reilly publishing house has earned significant revenue from books related to the open source concept.

Leveraging community software development

Leveraging the talents of the open source community allows companies to increase development productivity, with the added benefit that much work may be done for free. Thus, hundreds of Eclipse plug-ins have been developed. Also, Apple's initiative in starting the Darwin open source project to develop part of its operating system facilitates extra development contributions that for the most part are free. In addition, Apple's reputation in the open source community has improved. The phenomenon becomes circular, as the extra functionality increases the software's attractiveness to other developers. These, in turn, contribute additional functionality.

Leveraging the open source brand

While patents and copyrights are key issues with respect to free software, another IP mechanism, the trademark or brand, could become significant with OSS 2.0. For example, Oracle promotes the "unbreakable Linux" slogan. Also, an increasing number of government agencies and public administrations (traditionally the largest consumers of software) are mandating that open source be a priority option, even to the extent of requiring formal justification for not choosing an open source solution if one is available. This will ensure the open source brand becomes even more important in the future.

OSS 2.0 product support

In the past, developers have referred to the "exhilarating succession of problem-solving challenges" in installing open source products (Sanders 1998). As the OSS 2.0 model becomes more mainstream, however, time-impoverished professionals are unlikely to seek exhilaration in this manner. Further, many organizations have difficulty relying on bulletin boards for their support. As OSS 2.0 evolves, customers will want professional service—support, training, and certification—and will be prepared to pay for it.

The whole-product approach: from bazaar
process to bazaar product

The particular characteristics of OSS 2.0 position it as a good exemplar of the "whole-product" concept of a market-driven business approach that seeks to deliver a complete solution to the customer in terms of products and services (Moore 1999). The open source phenomenon is market-driven and, as discussed above, places a great deal of emphasis on services. It adopts a professional approach to achieving value by establishing a profitable business venture for which customers are willing to pay the going rate. In this scenario, developers do the coding. Others complete the business model by adding sales and marketing services—necessary activities but ones in which developers may not be interested. The OSS 2.0 whole-product approach is also larger than a single company or software product or service. Indeed, the network benefits of open source arise as a result of the size of the overall community and ecosystem. Thus, a network of interested parties with complementary capabilities can form an ecosystem to offer a professional product and service in an agile, bazaar-friendly manner. Customer service requests can be routed to the most appropriate expert partner in the network, perhaps even to the developer who wrote the actual code. In this manner, the OSS 2.0 brand increases trustworthiness to achieve market-leader status. Such convenience networks exist already in conventional business circles. The LVMH (Louis Vuitton Moet Hennessy) brand is an international network of almost 50 luxury brand leaders in fashion, wines and spirits, watches, jewelry, and cosmetics (www.lvmh.com). From a business perspective, this network of well-known brands creates the ultimate luxury brand status, LVMH. Nonetheless, individual businesses can still pursue their own interests independently.

In OSS 2.0, the bazaar metaphor therefore shifts from just being associated with the development process (Raymond, 1999), which becomes *less* bazaar-like, to product delivery and support, which becomes *more* bazaar-like. Many companies will find profitable opportunities in customer support.

The claim by large proprietary software companies that open source would stifle local software industries is proving unfounded. A more-likely scenario is that small service-centric software companies will thrive by providing training, technical support, and consultancy for local organizations that deploy open source products.

OSS 2.0 licensing

In OSS 2.0, a plethora of license types has emerged. The Open Source Initiative (OSI) and the Free Software Foundation (FSF) has approved almost 100 distinct licenses overall to date between them (but with little general agreement as only about one-third of these licenses are approved by

Table 2 A Typology of OSS 2.0 Licenses.

Reciprocal	GPL, LGPL, Open Source License (OSL)
Academic Style	Academic Free License, Apache License, BSD, MIT
Corporate Type	MPL, Qt Public License, Sun Public License, IBM Public License, Apple Public License, Eclipse Public License
Non-Approved (e.g., Shared Source family)	Microsoft Shared Source Initiative Licenses: (Microsoft Community License, Microsoft Permissive License), Sun Community Source License (SCSL)

both) (Lyddy-Collins 2005). The licenses can be grouped into four broad categories: reciprocal licenses (as per the FOSS era), academic-style licenses, corporate licenses, and non-approved (by FSF or OSI) licenses such as Microsoft's Shared Source family of licenses (Table 2).

In OSS 2.0, the term *viral* has been adjudged to have negative connotations. The preferred term is *reciprocal*. Reciprocal licenses such as the GPL and LGPL have already been discussed above in relation to FOSS licensing. Another variation, the Open Software License (OSL), was created in 2002 as an alternative to the GPL that would be more acceptable to corporate users and developers. Again, this emphasizes the continued progression toward corporate and commercial compatibility, which is at the heart of OSS 2.0. Interestingly, while the FSF has issued warnings against this license, Linus Torvalds has adopted it for open source development other than the Linux kernel.

Corporate-style licenses are central to OSS 2.0. They reveal a potential friction point in OSS 2.0, because they seek to benefit corporate interests rather than the open source development community. As mentioned already, these are generally based on the Mozilla Public License (MPL). Typically, they seek to allow open source code to be mixed with proprietary code and to ensure that corporate sponsors retain control of derivative works.

The non-approved category of licenses for OSS 2.0 is perhaps the most interesting. It pushes the boundaries of proprietary software as this sector seeks to accommodate the open source model. Two significant exemplars are the Sun Community Source License (SCSL) and the Microsoft Shared Source Initiative family of licenses.

The realization that "transparency increases trust" (Matusow 2005) has led to Microsoft's Shared Source Initiative. Microsoft has recently converged on three core shared source licenses:

• *Microsoft Reference License* allows licensees to merely view source code. This practice is regarded with deep suspicion by the open source community, which foresees potential transgressions of patents by developers who copy the code.

- *Microsoft Community License* is based on the Mozilla Public License and is intended for collaborative projects.
- *Microsoft Permissive License* is similar to the BSD license and effectively allows "licensees to review, modify, redistribute, and sell works with no royalties paid to Microsoft" (Matusow 2005).

Both the FSF and OSI originally agreed that the Shared Source Initiative was neither free nor open. Nonetheless, it will be increasingly difficult to exclude licenses, such as the Microsoft Permissive License, that comply with the hybrid model of OSS 2.0.

Microsoft is, therefore, likely to be a major player in OSS 2.0. It has already distributed an open source product for some time—Windows Services for Unix—and has publicly acknowledged that Windows 2000 and Windows XP use open source BSD code. Also, it has a number of high-profile open source projects on SourceForge. Microsoft has abstracted some of the key ideas from open source. Recognizing the power of the social and community identification aspects of open source, it has introduced the Most Valued Professionals (MVP) initiative. It has extended access to source code to this select group. The Open Value policy permits sales representatives to offer extreme discounts and zero percent financing to small businesses that might switch to zero-cost open source (Roy 2003).

Summary

The above discussion illustrates how the OSS 2.0 phenomenon is significantly different from its FOSS antecedent. The development process becomes less bazaar-like as strategic planning becomes paramount. Analysis and design are more deliberate as the model spreads to vertical product domains. Developers are increasingly being paid to work on open source. More sophisticated business models are emerging and employed in a hybrid fashion. Customers are willing to pay the going rate for the whole product in terms of support, which in turn can be delivered by a bazaar network of interested parties that provide varied but complementary services. Licensing also moves to the fore as proprietary companies produce licenses that comply with the open source definition, while open source companies seek to raise money through licensing. Given this complex melting pot, a number of significant implications and challenges for research and practice emerge.

Implications and challenges for research and practice

The discussion above indicates several issues that provide key challenges for research and practice (Table 3). As is appropriate in an applied discipline, these are not completely distinct. Challenges for practice have a research

Table 3 Key Issues for Research and Practice.

Research
- Transferring lessons from open source development to conventional development (inner source)
  - Offshoring—globally distributed software development
  - Open code-sharing, large-scale peer-review, community development model
- Expanded role of users and altered user-developer relationship
- Elaboration of business models
- Derivation of appropriate TCO models

Practice
- Achieving balance between value-for-money versus acceptable community values
- Implementing the whole-product approach
- Stimulating development in vertical domains
- Safeguarding against IPR infringement

---

angle and vice versa. Some research initiatives that appear relevant to addressing these challenges are also identified.

Implications and challenges for research

Transferring lessons from open source to conventional development

While open source may not represent a real paradigm shift in software development (Fitzgerald 2005), the model is an extremely successful exemplar of globally distributed development. It is attracting considerable attention in the current climate of outsourcing and off-shoring. Organizations are seeking to emulate open source success on traditional development projects, through initiatives variously labeled as *inner source, corporate source,* or *community source* (Dinkelacker and Garg 2001; Gurbani *et al.* 2005).

Other open source principles—such as open sharing of source code, large-scale independent peer review, the community development model, and the expanded role of users—also have important implications. In the traditional model of software development, users and developers are often located in separate departments. They sometimes have little mutual respect or voluntary interaction. The user–developer relationship in open source has typically been different. Early open source developers were often users of the products. As OSS 2.0 has emerged, this situation has changed. In the absence of a traditional vendor, users need to become involved more intimately in the development process, as technical staff cannot simply send a checklist of requirements to the vendor to ascertain if needs will be met. Deploying open source can lead to a sense of shared adventure that is not common in the proprietary software arena. Furthermore, users may be more willing to sacrifice certain desired functionality if open source products could not easily provide it (Norris 2004).

Elaboration of business models

Much research is already being undertaken to refine and elaborate the business strategies discussed earlier (e.g., Feller *et al.* 2006; Koenig 2004; Krishnamurthy 2005; Onetti and Capobianco 2005). Nonetheless, a more-careful definition of the concept is needed. For example, the term *business model* is frequently used loosely in the context of open source. A useful definition of business model suggests it comprises three components: value, revenue, and logistics (Mahadevan 2000). The value component represents the value proposition for customers and vendors, the revenue component focuses on how organizations can earn revenue, and the logistics component focuses on supply chain issues. Revenue generation has been the primary focus for most of the research on open source business models. As the earlier discussion of OSS 2.0 business strategies illustrates, however, the value proposition and the logistics of the whole product across the overall supply chain are paramount in OSS 2.0. More analysis is needed in these areas.

Deriving appropriate total cost of ownership (TCO) measures for OSS 2.0

Calculating the total cost of ownership (TCO) of software is a complex, multifaceted issue. It requires consideration of many factors, including software purchase, maintenance and upgrade costs, hardware purchase and maintenance costs, personnel training, and legal and administrative costs (Russo *et al.* 2005). Given this complexity, proprietary and open source advocates predictably have each claimed a lower TCO (Wheeler 2005). Nonetheless, conventional TCO measures may not be suited to the open source phenomenon. Less-obvious benefits accrue due to network externality effects and a more cooperative developer-user relationship.

A promising strand of research that could suit the dynamics of open source is based on the theory of real options investment analysis (Fichman 2004). Real options analysis is appropriate where high levels of flexibility and uncertainty exist (characteristics of open source environments). In terms of flexibility, considerable scope surrounds which products or functions may be implemented and how the software might be customized. Also, the zero-cost aspect offers considerable flexibility in terms of choosing when implementation occurs. Uncertainty arises because no "royal road" to fail-safe open source implementation exists.

Implications and challenges for practice

Value for money versus adhering to acceptable community values

The ambiguous term *free* may have been the key word for FOSS, where both its meanings (i.e., free as in *zero cost*, and free as in *unrestricted access*) were significant. *Value*, an even more ambiguous term, will be the key word for OSS 2.0. Two of the term's connotations are especially significant: *value for money* and *acceptable community values*. The integration of open source into the commercial arena and the associated desire to create profit represents a critical source of tension, given the concomitant need to achieve a balance with collectivist, public-good community values—an inevitable legacy from the more ideologically driven Free Software community. Both connotations of value are discussed here.

Value for money

OSS 2.0 can dramatically alter the economic dynamics of a marketplace. Despite the vast sums of money involved and the enormous economic potential of OSS 2.0, it erodes certain hitherto profitable markets, for example, the multibillion dollar operating system market. Such a market destruction strategy is captured in the mantra, "If you can't be the number one product in a sector, then open source it." As OSS 2.0 emerges, those involved are neither driven primarily by ideology nor seeking to make vast fortunes. They simply wish to earn a reasonable livelihood from their efforts (Everitt 2004). Both customers and developers need to perceive value for money in OSS 2.0. Free as in zero cost is replaced by a value-for-money concern, and OSS 2.0 customers are prepared to pay for a professional service. For instance, many companies are prepared to pay a fee for StarOffice with associated support and warranty, in preference to adopting the zero-cost, OpenOffice alternative.

Acceptable community values

OSS 2.0 blurs the distinction between open source and proprietary software. Key open source players such as Red Hat and Novell's SUSE Linux business unit position their Linux distributions to be more similar to a proprietary model. Traditional proprietary companies, such as HP, IBM, and Microsoft, move more toward open source. Nevertheless, in the OSS 2.0 model, these companies must still satisfy certain criteria in relation to acceptable community values (a significant challenge for OSS 2.0). Large commercial organizations are not always well perceived within the open source community. Companies such as IBM, Sun, and HP support open source initiatives, but their support for patents is clearly at odds with the open source philosophy. Also, the quintessential patron of open source, Red Hat, could struggle in future as its policies increasingly conflict with community spirit and values. Use of subscription agreements and effective customer lock-ins through confidential service bulletins are close to the boundary of acceptable community values. Also, MySQL's decision to port to SCO's OpenServer platform, although a profitable venture, has met with strong criticism because of the negative feelings toward the SCO group within the open source community. The power of community should not be underestimated. A telling example was the attempt by Caldera to sell its Linux distribution, which failed due to the extremely negative reaction of the open source community.

Within the overall community, the spirit of OSS 2.0 can lead to positive network externalities. In the Beaumont Hospital case (Fitzgerald and Kenny 2003), users of the same open source products in Finland traveled to Ireland to volunteer support and offer extra functionality that they had developed. The expectation was that Beaumont would reciprocate by making available any extra functionality they developed. Cooperation of this nature is rare in the proprietary marketplace, but it is symptomatic of the strong community value orientation of open source.

Implementing the whole-product approach

I have already discussed how a bazaar network of companies can collaborate to offer a whole-product approach to customers. In addition to providing a customized professional support service, the whole-product bazaar network can satisfy other emerging business needs. For instance, the plethora of open source products currently available and the lack of vendors to provide marketing information cause a large knowledge gap. An up-to-date catalog of high-quality open source products is needed which could provide details on the functionality offered by various products, the types of support available, training needs, reference sites of deployment, and companies offering support.

Stimulating open source in vertical domains

Early open source products tended to involve horizontal infrastructure where requirements are part of conventional wisdom. Developers with different backgrounds, or even students, could contribute. In vertical domains, however, business requirements are more complex and demand more-specialized knowledge. A significant challenge is to stimulate open source development in these domains. An example in the healthcare sector is the Beaumont Hospital case mentioned earlier. As more purposeful strategic planning takes place in OSS 2.0, complementary development strategies will be enacted to provide a complete portfolio of open source products.

Likewise, in the education sector, some cooperative initiatives have emerged to promote use of open source (e.g., www.osef.org; www.ossite.org; www.schoolforge.net).

Safeguarding against IPR infringement

While open source was a fringe phenomenon, its relative obscurity offered some safety from litigation. Once it entered the mainstream, the threat of litigation arising from IPR infringements became real—for example, the SCO Group's lawsuit against IBM over alleged patent infringement in Linux. The ultimate goal of IP protection mechanisms such as patents could be summarized as *the publication of nontrivial ideas, with an explicit guarantee of continued availability, which seeks to protect the interest of the small players, for the overall betterment of society, as others learn from and improve on the original ideas.* Interestingly, this definition also captures the open source phenomenon well. However, the stimulation of innovation and creativity, which should be the fundamental rationale behind IP protection, has failed abjectly in the software area (Bessen and Hunt 2004). Ironically, even though open source has often been about replicating proprietary products, the ingenuity of the global development community has allowed innovative new functionality to emerge—for example, the OpenOffice suite and the Mozilla Firefox browser.

Warranties and indemnification against IP infringements are key issues for OSS 2.0. A number of initiatives exist, but all are limited in scope. For example, Red Hat offers a warranty against any infringement in its Red Hat Enterprise Linux distribution (although this warranty just promises that Red Hat will replace any infringing code). Similarly, Novell has offered customers of its SUSE Linux an indemnification against copyright (but not patent) infringements. HP also offers its customers an indemnification, but only for claims made by SCO. JBoss offers indemnification to its customers, but limited to the value of the customer's contract. Meanwhile, some third parties, such as Open Source Risk Management, are selling indemnification protection.

Concluding remarks

The open source field today and the decision support systems (DSS) field in the past have interesting similarities. Both have drawn together a wide range of researchers from disparate disciplines. For DSS, however, the consequence has not been benign. For instance, Keen lamented DSS research having been "co-opted and trivialize . . . by lab-experiment-academics," and concluded that "identity is easily blurred and eroded when the purposive focus of the research is lost and the topic area then dominates" (Keen 1991, pp. 37–38). I believe a similar situation could occur in open source research

—indeed, the problems could be exacerbated as researchers take advantage of the ready availability of large online data repositories (where much of the data may be of little real value), and continue to focus their research efforts inward on the phenomenon to repeatedly study project characteristics and developer motivation, for example. Such research has been valuable, but a more purposive agenda is needed—one that also looks outward at the open source phenomenon in general and at the emergent OSS 2.0 phenomenon in particular.

Acknowledgments

I would like to record my gratitude to Joe Feller, Rishab Aiyer Ghosh, Carlo Daffara, Franco Gasperoni, and Maha Shaikh for feedback on this topic, and also the *MIS Quarterly* reviewers. The work was supported by EU project grants, CALIBRE and COSPA, and by a Science Foundation Ireland Principal Investigator Grant, 02/IN.1/I108.

Note

1 Because this article focuses on the evolution and transformation of the open source phenomenon, terminology is an issue. I use the term *FOSS* to refer to the initial era of Free and Open Source Software. I use *OSS* 2.0 to refer to the phenomenon which I see emerging now, and I use *open source software* to refer to the phenomenon in general.

References

Bessen, J., and Hunt, R. "An Empirical Look at Software Patents," Working Paper No. 03-17/R, Research on Innovation, Boston, 2004 (available online at http://www.researchoninnovation.org/swpat.pdf).

Bezroukov, N. "Open Source Software Development as a Special Type of Academic Research (Critique of Vulgar Raymondism)," *FirstMonday* (4:10), October 1999 (available online at http://www.firstmonday.org/issues/issue4_10/bezroukov/).

Dinkelacker, J., and Garg, P. "Applying Open Source Concepts to a Corporate Environment," in *Proceedings of 1st Workshop on Open Source Software Engineering*, Toronto, May 15, 2001 (available online at http://opensource.ucc.ie/icse2001).

Everitt, P. "Zope: Open Source, Revisited," First CALIBRE International Conference, Hague, November 19, 2004 (available online at http://www.calibre.ie/hague/docs/3_PEveritt_Zope.pdf).

Feller, J., Finnegan, P., and Hayes, J. "Open Source Networks: An Exploration of Business Model and Agility Issues," *Proceedings of the 14th European Conference on Information Systems*, Göteborg, Sweden, June 12–14, 2006.

Feller, J., and Fitzgerald, B. *Understanding Open Source Software Development*, Addison-Wesley; London, 2002.

Fichman, R. "Real Options and IT Platform Adoption: Implications for Theory and Practice," *Information Systems Research* (15:3), 2004, pp. 132–154.

Fitzgerald, B. "Has Open Source a Future?," in *Perspectives on Free and Open Source Software*, J. Feller, B. Fitzgerald, S. Hissam, and K. Lakhani (eds.), MIT Press, Cambridge, MA, 2005, pp. 121–140.

Fitzgerald, B., and Kenny, T. "Open Source Software in the Trenches: Lessons from a Large Scale Implementation," in *Proceedings of 24th International Conference on Information Systems*, S. T. March, A. Massey, and J. I. DeGross (eds.), Seattle, December 2003, pp. 316–326.

German, D. M. "GNOME: A Case of Open Source Global Software Development," in *Proceedings of the International Workshop on Global Software Development*, Portland, OR, May 9, 2003, pp. 39–43, gsd2003.cs.uvic.ca/gsd2003proceedings.pdf).

Gurbani, V. K., Garvert, A., and Herbsleb, J. D. "A Case Study of Open Source Tools and Practices in a Commercial Setting," in *Proceedings of the 5th Workshop on Open Source Software Engineering*, St. Louis, MO, May 17, 2005, pp. 24–29.

Hecker, F. "Setting Up Shop: The Business of Open-Source Software," June 2000 (available online at http://www.hecker.org/writings/setting-up-shop).

Keen, P. "Keynote Address: Relevance and Rigor in Information Systems Research," in *Information Systems Research: Contemporary Approaches and Emergent Traditions*, H. Nissen, H. Klein, and R. Hirschheim (eds.), Elsevier Publishers, Amsterdam, 1991, pp. 27–49.

Koenig, J. "Seven Open Source Business Strategies for Competitive Advantage," *IT Manager's Journal*, May 14, 2004 (available online at http://management. itmanagersjournal.com/article.pl?sid=04/05/10/2052216&tid=85&tid=4).

Krishnamurthy, S. "An Analysis of Open Source Business Models," in *Perspectives on Free and Open Source Software*, J. Feller, B. Fitzgerald, S. Hissam, and K. Lakhani (eds.), MIT Press, Cambridge, MA, 2005, pp. 279–296.

Lyddy-Collins, N. *Perspectives on Open-Source Software Licensing Policy in a Commercial Software Development Environment*, npublished Master's Thesis, University of Limerick, 2005.

Mahadevan, B. "Business Models for Internet-Based Ecommerce: An Anatomy," *California Management Review* (42:4), 2000, pp. 55–69.

Matusow, J. "Shared Source: The Microsoft Perspective," in *Perspectives on Free and Open Source Software*, J. Feller, B. Fitzgerald, S. Hissam, and K. Lakhani (eds.), MIT Press, Cambridge, MA, 2005, pp. 329–346.

Michlmayr, M., Hunt, F., and Probert, D. "Quality Practices and Problems in Free Software," in *Proceedings of First International Conference on Open Source (OSS2005)*, M. Scotto and G. Succi (eds.), Genoa, Italy, July 11–15, 2005, pp. 24–28.

Moore, G. *Crossing the Chasm*, Harper, New York, 1999.

Norris, J. "Mission-Critical Development with Open Source Software: Lessons Learned," *IEEE Software* (21:1), 2004, pp. 42–49.

O'Mahony, S. "Non-Profit Foundations and their Role in Community-Firm Software Collaboration," in *Perspectives on Free and Open Source Software*, J. Feller, B. Fitzgerald, S. Hissam, and K. Lakhani (eds.), MIT Press, Cambridge, 2005, pp. 393–414.

Onetti, A., and Capobianco, F. "Open Source and Business Model Innovation: The Funambol Case," in *Proceedings of First International Conference on Open Source (OSS2005)*, M. Scotto and G. Succi (eds.), Genoa, Italy, July 11–15, 2005, pp. 224–227.

Raymond, E. *The Cathedral and the Bazaar: Musings on Linux and Open Source by an Accidental Revolutionary*, O'Reilly, Sebastapol, CA, 1999.

Roy, A. "Microsoft vs. Linux: Gaining Traction," *Chartered Financial Analyst* (9:5), 2003, pp. 36–39.

Rusovan, S., Lawford, M., and Parnas, D. "Open Source Software Development: Future or Fad?," in *Perspectives on Free and Open Source Software*, J. Feller, B. Fitzgerald, S. Hissam, and K. Lakhani (eds.), MIT Press, Cambridge, MA, 2005, pp. 107–122.

Russo, B., Braghin, B., Gasperi, P., Sillitti, A., and Succi, G. "Defining TCO for the Transition to Open Source Systems," in *Proceedings of First International Conference on Open Source (OSS2005)*, M. Scotto and G. Succi (eds.), Genoa, Italy, July 11–15, 2005, pp. 108–112.

Sanders, J. "Linux, Open Source, and Software's Future," *IEEE Software*, September/October 1998, pp. 88–91.

Schach, S., Jin, B., and Wright, D. "Maintainability of the Linux Kernel," in *Proceedings of 2nd Workshop on Open Source Software Engineering*, J. Feller, B. Fitzgerald, S. Hissam, and K. Lakhani (eds.), Orlando, FL, 2002 (available at http://opensource.ucc.ie/icse2002).

Torvalds, L., and Diamond, D. *Just for Fun: The Story of an Accidental Revolutionary*, Harper Collins, New York, 2001.

Tushman, M., and Anderson, P. "Technological Discontinuities and Organizational Environments," *Administrative Science Quarterly* (31), 1986, pp. 439–465.

Wheeler, D. "Why Open Source Software/Free Software (OSS/FS, FLOSS, or FOSS)? Look at the Numbers!," November 2005 (available online at http://www.dwheeler.com/oss_fs_why.html).

Part 5

INEQUALITY AND THE DIGITAL DIVIDE

36

TOWARD A CRITIQUE OF THE INFORMATION ECONOMY

Patricia Arriaga

Source: *Media, Culture and Society* 7(3) (1985): 271–96.

Introduction

Over the past decade several scholars have argued that society is moving into a new stage of development: Dahrendorf's post-capitalist society; Barnet's post-petroleum; Brezinzky's technotronic; Etzioni's post-modern; and the most popular one, coined by Harvard sociologist Daniel Bell, the post-industrial society (Bell, 1980, 1973). One of the basic premises of the post-industrial society theories is that economic activity is moving into a new stage, the information stage. The basic idea is that knowledge and information are becoming the strategic resources and transforming agents in the post-industrial era. It is argued that the economy is shifting from a goods producing, industrial society to a service, information-based economy with the emergence of scientists, technicians and administrators as the pre-eminent social class, replacing business entrepreneurs and skilled workers.

This information economy is defined as one in which a very high percentage of the labour force is engaged in the production, processing and distribution of information goods and services; a considerable percentage of wages and salaries derive from information jobs and activities; and a high percentage of the gross national product (GNP) can be attributed to the production and distribution of information goods and services. One of the basic indicators used in the literature to analyse the transition of an industrial society to a post-industrial or information society is the composition of the labour force. The larger the employment in information activities, the closer an economy is to the post-industrial era. It is the purpose of this article to concentrate on this specific claim of information economy theory by analysing the nature of information labour within the debate on productive and unproductive labour and its impact on the process of capitalist accumulation.

The information economy: basic premises

As components of US domestic activity, the information industries have received a good deal of attention. Until recently there was little empirical evidence on the economic importance of information activities, with most researchers relying on Machlup's studies on the knowledge industries. As early as 1960 Machlup (1962) brought to light the significance of information industries in the national economy by formulating estimates of the proportion of the GNP accounted for by 'knowledge production' in the US. He concluded that total knowledge or information production accounted for almost 29 percent of the adjusted GNP in 1985 and that 32.4 percent of total employee compensation was accounted for by information occupations.

In an effort to overcome the limitations of previous studies and to generate a conceptual scheme that would distinguish an information sector, Porat (1973) broke down the National Income and Product Accounts and the Input-Output Matrix of the US economy for 1967. He concluded that 46 percent of the GNP was represented by information activity, and nearly half the labour force held some sort of 'informational' job, earning 53 percent of labour income. Porat argues that the structure of the labour force is a basic indicator of a nation's stage of development.

> Agricultural activities, which engaged 50% of the US labor force in the 1860's now occupy less than 4%. Industrial activities, which engaged nearly 40% of the workforce in the early 40's now occupy around 20%. And informational occupations, which engaged only 10% of the workforce at the turn of the century now account for 46% of all jobs. (Porat, 1978: 4)[1]

The OECD, wanting to establish the degree to which its member countries had already been transformed from industrial to information economies, conducted an analysis similar to Porat's (OECD, 1981, 1976). OECD findings point to the same trends observed for the US, showing that information jobs have increased at an average rate of 3 percent over five-year periods and that approximately 22 percent of the labour force in most OECD member countries is engaged in information activities.

The theoretical arguments and the empirical evidence presented by these studies, among others,[2] advance the hypothesis that the transition to the information economy is an irreversible and necessary process and that the only way to economic growth is the road to the information economy.

> The urgent need to go from an industrial stage to an information stage is, starting from today, valid in all places regardless of the level of industrialization, development or wealth of any society or any

nation. The transition from the old mode of production to the new one is valid in all places and in all times.

(Servan-Schreiber, 1982)

The US is now an information economy and Japan and most European countries are rapidly being transformed into information societies. Developing countries will have to emerge as information economies if they are to attain their long-desired development.

> Developed countries are rapidly evolving into information economies, and given the increasing internationalization of trade and interdependence, developing countries will also have to become information economies if they are to achieve higher economic growth rates.
>
> (Sweeney, 1981: 113)

If the composition of the Mexican labour force is analysed according to the four main divisions proposed by Porat it is possible to see that information labour in Mexico has continuously increased over the years, representing in 1980 29 percent of the Mexican labour force. If these data are compared to those obtained in the 1970s by the OECD, one can see that the participation of the Mexican labour force in information activities in 1970 (23.5 percent of the workforce) was as high as that of any OECD country in that year.

On the basis of this data one could argue that somehow Mexico is on the road to becoming an information economy. However, it is important to stress that there are still very significant differences between developed and developing countries. In developed countries agricultural labour represents the smallest part of the work force. In a developing country such as Mexico, although agricultural labour has decreased from 61.8 percent of the labour force in 1950 to 32.2 percent in 1980, it still represents the sector with the highest labour force participation. It is important to consider that in the Mexican agricultural sector a substantial amount of subsistence agriculture can still be found. Because this type of agriculture does not participate in the system of capitalist relations of production and/or distribution in a direct and substantive way, one would expect the official statistics to be conservative with respect to estimates of this type of labour. In addition the 2.3 percent of the US labour force engaged in agricultural activities is responsible for one of the largest agricultural trade surpluses in the world, while the 32.2 percent share of the Mexican work force devoted to agricultural activities does not produce enough to feed even the Mexican population, not to mention the trade deficit in this sector.

In developed countries, information activities, as well as services, tend to increase in relative and absolute terms, while industrial and agricultural labour tend to decrease. Analysis of the Mexican data shows that industrial labour tends to increase both in relative and absolute terms, although information activities and services increase at a faster rate. But the service sector in an advanced economy is formed mainly by business services while the same sector in a developing economy encompasses all kinds of services, including personal services which are usually very large and a useful category for dumping disguised unemployment.

As absurd as this might sound, the information economy arguments have been used already to justify the 'deindustrialization' processes in countries like Argentina and Chile. The argument has been to avoid wasting resources on industrialization when they can be devoted to the 'informatization' process and with it achieve modernization much faster (Fajnzylber, 1982). These arguments have also been used to justify intensive sales efforts of telecommunication goods and services as well as computers and data services to developing countries by the developed countries and their transnational corporations (TNCs). The nature of this information labour which seems to play such an important role on the 'road' to the information economy needs to be critically analysed.

On the nature of information labour

The Marxian definition of productive and unproductive labour

First we must define what is meant by information labour. Porat (1973) defined it as all labour related to information activities. Thus he included the following workers: (1) workers whose output or primary activity is the production and selling of knowledge, like scientists, inventors, teachers, librarians and journalists; (2) workers who handle information within firms such as secretaries, messengers, managers, clerks and typists; and (3) workers who operate information machines and information technology that support the two previous categories, such as telephone operators and drivers. For orthodox economic theory the specific characteristics of this information labour are irrelevant. The definition of labour poses no problems, mainly because everything is defined in the market. If someone is willing to pay for a good or service, and it is demanded in the market, the labour that produces it is considered to be productive labour. For orthodox theory there is no formal definition of unproductive labour.

Unlike neoclassical theory, for classical political economy the distinction between productive and unproductive labour is crucial, mainly because of its relation to the analysis of the accumulation and reproduction of capital. Labour that contributed to the creation of the 'wealth of nations' was considered productive, while labour that used up a portion of existing wealth without resulting in the creation of new wealth was considered unproductive labour.[3] Wealth considered in terms of its 'materiality' led Smith, Ricardo and even Malthus to agree that productive labour produced a material or physical object while unproductive labour produced a service.

In Marxian analysis the nature of the commodities into which labour is materialized is totally irrelevant. They can be 'physical' (goods) or 'non-physical' (services) use-values and they can be destined for reproductive or unreproductive consumption. The distinction between productive and unproductive is derived not from the nature of the commodity produced but from the social relations of production within which commodities are produced. Productive labour is exchanged against capital *and* results in the creation of surplus value. Hence the classical and now popular distinction between goods and services is irrelevant for the analysis of productive labour. The characterization of labour as productive or unproductive does not lie in the nature of labour nor of the commodities produced but in the nature of the social relationship of labour to capital.

The Marxian definition of labour considers three different levels of abstraction. At the first level[4] Marx deals only with the process of *capitalist production*, that is industrial capital per se. At this level productive labour is all labour exchanged against capital and productive of surplus value while unproductive labour is all labour exchanged against revenue. Productive workers use up use-values to create new wealth with their labour. The value of the final product can be divided into dead labour, C (the value of the means of production used in the labour process), and living labour, L. The latter in turn can be divided into necessary labour, that is, the value of the means of consumption that is consumed by workers, V, and surplus value (or surplus product), S. The ratio S/V is called by Marx the rate of surplus value. *Ceteris paribus*, the higher the rate of surplus value, the larger the amount of surplus value appropriated by the capitalists and the larger the profit.

It is very difficult to directly increase S by either lengthening the working day or reducing wages. Surplus value has to be increased in an indirect way by increasing the productivity of labour and lowering costs through the process of mechanization. When this process reaches those sectors devoted to the production of commodities that constitute the real wage, V, then the value of workers' consumption requirements is decreased, and with it the rate of surplus value is increased.

Marx argued that the production of 'physical' use-values made up most productive labour and that labour engaged in the production of services was so small that it could be left out of the analysis:

> [Sometimes] production cannot be separated from the act of its producer, as is the case with all performing artists, actors, teachers, doctors, parsons, etc. . . . All these manifestations of capitalist production in this sphere are so insignificant compared to total production that they can be left completely out of account.
>
> (Marx, 1979: 195)

Even though Marx does not deal directly with productive labour in the service sector, he examines in considerable depth unproductive labour in the service sector such as commercial activities. This leads to another level of analysis.

At a second level Marx deals with the process of the *reproduction of industrial capital* where he turns his attention to the sphere of circulation. For industrial capital there are two types of circulation labour. One is labour that operates in the sphere of actual circulation of commodities, such as transportation. When these circulation activities become independent branches of investment, they are constituted as spheres for the investment of productive capital.[5] Therefore the labour is productive. The other type of labour is engaged in pure circulation activities such as trading and accounting. This labour does not create any surplus value and, although unproductive, is a necessary activity for the reproduction of capital. When these activities become independent branches they maintain their unproductive character and give rise to unproductive capital.

At this level of analysis Marx is dealing with division of labour within industrial capital and even within the firm. His definition of productive labour is restricted to that labour exchanged only against productive capital. At the same time he extends his definition of unproductive labour to include not only labour exchanged against revenue but also labour exchanged against unproductive capital, that is, capital devoted to circulation and realization activities.

At a third level of analysis he deals with the process of the *reproduction of social capital* where unproductive activities, due to a process of social division of labour, get constituted as independent branches of investment, such as banking and trading. The definition of unproductive labour is further extended to include all labour engaged in a whole branch of unproductive economic activity. Thus the Marxian definition of productive labour includes all labour exchanged against *productive* capital that produces surplus value. Unproductive labour includes all labour paid out of revenue, for example, personal servants; all labour paid out of unproductive capital within the industrial sector, such as managers, accountants, supervisors and messengers; and all labour exchanged against unproductive capital in those sectors devoted to circulation activities like the trading sector.

Information labour: productive or unproductive labour?

Let us now examine the definition of information labour presented above in terms of the division between productive and unproductive labour. If the categories proposed by the OECD (1976), which are very similar to Porat's, are used, the results exhibited in Table 1 are obtained.

Almost all occupations in the information sector are unproductive. It will be recalled that the information society theories argue that information

Table 1 Information labour: productive and unproductive (OECD categories).

Categories	Productive labour	Unproductive labour
A. Producers of information	Technicians, scientific personnel	Social scientists, commercial agents, real estate agents, advertising executives, inspectors, business services
B. Processors of information		Administrators, supervisors, administrative personnel
C. Disseminators of information		Teachers and instructors,* communicators*
D. Operators of communications infrastructure	Printing workers, telecommunications operators	Calculating and accounting machine operators, messengers

*These workers could be productive workers if their labour power were bought by productive capital.

and service activities show the highest rate of growth in the post-industrial society. But if information labour is mostly unproductive, then the post-industrial society is a society made up of unproductive workers.

In order to study the information economy from this perspective, the US labour force will be divided between the production sector and the non-production sector. The production sector includes all industries where use-values are produced such as manufacturing, mining and construction. The non-production sector includes all economic branches devoted to the circulation and distribution of money and the use-values of production such as trade, finance, insurance, real estate and business services. All labour within the non-production sector is unproductive while labour in the production sector can be further divided into productive and unproductive labour (Shaikh, 1981).

Production sector		Non-production sector
Productive	Unproductive	Unproductive labour

An analysis of production and non-production activities in 1947 shows that 63.4 percent of the US labour force worked in the production sector while 36.6 percent worked in the non-production sector. For 1980 the percentages were reversed with only 46.1 percent in the production sector and 53.9 percent in the non-production sector. If labour in the production sector is now divided into productive and unproductive labour, that is, workers are differentiated from supervisory personnel, secretaries, messengers, etc., productive labour in 1947 consisted of approximately 15 million workers, representing 84 percent of production labour. For 1980 these productive workers had increased to 22 million. Nevertheless, they decreased in relative terms to represent a 61 percent participation of production labour and 28.4 percent of the total work force. What this means is that in 1947 unproductive labour (unproductive workers in the production sector and all workers in the non-production sector) represented 46.4 percent of the work force while in 1980 it had increased to 71.6 percent. The post-industrial society is a society of unproductive workers.[6] (See Tables 2 and 3.)

In the Mexican case, workers in the production sector represented 49 percent of the workforce in 1950 and decreased to 43 percent in 1980, a very slight decrease compared to the US economy. (See Table 4.) If the production

Table 2 Four sector aggregation of the US labour force.

Year	Information sector	Agriculture sector	Industry sector	Service sector	Total
1860	480.604	3,364.230	3,065.924	1,375.525	8,886.283
1870	601.018	5,884.971	4,006.789	2,028.438	12,821.216
1880	1,131.415	7,606.590	4,386.409	4,281.970	17,406.384
1890	2,821.500	8,464.500	6,393.383	5,074.149	22,754.032
1900	3,732.371	10,293.179	7,814.652	7,318.947	29.159.149
1910	5,930.193	12,377.785	14,447.382	7,044.592	39.799.952
1920	8,016.054	14,718.742	14,492.300	8,061.342	45,288.438
1930	12,508.959	10,415.623	18,023.113	10,109.284	51,056.979
1940	13,337.958	8,233.624	19,928.422	12,082.376	53,582.380
1950	17,815.978	6,883.446	22,154.285	10,991.378	54,844.087
1960	28.478.317	4,068.511	23.597.364	11,661.326	67,805.518
1970	37,167.513	2,466.883	22,925.095	17,511.639	80,071.130
1980[a]	44,650.721	2,012.157	21,558.824	27,595.297	95,816.999

Percentages

Year	Information sector	Agriculture sector	Industry sector	Service sector	Total
1860	5.8	40.6	37.0	16.6	100
1870	4.8	47.0	32.0	16.2	100
1880	6.5	43.7	25.2	24.6	100
1890	12.4	37.2	28.1	22.3	100
1900	12.8	35.3	26.8	25.1	100
1910	14.9	31.1	36.3	17.7	100
1920	17.7	32.5	32.0	17.8	100
1930	24.5	20.4	35.3	19.8	100
1940	24.9	15.4	37.2	22.5	100
1950	30.8	11.9	38.3	19.0	100
1960	42.0	6.0	34.8	17.2	100
1970	46.4	3.1	28.6	21.9	100
1980[a]	46.6	2.1	22.5	28.8	100

a. Bureau of Labor Statistics Projection.
Source: Bell, Daniel (1981) 'The Social Framework of the Information Society' in Michael Dertouzos and Joel Moses (eds), *The Computer Age: A Twenty-year View*. Cambridge, Mass.: The MIT Press.

Table 3 Employment by sectors, selected countries (percentages).

Country	Year	Information	Services	Industry	Agriculture
France	1954	20.3	24.1	30.9	24.7
	1975	32.1	28.1	29.9	9.9
Japan	1960	17.9	18.4	31.3	32.4
	1975	29.6	22.7	33.8	13.9
Sweden	1960	26.0	26.8	36.5	10.7
	1975	34.9	29.8	30.6	4.7
Great Britain	1951	26.7	27.5	40.4	5.4
	1971	35.6	27.0	34.2	3.2
United States	1950	30.5	19.1	38.4	12.0
	1970	41.1	24.1	31.5	3.3
Germany	1950	18.3	20.9	38.3	22.5
	1978	33.2	25.9	35.1	5.8

Source: OECD (1980).

Table 4 Employment by sectors, Mexico (in thousands).

	1950	%	1960	%
Information	1,225.505	15.3	2.195.335	19.5
Agriculture	4,939.449	61.8	6,184.018	54.9
Industry	1,272.713	15.9	1,995.607	17.7
Services	554.024	7.0	887.362	7.9
Total	7,991.391	100	11,252.317	100
	1970	%	*1980**	%
Information	2,870.665	23.5	5,704.192	25.3
Agriculture	5,173.267	42.3	6,338.882	32.2
Industry	2,505.227	20.5	4,693.585	23.7
Services	1.658.363	13.7	3,029.902	15.3
Total	12,207.512	100	19,766.511	100

*Preliminary data.
Source: Based on data from Censo General de Poblacion y Vivienda, Mexico.

sector is now separated into productive and unproductive labour it can be seen that, except for a drop in 1970 (in relative terms), productive labour in this sector has not decreased since 1950. It has maintained an approximate share of 86 percent of the labour in that sector. From the perspective of the overall Mexican labour force, productive labour in 1950 had a participation of 43 percent, which decreased to 37 percent in 1980.

If the data on the composition of the US labour force are compared to those of Mexico, it can be observed that both countries had a high percentage of unproductive workers in 1950. In both cases there is a relative increase of unproductive workers for 1980, although this is considerably sharper in

Table 5 Productive and unproductive labour, United States (in thousands).

	Production sector[1]		Non-production sector[2]	Total percentages		
Year	Productive labour	Unproductive labour	Unproductive labour	Productive labour	Unproductive labour	Total
1947	15,647	2,862	10,683	53.6	46.4	29,192
1950	15,440	5,785	11,274	47.6	52.4	32,499
1960	15,653	8,991	14,020	40.5	59.5	38,664
1970	21,421	11,994	30,233	33.7	66.3	63,648
1980	22,860	14,237	43,465	28.4	71.6	80,562

1. Includes all production workers in mining, construction, manufacturing, and transportation and public utilities.
2. Includes all production and non-production workers in wholesale and retail trade, finance, insurance and real estate, and services, as well as all non-production workers in mining, construction, manufacturing, and transportation and utilities.
Source: calculated from Employment and Training Report of the President, US Department of Labor, 1981.

the US than in Mexico.[7] In 1980 unproductive labour in the US represented 71.6 percent of the work force while in Mexico it was 63 percent.

In both countries there is a relative decline in the share of production workers, although the decline is relatively larger for the US (20%) than for Mexico (6%). This means that in the US there has been a sharp increase in the number of unproductive workers within the production sector. In 1947 there were seven productive workers for each unproductive worker in the US production sector. By 1980 there were only 1.5. (See Table 5.)

The importance of the above data lies in the fact that it shows very clearly that for the US economy the increase in unproductive workers can be significantly accounted for by the increase in unproductive workers within the firm. Curiously the OECD report showed that this category, that is, administrative personnel within the firm, made the largest contribution (58%) to the growth of information employment in OECD member countries.

In the case of Mexico the increase in unproductive workers comes mainly from employment in the non-production sector. (See Table 6.) This could be explained by the fact that this sector includes disguised unemployment, which usually appears under the category of services, as well as employment in the public sector,[8] an important employer in the Mexican economy. Obviously an analysis of the productivity of labour in both countries would shed important light on this issue, but it falls beyond the scope of this article.

It is evident that both societies are composed of a majority of unproductive workers but for different reasons and with different results. Therefore it cannot be assumed that the effect on capital accumulation of 'informatization' policies and programmes — that is, the massive introduction and utilization of information goods and services in all spheres of social life — would

Table 6 Productive and unproductive labour, Mexico (in thousands).

	Production sector[1]		Non-production sector[2]	Total percentages		
Year	Productive labour	Unproductive labour	Unproductive labour	Productive labour	Unproductive labour	Total
1950	1,343	199	1,577	43	57	3,120
1960	2,156	348	2,600	42	58	5,105
1970	2,714	627	3,761	38	62	7,104
1980	5,062	826	7,646	37	63	13,534

Notes: for a definition of productive and unproductive labour as used in this table see Shaikh (1981). The industry classification rules were those described in Table 5.
Source: calculated from Censo de Poblacion, Direccion General de Estadistica, Mexico, 1950, 1960, 1970, 1980.

be the same for every social formation regardless of any other economic, political and social determinants. To this we turn our attention now.

Unproductive labour and capital accumulation

The importance of the distinction between productive and unproductive labour lies in its relation to the process of capital accumulation. All kinds of labour use up use-values (goods and services) in the realization of their labour, but productive labour, as the only source of surplus value, not only replaces the use-values used up but also creates additional wealth. On the contrary, unproductive labour uses up society's wealth without replacing it, therefore creating a limit on the accumulation process.

An increase in the employment of productive workers brings about a net increase in the production of output while an increase in the employment of unproductive workers will actually absorb a portion of the net output and hence decrease the amount available for productive investment. Therefore the larger the number of unproductive workers, the greater the limits imposed on capital accumulation (Shaikh, 1980). For example, all workers use up inputs: a productive worker in a yarn factory will use machinery and wool to produce the yarn and an unproductive worker in the same factory will use pencils, paper, a desk and a computer to estimate a payroll. The hiring of an additional unproductive worker, *ceteris paribus*, means that those inputs are not available for the realization of productive labour. Therefore social consumption is increased but social production is not.

Why then have unproductive workers at all? Why not eliminate them altogether? As the scale of production is extended, unproductive operations required for the circulation and reproduction of industrial capital multiply accordingly. The process of production sets the limits to the scale of unproductive activities in two ways. To do packaging and selling in high volume, large inventories must be on hand. Unproductive activities depend on the quantity of commodities produced which are the object of these activities and not vice versa. On the other hand, unproductive capital is nothing but surplus value elsewhere created and transferred from the productive sphere of society to the unproductive one. For unproductive capital to make a profit, it is necessary to have surplus value already produced, and surplus value is only produced by productive workers in the process of production of commodities.

Although necessary for social reproduction, unproductive activities are similar to constant capital in the effect that they have over the rate of profit because they create no surplus value. Hence, other things being equal, the smaller the amount of unproductive capital employed as a whole the greater the profit for industrial capital and the higher the overall rate of profit.

> For this reason, the industrial capitalist endeavours to limit these expenses of circulation to a minimum, just as he (she) does with his (her) expenses of constant capital. Hence industrial capital does not maintain the same relations to its commercial wage laborers that it does to its productive laborers. The greater the number of productive wage laborers employed under otherwise equal circumstances, the more voluminous is production, the greater the surplus-value or profit. . . . The commercial laborer does not produce any surplus value directly. . . . He (she) adds to the income of the capitalist, not by creating any direct surplus value, but by helping him (her) to reduce the costs of the realization of surplus value.
>
> (Marx, 1977a: 353)

It will be recalled that the Marxian formula for computing the maximum rate of profit, r^*, given an annual turnover of capital is:

$$r^* = \frac{S}{C + V} \tag{1}$$

If U stands for unproductive capital (labour and use-values utilized to carry on unproductive activities) because it is a deduction from surplus value, acting at the same time as constant capital, the rate of profit is modified as follows:

$$r' = \frac{S - U}{C + V + U} \tag{2}$$

because U behaves as constant capital (Marx, 1977a). So that $r^* > r'$.

Obviously the smaller the unproductive expenses the higher the rate of profit. Assume, for example, that society as a whole invests $100 billion in variable capital and an equal amount in constant capital. Then if the rate of surplus value is set at 100 percent, productive workers will create another $100 billion as surplus value. Substituting Equation 1 and assuming there are no unproductive expenses, the rate of profit (r^*) will equal 50 percent ($100/$200).

If it is now assumed that unproductive expenses are $50 billion, by substituting in Equation 2, it can be seen that the rate of profit will go down to 20 percent ($50/$250). But if by some method capitalists are able to cut unproductive expenses in half, that is, $25 billion, the rate of profit will equal 33.3 percent ($75/$225).

The capitalist class as a whole obviously would benefit from a reduction in total unproductive expenses, including unproductive labour. Unproductive expenses cannot be eliminated altogether because they are a necessary link in the process of capitalist reproduction. Commodities are produced but they have to be distributed, advertised, sold and the money paid for them has to be collected. State activities are also necessary for the social and ideological reproduction of capitalist accumulation. But if unproductive expenses cannot be eliminated they can certainly be reduced, either directly or indirectly, to maximize profits. A direct way to do this would be to decrease the number of unproductive workers or to lower their wages. Working class resistance has made it more difficult for capitalists to attempt such measures for the reduction of unproductive expenses. Nevertheless, there are several indirect ways of achieving this.

The first, which has characterized the development of capitalism almost since its beginning, is the process of division of labour. When unproductive activities are constituted into independent branches of investment, such as the trading sector, one sector of unproductive capital becomes capable of handling the circulation needs of several sectors of productive capital. In this way the number of unproductive workers and overall unproductive expenses are reduced, with a positive effect on the profitability of capital.[9]

Another way of reducing unproductive expenses is by increasing the efficiency[10] of unproductive workers, or by reducing these expenses by decreasing the cost of the materials consumed by unproductive workers in their labour process. How is it possible to increase the efficiency of unproductive workers and reduce the cost of these materials? The information revolution is the answer.

Information revolution or profitability revolution?

The information revolution will affect significantly all aspects of social life, but it is probably the unproductive sector of economic activity that will undergo the most important transformation in this process. This is not mere chance. As seen above, unproductive sectors have increased continuously over the past thirty years in many countries. Computers and other automated devices are rapidly being adopted and utilized in unproductive branches such as banks, insurance companies, real estate agencies, retail stores and management offices. Small computers with access to databanks, multimode communication systems, word processors and telecommunications are sharply altering the nature of managerial labour and information occupations.

For the first time in fifty years the increase in the efficiency of unproductive workers seems to be at the top of the capitalist agenda. This has been of some concern in economic circles since the 1960s because it was found that, regardless of many problems of definition and comparability, the efficiency of unproductive workers was significantly lower than that of productive workers. Fuchs (1965, 1971) found a 1.17 percent per annum differential in the US while Briscoe (1975) found a 1.48 percent differential in Great Britain.

If we examine the office as the place, par excellence, for the development of unproductive activities, for example, in banking, trading, management, clerical work, etc., it is apparent that office labour has remained almost the same for the past fifty years. Even the invention of the electric typewriter was not really a great improvement as far as the efficiency of office labour is concerned. Capital investment per office worker has always been low compared to other sectors. Over the last decade a capital investment of $40,000 per agricultural worker has brought a 200 percent increase in labour productivity. In manufacturing every $30,000 spent per worker has seen a doubling of productivity. Only $2,500 has been invested per office worker and efficiency has increased by 5 percent (Predicasts, 1982).

With the information revolution the efficiency of office employees is set to increase, as investment in office automation more than triples to $18 billion in the next ten years. Teleconferencing equipment sales are expected to grow at 30 percent per year and electronic mail terminal sales will increase by more than seven times, not to mention the boom in sales of word processing equipment. Although the extent to which the information revolution will increase the efficiency of unproductive labourers is hard to determine at this point, it seems that it will affect it in a significant way. Werneke (1982) in a report on the impact of office automation on women's employment (women occupy the majority of lower clerical jobs in most countries) showed that as new technology has been introduced in the office, the rise in labour efficiency has allowed more work to be done with the same number or even fewer workers.

In the office the information revolution will also affect the cost of office equipment and materials.

> One word processor is cheaper than five typewriters and at the same time it can increase productivity by 150 to 400%. This is no empty sales talk. In those offices where word processors have been introduced office staffs have been cut by one-third to one-half.
>
> (Downing, 1981: 276)

The availability of more sophisticated and cheaper telecommunication services is also an important factor. Saunders *et al.* (1983) report that teleconferencing has been successfully used in the United States by different organizations such as NASA, Bank of America, Exxon, Procter and Gamble, among others. They report that IBM's teleconferencing system reduced travel costs by $414,000 in 1979, its first year of operation, and by $830,000 in 1980. A subsidiary of the RCA Corporation held a video conference for 450 sales people around the United States costing 15 percent of the cost of a similar size live conference involving travel expenses. In 1980 the US Post Office reported that business communications costs decreased when using digital data transmission in preference to regular mail. It was estimated that the cost of producing six minutes in a tie line network call was $0.74; the cost of teletype was $2.45 for sixty-six words; the cost of a letter mailed in the US would come to $6.41 per page. Computers are now available to almost any firm regardless of its size because of significant price reductions and processing capacity improvement. It will be recalled that the famous ENIAC (Electronic Numerical Integrator and Calculator) computer developed in 1946 at a cost of thousands of dollars had a capacity that today would cost under $100.

There is no question that the information revolution will bring about a significant reduction in the cost of those inputs that are used to a large extent by office employees. And this, together with an increase in the efficiency of unproductive workers, will affect profitability in a positive and direct way by liberating surplus value for capitalist appropriation. It could also be argued that the information revolution could affect profitability in an indirect way to the extent to which it contributes to a reduction in the unit costs of the commodities produced. If this reduction in costs reaches those commodities that form part of workers' consumption requirements the rate of surplus value could be positively affected.

But in order to understand the scope of this information revolution it is necessary to place it within the context of the rationalization of the labour process in capitalist production. The capitalist system is determined by the drive to maximize profitability. In order to achieve this capitalists have to control, rationalize and continually transform the labour process. This is achieved by subdividing it into increasingly specialized and highly defined tasks, reducing human labour to mechanical activities so that eventually real machines may indeed replace mechanized human labour. This tendency towards mechanization is the dominant force in the increase of the social productivity of labour and brings about a decrease in unit costs for the commodities produced. This has a double determination. In the first place it is the result of the struggle between capital and labour and the need for capitalist control over the labour process. In the second, it arises out of the struggle between individual capitals because capitalist competition forces them to mechanize in order to lower unit costs and gain an edge over their competitors.

The impact of the information revolution on the productive sectors of society is rather straightforward. A human hand hits a nail every two seconds. Soon a mechanized arm hits the nail every second and some years later a computerized robot arm hits it every tenth of a second. But the difference between the labourer hitting the nail and a robotized arm might just appear to be of a technological nature: the robotized arm has a longer reach, can carry a 200 lb load and can work continually. In the eyes of the capitalist the worker is an imperfect machine and the machine is a perfect worker. But the real difference is a much deeper and important one and lies in the essence of the capitalist system.

No matter how perfect a robot is, it will never be able to produce surplus value because surplus value can only be produced by productive workers. Information commodities in the workshop, such as fibre optics, computer-aided manufacturing systems (CAMS), computers, robots, etc., are introduced not to replace human labour but to increase its productivity and the control of capital over the labour process as dictated by the logic of capitalist production established long ago.

The effect of the information revolution on the unproductive sectors has to be analysed within the perspective of the rationalization of the labour process and its mechanization in capitalist production. Manual labour has been carefully specialized over the last 100 years; the turn of mental labour has finally arrived. Office labour will be broken down and transformed as much as manual artisans' labour was in the early period of industrial development. For example, the introduction of word processors in the office could result in a change in the organization of work by splitting secretarial work into typing, correspondence and administrative work. A separate word processing department could then be established which could receive the bulk of typing to be done within an organization, allowing the machinery to be continuously used, thus achieving the maximum use or capacity utilization of the word processing equipment. The change in work organization would result in the deskilling of the word processor operator compared to the traditional secretary. Less skill is required because the layout, accuracy, spelling and correction of work are done by the machine (Curnow and Curran, 1983). A similar case would be that of electronic mail and electronic filing systems. Their adoption in the office would probably mean an increase in the specialization of administrative personnel.

The introduction of new technology or information commodities in either the productive or unproductive branches of the economy is dictated by conditions of capitalist competition. It is not imposed by the technology itself because the technology is neither created nor adopted in a historical vacuum. If a new technology is introduced by a certain capitalist and he or she is successful, the innovator will gain a temporary advantage over the other capitals which operate in the same sphere of investment and will be in a position to ride the wave of higher profits. The new technology will eventually be adopted by all the competing capitals, if they are to survive the battle of competition. When these favourable conditions of operation are generalized the surplus profits accruing to the innovator will tend to disappear. This is the case, for example, in the banking sector. Computers and telecommunications were used at the beginning by a few banks in the industrialized nations, but today the international banking system as a whole makes use of these technologies in its everyday operations. This explains the existence, for instance, of a highly modernized banking sector in developing countries such as Mexico, Bolivia or even Bahrain when other branches of investment, whether productive or unproductive, are still operating under rather backward conditions.

The above analysis represents the theoretical space within which the information revolution, and the new technology brought about by it, will have to be studied in order to fully understand the scope and possible impact on economic life. Capitalists would certainly like to be able to impose their own rationality over other class interests, but history has proved that this is not always possible. The capitalist class is not a monolithic block. Divisions and struggles within capital itself will shape the dominance of some interests over others. For example, the fight of telecommunication firms to participate in the computer business, or the struggle between new direct broadcast satellites (DBS) with established television firms and the cable television industry (CATV) will in each case result in a different outcome.

Working-class resistance to the introduction of such technologies will certainly determine the extent to which they will be incorporated into economic life. The introduction of these technologies in the workshop and in the office implies not only changes in work practices and skill qualifications but also significant changes in the levels and composition of employment. For example, it is predicted that employment in the service sector will contract more and more as the new technologies are introduced (Henzies, 1982). Labour unions in industrialized countries, where 'information' processes are well on their way, are already fighting the effects of these technologies by demanding retraining programmes for workers, maintenance of previous employment levels and agreements between management and labour prior to their introduction. For example, delegates to the annual conference of the Banking, Insurance and Finance Union of the United Kingdom voted three to one to resist the introduction of these new technologies until employers sign agreements on the conditions of their introduction into the sector. Any attempt by the management to introduce the technology without first agreeing to the terms on which it is to be installed would result in the refusal of employees and workers to operate the equipment (*Microelectronics Monitor*, 1983).

Labour resistance to the adoption of these technologies is still rather unusual in developing countries where the 'informatization' process is just starting in an erratic and checkered way, but it will certainly appear on labour's agenda in the near future. Finally the incorporation of these technologies into social life will also be affected by other factors such as state policies, cultural elements and tradition, factors that will vary according to each social formation.

Conclusion

If the labour and employment data of any country were analysed today in terms of the theoretical premises advanced by the information economy theory, one would find that almost all societies are already on the path to the information society. Probably information labour and related activities would show significant increases over the past twenty years. Nevertheless, the road to the information economy is not as simple as it seems and if a critique of the information economy is to be developed it will have to address several aspects implicit in this information society theory.

First, it can be shown from a political economy perspective that information labour is unproductive labour. Further, by analysing employment data for the US and Mexico, it was made evident that the increase in information labour can stem from different sources having different effects on capitalist accumulation and social reproduction. In the case of the US this increase is due mainly to the growth of unproductive labour within the firm, that is, within the production sector of US economic activity, whereas in the case of Mexico it is due mainly to an increase in employment in the non-production sectors of the economy which include government employment. The paradox seems to be that the larger the number of unproductive workers the more developed the country. In 1980 over 70 percent of the US work force was unproductive labour whereas in Mexico 56 percent of the work force was productive labour. Obviously no final conclusions can be drawn without a detailed analysis on the productivity of labour in both countries.

Second, even though information labour appears to be so important for information economy theorists, the trend seems to be to aim at its reduction, or at the increase of its efficiency via the utilization of information technology. The extent to which the information revolution will be able to restore the productivity of labour and increase the efficiency of unproductive workers is hard to determine, but it will certainly be attempted.

The information society is not the clean, antiseptic and apolitical society we have been told it is, where democracy and freedom will rule. Capitalism is still the name of the game and profitability its main drive. The information society is a class society where the exploitation of the working class is still its main feature.

There is an important distinction that must be kept in mind when analysing the utilization of information commodities in a given social formation. Information commodities can be used in the workshop or in the office and in both cases their adoption can be analysed within the context of the rationalization of the labour process. When information commodities are used in the workshop they are used to increase the productivity of labour and to create surplus value. These commodities are then productively consumed, that is, they are utilized by productive workers, and this leads to the creation of wealth and the direct expansion of the process of capitalist accumulation. When information commodities are used in the office they are used up by unproductive workers and their consumption is unproductive, that is, although they help restore profitability, their use does not lead to the direct creation of new wealth.

Finally another distinction that has to be made when dealing with the effects of the so-called information revolution is related to the production of information commodities. A country that produces and productively consumes information commodities is better off than a country that imports these commodities and consumes them unproductively. The latter is the case of most Third World countries which have already 'joined' the information revolution mainly by importing large quantities of these information commodities to be used primarily by the public bureaucracies. This characteristic in particular merits further investigation if a thorough critique of the information economy theory is to be developed.

Because the information economy theses are part of a wider developmentalist approach, that links the process of 'informatization' of societies to that of modernization, this theory has to be carefully analysed in order to disentangle all the economic, political and social effects that will result from this 'information' process. Otherwise, on the grounds of modernization, the working class will be increasingly and continuously exploited; and on the grounds of development, developing countries will open their doors to foreign capital and the purveyors of 'informatization' the way they opened their doors in the 1950s and 1960s to the purveyors of industrialization with the economic and social consequences we all know.

Notes

1 For a more detailed treatment and presentation of the data on information labour in the US and Mexico see Arriaga (1984).
2 See the works of D. Bell, W. Dizard, Y. Masuda, S. Nora and A. Mine, E. Parket, M. Porat, I. Singh among others.
3 Smith has two definitions of productive labour but for the purpose of this article only one will be presented.
4 The three levels of abstraction at which Marx develops his concept of productive-unproductive labour are basically those in the three volumes of *Capital*.
5 See Marx (1977a).
6 For an alternative explanation to this phenomenon see Bowles *et al.* (1983).
7 These data, as well as those for Mexico, leave out agricultural labour. If included, in the case of the US the data would remain almost the same, while in the case of Mexico productive labour would probably increase considerably with respect to unproductive labour.

8 Employment in the public sector almost doubled between 1970 and 1982.
9 For further discussion see Marx (1977b), especially the chapters 'On Commercial Capital' and 'On Commercial Profit'.
10 Because orthodox economic theory does not distinguish between productive and unproductive labour, the concept of productivity of labour is applied to the production of goods and to the production of services. When making the distinction between both kinds of labour, one cannot talk of the 'productivity of unproductive labour'. I therefore use the concept of the 'efficiency' of unproductive labour and leave the concept of productivity to be applied exclusively to productive labour.

References

Arriaga, P. (1984) 'La informatización de México' in P. Arriaga (ed.), *La Revolución Informativa en México* Vol. 1. Mexico: CEESTEM-Nueva Imagen.

Bell, D. (1973) *El Advenimiento de la Sociedad Post-Industrial*. Mexico: Era.

Bell, D. (1981) 'The Social Framework of the Information Society' in M. Dertouzos and J. Moses (eds), *The Computer Age: A Twenty-Year View*. Cambridge: MIT.

Bowles, S., D. M. Gordon and T. Weisskoff (1983) *Beyond the Waste Land*. New York: Doubleday.

Briscoe, G. (1976) 'Recent Productivity Trends in the UK Service Sector', *Oxford Bulletin of Economics and Statistics*, 38 (4).

Curnow, P. and S. Curran (1983) 'The Technology Applied' in G. and Shaffia Friedrichs (eds), *Microelectronics and Society*. New York: The New American Library.

Dizard, W. (1982) *The Coming Information Age*. New York: Longman.

Downing, H. (1980) 'Word Processors and the Oppression of Women' in T. Forester (ed.), *The Microelectronics Revolution*. Cambridge: MIT Press.

Fajnzylber, F. (1983) 'Agotamiento de un patron industrial', mimeo.

Fuchs, R. (1965) 'Productivity Trends in the Goods and Service Sectors, 1929–1961, A Preliminary Survey', National Bureau of Economic Research, Occasional Paper 89.

Fuchs, R. (1967) 'The Growing Importance of the Service Industries'. National Bureau of Economic Research, Occasional Paper 96.

Fuchs, R. (1971) 'Productivity Differences Within the Service Sector', National Bureau of Economic Research, Occasional Paper 102.

Marx, K. (1975) *Capital*, Vol. I. New York: International Publishers.

Marx, K. (1977a) *Capital*, Vol. II. New York: International Publishers.

Marx, K. (1977b) *Capital*, Vol. III. New York: International Publishers.

Masuda, Y. (1980) *The Information Society*. Japan.

Nora, S. and A. Mine (1981) *The Computerization of Society: A Report to the President of France*. Cambridge: MIT Press.

OECD (1981) *Les Activites d'Information de l'Electronique et des Technologies de Telecommunication*, Vol. I. Paris.

Parker, E. (1981) 'Information Services and Economic Growth', *Information Society*, I (1).

Porat, M. (1973) 'The Information Economy', US Department of Commerce.

Porat, M. (1978) 'Communication Policy in an Information Society' in G. Robinson (ed.), *Communications for Tomorrow*. New Jersey: Praeger Publishers.

Predicasts (1982) 'The Office of the Future', mimeo.

Richeri, G. (1982) *L'Universo Telematico*. Italy: De Donato.

Saunders R., J. Warford and B. Wellenius (1983). *Telecommunications and Economic Development*. Washington DC: Johns Hopkins University Press.

Semmler, W. (1984) *Competition and Monopoly Power*. New York: Columbia University Press.

Shaikh, A. (1979) 'Notes on the Marxian Notion of Competition', unpublished paper.

Shaikh, A. (1981) 'On Production and Non-Production Labor', unpublished paper.

Singh, I. (1983) 'The Telematic Society: Implications for the Pacific Region', *PTC*.

Sweeney, G. (1981) 'Telematics and Development', *Information Society*, I (1).

Werneke, D. (1982) *Microelectronics and Office Jobs: The Impact of the Chip on Women's Employment*. Geneva: ILO.

37

INVENTING THE GLOBAL
INFORMATION FUTURE

Ernest J. Wilson III

Source: *Futures* 30(1) (1998): 23–42.

This essay analyses four possible outcomes of the transition to tomorrow's global information society. Using scenario building methods the essay describes and analyses the pathways the transitions may take, in the hopes of guiding proactive thinking about the most desirable information and communication strategies for developing countries.

For developing countries the Information Revolution is the key to their future. Some will seize the opportunities presented and prosper, while others will hesitate and lag behind. Still other governments will vigorously resist change and be shunted aside. Today, obtaining and using Information Technology (IT) effectively is a requirement for better education and health care at home, more competitiveness abroad, and more effective engagement with the global information society rapidly being linked together around the world.

It has been said that the future just doesn't happen, it has to be invented. The future is now mainly an invention of the industrialized countries. Through multilateral conferences, bilateral negotiations, joint public–private discussions and private meetings, the industrialized countries are urgently preparing for the information society of the next millennium. The G-7 countries, the most developed in the world, are unambiguous in their insistence on Information Technology's central role in their own future: "The smooth and effective transition toward the information society is one of the most important tasks that should be undertaken in the last decade of the 20th century."[1] For its part, the OECD has taken this message to heart and

284

prepared consensus documents carefully outlining specific steps that their members should take to create a viable IT future.[2]

The most powerful example to date of inventing the future is the recently-concluded World Trade Organization (WTO) treaty on basic telecommunications services.[3] The G-7 countries, especially the United States, insisted that the future should be very different from the past in this key sector. The Clinton administration reasoned that rapid technological changes in the IT supply industries, the desire of large private consumers to reduce their costs, and the predominant position of American consumer companies, would permit the US to develop a strategy to successfully restructure the basic rules of the entire international telecommunications regime.[4] Their strategy was successful, and as a consequence of the telecoms pact adoption, the future will no longer be the same as it was before the Geneva accord in mid-February 1997. The agreements reached in Geneva by nearly 70 nations will decisively shape the future contours and dynamics of the $500 billion plus global telecommunications markets. Accounting for about 90% of international telecoms sales, the signatories agreed to play by new pro-competitive rules governing market access, ownership and pro-market regulatory approaches.[5]

The most developed industrialized countries originally approached these negotiations with the very clear recognition that the outcomes of this multi-year process would reshape the future. Yet despite the definitive nature of these talks, most of the world's poorest countries never got seriously involved in the process; over 100 countries never participated at all. From the poorest continent, Africa, only seven out of over 50 countries participated seriously and made trade offers. Now that the negotiations are concluded, and the first stage is over, the implementation phase (the most difficult phase) lies ahead. The completion of these global talks provides an opportunity to speculate about what the future of the world of international telecommunications and information may hold, especially for developing countries.

While the industrialized countries are more attuned to the IT future than developing countries, it is senior managers in the poorest of the poor countries that most need to develop self-conscious strategies in order to maximize their access to new information technologies and services, with an even greater sense of urgency for their future.

This essay analyses four possible outcomes of the transition to tomorrow's global information society. It describes and analyses the pathways the transitions may take, in the hopes of guiding pro-active thinking about the most desirable information and communication futures for developing countries.

Why the future is so difficult to predict in the IT sector

An old truism says "it is always very difficult to predict, especially to predict the future". This is particularly true in the IT sector today, since so many of the fundamental 'certainties' of global IT markets have become uncertain and discontinuous, making prediction difficult.[6] The Information Revolution of industry convergence, digitalization and cost declines poses huge challenges to IT managers worldwide because the changes they bring are extremely fast-paced and very wide-ranging across many sectors and countries.[7] As award-winning business analyst C. K. Prahalad has warned managers, in today's fast moving world the dividing line between the present and the future is rapidly thinning.[8]

For example, the Computer System Policy Project (CSPP), an association of CEOs of the 13 largest computer manufacturers in the US report an extraordinary fact: 73% of their profits are earned from goods and services that were not yet on the market 18–24 months before. Another sign of hyper-acceleration—Texas Instruments, the huge chip maker and manufacturer of consumer electronics has moved to a '6–8–6' marketing system. Previously the time required to move from R&D, to production and on to sales took years. Today, the company requires only 6 months to get the product onto the market, it remains there for 8 months, and is then retracted from the market over the next 6 months as a new product is introduced.

It is not surprising therefore that corporations and governments have a difficult time predicting the future of the IT sector.[9] Private firms struggle just to understand current conditions, to get their products to market, and 24 months seems an eternity. Governments find it difficult even to comprehend the current situation, and efforts to lay down a widely accepted public framework for future IT expansion prove problematic.[10] Yet it is surprising that in the public domain—newspapers and journals—serious IT scenario building and forecasting is almost an overlooked subject. What is available in the popular press is often too hyperbolic or personalized.[11] More serious work is done privately by companies and consulting firms, but even among these proprietary documents one finds far less detailed forecasting than one would expect from such a future-oriented industry. The few exceptions are prepared for big organizations like Cable and Wireless or the World Bank,[12] and *Wired* magazine shows what could be done in this genre with its recent cover story.[13]

As tough as it is to devise forecasts and scenarios and to employ them strategically in developing countries, there are highly compelling reasons for a sharper sense of urgency about the future of developing countries in the global information society. The stakes are very high and countries need to plan for their IT future for several reasons. Firstly, IT has already become a central factor in the conduct of modern economic and political life. Studies show its introduction does not occur automatically; it requires vision and leadership at every level of society.[14] Unless LDC leaders provide a clear future-oriented IT strategy about how IT can serve economic and political priorities, then developing countries will be condemned to near-permanent second class citizenship.

Secondly, a future-oriented IT strategy is key because the shift towards a global information society is occurring at a time when the gap between most LDCs and the industrialized world is growing;[15] and the Information Revolution may well be accelerating the growth of the gap between the information have and have-nots. One World Bank economist wrote in a Bank publication that any talk of economic 'convergence' between rich and poor is completely misplaced. Between 1980 and 1993, he points out, "more than one half of the developing countries had negative growth."[16] Even for LDCs with positive growth, "in more than four-fifths of these countries growth rates were still lower than the average . . . the rates for many were still lower than the average (2.2%) registered by the high income countries."[17] Even for Brazil, at those low rates it would take 33 years just to reach that country's own earlier peak earnings, and "487 years before it achieved the current income level of the high-income countries" (which will themselves continue to grow).[18]

Therefore, more LDC managers need to think strategically about developing their domestic IT capabilities if they are even to slow the increasing gap. At a minimum, this requires designing and actively pursuing a pro-active 'National Information Infrastructure' strategy that is explicitly geared to moving the country into the digital future.[19] Without the rapid deployment of proactive national strategies to create 'wired economies', then the world's poor countries will be pushed more and more to the bottom of the global information society.

Thirdly, beyond the threat of marginalization, the IT revolution also brings the means to overcome marginalization. For perhaps the first time in the history of mankind, countries can choose to create the wealth they need to grow fast. Previously, wealth was extracted. It was mined and harvested from the mountains and subsoil. Gold, oil or rich fertile earth conveyed wealth to the citizens lucky enough to live above ample natural gifts. Now, with new global competitive conditions, what is found under a nation's land is less important than what is inside the heads of its citizens—IT education and 'hi tech' training.[20] Commodities, roads and ports, are being replaced with knowledge, information highways and teleports. These new resources can be created and installed anywhere in the world where the government has the vision, will power and long-term commitment to devise imaginative and effective ways to use IT to enrich its citizenry. History can now be driven more by active human choice, not merely by the passive facts of geography. These changes are causing a paradigm shift in the way smart countries approach development.[21]

A fourth reason for urgency is because as national governments operate today more and more within a tightly integrated global context, then IT has become both a *subject* of intense negotiation, as well as a *means* of bilateral and multilateral negotiation. LDCs must become more sophisticated about IT to obtain the best bargain when negotiating with transnational corporations or other governments. This includes anticipating future IT changes in order to obtain the best bargain possible in their negotiations with the international system.

Finally, the technological and commercial revolutions now require that governments redesign their national IT regulatory and legislative frameworks to anticipate global change. Rapid technical changes quickly make the best regulations outmoded. Rapid change has become permanent.[22] IT itself has altered some of the rock-solid 'certainties' of the modern international system, such as the certainties of state authority, the sanctity of borders, the subsidiary role of NGOs, etc. Politicians and policy-makers need to better understand future trends to redesign domestic institutions for greater flexibility.

Leading issues for the global information infrastructure

While there are relatively few formal 'futures' exercises in the IT sector, leading organizations like the OECD, the World Bank, the Global Information Infrastructure Commission, the International Telecommunications Union (ITU) and others have identified top priority issues they judge to be crucial for the future evolution of global information and communications markets.

Firstly, there is profound unease and concern among all players (public and private) about the lack of international agreement on the 'rules of the game'. By international 'rules of the game' we mean the laws, regulations, norms, expectations, institutions and incentives of the international telecommunications and information system. Concrete examples include the WTO General Agreement on Trade in Services (GATS) negotiations in Geneva, the EU telecoms market liberalization rules, and the IPR discussions at the World Intellectual Property Organization (WIPO). Without agreed-upon rules there is chaos; and chaos often has the most serious negative consequences for the developing states.

The global rules of the game have become a serious concern, mainly because global information markets have changed much more rapidly than existing laws and regulations of the relevant international organizations. With change so rapid, rules quickly become dangerously outdated. Technology changes faster than rules, and rules once designed to promote efficiency and cooperation now hamper good service instead of helping.

In response, informal but 'unauthorized' *de facto* private practices spring up overnight to replace formal rules, but they can be contradictory in impact and partial in coverage. This leaves company managers and government officials uncertain and confused, with each company making up rules as they go, leading to further confusion and conflict. One result can be less investment and less innovation.

The second vital issue of great concern to powerful international actors is the degree of competition in global information markets. How much competition is enough, how should it be achieved, and at what price? 'Degree of competition' matches standard economic definitions including shares of the market controlled by the top firms (monopoly, oligopoly or competition); barriers to market entry and exit; and the extent of government intervention.

The meaning and importance of competition to the 'North' is often different from its significance to the 'South'. There are also differences between the US and Europe. In the lead-up to the 1995 G-7 ministerial meetings in Brussels on the information society there were long debates between the US and EU delegations, with the US insisting that governments commit themselves to full scale 'competition', and the Europeans wanting a weaker, watered down version. The compromise was for 'dynamic competition'. [23]

The differences are even greater between countries of the 'North' and 'South'. Some of these differences were identified at the Second Annual meeting of the elite private body, the Global Information Infrastructure Commission (GIIC) meeting in Kuala Lumpur in July 1996. The GIIC Commissioner from Colombia, Fernando Restrepo, Chairman of the Board of RTI Television, said that "if competition connotes only 'open markets', 'free access' or 'universal service', it is perceived negatively in some developing countries, since it generally means that strong multinational players take over local operators."[24]

A nuanced 'Northern' perspective was offered by GIIC Commissioner Ray Lane, President and Chief Operating Officer of Oracle, who attempted to define different kinds of competition in a policy context. He identified three kinds of competition as understood in different parts of the world. "1) free competition, which implied the destruction of current structures for new, freewheeling competition; 2) competition where incumbents with a favorable position are unwilling to open markets to competition; and 3) competition where no one organization has a dominant position, but there is a willingness to take risks and build new structures."[25]

Other international disputes regarding competition arose at the Information Society and Development (ISAD) conference in South Africa in May, 1996, where representatives of leading industrialized countries pressed for competition for its own sake, while the developing countries insisted on defining competition as valuable to the degree that it contributes to wider social goods. 'Competition' and 'cooperation' are both necessary for an equitable, efficient global information society to emerge.[26] Their meaning and balance are contested and subject to sharp international debates; debating them with an eye towards future trends and outcomes is a fruitful approach.

Competition, cooperation and developing countries

Regrettably, while rule-making in the WTO and other organizations will continue to greatly shape developing countries' access to the valuable resources they need to develop their IT systems such as capital and new skills, developing countries are inadequately represented within the ongoing series of conferences, negotiations and forums where the new rules of the global game are being debated and decided. They should be more involved to represent their unique interests. Global compacts constructed only by the rich and powerful—the information *haves*—are unlikely to serve even their own long term interests if the information *have-nots* are not invited into the room to shape those rules. Countries that do not participate in the rule-writing will be less likely to play by the rules after they are written.[27]

Technologies for better understanding the future

As difficult as it is under chaotic conditions to understand one or more possible futures, there are several useful methods for doing so. They include trend projections, computer simulations, model-building, group consultation approaches such as the Delphi Technique, and scenario building.[28] In this report we concentrate on scenario building.

Scenario building

Scenario building is a means widely employed in companies and governments to concentrate the attention of managers on possible future outcomes, and to encourage them to consider their optimal responses. It has been widely used in industry, notably by Royal Dutch Shell which credits the technique with greatly enhancing its earnings and profits and is described in *The Art of the Long View* by former Shell forecaster Peter Schwartz.[29] Its successes in the public sector are described in *Changing Maps Governing in a World of Rapid Change*, by Steven Russell, an excellent and compelling description of the use of scenario building in the Canadian government.[30] Developing countries use this approach as well. The South Africans employed scenario building in the early 1990s to help bridge the chasm between black, white and colored groups, and to point out the future benefits of cooperation and the costs of conflict. Malaysia developed a far-sighted '2020' vision, and the Nigerian private sector uses it today to foster greater public–private cooperation.

The main purpose of the scenario process is to develop and build support in an organization for common responses to possible future outcomes. It is not used to predict the future, but to sensitize decision-makers to a range of plausible futures they may confront. By so doing, planners hope to achieve outcomes they prefer and to avoid outcomes they fear. Especially in uncertain times, when many of the most basic underlying factors that drive change are themselves changing, scenario building can be a very useful management technique in the public and private sectors. Scenarios are constructed by identifying relatively well-known, relatively invariable 'driving forces and predetermined elements', as well as 'key uncertainties' that do vary.[31]

Constructing the scenarios

Driving forces

Scenarios are driven by underlying forces that are expected to remain relatively consistent through time. We assume that for the four scenarios described below:

- technological change will continue but not necessarily at the same rapid rates as in the recent past (i.e. Moore's law may no longer hold);
- information will continue to create vast new wealth, but not equally— inequality will continue to grow;
- commercial and technological convergence continues;
- the capacity of states and civil society to absorb and direct IT innovations will be severely stretched; and
- the limiting factors in the successful applications of IT will continue to be organization, training, leadership and 'vision', not money or technology.

Critical uncertainties

There are other elements which are much more difficult to anticipate:

- Which technologies will be dominant?
- What IT are consumers willing to pay for?
- Will world politics be stable or volatile?
- Will nations reach agreement on international 'rules of the game' for IT?
- Will IT markets be competitive, oligopolistic or monopolistic?

From these conditions flow other second-order questions:

- Will capital investment in IT rise or decline?
- Will sectoral growth be high or low?
- Will international organizations continue to support LDCs or not?
- Will the opportunities for participation and the distribution of power in the international system spread or narrow?

Scenario design

For the sake of simplicity and transparency, the four scenarios are built mainly around world telecommunications markets. While we want to

291

convey the contours and dynamics of all information and communications markets, from software to satellites, it would be much too unwieldy and impractical to try to construct scenarios of every single industry and every sub-sector of information and communications technology and services (ICTS). Therefore, we focus on the largest core market, the fully global, $400 billion telecommunications market. Besides being the largest component of the GII, international telephony is also the backbone along which other ICTS services are transmitted, especially the Internet. It is also the most politically problematic domestic market since its workers and managers are at risk of losing jobs and status through competition-promoting reforms. It is the telecommunications market that has recently concluded unprecedented global agreements, but which remains highly sensitive to commercial, political and national security concerns.

Still, we recognize that this approach somewhat skews the scenario since there are very real differences between telecoms and other IT markets. Not all the elements of telecommunications competition and rule-making apply equally to other industries like software or computers. Still, providing a broad birds-eye view enhances our understanding of the stakes involved for LDCs and other players in the emerging GII. A useful complement would be to construct a separate scenario matrix for each major IT market— software, satellites and so forth.[32] Government officials could also use scenarios to model their own national level information policies.

Below in *Figure 1* is a simple illustration that arranges the two central goals of competition and rule agreement as two dimensions of a four-cell

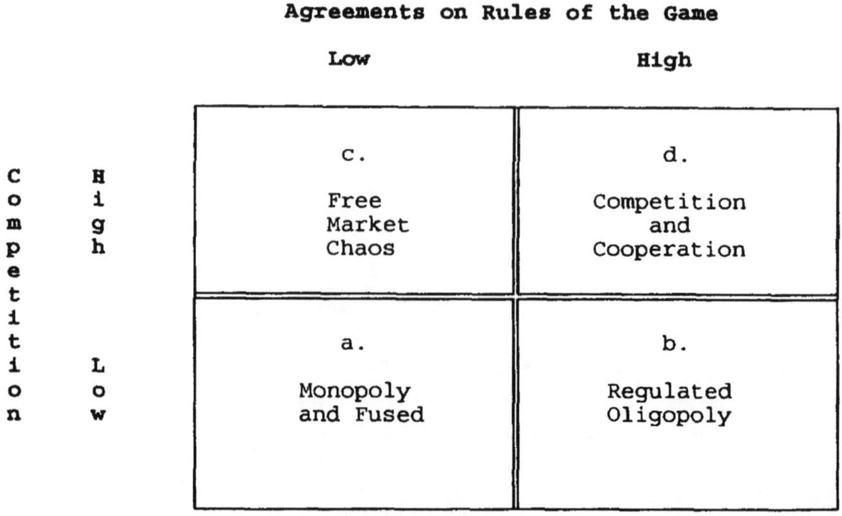

Agreements on Rules of the Game

| | **Low** | **High** |

		Low	High
Competition High		c. Free Market Chaos	d. Competition and Cooperation
Competition Low		a. Monopoly and Fused	b. Regulated Oligopoly

Figure 1 Four scenarios.

matrix. At the top, 'Agreement on Rules of the Game'; along the side, 'Degree of Competition'. They represent potential end-states in the evolution of the global information society.

Each of these four cells—Monopoly and Fused, Regulated Oligopoly, Free Market Chaos and Competition and Cooperation—represents a very plausible future state of the Global Information Society. There is absolutely no guarantee that the world will settle into any one of these outcomes. Each alternative cell is equally plausible, with differing opportunities for developing countries to win and to lose:

- Cell A: the Monopoly and Fused scenario with low agreement and low competition, represents a world where regulatory, ownership and management structures remain fused and undifferentiated.
- Cell B: the Regulated Oligopoly scenario with high agreement and low competition, indicates greater international agreement, but low levels of competition.
- Cell C: the Free Market Chaos scenario with low agreement and high competition, shows more competition in global and national markets, but low agreement on the basic rules of the game.
- Cell D: the Competition and Cooperation scenario with high agreement and high competition, maximizes both dimensions.

The scenarios

Cell A: monopoly and fused, low rules, low competition

Summary

This scenario provides a base scenario of low competition and low agreement on rules of the game. Almost all countries in this scenario still rely on monopoly suppliers for basic telephone services allowing limited competition in value added markets like cellular and paging. Domestically, most countries rhetorically commit to liberalization, and they seek modest regulatory and legislative reforms in their own domestic laws and institutions —but the ownership, policy and regulatory structures too often remain fused in a single government ministry with only a few halting steps toward independent regulatory bodies. Internationally, negotiations on liberalization conclude successfully, but real operational results are much more limited. Governments are very hesitant to liberalize. There is considerable rhetorical commitment to liberalizing markets—public and private sectors go on record committing themselves to greater openness, but they fail to implement. Both competition and agreement are relatively low in contrast to what they could be under a more favorable future. Not only are formal agreements left unenforced, but China and Russia's fast growing markets remain outside all international agreements altogether.

Driving factors in this scenario

This scenario shares many features with today's global situation. It is still the case that outside the United States about 96% of the $400 billion international telecommunications market comes from countries with a monopolistic supplier or a supplier with a substantially dominant market position.[33] These conditions will not disappear overnight, and this *de facto* immobility drives the scenario. There remain substantial national restrictions on market access, and copyright and intellectual breaches and disagreements are rampant. There are sharp and enduring conflicts over how best to promote cultural diversity without violating trade norms. Formal WTO accords were reached, but in this scenario the apparent WTO successes prove to be hollow victories. A positive scenario does not automatically emerge from today's high uncertainty.

One cannot exclude the possibility that both competition and cooperation could seriously deteriorate below even today's modest levels. Indeed, governments need to consider such a 'doomsday' or collapse scenario of bitter conflicts over the rules of the game, combined with far lower levels of competitive openness and exchange. The Asian crisis worsens. Trade wars, collapsing value of IT firms on national stock exchanges and beggar-thy-neighbor policies result. The costs to LDCs of a collapse in both competition and in rules of the game would be enormous.

In summary form, in the 'Monopoly and Fused' scenario:

- Power of state-owned telecoms PTT managers remains high; they veto or slow expansion of national information systems.
- Public–private relations are mistrustful and hostile.
- Ideas of market expansion lose out to cultural and national protection.
- Islands of connectivity grow within global markets, but do not spread.
- LDC influence is mainly in intergovernmental forums, but with little influence over investment and trade.

Trends

- Technological Innovation   Low
- Growth   Low
- Investment   Low
- Income Inequality   High
- International Organizations' Support for LDCS   Medium

Cell B: regulated oligopoly, high rules, low competition

Summary

The 'Regulated Oligopoly' world is one where LDC investment and trade stagnate, and regional blocs compete in a cartelized world of low competition but high agreement on conservative global rules.

Countries, international organizations and firms reach global agreements on key issues such as IPR, interconnectivity and standards, but market competitiveness is low as companies pursue conservative market strategies, consolidating current niches and resisting aggressive technological and commercial expansion. New IT investment rates fall, including direct foreign investment (DFI), and IT sales to developing countries rise only slowly. With less investment, technological innovation drops and costs rise for the final consumer.

Driving factors in this scenario

These conditions result from endogenous factors within the IT sector and exogenous factors beyond. Externally, the IT sector experiences hard shocks from an overall macroeconomic slowdown, an eruption of conflict in large unstable states like China and Russia, and the re-emergence of nationalism in Japan. These political changes increase investor worries and badly depress growth rates. The US retreats further from global engagements.

Internally, the sector experiences discontinuities in the historical rates at which firms move products from innovation through commercialization to amortizing investments. Moore's law and other 'constants' change as new and unexpected threshold points are reached. The capacity of IT firms to easily process and master convergence and competition peaks and commercial progress slows to a crawl. Consumers react to 'information overload' and cut back their IT purchases.

With a market of regulated oligopolies, market-subverting government-to-government agreements multiply. Rules of market access, interconnections and IPR are more widely accepted—but so are cartels, restrictive agreements and closed markets. Markets are 'opened' but only to special suppliers with political ties.

Implications for LDCs

LDC governments recognize there is no guarantee that they will be effective participants in rule-making forums, and that global rules will not automatically reflect their concerns, putting them in double jeopardy as both markets and rules work to their disadvantage.

On the upside for LDCs, less multinational competition permits more niches for local private market entrants to get involved in IT activities. Favored with special privileges, local firms grow. Multilateral organizations like the ITU and the World Bank lend support to the LDCs, including more training.

On the downside, cartelization strengthens the hand of national PTT managers who oppose job-threatening technological or policy innovation, risking further IT stagnation. A slowdown in global markets brings lower investment in marginal markets like Africa.

Larger LDCs with an IT export base grow less quickly, and/or are incorporated into regional cartels which greatly limit their freedom of manoeuvre. With more agreements on rules of the game, the IT sector witnesses the rise of many more restrictive commercial agreements designed to reduce or limit effective market competition. This includes anticompetitive *regional blocks* for Asia, the Americas and Europe, built around a large regional champion. In this future convergence leads not to greater competition but to greater market concentration and control. The once-rapid growth of the IT sector slows, as companies seek to protect and defend their gains rather than seek new markets, products and competitive opportunities. Large oligopolies dominate global, regional and national markets. Domestically, dominant telephone service suppliers remain dominant with only minimal competition in core services. This is a slower, cartelized future where companies like Microsoft and Fujitsu control two thirds of the global markets.

To summarize, the world of 'Regulated Oligopolies' shows us:

- A balkanized, cartelized GII. Parties prefer stability over risk, even if it means lower growth and stagnation for many. Risk aversion.
- Diffusion of IT technology slows and occurs much more selectively.
- Rule agreement on dividing up global markets is controlled mostly by G-7 nations.
- Big countries and big firms dominate local societies and global markets.
- Regional blocs slow cross-border investments and trade.
- Capital investment in IT slumps.
- Costs rise to consumers (or fall more slowly).
- The hand of domestic interests favoring continued dominance of single supplier PTTS is strengthened.
- Political conflicts explode over access, controls (especially US, UK vs others).
- 'Agreements' are made mostly among the powerful states and companies, but LDCs have some voice.

Trends

• Technological Innovation	Low
• Growth	Low

- Investment   Low
- Income Distribution   Medium
- Support for LDCS   Medium
- Power Distribution   Same

Cell C: free market chaos, low rules, high competition

Summary

This 'Wild West' scenario occurs when market competition explodes with very aggressive private sector activities, accompanied by the failure of the major actors to reach agreement on the global issues. 'Free market chaos' rules. IT investment flows and sales remain vigorous, but mainly to OECD countries and to the most secure and reliable markets in developing areas. Some LDCs complain of being ignored, while others complain of 'predatory' behavior unrestrained by good business norms or effective international dispute resolution mechanisms. Developed countries and their firms complain about unreliable national rules and unfair expropriation or broken contracts in LDCs. International organizations like the WTO and World Bank lose clout and legitimacy.

Driving factors in this scenario

In a series of unanticipated defeats, in Geneva, Brussels and Rome, in global meeting after global meeting, the world's nations fail to reach agreement on IT trade and investment, copyright, encryption and intellectual property. Agreements signed on paper are not implemented. Not only do the developing countries fail to achieve satisfaction in these forums, but there are serious splits among the governments of Japan, the EU and the United States. China, excluded from the WTO and with aggressive new leadership, retaliates by refusing to adhere to intellectual property rights and encourages their factories to produce pirated CDs. Canada and France toughen their stance by restricting cross-border movement of foreign content, leading to severe Franco-American and Franco-British conflicts that poison relations among these countries. Russia's political deterioration makes it more difficult to reach agreements. Private firms pursue vigorous competition strategies. At the same time, in the absence of formal intergovernmental agreements, private firms create *de facto* international standards (as did Microsoft), and through coalitions of companies that establish industry standards.

Companies from industrialized countries rush to replace mature markets at home with fast growing ones, and invest in those LDCs with larger, more secure markets. Important for poorer countries, international development initiatives like the World Bank's InfoDev and international agreements through the WTO, collapse, reducing multilateral resources for IT development and hurting the most vulnerable. International stalemate occurs on many IT issues, deterioration on others. Thus a return to the unproductive vitriol and hostility of the 1970s 'New International (Information) Order', with a severe North–South split. In weaker areas like Africa, with tenuous positions in international markets, individual countries' leverage is greatly diminished since their membership in large international organizations counts for less as these bodies are weakened. Ignored by big states and big companies, in this future the smaller developing countries are hurt the most.

Implications for developing countries

Consumers of information technology in developing countries can expect to benefit from falling IT prices and improvements in technology. With competition high and firms seeking their own commercial advantage, sophisticated LDC managers try to play off one vender or investor against another in bargaining for IT market entry or expansion.

There are downsides in this scenario for developing countries. A breakdown of international agreement on rules slows investments in marginal markets as private firms fear Third World risks. A global system with cut-throat competition and disagreement on regulatory procedures is more subject to sharper business cycle booms and busts harmful to all actors. Also, the global environment allows bigger more powerful MNCs to gain leverage *vis-a-vis* poor governments.

Inability to decide on the timing of deregulation and privatization, on the extent of intellectual property rights coverage, or even technical standards for new technologies, harms political and commercial relations among nations. Disputes over IT issues bleed into other bilateral negotiations, with countries linking their failures to resolve differences in one area with their contested position in another, as has already occurred for example in IPR disputes between the US and China.

A world of chaotic rules and frequent stops and starts disadvantages countries without adequate and sophisticated manpower to track constant rule changes and abrupt changes of course in international negotiations. The more fragmented the international regime and its rules, the more costly and difficult it is for LDC managers to keep up with the changes, especially in critical areas like electronic commerce and electronic banking. 'Cybercrime' grows exponentially, based in small, vulnerable LDCs that provide a haven for international criminals.

Stalemate or deteriorating international cooperation impacts on commercial conditions and competition as well. The negative impact will be especially severe in global markets for satellite services, among firms like Iridium and Teledesic that require basic agreements across many nations. Inability to reach agreement on cellular telephone standards proves costly, as between GSM and other systems.

Programs targeted to advance poorer countries' IT sectors, such as WorldTel or InfoDev, lose support. A decline in commitments to management training will be especially harmful, since the key to successful NIIs is not just investment in hardware or software but in 'peopleware'. Their political and economic stability deteriorates and emigration flows grow.

In summary this scenario shows us:

- The 'Wild West' revisited as international cooperation declines, and information and income gaps grow very wide, very fast.
- Big powers can't agree on global rules either bilaterally or multilaterally.
- A lack of collective leadership globally.
- High uncertainty about overall global investing, and about national and local rules.
- The production of islands of Internet connectivity. Poorer regions are bypassed by the information revolution.
- A boom and bust pattern of investment and company performance.
- Multimedia skyrockets in popularity.
- A rapid product cycle, 'policy cycle'.
- LDC influence is very marginal.
- Support for LDC IT training, etc. declines sharply.
- Gradual breakdown of social order in some countries.
- Cybercrime explodes, low Internet security.

Trends

Technological Innovation	Low
Growth	Mixed
Investment	Mixed
Income Distribution	Worsens
Support for LDCS	Low
Power Distribution	Skewed

Cell D: competition and coordination, high rule, high competition

Summary

Under these conditions countries seek ways to capture the benefits and meet the challenges of high competition and high rule agreement. The combination of substantial competition and widespread rule agreement accelerates capital investment, innovation, the creation of new greenfield industries and the further radical restructuring of existing industries and the links and alliances among them. Customers get more choice and better service, at lower prices.

Driving factors in this scenario

This scenario comes about through sustained, difficult and high profile negotiations in a variety of international forums, where the leading parties are
able to reach agreement. Private industry associations accelerate agreement
of rules governing Internet standards and IT market access. The US continues the leadership role staked out in the WTO talks. The G-7 governments
reach common accords, and agree to reach out to the developing world in
the design of the global information society. Nations in the developing world
also exercise new independent leadership to advance their interests while
seeking a common cause with industrialized countries and more liberal
relations with private sector firms. Because there is political agreement on
institutional, regulatory and legal frameworks, these private firms expand
their investments.

Implications for developing countries

The positive experiences of residential telephone users in Chile and Argentina, corporate customers in Europe, and small- and medium-sized businesses
in the US support the claim that a wide range of consumers and suppliers
benefit from growing market competition. The positive demonstration effect
encourages more LDCs to liberalize markets and regulatory systems.

With agreements on IPR, this scenario brings an explosion of new media
content in a variety of forms. The cinema industry grows within developing
countries and finds markets in other LDCs and in the industrialized world.
Trade in content in many forms—CD ROMs, book publishing, cinema
and Internet traffic—accelerates globally. Prompted by international and
interfirm agreements over e-cash and EDI, the volume of world trade grows
substantially.

In short, while all countries gain, it appears that developing countries
gain the most from this D Cell scenario, since it provides the greater
certainty (rules) and the greatest growth (through enhanced trade and
investment) required to halt the precipitous slump to a world divided into
the information haves and have-nots.

There are indications that countries are seeking the upside gains of the
D scenario. The acceleration of private companies creating or joining
commercial consortia to establish internationally accepted standards of
operation, manufacture and interconnection attest to the need that leading
corporations feel for greater rule agreement globally. One can infer the
same from the number of meetings and conferences among a wide range of
countries, from industrialized to developing, at which both competition and
rule agreement are central.

On the other hand, accelerated rule and market growth substantially
threatens the status of the powerful PTT managers, perhaps producing a

political backlash against further LDC market liberalization and PTT commercialization. For example, accelerated job losses in the PTT sector poses severe political problems for LDC national governments.

There will be some continued nationalist backlash against accelerated exports of foreign cultural artifacts through a variety of media. One could especially expect this kind of backlash against the world market leader, the US, which has 75% of the $100 billion global software industry (Germany and Britain are the next largest with only %10 between them).

Countries marginal to markets and rule making will find it difficult to stay abreast of future changes if indeed the rate, breadth and depth of change truly speeds up. But greater cooperation with the industrialized countries and higher earnings encourages them to create programs for training, capacity building, subsidized loans and so forth.

This scenario brings:

- Re-balancing of telecommunications and information technologies.
- More harmonious, cooperative and complementary public–private sector relations.
- Falling prices to the final consumers.
- Markets open to world suppliers.
- Basis of 'knowledge' defined as requiring collective input and interpretation; joint production of knowledge.
- High rates of interconnection.
- Participatory rule making.
- Investment spreads to many LDC markets.
- More training of LDC officials in, e.g. regulatory reform.

Trends

•	Technological Innovation	High
•	Growth	High
•	Investment	High
•	Income Distribution	Better
•	Support for LDCS	High
•	Power Distribution	More Positive

Getting from here to there: the future is path dependent

For the sake of analysis we have treated the four scenarios as separate and discrete. In the real world, they are combined and interconnected. Indeed, for governments and firms, the path to the future(s) is as important as the destination. The transition from the current rules and market conditions to the new end-state conditions will profoundly shape the future state of the global information society. History, even future history, does makes a difference—Japan is a market society and Italy is a market society, but their unique histories have given them very particular rules and very particular forms of the relations between market and government. The future is heavily path dependent.

For example, even if we assume that Cell D is the preferred target and is reached successfully, will the path of least resistance go easily and steadily on the diagonal from Cell A to Cell D? Or will the global system move more circuitously and first pass through the less desirable and more difficult Cell C or Cell B before reaching destination D? Senior policy makers therefore need to consider the implications for their countries of alternative paths to the future—whether an A–C–B–D path or an A–B–C–D path. Nor should we automatically assume our arrival at D. Some countries may be caught in B and remain there.

Decision makers therefore should develop path scenarios for the transition, as well as destination scenarios. There are two critical aspects of path scenarios that should be considered.

First, will the transition be fast or slow? Will the powerful telecoms and communications actors gather themselves up and shift quickly out of our presently slow, fused and monopoly world in 3 years, or will it take the system 30 years to make a full and complete transition? On the answer to this question hangs the national plans and the corporate strategies of countries and companies. Some companies will make the correct analysis, and they will prosper; others will make the wrong analysis, assuming 3 years of transition when it is 30, and their fortunes will suffer. Similarly with governments.

Second, will the transition be fractured or coherent? We can imagine a future in which countries make the transition at roughly the same pace, moving in roughly similar directions. For example, while France and Senegal have very different starting points, they nonetheless move steadily toward Cell D with similar levels of commitments. This is a coherent transition. We can also imagine a more fractured transition, a more likely one, in which countries move toward their own 'Nirvanas' at very different rates, with very different levels of commitment, and probably with very different Nirvanas. Along this path—or these paths—uncertainty is greater, and some countries move towards and eventually occupy virtually every quadrant of the matrix. In this world, the global information society becomes very complex and contradictory, with an extended 'transition' that may go on for decades.

Other scenarios

There are several other ways to conceive and design IT scenarios. We noted above that scenarios could be constructed for each IT industry—one separate scenario for computer hardware, another for software, etc. One could also create separate 'customized' multi-sector transition scenarios country by country. Also, while we described the four scenarios above as distinct alternatives for the GII as a whole, they can also be seen as co-existing simultaneously as different sub-areas or neighborhoods in the global information society, with some countries already operating under 'Competitive and Cooperative' conditions, while others remain in the 'Monopoly and Fused' circumstance.

There are other scenarios beyond telecommunications. For example, the Secretary General of the ITU, Pekke Tarjanne, recently proposed four scenarios for Internet development. They are:

- The future will be much like today, 'with incremental improvements in bandwidth availability and performance.' Supply–demand balances would be the principal regulators.
- The current Internet 'will splinter into a series of interconnected, privately owned, parallel Internets that may be application-specific' and perhaps 'each . . . owned by a service provider who will guarantee minimal level of service in return for a usage fee.'
- The net collapses under its own weight as more people leave in frustration than join as new subscribers.
- Some new core information infrastructure emerges perhaps based on other protocols and better services. These different scenarios will have different impacts on developed and developing countries.[34]

Walter Baer of the RAND Corporation has conjectured about possible institutional responses to the emerging conditions of international convergence and competition.[35] He foresees three possible scenarios based on the form of international coordination that emerges—international coordination mainly through national-level initiatives; coordination through formal international organizations; or coordination through less formal, specialized private standard-setting coalitions. His scenario-building reminds us that an important component of cooperation and rule-making will be strengthening appropriate international institutions through which developed and developing countries can work effectively together for common purposes. LDC access to international resources will differ substantially under each scenario; LDCs will find it more difficult to monitor and influence change under the third Baer scenario, for example.[36]

Barbara Cross hypothesizes information futures in her work on *Netciety*.[37] Instead of alternative futures, she discusses a single possible future, sketching the evolution of global information society, describing it from the vantage point of the year 2010. She divides the world into four groups. While in her analysis these groups are meant to coexist simultaneously with one another, we can also consider them as alternative scenarios for some countries in the South. There are:

- countries 'so threatened by internal chaos that only tiny pockets of connectivity have been established;
- those where governments had refused to accept the consequences of connectivity in terms of increased transparency of government and decentralization of power and had therefore limited access to a few privileged or acceptable constituencies;
- those which recognized the benefits of connectivity to economic and social development but were nonetheless aware of the threat posed to traditional culture and which attempted to develop and apply technologies to limit access to information considered inimical to the maintenance of national characteristics and social stability; and
- the majority which had embraced access to the global information highway as a means of enhancing the development potential of their citizens; these still faced substantial development problems but could envisage the possibility of their solution.' (p. 5, Rath).

Conclusion

Developing country national IT managers should not underestimate the synergies created from market expansion and rule agreement, which is at the heart of this project's scenarios. On the one hand, wider agreement on the rules of the game can provide a boost to competition. New rules, agreements and institutions can:

- provide more reliable and timely information about markets;
- reduce uncertainty about the behavior of other competitors, strategic allies and regulators;
- better structure rewards and punishments; and
- define property rights and responsibilities of various actors in the global market/society.

In other words, agreeing on the rules of the game will clarify expectations governing core competition activities – market entry and exit; competitive/ anti-competitive behavior; foreign vs domestic ownership rights.

As a consequence of greater certainty about the behavior of other firms or governments, and about their own rights and responsibilities (including dispute resolution), private investors are more likely to significantly expand their investment, including that in new technologies.

Conversely, greater competition can impact positively on rule making. For example, the growing size of the market likely to result from growing competition will expand the size of the pie available to all actors. Growth provides the economic surplus to create win–win, positive sum outcomes, and hence reduces cut-throat competition and pressures to cheat, shirk or otherwise bend and break international rules in a shrinking market. Slower or negative growth is more likely to produce dog-eat-dog zero-sum behavior and to block progress on devising rules of the game. Furthermore, enhanced international competition is also likely to expand the number of private sector consortia seeking inter-firm agreement on rules, especially on international standards. This can create a richer texture of international cooperation that complements (and may replace) slower government-to-government arrangements. Thus, greater competition and greater rule adherence can be complementary. Whether this positive outcome occurs will depend in part on the quality of leadership among the main actors.

The conclusion of the WTO talks certainly does not mean the end of the invention of the future; this is not the 'end of history'. In important ways, this is just the beginning of a possible future, but the hard work lies ahead. Through this on-going iterative process, conflicts over access to the magnetic spectrum for broadcasts, access to capital, access to orbital slots for satellites and rules in standards-setting remain to be continually managed and resolved. Even the WTO agreements are only agreements on paper, and the actual contours of the future hinge on translating paper accords into actual practice. If that practice can be equitably designed and implemented, the entire global information society can benefit.

Developing country officials should not underestimate the costs of their exclusion from global rule negotiations, nor the costs of refusing to make their domestic economies and regulatory structures more flexible, open and competitive. As the core developed and developing countries of the WTO group reach a global deal incorporating 95% of the world's telecom markets, the other non-participants risk finding themselves marginalized and their national IT systems under-capitalized and uncompetitive. The stakes are high. The most positive path ahead is greater LDC proactive engagement in the invention of the global information future. When this happens, the entire global information society will benefit.

Acknowledgements

The author wishes to thank the following colleagues for their helpful comments: Carlos Bragga, Walter Baer, Carol Charles, Bowman Cutter, William Garrison, Odvaar Kvale, Brian Levy, David Olive, Dennis Pirages, Walda Roseman and Joe Young.

Notes and references

1 G-7, *Chair's Conclusions*, G-7 Ministerial Conference on the Information Society, Brussels, 1995.
2 Organization for Economic Co-operation and Development (OECD), *Interfutures Facing the Future: Mastering the Probable and Managing the Unpredictable.* OECD, Paris, 1979; and *L'interdépendance Mondiale: Les liens entre l'OCDE et les principales économies en développment.* OECD, Paris, 1995.

305

3 Petrazzini, B. A., *Global Telecom Talks: A Trillion Dollar Deal.* Institute for International Economics, Washington, DC, 1996.

4 Cowhey, P. F., The international telecommunication regimes: the root of regimes for high technology. *International Organization*, Spring 1990, **44**(2), 169–200.

5 Petrazzini, B. A., *op cit*, ref. 3.

6 Morrison, J. L., Renfro, W. L. and Boucher, W. I., *Applying Methods and Technique of Futures Research*, Jossey Bass, San Francisco, CA, 1983.

7 Institute for Information Studies, *Crossroads on the Information Highway Convergence and Diversity in Communications Technologies.* The Aspen Institute and Northern Telecoms, 1994.

8 Hamel, G. and Prahalad, C. K., *Competing for the Future.* Harvard Business School Press, Boston, MA, 1994.

9 *Business Week.* Strategic planning—after a decade of gritty downsizing, big thinkers are back in vogue (Cover Story), 26 August 1996.

10 Russell, S., *Changing Maps Governing in a World of Rapid Change.* Carleton University Press, Ottowa, 1995.

11 Diamond, D., What comes after what comes next. *Fast Company* December–January 1997, p. 72–80.

12 Forge, F., *The Macro-Economic Effects of Near-Zero Tariff Telecommunications Rethinking Infrastructure and Society with Telecommunications.* Project NEAR ZERO, CSC, 1994.

13 Schwartz, P. and Leyden, P., The long boom, *WIRED*, July 1997, p. 115.

14 United Nations Commission on Science and Technology for Development, *Strategies for ICT and Development: Accumulating National Capabilities*, Typescript, December 1996.

15 Pritchett, L., Forget convergence: divergence past, present, and future. *Finance and Development*, June 1996, p. 40–43.

16 *Ibid*, p. 41.

17 *Ibid*, p. 41.

18 *Ibid*, p. 42.

19 Kahin, B. and Wilson III, E. J. (eds.), *National Information Infrastructure Initiatives Vision and Policy Design.* MIT Press, Cambridge, 1996.

20 Talero, E. and Caudette, P., *Harnessing Information for Development*, World Bank, Washington DC, May 1995.

21 Tapscott, D. and Caston, A., *Paradigm Shift: The New Promise of Information Technology.* McGraw Hill, New York, 1993.

22 Rosenau, J. N., Governance in the twenty-first century. *Global Governance*, 1995, **1**(1), 29–32.

23 G-7, *op cit*, ref. 1.

24 Global Information Infrastructure Commission, *GIIC Annual Meeting Report.* Kuala Lumpur, 30–31 July 1996.

25 Global Information Infrastructure Commission, *ibid*, p. 5.

26 Mansell, R., *The New Telecommunications: A Political Economy of Network Evolution.* Sage, London, 1993.

27 Wilson III, E. J., *Mapping the Global Information Infrastructure.* Report prepared for the United Nations Commission on Science and Technology for Development, 1997.

28 Millett, S. M. and Honton, E. J., *A Manager's Guide to Technology Forecasting and Strategy Analysis Methods.* Battelle Press, Columbus, OH, 1991.

29 Schwartz, P., *The Art of the Long View.* Doubleday, New York, 1991.

30 Russell, S., *Changing Maps Governing in a World of Rapid Change.* Carleton University Press, Ottowa, 1995.

31 Masuda, Y., *The Information Society as Post-Industrial Society.* World Future Society, Bethesda, MD, 1981.
32 Kvale, O., Personal Communication.
33 Hundt, R., Speech before the Institute of International Economics, March 1997.
34 Tarjanne, P., Secretary General, International Telecommunications Union, at the Pacific Telecoms Council 18th Annual Conference, *The Information Infrastructure: Users, Resources and Strategies,* Honolulu, 1966, as summarized by National Computer Board.
35 Baer, W., Will the global information infrastructure need transnational (or any) governance? In *National Information Infrastructure Initiatives Vision and Policy Design,* eds. B. Kahin and E. J. Wilson III. MIT Press, Cambridge, 1996.
36 *Ibid,* p. 33.
37 Cross, B., *Netciety,* Typescript, 1996, p. 23. For a base-line analysis of the Information Revolution's impacts on the world's poorest nations, see Wilson III, E. J., The information revolution comes to Africa. CSIS Africa Notes, Center for Strategic and International Studies, Washington, D.C., June 1996.

38

AN INVESTIGATION OF THE IMPACT OF INFORMATION AND COMMUNICATION TECHNOLOGIES IN SUB-SAHARAN AFRICA

Lishan Adam and Frances Wood

Source: *Journal of Information Science* 25(4) (1999): 307–18.

Abstract

Information and communication technologies (ICT) have been in use for over three decades in different settings in Africa, but the impact of ICT on users in the region is not well documented. This paper attempts to examine the impact of ICT in sub-Saharan Africa, based on a study using a grounded theory approach. It was aimed at understanding users within their ICT applications context. Four main aspects of the impact of ICT were identified: 'Actual impact', 'Potential impact', 'Constraints' and 'Actions centred around users and their reactions'. The research indicates that an understanding of ICT users' iterative and adaptive behaviour and their day-to-day pains in coping with problems of ICT in the local context is necessary for impact assessment.

The constructionist behaviour in which individuals, organisations, professionals and groups map their world and situation, and the complex action and interaction between them, imposes the structure of ICT use. This paper discusses the impact of ICT in the context of its use and the concrete circumstances of the individuals involved and the tasks undertaken, together with historical and environmental perspectives.

1. Introduction

The rapid advances in information and communication technologies (ICT) have, according to Michael [1], resulted in a 'new social condition' that is

308

affecting the day-to-day activities of individuals, organisations and society. Although the effects of ICT are global, there has been little investigation into the specific impact of ICT in Africa. There has, however, been a growing concern about the limited exploitation of the potential of ICT in Africa. Policy makers, for example, were 'increasingly searching for in-depth analysis that informs decisions' [2]

A growing body of research exists in the developed world under the rubric of 'social informatics', but adapting these studies to developing countries creates a number of problems. First, studies in developed countries cover only a small portion of the problems that face developing countries. Second, most of the results are not applicable to the situations in developing countries. In an evaluation of the suitability of impact studies to developing countries, McConnell [3] concluded that the literature in the developed world:

(1) focuses on northern perspectives where countries have other information traditions and infrastructures than developing countries;
(2) treats particular organisations or sectors, as opposed to a comprehensive assessment of the larger impact question;
(3) often uses simple quantitative tools to measure impact, instead of a generalised and expanded treatment of both qualitative and quantitative techniques;
(4) interprets impact as a simplified transformation in a small user community, rather than examining the long-term consequences on the society as a whole.

The existing literature that discusses ICT in Africa is mainly scattered, superficial, or written from business, information processing or library and archiving angles [4–6]. In addition, it often lacks a methodological framework [7, 8]. Related to the paucity of ICT impact research in Africa is a growing gap between expectations of ICT and realisations. The prediction that personal computers could have an impact on development in Africa did not hold – efforts have not been successful, at least for a decade [9]. For example, in 1985, the Third World Academy of Sciences conference on information technology in developing countries called for urgent measures, stating:

> Either the developing countries adapt and use the knowledge to enhance their drive for socio-economic development, or they fall back even further – this is harsh rule of survival in an increasingly competitive world marketplace [10].

Many of those in developed countries that thought microcomputers could facilitate their work or transform their countries' economies were unable to fulfil these expectations. A decade later, the same message was repeated at a regional symposium on telematics for development in Africa:

> Unless African countries become full actors in the global information revolution, the gaps between haves and have-nots will widen, opening the possibility of increased marginalization of the continent [11].

Why have African countries not been successful in realising minimum levels of application or benefits? Although this issue is beyond a single study, an interpretative understanding of the impact of ICT in the region could be a step towards building a body of knowledge in the area.

2. Research methodology

Quantitative methods were not considered appropriate for analysing the impact of ICT, which is largely a social construction and based on the understanding of people, their drive, knowledge structures and social interactions. The study therefore relied on qualitative methods, so as to examine the interpretative understanding of users. The focus of user perceptions made grounded theory an appropriate methodology to employ.

The choice of qualitative methodology and grounded theory in the study was reinforced by ongoing debate over impact measurement. Thorngate [12], for example, was opposed to the emerging fields of study based on quantitative methods, as he believed that impact cannot be assessed outside the context of use. Selecting a qualitative approach led to adopting the grounded theory to emerge inductively with findings based on data. Experience in the use of the grounded theory approach at the University of Sheffield contributed to this choice [13–15].

Proposed by Glaser and Strauss, grounded theory advocates the generating of theory that is 'grounded' in data rather than working with a preconception [16]. The inadequacy of previous studies in the area of impact of ICT was also a contributory factor in choosing to use grounded theory. This was partly because there was only limited data to rely on as the basis of a testable hypothesis. Empirical studies on the impact of ICT have produced conflicting results, due to the lack of a theoretical base, measurement problems and lack of data. Testing existing conflicting speculations and hypotheses from conference papers and literature was ruled out, as this was deemed to cause more confusion. Martin and Turner suggested the use of grounded theory on these occasions:

> Frequently when no relevant theory exists and even when theories concerned with a topic do exist, they may be too remote or abstract to offer much detailed guidance and assistance. Under such circumstances, the researcher will want to develop a theoretical account that facilitates the discussion of general features of the topics under

study and is firmly based or grounded in the data collected – a grounded theory [17].

There has been criticism of grounding theory on data, especially on the influence of existing theory and the need to limit the use of grounded theory to substantive areas. Much of the criticism seems to emerge from lack of understanding and misuse. Although a considerable volume of theoretical work seems to be missing which incorporates existing human understandings while grounding theory in data [18], grounded theory has been found useful in providing insights that closely conform with the interpretative under-standing of ICT users [19].

3. Data collection and analysis

The study began in October 1995 as a PhD research project by the first author. It was completed in November 1997. The fieldwork took place in two rounds: the first round between March and August 1996 and the second between January and May 1997. The sampling was based on emerging con-cepts (theoretical sampling) – the ideas that emerged guided the decisions as to what data to collect and where to find it [20]. Nevertheless, rigorous theoretical sampling was delayed until the second phase, due to the paucity of research in this area. It was felt that the emergent concepts identified during the first phase could assist further systematic sampling for the second round. Charmaz suggested that this type of delay of theoretical sampling is useful, especially when little is known of the phenomenon [18]. She asserted that 'by the time theoretical sampling is planned, a researcher would have hunches or even hypotheses that he or she wishes to check'.

Two groups of informants were covered:

•   local ICT users in Ethiopia; and
•   opportunity informants from other African countries.

Participants in the interviews consisted of senior civil servants, high-level managers in business, education and services, technicians and support staff. These were very crucial, due to their exposure to different situations, jobs that require them to solve complex problems and their responsibilities in the implementation of ICT. Fifteen per cent of the interviewees were senior government officials involved in the development of national ICT policy (Table 1). Effort was made to interview two to three participants from the same organisation across various management levels. Although the number of women in the ICT field in Africa is very limited compared to developed countries, ten (14%) have been included. Three women held managerial positions, five were at professional levels and two others worked as support and administrative staff.

311

Table 1 Distribution of samples.

| Position | International | Ethiopia | | Education | Total | Percentage |
		Business	Economy*			
Senior	5	2	4	–	11	16%
High-level managers	6	6	6	5	23	33%
Technical (professional)	7	5	11	5	28	40%
Support	1	–	4	3	8	11%
Total	19	13	25	13	70	100%

*agriculture, industry, etc.

The sample included non-Ethiopians with experience in ICT in Africa and the developed world. This was intended to widen the impact of the study from different perspectives. Five of these worked for international organisations in Ethiopia, two for non-governmental organisations and three for the local government. Four were graduate students from eastern and southern Africa. The rest worked for their own governments in African countries.

The data were transcribed and analysed using the comparative analysis method suggested by Glaser and Strauss [16]. The core data analysis, using the comparative analysis method, can be broken down into four sets of non-linear and interdependent procedures, including:

(1) the generation of descriptive codes from interviews and field notes;
(2) the development and linking of conceptual categories by comparing incidents;
(3) theoretical interpretation;
(4) the testing, verification and refining of the emergent interpretation.

4. Results

A wide range of issues was raised in the interview schedule. These included the function of the informant in his/her organisation, the influence of ICT on his/her work, his/her understanding of ICT, the type of infrastructure available at his/her institution, the commitments and relationships between various actors in his/her organisation, the level of negotiation between various actors in the implementation of ICT, the constraints encountered and his/her opinions on the applications and the impact of ICT at individual, organisational and national levels. Analysis of the informants' interpretative statements in response to these questions resulted in four core categories that explain the impact of ICT in Africa:

- actual impact;
- potential impact;
- constraints;
- actions centred on users and their reactions.

The *actual impact* of ICT refers to its current value, benefits, transformation and consequences in a complex social and organisational setting. The historical and cultural context and the infrastructure available influence the actual impact of ICT.

Potential impact refers to potential gains or values and the negative or positive consequences achievable through learning, development and by current actions, strategies and applications. Potential impact rests on a number of factors: current actual impact, organisational setting, resources, the attitudes of policy makers and the other stakeholders and, importantly, on the constraints which operate in the particular situation.

Constraints stand as barriers between actual and potential impact. Constraints are the various inhibiting factors, ranging from social and technical problems to the commitment levels in organisations and government. Constraints and the actions centred around users and users' reactions dynamically alter the interaction between actual and potential impact.

Action centred around users and users' reactions act as a feedback loop between actual and potential impact (Fig. 1). The phrase refers to the ecology of participation, the social relationship between various actors and the creativity of users in dealing with constraints. The creativity of users, their actions, why they act, what implications their actions bring to the development and use of ICT within a variety of cultural, social, political and economic settings are crucial elements in the application of ICT, yet they are the least addressed. Various actors are involved in the application and use of ICT in Africa at different levels and different times. These include:

- policy makers;
- public and private institutions that implement ICT;
- external bodies, such as United Nations agencies and bilateral and multilateral donors;
- coordinating bodies at national and regional levels;
- scientific and academic institutions that carry out research or implementations related to the projects;
- local governments that often receive the funds;
- communities or organisations that receive the ICT;
- individual users and their families.

The study also found external factors that play a considerable role in stimulating and inhibiting the interaction among the four core categories. Some of the external factors that were identified and that cannot be

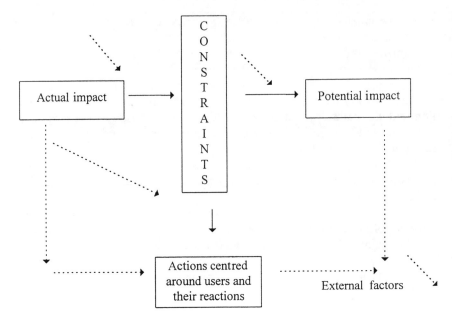

Figure 1 A social feedback model of four core categories and external factors.

controlled locally include withdrawal or increase of external funding (due to bad or good bilateral relations between countries), new marketing strategies, foreign direct investment, joint venture agreements, new products or technological breakthroughs, natural or political crises. External factors fall within the larger matrix of social and economic relations between nations, institutions and groups and are often difficult to control by actions centred around users and users' reactions.

4.1. The actual impact of ICT in sub-Saharan Africa

The actual impact of ICT appears at five levels: on government, within the business sector, at organisational and at individual levels. The overall findings of the actual impact of ICT in sub-Saharan Africa are discouraging. Table 2 summarises the actual impact of ICT in sub-Saharan Africa at these levels.

In sub-Saharan Africa, there was an increase in awareness of the value of ICT during the last decade. Changes in perception, from initial resistance and mystification to understanding of the value of various technologies, had been witnessed by informants. However, awareness did not lead to the immediate application of ICT. Introduction of ICT had not yet moved beyond substitution – for many informants, the impact was 'simply replacement of typewriters with computers'.

Table 2 Actual impact of ICT in sub-Saharan Africa.

Government	Education	Business	Organisations	Individuals
• Demystification of ICT in public institutions. • Improved communication and delivery of services.	• Increasing use of computers in education. • Pressure for new ways of teaching and learning in higher education. • Improving communication among researchers and research institutions.	• Emergence of a new breed of information workers. • Spread of ICT knowledge through or by business institutions. • Opportunities for employment.	• Improved awareness of ICT. • Greater opportunities in cost savings and new areas of ICT application. • Changes in the roles of professionals in organisations. • Increased numbers of outlets for access to information.	• Cost saving. • Possibilities to participate in global lists. • Professional diversification and job satisfaction.

The adoption of ICT involved a substantial learning cycle and a level of investment that were difficult to achieve in sub-Saharan Africa. For many institutions and nations, it was difficult to cope with the need for continuous changes in skills. Resources were mostly available through donor agencies. Donor support was given with various strings attached, sometimes with the result that the growth of ICT at the national level was affected, usually negatively. The consequence of dependency can be summed up as under-utilisation of existing technology, reinforced by inappropriate education, lack of awareness and by subscription to inappropriate tools. Consequently, indigenous knowledge and capacity have not been fully developed in sub-Saharan Africa. This has been the major cause of backwardness in the application of ICT in Africa.

Profound changes were difficult to achieve on the organisational front. For example, there were not reports on using ICT to gain competitive advantage at the level of organisations. Management remained the main hindrance to growth. Limited maturity in organisational management and lack of good planning and control made the process of investment in ICT difficult. The organisations surveyed suffered from resource problems and the lack of academically qualified managers.

The main positive impact of ICT in sub-Saharan Africa has been in the area of information system development. Initially, information services were set up in large government institutions with the expectation of achieving centralised management and control of information. This had mixed results, with success recorded in transaction processing, especially in running pay-rolls and utility bills, as well as in building databanks. Centralisation was followed by decentralisation when the cost of the technology decreased as personal computers became available. However, full advantage was not taken of the decentralisation, mainly because of limited networking.

The impact of ICT on individuals working in information services and computer business was high compared to other users. Frequent users were able to achieve efficiency and cost reductions in document processing. Electronic mail was found to be an empowering tool for individual users, regardless of their profession. Those in the ICT and information sector found ICT to be rewarding in terms of income, but highly stressful, due to the difficulty of coping with the rapid changes involved.

4.2 The potential impact of ICT in sub-Saharan Africa

The potential impact of ICT is dependent on current technologies as well as those of the future, thus making predictions difficult. Most predictions in the study were based on extrapolation of the current impact of ICT in developed countries. Nevertheless, it was argued that the potential impact of ICT is a function of the accessibility of ICT to a wide range of users and its applicability to local settings. This requires the development and introduction of sound policies that enable growth. In addition, there needs to be a willingness and the ability to tailor ICT to national requirements.

Potential impact was envisaged at five levels: government (national level), education, public sector institutions, institutions in the private sector and individuals (Table 3). At the national level, the potential impact of ICT can be constructive and/or disruptive, but the constructive aspects were highlighted in the study. The main opportunity for developing countries lies in transmitting and exchanging information and *knowledge* to individuals, regardless of location, education, social and ethnic background and economic status. The use of ICT could lead to either a reduction or an expansion of the gap between the information poor and the information rich.

ICT have the potential to increase coordination in government operations. Growing use of digital archiving and information management could lead to the increased effectiveness of government bureaucracy. Governments could use ICT in areas that require automation. For example, interviewees argued that ICT would have an effect in speeding up such activities as invoicing and payments. The intensive application of ICT in traditional sectors such as agriculture could enhance the delivery of social, economic and infrastructural services.

Social applications of ICT in learning, telemedicine, land and environment management are also potential areas of value to governments. These applications require considerable resources that have been difficult to obtain; consequently, they are areas that have enjoyed limited attention. Applications have been fragmented, so that unnecessary duplication has occurred. However, reduction in cost could lead to the application of ICT in society on a wider scale.

Capacities exist for all countries to develop a software sector that caters to local markets and for exchanges with developing countries. Openness in software development could enable those who take the pains to reap the benefits. Such potential will remain a dream without adequate investments in education and especially in computer science and engineering.

Improved coordination among organisations and a widening gap between public and private institutions were cited as potential implications of ICT for organisations. In banks, for example, ICT could lead to better coordination by increasing response speed. Decentralisation and restructuring are expected in private organisations, leading to changes in practices that fit with growing ICT. However, this could be difficult to achieve in public institutions in sub-Saharan Africa in the medium term.

The potential impact on individuals is somewhat comparable to the current and actual impact of ICT – the changes will be more of a quantitative nature than qualitative, i.e. more people with computers rather than people doing more with computers. While ICT continue to empower individuals, especially those working in the information and computing field, they could also lead to information and knowledge anxiety.

317

Table 3 Potential impact of ICT in sub-Saharan Africa.

Government	Education	Business	Organisations	Individuals
• Intensive application of ICT in substantive sectors.	• Access to global information to researchers and research institutions.	• Advanced information processing, e.g. electronic commerce.	• Growing decentralisation of applications in organisations.	• Greater and continuous empowerment of individuals.
• Cost saving and availability of tools within the range of public institutions.	• Distance education and lifelong learning.	• Growth from focus on primary products to information products.	• Improved coordination among organisations.	• Improved desires for learning and career advancement.
• Reduction of gaps between poor and rich, urban and rural.	• Increased role of research and academic institutions in disseminating technology.	• Access to communication facilities and improved competitiveness.	• Changes to organisational structure to adapt to ICT.	• Growing stress for those involved in ICT and individuals accessing large amounts of information.
• Improvement of horizontal communication in government institutions.	• Diffusion of technology to elementary schools.	• Improved customer/client relationships.	• Widening gap between those who act (private institutions) and those who lag.	
		• Improved information brokerage roles.		
		• Competition in new areas of information services (cyber cafes, data entry, software development, etc).		

Table 4 Number of low-level concept categories.

Categories	*Actual impact*	*Potential impact*	*Constraints*	*User-centred action and strategies*
No. of categories	43	63	191	66
Percentage	11.8%	17.4%	52.6%	18.2%

Arguments were made in the study against the growing pressure from market and development agencies to ascribe only positive attributes to ICT. In contrast, participants thought that ICT could exacerbate social stratification and that countries needed to develop strategies for the use of ICT to bring overall human development, especially in rural areas, to avoid this consequence.

4.3. Constraints

Participants identified far more constraints than they did either actual or potential impacts of ICT (Table 4). The large number of constraints explains why the gap between the expectation and the realisation of ICT is so wide. This suggests significant difficulties in the use of ICT in sub-Saharan Africa. The following constraints were frequently stated: political (policy), management aspect, lack of information (learning and content), underutilisation, resource limitations and weak infrastructure.

The findings suggest that utilisation of ICT alone cannot solve the overall development problems in sub-Saharan Africa. The impact of ICT lies in their ability to stimulate existing institutions and infrastructure so as to lay sounder economic foundations. Significant impact could also result from applying information technologies to human development by improving education and learning. There is a need to develop the infrastructure in parallel with increased use of ICT.

High cost is one of the barriers to effective access to new ICT in sub-Saharan Africa. Operational costs have not fallen with the introduction of technology, but have been exacerbated by mounting taxes, running and reskilling costs. Added to existing resource difficulties, the high cost of information technologies has left institutions in a cycle of dependency, moving from one donor to the other.

Limited management understanding, lack of information on hardware and software, limited networks to exchange experiences and lack of recognition of human and organisational factors in systems development are recurring difficulties. These are intensified by isolation. Many key decision-makers were unable to keep up with the advancement of ICT. Resources, time and an analytical approach are all in short supply to decision makers in sub-Saharan Africa, whose ultimate decisions and plans affect not only ICT growth but also the development of their countries.

Infrastructural constraints, such as unreliable telecommunications and energy supplies, pose serious problems for the full utilisation of ICT. Local telecommunications are characterised by a large gap between demand and supply, poor connectivity, low level of maintenance, inadequate management and limited access in rural areas. Telephone line failures are as common as electrical blackouts. Since infrastructure problems affect all social, political, technical and economic growth, they also inhibit development.

A further constraint brought up was the mis-match between imported systems and the local environment. Imported technology is generally designed to operate in air-conditioned, dust-free environments, with a good maintenance and support network. In many sub-Saharan African countries, the equipment has to work in hot and humid weather, with very unreliable power supplies and where maintenance support is exceptionally poor. Some of the causes of equipment failure are due to a lack of understanding of basic concepts, such as differences in line voltages. Much equipment has failed simply because of a lack of knowledge of how to switch between 110/220 volts. Maintenance engineers who participated in the study reported that most equipment failures are due to the continuous fluctuation of electric currents.

The limited education infrastructure poses a serious problem for ICT deployment. Not only is the quality of education needed to build a solid foundation absent, but also the quality of training in ICT is unsatisfactory. Widespread illiteracy is one of the main problems to have limited the effectiveness of ICT within the wider population in sub-Saharan Africa.

Analysis of the range of constraints showed the solution to some of the problems is within the reaches of government, individuals and organisations. What seems to be lacking is awareness of what is possible. International support, to date, does not seem to focus on enabling countries and institutions to solve their own problems by using local means. Development support often follows those prescriptions applied in the developed countries that have different economic, social and cultural orientations.

4.4. Action centred around users and users' strategic reactions

Analysis also showed that the constraints cited above have not been set aside as problems and difficulties, but rather have been faced as challenges by users and actors. Various actors have made contributions to facing these challenges despite a lack of coordination. Limited understanding and cooperation among management, systems designers, local users and donors, business people and educators are widespread.

The opinions found in the study were, in the view of the main researcher, as valuable as, and often better than, 'expert advice'. Firstly, informants' understandings were based on action research (action learning) and not on experts' surveys or opinions. Secondly, in-depth analysis revealed their constructionist understanding of the applications of ICT – the users' space continuum that is constantly changing and refining with exposure to ICT [21, 22].

Partly, the problem in applications of ICT in sub-Saharan Africa lies in the difficulty in tapping the opinions and understandings of users and local actors to inform policy making, project implementation and understanding. People adapt and learn, thus it is important to take these capabilities into account in analysing impact and in the implementation of projects. Table 5 provides lists of constraints which emerged in the study and informants' interpretation of actions and strategies against these constraints.

5. Discussion

The results presented above show that, although ICT have a considerable potential role in sub-Saharan Africa, the gaps between actual and potential impact are (and are likely to remain) wide, due to insurmountable constraints. Probably, any impact will be achieved gradually. The extent of the use of ICT will continue to be based on the pace of development locally and the attitudes of those implementing it. Any leapfrogging in ICT will depend on the attitudes and abilities of the users and policy makers and the ability of each country to overcome the large number of social, political, technical, infrastructural and economic challenges. Although efficiency and growth are expected at various levels, the history, and current circumstances, of many of these countries makes it difficult for them to benefit fully from the technology.

Underutilisation, as a core finding in the study, signals the need for indigenous capacity-building. The introduction of physical equipment and physical infrastructure has not solved the development challenges; at least, not in the last 30 years. What have been lacking are human capacity and skills in innovation, which are major factors that lead to impact, but which are often overlooked in impact analysis. Changes in policies and increasing management awareness, application to local context, improving local content, knowledge and learning and the development of the infrastructure were believed by the participants to be crucial to bringing changes in the quality of life.

5.1. Policy and management awareness

Although a number of studies indicate that lack of, or inappropriate, policies are the main problem in sub-Saharan Africa [23], there is little to indicate how this situation could be improved. Undoubtedly, government policy has been playing, and will continue to play, a bigger role in unleashing or hindering the ability of communities, individuals and organisations to benefit from ICT. The argument that can be derived from this study is that

Table 5 Informants' interpretations of actions and strategies against constraints.

Challenges	Informant responses
Political: • non-enabling government policies; • obstruction of access to information; • lack of political stability; • lack of management understanding of effective ICT use; • incompetent management and lack of commitment from management; • weak status of information systems; • weak information and communication policies; • institutional rigidities and constraints to learning; • inappropriate regulatory framework; • underdeveloped legal framework for information sharing and intellectual property rights; • weak civil services.	• involve stakeholders in policy formulation process; • promote enabling environment; • disseminate information on best practices; • improve education of management; • democratise access to information; • establish a lead agency to work on ICT policy, bringing in multiple users and stakeholders; • increase the role of media and other public and private information sources to educate on ICT; • improve government systems using ICT, including tax and customs management, socio-economic information and financial management.
Infrastructural: • inadequate human resources; • inadequate and unreliable electric power; • unreliable and very limited telecommunications infrastructure, with non-enabling regulatory framework; • inadequate educational infrastructure; • bad social infrastructure (health, social services, public administration, etc); • poor connection to worldwide networks.	• build community centres and relevant tools for the majority; • increase private sector participation in infrastructure, and privatise energy and telecommunications; • improve the quality of system design when applying ICT in the public sector; • use ICT to plan and coordinate social infrastructure; • improve links to the worldwide networks.

Technical:
- maintenance problems, poor delivery of services and inadequate technical support;
- weak research and development; slowly responding university education;
- low standards in private institutions;
- inadequate knowledge of systems and poor systems design;
- inadequate documentation and insufficient training;
- lack of standards;
- poor ICT planning;
- inadequate use of existing ICT;
- lack of access to ICT by rural communities.

- improve effective use of existing ICT;
- use multiple technologies, e.g. radio, satellite, PCs and terminals;
- increase the roles of private institutions in delivery of support through adequate competition and exposure;
- improve users' actions through associations and user groups;
- organise associations around various standards and encourage standardisation;
- provide training to private ICT sector on business management.

Economic:
- financial resource problems;
- high taxes that mount high costs;
- increased dependency on donors;
- low level of partnerships between government and business;
- poor access to credit, limited venture capital, non-enabling environment to invest in ICT.

- use innovative and all-involving funding mechanism to improve the infrastructure;
- improve public investment, procurement;
- innovative funding of ICT projects, e.g. cost sharing;
- increase competitiveness in the private sector.

Social:
- gender, ethnic and class inequalities;
- islands of sophisticated users;
- weak analysis of information requirements and user needs;
- lack of information culture;
- lack of motivation to improve performance;
- language and alphabet problems;
- human factors, e.g. lack of desire to experiment;
- age factors;
- mobility (skill movement from public to private);
- information asymmetry between local users and multinational companies, donor agencies and island of sophisticated users.

- provide information on domestic and foreign markets;
- improve education and awareness;
- work on language interfaces;
- improve access to information for communities to use ICT to improve efficiency of social services;
- improve innovative learning, including parent education.

policy should not be forced, but rather designed, to derive social benefits from the application of ICT. This requires the managements of organisations and governments to emerge with innovative and flexible policies. Continuous learning, participation of citizens and stakeholders in the policy formulation process and diligent implementation are ingredients of successful ICT application. Policy makers and other managers should have increased understanding of the potential application of ICT. Education, including continuing professional development at all levels, is vital to achieve this.

5.2. Application in local communities

There have been few applications of ICT which are appropriate to the special needs of local communities in sub-Saharan Africa, although implementation of ICT should take into account the society in which it is to operate. Human development through education and lifelong learning for both children and adults was considered by participants to be the primary application area for local communities.

5.3. Application in the wider context

Information generation or exchange based on ICT can foster job creation and business and improve governance and social cohesion. In particular, ICT can have an impact on the growth of substantive sectors such as transport, electricity, clean water, agriculture, industry and health. These technologies have the potential to facilitate general economic activity, especially on small and medium-sized enterprises; to foster global competitiveness in trade; to improve the management of macroeconomics structure; to help in combating poverty and to aid preservation of the natural environment. Underutilisation cannot be fought by simply adding new technology, but only by incremental learning, so that the technologies used can be tailored to meet social imperatives.

5.4. The infrastructure

The infrastructure remains the main bottleneck to the development of ICT in the region. Technical infrastructure, such as electricity and transportation, is often inadequate. Better support infrastructure, such as trainers, troubleshooters, system designers and implementers, is desperately needed in sub-Saharan Africa. The technical capability of some of the people using ICT is insufficient. Lack of qualified human resources and institutional capacity is a core problem that emerged in this study.

Building indigenous content and developing greater access to global information resources are also important to attain improved economic activities and to empower individuals and communities. Investment in ICT alone cannot yield results without investment in social, technical and human resources infrastructures.

6. Further areas of research and conclusions

Technological changes are not deterministic. Development is the ability of people to better, in their own terms, cope with the world in which they live. ICT impact relates to people's communication and learning; therefore what was investigated in this study is how people make sense of, and take advantage of, ICT. Further careful research, proactive thinking, action learning and tapping the reactions of users could lead to explicit policy actions that could minimise the undesirable effects, and maximise the potential benefits, of ICT.

However, research is less of a tradition in sub-Saharan Africa. Nevertheless, research on the social impact of ICT is necessary to maximise the favourable impact of ICT and reduce the gap between expectations of ICT and their realisation. At the macro level, the implementation of ICT needs continuous interdisciplinary investigations. As their user communities emerge, the scale, complexity and dynamism of ICT make interdisciplinary research, involving computer scientists, systems engineers and social scientists, crucial. In the medium term, a network that brings together individuals, research teams, institutions, donors and scientific and professional communities should be created. Multidisciplinary investigations of users' adaptability and of the social context in which ICT are expected to operate should be used to help planners and implementers to design, evaluate and make use of ICT. The results of investigations should be used also to inform and develop education at all levels.

In the long term, studies of the social implications of ICT within the complex social, political and economic environment of developing countries require longitudinal anthropological studies and sustained research investment. This study found that impact is too complex for macro studies. Taking one subject or constituency in a given social context is beyond a PhD research project. Apart from the specificity of each milieu, there are common traits across countries thus developing a regional and international research front is essential. Such global interdisciplinary research may necessitate the creation of a centre for social informatics research in a developing country, specifically to serve such countries.

The increasing impact of ICT in Africa requires political, economic and organisational commitments that match developments in ICT to local needs and that help to reduce the effect of the various constraints. The ability to change and make compromises is crucial. A wide range of ICT tools for communications and information management could help individuals, communities and organisations to organise local cooperative activities, to seek innovative solutions to local problems, to gather reliable, basic and empirical data and to enter into relationships with other individuals, institutions, regions and nations. If proper actions are not taken, the same tools could disenfranchise individuals, communities, organisations and nations.

To promote the positive impact of ICT, the following actions are required. Firstly, users of technology should be central to, and involved in, all developments. Secondly, education should increase and enhance basic competence in reading and writing and stimulate critical thinking. Imaginative efforts are required to increase access to ICT and develop tools that bring change on a human scale. Such imagination cannot occur without ongoing research pertaining to less developing nations that provides insightful feedback to the various actors and that helps to develop original applications.

References

[1] M. Michael, Some questions for the information society. In: T. Forester (ed.), *The Information Technology Revolution* (Basil Blackwell, Oxford, 1983).

[2] M. Menou, *Measuring the Impact of Information on Development* (IDRC, Ottawa, 1994).

[3] P. McConnell (ed.), *Making a Difference: Measuring the Impact of Information on Development* (IDRC, Ottawa, 1995).

[4] S. Zulu, Africa's survival plan for meeting the challenges of information technology in the 1990s and beyond, Libri 44(1) (1994) 77–94.

[5] L. Moyo, Information technology strategies for Africa's survival in twenty-first century: IT all pervasive, *Information Technology for Development* 7 (1996) 17–27.

[6] J. Chisenga, *User's Needs for Electronic Connectivity: Libraries and Other Information Centers* [Paper presented at a workshop on Telematics for Development in Africa, Addis Ababa, April 1995] (UNECA, Addis Ababa, 1995).

[7] S. Sahay and J. Walsham, Information technology in developing countries: a need for theory building, *Information Technology for Development* 6 (1995) 111–124.

[8] J. Walsham, The emergence of interpretivism in information systems research, *Information Systems Research* 6 (1995) 376–393.

[9] M. Stone, *National Information Policies: Are These Possible to Formulate?* (1996) Available at: http://wn.apc.org/ecis/global.htm (site visited on 22 November 1997).

[10] M. Munasinghe, *Computers and Informatics in Developing Countries* (Butterworths, London, 1987).

[11] UNECA, *Report of Telematics for Development in Africa* (UNECA, Addis Ababa, 1995).

[12] W. Thorngate, Measuring the effects of information on development. In: P. McConnell (ed.), *Making a Difference: The Impact of Information on Development* (IDRC, Ottawa, 1995).

[13] D. Ellis, *The Derivation of a Behavioural Model for Information Retrieval System Design* (PhD Thesis) (University of Sheffield, 1987).

[14] A. Brown, *Information, Communication and Organization of Culture: Grounded Theory Approach* (PhD Thesis) (University of Sheffield, 1990).

[15] S. Soto, *Information in Dentistry: Patterns of Communications and Use* (PhD Thesis) (University of Sheffield, Department of Information Studies, 1992).

[16] B. Glaser and A. Strauss, *The Discovery of Grounded Theory* (Aldine, Hawthorne, New York, 1967).

[17] P. Martin and B. Turner, Grounded theory and organizational research, *The Journal of Applied Behavioural Science* 22(2) (1986) 141–157.

[18] K. Charmaz, Discovering chronic illness: using grounded theory, *Social Science and Medicine* 30(11) (1990) 1161–1172.

[19] B. Turner, Some practical aspects of qualitative data analysis: one way of organising the cognitive process associated with the generation of grounded theory, *Quantity and Quality* 15 (1981) 225–247.

[20] C. De la Cuesta, Marketing: a process in health visiting, *Journal of Advanced Nursing* 19 (1994) 347–353.

[21] R. Morrison, Towards a user-centered information service, *Journal of the American Society for Information Science* 45(1) (1994) 20–30.

[22] B. Dervin, Information democracy: an examination of underlying assumptions, *Journal of the American Society for Information Science* 45(6) (1994) 369–385.

[23] Reference paper for the World Bank Electronic Conference on harnessing information for development (The World Bank, Washington DC, 1995).

39

WEAVING THE WESTERN WEB

Explaining differences in Internet
connectivity among OECD countries

Eszter Hargittai

Source: *Telecommunications Policy* 23(10–11) (1999): 701–18.

Abstract

Despite the Internet's increasing importance, there is little
social scientific work that addresses its diffusion. Our knowledge is especially limited with respect to the conditions that
encourage its spread across nations. This paper takes a first
step in explaining the differences in Internet connectivity among
OECD countries. After examining the impact of economic
indicators, human capital, institutional legal environment, and
existing technological infrastructure, the empirical analyses
show that economic wealth and telecommunications policy are
the most salient predictors of a nation's Internet connectivity.

The Internet is a major technological innovation of the 20th century with
key political, social, and economic consequences (Castells, 1996). Politically,
the Internet is expected to revive participatory democracy (Anderson, Bikson,
Law & Mitchell *et al.*, 1995; Naisbitt, 1982; Deaken, 1981; Rheingold, 1993;
Geser, 1996) and has even been used as an indicator of a country's level of
democracy (Anderson, Bikson, Law & Mitchell *et al.*, 1995). Socially, the
new medium is expected to act as a moderator of inequality by making low-
cost information available to everyone without discrimination (Anderson,
Bikson, Law & Mitchell *et al.*, 1995; Hauben & Hauben, 1997). Yet, others
have argued that the technology contributes to increasing inequality given
that it is unequally distributed among the population (NTIA, 1995, 1998,
1999; Novak & Hoffman, 1998). Research has also shown that people use

the Internet as a complement to traditional media rather than a substitute for them, thereby increasing information gaps across the population (Robinson, Barth & Kohut, 1997; Robinson, Levin & Hak, 1998).

Although several of the above-mentioned claims regarding the effects of the Internet have also been contested (Calhoun, 1998; Etzioni, 1992; Stoll, 1995), the far-reaching impact of the Internet is uncontroversial. Despite its overarching importance, little attention has been devoted to the study of its spread, especially on an international level. Given the potential wide-ranging effects of the technology, the level of diffusion in a country can influence the degree to which a country can hold its place in the global economy. This paper explores what circumstances explain international variation in Internet connectivity among the member countries of the Organization for Economic Cooperation and Development (OECD).[1]

In the next section, I provide a brief background of the Internet with particular emphasis on its recent exponential growth. Then, I summarize relevant literature on communication technology diffusion that leads to testable propositions. The data and methods section presents details of the data set and modes of operationalization. That section is followed by a discussion of findings and a conclusion that also highlights avenues for future research.

1. Background

The Internet is a world-wide network of computers, but sociologically it is also important to consider it as a network of people using computers that make vast amounts of information available to users. Given the two services of the system — computer-mediated communication and information retrieval — the multitude of services allowed for by the network is unprecedented. Although the system was first implemented in the 1960s, it was initially restricted to a small community of scientists and scholars in just a few nations. Moreover, the World Wide Web, — the key aspect of the Net concerning its wide popularity — was invented only in 1990 and the graphical interface that made its use accessible to the layperson, the Web browser, was created only in 1993. It was this addition to the technology that significantly accelerated its spread both nationwide in the United States and internationally. Thus, significant Internet diffusion can be observed world-wide only in the past few years with the global number of network connected computers surpassing 35 million in 1998 compared to less than 1.5 million in 1993.

Similar to infrastructure innovations of the past such as railroads and the telegraph, the Internet contributes significantly to the convergence of space and time by making various types of communication — regardless of geographical proximity — quicker than ever before. The ramifications of this spatio-temporal convergence are profound and not well understood because no previous technology has embraced and allowed for as many communication services as the Internet. Since knowledge-intensive activities are an increasingly important component of OECD economies (Reich, 1992) and since today's telecommunication infrastructure underlies virtually all domains of economic activity (Drake, 1995, p. 22), exploring the spread of the network is imperative for understanding which nations will be able to advance their economies the most. The presence of the Internet in a society may create new economic activities and jobs, and may also allow for potential improvements in social benefits by offering new educational opportunities, improving health care delivery, and access to cultural and leisure activities (OECD, 1997a). More generally, the network functions — and will do so increasingly with technological innovations — as a link between all sectors of the economy affecting also social, political and cultural relationships. Given such potential wide-ranging consequences, the Internet's level of diffusion in a country can influence many of its economic and socio-cultural spheres. Conversely, its absence can have negative impacts with equally important implications.

During the last five years, the rate of growth in the network's global diffusion has exceeded fifty percent annually (Network Wizards, 1998). Between the years 1994 and 1998, the use of the system more than quadrupled in the United States to include between 30% and 35% of Americans over the age of sixteen (Pew, 1998; CommerceNet, 1998). The system has seen similar popularity in several other nations such as Finland, Sweden, New Zealand, and Australia. However, other nations such as France, Spain, Italy and Greece have been much slower in embracing this new technology. Existing literature about diffusion data is often descriptive (ITU, 1997, 1999; OECD, 1997a, 1998a, 1999a; Paltridge & Ypsilanti, 1997) and does not use methods that allow us to isolate the impacts of indicators controlling for other factors and thus understand their relative importance in explaining connectivity. Alternatively, existing studies only focus on the impact of information technologies on the economy, ignoring the conditions that shape information technology landscapes across countries. Although some literature does exist regarding the Internet's unequal spread to lesser developed nations (Goodman, Press, Ruth & Rutkowski, 1994; Hargittai, 1996, 1998; ITU, 1997, 1999; Press, Burkhart, Foster, Goodman, Wolcott & Woodard, 1998; Rao, 1995), there has been surprisingly little discussion of the Internet's unequal spread among developed countries, i.e. those with resources to accelerate adoption.

By concentrating on a group of nations with approximately similar levels of social and economic development, i.e. the OECD, it is possible to examine the more intricate details influencing the spread of the medium. The OECD is an ideal case for investigating the details leading to differences in international Internet diffusion among countries of approximately similar socio-economic development. The members of the organization represent advanced capitalist countries and thus membership controls for a general level of development. In this case, the top-tier nations — as classified by the United Nations Development Programme's Human Development Report (UNDP, 1998) — of the high development level category are examined. This paper fills a gap in the literature by exploring what factors explain the level of Internet connectivity among OECD countries by teasing out the particularities affecting the technology's diffusion among countries witnessing the greatest spread.

2. Theoretical considerations

In this section, I summarize existing literature about important predictors of Internet connectivity. Specifically, I discuss how the economic situation of a country, the education level of its inhabitants, the institutional legal environment governing communication technologies, and the existing communication technology infrastructure may be related to Internet connectivity.

2.1. Findings from previous research

Some studies have attempted to explain differences in international Internet connectivity generalizing to the entire global landscape. Using the Human Development Index (HDI) measure from the UNDP's Human Development Report, Hargittai (1996, 1998) found that a country's human development level is correlated with its level of Internet connectivity. HDI uses information on adult literacy rate, education, Gross Domestic Product, and life expectancy to create an index of countries' level of development. The International Telecommunications Union (ITU, 1997) used the same measures and found a similar relationship between the two variables. The limitations of these studies lie in the fact that they only include one overarching measure of development, which leaves little room for understanding the specifics of what factors lead to differentiated Internet connectivity. Moreover, these analyses cannot isolate explanatory factors among countries of similar development levels. The conclusion that general level of development influences Internet connectivity is not helpful in understanding how and why countries with similar levels of development have unequal levels of connectivity.

Kelly and Petrazzini (1997) included more variables, such as information on connectivity prices and language in addition to wealth and education, in their discussion of differentiated connectivity levels. However, their methods were restricted to simple correlations between two variables at a time. Thus, their findings do not provide a comprehensive understanding of what factors determine a country's level of network connectivity. Nonetheless, Kelly and Petrazzini's analysis does suggest that wealth, education, language and pricing are important correlates of Internet connectivity.

331

2.2. Economic factors

Studies on technology diffusion have found that economic wealth strongly predicts a population's adaptation of new technologies (Rogers, 1983). A country's overall economic strength will affect Internet diffusion in that the necessary resources are more likely to be present, and capital required for the expansion of the technology is more available, in richer countries. Another economic factor that influences Internet connectivity is the level of inequality in a country. The more egalitarian, the more people will be able to afford the new technology, thus increasing the probability of a high level of diffusion.

2.3. Human capital

There are two ways in which the level of human capital may be relevant to Internet connectivity: the population's level of education and its English language proficiency. Most studies that have examined the education level of adopters of new technologies find that more educated people are quicker to adopt new innovations than people with comparatively less education (Rogers, 1983). In the case of the Internet's global spread, this suggests that countries with better educated populations will be more likely to show higher rates of Internet diffusion than nations with less educated citizens. Kelly and Petrazzini (1997) also suggest that academic institutions often play an important role in spreading the Internet since they are often among the first institutions in a nation to be wired. This provides another reason for considering the education level of a nation in understanding the necessary and sufficient conditions for Internet connectivity. Higher scores on the education measure are likely to reflect a higher number of academic institutions because the scores reflect gross enrollment ratios.

Individual knowledge may affect the spread of a communication technology in yet another way. Laponce (1987) suggests that some languages have greater status than others and they dominate certain areas of life such as English language having a prominence in the computer industry and even international media sphere. Weinstein (1983) argues that English is especially dominant in the realm of international communications. Barnett and Choi (1995) claim that English is so important in some areas that not speaking the language leads to a serious barrier in access to telecommunications technology. Given the prominence of the English language on the content of the World Wide Web, level of English proficiency may affect the number of people interested in using the medium. The prominence of English on the Web is not due to a higher rate of diffusion in the United States, but the relative size of the U.S. population compared to other countries. There is evidence that the US dominates content on the Web with a large percentage of the most visited Web sites being created and located in the United States

332

(OECD, 1997e). Because English is the major international language linking people of different origins (Fishman, Cooper & Conrad, 1977), even non-Americans on the Web may contribute to English content as long as their Web content is directed at viewers from other nations. English is by far the most pervasive language on sites hosted outside of the United States excluding the native language of the host country (OECD, 1999c). Overall, the two aspects of human capital relevant to Internet connectivity are education level and familiarity with English.

2.4. Institutional legal environment

The institutional legal environment in a country is also relevant to the Internet's spread because national policies can enhance or hold back diffusion of a technology, depending on their approach to regulating mechanisms, privatization, and free competition. The Information, Computer and Communications Policy Division of the OECD's Directorate for Science, Technology and Industry has published several reports advocating the importance of free competition in the telecommunications sector (OECD, 1996, 1997a–c, 1998b, 1999b). The International Telecommunications Union has contributed to the literature in similar ways (ITU, 1997, 1999). These reports suggest that free competition in the telecommunications sector will improve the options for telecommunications services and reduce the price of access charges. These arguments suggest that countries with free competition in the telecom sector will have higher Internet connectivity than countries with monopolies in this sector of their economies.

2.5. Existing technologies

In his work on the diffusion of the telephone in Germany, Thomas (1988) found that the spread of technology is contingent upon certain technological and infrastructural factors being present in the target nation. Kelly and Petrazzini (1997) also emphasize this point when explaining the large differences between connectivity among countries of different income categories. With respect to the Internet, existing telecommunication facilities may be crucial for understanding variation in the spread of the Internet.

2.6. Testable propositions

In sum, the review of related studies identifies several important factors in the discussion of international Internet connectivity and suggests the following testable propositions. Greater economic wealth and a higher level of economic equality will lead to higher connectivity, whereas less wealth and larger inequality is likely to have an opposite effect. A country whose population has high levels of education is likely to be more densely connected than a country with lower levels of general education. English language exposure will influence connectivity by favoring native speakers most, followed by countries with populations exhibiting high levels of English training, and discriminating most against populations with low English exposure and proficiency. Free competition in the telecommunication sector will have a positive effect on Internet density while telecom monopolies will impede the network's spread. Lower Internet access charges will act as a catalyst for network diffusion. Finally, claims based on the importance of existing telecommunications infrastructure predict that telephone density affects Internet connectivity positively. The following section presents the data and methods, and is followed by a discussion of these propositions based on empirical results.

3. Data and methods

The study includes 18 member countries of the OECD.[2] The unit of analysis is the nation-state.[3] As Fig. 1 shows, there is considerable amount of variance in Internet connectivity among OECD countries to warrant exploration and explanation. Data were collected from various sources on the aggregate country level. (See Appendix A for details about the sources of the data set.) Data are lagged: the outcome variable is reported in January 1998 figures, whereas explanatory variables are reported for 1994–1996 (depending on availability) with the exception of the Gini coefficient, which is only available for earlier years (see Appendix A for information on specific years).[4]

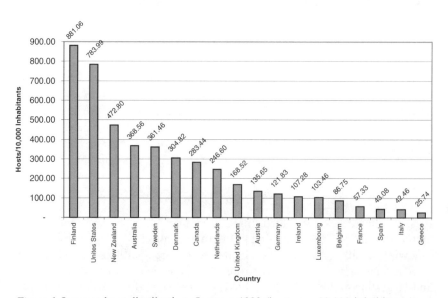

Figure 1 Internet host distribution, January 1998 (hosts per 10,000 inhabitants).

The lag in the data is necessary because the question involves explanatory variables for diffusion and attempts to understand what country attributes lead to adaptation of the Internet.[5]

3.1. Outcome variable

Internet connectivity is measured as number of hosts per 10,000 inhabitants in January 1998 where hosts are individual computers with network access.[6] Because multiple users may use a single host computer, this is not a measure of number of users, and can be regarded as the most conservative measure of Internet presence in a country.[7] One can only estimate the number of users from information about hosts, but, unfortunately, such estimates are much less reliable than host count measures and no such systematic measures exist. Therefore, host count is the most precise available data on the presence of the Internet in a country (OECD, 1998a). Since the outcome variable reveals a somewhat skewed distribution, it was logged for the regression analyses in order to make it meet the assumptions of the OLS regression analysis.[8]

3.2. Explanatory factors

Characteristics of the countries are explored with respect to their economic situation, human capital, related institutional legal environment, and existing technological infrastructure. Gross Domestic Product is used as a measure of economic wealth. The Gini coefficient represents a country's level of inequality.[9] General level of education was derived from the UNDP's Human Development Report and stands for combined first-, second-, and third-level gross enrollment ratio. English language proficiency was coded as dummy variables. Its values are derived from information about the percentage of students in general secondary education learning English as a foreign language. Countries where English is the dominant language were coded as Native speakers and represent the baseline, whereas all others were split into high and low English exposure (see Table 1 for details).

To address the hypotheses regarding a nation's legal institutional environment, information on the telecommunications sector and on Internet access charges is included in the analysis. Telecommunications policy was coded as a dichotomous variable distinguishing between countries that have monopolies in the telecommunications sector and those that have some level of competition in the year studied. The average cost of a twenty hour monthly Internet access basket is used to indicate pricing.[10] Existing telecommunications infrastructure is measured by information on phone density. This composite variable was constructed by including information on both mainlines per 100 inhabitants and cellular phone subscribers per 100 inhabitants.[11]

Table 1 Descriptive statistics of variables (*N* = 18).

	Minimum	Maximum	Mean	Std. Deviation
Internet hosts[a,b]	25.74	881.06	255.26	247.46
GDP[a]	139.45	33202	21941.61	4299.08
Gini coefficient	25.91	41.72	32.32	4.66
Education	58	100	86	9.71
Pricing	20.59	89.81	43.74	15.6
Phone density[a]	40.39	90.85	60.18	13.45

		frequency
English proficiency	dummy variables:	
	Native[c] (base in models)	6
	High level (> 90% of high school students)	8
	Low level (64–76% of high school students)	4
Telecom Policy	dichotomous variables:	frequency
	Competition (partial or free)	7
	Monopoly (base in models)	11

[a]Per capita figures (see Appendix A for per capita specifics, description of variables, and data sources).
[b]US includes figures for .com, .edu, .gov, .mil, .org, .net, .us
[c]Canada is coded as an English speaking country given that English is a national language, it is the first language of the majority of its population, and the rest of the population studies it extensively in school.

Table 1 presents descriptive statistics for all the variables. Despite general similarities among the members of the OECD, most variables exhibit considerable amount of variance. Finland has the highest level of Internet connectivity with the United States following close behind. Spain, Italy, and Greece exhibit the lowest levels of network connectivity among the 18 countries included in the analysis. On the wealth measure, Luxembourg and the United States lead the group whereas Spain and Greece show figures half the per capita value of the wealthiest nations. Finland and Spain have the lowest levels of inequality according to the Gini coefficients whereas New Zealand and Australia represent relatively greater levels of inequality although the overall variance is not large for this measure. Luxembourg scores far below the other 17 nations in education although this is probably due to the fact that the majority of the people in this country pursue post-secondary education abroad. Italy also occupies a low rank on this measure. In contrast, Canada, Finland, and the United States have larger populations with higher levels of education.

There are six native English speaking countries included in the study. Eight countries exhibit high exposure to English whereas four (Greece, Belgium, Italy, Luxembourg) have populations with low exposure to English. Seven countries had competition in their telecom markets for the year studied: Australia, Canada, Finland, New Zealand, Sweden, the United Kingdom, and the United States, whereas the remaining eleven countries all had monopolies at this time. Not surprisingly, countries without monopolies have the lowest off-peak Internet access tariffs: Canada, Australia, Finland, and the US. Austria's prices are far higher than any other nation's with rates in Greece and Germany also quite high in comparison to most others. Ireland and Spain have the lowest levels of phone density whereas Sweden is far ahead of the group followed by other Scandinavian countries and the United States, Canada and Australia.

Appendix B presents a correlation matrix for the outcome and all explanatory variables. Although several variables are highly correlated, the correlation coefficient is rarely prohibitively high. Among the predictor variables, of particular concern is the high correlation between telecommunications policy and phone density, which yields a correlation coefficient of -0.633. The strength of this relationship is not surprising given that telecommunications policy can have a direct impact on phone density. Free competition in the telecom market can be expected to encourage phone diffusion in contrast to the hindering effects of a telecom monopoly. Given the high value of the relationship between these two variables, their inclusion together in one model should be interpreted with caution.

4. Findings

Table 2 presents the results of OLS regression models. The first set of models (Models 1–4) show the individual explanatory power of the hypothesized variables. The second set of models (Models 5–8) address the impact of the variables in relation to other explanatory factors. The nested models are presented with respect to propositions suggested in the review of prior studies. Model 5 considers the hypotheses regarding the effect of human capital indicators — general level of education and English language exposure — in addition to economic variables on Internet connectivity. Model 6 looks at the additional importance of telecommunications policy in explaining the level of Internet spread in a country. Model 7 explores the significance of existing telephone infrastructure. Finally, Model 8 is presented to demonstrate that having both policy and phone density measures in the model does not add to the model's explanatory value.

Although economic wealth of a country is a significant predictor of Internet connectivity, it is clear from Model 1 that among rich nations, economic factors alone do not explain the level of Internet connectivity. Adding information on human capital (Model 5) — both level of education and English language proficiency — significantly improves the fit of the model. However, adding information on policy (Model 6) adds even more to the fit of the model and the effects of both education and language competency disappear. The positive value of high English proficiency is contrary to the

Table 2 OLS regression results for Internet hosts[a] (Standardized betas with significance reported in parentheses).

	Model 1	Model 2	Model 3	Model 4	Model 5	Model 6	Model 7	Model 8
GDP	0.383				0.521*	0.491**	0.278	0.494*
	[0.123]				[0.028]	[0.007]	[0.155]	[0.036]
Gini coef	0.259				0.155	0.173	0.015	0.175
	[0.286]				[0.523]	[0.310]	[0.939]	[0.397]
Education		0.094			0.378	0.298	0.286	0.299
		[0.734]			[0.190]	[0.148]	[0.209]	[0.172]
English high		-0.250			-0.062	0.338	-0.208	0.344
		[0.315]			[0.816]	[0.136]	[0.341]	[0.358]
English low		-0.638			-0.384	0.049	-0.376	0.053
		[0.054]			[0.261]	[0.848]	[0.166]	[0.872]
Monopoly			-0.768**			-0.667**		-0.673
			[0.003]			[0.007]		[0.082]
Prices			0.029			-0.011		-0.012
			[0.894]			[0.950]		[0.950]
Phone density				0.699**			0.497*	0.007
				[0.001]			[0.013]	[0.983]
Adjusted R^2	0.080	0.262	0.506	0.457	0.435	0.736	0.657	0.707
F-test significance					0.031[b]	0.009	0.013[c]	0.983

[a]N = 18, Hosts per 10,000 inhabitants logged.
[b]Significance change from Model 1 to Model 5.
[c]Significance change from Model 5 to Model 7.
*$p < 0.05$
**$p < 0.01$ (2-tailed).

expected direction of this correlate since it was hypothesized that a native English speaking population (i.e. the base value in this model) would encourage Internet spread compared to countries' with other native languages. However, it seems that having a population of native speakers versus good English speakers does not make a difference. The reason for this could be that browsing the large amounts of information available on the Web only in English requires no more than an exposure to and familiarity with the language because most browsing activity involves reading. However, having even lower levels of English exposure also does not have a large impact on connectivity. This may be due to the fact that people use the Internet as much for one-to-one communication as for browsing. It is fair to assume that most people will engage in personal communication with others that share a common language in which case exposure to English may not be an important concern in deciding whether to become connected.[12]

In contrast to the low influence of English language competency, the results show evidence in support of telecommunication policy's role in the puzzle. The existence of a monopoly in the telecom sector of a nation seems to have a considerable negative impact on that country's Internet connectivity. Interestingly, price of access is not a significant predictor of Internet connectivity and has a very small β value. This small effect is probably due to high correlation with the policy variable.[13]

Model 7, which does not include information on telecom policy, adds information on phone density. This proves to be an important addition to only having wealth and human capital measures. However, the explanatory value of this model is lower than the one obtained with the inclusion of telecommunications policy, suggesting that policy exhibits a more salient influence on Internet connectivity than does phone density. This is not surprising given that phone density may be just as dependent on telecom policy as Internet density.[14] This suggests that telecom policy is not only related to directly making Internet services available to users through encouraging affordable pricing, but it also contributes to the development of the necessary telecommunications infrastructure of a country, which in turn facilitates connectivity. Overall, the findings lend support to the hypotheses that economic wealth and especially telecommunications policy are important predictors of a country's level of Internet connectivity among OECD nations.[15] The results also show that presenting simple correlations for predictor and outcome variables (Kelly & Petrazzini, 1997; Hargittai, 1996, 1998; ITU, 1997) is not sufficient for understanding the interplay of the various factors that may influence Internet connectivity.

5. Discussion

The aggregate quantitative analyses provide a good sense of the overarching explanatory factors regarding countries' Internet connectivity in OECD nations. However, the quantitative aspects discussed so far need to be supplemented by qualitative information about country-specific attributes that may also affect connectivity. Of particular interest is the parallel topic of telephone diffusion that was explored by Rammert in his paper comparing the telephone's diffusion in the US, France, the UK and Germany (Rammert, 1990). His departing premise is that the rate of telephone diffusion across these societies was very different during the first years of the diffusion process, despite the fact that all four of these countries were similar in their industrial advances and available capital. Therefore, Rammert argues that cultural considerations need to be examined to understand how the telephone was first perceived, how it fit the lifestyles of a society, and thus, how it was adopted.

In the United Kingdom, for example, face-to-face encounters in business dealings were essential in determining the other party's social status. Because such information was paramount for business transactions, adapting to business interactions over the phone was difficult. In contrast, Rammert argues that the entrepreneurial spirit characteristic of the United States at the time was much more conducive to incorporating the telephone in everyday life. Although the article only contains descriptive statistics, the author's observation about affinity towards the use of a technology may be relevant to understanding differences in Internet diffusion among countries of similar levels of development.

Currently, few systematic studies exist on people's use of the Internet with such basic questions left unanswered as to what proportion of Internet use involves computer-mediated communication services (e.g. e-mail) as opposed to information retrieval use (e.g. Web browsing). We know even less about how people incorporate these specific services into their lives and what previous activities they substitute or complement with network applications. Once such information becomes available, it will be possible to incorporate cultural aspects of Internet use into the study of the network's diffusion across nations. However, even when such data become available, they may not be the type that can easily be included in a statistical equation. This justifies the inclusion of qualitative descriptions of country specific approaches to Internet technology (Press, Burkhart, Foster, Goodman, Wolcott & Woodard, 1998). Therefore, I present two cases that draw on the above empirical findings to explain the Internet connectivity of a nation complemented by country-specific information that is not possible to quantify for systematic inclusion in regression analyses.

Fig. 1 shows Finland's striking position in the diffusion hierarchy as being by far the most wired nation. Information on telephone density also underlines Finland's strength with respect to communication technologies. Finland is one of the few European nations with open competition in its telecommunications sector over several years. This is probably the reason for Finland's Internet access charges being among the lowest across the countries included in this study. With respect to flat rate versus measured access charges, Helsinki Telecom had flat rate off-peak charges during this period which may have also contributed to higher use. Moreover, the Finnish government initiated a national information society strategy as early as 1994, leading to the full-time connectivity of all higher education institutions and the majority of government organizations (Mosaic, 1998). The country's per capita information technology production is also among the highest in the world (Lyytinen & Goodman, 1999) thanks to being home to such major players in the telecommunications equipment industry as Nokia, supplying local know-how and equipment to encourage the spread of communication networks.

The position of France on the connectivity hierarchy is surprising in the opposite direction. Although the country has internationally recognized research institutions in the field of information technologies (e.g. INRIA), the nation has been slow at gaining widespread connectivity to the Internet. In contrast to the Finnish government's early efforts in playing an active role regarding the creation of a national information infrastructure, France's leaders have done much less to encourage the spread of the Internet. Not until 1997 did a top official express support of the technology (Giussani, 1997). All of this is not to say that French citizens are not networked. Since 1982, the French have had their own national network — the video-text system Minitel. It provides users with many of the services currently available on the Internet. However, it does so on a text-based system (no graphics). Moreover, it is an isolated network that does not have any international connections, so its proliferation cannot be easily translated into high-level national Internet connectivity. Rather, it can almost be seen as an impediment to that process. France's telecommunications policies also do not encourage the diffusion of the Internet. Monopoly in the telecom sector had restricted competition and had kept Internet access charges high. Moreover, France has had a strict approach to policies regarding national security with respect to encryption software, which may have also added to the slow spread of the Internet (Fletcher, 1998; Giussani, 1997).

As the examples of Finland and France show, nation-specific postures and policies need to be considered when assessing the full range of issues that affect the Internet connectivity of a nation. Nonetheless, the findings of the quantitative analysis in this paper provide a basis for what factors are necessary to consider in understanding Internet connectivity, in addition to possible other factors. Both Finnish and French cases underscore the role of telecommunications (and possibly other) policies in Internet diffusion, and illustrate the importance of case-specific studies to understand the pace of Internet connectivity worldwide.

6. Conclusion

There are several implications of the above findings. First of all, it is important to recognize that the current spread of the Internet indicates that even among the richest countries of the world, general economic strength does matter in predicting Internet connectivity. This is important to keep in mind when making overarching optimistic claims about the Internet's potential role in eliminating international differences. The finding about the importance of telecommunication policy suggests that if governments are interested in keeping afloat an increasingly knowledge-intensive economy with a large reliance on information, they may need to consider the implications of their telecommunication policies with respect to Internet connectivity in particular.[16] The findings of this paper lend empirical support to the message conveyed in several publications of the OECD regarding the role of competition in assisting the spread of the Internet (OECD, 1996; Paltridge, 1996; Paltridge & Ypsilanti, 1997).

Regarding future research on this topic, an important next question needs to address what it is about the societies with competition in their telecom markets that has led them to adopt their particular policies. More qualitative information about each nation will help uncover the answers to this question. Moreover, as more relevant data become available, time-series analysis will tell us how the current changes in policy regulations are influencing Internet connectivity.[17]

The macro-level analyses presented above should eventually — when such data become available — be supplemented by more detailed information on national diffusion patterns. Future research needs to examine specific implementation and use in more detail. Whether there is an equal distribution of technology in a country may significantly affect its final impacts for that society. Although host distribution is a good raw measure of Internet connectivity, once data are available, it should be supplemented by information on the number of users, their time spent online, the quality of connectivity, the amount and type of data transferred, and the technology's distribution among the population.[18] With respect to individual characteristics, information on age, socio-economic status and political affiliation may tell us more about who within a nation is adopting the technology. Now that we have a sense of what overarching factors explain the network's spread to certain nations, we can start focusing in on the particularities in order to have an even better understanding of the process.

Documenting the level of connectivity across long-standing democratic societies is a first step in understanding the potential global impact of the Internet. The findings can be used to guide research on network diffusion to other areas of the world, although data availability problems make this a difficult task at the present. By identifying the key predictors of Internet connectivity among OECD countries, this paper has set the agenda for more detailed analyses regarding this important social phenomenon on a world scale.

Acknowledgements

I would like to thank Marta Tienda, Miguel Centeno, Martin Dodge, Bruce Western, the members of Princeton University's 1998/99 Sociology Empirical Research Seminar and an anonymous reviewer for their helpful comments on earlier drafts of this paper. I am grateful to Tim Kelly, Ben Petrazzini and Sam Paltridge for their help in providing data.

Appendix A

As mentioned this appendix provides details about sources of the data set (Table 3).

Appendix B

As mentioned in text we provide in this appendix all explanatory variables and correlation between them (Table 4).

Table 3 Description of variables, data sources.

Variable	Description	Measurement	Year	Source
Internet hosts	Individual computers connected to the Internet	Per 10,000	1998	Network Wizards (1998)
GDP	Gross domestic product	Per capita	1996	OECD Communications Outlook (1997)
Gini coefficient	Gini coefficient for income inequality	Score	Various[a]	Deininger and Squire Data Set (1996)
Education	Combined first-, second-, and third-level gross enrollment ratio	Percentage	1995	UNDP Human Development Report (1998)
English	Percentage of students in general secondary education learning English as a foreign language; Native speakers	Percentage	1995	Eurostat Yearbook (1997)
Telecom policy	Competition vs. monopoly	Y/N dichotomy	1990s	ITU (1997); OECD (1997d)
Pricing	The cost of a 20 h monthly Internet access basket	PPP$	1995	OECD Communications Outlook (1997)
Phone density	Composite variable consisting of:		1995	OECD Communications Outlook (1997)
	mainlines	Per 100	1995	
	cellular phone subscribers	Per 100	1995	

[a]France, Germany 1984, Luxembourg 1985, Austria, Ireland 1987, Greece 1988, Spain 1989, Australia, New Zealand 1990, Canada, Finland, Italy, Netherlands, United Kingdom, United States 1991, Belgium, Denmark, Sweden 1992.

Table 4 Correlation coefficients for all variables: Pearson's correlation coefficient (Significance; 2-tailed test on second line)

	Hosts	GDP	Gini coef	Education	Native Eng	High Eng	Low Eng	Telecom policy	Prices
GDP	0.350 / 0.155								
Gini coef	0.210 / 0.403	-0.129 / 0.611							
Education	0.447* / 0.063	-0.323 / 0.191	0.038 / 0.881						
Native Eng	0.437* / 0.074	0.070 / 0.784	0.536** / 0.022	0.337 / 0.171					
High Eng	0.075 / 0.767	-0.150 / 0.553	-0.315 / 0.203	0.213 / 0.396	-0.632*** / 0.005				
Low Eng	-0.578* / 0.012	0.100 / 0.692	-0.231 / 0.356	-0.637*** / 0.004	-0.378 / 0.122	-0.478* / 0.045			
Telecom policy	-0.751* / 0.000	-0.031 / 0.902	-0.308 / 0.214	-0.386 / 0.113	-0.645*** / 0.004	0.255 / 0.307	0.426 / 0.078		
Prices	-0.435* / 0.071	-0.152 / 0.548	-0.091 / 0.720	-0.221 / 0.377	-0.470** / 0.049	0.391 / 0.109	0.065 / 0.797	-0.604*** / 0.008	
Phone density	0.699*** / 0.001	0.347 / 0.158	0.136 / 0.590	0.110 / 0.663	0.067 / 0.791	0.178 / 0.480	-0.289 / 0.245	-0.633*** / 0.005	-0.404* / 0.097

Note: Hosts/10,000 logged, GDP/cap; $p < 0.1*$, $p < 0.05**$, $p < 0.01***$.

Notes

1 As Section 3 on Data and Methods will elaborate, only 18 countries of today's 29 member nations were included in this analysis.

2 Although every attempt was made to include all member countries of the OECD, due to lack of data on several important variables (most notably access charges and English competence), only 18 countries could be included. Data were missing for the most recent members of the OECD (Czech Republic, Hungary, Korea, Poland, and Mexico) and some other nations (Iceland, Japan, Norway, Portugal, and Switzerland). I used t-test significance testing for means differences to determine whether the excluded cases are significantly systematically different from the ones that were included in the analysis. Only one variable showed systematic difference; all excluded countries had monopolistic telecommunications markets in the year studied. This should be kept in mind when interpreting the results with respect to the overall OECD population.

For demographic information on OECD nations, see http://www.oecd.org/publications/figures.

3 In the future, when comparable data become available for sub-national geographical units, analysis on cross-border regions/cities would also be important and revealing. Such work would be especially helpful in understanding national inequalities.

4 The use of earlier figures as inequality measures is not a serious problem because level of inequality does not change quickly in these long standing democratic countries.

5 Studies of diffusion often look at data over time in order to include the rate of diffusion in the model with special importance attributed to the starting point of the diffusion. Although there is a difference in timing regarding countries' initial connection to the Internet, most connections (with the exception of Luxembourg) took place relatively close to each other all between 1988–1990 (OECD, 1996). Given that this study looks at 1998 connectivity levels, these initial differences are likely not to be an overarching explanatory factor concerning the differences in the outcome variable. Regarding the specific theories addressed in this paper, lack of sufficient data on predictor variables made over-time analysis impossible.

6 Hosts are measured by top-level domain names, the United States includes figures for generic top-level domain names (.com, .edu, .gov, .mil, .org, .net) and .us. Although weighted host data are available that account for the number of top level domain names registered by countries other than the United States (OECD, 1998b, OECD, 1999a), these data were less suited for meeting the assumptions of regression analysis and thus results of the other data are reported. Nonetheless, the tests were run on the weighted data as well and the findings are robust.

7 There is no systematic information available on the number of users per host across nations. The Discussion section elaborates on what this lack of data implies for the findings of this study and its implications for future research.

8 I experimented with different scales for the dependent variable for performing the log transformation and the results are robust. The regression results are only discussed with respect to standardized coefficients so the log transformation does not affect the discussion of the outcome. The results are also robust without logging the dependent variable.

9 Gini coefficients are difficult to collect, represent measures for varying years, and the data source acknowledges the questionable quality of some of the figures

(Deininger & Squire, 1996). Nonetheless, they are the only available source of income inequality. The quality of the data must be kept in mind when interpreting the effects of this variable. Lower coefficients denote lower inequality.

10 It is important to note that this information on pricing does not distinguish between flat-rate versus measured charges. A flat-rate connection fee may seem more with respect to a twenty-hour connection charge, but it may become more preferable when compared with the forty-hour fee of measured charges. Twenty-hour rates were used in this analysis because that is the way data are available for this measure (OECD, 1997d).

11 Personal computers could also be used to measure related existing technologies. However, given the close conceptual relationship between computer ownership and Internet connectivity, the use of that variable would be problematic for this purpose.

12 Why these ideas are merely hypothetical is elaborated in the final section, which discusses what we know about people's actual use of the Internet.

13 Note that dial-up pricing and not leased line pricing was included in this analysis. The model was also run with the inclusion of data on leased line pricing, but similarly to the model reported here, the policy variable was the most salient predictor of connectivity level.

14 As stated earlier, because of the high correlation between telecom policy and phone density, including both in the same model leads to unstable results. Model 8 demonstrates that this is, in fact, the case given that the model is not significantly improved by the inclusion of both factors, and the explanatory value (adjusted for the increased number of variables) is lower than that of the model with information only on telecom policy.

15 Recall that the 11 excluded OECD countries have monopolies in the telecom sector. Given that this is coupled with a slight means difference in Internet connectivity with excluded countries exhibiting lower levels of connectivity, if anything, the findings of this analysis are likely to be conservative with respect to policy's influence on Internet connectivity with respect to all OECD nations.

16 As this paper does not address the question of national patterns of diffusion, the findings have no specific implications for what types of policies need to be considered in order to allow for equal distribution within a nation preventing the possible rise of national inequalities.

17 The OECD Communications Outlook reports publish relevant data (OECD 1997a, 1999a) so it is clear that over the years the necessary lagged data will be available for use in time-series analyses.

18 Although some work has been done at this level in the United States (e.g. see Kraut et al., 1998), data are yet to be collected on a random sample of the population (even just online population) that would allow for generalizability.

References

Anderson, R. H., Bikson, T. K., Law, S. A., & Mitchell, B. M., et al. (1995). Universal access to e-mail — feasability and societal implications. Santa Monica, CA: Rand.

Barnett, G. A., & Choi, Y. (1995). Physical distance and language as determinants of the international telecommunicatoins network. International Political Science Review, 16(3), 249–265.

Calhoun, C. (1998). Community without propinquity revisted: Communications technology and the transformation of the urban public sphere. *Sociological Inquiry*, *68*(3), 373–397.

Castells, M. (1996). *The rise of the network society*. Cambridge, MA: Blackwell Publishers.

The CommerceNet/Nielsen Internet Demographic Survey June 1998 Internet Demographic Highlights (1998). http://www.commerce.net/research/stats/highlights.html. Number of Internet Users and Shoppers Surges in United States and Canada. http://www.commerce.net/news/press/19980824b.html.

Deaken, J. (1981). The electronic cottage. New York: Morrow.

Deininger, K., & Squire L. (1996). A new data set measuring income inequality. *The World Bank Economic Review*, *10*(3), 565–691.

Drake, W. J. (1995). *The new information infrastructure: Strategies for U.S. policy*. New York: The Twentieth Century Fund Press.

Etzioni, A. (1992). Teledemocracy: the electronic town meeting. *The atlantic*, *270*(4), 34–39.

Eurostat Yearbook (1997). Luxembourg.

Fishman, J. A., Cooper, R. L., & Conrad, A. (1977). The spread of English. Rowley, MA: Newbury House.

Fletcher, A., (1998). Markets and states in the information society: A comparative institutional analysis of telecommunications policy in the United States and France. *Political Communication*, July–Sep V15N3:413(2).

Geser, H. (1996). Auf dem Weg zur "Cyberdemocracy?" http://www.unizh.ch/~geserweb/komoef/ftext.html.

Giussani, B. (1997). France gets along with pre-web technology. *The New York Times CyberTimes*. September 23 (http://www.nytimes.com/library/cyber/euro/092397euro.html).

Goodman, S. E., Press, L. E., Ruth, S. R., & Rutkowski, A. M. (1994). The global diffusion of the internet: Patterns and problems. *Communications of the ACM*, *37*(8).

Hauben, M., & Hauben, R. (1997). Netizens: On the history and impact of Usenet and the Internet. Los Alamitos, CA: IEEE Computer Society Press.

Hargittai, E. (1996). Holes in the net: The internet and international stratification. Senior honors thesis. Smith College (http://cs.smith.edu/~hargitta/Thesis).

Hargittai, E. (1998). Holes in the net: The internet and international stratification revisited. *Proceedings of the internet society's internet summit meetings*. (http://www.isoc.org/inet98/proceedings/5d/5d_1.htm).

ITU (1997). Challenges to the network: Telecoms and the internet. Geneva.

ITU (1999). Challenges to the network: Internet for development 1999. Geneva.

Kelly, T., & Petrazzini, B. (1997). What does the internet mean for development? Telecom interactive development symposium, Geneva, 11 September.

Kraut, R., Patterson, M., Lundmark, V., Kiesler, S., Mukophadhyay, T., & Scherlis, W. (1998). Internet paradox: A social technology that reduces social involvement and psychological well-being?. *American Psychologist*, *53*.

Laponce, J. A. (1987). Languages and their territories. Toronto: University of Toronto Press.

Lyytinen, K., & Goodman, S. (1999). Finland: The unknown soldier on the IT front. *Communications of the ACM*, *42*(3), 13–17.

The MOSAIC Group (1998). The global diffusion of the internet project, An initial inductive study. Fairfax, VA: The MOSAIC Group (http://www.agsd.com/gdi97/gdi97.html).

Naisbitt, J. (1982). Megatrends. New York: Warner Publications.

Network Wizards (1998). (http://www.nw.com).

Novak, T. P., & Hoffman, D. L. (1998). Bridging the digital divide: The impact of race on computer access and internet use. *Science, 280,* 390–391.

NTIA (1995). Falling through the net: A survey of the 'have nots' in rural and urban America. Washington, DC: US Department of Commerce.

NTIA (1998). Falling through the net II: New data on the digital divide. Washington, DC: US Department of Commerce.

NTIA (1999). Falling through the net III: Defining the digital divide. Washington, DC: US Department of Commerce.

OECD (1996). Information infrastructure convergence and pricing: The internet. Paris: OECD (http://www.oecd.org/dsti/sti/it/cm/prod/e_96-73.htm).

OECD (1997a). Global Information Infrastructure — Global Information Society (GII-GIS): Policy Requirements OCDE/GD(97)139 (http://www.oecd.org/dsti/sti/it/infosoc/prod/e_97-139.htm).

OECD (1997b). Global Information Infrastructure — Global Information Society (GII-GIS): Policy recommendations for action. Paris: OECD OCDE/GD(97)138. (http://www.oecd.org/dsti/sti/it/infosoc/prod/e_97-138.htm).

OECD (1997c). Information technology outlook 1997. Paris: OECD. (http://www.oecd.org/dsti/sti/it/prod/itblurb.htm).

OECD (1997d). Communications Outlook 1997. Paris: OECD.

OECD (1997e). Webcasting and convergence: Policy implications. Paris: OECD (http://www.oecd.org/dsti/sti/it/cm/prod/e_97-221.htm).

OECD (1998a). OECD Internet infrastructure indicators. Paris: OECD.

OECD (1998b). Internet traffic exchange: Developments and policy. Paris: OECD (http://www.oecd.org/dsti/sti/it/cm/prod/traffic.htm).

OECD (1999a). Communications outlook 1999. Paris: OECD.

OECD (1999b). Building infrastructure capacity for electronic commerce — leased line developments and pricing. Paris: OECD.

OECD (1999c). Internet indicators. Online component of communications outlook 1999. Paris: OECD (http://www.oecd.org/dsti/sti/it/cm/stats/indicators.htm).

Paltridge, S. (1996). How competition helps the internet. *The OECD Observer.* August–September p. 25.

Paltridge, S. & Ypsilanti, D. (1997). A bright outlook for communications. *The OECD Observer.* No. 205. April/May, pp. 19–22.

Pew Research Center For People and The Press. 1998. Internet news takes off. Washington, DC: The Pew Research Center For The People and The Press (http://www.people-press.org/med98rpt.htm).

Press, L., Burkhart, G., Foster, W., Goodman, S., Wolcott, P., & Woodard, J. (1998). An internet diffusion framework. *Communications of the ACM, 41*(10), 21–26.

Rammert, W. (1990). Telefon und kommunikationskultur. *Kölner Zeitschrift fur Soziologie, 42,* 20–40.

Rao, M. (1995). North vs. South. *OnTheInternet.* September/October.

Reich, R. (1992). The work of nations: Preparing ourselves for 21st century capitalism. New York: Vintage Books.

Rheingold, H. (1993). The virtual community: Homesteading on the electronic frontier. Reading, MA: Addison-Wesley.

Robinson, J., Barth, K., & Kohut, A. (1997). Personsal computers, mass media, and use of time. *Social Science Computer Review, 15*, 65–82.

Robinson, J., Levin, S., & Hak, B. (1998). Computer time. *American Demographics*, 18–23.

Rogers, E. M. (1983). Diffusion of innovations. New York: The Free Press.

Stoll, C. (1995). Silicon snake oil: Second thoughts on the information highway. New York: Doubleday.

Thomas (1988). The politics of growth: The German telephone system. In M. Renate, & T. P. Hughes, *The development of large technical systems* (pp. 179–213). Boulder, CO: Westview Press.

UNDP (1998). Human development report. New York: Oxford University Press.

Weinstein, B. (1983). The civic tongue: Political consequences of language choice. New York: Longman.

40

FROM DIGITAL DIVIDES TO DIGITAL ENTITLEMENTS IN KNOWLEDGE SOCIETIES

Robin Mansell

Source: *Current Sociology* 50(3) (2002): 407–26.

1. Introduction

'New media' technologies and services are being developed as a result of the spread of digital networks and software platforms. In the first article in this special issue, Judy Wajcman (2002: 360) points out that 'revolutions in technology do not create new societies, but they do change the terms in which social, political and economic relations are played out'. New media are implicated in these changes in a variety of ways. One of these has caught the attention of policymakers worldwide. This is the way the uneven spread of the new media or the so-called 'digital divide' and its consequences are a threat to those citizens who, for one reason or another, are not participants in electronically mediated networks. This paper suggests that most interpretations of the causes and consequences of this 'divide' are inadequate. Correspondingly, the appropriate actions to alleviate the manifestations of this 'divide' remain to be identified. These shortcomings are a consequence of failing to fully address issues of how new media applications may be used to empower those who are disadvantaged, disadvantages that stem from the way social and technical relations are working themselves out at the start of this century.

Paradoxically, the sociology of globalization and its consequences is bifurcated between studies at the macro-analytical level such as those by Beck (1992/1986), Giddens (1999), and Held *et al.* (1999), and studies at the micro-analytical level which suggest how social decision processes yield particular configurations of the technical (for instance, Bijker *et al.*, 1989; Bijker and Law, 1994; and MacKenzie and Wajcman, 1999). Just as it is revealing to examine the mutually constituted relation between the technical

351

and the social at the micro- and macro-analytical levels, it is similarly interesting to examine this relation at the 'meso' or institutional level. Most studies of new media policy at this level take the technological configuration of the new media as a 'given' or prefigured system that needs to become more widely diffused to citizens (see Mansell and Steinmueller, 2000, and MacKenzie, 1996, for a critique of this view). Exceptions are to be found in examinations of Internet policy as, for example, in Lessig's work (2000, 2001). However, his research does not examine the rhetorical forms that help to sustain the configurations of the new media that are favoured by an influential minority of technology developers and producers.

There are comparatively few accounts of how those who inhabit the 'meso-level' institutions of policy are constructing prevailing conceptions of the new media and the associated norms for social organization. Some of these conceptions are examined in this article to illustrate how they are informing new media policy associated with the 'digital divide'. The analysis suggests that many of the actors who participate in intergovernmental discussions tend to promote particular configurations of the new media. These configurations come to be regarded as the most effective way to develop new media applications and it becomes more difficult to envisage alternatives that are consistent with a goal of empowering the majority of citizens in their interactions with the new media.

Seeking greater variety in the configurations of the new media is desirable. To encourage this, however, there must be a shift in the emphasis of most social science analysis and policy debate about the causes of new media developments and their consequences for society. The contention in this article is that a change in the rhetorical form of the 'digital divide' debate is essential. This means that much greater attention must be focused on alternative ways in which the new media might be configured so that the majority of citizens can begin to strengthen their abilities to make choices about alternative ways of living their lives.

The focus of policy debate on the 'digital divide' is overwhelmingly on macro-level issues of technology access and social exclusion. To a lesser extent there is consideration of micro-level issues but this focuses mainly on a narrow conception of the capabilities needed to function in a society that increasingly favours social interaction mediated by the Internet. This narrow conception of capabilities links issues of individual learning and cognitive development principally to human capital formation aimed at strengthening the contribution of the work force to the achievement of efficiency and productivity gains associated with the use of new media (see Mansell and Wehn, 1998; Mansell, 2001a). But if new media applications are also envisaged as offering tools for the empowerment of the majority of citizens it is essential to redefine the concept of capability to encompass forms of learning and cognitive development that are necessary for making sense of a social world of on-line spaces created by the new media. In this article, the work of Amartya Sen (1999) provides a basis for considering capabilities in a much broader context and for examining whether the dominant configurations of new media are consistent with a social goal of empowering the majority of citizens. This suggests the foundation for a rights-based approach to new media policy.

In section 2, the reason that it is essential to examine the specificity of the relation between new media and society is discussed. Section 3 then examines the rhetorical form used by participants in intergovernmental forums in their discussions of the problem of the 'digital divide' and appropriate policy choices. This analysis illustrates the extent to which the rhetoric forecloses an assessment of the need for greater variety in the deployment of new media configurations. In section 4, evidence of the biases of new media configurations based on the Internet is used to demonstrate the predominance of a familiar 'broadcast' mode of information provision over new media applications that would favour citizen acquisition of new media literacies. Amartya Sen's framework for evaluating capabilities and the entitlements of citizens is discussed in section 5 together with an exploratory analysis of new media developments that appear to be consistent with a goal of enabling the majority of citizens to acquire new media capabilities that may empower them. Finally, in the conclusion, the likelihood of a much needed shift in the rhetorical form and associated actions of new media policy is assessed.

2. New media technologies and society

For the most part, new media policy discussions focus on market dynamics, governance procedures and regulation of the new technologies and services. These discussions are conducted in forums where the participants generally presume that the relation between the new media and the citizen is beneficial and that the main barrier to ensuring that all citizens benefit is created by an unequal distribution of new media (Internet) access. However, the implications of the new media need to be understood more deeply because of the way in which innovations in digital technologies are contributing to the exercise and the distribution of power in society (Silverstone, 1999). The implications of the new media are contradictory. Once connected, there are no grounds for simply assuming that citizens will be empowered to conduct their social lives in meaningful ways. There is, therefore, a growing need to examine whether the deployment of new media is consistent with ensuring that the majority of citizens acquire the necessary capabilities for interpreting and acting upon a social world that is intensively mediated by the new media. New media literacies are crucial for sustaining a democratic dialogue (Silverstone, 1999). These literacies or capabilities entail far more than knowing how to read and understand digital information products. This is because it is difficult to make sense of a social world that is mediated by the new media. The provenance of much information is increasingly unclear and the opportunities for citizens to contribute information and to engage in public dialogue are not promoted by the dominant configurations of the new media services.

For citizens to make sense of the information they receive, they need skills. In particular, they need the skills to discriminate between authoritative information and information whose provenance is detached from its originator. This is characteristic of most of the new media and it creates a need for citizens to acquire new capabilities for assessing the value, veracity and reliability of information if they are to participate effectively within the fabric of a global society. If, as Castells (2001: 1) suggests, 'the Internet is the fabric of our lives', and if those living within this fabric are to have the freedom to achieve the lifestyles they desire, then they must be able to acquire new media literacies. Without such literacies, social problems of alienation, poverty and ignorance are likely to worsen with the spread of the new media since the majority of citizens will not have acquired the capabilities needed to make choices or to express opinions about what they value. Castells (2001: 161) suggests that informational strategies are 'the new, and most effective, frontier for the exercise of power on the world stage'. Democratic processes, constructed around new media literacies, are essential. As electronic sources of information become pervasive, achieving improved control over the social and technical relation that is configured by the Internet and its digital information flows is, arguably, one of the most fundamental political issues at the beginning of the 21st century (Castells, 2001).

The problem of the social control of media and communication networks is not new. Williams linked issues of control of the structure and content of the older generations of media and communication technologies to the organization of society. He suggested that matters concerning the forms of communication are closely associated with institutional form and with the organization of social relationships (Williams, 1976). But Thompson's (1995) analysis two decades later suggests that the social science community continues to display a profound neglect of how specific forms of media and communications are influencing the way that citizens experience their lives. Much research in the genre of 'Internet Studies' is not concerned with how alternative configurations of the new media might augment people's capabilities for living their lives (see Dawson, 1999; Gauntlett, 2000; Simon, 2000). There has so far been little consideration of the conditions of people's lives or of their freedom to create positive changes in their lives within the fabric of the 'global information society'. In many cases, it is simply assumed that the new technologies will facilitate democratic processes (see Dutton, 1999 for a critique of this view).

The spread of the new media means that social processes of identity formation are being enriched by the new media's vast symbolic content. But, at the same time, social actors are becoming more dependent upon electronically mediated information flows that are largely beyond their control. Thompson (1995: 37) refers to this phenomenon as the 'double bind of mediated dependency'. The vast majority of citizens make no contribution to the way that new media networks and their content are developed. The majority of citizens have few opportunities to express their views about whether the prevailing new media configurations are consistent with enabling them to acquire new media capabilities. Thompson suggests that the media are biased in various ways. In particular, he argues that they tend to disempower local forms of political organization. They render traditional forums for democratic dialogue very difficult to sustain. There is, he suggests, a need to encourage a new form of 'publicness' (Thompson, 1995: 10) and the new media, based in part on the Internet, are implicated along with other digital technologies and services.

Habermas's (1992/1962) advocacy of the creation of a public sphere within which informed public discourse might flourish has proved to be elusive. Thompson advocates legislation and regulation to create a foundation for new forms of publicness through 'regulated pluralism' and a 'deconcentration' of the new media through policy intervention (Thompson, 1995: 225). His expectation is that such policy action will encourage new media providers to offer greater variety in the structure and content of their services thereby encouraging information flows and debates that sustain a 'deliberative democracy'. New media market structures undoubtedly influence the variety of content that is produced and the extent to which public dialogue is encouraged. But this is only one aspect of new media development. Equally important are the specific new media configurations that emerge as dominant forms. At present, the dominant configuration of new media supported by the Internet appears to favour a minority of citizens. This is because it is only a minority of citizens who are being provided with learning experiences consistent with functioning in a highly technologically mediated world.

There is a need to foster new media developments that will enable the majority of citizens to acquire the capabilities or new media literacies they need for functioning in such a world. This could be achieved by extending and deepening the capabilities for critical discourse about the origins and validity of information provided through access to Internet-based new media environments. However, policy intervention is necessary to ensure that the new media provide the kinds of electronic spaces where people can acquire capabilities to evaluate information, to offer their own views, and to discriminate between alternative choices. These capabilities are learned. They involve the cognitive capacities to recognize and evaluate choices and alternatives. In section 5, this observation is developed and linked to an argument in support of a rights-based approach to new media policy. It is first necessary, however, to examine the extent to which the rhetorical form (section 3) and the predominant configuration of the new media (section 4) are biased in ways that favour economic growth more strongly than citizen empowerment and new forms of 'publicness'.

3. Constructing the digital divide

The participants in intergovernmental forums on the 'digital divide' are drawn from the public and private sectors and civil society organizations. They tend to portray the causes and consequences of the 'digital divide' and the appropriate policy actions in ways that favour the extension of access to the new media mainly to support the development of the 'digital economy'. The evidence in support of this claim is drawn from the writer's experience as a participant in various policy forums. In these forums, the problem of how to overcome uneven access to the new media is often discussed along-side measures to promote the use of services for electronic commerce or electronic government.[1] The argument in this paper is that the rhetorical form of participants' contributions to such forums encourages a focus on 'digital divide' issues that are predominantly concerned with how the new media create a need for capabilities that will enable people to participate more effectively in the economy. Consequently, the rhetoric rarely gives rise to a consideration of the new media literacies that might sustain a broadly-based deliberative democratic dialogue.

Since its initial use in the USA to describe uneven access to advanced information and communication technologies, and particularly to the Internet (US Department of Commerce, 1995), the 'digital divide' has become a rhetorical device for focusing policy discussion in intergovernmental forums on how disparities in access to the new media between and within countries can be overcome. Although many acknowledge that the 'digital divide' is not a new problem, this terminology is used to mobilize financial and other resources in an effort to remove barriers to wider adoption of the new media. As Schwab suggests,

> . . . you can't eat computers – and you can't prevent malaria with software. The debate over the so-called digital divide has taken many forms. It's not a new discussion, or a new global issue. It is, perhaps, more like a social and economic challenge with a new name – and with different actors and an invigorating sense of optimism.
>
> (2001: 3)

The new media, and especially the Internet, are often portrayed by participants in such forums as offering new opportunities for enabling improved access to skills acquisition and knowledge. As a senior speaker from one intergovernmental organization observed:

in a globalizing world, no government can regulate based on its own sovereignty . . . The world has become a real global place; not just a global market place . . . The global distribution of skills and knowledge will be the precondition for the distribution of wealth in the world economy.

He added that 'it is important to listen . . . not just to transfer best practice policies'.

In 2000, representatives of the Group of Eight countries released the Okinawa Charter on the Global Information Society and created a Digital Opportunities Task (DOT) Force. This group reported in July 2001 (DOT Force, 2001b). The motivation for this initiative was the realization that the expansion of global trade and investment depends upon economic growth and global stability and that it is in the 'enlightened self-interest' of the wealthy countries to address problems that lead to the risk of instability. One means of addressing such problems is believed to be encouragement of the spread of an inclusive global Internet fabric and the removal of barriers to its use. In the context of the DOT Force deliberations and in associated forums for discussion about the global information society, there has been consideration of a collective vision of the way the new media can be used to enable all people to improve their social and economic circumstances. But the emphasis in these discussions is on the role of the new media in enabling productivity and efficiency gains in the economies and regions that are disadvantaged. Thus, for example,

. . . poor countries (and within them poorer segments of the population) are being further marginalised, as their access to opportunities for wealth creation is being reduced; considerable development opportunities are being missed, as productivity and efficiency gains are not being transmitted from rich to poor countries.

(DOT Force, 2001a: 3)

The DOT Force participants were seeking to mobilize action that will contribute to bridging the 'digital divide', to secure the participation by non-members of the Group of Eight, and to integrate digital technology initiatives within more broadly based development initiatives. In this context, it was recognized that 'one size fits all' policies are inappropriate and that simply acquiring knowledge of 'best practice' is an insufficient foundation for development because certain human capabilities are essential in order to absorb knowledge and put it to effective use. A senior public sector spokesperson attending one intergovernmental forum extended the discussion of policy issues beyond those of capabilities for economic development. He observed that

> ... ICTs [information and communication technologies] must be seen as a tool for empowerment of people and which could help bridge other divides of society ... Services must be citizen focused and fully integrated. Delivery must start from needs of citizens and business ... Special attention must be given to human capital development through knowledge advancement and training.

He emphasized the needs of citizens and business, but this balanced treatment of the issues by a senior representative of government was a somewhat unusual occurrence in the context of such forums.

When representatives of government, firms, and civil society organizations from around the world meet in these institutional settings, they often compare their common interests and different experiences with new media and the 'digital divide'. They often agree about the importance of investment in the technical infrastructure of the new media and in content to achieve a range of economic and social goals. They also frequently observe that the opportunities associated with the new media must be considered in the light of the risk of reinforcing existing economic and social problems. But above all, they tend to suggest that knowledge gaps are the greatest barriers to economic development and that these must be alleviated through the provision of efficient infrastructure, affordable access to new media, the production of relevant content, and increased attention to education provision and skills development. In addition, they generally insist that policy measures to promote more inclusive access to the new digital technologies must be linked to overarching policy goals for development.

The rhetorical form that tends to be adopted in such policy forums is not only constructed to promote convergent viewpoints. The differences in the views of participants representing various organizations are not entirely swept away. But the rhetoric tends to acknowledge and encourage the use of the dominant technological configurations of the new media. These configurations are strongly biased to give priority to building capabilities consistent with the goal of strengthening the contribution of new media users to economic growth and development.

And, as a senior public policy representative from the industrialized world put it during one forum, 'the danger of the digital divide is real. There are possibilities to use these technologies to close the gap. We need to turn possibilities into probabilities.' Education is essential and international cooperation and sharing of experience can help governments to avoid mistakes and adopt 'best practices'. Although a senior government representative of a developing country might argue for legislative reforms 'with a human face', he or she might also observe that 'this decade belongs to software and other services'. Little attention is given to whether the technical configuration of the new software and services is itself consistent with building capabilities that will empower citizens. Instead, the visions of the global new media and their consequences are informed by the premise that the 'digital divide' manifests itself in many ways, 'dividing one business, region, or social group from another and affecting the ability of some countries to participate in the development process and market growth that others enjoy'. Problems can therefore be addressed by providing access to technology.

Occasionally, the issue of human needs comes onto the agenda, as in the case of a DOT Force discussion forum in South Africa:

> Looking at the 'new economy' in isolation (dot.com fascination syndrome) is a recipe for failure: rooting efforts in good management, good governance and *'real needs'* is the proper way to contribute to various countries' development efforts while respecting their differences.
>
> (DOT Force, 2001a: 10, emphasis added)

During one policy forum, a South African researcher suggested that the 'digital divide' discussion was overly focused on 'costs and affordability', arguing that the most important question is 'not what use of the internet, but whether initiatives are addressing community needs for information'. Another spokesperson from a northern African country argued that there is a 'need to deliver the hope and the opportunity provided by equitable access to new technology. An emphasis on people.com is better than dot.com.' He went on to observe that 'the world will not be that different just by having the "e" in front of commerce or government'. A spokesperson for a global technology and service provider also emphasized the importance of 'lifelong' learning, but he argued that this was the responsibility of employees who should take advantage of the re-skilling opportunities offered by their employers. Again, the discussions and the rhetoric are mainly concerned with economic development and the contributions of the existing new media network configurations to this goal. Very occasionally the rhetorical form of these discussions highlights the possibility that the technological configurations of the new media may themselves be inappropriate to promote learning and the acquisition of the cognitive capacities necessary for citizens to achieve their goals and aspirations in society. Insofar as new media configurations are considered, it is only to the extent that it is recognized that 'the choice of technical components must take into consideration the specific infrastructure, demographic conditions, organizational capacities, and policy contexts of the region' (TeleCommons Group, 2000: 23).

Issues of culture and differences in perceptions of trust in the products and services supported by digital technologies surface in these policy discussion forums from time to time. For instance, a spokesperson from South Africa observed that 'many leaders of developed countries do not understand the need to recognise cultural differences' or the desire of Africans to assert their 'Africanness'. 'Developing countries want to be equal citizens in a global information society, not just citizens; and to develop a vision to provide a better and full life for all our citizens.' The view of the problem of the 'digital divide' that tends to prevail is captured by a contribution of a private sector representative who claimed that the only response to the technological changes in the new media is to 'adopt or perish! There are not many choices, there is only one way to go.'

The social construct, trust, is an important factor that influences whether citizens are likely to regard new media developments as enhancing their ability to participate in society. The more or less taken-for-granted trust that citizens place in banks, credit agencies and governments in the industrialized countries is sometimes compared, in these policy discussions about the 'digital divide', with the different conditions that are present in other countries. In one forum, for example, a private sector representative from an eastern European country pointed out that for more than two years the banks in his country had been considering the use of electronic payment systems but 'most people simply do not use a credit card'. He suggested that there are other systems that are not based on credit cards but that little effort was being given to the development of any technological alternatives.

Another commentator representing a civil society organization in a discussion forum observed that 'there are questions about the extent to which consumers are sophisticated enough not to sign away rights because they may not be aware of the implications'. He suggested that there is a need to 'rethink the underlying structure of consumer protections. Not as a way of promoting e-commerce, but rather as *rights* in the marketplace' (emphasis added). In this instance, the issue of human rights becomes incorporated within the rhetorical form but only insofar as this applies in the economic sphere of producers and consumers.

An emphasis on education and skills acquisition in these discussion forums occurs frequently in the rhetorical form of the debates, but these issues are often framed in terms of a skills crisis or in terms of the potential for the new media to support economic 'leap-frogging'. As one participant from an intergovernmental organization suggested, 'preventing the digital divide means that time is of the essence, but time is becoming shorter and shorter' if leapfrogging is to occur in a way that stimulates economic growth and a catch-up of poor countries with the wealthy ones. Another participant with expertise in international trade commented that 'the key factor is e-competency . . . Leapfrogging is real, not just conjecture. We have moved onto e-management; it is a fast charging train.' Here the emphasis is on speed, rapid investment in access to the new media, and in learning and capabilities development oriented towards growth.

These illustrations of the rhetoric employed by those who participate in the intergovernmental policy community that is concerned with the 'digital divide' are to a degree anecdotal. Greater insight could be derived from a more systematic analysis of the content of such debates. Nevertheless, the evidence presented here does suggest that in the race to remove barriers to global information society access, the emphasis is on the new media configurations that are achieving the widest diffusion in the industrialized countries and their transfer to bridge gaps in disadvantaged regions and countries. The use of these configurations of new media is expected to benefit users because of their improved access to digital information. The rhetoric is consistent with an emphasis on the economic importance of the global interconnection of people and markets. It is consistent with a focus on the knowledge economy where hardware, software, and human capital become replacements for raw materials and for certain kinds of workers (Romer, 1995). The rhetoric privileges the 'new' economy and implies that policy should focus mainly on how the workforce can acquire new capabilities for managing electronic businesses since the prospects for economic growth depend on reaping benefits from the organization of commerce around networks (Romer, 1986). The rhetorical form of the 'digital divide' discussion echoes this narrow conception of issues that are at stake in the global information society. It emphasizes economic growth and the deployment of prefigured technologies, over issues of equity, social development and the need for a broader conception of the potential of the new media.

Cultural differences and social needs are not entirely absent from the dominant rhetoric of the 'digital divide' debate. But these issues do not inform the overall vision of what must be done in terms of new media policy intervention. Policy interventions to reduce the 'digital divide' are understood to involve a process whereby, as a private sector spokesperson in one forum stated, 'implementation is rapid; there are no decades any more . . . Countries are expected to set targets and begin to move.'

As a representative of one global company put it, 'you cannot win by stopping, but you can *choose* where to move' (emphasis added). This spokesperson is assuming that the capacity to choose exists, that is, that the majority of people do have the capabilities to choose between alternative ways of incorporating new media into their lives. It is also implicitly assumed that there is scope for choice in the technological configuration of the new media and over the types of information environments that emerge as a consequence of such choices. Yet a United Nations Human Development report states clearly that 'a global map for the new technologies is being drawn up faster than most people are able to understand the implications – let alone respond to them – and faster than anyone's certainty of the ethical and developmental impacts' (UNDP, 1999: 1). The next section assesses the issue of whether the dominant configurations of new media provision are consistent with enabling the majority of citizens to acquire new media literacies.

4. Dominant new media configurations

A growing minority of policymakers, businesses, consumers and citizens is benefiting from Internet-based discussions and information resources that comprise a significant portion of new media activity (Commonwealth Secretariat, 2001). In August 2001 there were an estimated 512.41 million users of the Internet (Nua Internet Surveys, 2001). In some developing countries, the growth rate in users is faster than the rate of growth in the industrialized countries. However, as the preceding discussion suggests, the biases in the configuration of the new media and their implications for building capabilities for informed debate are rarely acknowledged. To the extent that the bias of new media configurations is considered, this is usually only with respect to the statistic that some 68 percent of the Internet's content is in the English language. This creates an obvious barrier for people who may wish to acquire capabilities through their use of new media (Global Reach, 2001). However, other biases of the new media are deeply embedded in the specific technical configurations that are becoming predominant, especially in the case of the Internet and the development of information applications using the World Wide Web.

An examination of Internet-based information intermediaries offers insight into the way that technical design decisions reflecting the social and economic interests of new media developers are favouring certain new media applications and discouraging others. A vast number of information intermediaries are establishing sites on the World Wide Web. The private sector owners of these sites often claim that they support commercial transactions by any individual or firm seeking to buy or sell goods and services, regardless of their geographical location. Yet Paré's (2001) analysis of over 350 sites in the horticulture and garment sectors shows that the majority of these are 'walled' sites, that is, they are for members only.[2] Even when these sites are open to all potential buyers and sellers, they do not always deliver the information and business support services they claim to provide at their home pages. It may appear that the owners of these web sites offer services such as logistics, assistance for goods producers to meet industry standards for quality or environmental protection, or help in verifying the identities of firms. But scrutiny of these sites indicates that few actually provide all these services and that the services offered are available mainly to a minority of firms that are members of closed clubs. Thus, the dominant trend or configuration bias of new media services in the commercial world of electronic commerce and electronic markets is exclusivity. This is inconsistent with the goal of ensuring that the new media offer opportunities for learning and participating in the global economy that are inclusive.

A new media configuration bias is also suggested by the dominant forms of new media provision of services for citizens. Examination of information intermediary web sites in the health and education sectors and of web sites focusing on issues of environmental protection or globalization suggests that these sites, operated by institutions including governments, schools and development agencies, mainly provide structured, authoritative information.[3] Although some of the sites in the sample examined appeared to support limited interactivity between citizens and public organizations, few were designed to enable citizens to contribute their own information, or indeed, to participate in a learning process that would enable them to acquire capabilities for deciding how the information that is available should be valued or acted upon.

There is also a growing number of web sites of organizations that claim to represent citizens (Centre for Civil Society and Centre for the Study of Global Governance, 2001). These civil society organizations confer authority on the information they provide through their web sites, but a cursory examination of many of these sites suggests that they are mainly 'pushing' information *to* users.[4] They do not appear to be configuring their new media applications in ways that will support the majority of citizens to acquire capabilities for making their own information contributions or to learn how to employ available information to choose between alternative courses of action. Most Internet-based information intermediaries keep track of information or enhance it with annotations and various kinds of personalization. But these web-based intermediaries appear to be providing very few resources that enable the majority of citizens to acquire the cognitive capacities for discriminating between alternative social choices. Yet this is essential if the new media are to assist in fostering new forms of 'publicness'.

These biases of new media configurations are inconsistent with claims that the new media are technological innovations with the potential to empower the majority of citizens. This suggests that there is a need to move the rhetoric of debates about the new media and social relations towards an examination of the range of capabilities and associated new media configurations that would be more consistent with the encouragement of deliberative democracy.

5. Towards new media rights and entitlements

Too little emphasis is being given to whether the new media can be developed in ways that are likely to contribute to the reduction of poverty and to support socially productive networking among informed citizens (Pratt and Gill, 2001). Policy intervention is required to encourage new media developments that can help to encourage the majority of citizens to acquire the capabilities or new media literacies necessary for a democratic dialogue.

As Amartya Sen (1999) argues, citizens have an entitlement to acquire such capabilities and this is a fundamental human right. 'Functionings', he suggests, are what people value doing or being, and they may be basic such as being free from hunger or illness. They may also be complex such as being able to participate in the life of a community or having self-respect. Sen argues that 'capabilities' should be understood as the functionings that an individual is actually able to achieve. Capabilities in this sense are the underpinning of the freedom of citizens to construct meaningful lives.

Extending the idea of capabilities to the issue of new media development and policy requires a shift away from a focus on the causes and consequences of the 'digital divide'. It suggests the need for a focus on what citizens are able to do as a result of their interactions with the new media and what capabilities they are able to acquire as a result of those interactions. Sen's (1999: 293) capabilities approach focuses on 'the substantive freedom – of people to lead the lives they have reason to value and to enhance the real choices they have', in this instance, through the dynamic of the relation between new media and social organization.

Sen's approach starts with a concern for human well-being and from the view that human choice and the freedom to act are essential human rights.[5] The main concern is with the individual's capacity for social growth and with the acquisition of cognitive capabilities through learning. If the use of these cognitive capabilities is threatened so too is the satisfaction of basic human needs. If the configuration biases of the new media are not enabling the majority of citizens to acquire the cognitive capabilities for participating in deliberative democratic processes then there is an argument for a rights-based approach to new media policy.

In the field of telecommunications policy, Garnham (2000) has drawn upon Sen's work to argue that policy decisions about citizens' entitlements to telecommunications service access should not be based upon assessments of merit or absolute wealth. Instead, they should be based upon an assessment of whether citizens should be entitled to such access in order to develop their capabilities. A similar argument applies in the case of the new media. There is a need for an evaluation process which is an exercise in social choice that requires public discussion, understanding and democratic acceptance. In his work on *Development as Freedom*, Sen (1999) observes that communication and exchanges between people that are valued require basic education and training. He suggests that capabilities for being well-informed and able to participate freely in society are essential. However, in the absence of an assessment of how the new media can be configured to support the acquisition of such capabilities, the application of Sen's argument about entitlements yields little more than a call for the new media to play a greater role in fostering informed dialogue. It does not provide insight into the actions that would be essential to encourage the configuration of new media in ways that foster the capabilities that Sen regards as being essential.

Research on the development of capabilities required for using new media services provided by the public and private sectors is being undertaken (see Mansell, 2002) and there is discussion about the biases of the configuration of the Internet's technical architecture (David, 2001). But research that would specify how the majority of the citizens can best use the new media to strengthen their freedoms to decide between alternative social choices and which takes account of the configuration biases of the new technologies and services is virtually non-existent. A starting point for a research agenda that would contribute to a debate about the new media that embraces citizen's rights and entitlements is outlined below.

Social science analysis of the role of the new media in fostering 'capability acquisition' should focus on the development of new media applications that could provide alternatives to the dominant 'broadcast' or 'advertising-supported' mode of digital information provision. For instance, some new media developers are providing free 'toolkits' for producing and sharing information in the public spaces of the Internet. The Internet Scout project, supported by the National Science Foundation and the Mellon Foundation in the USA, offers such a toolkit at its web site. This is designed to simplify the technical hurdles involved in creating and sharing web-based information and discussions (Scout Project, 2001). The software package allows individuals or organizations with a minimum level of technical expertise and resources to set up a web site and to manage it. This application relies on open source software and provides access to information that is available in the public domain.

A web-based intermediary that solicits contributions of information from those who are not highly skilled in the use of the Internet is ID21 (2001), a development research site on the Web. Information can be copied or quoted without restriction and the originating authors are acknowledged so that the viewer can discern the provenance of the information. The Hansard Society (2001) is also developing new media applications that provide resources for all citizens to interact with electronic democracy initiatives.

Initiatives that offer citizens new media tools for making contributions to public discussion or for sharing information are being developed in ways that support the acquisition of the cognitive capacities that citizens need if they are to develop new media literacies and to participate in a democratic dialogue. But most of these alternative new media configurations are inadequately funded compared to those services that 'push' information at viewers. Most publicly sponsored and civil society organization web sites are offering authoritative information in a 'broadcast' or 'advertising' mode. They do not foster new media applications that will encourage the capabilities acquisition that Sen has in mind.

The under-resourcing of alternative new media initiatives, such as those described in this section, can be addressed through policy intervention. However, this is unlikely to occur without a major shift in the rhetorical form of discussions about the relation between innovations in digital technologies and society. New media policy aimed at encouraging these developments will need to be presented in a rhetorical form that persuasively makes the case for a rights-based approach to policy based on the citizen's entitlement to acquire capabilities for informed social dialogue. Since much of the discussion is conducted in intergovernmental forums, there is a need not only for more systematic social science research on the social and technical relation in this area, but also for rights-based arguments to filter into the rhetoric employed by participants in the influential policy institutions.

6. Conclusion

Much can be done by extending existing new media initiatives to citizens through creative organizational and investment strategies (Heeks, 2001). But it is important to decompose new media configurations to ensure that investment is encouraged in alternative new media applications that do not simply favour the dominant 'broadcast' mode of new media provision. The 'digital divide' rhetoric encourages a 'blind spot' in thinking about the new media and society relations. Innis (1951: 191) argued that 'civilisation has been profoundly influenced by communication' and that 'oral discussion inherently involves personal contact and a consideration for the feelings of others'. The new media may offer the potential to foster democratic dialogue but, for the majority of citizens to participate, it will be essential for them to acquire capabilities for contributing information and for making decisions about the value and provenance of information.

Most new media configurations favour exclusive electronic spaces for commercial activity and a 'broadcast' mode of authoritative information provision in the non-commercial sphere. The social and technical characters of the new media are mutually constituted and this relation will continue to be malleable. Much greater attention should be given to policy intervention that favours Internet-based tools to support the acquisition of new media literacies by the majority of citizens. This could be encouraged through a debate that embraces a rights-based approach to policy and the actions that are required to respond to citizen entitlements in a global information society. The power of the new media could then be used to reshape social bonds and to foster a greater sense of community in a way that assists people in resolving profound social problems that are facing humanity (Lévy, 1997: xxi).

New media policy debates tend to be centred on legal issues, regulation, and the means to reduce the 'digital divide'. These debates encourage policy measures aimed at the supply side of the new media industry and at efforts to control the market power of the largest firms. A rights-based approach to new media policy would encourage discussion and the formation of a consensus on the new media capabilities (or literacies) that all citizens are entitled to acquire. What policy measures would foster the growth of new media configurations that are responsive to the freedoms that people are entitled to in the Internet age? The public consensus on the answer to this question will vary from place to place. But if the bias of new media developments is responsive mainly to the needs of the minority of the population, then an alternative is necessary. Public policy encouragement of investment in information intermediaries that are developing new media applications that enable most citizens to acquire the capabilities to become critical, informed participants in democratic processes is one place to begin to develop a rights-based policy approach.

Policies for the new media are encouraging the development of new media configurations that are responsive to the needs of a minority of citizens who are able to acquire capabilities for valuing information and contributing to public debates. Some citizens are using the new media to support their choices about their lives. For instance, they are using existing new media sites on the Internet to find and assess information about treatments for illness, about new skills and jobs, or about like-minded people. But, for those who are unable to use the new media in this way, much human potential is being lost. This is an infringement of human rights.

Policies to reduce disparities in access to the new media are important. However, such policies do not address issues of citizen entitlements and rights in the global information society. The bias of new media configurations favours the minority of citizens: those who are best positioned to live their lives in an intensely technologically mediated world. A rights-based approach to new media policy has the potential to support and encourage new media developments that are consistent with aspirations to develop new forms of 'publicness' that embrace the majority of citizens.

Notes

1 Such forums are usually open in the sense that the sponsors invite government, private sector and non-governmental organization representatives, but the proceedings are generally conducted on the understanding that the discussion is non-attributable. The material in this section is a compilation of comments offered by such participants over the period from 1997 to 2001. Contributors to the discussions are identified only in terms of their status and type of organization. The main source of evidence is drawn from the OECD Emerging Market Economy Forum on Electronic Commerce, held in Dubai, UAE, in January 2001 (see Mansell, 2001b, c for formal reports). Evidence is also drawn from discussions between experts on matters associated with the 'digital divide' in connection with the UN Commission on Science and Technology for Development in 1997 and the Commonwealth Agencies in 2001.
2 The methodology for this analysis of web sites is documented in Paré (2001).
3 The writer surveyed about 300 web sites across these sectors that appeared to be hosted in the UK in early October 2001 to assess the nature of the content and the degree to which the sites provided either interactive opportunities for learning how to use the information or opportunities to those accessing the sites to learn how to use web authoring or related tools.
4 The writer surveyed on a random basis 10 percent of the sites listed in Centre for Civil Society and Centre for the Study of Global Governance (2001).
5 Sen's capabilities approach is similar to the concept of self-actualization (Maslow, 1954, 1968) which is concerned with people's needs, functions and motivations.

References

BECK, U. (1992/1986) *Risk Society: Towards a New Modernity*. London: Sage.

BIJKER, W. E. and LAW, J. (1994) *Shaping Technology/Building Society (Inside Technology)*. Cambridge, MA: The MIT Press.

BIJKER, W. E., HUGHES, T. P. and PINCH, T. F. (1989) *The Social Construction of Technological Systems*. Cambridge, MA: The MIT Press.

CASTELLS, M. (2001) *The Internet Galaxy: Reflections on Internet, Business and Society*. Oxford: Oxford University Press.

CENTRE FOR CIVIL SOCIETY and CENTRE FOR THE STUDY OF GLOBAL GOVERNANCE (2001) *Global Civil Society Yearbook 2001*. Oxford: Oxford University Press.

COMMONWEALTH SECRETARIAT (2001) 'A Commonwealth Action Programme for the Digital Divide: Report of the Commonwealth Expert Group on Information Technology for the Commonwealth High Level Review Group', prepared by S. K. Rao and S. Raju with the assistance of R. Mansell and N. Couldry. London: Commonwealth Secretariat.

DAVID, P. A. (2001) 'The Beginnings and Prospective Ending of "End-to-End": An Evolutionary Perspective on the Internet's Architecture', *Oxford Review of Economic Policy* 17(2): 159–87.

DAWSON, A. C. (1999) 'The Internet: Towards a Global Political System', *Policy* 15(1): 29–33.

DOT FORCE (Digital Opportunities Task Force) (2001a) 'Global Bridges: Digital Opportunities', draft report for discussion at Cape Town meeting, 1–2 March 2001 http://www.dotforce.org/reports/dotforce-draft-report-v1.doc, accessed 30 March 2001.

DOT FORCE (Digital Opportunities Task Force) (2001b) *Digital Opportunities for All: Meeting the Challenge*, Report of the Task Force, 21 July, http://www.uspolicy.be/Issues/E-commerce/dotreport.072101.htm, accessed 23 November.

DUTTON, W. H. (1999) *Society on the Line: Information Politics in the Digital Age*, Part IV. Oxford: Oxford University Press.

GARNHAM, N. (2000) 'Amartya Sen's "Capabilities" Approach to the Evaluation of Welfare: Its Application to Communications', in B. Cammaerts and J. C. Burgelman (eds) *Beyond Competition: Broadening the Scope of Telecommunications Policy*, pp. 25–36. Brussels: VUB University Press.

GAUNTLETT, D. (2000) *Web.studies: Rewiring Media Studies for the Digital Age*. London: Arnold.

GIDDENS, A. (1999) *Runaway World: How Globalisation is Reshaping our Lives*. London: Profile.

GLOBAL REACH (2001) http://www.glreach.com/globstats/ accessed 28 September 2001.

HABERMAS, J. (1992/1962) *The Structural Transformation of the Public Sphere: An Inquiry into a Category of Bourgeois Society*, trans. Thomas Burger with Frederick Lawrence. Cambridge: Polity Press.

HANSARD SOCIETY (2001) http://www.hansard-society.org.uk/eDemocracy.htm, accessed 26 September 2001.

HEEKS, R. (2001) 'Overestimating the Global Digital Divide', 12 February 2001, http://www.iicd.org/news/ accessed 15 April 2001.

HELD, D., MCGREW, A., GOLDBLATT, D. and PERRATON, J. (1999) *Global Transformations: Politics, Economics and Culture*. Cambridge: Polity Press.

ID21 (2001) http://www.id21.org, accessed 26 September 2001.

INNIS, H. A. (1951) 'Minerva's Owl', in *The Bias of Communication*. Toronto: University of Toronto Press.

LESSIG, L. (2000) *Code and other Laws of Cyberspace*. New York: Basic Books.

LESSIG, L. (2001) *The Future of Ideas: The Fate of the Commons in a Connected World*. New York: Random House.

LÉVY, P. (1997) *Collective Intelligence: Mankind's Emerging World in Cyberspace*. Cambridge, MA: Perseus Books.

MACKENZIE, D. (1996) *Knowing Machines: Essays on Technical Change*. Cambridge, MA: The MIT Press.

MACKENZIE, D. and WAJCMAN, J. (1999) *The Social Shaping of Technology*, 2nd edn. Buckingham: Open University Press.

MANSELL, R. (2001a) 'Digital Opportunities and the Missing Link for Developing Countries', *Oxford Review of Economic Policy* 17(2): 282–95.

MANSELL, R. (2001b) 'Issues Paper' for the OECD Emerging Market Economy Forum on Electronic Commerce, Dubai, UAE, 16–17 January http://www1.oecd.org/dsti/sti/it/ec/act/dubai_ec/products/Dubai_issues.pdf, accessed 13 March 2002.

MANSELL, R. (2001c) 'Summary Report of the OECD Emerging Market Economy Forum on Electronic Commerce, Dubai, UAE, 16–17 January', OECD, Paris, DSTI/ICCP(2001)4, 12 February http://www1.oecd.org/dsti/sti/it/ec/act/dubai_ec/products/Dubai_summary.pdf, accessed 13 March 2002.

MANSELL, R., ed. (2002) *Inside the Communication Revolution: New Patterns of Technical and Social Interaction*. Oxford: Oxford University Press.

MANSELL, R. and STEINMUELLER, W. E. (2000) *Mobilizing the Information Society: Strategies for Growth and Opportunity*. Oxford: Oxford University Press.

MANSELL, R. and WEHN, U., eds (1998) *Knowledge Societies: Information Technology for Sustainable Development*, published for the United Nations Commission on Science and Technology for Development. Oxford: Oxford University Press.

MASLOW, A. H. (1954) *Motivation and Personality*, 2nd edn. New York: Harper & Row.

MASLOW, A. H. (1968) *Toward a Psychology of Being*, 2nd edn. New York: Van Nostrand Reinhold.

NUA INTERNET SURVEYS (2001) http://www.nua.ie/surveys/how_many_online/ accessed 23 November 2001.

PARÉ, D. J. (2001) 'Does This Site Deliver? B2B E-commerce Services for Developing Countries', prepared for a project supported by the UK Department for International Development, Media@lse, London School of Economics, 28 October, mimeo.

PRATT, A. and GILL, R. (2001) 'Social Exclusion Goes Digital?', London School of Economics, draft mimeo, London.

ROMER, P. (1986) 'Increasing Returns and Long-run Growth', *Journal of Political Economy* 94(5): 1002–37.

ROMER, P. (1995) 'Beyond the Knowledge Worker', *World Link*, Jan–Feb: 3.

SCHWAB, K. (2001) 'Wiring the Third World', World Economic Forum, January, http://Europe.thestandard.com/article/article_print/0,1151,13797,00.html, accessed 30 March 2001.

SCOUT PROJECT (2001) http://scout.cs.wisc.edu/ accessed 26 September 2001.

SEN, A. (1999) *Development as Freedom*. Oxford: Oxford University Press.

SILVERSTONE, R. (1999) *Why Study the Media?* London: Sage.

SIMON, L. D. (2000) *NetPolicy.Com: Public Agenda for a Digital World.* Washington DC: Woodrow Wilson Center Press, distributed by Johns Hopkins University Press.

TELECOMMONS DEVELOPMENT GROUP (2000) *Rural Access to Information and Communication Technologies: The Challenge for Africa*, IBRD/World Bank report prepared for the African Connection Secretariat, http://www.telecommons.com/documents.cfm, accessed 30 March 2001.

THOMPSON, J. B. (1995) *The Media and Modernity: A Social Theory of the Media.* Cambridge: Polity Press.

UNDP (1999) UN Human Development Report 1999, chapter 2 'New Technologies and the Global Race for Knowledge', http://www.undp.org/hdro/Chapter2.pdf, accessed 30 March 2001.

US DEPARTMENT OF COMMERCE (1995) *Falling through the Net: A Survey of the 'Have Nots' in Rural and Urban America*, Washington, DC, July at http:www.ntia.doc.gov/ntiahome/fallingthru.html, accessed 19 July 2001.

WAJCMAN, J. (2002) 'Addressing Technological Change: The Challenge to Social Theory', *Current Sociology* 50(3): 347–63.

WILLIAMS, R. (1976) *Communications*, 3rd edn. Harmondsworth: Penguin.

41

RECONCEPTUALIZING THE DIGITAL DIVIDE

Mark Warschauer

Source: *First Monday* 7(7) (2002): n.p.

Abstract

Reconceptualizing the Digital Divide by Mark Warschauer. This paper examines the concept of a digital divide by introducing problematic examples of community technology projects and analyzing models of technology access. It argues that the concept provides a poor framework for either analysis or policy, and suggests an alternate concept of technology for social inclusion. It then draws on the historical analogy of literacy to further critique the notion of a divide and to examine the resources necessary to promote access and social inclusion.

As the Bush administration takes steps to dismantle the digital divide initiatives of the Clinton-Gore era, those who advocate technology access programs must consider their lines of defense and the rationale for their views. Is the "digital divide" a useful construct as originally conceived? Or should the notion be broadened or reconceptualized toward a different framework for analyzing technology access and social inclusion? I argue that a reconceptualization is in order. I begin the discussion with three vignettes, and then I turn to models of access for social inclusion, drawing on discussions of literacy.

A slum "Hole in the Wall"

In 2000, the Government of New Delhi, in collaboration with an information technology corporation, established a project, known as the

"Hole-in-the-Wall" experiment, to provide computer access to the city's street children[1]. An outdoor five-station computer kiosk was set up in one of the poorest slums of New Delhi. Though the computers themselves were inside a booth, the monitors protruded through holes in the walls, as did specially designed joysticks and buttons that substituted for the computer mouse. Keyboards were not provided. The computers were connected to the Internet through dial-up access. A volunteer inside the booth helped keep the computers and Internet connections running.

No teachers or instructors were provided, in line with the concept called *minimally invasive education*. The idea was to allow the children unfettered 24-hour access, and to learn at their own pace and speed, rather than tie them to the directives of adult organizers or instructors.

According to reports, children who flocked to the site taught themselves basic computer operations. They worked out how to click and drag objects; select different menus; cut, copy, and paste; launch and use programs such as Microsoft Word and Paint; get on the Internet; and change the background "wallpaper". The program was hailed by researchers (e.g., Mitra, 1999) and government officials alike[2] as a ground-breaking project that offered a model for how to bring India's and the world's urban poor into the computer age.

However, visits to the computer kiosk indicated a somewhat different reality. The Internet access was of little use since it seldom functioned. No special educational programs had been made available, and no special content was provided in Hindi, the only language the children knew. Children did learn to manipulate the joystick and buttons, but almost all their time was spent drawing with paint programs or playing computer games.

There was no organized involvement of any community organizations in helping to run the kiosk, since such involvement was neither solicited nor welcomed[3]. And, indeed, the very architecture of the kiosk – based on a wall rather than a room – made supervision, instruction, and collaboration difficult.

Parents in the neighborhood had ambivalent feelings about the kiosk. Some saw it as a welcome initiative, but most expressed concern that the lack of organized instruction took away from its value. Some parents even complained that the kiosk was harmful to their children. As one parent stated, "My son used to be doing very well in school, he used to concentrate on his homework, but now he spends all his free time playing computer games at the kiosk and his schoolwork is suffering." In short, parents and the community came to realize that "minimally invasive education" was, in practice, minimally effective education.

An Information Age Town

In 1997, Ireland's national telecommunications company held a national competition to select and fund an "Information Age Town"[4]. A rationale of the effort was to help overcome the gap between Ireland's emerging status as a multinational business center of information and communication technology (ICT) *production* and the rather limited *use* of ICT among Ireland's own people and indigenous small businesses.

Towns of 5,000 people and more across Ireland were invited to compete by submitting proposals detailing their vision of what an Information Age Town should be and how they could become one. The winning town was to receive 15 million Irish pounds (at that time roughly $22 million U.S. dollars) to implement its vision.

The sponsor of the competition, Telecom Eirann (later renamed Eircom), was getting ready to be privatized. The company naturally had an interest in selecting the boldest, most ambitious proposal so as to showcase the winning town as an innovative example of what advanced telecommunications could accomplish for the country under the company's leadership. Four towns were chosen as finalists, and then Ennis, a small, remote town of 15,000 people in Western Ireland, was selected among them as the winner. The prize money that Ennis received represented over $1,200 U.S. dollars per resident, a huge sum for a struggling Irish town.

At the heart of Ennis's winning proposal was a plan to give an Internet-ready personal computer to every family in the town. Other initiatives included an ISDN line to every business, a Web site for every business that wanted one, smart card readers for every business (for a cashless society), and smart cards for every family. Ennis was strongly encouraged by Telecom Ireland to implement these plans as quickly as possible.

Meanwhile, the three runners up – the towns of Castlebar, Kilkenny, and Kilarney – each received consolation prizes of 1 million Irish pounds (about $1.5 million U.S. dollars). These towns were given us much time as they needed to make use of the money.

How did the project turn out? A visit to Ennis three years later by a university researcher indicated that the town had little to show for its money. Advanced technology had been thrust into people's hands with little preparation. Training programs had been run, but they were not sufficiently accompanied by awareness programs as to why people should use the new technology in the first place. And in some instances, well-functioning social systems were disrupted in order to make way for the showcase technology.

For example, as is the case in the rest of Ireland, the unemployed of Ennis had been reporting to the social welfare office three times a week to sign in and receive payments. Following their visits, the people usually stayed around the office to chat with other unemployed workers. The sign-in system thus facilitated an important social function to overcome the isolation of the unemployed.

As part of the "Information Age Town" plan, though, the unemployed received computers and Internet connections at home. They were instructed to sign in and receive electronic payments via the Internet rather than come to the office to sign in. But many of the unemployed couldn't figure out how to operate the equipment, and most others saw no reason to do so when it deprived them of an important opportunity for socializing. A good number of those computers were reportedly sold on the black market, and the unemployed simply returned of their own accord to coming to the social welfare office to sign in.

Meanwhile, what happened in the other three towns? With far fewer resources, they were forced to carefully plan how to make use of their funds, rather than splurging for massive amounts of equipment. Community groups, small businesses, and labor unions were involved in the planning process. Much greater effort and money were spent on developing awareness, planning and implementing effective training, and setting up processes for sustainable change, rather than merely on purchase of equipment. The towns built on already existing networks among workers, educators, and businesspeople to support grassroots uses of technology for social and economic development.

Information about social services and job opportunities was put online. Small businesses and craft workers learned how to pool their resources to promote their products through e-commerce. Technology coordinators were appointed at schools and worked with other teachers to develop plans for better integration of ICT in classrooms. In the end, according to a researcher from University College Dublin[5], the three runners-up – which each received only 1/15 of the money that Ennis received – actually had more to show for their efforts to promote social inclusion through technology than did the winner.

A model computer lab

An international donor project funded by the United States Agency for International Development (USAID) decided to donate a computer laboratory to the college of education at a major Egyptian university[6]. The purpose of the donation was to establish a model teacher-training program in computer-assisted learning in one of the departments of the college. State-of-the-art equipment was selected, including more than 40 Pentium III computers, an expensive video projection system, several printers and scanners, and tens of thousands of U.S. dollars worth of educational software. This was to be a model project that both the U.S. and Egyptian governments would view with pride. To guarantee that the project would be sustainable, the Egyptian university would be required to manage all the ongoing expenses and operations, including paying for Internet access, maintaining the local area network (LAN), and operating the computer laboratory.

Under a paid contract from USAID, a committee from the college of education within the Egyptian university put together a detailed proposal on how the laboratory would be used, run, and maintained. Based on this proposal, USAID purchased all the hardware and software. However, well before the equipment was installed, it became clear that the college would have difficulty absorbing such a huge and expensive donation. Other departments within the college – which, together, had access to only a handful of computers – became envious that a single department would have such modern and expensive equipment, and they attempted to block the university's support for the lab. The college and university could not easily justify spending the money to house and maintain such an expensive laboratory for a single program when other programs were poorly funded. No money was available to hire an outside LAN manager or provide Internet access at the level agreed upon in the proposal. Faculty relations problems also arose, as a key department chair resented the involvement and initiative of less-senior faculty members who were taking computer training and working together to plan new curricula. Due to all these difficulties, the expensive state-of-the-art computers sat in boxes in a locked room for more than a year before they were even installed, thus losing about one-third of their economic value.

Rethinking the digital divide

Each of the programs described in the preceding vignettes was motivated by a sincere attempt to improve people's lives through ICT. But each program ran into unexpected difficulties that hindered the results. Of course any ICT project is complicated, and none can be expected to run smoothly. But the problems with these projects were neither isolated, nor random. Rather, these same types of problems occur again and again in technology projects around the world, which too often focus on providing hardware and software and pay insufficient attention to the human and social systems that must also change for technology to make a difference. As seen in these three vignettes, meaningful access to ICT encompasses far more than merely providing computers and Internet connections. Rather, access to ICT is embedded in a complex array of factors encompassing physical, digital, human, and social resources and relationships. Content and language, literacy and education, and community and institutional structures must all be taken into account if meaningful access to new technologies is to be provided.

Some would try, as I myself have in the past, to stretch the notion of a digital divide to encompass this broad array of factors and resources. In this sense, a digital divide is marked not only by physical access to computers and connectivity, but also by access to the additional resources that allow people to use technology well. However, the original sense of the digital divide term – which attached overriding importance to the physical availability of computers and connectivity, rather than to issues of content, language, education, literacy, or community and social resources – is difficult to overcome in people's minds.

A second problem with the digital divide concept is its implication of a bipolar societal split. As Cisler (2000) argues, there is not a binary division between information "haves" and "have-nots", but rather a gradation based on different degrees of access to information technology. Compare, for example, a professor at UCLA with a high-speed connection in her office, a student in Seoul who occasionally uses a cyber-cafe, and a rural activist in Indonesia who has no computer or phone line but whose colleagues in her women's group download and print out information for her. This example illustrates just three degrees of possible access a person can have to online material.

The notion of a binary divide between the haves and the have-nots is thus inaccurate and can even be patronizing as it fails to value the social resources that diverse groups bring to the table. For example, in the United States, African-Americans are often portrayed as being on the wrong end of a digital divide (e.g., Walton, 1999), when in fact Internet access among Blacks and other minorities varies tremendously by income group – with divisions between Blacks and Whites decreasing as income increases (National Telecommunications and Information Administration, 2000). Some argue that the stereotype of disconnected minority groups could even serve to further social stratification, by discouraging employers or content providers from reaching out to those groups. As Henry Jenkins, director of comparative media studies at the Massachusetts Institute of Technology, argues, "The rhetoric of the digital divide holds open this division between civilized tool-users and uncivilized nonusers. As well meaning as it is as a policy initiative, it can be marginalizing and patronizing in its own terms"[7].

In addition, the notion of a digital divide – even in its broadest sense – implies a chain of causality, i.e., that lack of access (however defined) to computers and the Internet harms life chances. While this point is undoubtedly true, the reverse is equally true; those who are already marginalized will have fewer opportunities to access and use computers and the Internet. In fact, technology and society are intertwined and co-constitutive, and this complex interrelationship makes any assumption of causality problematic.

Finally, the digital divide framework provides a poor roadmap for using technology to promote social development since it overemphasizes the importance of the physical presence of computers and connectivity to the exclusion of other factors that allow people to use ICT for meaningful ends. Rob Kling, director of the Center for Social Informatics at Indiana University, explains well this shortcoming[8]:

"[The] big problem with "the digital divide" framing is that it tends to connote "digital solutions," i.e., computers and telecommunications, without engaging the important set of complementary resources and complex interventions to support social inclusion, of which informational technology applications may be enabling elements, but are certainly insufficient when simply added to the status quo mix of resources and relationships."

The bottom line is that there is no binary divide, and no single overriding factor for determining such a divide. ICT does not exist as an external variable to be injected from the outside to bring about certain results. Rather, it is woven in a complex manner in social systems and processes. And, from a policy standpoint, the goal of using ICT with marginalized groups is not to overcome a digital divide, but rather to further a process of social inclusion. To accomplish this, it is necessary to "focus on the transformation, not the technology"[9]. For all these reasons, I join with others (e.g., DiMaggio and Hargittai, 2001; Jarboe, 2001) in recognizing the historical value of the digital divide concept (i.e., that it helped focus attention on an important social issue) while preferring to embrace alternate concepts and terminology that more accurately portray the issues at stake and the social challenges ahead.

Technology for social inclusion

The alternate framework I suggest is that of *technology for social inclusion*. Social inclusion and exclusion are prominent concepts in European discourse[10]. They refer to the extent that individuals, families, and communities are able to fully participate in society and control their own destinies, taking into account a variety of factors related to economic resources, employment, health, education, housing, recreation, culture, and civic engagement.

Social inclusion is a matter not only of an adequate share of resources, but also of "participation in the determination of both individual and collective life chances" (Stewart, 2000). It overlaps with the concept of socioeconomic equality, but is not equivalent to it. There are many ways that the poor can have fuller participation and inclusion, even if they lack an equal share of resources. At the same time, even the well-to-do may face problems of social exclusion, due to reasons of political persecution or discrimination based on age, gender, sexual preference, or disability. The concept of social inclusion does not ignore the role of class, but recognizes that a broad array of other variables help shape how class forces interact. Though an historical treatment of the term is beyond the scope of this article, one could argue that the concept of social inclusion reflects particularly well the imperatives of the current information era, in which issues of identity, language, social participation, community, and civil society have taken central stage (Castells, 1997).

Models of access

What role, then, can access to technology play in promoting social inclusion? That depends in large measure on how we define "access." The most common model for thinking about access to technology is that based on ownership of, or availability of, a device, in this case a computer. Physical devices can diffuse relatively quickly, and, in some cases, equally; note for example the almost universal degree of television ownership in the U.S. among both rich and poor. However, the device model has several flaws, starting with the fact that the actual purchase price of a computer is only the small part of what can be considered the *total cost of ownership*, which includes the price of software, maintenance, peripherals, and, in institutional settings, training, planning, and administration (see comments by Kling in Patterson and Wilson, 2000) – not to mention the price of replacement hardware and software due to corporate-planned product obsolescence. More importantly, other barriers beyond affordability of computers (or of the broader computing package) will continue to play a major role in fostering digital inequality. These barriers include differential access to broadband telecommunications; differences in knowledge and skills in using computers, or in attitudes toward using them; inadequate online content available for the needs of low-income citizens, especially in diverse languages; and governmental controls or limitations on unrestricted use of the Internet in many parts of the world (see discussion in DiMaggio and Hargittai, 2001).

The device model is improved somewhat by a *conduit* model[11]. While a device can be acquired through a one-time purchase, access to a conduit necessitates connection to a supply line that provides something on a regular basis, such as electricity, telephone service, or cable television. Diffusion of conduits is slower than that of devices, either because a delivery infrastructure must be established first (such as the installation of telephone lines or fiber optic cables) or because the cost of a regular monthly fee is a disincentive to access. For example, conduits such as electricity, telephone service, and cable television service have diffused more slowly than devices such as television sets, radios, and videocassette recorders.

The diffusion of conduits often involves a high degree of social mobilization and struggle to insure equal access. This occurred most notably in regard to electricity, where different countries chose different paths to mass (or selective) electrification due in large part to the balance of social and class forces in the country[12]. Similarly, in many countries, lengthy social struggles have been carried out on behalf of universal telephone access.

Though conduits provide a better comparative model for ICT than do devices, neither category captures the essence of meaningful access to information and communication technologies. What is most important about ICTs is not so much the availability of the computing device or the Internet line, but rather people's ability to make use of that device and line to engage in *meaningful social practices*. Those people who cannot read, who have never learned to use a computer, and who do not know any of the major languages that dominate available software and Internet content will have difficulty even getting online much less using the Internet productively.

Literacy

A better model of access is provided by the concept of literacy. While the common sense definition of literacy is the individual skill of being able to read and write, many theorists prefer a broader definition that takes into account the social contexts of literacy practice. They point out that what is considered skillful reading or writing varies widely across historical, political, and sociocultural contexts (Gee, 1996). Witness, for example, the well-known example of changing literacy practices before and after the diffusion of the printing press (see discussion in McLuhan, 1962; Eisenstein, 1979), or the differences between the types of literacy valued in a Pakistani *madrassa* (religious school) as compared to a U.S. university. In this broader sense, then, literacy involves "having mastery over the processes by means of which culturally significant information is coded"[13].

There are many similarities between literacy and ICT access (see Table 1). First, both literacy and ICT access are closely connected to advances in human communication and the means of knowledge production. Second, just as ICT access is a prerequisite for full participation in the informational stage of capitalism, literacy was (and remains) a prerequisite for full participation in the earlier industrial stages of capitalism. Third, both literacy and ICT access necessitate a connection to a physical artifact (i.e., a book or a computer), to sources of information that get expressed as content within or via that physical artifact, and to a skill level sufficient to process and make use of that information. Fourth, both involve not only receiving information but also producing it. Finally, they are both tied to somewhat controversial notions of societal divides: the *great literacy divide* and the *digital divide*.

Table 1 Comparing Literacy and ICT Access.

	Literacy	*ICT Access*
Communication Stage	Writing, print	Computer-mediated communication
Economic Era	Industrial capitalism	Informational capitalism
Physical Artifact	Books, magazines, newspapers, journals	Computer
Organization of Content	Novels, short stories, essays, articles, reports, poems, forms	Web sites, e-mail, instant messages
Receptive skills	Reading	Reading + multimedia interpretation, searching, navigating
Productive skills	Writing	Writing + multimedia authoring and publishing
Divides	A great literacy divide?	A digital divide?

The literacy divide

One of the most important theoretical questions related to the social practice of literacy, and one that corresponds to current debates over a digital divide, is whether there exists a *great literacy divide*. Literacy is distributed and practiced on a highly unequal basis, and is highly correlated with income and wealth at both an individual and a societal level. So the importance of literacy in social and individual development is broadly recognized.

What is disputed, though, is the issue of causality, that is, whether literacy enables development, or whether unequal development (and corresponding unequal distribution of political, economic and social power) restricts people's access to literacy. Some advocates of the former notion posit the existence of a literacy divide. From this perspective, there are fundamental cognitive differences in individuals who are literate and who are not, resulting in a great literacy divide at both the individual and societal levels. Literacy has been said to separate prehistory from history (Goody and Watt, 1963), primitive societies from civilized societies (Levi Strauss, in Charbonnier, 1973), and modern societies from traditional societies (Lerner, 1958; see discussion in Scribner and Cole, 1981). At the individual level, literacy has been said to allow people to master the logical functions of language (Goody, 1968; Olson, 1977) and to think abstractly (Greenfield, 1972; Luria, 1976).

The imputed cognitive benefits of literacy have proven difficult for researchers to investigate. The problem is that literacy is almost always confounded with other variables, particularly with schooling. For the most part, those who are completely illiterate tend to have had little or no schooling, whereas those with high levels of literacy tend to have had a good deal of schooling. And amount of schooling usually correlates directly with income levels of a child's family, or the work engaged in by the child's family.

Two educational psychologists, Sylvia Scribner and Michael Cole, developed a creative solution to the research problem of determining the particular cognitive benefits of literacy in isolation from its covariants. They identified a tribe in Liberia, the Vai, that had developed its own written script in the tribe's own local language. Literacy in the Vai script was passed on through informal tutoring, not through formal schooling. Vai writing was used in very limited ways, mostly for personal correspondence and business records. By carrying out a three-way study that compared illiterate tribal members, those literate only in the Vai language (through personal tutoring), and those with broader English or Arabic literacy skills gained through schooling, Scribner and Cole (1981) were able to separate which cognitive benefits could be most likely attributed to literacy and which others were most likely due to the broader environment of formal education.

Interestingly, Scribner and Cole found virtually no generalizable cognitive benefits from Vai literacy. Individual differences on a range of cognitive tasks, in areas such as abstraction, classification, memory, and logic, were instead due to other factors, such as schooling, or, in some cases, living in an urban (as opposed to rural) area. Scribner and Cole's study helped settle the question whether or not there is a great literacy divide, at least at the individual level. Their work showed that there is no single construct of literacy that divides people into two cognitive camps. Rather there are gradations and types of literacies, with a range of benefits closely related to the specific functions of literacy practices. Literacy, in a general sense, cannot be said to cause cognitive or social development; rather literacy and social development are intertwined and co-constituted, as are technologies and society in general.

Acquisition of literacy

If literacy is understood as a set of social practices rather than a narrow cognitive skill, this has several important consequences for thinking about the acquisition of literacy, and important parallels with the acquisition of access to ICT. Literacy acquisition, like access to ICT, requires a variety of resources. These include physical artifacts (books, magazines, newspapers, journals, computers, etc.); relevant content transmitted via those artifacts; appropriate user skills, knowledge, and attitude; and the right kinds of community and social support.

The physical availability of books or other reading material is of course essential for the acquisition of literacy, but the other resources are equally important. As for relevant and accessible content, one of the major obstacles toward literacy acquisition is the dearth of published material in many if not most of the 7,000 languages that are spoken around the world. In addition, Paolo Freire (1994) and others have shown that literacy instruction is most effective when it involves content that speaks to the needs and social conditions of the learners. And, as with ICT-related material, this content is often best developed by the learners themselves.

Literacy acquisition obviously requires the development of a variety of skills, knowledge, and attitude, including cognitive processing skills; background knowledge about the world; and the motivation, desire, and confidence to read – and this has important parallels to the kinds of skills, knowledge, and attitudes necessary to make meaningful use of ICT.

Finally, learning to read is a social act that intersects in a myriad a way with social structure, social organization, and social practices. People learn to read (and to read in certain ways) when they are surrounded by people who support them in the process, ranging from parents that read to them, to schoolmates that discuss comic books together, to village elders that value children's education.

The multifaceted nature of literacy, the range of resources it requires, and the social nature of its practice and mastery all point to conclusion that the acquisition of literacy is a matter not only of cognition, or even of culture, but also of power and politics (Freire, 1970; 1994; Freire and Macedo, 1987; Gee, 1996; 1984; Street, 1995). From South Africa to Brazil to the impoverished ghettos of the United States, access to literacy intersects with unequal opportunities to attend school, inequitable distribution of resources within the educational system, and curricula and pedagogy that meet the needs of certain social groups more than others. Perhaps the most obvious evidence of this phenomenon is the appallingly low rate of women's literacy in many countries in the world today. Because of the politicized nature of literacy, campaigns that focus exclusively on individual skill while ignoring broader social systems that support or restrict extended literacy are not always the most effective. In many cases literacy is not so much granted from above, as seized from below through the social mobilization and collective action of the poor and dispossessed.

Literacy and ICT access

A synthesis of the above discussion yields six principal conclusions about literacy:

1 There is not just one, but many types of literacy;
2 The meaning and value of literacy varies in particular social contexts;
3 Literacy capabilities exists in gradations, rather than in a bipolar opposition of literate versus illiterate;
4 Literacy alone brings no automatic benefit outside of its particular functions;
5 Literacy is a social practice, involving access to physical artifacts, content, skills, and social support; and,
6 Acquisition of literacy is a matter not only of education, but also of power.

These points serve well as the basis of a model of ICT access: There is not one type of ICT access, but many; the meaning and value of access varies in particular social context; access exists in gradations, rather than in a bipolar opposition; computer and Internet use bring no automatic benefit outside of particular functions; ICT use is a social practice involving access to physical artifacts, content, skills, and social support; and, acquisition of ICT access is a matter not only of education, but also of power.

Access to ICT for the promotion of social inclusion cannot rest on the provision of devices or conduits alone. Rather, it must entail the engagement of a range of resources, all developed and promoted with an eye toward enhancing the social, economic, and political power of the targeted clients and communities. Any attempt to categorize these resources is by nature arbitrary, but an analysis based on four general categories serves the purposes of both analysis and policy-making. These categories have emerged from my ethnographic research in Hawai'i (e.g., Warschauer, 1999) and Egypt (Warschauer, in press) as well in my case study research in California, Brazil, and India, and have been pointed to in similar terms by other researchers and theorists who have examined issues of technology and social inclusion in various contexts (see, for example, Aichholzer and Schmutzer, 2001; Carvin, 2000; Wilson, 2000). They can be labeled (1) Physical Resources, (2) Digital Resources, (3) Human Resources, and (4) Social Resources (see Figure 1). Physical resources encompass access to computers and telecommunication connections. Digital resources refer to digital material that is made available online. Human resources revolve around issues such as literacy and education (including the particular types of literacy practices that are required for computer use and online communication). Social resources refer to the community, institutional, and societal structures that support access to ICT.

In considering these four sets of resources, it is important to realize their iterative relation with ICT use. On the one hand, each of the resources is a *contributor* to effective use of ICTs. In other words, the presence of these

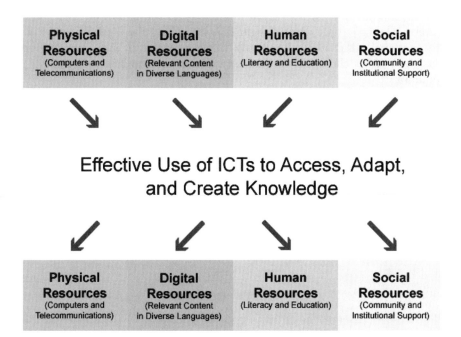

Figure 1 Effective Use of ICTs.

resources helps ensure that ICT can be well used and exploited. On the other hand, access to each of these resources is a *result* of effective use of ICTs. In other words, by using ICTs well, we can help extend and promote access to these resources. If handled well, these resources can thus serve as a virtual circle that promotes social development and inclusion. If handled poorly, these elements can serve as a vicious cycle of underdevelopment and exclusion.

Conclusion

Given the Bush administration's cutbacks of technology access programs, there are those who might say that now is not the time to question the idea of a digital divide. Here again, though, the analogy of literacy serves a lesson. Challenging the notion of a great literacy divide, and developing a more sophisticated understanding of literacy, did not lead to a downplaying of literacy's importance. Rather, by better understanding literacy, educators and policy-makers could better promote it. Those who have critiqued simplistic asocial frameworks of literacy have been at the forefront of efforts to extend literacy, starting with the Paolo Freire, who both put forward a socially-rooted critical concept of literacy and also helped devise mass literacy campaigns in several countries around the world.

Similarly, a critique of the notion of a digital divide is necessary to fully inform and unleash efforts to use technology to promote social inclusion. Overly simplistic notions of a digital divide lead to the kinds of problematic outcomes discussed in the above vignettes, which in turn provide grist for the mill of those who would like to end all community technology funding.

A framework of technology for social inclusion allows us to re-orient the focus from that of gaps to be overcome by provision of equipment to that of social development to be enhanced through the effective integration of ICT into communities and institutions. This kind of integration can only be achieved by attention to the wide range of physical, digital, human, and social resources that meaningful access to ICT entails.

Those who popularized the term "digital divide" have helped focus public attention on the important social issue of technology and inequality. It is now time to deepen public understanding of this issue through a more thorough appraisal of what access to ICT entails and of the ends that such access serves.

Acknowledgments

This article draws on the author's broader discussion of these issues in the forthcoming book, *Technology and Social Inclusion: Rethinking the Digital Divide,* to be published by MIT Press in fall 2002.

Notes

1 Information on this project comes from a paper by Sugata Mitra (1999), personal communication with Chetan Sharma (July 2001), and my own visit to the site and interviews with users and community residents in July 2001.
2 Personal communication, S. Regunathan, Principal Secretary for Information Technology, Government of New Delhi, July 2001.
3 The director of the project told me that he intentionally eschewed the involvement in the kiosks of neighborhood organizations, since he preferred working "directly with the people." Based on an interview with S. Regunathan, Principal Secretary for Information Technology, Government of New Delhi, July 2001.
4 Information on this competition and its results comes from the Web site of Eircom (http://www.eircom.ie/); the Web sites of the four winning towns (http://www.ennis.ie/, http://www.castlebar.ie/, http://www.kilkenny.ie/, and http://kerry.local.ie/killarney) and personal communication from John Mooney, University College Dublin, May 2001.
5 Personal communication, John Mooney, May 2001.
6 Information on this project comes from my personal involvement as a staff member on a USAID-funded program in Egypt.
7 Quoted in Young, 2001, p. A51.
8 Personal communication, January 2002.
9 Jarboe, 2001, p. 31.
10 For general overviews, see Askonas and Stewart (2000), Byrne (1999), and Littlewood , Glorieux, Herkommer, and Jonsson (1999). For particular discussion of relationship to technology, see Commission of the European Communities (2001).
11 For a discussion of the conduit model and its limitations, see Lievrouw (2000).
12 See, for examples, discussion of electrification in South Africa, by Renfrew (1984); in the Soviet Union, by Abamedia (1999), and Nye (1990); in Western Europe, by Nye, (1990); and in the U.S., by Brown (1980).
13 de Castell and Luke, 1986, p. 374.

References

Abamedia, 1999. "Propaganda in the propaganda state," at http://www.pbs.org/redfiles/prop/inv/prop_inv_ins.htm, accessed 10 May 2001.

George Aichholzer and Ruper Schmutzer, 2001. *The Digital Divide in Austria*. Vienna: Institute of Technology Assessment.

Peter Askonas and Agnes Steward (editors), 2000. *Social Inclusion: Possibilities and Tensions*. London: Macmillan.

D. Clayton Brown, 1980. *Electricity for Rural America: The Fight for the REA*. Westport, Conn.: Greenwood Press.

David Byrne, 1999. *Social Exclusion*. Buckingham, Eng.: Open University Press.

Andy Carvin, 2000. "Mind the gap: The digital divide as the civil rights issue of the new millennium," *Multimedia Schools*, volume 7, number 1 (January), at http://www.infotoday.com/MMSchools/Jan00/carvin.htm, accessed 10 May 2001.

Manuel Castells, 1997. *The Power of Identity*. Malden, Mass.: Blackwell.

George Charbonnier, 1973. "'Primitive' and 'civilized' peoples: A conversation with Claude Lèvi-Strauss," In: R. Disch (editor). *The Future of Literacy*. Englewood Cliffs, N.J.: Prentice-Hall.

Steve Cisler, 2000. "Subtract the digital divide," *San Jose Mercury* (15 January), at http://www.mercurycenter.com/svtech/news/indepth/docs/soap011600.htm, accessed 28 December 28 2001.

Commission of the European Communities, 2001. "e-Inclusion: The Information Society's potential for social inclusion in Europe," at http://europa.eu.int/comm/employment_social/soc-dial/info_soc/esdis/eincl_en.pdf, accessed 8 December 2001.

Suzanne de Castell and Allan Luke, 1986. "Models of literacy in North American schools: Social and historical conditions and consequences," In: S. de Castell, A. Luke, and K. Egan (editors). *Literacy, Society, and Schooling*. New York: Cambridge University Press, pp. 87–109.

Paul J. DiMaggio and Ezster Hargittai, 2001. "From the 'digital divide' to 'digital inequality': Studying Internet use as penetration increases," *Working Paper 19, Center for Arts and Cultural Policy Studies, Woodrow Wilson School*. Princeton, N.J.: Center for Arts and Cultural Policy Studies, Woodrow Wilson School, Princeton University.

E. L. Eisenstein, 1979. *The Printing Press as an Agent of Change: Communications and Cultural Transformations in Early Modern Europe*. Cambridge: Cambridge University Press.

Paolo Freire, 1994. *Pedagogy of the Oppressed*. Third edition. New York: Continuum.

Paolo Freire, 1970. "The adult literacy process as cultural action for freedom," *Harvard Educational Review*, volume 40, pp. 205–212.

Paolo Freire and D. Macedo, 1987. *Reading the Word and the World*. Hadley, Mass.: Bergin and Garvey.

James P. Gee, 1996. *Social Linguistics and Literacies*. London: Taylor and Francis.

J. Goody (editor), 1968. *Literacy in Traditional Societies*. Cambridge: Cambridge University Press.

J. Goody and I. Watt, 1963. "The consequences of literacy," *Comparative Studies in History and Society*, volume 5, pp. 304–345.

P. M. Greenfield, 1972. "Oral and written language: The consequences for cognitive development in Africa, the United States, and England," *Language and Speech*, volume 15, pp. 169–178.

K. P. Jarboe, 2001. "Inclusion in the information age: Reframing the debate," at http://www.athenaalliance.org/inclusion.html, accessed 15 December 2001.

D. Lerner, 1958. *The Passing of Traditional Society*. New York: Free Press.

A. L. Lievrouw, 2000. "The information environment and universal service," *Information Society*, volume 16, pp. 155–159.

P. Littlewood, I. Glorieux, S. Herkommer, and I. Jonsson (editors), 1999. *Social Exclusion in Europe: Problems and Paradigms*. Aldershot, Eng.: Ashgate.

A. R. Luria, 1976. *Cognitive Development: Its Cultural and Social Foundations*. Cambridge, Mass.: Harvard University Press.

M. McLuhan, 1962. *The Gutenberg Galaxy: The Making of Typographic Man*. Toronto: University of Toronto Press.

S. Mitra, 1999. "Minimally invasive education for mass computer literacy," *CSI Communications* (June), pp. 12–16.

National Telecommunications and Information Administration, 2000. *Falling Through the Net: Toward Digital Inclusion*. Washington, DC: NTIA.

D. Nye, 1990. *Electrifying America: A Social Meaning of New Technology, 1880–1940*. Cambridge, Mass.: MIT Press.

D. R. Olson, 1977. "From utterance to text: The bias of language in speech and writing," *Harvard Educational Review*, volume 47, number 3, pp. 257–281.

R. Patterson and E. J. Wilson, 2000. "New IT and social inequality: Resetting the research and policy agenda," *Information Society*, volume 16, number 1, pp. 77–86.

C. Renfrew, 1984. *Electricity, Industry, and Class in South Africa*. Albany, N.Y.: State University of New York Press.

Sylvia Scribner and M. Cole, 1981. *The Psychology of Literacy*. Cambridge: Harvard University Press.

A. Stewart, 2000. "Social inclusion: An introduction," In: P. Askonas and A. Stewart (editors). *Social Inclusion: Possibilities and Tensions*. London: Macmillan, pp. 1–16.

Brian Street, 1995. *Social Literacies: Critical Approaches to Literacy in Development, Ethnography and Education*. London: Longman.

A. Walton, 1999. "Technology vs. African-Americans," *Atlantic Monthly* (January), at http://www.theatlantic.com/issues/99jan/aftech.htm, accessed 7 October 2000.

Mark Warschauer, in press. "The allures and illusions of modernity: Technology and educational reform in Egypt," manuscript submitted for publication.

Mark Warschauer, 1999. *Electronic Literacies: Language, Culture, and Power in Online Education*. Mahwah, N.J.: Lawrence Erlbaum Associates.

E. Wilson, 2000. "Briefing the President," at http://www.internetpolicy.org/briefing/ErnestWilson0700.html, accessed 10 May 2001.

J. R. Young, J. R., 2001. "Does 'digital divide' rhetoric do more harm than good?" Chronicle of Higher Education (9 November), p. A51, at http://chronicle.com/free/v48/i11/11a05101.htm, accessed 10 December 2001.

42

AFRICA AS A
KNOWLEDGE SOCIETY

A reality check

J. J. Britz, P. J. Lor, I. E. M. Coetzee and B. C. Bester

Source: *International Information & Library Review* 38(1) (2006): 25–40.

Summary

This paper investigates the question of whether Africa is moving towards a knowledge society. An analysis is made of the current initiatives that are undertaken in Africa to put the continent on the road towards a knowledge society. The content of the paper is structured in the following manner. Firstly, we explain what a knowledge society means and based on this definition we describe the technological and economic landscapes that shape the knowledge society. We also identify and discuss four interrelated pillars of a knowledge society which we coined as follows, information and communication technology (ICT) and connectivity; usable content; infrastructure and deliverability and human intellectual capability. We then use these four pillars to analyze the African content as a knowledge society. Our main findings are that Africa has still a far way to go to become a true knowledge society, but that there is hope to successfully transform Africa into a knowledge society. We argue that this success is based on certain preconditions amongst other investment in human capital, effective stopping of brain draining as well as the effective development and maintenance of a physical infrastructure.

Introduction

As humankind is entering into the new era of an information and knowledge economy, characterized by advanced medical research (e.g. stem cell research), digital convergence, development of nano-technology, the use of space for commerce and an increased spending on research and development (R&D) by most developed countries, Africa is losing its scientists and researchers at an alarming rate, failing to educate its own people, hardly budgeting for R&D and, it would seem, not shopping around for intellectual capital to innovate and produce new technologies. No country on the African continent is listed among the world's rising innovation hot spots (these countries include Russia, India, Taiwan, China, Singapore and South Korea) and Africa's inventors have secured very few patents (BusinessWeek, 2004).

In many respects, Africa is worse off than in 1960 and according to a report on Africa by the G8 countries, Sub-Saharan Africa is the only region of the world that has actually become poorer in the last generation (G8 Gleneagles, 2005). The average per capita income of sub-Saharan Africa is less than it was in 1960 (Ellis & Padmore, 2003; Human Development Report, 2003). Africa has a huge debt burden. In 1999 it amounted to US$231 thousand million, which translates into 76% of the Gross Domestic Product. Currently only a small percentage of this debt has been cancelled. In the past decade aid to African countries dropped from US$17.2 thousand million to only US$12.2 thousand million in 1999. As Ellis and Padmore put it, "Such a situation spells out the conditions for a self-defeating cycle" (2003, p. 19). In a thought-provoking article published in the *Economist* it was stated that Africa is simply too poor to grow and too poor to save (Economist, 2005).

Criticism that Africa is in a particularly weak position to respond to the new move towards the information and knowledge economy and to become a true knowledge society seems to be justified. One can indeed ask the question, as was put forward in the *Economist*, namely, What happened to the $450 billion of aid that the West made available to Africa over the past 40 years? However, a number of recent events raise hopes that there may be a possible turnaround in the history of Africa. One of these is the recent meeting of the G8 countries in Scotland where Africa was put at the top of the agenda by Tony Blair, prime minister of Britain. Africa's current economic performance, specifically that of countries such as Uganda, Botswana, South Africa and Mozambique, is worth noting. Political initiatives and reforms are also promising. Recently 40 of the 56 countries on the continent have had multi-party elections. In 1973 the number was only three. The Commission for Africa, set up by Tony Blair, published a report on Africa (Commission for Africa, 2005), that called for another $25 billion of aid for Africa every year over the next 3–5 years. At the meeting, the G8 countries committed themselves to an even bigger financial support to Africa. There is also evidence that the continent is slowly but surely taking its first steps towards better governance as well as entering the new information based economic paradigm (a notion that we will explain later in the text) and moving towards becoming a knowledge society.

This is happening at a time when the United Nations (in its Millennium Declaration) and the World Summit on the Information Society (WSIS) aim to bridge the digital divide. They are concerned with promoting the use of information and communication technologies (ICTs), putting the potential of knowledge at the service of development and addressing the challenges of the information and knowledge society. This constitutes recognition of the importance of ICTs as an essential foundation for the information and knowledge society, and for access to information and knowledge and capacity building, specifically through education (WSIS, Plan of Action, Geneva, 2003).

It is the convergence of these developments with a possible turnaround in the history of Africa that motivated us to write this article and specifically to analyze some of the current initiatives undertaken in Africa to put it on the road towards a knowledge society. In order to do this we structured the article in the following manner. Firstly, we explain what is meant by a knowledge society, and following from this we discuss the technological and economic landscapes that shape the knowledge society. We also identify and discuss the four interrelated pillars of a knowledge society. Using these four pillars as criteria we then analyze Africa as a knowledge society. We end the article with some comments regarding the road ahead.

The technological and economic landscape of a knowledge society

In discussing Africa's road towards a knowledge society one assumes a mutual understanding and agreement on what is meant by a 'knowledge society.' However, an overview of recent literature showed that the notion of a 'knowledge society' is used in a rather ambiguous way. For example,

- It is used, specifically in the popular literature, without defining it (Smith, 2002).
- It has become a 'fashionable' concept increasingly replacing the so-called 'information society' (WSIS, Plan of Action, Geneva, 2003; Drucker, 1998; Evers, 2000; Servaes, 2003).
- It is used interchangeably with notions such as 'knowledge economy', 'knowledge driven economies', 'economies of innovation', and the 'information society' (Evers, 2000; Servaes, 2003; Smith, 2002).

It is normally characterized as a society where,

- knowledge has become the most important production factor (Davenport & Prusak, 1998; Drucker, 1998; Mansell & When, 1998; McInerney, 2002; OECD, 1999; Smith, 2002). According to Peter Drucker knowledge has sidelined both capital and labour (Drucker, 1998, p. 15);
- there is a culture of knowledge production underpinned by a higher level of education; and

390

- the focus is not only on the use of modern ICTs, but also on "content, meaning and knowledge" (Evers, 2000).

A number of knowledge society indicators have been developed (Mansell & When, 1998; United Nations University, 1998; The World Development Report, 1999). The most popular indicators used are,

- qualitative measurement of the use of, and access to, modern ICTs;
- the number of scientists in a country;
- the amount spent on R&D as a percentage of the gross domestic product (GDP);
- the ability to produce and export high technology;
- the number of patents filed in a country; and
- the number of articles published in highly ranked scholarly journals.

Although we agree with most of the above-mentioned characteristics of a knowledge society as well as with the listed 'knowledge society indicators,' we prefer to approach the notion of a knowledge society from both a technological and an economic perspective. We argue that modern ICTs, defined by Preston (2003, p. 35) as "the cluster or interrelated systems of technological innovations in the fields of microelectronics, computing, electronic communications including broadcasting and the Internet," bring about a profound transformation in the information and knowledge landscape. These technologies are indeed the most spectacular and revolutionary technologies ever developed when it comes to the creation, distribution, dissemination and repackaging of information as well as the interactive sharing of knowledge. What has changed is not the fact *that* people create, manipulate and use knowledge—this has always been the case. However, a fundamental change has taken place in the *way* in which knowledge is created, manipulated and used.

Evans and Wurster (1997) as well as Clarke (2003) explain the impact of these new ICTs in terms of a shift from the economics of things to the economics of information. It has become possible for information to become unbundled from its original physical carriers and it is no longer bound to a linear flow—it can travel by itself and documents become interlinked. As Evans and Wurster explain,

When information is carried by things—by a salesperson or by a piece of direct mail, for example—it goes where the things go and no further. It is constrained to follow the linear flow of the physical value chain. But once anyone is connected electronically information can travel by itself . . . what is truly revolutionary about the explosion in connectivity is the possibility it offers to unbundle information from its physical carrier".

(1997, p. 73)

This has made possible a weightless and dematerialized economy (Clarke, 2003, p. 1). The Internet, specifically the World Wide Web, is a manifestation of the new economics of information. As a nonlinear structure of unbundled information it allows more people to reach more information, in an interactive and customized manner.

This shift from the economics of things to the economics of information for the first time makes the following possible,

*   More people can be reached simultaneously and be exposed to more information in an interactive way (for example e-mail).
*   Information itself can be customized, integrated, altered, copied and destroyed at essentially zero cost.
*   Knowledge can be shared in real time without time and space barriers.

What has changed is therefore not the fact that people suddenly discover and start using knowledge in economic activities. It is more about an economy, driven by modern ICTs, that has profoundly changed the way in which information and knowledge are produced, reproduced, reconfigured and disseminated.

This paradigm shift towards the economics of information introduced advanced capitalism as well as the process of globalization. Through globalization a network of economic and social networks is created and the gap between the rich and the poor countries is no longer a 'physical object gap', but has become rather an 'immaterial information gap.' Open markets and competitiveness make it an imperative to invest in innovation and knowledge production. R&D and higher education increasingly play a crucial role in knowledge production and innovation to meet these new demands. This has led to greater investment in knowledge production.

Defining a knowledge society

Based on the above discussion it is possible to define a knowledge society as

> a society that operates within the paradigm of the economics of information. It values human capital as the prime input to production and innovation. A knowledge society is well connected via modern ICTs to the dematerialized economy, and has access to relevant and usable information. A highly sophisticated physical infrastructure underpins this economic model and allows the delivery of the material objects that are accessed and manipulated in the dematerialized world of modern ICTs.

The four pillars of a knowledge society

For a society to become a knowledge society and to be part of the new economics of information, it must meet four interrelated criteria which we refer to as the four pillars of a knowledge society. We label these criteria as follows:

*   ICTs and connectivity;
*   usable content;
*   infrastructure and deliverability; and
*   human intellectual capability

ICTs and connectivity

Participation in a knowledge society in the era of the information economy is based on connectivity to modern ICTs. The backbone of a knowledge society is therefore a well-developed, well-maintained and affordable information infrastructure that allows access to, and manipulation of the dematerialized economy. Kularatne (1997, p. 119) expresses his concern about Third World countries' inability to become knowledge societies by commenting that, "Whether a coordinated and organized national information policy exists in a country or not, there are certain fundamental inadequacies in the information infrastructure of many Third World countries." The African Information Society Initiative (AISI) strongly argues that modern ICTs have become a necessity for the masses in the developing world (http://www.ueca.org/aisi).

Usable content

Access to, and accessibility of information to enable participation in the dematerialized economy alone is not enough. The information available should be affordable, available, timely, relevant, readily assimilated, and in a language users can understand. Herbert Schiller (1991) in particular criticizes the fact that there is so much irrelevant information available and that the really valuable information is proprietarized. Schiller (1983, 1996) also accused the Western media of cultural and information imperialism and of making non-relevant information available to the third world. Cullen (2003) found that non-Western cultures have no real need to search for information on the Internet as it is in many cases irrelevant to their needs.

Infrastructure and deliverability

What many policy makers forget is that this new dematerialized and weightless economy is underpinned by a 'materialized' and top-heavy infrastructure comprising of airports, railways, roads, trucks, warehouses and physical addresses of people. Access to the 'unbundled' products and services offered via modern ICTs in most cases (education and banking are for example excluded) does not allow access to the physical object itself. Medicine, cars, food and household items such as refrigerators cannot be shipped as e-mail attachments. Delivery of these products requires a highly sophisticated and efficient physical infrastructure. A dematerialized economy without a physical infrastructure is of little use and can even create unmet expectations. For example, there is not much merit in making information on how to purify water available on the Internet when the tablets used for purifying the water cannot be delivered (Britz, 2004).

Human intellectual capability

The development of human capital represents one of the most important factors that facilitate development and economic growth. As Norris puts it, "Human capital represents that property that allows people to live and work productively" (Norris, 2001, p. 59). One can therefore state that the most valuable asset of a knowledge society is its intellectual capital. Such a society must invest in its people. Van Audenhove, in his analysis of the information society (which, for the purpose of this article can also be translated to the 'knowledge society') powerfully states that

> One fundamental danger then of the rhetoric—and theory—of the information society is that it mainly focuses on the technical capacity of countries and sees education as a facilitator in the information society. I would argue that the central element in the information society is knowledge and that technology is merely the facilitator in development. The main focus in the development effort has in recent years dangerously shifted towards the technological to the detriment of the educational".
>
> (2003, p. 65)

Mansell and When (1998) echo this view by stating that investing in mere technology and not in human capability will only lead to an increase in electricity consumption and not in economic growth.

Castells (1998) as well as Freeman and Soete (1997) focus on R&D as the core theme of their analysis of the information/knowledge society and technological innovation. They argue that, although the formal (primary, secondary and tertiary) educational systems are important for the creation and spreading of knowledge, the growth of professional R&D in the industrial sector has been one of the most important factors that brought about economic and social changes.

Of relevance here is the concern expressed by Freeman and Soete (1997) that, if the developing countries do not invest more in education and specifically in R&D, they will be excluded from the triadic knowledge and innovation networks, which are mainly concentrated in the USA, Europe and Asia. This concern is well-founded. A knowledge society needs people who can create as well as utilize knowledge. Studies also found that more highly educated people adapt more rapidly to new innovations (Rogers, 1995). It is for this reason that the European Union (EU) has recently set out plans to double its research budget to €70 billion. It is not only to bolster growth but also to catch up with Japanese and American spending on innovation. The current spending on R&D in the EU is only 1.93% of the GDP. This is far below the 2.76% by the USA and 3.12% by Japan (Financial Times, April 4, 2005).

The challenge to Africa

It is clear that this new economics of information is significantly different from the old economic paradigm and that a fundamentally different global environment is created in which development, and economic growth occurs. Knowledge has become the primary input in economic activities and has allowed sustainable growth.

The ability of Africa to become a knowledge society will largely be determined by the continent's response to this new economic paradigm. New strategies are needed and Africa must "... recognize and incorporate this new reality and focus on achieving knowledge-intensive development" (Clarke, 2003, p. 1). Amongst others, there needs to be a massive investment in human capital, a reassessment of the value of knowledge, the development of an information infrastructure to accommodate the new economic landscape as well as a large-scale investment in new ICTs. Such initiatives will support and encourage Africa's progress towards becoming a knowledge society. The new economics of information has indeed opened a window of opportunity for Africa. The question is, will Africa embrace this opportunity? In the next part of the paper we will evaluate Africa's route towards a knowledge society. Our evaluation is based on the four identified pillars.

In assessing Africa's route towards a knowledge society it is important to first and foremost make the comment that there is a strong political will and commitment by most African leaders to succeed in the attempts to make Africa a knowledge society and an important economic and political force in the world. There is furthermore a realization that Africa is responsible for its own destiny and future. It is worthwhile quoting Thabo Mbeki, President of South Africa, who made the following closing remarks in this famous *I am an African* speech, "When once the saying is recalled, *Ex Africa simper aliquid novi*, this must be so, because out of Africa's rebirth must come modern products of human economic activity, significant contributions to the world of knowledge, in the arts, science and technology, new images of an Africa of peace and prosperity" (Mbeki, 1998). As Cleary (1998, p. 21) puts it, such a rebirth "encapsulates the tension between the rediscovery of an earlier, higher civilization and a great leap forward from the platform provided by the antique philosophical, legal, scientific and aesthetic verities." It is not only a matter of rediscovering the continent's historical roots and cultural values before colonialism, but also of turning those values and abilities into competitive advantages and ensuring that Africa can take its place along the world of nations as a knowledge society. But this rather simple notion of the rebirth of a continent needs to be translated into a coherent plan of action and practical implementation. Apart from the political will there need to be action plans and imagination to give content to the African renaissance (Kornegay & Landsberg, 1998, p. 29).

Africa and the four pillars of a knowledge society

In the next part of the paper we will examine, based on the selected criteria, some of these activities that are undertaken in Africa.

ICTs and connectivity

We have pointed out that connectivity to modern ICTs is one of the prerequisites for becoming a knowledge society. In comparison to the developed world, Africa is still significantly behind when it comes to connectivity and the use (specifically the economic application) of modern ICTs. During a meeting in February 2005 at the Africa Regional Preparatory Conference for the World Summit on the Information Society, held in Accra, Ghana, the Executive Secretary of the UN Economic Commission for Africa, Kingsley Y. Amoako, warned that the underdeveloped information infrastructure "... continues to be the Achilles heel of Africa's information society" (UNECA, 2005).

The question then is, What is Africa's response to the challenge of getting connected? It is true that many of the early post-colonial initiatives to get Africa connected to information and communication technologies were not that successful. The Pan-Africa telecommunications Network (Panaftel) serves as one example. It started in 1962 as an initiative to better the communication and information infrastructure of post-colonial Africa and was funded by the United Nations Development Program (Okundi, 1976, pp. 749–754). Panaftel was initially successful, specifically between 1970 and 1980, but it eventually got derailed due to political and economic mismanagement. The project ended officially in 1995 (Schaeffer, 2004). Other projects such as Africa One (a project aimed to connect Africa via a fiber optic cable) as well as TELEDESIC (a project initiated by McCaw Cellular Communications and Microsoft) also did not meet the expectations. (Africa ONE, 2002; ATU, 2002; TELEDESIC Streaming Media World, 2001).

However, there are three encouraging trends regarding ICTs in Africa that we want to highlight. Firstly, there is a broad consensus in Africa that modern ICTs play a major role in boosting economic growth prospects. It seems, at least at policy level, that since the late 1990s there are much better coordinated efforts in Africa to implement and utilize modern ICTs. During 1996 the Economic Commission for Africa (ECA) initiated the AISI. One of the main aims of the AISI is to build Africa's *information highway* and to investigate the use of ICTs for development in Africa. Countries on the continent were therefore encouraged to develop national information and communication infrastructures (NICI). According to Barka (2004) more than 30 countries in Africa have embarked on a NICI to ensure that sound ICTs policies are in place. The AISI was followed by the establishment of the New Economic Partnership for African Development (NEPAD). NEPAD can in short be described as a vision and strategic framework for Africa's renewal. It was founded in 2001 as one of the programmes of the newly formed African Union (AU). NEPAD was designed specifically to address challenges such as poverty, economic marginalization and the acceleration of the empowerment of women on the African continent. One of the main priorities of NEPAD is "building and improving infrastructure including ICT" (NEPAD, 2004). One of the first projects of NEPAD was a survey on the current status of ICTs in Africa. The study's findings were amongst others that enabling laws to drive e-strategies in Africa are nearly non-existent. Mauritius is the exception with a good e-strategy to become a "cyber island". The study also concluded that in those countries where projects such as e-learning, e-health and e-commerce are started it is mostly done without a policy framework. Following from this NEPAD adopted a recommendation of a continental ICT survey to identify current technical and regulatory obstacles that can jeopardize the development of an ICT infrastructure on the continent. One way to identify these obstacles will be by means of a database on ICTs in Africa. According to Shola Taylor, one of the major role players in this study, the idea would then be to develop an ICT master plan for Africa (Baradu, 2005).

The second positive trend is the exponential growth of ICTs on the continent—in terms of both implementation and applications. This is mainly due to huge financial support from the World Bank, the G8 countries as well as the United Nations. Up to 1995 only six countries in Africa were connected to the Internet. Now nearly all the countries on the continent are connected (Ya'u, 2002, p. 8). Not only is there an exponential growth of ICTs on the African continent, but to a certain extent Africa has leap-frogged into new technologies. This is specifically true of cell phone use. Africa was the first continent where the use of cell phones outnumbered the use of landlines (www.newsbatch.com/africanews.html). Of more importance than the ability to leapfrog into new technologies is the fact that ICTs allow Africa to avoid to a certain extent the first socio-economic effects of radical technological changes. These effects are mostly negative, for example unemployment as well as initial slower economic growth. By leap-frogging and avoiding the errors made by the developing nations with regards to the development and applications of new ICTs, Africans can directly benefit from the so-called secondary (rebound) effects of innovation namely job creation and sustainable economic growth. Access to and the use of modern ICTs on the continent has also become more affordable, and with the growing application and use of open source software, it has in many cases become free.

Thirdly, the African continent has its best ever representation on the World Economic Forum's Global IT ranking which was published during March 2005. This ranking is based on the Forum's Readiness Index Ranking. Amongst others it measures countries' ability to take advantage of ICTs. The ranking covers technical infrastructure, government policies on information technology, the quality of education, and the affordability of telephone and Internet services. Twenty-one African countries made it to the top one hundred list.

A comparative ranking in 2003 is listed to illustrate Africa's increased performance according to the index (Table 1).

Based on the above there is indeed enough reason to be optimistic about Africa's 'connectivity to ICT' future. Not only is there a clear political will to be successful, but much progress has been made to connect the continent to modern ICTs. In purely statistical terms there is a general trend over the

Table 1 Africa's position on the top 100 list of the The Networked Readiness Index Ranking 2003 and 2004 (Networked readiness index rankings, 2003, 2004).

Country	Rank 2004	Rank 2003
Tunisia	31	40
South Africa	34	37
Botswana	50	55
Morocco	54	64
Namibia	55	59
Egypt	57	65
Ghana	65	74
Gambia	74	82
Kenya	75	85
Uganda	77	80
Algeria	80	87
Zambia	81	85
Tanzania	83	71
Nigeria	86	79
Mali	91	96
Malawi	93	88
Zimbabwe	94	95
Mozambique	96	97
Angola	Not listed	99

past 4 years of a narrowing of the digital divide between the most developed countries and the least developed countries, most of which are in Africa (World Economic Forum, 2002).

Statistics can, however, be misleading and a strong political will might not be enough. There seems to be a growing concern amongst scholars that the gap (digital divide) between the developed and developing countries is actually increasing and that it will be getting more difficult for the ICT-poor countries to catch up or even keep pace with the technology advanced countries (Ya'u, 2002, p. 8; Norris, 2001). There are two main reasons for this concern. Firstly, the development and application of modern ICTs are growing exponentially. The problem is that most of the ICT-poor countries, although connected, do not have the ability to constantly upgrade their current ICT infrastructure. The second concern relates to the economic application of modern ICTs. We have already argued that the real benefit of modern ICTs is that they allow the manipulation of a digital economy to gain a competitive advantage in the market place. The question then arises, how many individuals on the African continent can log on the Internet, access the website of an electronic journal publisher and use a credit card to download articles from research journals? To what extent has the African continent, in the application and use of modern ICTs, succeeded in benefiting from this new economic landscape? Are these new technologies used to their full economic capacities, or is their use limited to mere *communication* technologies between groups and individuals?

Usable content

To be connected does not necessarily mean to be informed. In describing the four pillars of a knowledge society we pointed out that available information also needs to be affordable, timely, relevant, readily assimilated, and in a language users can understand. In the next paragraphs we will briefly address these criteria.

Affordability

A number of factors affect the affordability of content on the African continent. Here a distinction has to be made between African and non-African content. Lack of financial resources affects both, but in different ways. Affordability of African-produced content is not an issue if seen in isolation. Books and journals produced in Africa are generally inexpensive by West European or North American standards. The problem here is rather one of infrastructure, logistics and availability. In contrast, given the connectivity discussed above, the availability of content from other parts of the world can be taken for granted but its affordability is a serious problem.

The main barrier to the importation of content from the developed countries is lack of funds. It is well known that the libraries of African institutions of higher learning lack funds for subscribing to conventional printed journals or purchasing monographs, student texts and other printed materials from the developed countries (Arunachalam, 2003; Britz & Lor, 2003; Rosenberg, 2002). Lack of money is frequently exacerbated by shortages of foreign exchange, punitive customs duties and bureaucratic impediments.

Access to electronic content at first sight appears to offer a solution. After all, once scientific and scholarly material has been put on a publisher's Web server, few additional costs are generated if the number of document accesses increases. Thus one would expect that modern ICTs would help to narrow the divide between information-rich and information poor. However, publishers of electronic content are no less driven by profit than print publishers. They guard their intellectual property vigilantly. The normal commercial cost of electronic journals, handbooks and databases are beyond the reach of many African institutions.

To remedy this, various programmes have been launched to make access to usable scientific and scholarly content affordable to African institutions. Examples are HINARI, AGORA and PERI. The success of these programs is mainly due to the progress made with the development of the ICT infrastructure in Africa over the past few years.

HINARI, the Health Internetwork Access to Research Initiative, is an initiative of the World Health Organization (WHO) that focuses on the distribution of health information to developing countries. It provides free or highly subsidized access to major journals in biomedicine and related fields to non-profit organizations such as universities, hospitals, medical libraries and government offices in developing countries that meet eligibility criteria based on per capita GDP (HINARI, 2005). A number of major international journal publishers, such as Blackwell, Elsevier and John Wiley make their titles available to the programme. The total number of titles available exceeds 2000. The retrieval of full text articles is allowed. Currently more that 1100 institutions, in more that 100 countries are benefiting from the program. The criteria are designed to separate the poor developing countries from the not so poor. Hence African countries such as Ethiopia and Sudan are eligible for free access (Aronson, 2003) but South Africa is not. There are limits to the generosity of the major journal publishers. A number of countries of which the per capita GDP falls below the threshold are nevertheless excluded from HINARI because participating publishers already have a lucrative market there (Chan & Costa, 2004).

AGORA (Global Online Research in Agriculture) is a similar programme to HINARI, but focuses on agriculture. It is administered by the United Nations Food and Agricultural Organization and the aim is to provide institutions in the developing world with free or low cost access to over 400 scientific journals in the hope that this will help reduce famine and improve food and nutrition quality in these countries (AGORA, 2005).

Chan and Costa (2004) have pointed out that programmes such as HINARI and AGORA are mainly palliative in effect and do not reduce the underlying dependence of developing countries on the supply of information from developed countries. An exception to this is the Programme for the Enhancement of Research Information (PERI), a worldwide research initiative coordinated by the International Network for the Availability of Scientific Publications (INASP). Its main objective is to "support capacity building in the research sector in developing and transitional countries by strengthening the production, access and dissemination of information and knowledge" (INASP, 2005). Like HINARI and AGORA, PERI helps developing countries to obtain affordable or even free access to publications published by commercial publishers. What is different is that PERI puts more emphasis on the development of programs to assist journals from developing countries to become more professional and improve their scientific and editorial quality.

Availability

Although Africa has made significant progress in the establishment of its ICT infrastructure, there are still serious infrastructural and logistical barriers that impede the printed as well as electronic availability of African content within and between African countries. African authors who wish to publish locally face the problem that there are not many African scholarly journals of good quality, and the number is declining. Most of these publications are also not available in electronic format. Many are poorly run and edited and appear irregularly, so that libraries in the North do not want to subscribe to them (Rosenberg, 2002). Omekwu (2003) states that journal publication in Africa is "highly unsustainable" and according to Tonukari (2004, p. 124) "In sub-saharan Africa, traditional print journals have not lived up to expectations because these journals mostly survive on grants and few fortunate African universities rely again on grants to buy them. Their subscription record is pathetic at best." The journals lack a steady subscriber base and are financially insecure. Marketing is minimal and distribution is poor. Many lack a consistent supply of articles (Omekwu, 2003), possibly because of a tendency of authors to seek publication in more prestigious titles published in the North (Britz & Lor, 2003).

When scholars from developing countries publish in national or regional journals, their output does not easily enter the mainstream of science and scholarship (Arunachalam, 2003). Partly as a result of their irregular publication and indifferent standard, coverage of these journals in international indexing and abstracting services is inadequate. And since bibliographic control at the national or regional (African) level leaves much to be desired, the contributions of African scholars may fail to reach readers in their own countries or elsewhere in Africa (Lor & Britz, 2005).

Timeliness

Modern ICTs allow information content to be disseminated on the World Wide Web in the twinkling of an eye. Given electronic content and the connectivity that was discussed above, the requirement of timeliness can, at least in theory, readily be met. It is mostly non-African content that can be made readily available in Africa. However, as we have already pointed out, it is very expensive and most university and research libraries in Africa cannot afford it.

Locally created knowledge is mostly limited to hard copies and the distribution thereof is not effective due to infrastructural limitations (an issue we will address later in the paper). Indigenous oral knowledge, part of the wealth of Africa's knowledge base, is only rapidly accessible to people sharing the same context, space and time.

Relevance

Following from this one has also to ask, to what extent can people really benefit from the information that they access electronically or via the Internet? Chan and Costa justifiably ask, "Is it useful for doctors in Nigeria to read about the latest high-tech treatments for infertility published in a western journal when it is not economically feasible to implement these procedures in a cash-strapped public hospital in Nigeria?" (2004) This comment underscores the problem with so-called relevant information that is made available on the Internet and other media. In many cases available and relevant information is not backed up by the availability of the resources to which the information has a bearing. This can even create unmet expectations (Britz, 2004, p. 200). Information alone in many cases does not solve problems. The actual resources, to which the information refers, must also be available.

Consequently one can also argue that content produced in Africa is potentially of higher relevance than non-African content, but this depends on the mindset of African scholars. In a previous article Britz and Lor (2003) listed a number of obstacles that prevent African scholars from making a contribution to the body of knowledge that is published in the leading international scientific journals. Research done in Africa does not always meet the international quality standards set by scientific journals. This can be attributed to a variety of reasons, varying from poor education to poor command of English as well as inadequate access to other published research. Therefore some relevant research done in Africa never gets published and is effectively lost to the global body of knowledge.

However, some initiatives have been taken to make Africa's own body of scientific knowledge more accessible. One example is the initiative by INASP, which in 1998 launched the African Journals Online project (AJOL). AJOL displays the tables of contents of African journals and provides an article delivery service which is free to African scholars. AJOL, running on open source software, is now managed from South Africa and currently covers over 220 titles, including French titles (AJOL, 2005). The Michigan State University also took the initiative to make African scholarly journals available electronically through its African eJournals Project (AEJP), with the focus on biomedical information (Rosenberg, 2002, p. 54). Within Africa, mention should be made of the Africa Knowledge Networks Forum (AKNF), an initiative led by the UN Economic Commission for Africa (ECA). Its main aim is to facilitate knowledge sharing and research partnerships in Africa. It seeks to address shortcomings such as

- duplication of research,
- absence of a knowledge gateway to access the best research knowledge products,
- limited local content in training programs at all levels of education, and
- limited impact of research on public policy.

AKNF aims to link knowledge creators and knowledge users in Africa in order to "strengthen[. . .] indigenous policy-oriented research and analysis for more effective use by African decision-makers" (AKNF, 2001).

Language

When it comes to language and access to the global body of knowledge, Africans are in a privileged position. Most educated people on the continent can speak or understand either French or English, two of the languages that have a prominent representation on the Internet. Furthermore, English is the dominant political, economic as well as scientific language on the continent. The drawback is, however, the low level of literacy.

However, the problem is not so much the ability of Africans to understand foreign languages as the preservation and advancement of their own indigenous languages. There are more than 1000 languages spoken on the African continent and some of these do not have a written form. Also, very little scholarly work gets published in local languages. There are some initiatives to preserve and distribute African languages. The African Language Materials Archive (ALMA) is an initiative of the West African Research Association (WARA), the Council of American Overseas Research Centers (CAORC), the Columbia University Libraries for African Studies, and the Information Society Division of the United Nations Educational, Scientific and Cultural Organization (UNESCO). This initiative aims at increasing dissemination of, and access to materials published in indigenous African languages through digital formats (ALMA, 2005).

There is also the recognition and reaffirmation that African languages must play a pivotal role in the development of Africa, specifically in terms of science and technology. After the first ever conference by African authors and scholars held in Asmara, Eritrea in January 2000 the Asmara Declaration on African Languages and Literatures was issued. It stated amongst other points that,

- Equality of African languages must be recognized as a basis for future empowerment of Africa.
- African research must be done and documented in African languages (The Asmara declaration on African languages and literatures, 2000).

Infrastructure and deliverability

The importance of a well developed and maintained infrastructure, including roads, railways, and airports cannot be over-emphasized. It is an input to all other economic activities and allows consumption as well as economic participation. We have pointed out that the new dematerialized and weightless economy is even more dependent on a well developed and maintained infrastructure to allow the effective flow of products and services and to accelerate economic growth.

The World Bank, in one of its official documents *Ten things you never knew about the World Bank in Africa* (World Bank, 2005), specifically points out that an adequate infrastructure in Africa is a prerequisite to increase trade and will consequently spur economic growth. According to this report an improved infrastructure across the region will not only lower transportation and energy costs, but will also make African products and services more competitive in the global economy. More than 40 percent of World Bank lending is therefore for infrastructure development in Africa and comprises the financing of road construction, harbour modernization, and increased supply of energy.

One of the biggest barriers to Africa's entry into the new knowledge economy is therefore not the lack of computers or access to the Internet, but the lack of the ability to provide and maintain an effective infrastructure to deliver necessary products and services to its people. Based on World Bank reports as well as NEPAD's documentation we highlight a few of the horrific statistics regarding Africa's infrastructure,

- In 1997 Africa had only 171,000 km of paved roads—18 percent less than Poland. What makes these statistics even worse is the fact that in Africa most people are further away from a road than anywhere else in the world. Not only does Africa have a very difficult geography in terms of rivers and landlocked countries, but the continent has a very low population density. In a country such as Ethiopia more than 70% of the population does not have access to all-weather roads. People are therefore marginalized from nearly all major economic activities.

- When there is quantity, it does not guarantee quality. In 2000 only 16% of the roads were paved. Most of the unpaved roads are only in fair to poor condition and in many cases access is possible only in the dry seasons. One-third of the roads built in Sub-Sahara Africa during the past 20 years have eroded due to a lack of maintenance.

- Transportation is unreliable and costly. The World Bank estimates that transportation cost in Africa is of the highest in the world and is marginalized from all major air and maritime routes. Landlocked countries are specifically hard hit and in some cases air-transport is just not available or extremely expensive. It is for example in many cases cheaper to fly between Johannesburg (South Africa) and Europe, covering a distance of 12,000 km, than flying between Johannesburg and Harare (Zimbabwe)—which is a mere 1800 km. There are many reasons for higher transportation cost. Some of the main reasons are lack of economics of scale; poor transport systems, corruption, high fuel prices and vehicle prices. Bribes contribute to one-third of transportation cost in some West African countries.

- In 1999 less than 1 out of 5 Africans had access to electricity and less than half had access to clean running water.

- The administrative, fiscal, legal and security infrastructure in Africa is not well developed and is even totally lacking in some cases. NEPAD specifically expressed concerns regarding bureaucratic impediments, customs difficulties, corruption, insecurity, political instability and the lack of sound and accountable governance. A big problem in some instances is the lack of political will to utilize the infrastructure that does exist. A good example is the failure of the South African government to effectively roll out antiretrovirals for persons affected by HIV-AIDS, in spite of winning a much publicized court case which opened the way to the local manufacture of generic drugs. It is ironic that Coca-Cola and (South African) Castle Beer can be found in some of the smallest and most isolated communities in Africa. Commercial undertakings have found ways to deliver goods to the most remote places in Africa while governments seemingly remain unable to deliver education, health and other services to the same communities.

- Many economies in Africa are war-effected economies and are the hardest hit by the inadequate provision of infrastructural services (Angola, Mozambique, Democratic Republic of Congo, Burundi, etc.). Money is spent on war and not on the maintenance or development of new infrastructure. In the Democratic Republic of Congo, which is being torn apart by a civil war, the entire road and railway infrastructure has practically disappeared.

However, Africa has not figuratively speaking reached the 'end of the road'. There is indeed some light at the end of the long tunnel and it is not an on-coming train. All the major stake-holders realize the importance of a strong and well maintained infrastructure in Africa and most of these role players are not only morally, but also economically committed to bring about change. It is estimated that Africa will need more or less 6% of its Gross Domestic Product per year to develop and maintain an effective infrastructure (World Bank, 2000).

Recently the World Bank provided US$409 million to the eight countries of the West Africa Economic and Monetary Union to improve 1300 km of cross-country roads. This allowed for the creation of a regional market that enabled these countries more competitive advantages (World Bank, 2000). The World Bank has also committed itself to lend $1.8 billion a year for infrastructure development in Africa. Currently Britain is urging the member states of the G8 countries to embrace what is called a new Marshall Plan for Africa. It includes a financial contribution of $25 billion over the next 3–5 years as well as plans to write off the debt of most of the poorest countries on the continent. This initiative is part of the G8 Africa Action Plan which was agreed to by the G8 countries in 2002. It includes commitments on promoting economic growth (include infrastructure development) as well as expanding knowledge and improving health on the continent (Commission for Africa Report, 2005).

The Southern African Development Community (SADC) countries are also involved in major and imaginative road-construction projects, including the Maputo Corridor, which links Maputo (Mozambique) to Walvis Bay (Namibia) via the Trans Kalahari Highway. Siemens Southern Africa is also highly involved in implementation and upgrading of power-station infrastructure in Southern Africa (ESI Africa, 2003).

Human and intellectual capacity

We have already argued that the most valuable asset of a knowledge society is its intellectual capital and that societies, to be able to become knowledge societies, must invest in their people. Knowledge constitutes a very central part in the techno-economic paradigm and is seen as the most important production factor in all economic spheres. We are convinced that education and the investment in human capital are fundamental in the creation of a knowledge society and a knowledge economy. It should be more than literacy and e-literacy—a knowledge society and knowledge economy requires knowledge workers that have the ability to innovate and do scientific discoveries. This will allow Africans to find their own solutions to their own problems.

Hans van Ginkel, the Rector of the United Nations University, correctly observed that without a sustainable, strong knowledge sector of its own, Africa will always remain in a dangerously dependent position (United Nations University, 1998). In his opening speech at the Conference on Education for African Renaissance in the twenty-first century Thabo Mbeki, the South African President echoed this view with the following remark (quoted by Butcher),

> If the next century is going to be characterized as a truly African century, for social and economic progress of the African people, the century of durable peace and sustained development in Africa, then the success of this project is dependent on the success of our education systems. For nowhere in the world has development been attained without universal and sound primary education, without an effective higher education and research sector, without equality of educational opportunity.
>
> (Mbeki, in Butcher, 2003, p. 11)

This raises some intriguing questions, To what extent does Africa invest in its education and R&D programs and to what degree are people in Africa able to utilize and create new knowledge?

It is clear, based on the education budgets of some African countries and on the list of priorities set by NEPAD as well as the G8 countries, that education and human development are very high on the priority list of the continent (NEPAD, 2004). One of the top 10 priorities of NEPAD is *human development*, with specific reference to education. As part of the Human Capacity Development strategy NEPAD has also launched an e-school initiative focusing on teaching school children as well as teachers ICT skills (Commission for Africa Report, 2005). Some countries in Africa have made remarkable progress in education. Mozambique for example doubled the number of children in school over the past 5 years and Kenya recently introduced free primary education. This has brought more that 1.2 million children back to school. In Tanzania 1000 new schools have been built and 18,000 new teachers were recruited (G8 Gleneagles, 2005).

There is a general consensus that, without proper education of its people, Africa will not survive this millennium. However, the education and human development pictures in Africa look still very bleak and we highlight some of the alarming trends.

Lack of educated people and educators as well as low school completion rate

According to the NEPAD Secretariat weekly newsletter (8 September 2005) there are more that 40 million children in Africa not in school and who have never been exposed to any formal education. There is an estimated shortage of 3 million teachers on the continent. Furthermore Africa is the continent with the lowest average school completion rate—it is on average 60% or less and Africa has also the highest number of girls not attending school (23 million). Another example to illustrate the education crises in Africa is the fact that in 2000 Nigeria (the most populous country in Africa and one of the richest in terms of natural resources) had only the capacity to accommodate 12% of qualified candidates for higher education (Commission for Africa Report, 2005; World Economic Forum, 2003).

South Africa, the richest and most advanced country on the continent, has some serious educational drawbacks. This is mainly due to the apartheid system and its legacy. According to the 1996 census 3.2 million of the 24 million adults in South Africa have had no schooling and a further 9.4 million have not completed grade 9. More than 12 million adults (more than half) have not completed a general education (grade 12). During the apartheid era more that 24% of black adults did not have access to education compared with the mere 1.4% of whites (Puonti & Puranen, 2002).

Research and development

R&D is crucial to any economic development. In the Introduction we already pointed out how highly the EU values R&D. Reflecting the priorities of the AU it is clear that R&D is also valued in Africa. NEPAD for example organized a meeting of African ministers of science in 2004. At this meeting it was agreed that Africa should increase its spending on R&D to at least 1% of GDP in the next decade. The current spending is less that 0.1% (Science and Development Network, 2003). The question is of course, is this goal obtainable? In his analysis Dickson observes, "This was put forward less as a realistic goal than as an aspiration intended to highlight the extra political commitment required to secure an effective scientific infrastructure" (Dickson, 2004).

In their analyses of development of R&D in Africa, the Commission for Africa comments that there are some excellent R&D facilities in Africa (2005). Specific mention is made of the African Economics Research Consortium, the Bio Sciences Facility for Central and Eastern Africa as well as the Community and Individual Development Association (CIDA) City Campus in South Africa. However, the resources and research capabilities are limited. Furthermore, 60% of all R&D activities in Africa are centered in South Africa and in the greater Congo basin there is virtually "no science at all" (Commission for Africa Report, 2005, p. 138).

The brain drain

The brain drain, or the migration of well-educated people from Africa to the developed world, can be seen as a significant contributor to Africa's inability to move towards becoming a knowledge society.

According to a study by the Population Research Group at the South University of Natal (South Africa) some 60,000 plus middle and high level managers left Africa between 1985 and 1990. Figures released by the International Organization for Migration (IOM) and the UN's Economic Commission for Africa confirms this trend. According to these statistics

- An estimated 27,000 highly qualified Africans left the continent between 1960 and 1975.
- This number increased to 40,000 between 1975 and 1984.
- The number doubled in 1987. It then represented 30% of the highly skilled labour force.
- Africa lost more than 60,000 professional people between 1985 and 1990 and an estimated 20,000 every year since then.

Another study by the World Bank reported that some 70,000 highly qualified African scholars and experts leave their home countries every year in order to work abroad. Africa spends an estimated US$4 thousand million annually on recruiting some 100,000 skilled expatriates (World Markets Research Centre, 2002). The Commission for Africa Report estimates that more African scientists and engineers are working in the USA than in the whole of Africa. In Ghana, more that 70% of the trained medical officers left the country during the 1990s (2005, p. 137).

Apart from the direct economic impact of the brain drain, it also has a profound effect on efforts to prevent HIV/AIDS as well as health care. After a week-long visit to Southern Africa during June James Morris, the UN special envoy for humanitarian needs in Southern Africa, said, "The number of trained health practitioners, teachers, and other professionals that are succumbing to HIV/AIDS is causing a truly extraordinary human resources vacuum in societies across the region," and "It is impossible to counter the crisis if people aren't on the ground to implement effective programming, or to deal with the sick and dying, or to care for the unprecedented number of orphans and other vulnerable groups." (HIV/AIDS seriously impacts social service delivery, 2004).

However, there are some brain-gaining initiatives in Africa. It is clear that Africa is aware of the brain drain which can end up in a "brain dead" continent. Meyer, Kaplan, and Charum (2001) report that there are more that 40 countries in Africa that are part of 'intellectual diaspora networks' whose general aim is to utilize the skills and knowledge of expatriates in such a way that they can contribute to the country's development. It is based on the idea that a pool of knowledge must be potentially available without the expatriates having to return to their home countries permanently (Brown, Kaplan, & Meyer, 2001). The United Nations Development Program initiated a program called 'Transfer of Knowledge through Expatriate Networks (TOTKEN)'. The aim of this program is to promote the greater use of well-skilled expatriates to train Africans. In South Africa, such a program, known as the South African Network of Skills Abroad (SANSA) has also been initiated. The idea is also to encourage expatriate South Africans to make their body of knowledge available to continue contributing to the South Africa's development without having to return (S.A. National Research Foundation, 2002). South African universities are also playing a leading role in initiating projects to enhance higher education in Africa. In association with the Association of African Universities and the Association of Commonwealth Universities, a 10-year partnership program has been launched. The project is named 'Renewing the African University'. The estimated cost of the ambitious project is estimated at $500 million per annum and the G8 Commission on Africa Report strongly recommends that the international community support this initiative (Rowett, 2005; Commission for Africa Report, 2005, p. 138).

Conclusion: the road ahead

Based on new initiatives in Africa, as well as increased financial aid to Africa, one can indeed argue that there is enough evidence that the continent is slowly but surely taking some steps towards better governance, entering the new economic paradigm and moving towards becoming a knowledge society.

Although new ICTs certainly do not provide the 'magic bullet' to solve all Africa's problems, they offer a new and challenging opportunity for Africa to become a knowledge society and to participate as an equal partner in the competitive information-based economy. It is evident that the African leaders, educators and other important role players understand the importance of fully embracing this challenge. It is also clear that the agenda for Africa to become a knowledge society is increasingly driven by Africans. The African Union and more specifically NEPAD are setting the agenda. There are also improved partnerships between Africa and donor organizations and nations (specifically the G8) in the effort to develop Africa into a knowledge society and to make it part of the global economy.

Based on our definition of a knowledge society as well as the four interrelated pillars of a knowledge society we argue that Africa can successfully be transformed into a knowledge society if the continent succeeds in,

* Investing effectively in its human capital, allowing people not only to access and use new ICTs, but also to utilize it to create new knowledge. The focus should therefore not only be limited to primary and secondary

education, but also on tertiary education as well as R&D. Investment in its people and in education will allow Africa to move away from 'borrowing money to making money'.

• Effectively stopping the brain drain out of Africa, and turning it around to become a 'brain gain'.

• Developing and maintaining an effective and efficient physical infrastructure that will allow the delivery of goods and services. Such an infrastructure is a precondition for the successful functioning of a dematerialized information economy.

It is furthermore clear, based on available statistics, that Africa is indeed leapfrogging into the new technologies and thereby entering the mainstream of the global information economy. In this paper, we have pointed out that this 'leap-frog-ability' may help Africa to avoid the first socioeconomic effects of radical technological changes, to benefit from secondary (rebound) effects, and to gain a clear economic advantage. However, we have raised two specific concerns in the paper. Firstly, once leapfrogged into new technologies the question arises, will Africa be able to constantly upgrade their technology? Secondly, to what extent will Africa be able to fully utilize modern ICTs for their economic benefit? Thirdly, to what extent will Africa be able to solve fundamental problems such as undemocratic regimes, maladministration, corruption, shortsighted economic policies, huge gaps between rich and poor, and armed conflicts between groups. Positive answers to these issues might put Africa on route towards becoming a true knowledge society.

References

AKNF. (2001). *About AKNF: What is, and why AKNF? (2001)*. Retrieved November 22, 2004 from http://www.uneca.org/aknf/about/index.htm.

Africa ONE. (2002). *Africa ONE: Wiring a continent for the 21st century: The Africa ONE project overview*. Retrieved January 19, 2005 from http://www.africaone.coni/english/about/about.cfrn.

AGORA. (2005). *AGORA: Access to global online research in Agriculture*. Retrieved September 25, 2005 from http://www.agInternetwork.org/en/.

AISI. (n.d.). *The African Information Society Initiative (AISI)*. Retrieved October 17, 2005 from http://www.uneca.org/aisi.

AJOL. (2005). *AJOL: African Journals OnLine*. Retrieved September 25, 2005 from http://ajol.info/.

ALMA. (2005). *African Language Materials Archive: A multilingual public digital library of West African language publications*. Retrieved July 24, 2005 from http://portal.unesco.org/ci/en/ev.php-URL_ID=12753&URL_DO=DO_PRINTPAGE&URL_SECTION=201.html.

Aronson, B. (2003). Improving online access to medical information for low income countries [Electronic version]. *New England Journal of Medicine, 350*(10), 966–968.

Arunachalam, S. (2003). Information for research in developing countries: Information technology, a friend or foe? *International Information and Library Review*, *35*(2/4), 133–147.

The Asmara declaration on African languages and literatures. (2000). Retrieved September 25, 2005 from http://www.queensu.ca/snid/asmara.htm.

ATU. (2002). *African Telecommunications Union: Projects.* Retrieved October 17, 2005 from http://www.atu-uat.org/.

Audenhove, L. (2003). Theories of the information society and development: Recent theoretical contributions and their relevance for the developing world. *Communication*, *29*(1&2), 48–67.

Baradu, S. (2005). *Nepad survey proposed African ICT—Database.* Retrieved February 18, 2005 from http://www.nepad.com/2005/news/wmview.php?ArtID=6.

Barka, L. B. (2004). *Africa and the knowledge society.* Retrieved January 15, 2005 from http://www.uneca.org/eca_resources/Speeches/2004_speeches/042704speech_ms_ben_ba.

Britz, J. J. (2004). To know or not to know: A moral reflection on information poverty. *Journal of Information Science*, *30*(3), 195–207.

Britz, J. J., & Lor, P. J. (2003). A moral reflection on the information flow from South to North: An African perspective. *Libri*, 53(3), 160–173.

Brown, M., Kaplan, D., & Meyer, J. B. (2001). *Counting brains: Measuring emigration from South Africa, Southern African Migration Project.* Kingston, Ontario: Queen's University.

BusinessWeek. (2004). The innovation economy. Special report. The technologies and new ideas that are changing the world. *BusinessWeek*, October 11.

Butcher, N. (2003). *Technological infrastructure and use of ICT in education in Africa: An overview. Working group on distance education and open learning (WGDEOL).* Paris: Association for the Development of Education in Africa.

Castells, M. (1998). End of millennium, the information age. In *Economy, society and culture* (Vol. III).

Chan, L. & Costa, S. (2004). Participation in the global knowledge commons: Challenges and opportunities for research dissemination in developing countries. *Social Sciences*. Retrieved October 17, 2005 from http://hdl.handle.net/1807/2388.

Clarke, M. (2003). e-Development: Development and the new economy. UNU World Institute for Development Economics Research, Policy Brief no. 7. Helsinki: United Nations University.

Cleary, S. M. (1998). African renaissance: Challenges for South Africa. South African–German Chamber of Commerce and Industry, November 25, 1997. In *The African renaissance. Occasional papers* (pp. 21–27). Johannesburg: Konrad Adenauer Stiftung.

Commission for African Report. (2005). Retrieved October 19, 2005 from http://www.commissionforafrica.org/english/report/introduction.html.

Cullen, R. (2003). The digital divide: A global and national call to action. *The Electronic Library*, *21*(3), 247–257.

Davenport, T. H., & Prusak, L. (1998). *Working knowledge: How organizations manage what they know.* Boston: Harvard Business School Press.

Dickson, D. (2004). Scientific output: The real 'knowledge divide." *SciDevNet*, July 19.

Drucker, P. F. (1998). *Peter Drucker on the profession of management.* Boston: Harvard Business School Press.

Ellis, V., & Padmore, L. (2003). An African imperative: Will Nepad succeed or stumble? *Convergence, 3*(3), 18–27.

Economist. (2005). Special report: The $25 billion question—Aid to Africa. *The Economist, 376* (8433), 25.

ESI Africa. (2003). *Siemens implements Africa's infrastructure*. Retrieved October 17, 2005 from http://www.esi-africa.com/last/esi_2_2003/032_36.htm.

Evans, P. B., & Wurster, T. S. (1997). Strategies and the new economics of information. *Harvard Business Review, September*, 71–82.

Evers, H. (2000). Die Globalisierung der epistemischen Kultur, Entwicklungstheorie und Wissengesellschaft. In Ulrich Menzel (Ed.). *Vom Ewigen Frieden und vom Wohlstand der Nationen*. Frankfurt am Main: Suhrkamp Verlag.

Financial Times. (2005). Brussels to outline €70bn spending plan on research to close the gap with its rivals. *Financial Times*, April 4.

Freeman, C., & Soete, L. (1997). *The economics of industrial innovation* (3rd ed.). London: Continuum.

G8 Gleneagles 2005. Policy issues. (2005). Retrieved September 19, 2005 from http://www.g8.gov.uk/servlet/Front?pagen-ame=OpenMarket/Xcelerate/Showpage&c+Page.

HINARI. (2005). *Health internetwork access to research initiative*. Retrieved September 15, 2005 from www.healthInter-network.org/.

HIV/AIDS seriously impacts social service delivery. (2004). Retrieved October 19, 2005 from http://irinnews.org/report.asp?ReportID=41814&SelectRegion=Southern_Africa&SelectCountry=SOUTHERN_AFRICA.

Human Development Report. (2003). Retrieved October 17, 2005 from http://hdr.undp.org/reports/global/2003/.

INASP. (2005). *Programme for the enhancement of research information (PERI)*. Retrieved September 25, 2005 from http://www.inasp.info/peri/index.shtml.

Kornegay, F. A., & Landsberg, C. (1998). Can South Africa lead an African Renaissance? In M. Lange (Ed.). *The African renaissance. Occasional Papers* (pp. 29–48). Johannesburg: Konrad Adenauer Stiftung.

Kularatne, E. D. T. (1997). Information needs and information provision in developing countries. *Information for Development, 13*(3), 117–121.

Lor, P. J., & Britz, J. J. (2005). Knowledge production from an African perspective: International information flows and intellectual property. *International Information and Library Review, 37*(2), 61–76.

Mansell, R., & When, U. (Eds.). (1998). *Knowledge societies: Information technology for sustainable development*. Oxford: Oxford University Press.

Mbeki, T. (1998). *The African Renaissance, South Africa and the world: South African Deputy President Thobo Mbeki speaks at the United Nations University*. Retrieved October 17, 2005 from http://www.unu.edu/unupress/mbeki.html.

McInerney, C. (2002). Knowledge management and the dynamic nature of knowledge. *Journal of the American Society for Information Science and Technology, 53*(12), 1009–1018.

Meyer, J. B., Kaplan, D., & Charum, J. (2001). Scientific nomadism and the new geopolitics of knowledge. *International Social Sciences Journal, 168*, 309–321.

NEPAD. (2004). *NEPAD: Three years of progress*. Retrieved July 24, 2005 from http://www.sarpn.org.za/documents/d0000982/P1091-NEPAD_3Years_Oct2004.ppt#256,1,NEPAD.

Networked readiness index rankings. (2003). Retrieved January 12, 2005 from http://www.weforum.org/pdf/Gcr/GITR_2003_2004/Rankings.pdf.

Networked readiness index rankings. (2004). Retrieved January 12, 2005 from http://www.weforum.org/pdf/Global_Competitiveness_Reports/Reports/GITR_2004_2005/Networked_Readiness_Index_Rankings.pdf.

Norris, P. (2001). *Digital divide: Civic engagement, information poverty, and the Internet worldwide*. New York: Cambridge University Press.

OECD. (1999). *The knowledge based economy: A set of facts and figures*. Paris: OECD.

Okundi, P. O. (1976). Pan-African telecommunication network: A case for telecommunications in the development of Africa. *IEEE Transactions on Communications*, *24*(7), 749–754.

Omekwu, C. (2003). Current issues in accessing documents published in developing countries. *Interlending & Document Supply*, *31*(2), 130–137.

Preston, P. (2003). European Union ICT policies. In J. Servaes (Ed.), *Neglected social and cultural dimensions in the European information society: A reality check*. Bristol: Intellect Books.

Puonti, P. & Puranen, P. (2002). *South Africa: Country analyses. Finish Ministry for Foreign Affairs*. Retrieved October 13, 2004 from http://global.finland.fi/koyhyys/aineisto/doc_educationea.doc.

Rowett, J. S. (2005). *Renewing the African University*. Retrieved October 13, 2004 from http://www.aau.org/gc11/adocs/pdf/eng/aau-acu-sauvcaprog.pdf.

Rogers, E. (1995). *Diffusion of Innovations*. New York: Free Press.

Rosenberg, D. (2002). African journals online: Improving awareness and access. *Learned Publishing*, *15*(1), 51–57.

Schaeffer, S. J. (2004). Information Ethics in the Electronic Age. Current issues in Africa and the world. In T. Mendina, & J. J. Britz (Eds.), *Telecommunications infrastructure in the African continent* (pp. 22–27). North Carolina: McFarland.

Schiller, H. I. (1983). The communication revolution: Who benefits? *Media Development*, *4*, 18–20.

Schiller, H. I. (1991). Public information goes corporate. *Library Journal*, *1*(8), 42–45.

Schiller, H. I. (1996). *Information inequality: The deepening social crisis in America*. New York: Routledge.

Science and Development Network. (2003). *African nations agree on science spending targets*. Retrieved October 19, 2005 from http://www.scidev.net/News/index.cfm?fuseaction=readNews&itemid=1095&language=1.

Servaes, J. (2003). The European information society: A wake-up call. In J. Servaes (Ed.), *The European Information Society, a reality check* (pp. 11–32). Bristol: Intellect.

Smith, K. (2002). What is the 'Knowledge Economy'?: Knowledge intensity and distributed knowledge bases. INTECH. Discussion Paper Series. Maastricht: United Nations University.

Smith, R. (2002). Publishing research in developing countries. *Statistics in Medicine*, *21*, 2869–2877.

S.A. National Research Foundation. (2002). *SANSA: South African network of skills abroad*. Retrieved September 1, 2002 from http://sansa.nrf.ac.za/interface/AboutSANSA.htm.

TELEDESIC Streaming Media World. (2001). *Teledesic: A space based Internet.* Retrieved October 19, 2005 from http://www.streamingmediaworld.com/yours/docs/tele-desic/index.html.

Tonukari, N. J. (2004). Research communications in the 21st century. *African Journal of Biotechnology, 3*(2), 123–126.

UNECA. (2005). *United Nations Economic Commission for Africa.* Retrieved October 19, 2005 from http://www.uneca.org/.

United Nations University. (1998). *United Nations University: Higher education and knowledge.* Retrieved October 17, 2005 from http://www.unu.edu/africa/00sps-strengthen.html.

World Bank. (2000). *Can Africa claim the 21st century?* World Bank Report. Washington, DC: The World Bank.

World Bank. (2005). *Ten things you never knew about the World Bank in Africa.* Retrieved June 30, 2005 from http://worldbank.org/tenthings/AFR10-afr.htm.

The World Development Report. (1999). *Entering the 21st century: The World Development Report, 1999/2000.* Retrieved October 19, 2005 from http://www.worldbank.org/wdr/2000/.

World Economic Forum. (2002). *Intellectual infrastructure for the NEPAD: Exploring Africa's advanced knowledge requirements, African Economic Summit.* Retrieved October 12, 2004 from http://www.weforum.org/site/knowledgenavigator.nsf/Content/Intellectual%20Infrastructure%20.

World Economic Forum. (2003). *Gearing Africa for the knowledge economy, African Economic Summit.* Retrieved October 13, 2004 from http://www.weforum.org/site/knowledgenavigator.nsf/Content/Gearing%20Africa%20.

World Markets Research Centre. (2002). *The world in focus 2002.* Retrieved October 19, 2005 from http://www.worldmarketsanalysis.com/InFocus2002/articles/global_overview.html.

World Summit on the Information Society, Plan of Action, Geneva. (2003). Retrieved October 17, 2005 from http://www.itu.int/wsis/docs/geneva/official/poa.html.

Ya'u, Y. Z. (2002). *Confronting the digital divide: An interrogation of the African initiatives at bridging the gap.* Retrieved October 17, 2005 from http://www.codesria.org/Links/conferences/Nepad/yau.pdf.

Further reading

AITECH. (2002). *African IT exhibitions and conferences (AITECH): AITEC releases African communications infrastructure and services report.* Retrieved November 24, 2004 from http://aitecafrica.com/reports/infrastructure/html.

Evers, H. (2001). *Towards a Malaysian knowledge society.* Retrieved October 20, 2004 from http://64.233.161.104/search?q=cache,FfWtZQ3PgCMJ,home.t-online.de/home/hdevers/htm.

United Nations. (2003). *United Nations: Human development report.* New York: Oxford University Press.

World Internet usage and population statistics Internet usage statistics: The big picture. (2004). Retrieved July 24, 2004 from http://www.Internetworldstats.com/stats.htm.

43

DIGITAL DIVIDE RESEARCH, ACHIEVEMENTS AND SHORTCOMINGS

Jan A. G. M. van Dijk

Source: *Poetics* 34(4–5) (2006): 221–35.

Abstract

From the end of the 1990s onwards the digital divide, commonly defined as the gap between those who have and do not
have access to computers and the Internet, has been a central
issue on the scholarly and political agenda of new media
development. This article makes an inventory of 5 years of
digital divide research (2000–2005).

The article focuses on three questions. (1) To what type
of inequality does the digital divide concept refer? (2) What
is new about the inequality of access to and use of ICTs as
compared to other scarce material and immaterial resources?
(3) Do new types of inequality exist or rise in the information
society?

The results of digital divide research are classified under
four successive types of access: motivational, physical, skills
and usage. A shift of attention from physical access to skills and
usage is observed. In terms of physical access the divide seems
to be closing in the most developed countries; concerning
digital skills and the use of applications the divide persists or
widens.

Among the shortcomings of digital divide research are its
lack of theory, conceptual definition, interdisciplinary approach,
qualitative research and longitudinal research.

1. Introduction

In the second half of the 1990s the attention for the subject of unequal
access to and use of the new media started to focus on the concept of the
so-called digital divide. Before that time more general concepts were used
such as information inequality, information gap or knowledge gap and

416

computer or media literacy. The origin of the term digital divide goes back to an unknown American source in the middle of the 1990s and was first used in an official publication by the US Department of Commerce's National Telecommunications and Information Administration (NTIA, 1999). [See Gunkel (2003) for more details about the origin of the term.] The digital divide commonly refers to the gap between those who do and those who do not have access to new forms of information technology. Most often these forms are computers and their networks but other digital equipment such as mobile telephony and digital television are not ruled out by some users of the term.

The term digital divide probably has caused more confusion than clarification. According to Gunkel (2003) it is a deeply ambiguous term in the sharp dichotomy it refers to. Van Dijk (2003, 2005) has warned against a number of pitfalls of this metaphor. First, the metaphor suggests a simple divide between two clearly divided groups with a yawning gap between them. Secondly, it suggests that the gap is difficult to bridge. A third misunderstanding might be the impression that the divide is about absolute inequalities, that is between those included and those excluded. In reality most inequalities of the access to digital technology observed are more of a relative kind (see below). A final wrong connotation might be the suggestion that the divide is a static condition while in fact the gaps observed are continually shifting (also see below). Both Gunkel and van Dijk have emphasized that the term echoes some kind of technological determinism. It is often suggested that the origins of the inequalities referred to lie in the specific problems of getting physical access to digital technology and that achieving such access for all would solve particular problems in the economy and society. In the last suggestion not only a technological bias but also a normative bias is revealed.

The great merit of the sudden rise of the term digital divide at the turn of the century is that it has put the important issue of inequality in the information society on the scholarly and political agenda. Between the years 2000 and 2004 hundreds of scientific and policy conferences and thousands of sessions on regular conferences have been dedicated to this issue under the call of the term digital divide. In the years 2004 and 2005 attention started to decline. In terms of policy and politics many observers, particularly in the rich and developed countries, reached the conclusion that the problem was almost solved as a rapidly increasing majority of their inhabitants obtained access to computers the Internet and other digital technologies.

From a scientific point of view the concept ran into difficulties; ever more expressions such as 'redefining the digital divide' and 'beyond access' appeared. However, this does not mean that the concept has become an empty cover. On the contrary, it is more of a container concept carrying too many meanings. Therefore, as will be done in this article, one should carefully distinguish between different kinds of digital divide, for example in the shape of a number of types of access.

The ambitious purpose of this article is to list and describe the *main* achievements and shortcomings of 5 years of digital divide research (2000–2005). Completeness cannot be attained as the database of articles and books on this topic reaches into the thousands by now. The focus of attention will be both theoretical conceptualisation or model building and empirical investigations. Listing the achievements, the most important facts observed will be summarized. Explaining the shortcomings, ways to go forward with empirical research on this issue will be proposed at the end of this contribution. First, a number of basic questions have to be addressed. Why is the presumed problem of the digital divide an interesting or perhaps even important scientific issue?

2. Three basic questions

According to Amartya Sen every investigator of a problem concerning equality has to answer the question: "Equality of *what*?" (Sen, 1992, p. ix). So, a first basic question would be: *What inequality does the digital divide concept refer to?* A first glance through the social-scientific and economic literature already results in 10 potential answers that can be listed as technological, immaterial, material, social and educational types of (in)equality:

Technological	*Technological opportunities*
Immaterial	Life chances
	Freedom
Material	Capital (economic, social, cultural)
	Resources
Social	Positions
	Power
	Participation
Educational	Capabilities
	Skills

All of these types of inequality can be observed in digital divide research. The most popular still is technological opportunities because physical access to computers, networks and other technologies has achieved the biggest attention. In considering the demographics that are related to digital divides the three forms of capital and resources have been amply used. In the last few years the focus of attention has also shifted to capabilities and skills, particularly when educational solutions to the digital divide problem are proposed.

The presence of all these types of inequality in current digital divide research shows that classical sociological concepts of inequality could still serve as a background. Concepts of inequality in terms of possessions (Marx), status and profession (Weber) or relationship and power (Simmel and Dahrendorf) still prove to be relevant. However, we will notice that they scarcely play any role in digital divide research as it is relatively poor in theory. We may also ask whether these classical sociological concepts are still adequate to explain inequality in the information society. This general question might lead to two other basic questions.

The suggestion in many digital divide investigations is that this phenomenon is just as new as the technology it is linked to. The divides observed are related to age-old demographics of income, education, age, sex and ethnicity but no comparison is made with other things that are unequally divided in contemporary or past societies. Most often a historical perspective is lacking. The following basic question urges itself: *What is exactly new about the inequality of access to and use of information and communication technology as compared to other scarce material and immaterial resources in society?*

When this second question is answered in an affirmative way (there are new aspects to be observed) this could lead to a third question: *Do new types of inequality rise or exist in the information and network society? If so, what are these types?*

These three basic questions will serve as a touchstone for the following summary of results of digital divide research.

3. Achievements of digital divide research

3.1. Types of access

Digital divide research started with the observation of the number and categories of persons who have a computer and network connection at their disposal. This is a case of having a particular technological opportunity. The technological orientation of this early digital divide research led to the equalization of media or technology access with physical access. Currently, the majority of this research still focuses on physical access. However, since the year 2002, an increasing number of researchers suggests to go 'beyond access', to reframe the overly technical concept of the digital divide and to pay more attention to social, psychological and cultural backgrounds. Some have extended the concept of access for this purpose, others have added the concepts of (digital) skills or competencies and media or technology use and applications.

Here, a model that extends the concept of access will be used as a framework to reveal the main achievements of digital divide research (van Dijk, 2003, 2005). See Fig. 1. The succession of types of access that characterizes this model is validated in multivariate research (de Haan and Iedema, in

419

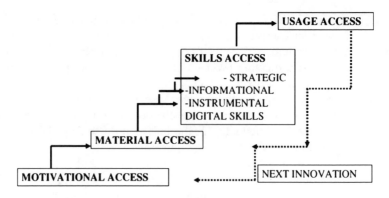

Figure 1 A cumulative and recursive model of successive kinds of access to digital
   technologies.
Source: van Dijk (2005), p. 22.

preparation). This succession is elaborated because media or technology
access should be seen as a *process* with many social, mental and technological causes and not as a single event of obtaining a particular technology
(Bucy and Newhagen, 2004). In this model material access is preceded by
motivational access and succeeded by skills access and usage access. When
the full process of technology appropriation is completed, according to this
ideal scheme, a new innovation arrives and the process starts again, wholly
or partly.

   The concept of material access to appear comprises physical access and
other types of access that are required to reach complete disposal and connections such as conditional access (subscriptions, accounts, pay-per-view).
The concept of skills access is divided into three types of skills that often
assume the following order: first a computer user has to acquire operational
skills, then s(he) has to develop and apply information skills and finally
strategic skills (the capacity to use computer and network sources as means
for particular goals in society). Usage access is the final stage and ultimate
goal of the process of technological appropriation in the shape of particular
applications.

3.2. *Material access*

I will start with the research that has produced data about material access
because this was the predominant focus of attention until fairly recently.
The largest part of digital divide research is devoted to the observation of
divides of physical access to personal computers and the Internet among
demographical categories that are obvious in this respect: income, education, age, sex and ethnicity. The first nation-wide surveys in the developed

countries at the end of the 1990s and the turn of the century all showed growing gaps of access between people with high and low income or education and majority ethnicities as compared to minority ethnicities. However, the gender physical access divide closed in those years, although complete closure only happened in the Northern American and North-Western European countries. Considering age the relationship is curved: physical access culminates in the age group of 25–40 to sharply decline afterwards. Clearly, the youngest generation and women benefit from the household possession of computers, as households are the most familiar survey unit of measurement. The best representative surveys of that period are the first four American NTIA reports (NTIA, 1995, 1998, 1999, 2000, 2002), parts of the annual Eurobarometers (see http://europa.eu.int/comm/public_opinion/index_en.htm) summarized by the SIBIS-project (www.sibis-eu.org), and two OECD-reports (2000, 2001). From the years 2000–2002 onwards the physical access divides in the northern developed countries started to decline as the categories with high income and education reached a partial saturation and people with lower income and education started to catch up (NTIA, 2002; Horrigan and Rainie, 2002a,b; Eurobarometer 56–63, 2001–2005). However, in the developing countries the physical access divide kept widening and is still widening (United Nations Statistics Division, 2004; van Dijk, 2005). In 2000 Norris (2001) surveyed the extent of access to and use of the Internet in 179 nations across the world. A global divide appeared to be evident between industrialized and developing societies. A social divide was apparent between rich and poor within each nation. And within the online community, evidence for a democratic divide was emerging between those who do and do not use Internet resources to engage, mobilize and participate in public life.

Probably, the path of the physical access divide follows the familiar S-curve of the adoption of innovations. However, the path is much more complex and differentiated among groups of the population than the S-curve projects and there are serious problems with mainstream diffusion theory considering computer and Internet technology (see van Dijk, 2005, p. 62–65). One of these problems is treated by Norris (2001) who makes a distinction between a normalization and a stratification model of diffusion. In the normalization model it is presupposed that the differences between groups only increase in the early stages of adoption and that differences disappear with saturation in the last stages. The stratification model assumes that (1) there is a different point of departure of the access curve for the higher and the lower social strata and (2) a different point of arrival: for some strata it might never reach 90–100%.

The two models lead to quite different projections of the evolution of the digital divide from the current situation. Fig. 2 compares the curves of adoption of the highest and the lowest social strata in the developed countries and it suggests a potential trend. Fig. 2 shows how the curves are becoming

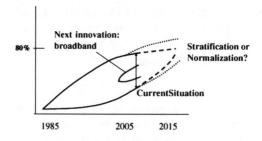

Figure 2 Real and potential trend of the digital divide in terms of physical access to computers and the Internet according to a stratification model versus a normalization model of development.
Source: van Dijk (2005), p. 68.

more convex suggesting the (almost complete) closure of the physical access divide if a normalization model applies, and the continuation of a gap in case the stratification model applies.

At the time of writing (2005) I would estimate from all the available statistics that there is still a gap of about 50% between the highest and the lowest social strata (90% diffusion as compared to 40% diffusion) in the *most developed* countries and that in these countries approximately 25–30% of the total population still has no home access to computers and the Internet at all. In less developed countries this figure swiftly increases to reach a majority and in Third World countries it is a vast majority of 90, 95 or even more percent of the population.

What are the most important background characteristics of the physical access divide? Usually they are presented in descriptive statistics of simple correlations. Then it appears that the highly correlated variables of income, education and occupation are the most important ones. Multivariate regression analyses with structural equation models are much less frequent. Such analysis was made in a large-scale representative Dutch survey in 2000 (van Dijk, L. *et al.*, 2000) later summarized in English (de Haan, 2003). It appeared at that time that income was the most important factor for physical access, followed by age (with as mentioned above its curvilinearity), and then education. With the declining costs of computer equipment in recent years the importance of income has been somewhat reduced but it remains the most important factor for material access because total computer and Internet access costs (peripherals, printing costs, software, subscriptions and connection costs) barely diminish. In poor countries lack of income remains the decisive barrier.

The background variables mentioned reveal that types of inequality such as those based on differences in economic, social, and cultural capital are prevalent in digital divide research aimed at explaining differences in physical access. Other researchers defend a resource based approach (van Dijk,

2000; de Haan, 2003; Dutta-Bergman, 2005). Van Dijk (2005) combines a resource based and a social position or network approach. Differences in physical access are related to a distribution of resources (temporal, mental, material, social and cultural) that in turn can be accounted for by ascribed categories such as age, sex, intelligence, personality and ability and positions in society (labour, education and household position). The main consequence of the digital divide, defined in this way, is more or less participation in the most relevant fields of society (economy, politics, culture, spatial mobility, social institutions, social networks and communities). For example, as Dutta-Bergman shows, a particular type of physical access, (easy) public Internet access in communities is related to participation in this community.

3.3. Motivational access

Prior to physical access comes the wish to have a computer and to be connected to the Internet. Many of those who remain at the 'wrong' side of the digital divide have motivational problems. With regard to digital technology it appears that there are not only 'have-nots', but also 'want-nots'. In the age of the Internet hype this was a much neglected phenomenon. Research among non-users and the unconnected is relatively scarce. At the turn of the century German and American surveys (ARD-ZDF, 1999a and NTIA, 2000) showed that the main reasons for the refusal to use computers and get connected to the Internet were:

* no need or significant usage opportunities;
* no time or liking;
* rejection of the medium (the Internet and computer games as 'dangerous' media);
* lack of money;
* lack of skills.

In several European and American surveys reported between 1999 and 2003 it was revealed that half of the respondents unconnected to the Internet at that time explicitly responded that they would refuse to get connected, for the list of reasons just mentioned (e.g. ARD-ZDF, 1999b and a Pew Internet and American Life survey (Lenhart et al., 2003).

One of the most confusing myths produced by popular ideas about the digital divide is that people are either in or out, included or excluded. The Pew survey revealed that the Internet population is ever shifting (Lenhart et al., 2003). First, there are so-called intermittent users: in 2002 between 27 and 44% of American Internet users stated that they had gone offline for extended periods. A second, often unnoticed, group is the dropouts that lost connection to the Internet. Their number was 10% of the American population in 2002. The next group is the 'net-evaders' (about 8% in this survey) that simply refuses to use the Internet, whether they have the resources or not. Among them we find older managers ordering their secretaries to use email and search the Internet and persons being proud of not using that 'filthy medium' or computers that are related to 'women's work').

The ever-shifting Internet population focuses our attention on a second, perhaps even more influential myth produced by the misleading dichotomy of the digital divide. This is the assumption that those who have a computer or Internet connection are actually using it. Many presumed users use the computer or the Internet only once a week or a couple of times a month, a few people never use them. Measuring computer and Internet access in survey questions often conflates possession or connection with use or usage time. Time diary studies and the like show much larger differences or divides between categories of people as will be argued with usage access below (see Section 3.5, below). Here the (allegedly vanished) physical access gap of gender in some Western countries appears to be all but closed. On the contrary, with actual computer and Internet usage gender differences are getting more pronounced.

The factors explaining motivational access are both of a social or cultural and a mental or psychological nature. A primary social explanation is that "the Internet does not have appeal for low-income and low-educated people" (Katz and Rice, 2002, p. 93). To dig deeper into the reasons for this lack of interest it seems appropriate to complete large-scale surveys with qualitative studies in local communities and cultural groups. This was done for instance by Laura Stanley in a San Diego study in poor Latino and African American working class neighbourhoods (Stanley, 2001), and by the University of Texas in poor communities of Austin (Rojas et al., 2004). They discovered the importance of traditional masculine cultures (rejecting computer work that is not 'cool' and 'something girls do') and of particular minority and working class lifestyles.

However, most pronounced are mental and psychological explanations. Here the phenomena of computer anxiety and technophobia come forward. Computer anxiety is a feeling of discomfort, stress, or fear experienced when confronting computers (Brosnan, 1998; Chua et al., 1999; Rockwell and Singleton, 2002). Technophobia is a fear of technology in general and a distrust in its beneficial effects. According to a representative UCLA survey of 2003 more than 30% of new American Internet users reported that they were moderately to highly technophobic and the same applied to 10% of experienced Internet users (UCLA, 2003, p. 25). Computer anxiety and technophobia are major barriers of computer and Internet access, especially among seniors, people with low educational level and a part of the female population. These phenomena do not completely disappear with a rise in computer experience.

The continuation of anxiety is partly explained by personality character-istics. The Big Five personality dimensions (agreeableness, conscientiousness, neuroticism, extraversion, and openness) are known to be related to computer use, attitude and stress. For example, neuroticism aggravates problems experienced in approaching and using computers and extraversion alleviates them. See Hudiburg (1999) and Finn and Korukonda (2004) for the person-ality dimensions related to computer use.

3.4. Skills access

After having acquired the motivation to use computers and some kind of physical access to them, one has to learn to manage the hardware and software. Here the problem of a lack of skills might appear according to the model in Fig. 1. This problem is framed with terms such as 'computer, information or multimedia literacy' and 'computer skills' or 'information capital'. Steyaert (2000) and van Dijk (1999, 2003, 2005) introduced the concept of 'digital skills' as a succession of three types of skill. The most basic are 'instrumental skills' (Steyaert) or 'operational skills' (van Dijk), the capacities to work with hardware and software. These skills have acquired much attention in the literature and in public opinion. The most popular view is that skills problems are solved when these skills are mas-tered. However, many scholars engaged with information processing in an information society have called attention to all kinds of information skills required to successfully use computers and the Internet. Steyaert distin-guishes between 'structural skills' and 'strategic skills'. van Dijk proposes a comparable distinction between 'information skills' and 'strategic skills'. Information skills are the skills to search, select, and process information in computer and network sources. Two types of information skills are required: formal information skills (ability to work with the formal charac-teristics of computers and the Internet, e.g. file and hyperlink structures) and substantial information skills (ability to find, select, process, and evaluate information in specific sources following specific questions). See van Dijk (2005, p. 81). Strategic skills can be defined as the capacities to use computer and network sources as the means for particular goals and for the general goal of improving one's position in society.

Research on these kinds of digital skills is scarce. Actually, the only data available bear on people's command of operational skills. Institutions offering computer courses sometimes record the achievements of course takers. Some national surveys that ask population samples to report about their computer and Internet skills are available (for example van Dijk, L. *et al.*, 2000; Park, 2002; UCLA, 2001, 2003). Mostly, they only pay attention to the command of hardware and software, not to information skills. However, the biggest problem of these surveys is validity: are self-reports valid measurements of actual skills possessed? In one of the UCLA Internet studies 63% of respondents declared they had good or excellent abilities to use the Internet (UCLA, 2003, p. 24), while a much more specific Dutch measurement of (mainly operational) digital skills by self-reports showed that actually only working young males below 40 reached a 6 on a nine-point scale and other groups a 2 to 5 (CBS/SCP, 2001).

The other, much better, scientific approach is to organize performance tests in controlled environments. So far, the only experiments we know of are those by the new media researcher and sociologist Eszter Hargittai. For her dissertation, she conducted a series of experimental tests with American user groups charged with the task of finding particular types of information on the Internet (Hargittai, 2002, 2003, 2004). Thus, she was able to measure both formal and substantial information skills. Subjects were selected and matched according to age, sex and education. Enormous differences were found in the measure of accomplishment and time needed to finish these tasks. Only half of the experimental group was able to complete all tasks in the first experiment, but for some subjects time required for a particular task was a few seconds while others needed 7–14 min (Hargittai, 2002).

The general impression of these skills investigations, both surveys and tests is (1) that the divides of skills access are bigger than the divides of physical access and (2) that, while physical access gaps are more or less closing in the developed countries, the skills gap (in particular, regarding information skills) tends to grow. A striking result is that those having a high level of traditional literacy also possess a high level of digital information skills (van Dijk, L. *et al.*, 2000; de Haan, 2003). These skills appear to be more important for computer and Internet use than technical know how and the capacity to deal with numerical data.

Another striking result from digital skills research is that people learn more of these skills in practice, by trial and error, than in formal educational settings (de Haan and Huysmans, 2002; van Dijk, 2005). The social context and social networking of computer and Internet users appear to be decisive factors in the opportunities they have for learning digital skills.

Asking for differences in strategic skills has not been an explicit research question yet. Talking about these skills means making a transition to the actual usage of digital media and how this usage may lead to more or less participation in several fields of society.

3.5. *Usage access*

Actual usage of digital media is the final stage and ultimate goal of the total process of appropriation of technology that is called access in this article. Having sufficient motivation, physical access and skills to apply digital media are necessary but not sufficient conditions of actual use. Usage has its own grounds or determinants. As a dependent factor it can be measured in at least four ways:

1   usage time;
2   usage applications and diversity;
3   broadband or narrowband use;
4   more or less active or creative use.

Current computer and Internet use statistics are notoriously unreliable with their shifting and divergent operational definitions of use (see below), most often made by market research bureaus. They only give some indication of how much actual use differs from physical access. For example, according to the market researcher Nielsen/NetRatings, between one-third and two-thirds of those connected to the Internet in a large number of countries are using the Internet only once a month (see: http://www.clickz. com/stats/web_worldwide/). Though one may doubt these low figures, most observers would agree that actual use diverges from potential use. More exact measures of daily, weekly or monthly Internet use are reported in the annual surveys of the Pew Internet and American Life Project (www. pewinternet.org) and the UCLA Internet Reports (www.digitalcenter.org). However, the most valid and reliable estimations of actual usage time are made in detailed daily time diary studies that are representative for a particular country. They sometimes produce striking results. For example, the Dutch Social and Cultural Planning Agency found in a 2001 time diary study that the number of weekly hours of computer and Internet use of males was double that of females (SCP, 2001). The gender physical access gap may have almost been closed in the Netherlands, but this certainly does not apply to the usage gender gap.

Comparable results appear in surveys relating usage applications to demographic characteristics of users (see for the US Howard *et al.*, 2001; Horrigan and Rainie, 2002a; UCLA Center for Communication Policy, 2003). Specific social categories of users prefer different kinds of applications. These studies all show significant differences among users with different social class, education, age, gender and ethnicity. Some investigators (van Dijk, 1999, 2000, 2003, 2004; Bonfadelli, 2002; Park, 2002; Cho *et al.*, 2003) even perceive a so-called *usage gap* between people differing in social class and education that is comparable to the phenomenon of the knowledge gap that has been observed from the 1970s onwards. While the knowledge gap is about the differential derivation of knowledge from the mass media, the usage gap is a broader thesis about a differential use of whole applications in daily practices. Van Dijk (2005, p. 130) observes 'the first signs of a usage gap between people of high social position, income, and education using the advanced computer and Internet applications for information, communication, work, business, or education and people of low social position, income, and education using simpler applications for information, communication, shopping, and entertainment'.

Usage of narrowband versus broadband connections appears to have a strong effect on usage time and on the type and range of applications. People with broadband connections take much more advantage of the opportunities of the new media. They are much less deterred by the costs of connection time; they use many more applications and for a longer time (Horrigan and Rainie, 2002b; UCLA, 2003). A 'broadband elite' arises that uses the connection for 10 or more online activities on a typical day (Horrigan and Rainie). Finally, broadband stimulates a much more active and creative use of the Internet (Idem).

Despite its image of being interactive, most Internet usage, apart from emailing, is relatively passive and consuming. Active and creative use of the Internet, that is, contributions to the Internet by users themselves, is a minority phenomenon. Active contributions are publishing a personal website, creating a weblog, posting a contribution on an online bulletin board, newsgroup or community and perhaps, in a broad definition, exchanging music and video files. In USA, 20% of online Americans produced such content in 2002 in a narrow definition and 44% in 2003 in a broad definition (Lenhart et al., 2003, 2004).

A general conclusion from a number of investigations of usage is that, increasingly, all familiar social and cultural differences in society are reflected in computer and Internet use.

4. Starting to find answers to the basic questions

In light of the information of access types, we may consider whether and to what extent current digital divide research has addressed the basic questions mentioned in Section 2. A general qualification is that it has only started to address these issues. This is due to the theoretical weakness of digital divide research, the main shortcomings of which will be discussed in the next section. In digital divide research, the notion of inequality mostly refers to inequality of technological opportunities. This is due to the fact that in the first years of digital divide research priority was given to physical access; besides, technological determinism, the view that everything could be fixed through a technological approach, played a role. From 2002 onwards the calls to go beyond (physical) access have led to social scientific, communication and educational research emphasizing inequality of social, cultural and information capital and resources. Additionally, some have called attention to the inequality of positions and power in social networks that could lead to unequal participation in several fields of society. Subsequently, attention shifted to inequalities of skills, capabilities and interests when research started to deal with the large-scale incorporation of digital media in daily life, in this way reflecting all social and cultural differences in society.

Contemporary digital divide research has much more difficulty in providing answers to the second basic question, the question of what is exactly new about the inequality of access to and use of information and communication technology as compared to other scarce material and immaterial resources in society. In seeking to answer this question, we presume the characterization of contemporary society as an information society to be fruitful. In that context we can call attention to the effects of information as a source of inequality. The literature refers to three effects of information that serve as a basis of inequality.

First, information is considered to be a *primary good* (see Rawls, 1971 and Sen, 1985). Primary goods are material and immaterial goods that are so essential for the survival and self-respect of individuals that they can not be exchanged for other goods, such as a basic (survival) level of income, life chances, freedoms and fundamental rights. Information has become a primary good in contemporary society even though the minimum amount that is required appears hard to assess and is likely to differ according to the type of society. Not all people possess such a minimum, for example (functional) illiterates. When digital media are gradually replacing and surpassing analogue print media, traditional illiterates are joined by a new category, the 'digital illiterates'.

Even more important than this absolute type of inequality in processing information is the increasing role of relative differences in possessing and controlling information in an information society. According to Castells (1996) information has become an independent source of productivity and power. Van Dijk (2005) adds that the relative differences between social categories, that were already unequal in terms of 'old' types of resources and capital, are amplified by the use of digital media. This happens because the control of positions in an increasingly complex society and the possession of information and strategic skills to acquire and maintain these positions are increasingly unequally divided. In this way digital media usage contributes to new types of absolute and relative inequality on top of the old ones, or they reinforce them.

This is backed by another characteristic of information. It can also be a *positional good* (Hirsch, 1976). These are goods that, by definition, are scarce. Despite the phenomenon of information overload in society, information can be scarce in particular circumstances. Some positions in society create better opportunities than others in gathering, processing and using valuable information. This condition appears to be becoming increasingly important in the nascent network society (van Dijk, 1999, 2005). In this kind of society, the positions people have in social and media networks determines their potential power. As the importance of the media networks created by computers and their networks increases in contemporary society, having no position in these networks, or a marginal one, entails social exclusion. Contrary to that, those that are very much included because they do have a central position, the so-called information elite, increase their power, capital and resources. So, this is a second effect of the possession of information in the information and network society that amplifies old inequalities.

A third amplifying effect comes from *information as a source of skills*. Investigators of the Dutch CPB (Netherlands Bureau of Economic Policy Analysis) have shown in an international comparative and historical survey of labour markets that the successful appropriation of ICTs creates a so-called 'skills premium' (Nahuis and de Groot, 2003). On the basis of very extensive quantitative longitudinal data of a large number of countries they argue that the skills premium of having ICT skills is one of the main causes of increasing income inequality in these countries in the 1980s and 1990s.

5. Shortcomings of digital divide research and ways to compensate them in empirical research

Attempts to answer the basic questions discussed above are very scarce. The main reason is that digital divide research suffers from a *lack of theory*. In the past 5–10 years, it has remained at a descriptive level, emphasizing the demographics of income, education, age, sex, and ethnicity. The deeper social, cultural, and psychological causes behind the inequality of access have not been addressed so far. The most conspicuous fact is that the digital divide has not been discussed against the background of a general theory of social inequality, other types of inequality, or even a concept of human inequality in general. A theoretical background that has played a minor role is the diffusion of innovations theory. (See Mason and Hacker (2003) for the small role of communication theory.) However, many criticisms of innovations theory can be listed when applied to digital divide research (see van Dijk, 2005, p. 62–66). Its most important popular expressions, the so-called S-curve and the trickle-down principle of the adoption of innovations – from the higher to the lower social strata –, pose serious problems, and they bear a determinist flavour. Recent digital divide research has reached the stage of causal model building and structural equation modelling. This is the most important way to go ahead. However, for this purpose explicit theories are urgently required.

A second problem is the lack of *interdisciplinary research*. Following the usual demographics and the emphasis on physical access, there is a preponderance of sociological and economic research. Contributions from psychology and even from communication and education studies are relatively small (Bucy and Newhagen, 2004; Mason and Hacker, 2003). However, the summary of achievements of digital divide research in Section 3 has shown that the digital divide cannot be understood without addressing issues such as attitudes toward technology (e.g. technophobia and computer anxiety), the channels used in new media diffusion, educational views of digital skills, and cultural analyses of lifestyles and daily usage patterns.

The next lacuna is a lack of *qualitative research*. Most digital divide research is based on quantitative data collection and tries to describe the large picture of the problem. Although this produces vast amounts of correlations, it does not bring forward the precise mechanisms explaining the appropriation and division of the technology concerned in everyday life. Qualitative research, such as that of Laura Stanley in poor San Diego communities mentioned above is able to show how attitudes to computer and Internet use are created and how inequalities of motivational, physical, skills and usage access are maintained in particular small individual and group settings where interpersonal relations and particular cultures dominate.

The fourth basic problem with digital divide research is that it is rather static, both in arguments produced and in empirical data used. There is a lack of *dynamic approach* (van Dijk and Hacker, 2003). For example, according to the trickle-down principle of diffusion theory, present technologies such as personal computers and an Internet connection will soon be available to all because they are getting cheaper and easier to use by the day. Such reasoning seems dynamic, but actually it is static, because one forgets that the technology is changing fast and that the people who first adopted it do not stop to obtain new technologies and skills. As soon as the laggards have caught up, the forerunners have already moved further ahead and are using a more advanced technology. Concerning the data used in digital divide research, annual cross-sections in time are common, but longitudinal data are scarce. They are only starting to appear now in regular or annual replicated survey research.

A fifth flaw of digital divide research is insufficient attention paid to the consequences of the digital divide(s) observed. Are these consequences to be sought in more or less participation in several fields of society, or in more or less utilization of new technological opportunities? The solution of this problem requires answers to the three basic questions discussed in this article. Simultaneously it calls for extensive empirical research, first of all longitudinal research and multivariate analyses, of the relationships between all kinds of access explained above and social behaviour.

A final and most serious omission of current digital divide research is the lack of *conceptual elaboration and definition*. Filling this gap is the most urgent task. Unfortunately, even the most basic terms and concepts are still ill defined. The most important seems to be the concept of access itself (see Bucy and Newhagen, 2004). Others are exact definitions of the technology concerned and the way it is used. What exactly is a computer and an Internet connection? What precisely is having access to the Internet and what parameters are insufficient to the phrase having access? What is computer literacy or what are the so-called digital skills and similar terms? What exactly is Internet use? Better definitions of these concepts backed by theory and valid operational definitions for empirical research would considerably support the achievements of digital divide research in the next 5 years.

References

ARD/ZDF-Arbeitsgruppe Multimedia, 1999a. ARD/ZDF-online-studie 1999: Wird online alltagsmedium? [ARD/ZDF online study: Is online becoming an everyday medium?]. Media Perspektiven, 1999. Nr. 8, 388–409.

ARD/ZDF-Arbeitsgruppe Multimedia, 1999b. Nichtnutzer von online: Einstellungen und zugangsbarrieren. Ergebnisse der ARD/ZDF-offline-studie 1999 [Online non-users: Attitudes and access barriers. Results of the ARD/ZDF offline study 1999]. Media Perspektiven, 1999. Nr. 8, 415–422.

Bonfadelli, H., 2002. The Internet and knowledge gaps: a theoretical and empirical investigation. European Journal of Communication 17 (1), 65–84.

Brosnan, M. J., 1998. The impact of computer anxiety and self-efficacy upon performance. Journal of Computer Assisted Learning 14, 223–234.

Bucy, E., Newhagen, J. (Eds.), 2004. Media Access: Social and Psychological Dimensions of New Technology Use. LEA, London.

Castells, M., 1996. The Information Age: Economy, Society and Culture. Vol. I. The Rise of the Network Society. Blackwell, Oxford, England.

CBS/SCP (Centraal Bureau voor de Statistiek/Sociaal-Cultureel Planbureau), 2001. ICT-Pilot 2001. CBS/SCP, Rijswijk, Netherlands.

Cho, J., de Zúñiga, H., Rojas, H., Shah, D., 2003. Beyond access: the digital divide and Internet uses and gratifications. IT & Society 1 (4), 46–72.

Chua, S. L., Chen, D. T., Wong, A. F. L., 1999. Computer anxiety and its correlates: a meta-analysis. Computers in Human Behavior 15, 609–623.

de Haan, J., Huysmans, F., 2002. Van huis uit digitaal: Verwerving van digitale vaardigheden tussen thuismilieu en school [Raised digital: The acquisition of digital skills between home and school environment]. The Hague: Sociaal en Cultureel Planbureau. Retrieved June 25, 2004. from http:/www.scp.nl/publicaties/boeken/9037700896.shtml.

de Haan, Jos, 2003. IT and social inequality in the Netherlands. IT & Society 1 (4), 27–45.

de Haan, Jos, Iedema, J. (in preparation). Models of access to the information society. New Media & Society.

Dutta-Bergman, M., 2005. Access to the Internet in the context of community participation and community satisfaction. New Media and Society 7, 89–109.

Eurobarometer, 2002–2005. Standard Eurobarometer 56–63. Retrieved September 8, 2005, from http://europa.eu.int/comm/public_opinion/index_en.htm.

Finn, S., Korukonda, A. R., 2004. Avoiding computers: does personality play a role? In: Bucy, E., Newhagen, J. (Eds.), Media Access: Social and Psychological Dimensions of New Technology Use. LEA, London, pp. 73–90.

Gunkel, D., 2003. Second thoughts: toward a critique of the digital divide. New Media & Society 5 (4), 499–522.

Hargittai, Eszter, 2002. The second-level digital divide: differences in people's online skills. First Monday: Peer-Reviewed Journal on the Internet, 7(4). Retrieved August 31, 2004, from http://firstmonday.org/issues/issue7_4/hargittai/.

Hargittai, Eszter, 2003. The digital divide and what to do about it. In: D. C. Jones (Ed.). The New Economy Handbook. Academic Press, San Diego, CA. Retrieved August 31, 2004, from http://www.princeton.edu/~eszter/research/c04-digitaldivide.html.

Hargittai, Eszter, 2004. How wide a web? Social inequality in the digital age. Ph.D. dissertation, Princeton, NJ, Princeton University, Sociology Department.

Hirsch, F., 1976. The Social Limits to Growth. Routledge & Kegan Paul, London.

Horrigan, J., Rainie, L., 2002a. Getting serious online: as Americans gain experience, they pursue more serious activities. Washington DC: Pew Internet and American Life Project. Retrieved August 28, 2004, from http://www.pewinternet.org.

Horrigan, J., Rainie, L., 2002b. The broadband difference: how online behavior changes with high-speed Internet connections. Washington DC: Pew Internet and American Life Project. Retrieved August 28, 2004, from http://www.pewinternet. org.

Howard, P., Rainie, L., Jones, S., 2001. Days and nights on the Internet: the impact of a diffusing technology. In: Wellman, B., Haythornthwaite, C. (Eds.), The Internet in Everyday Life. Blackwell, Oxford, England, pp. 45–73.

Hudiburg, R. A., 1999. Preliminary investigation of computer stress and the big five personality factors. Psychology Reports 85, 473–480.

Katz, J. E., Rice, R. E., 2002. Social Consequences of Internet Use, Access, Involvement and Interaction. MIT Press, Cambridge, MA.

Lenhart, A., Horrigan, J., Rainie, L., Allen, K., Boyce, A., Madden, M., et al., 2003. The ever-shifting Internet population: A new look at Internet access and the digital divide. Washington, DC: Pew Internet and American Life Project. Retrieved August 28, 2004, from http://www.pewinternet.org.

Lenhart, A., Fallows, D., Horrigan, J., 2004. Content creation online. Washington, DC: Pew Internet and American Life Project. Retrieved August 28, 2004, from http://www.pewinternet.org.

Mason, S., Hacker, K., 2003. Applying communication theory to digital divide research. IT & Society 5 (5), 40–55.

Nahuis, R., de Groot, H., 2003. Rising skill premia: you ain't seen nothing yet (CPB discussion paper no. 20). The Hague, Netherlands: Centraal Plan Bureau, Netherlands Bureau for Economic Policy Analysis. Retrieved February 7, 2004, from http://ideas.repec.org/p/cpb/discus/20.html.

Norris, P., 2001. Digital Divide, Civic Engagement Information Poverty and the Internet Worldwide. Cambridge University Press, Cambridge, England.

NTIA (National Telecommunications and Information Administration), July 1995. Falling through the Net: A survey of the "have nots" in rural and urban America. Retrieved September 29, 2004, from http://www.ntia.doc.gov/ntiahome/ fallingthru.html.

NTIA (National Telecommunications and Information Administration), 1998. Falling through the Net II: New data on the digital divide. Retrieved September 29, 2004, from http://www.ntia.doc.gov/ntiahome/net2/.

NTIA 1999 (National Telecommunications and Information Administration), 1999. Falling through the Net: defining the digital divide. Retrieved September 29, 2004, from http://www.ntia.doc.gov/ntiahome/fttn99/contents.html.

NTIA 2000 (National Telecommunications and Information Administration), 2000. Falling through the Net II: toward digital inclusion. Retrieved September 29, 2004, from http://www.ntia.doc.gov/ntiahome/fttn00/contents00.html.

NTIA (National Telecommunications and Information Administration), 2002. A nation online: how Americans are expanding their use of the Internet. Retrieved September 29, 2004, from http://www.ntia.doc.gov/ntiahome/dn/index.html.

OECD, 2000. The digital divide: diffusion and use of ICT's. Paris, OECD.

OECD, 2001. Understanding the digital divide. Paris, OECD.

Park, Han W., 2002. The digital divide in South Korea: closing and widening divides in the 1990s. Electronic Journal of Communication/Revue de Communication Electronique, 12(1 & 2). Retrieved September 28, 2004, from http://www.cios.org/www/ejc.

Rawls, J., 1971. Theory of Justice. Harvard University Press, Cambridge, MA.

Rockwell, S., Singleton, L., 2002. The effects of computer anxiety and communication apprehension on the adoption and utilization of the Internet. Electronic Journal of Communication/Revue de Communication Electronique, 12(1). Retrieved June 12, 2004, from http://www.cios.org/www/ejc.

Rojas, V., Straubhaar, J., Roychowdhury, D., Okur, O., 2004. Communities, cultural capital and the digital divide. In: Bucy, E., Newhagen, J. (Eds.), Media Access: Social and Psychological Dimensions of New Technology Use. LEA, London, pp. 107–130.

SCP (Sociaal en Cultureel Planbureau), 2001. Trends in de tijd [Trends in time] The Hague, Netherlands SCP.

Sen, A., 1985. Commodities and Capabilities. North-Holland, Amsterdam.

Sen, A., 1992. Inequality Reexamined. Oxford University Press, Oxford, England.

Stanley, L., 2001. Beyond access. Retrieved March 11, 2004, from www.mediamanage.net/Beyond_Access.pdf.

Steyaert, J., 2000. Digitale vaardigheden: Geletterdheid in de informatiesamenleving [Digital skills: Literacy in the information society]. Rathenau Instituut, The Hague, Netherlands.

UCLA, University of California, Los Angeles, Center for Communication Policy, 2001. The UCLA Internet report 2001: Surveying the digital future, year two. Los Angeles: Author. Retrieved March 2, 2004, from http://www.ccp.ucla.edu/pages/internet-report.asp.

UCLA, University of California, Los Angeles, Center for Communication Policy, 2003. The UCLA Internet report: Surveying the digital future, year three. Los Angeles: Author. Retrieved March 2, 2004, from http://www.ccp.ucla.edu/pages/internet-report.asp.

United Nations Statistics Division, 2004. Millennium indicators database: Personal Computers and Internet users per 100 population (ITU estimates). Retrieved March 11, 2004, from http://millenniumindicators.un.org/unsd/mi/mi_indicator_xrxx.asp?ind_code=48.

van Dijk, Jan, 1999. The Network Society: Social Aspects of New Media. Sage Publications, London.

van Dijk, Jan, 2000. Widening information gaps and policies of prevention. In: Hacker, K., van Dijk, J. (Eds.), Digital Democracy: Issues of Theory and Practice. Sage Publications, London, pp. 166–183.

van Dijk, Jan, 2003. A framework for digital divide research. Electronic Journal of Communication/Revue de Communication Electronique, 12(1). Retrieved September 30, 2004, from http://www.cios.org/getfile/vandijk_.

van Dijk, Jan A. G. M., 2004. Divides in succession: possession, skills, and use of new media for societal participation. In: Bucy, E., Newhagen, J. (Eds.), Media Access: Social and Psychological Dimensions of New Technology Use. LEA, London, pp. 233–254.

van Dijk, Jan A. G. M., 2005. The Deepening Divide Inequality in the Information Society. Sage Publications, Thousand Oaks CA/London/New Delhi.

van Dijk, Jan A. G. M., Hacker, K., 2003. The digital divide as a complex and dynamic phenomenon. Information Society 19, 315–326.

van Dijk, Liset, J., de Haan, J., Rijken, S., 2000. Digitalisering van de leefwereld: Een onderzoek naar informatie en communicatietechnologie en sociale ongelijkheid [Digitization of everyday life: A survey of information and communication technology and social inequality]. The Hague, Netherlands: Sociaal en Cultureel Planbureau. Retrieved June 25, 2004, from http://www.scp.nl/publicaties/boeken/905749518X.shtml.

Part 6

WIDESPREAD ORGANIZATIONAL CHANGE

44

COMPUTERIZATION AND SOCIAL TRANSFORMATIONS*

Rob Kling

Source: *Science, Technology, & Human Values* 16(3) (1991): 342–67.

This article examines the relationship between the use of computer-based systems and transformations in parts of the social order. Answers to this question rest heavily on the way computer-based systems are *consumed* — not just produced or disseminated. The discourse about computerization advanced in many professional magazines and the mass media is saturated with talk about "revolution," and yet substantial social changes are often difficult to identify in carefully designed empirical studies. The article examines qualitative case studies of computerization in welfare agencies, urban planning, accounting, marketing, and manufacturing to examine the ways that computerization alters social life in varied ways: sometimes restructuring relationships and in other cases reinforcing existing social relationships. The article also examines some of the theoretical issues in studies of computerization, such as drawing boundaries. It concludes with some observations about the sociology of computer science as an academic discipline.

The question of social transformation

One of the fascinating and important sociological questions surrounding computerization is the extent to which the use of computer-based systems really transforms any part of the social order — and if so, how? Answers to this question rest heavily on the way computer-based systems are *consumed* — not just produced or disseminated. This question differs from the central focus of the sociology of technology on the conditions that produce differing technologies and the character of technological alternatives (e.g., Bijker, Hughes, and Pinch 1987).[1] In my view, it is a fundamental question, since social studies of technology gain their public value by shedding light on the consequences of social groups using various technologies. Moreover, if we want technologists to take the social consequences of their designs into account, some group should be producing reliable studies to help inform their actions. Whether and how the widespread use of computer-based systems transforms parts of the social order are just two of the fascinating questions about the social consequences of computerization. But they have attracted attention and stimulated significant discussion.

Studies of computerization and the quality of working life are one domain in which scholars and professionals have raised questions about social transformations attributable to computerization. In addition to a large body of specialized research studies (cf. Attewell 1987a, 1987b; Dunlop and Kling forthcoming; Danziger and Kraemer 1986), several authors have addressed this question in books with a broad historical sweep and bold theorizing. In *Information Payoff: The Transformation of Work in The Electronic Age*, Strassman (1985) argues that computerization will make work more varied, interesting, and flexible. In contrast, in *Work Transformed*, Shaiken (1986) argues that (under capitalism), managers routinely computerize so as to increase their control by fragmenting and deskilling jobs. Zuboff's (1988) *In the Age of the Smart Machine: The Future of Work and Power* describes case studies of clerks and blue-collar workers — all of whom found their work made more abstract, confusing, and socially isolating after computerization projects. Each of these authors argues that computerization transforms work, but each identifies different typical changes. Each of these authors attempts to characterize computerization within a single overarching logic. The boldness of the accounts is daunting, and yet each author's evidence seems carefully selected to fit his or her logic of social change.[2]

There are now a large number of social studies of topics such as computerization and work, the practices of software developers using artificial intelligence, the use of computer-based models in policy making, the relationship between computerization and the structure of organizations, and computerization and shifts of power. I find the best-quality studies are often relatively micro in scale. There are tens of thousands of settings in which people and organizations computerize; these vary in social scale, ecology of social interests and their balance of power, relevant ideologies, technical and economic options, and so on. We therefore have trouble assembling a credible composite historical portrait of the links between computerization and the larger social order.

Although their social roles are the subject of immense hype, computer-based technologies are potentially socially transformative (Kling and Iacono 1990). By transformative, I mean that they can play key roles in restructuring major social relationships — interpersonal, intergroup, and institutional. Computer systems can restructure social relationships by altering the kinds of information readily available, reorganizing patterns of access to information, altering the cost and work of organizing information, and shifting patterns of social dependencies for key resources, such as computing and skilled computing staff. Whether computer-based systems have been integrated into social settings so as to transform them, reinforce patterns of preexisting social relationships, or have negligible influence is still the subject of research. Moreover, the systemic character of the transformations that do occur is still unclear. Computerization also raises questions about value conflicts and social choices that participants often do not seem to understand very well. Articulating these social choices is a potential contribution of scholars who do social studies of science and technology.

I will examine some of the attempts my colleagues and I have made to work on questions like these through a 20-year program of research at the University of California, Irvine (UCI), on the social aspects of computerization. We did not conduct these in scholarly isolation, although the active research community was tiny when we began. I have published integrated reviews of social studies of computerization elsewhere that identify key lines of work and theoretical perspectives of the larger research community (Kling 1980, 1989; Dunlop and Kling forthcoming).

In the early 1970s, I teamed up with Kenneth Kraemer, a scholar of public administration, and Jim Danziger, a political scientist, to study the social impacts of computing through a series of empirical studies of computerization in organizations. The researchers at UCI, including Kenneth Kraemer, Jim Danziger, John King, Suzanne Iacono, Nick Vitalari, and me, have examined how computer-based information systems are adopted, what interests they serve, and what consequences they have for organizational practices, decision making, and work life. We have studied computerization in a variety of institutional sectors — including government agencies, factories, banking, schools, offices, and homes. We have tried to amplify the level of social realism in studies of computerization, while avoiding the tendencies to create captivating, but oversimplified and ungrounded, narratives (Kling forthcoming). These studies have focused on computerization within organizations — the primary setting of computer use in the 1970s and 1980s. Much of our work is therefore anchored in theories of organizations.[3] I draw upon some of that research in this article.

Discourse about computer revolutions — popular and academic

Social change is sometimes treated as a specialty topic within sociology. Yet ideas about social change so permeate the discourse and images of computerization that they should be at the center of attention for sociological inquiry. I do not mean that sociologists should uncritically accept glossy images of "information societies" or "computer revolution" or "revolutionary this and that," which are part of the official story of computerization — pushed by the marketing arms of computer vendors as well as futurists like Alvin Toffler and John Naisbitt and sympathetically amplified by journalists in the mass media.

441

Toffler (1980) helped stimulate enthusiasm for computerization in these popular terms in his best seller *The Third Wave*. He characterized major social transformations in terms of large shifts in the organization of society driven by technological change.[4] Toffler is masterful in describing major social changes in energetic prose, for example:

> Today, as we construct a new info-sphere for a Third Wave civilization, we are imparting to the "dead" environment around us, not life, but intelligence. A key to this revolutionary advance is, of course, the computer.
>
> (P. 168)

> As miniaturization advanced with lightening rapidity, . . . [e]very branch factory, laboratory, sales office, or engineering department claimed its own. . . . The brain-power of the computer . . . was "distributed." This dispersion of computer intelligence is now moving ahead at high speed.
>
> (P. 169)

> The dispersal of computers in the home, not to mention their interconnection in ramified networks, represents another advance in the construction of an intelligent environment. Yet even this is not all. The spread of machine intelligence reaches another level altogether with the arrival of microprocessors and microcomputers, those tiny chips of congealed intelligence that are about to become a part, it seems, of nearly all the things we make and use.
>
> (P. 170)

> What is inescapably clear . . . is that we are altering our info-sphere fundamentally. . . . we are adding a whole new strata of communication to the social system. The emerging Third Wave info-sphere makes that of the Second Wave era — dominated by its mass media, the post office, and the telephone — seem hopelessly primitive by contrast.
>
> (P. 172)

In all previous societies, the infosphere[5] provided the means for communication between human beings. The Third Wave multiplies these means. But it also provides powerful facilities, for the first time in history, for machine-to-machine communication, and, even more astonishing, for conversation between humans and the intelligent environment around them. When we stand back . . . it becomes clear that the revolution in the info-sphere is at least as dramatic as that of the technosphere — in the energy system and the technological base of society. The work of constructing a new civilization is racing forward on many levels at once.

(Pp. 177–78)

Toffler's breathless enthusiasm can be contagious — but it also stymies critical thought. Toffler opens up important questions about the way information technologies alter how people perceive information, the kinds of information they can get easily, and how they handle the information they get. But his account — like many popular accounts — caricatures the answers by using only illustrations that support his generally buoyant theses. And he skillfully sidesteps tough questions while titillating readers with sentences like "The work of constructing a new civilization is racing forward on many levels at once."

Toffler's vision is not dated, however. This is an excerpt from a recent article by two respected information systems scholars:

> The office of the late 1990s can now be envisioned. Its staff of professionals and managers are surrounded by intelligent devices that speak, listen, or interact with them to determine what is to be accomplished and how it is to be done. Contacts with other departments, other divisions, customers, vendors, and other organizations are made with little effort and without human intervention. Behind the scenes, systems are being developed by system developers equipped with versatile and highly integrated software.
>
> (Straub and Wetherbe 1989, 1338)

This vision has a character similar to a spaceship in which the crew is highly automated and staffed with robots. But the problematic that these people and organizations suggest — that computerization plays an important role in transforming our social worlds — is too important to ignore. Moreover, this is a pivotal time in which key social choices might still be influenced by sharp and sensitive social analysis.

Sometimes good social analysts get caught up in the rhetorical fervor. For example, in his book on scientific revolutions, the historian Cohen wrote:

> As I was writing this chapter, a glance at a single shelf in my study showed almost a dozen books on computers had 'revolution' in the title. Who would deny that there has been a computer revolution?
>
> (1985, 21–22)

I have examined numerous books with terms like *computer revolution* or *information revolution* in their titles. Remarkably, none of these books carefully characterizes computer revolutions analytically or behaviorally. They do not explain how we would know one when we saw it. They usually refer to the pervasiveness of computer systems in social life and suggest that when powerful technologies become commonplace, social life must be altered. I do not mean that a case could not be made. But to my knowledge, no one has tried to make a careful case — indicating what kinds of social relations have been transformed, at what level of social activity, under what conditions, and what has *not* changed.

I believe that a careful assessment would show that the restructuring of social relations because of computerization has been much more important in some institutional areas than in others. For example, computer-based systems have been part of larger and more far-reaching structural transformations in travel reservations and banking than in the instructional aspects of schooling (unless one considers mass testing). As we know from studies of other social revolutions, such as the industrial revolution and the transition from feudalism to capitalism, major social transformations differ in their timing and depth in different places and social sectors.

I have become skeptical of stories of computerization and social transformations that absorb all changes into one dominant logic — whether it is the blooming of a knowledge-based society (Strassman 1985), a progressive expansion of monopoly capitalism and the domination of the working class (Noble 1984), or a "control revolution" (Beniger 1986).

These single logics have compelling simplicity. They are useful starting points for more subtle inquiries. But as total frameworks, they often mislead. In our studies at UCI, we have taken a position that is *open to the possibility* of social transformations facilitated by computerization. Simultaneously, we have been skeptical of many of the technologically utopian and dystopian claims.

The varied character and conditions of social transformations

Transformed images

Between 1973 and 1979, my colleagues at UCI and I conducted a series of studies about the social impacts of computer-based information systems on the character of work, the nature of decision making, and shifts in the character of services in American local governments. This is a complex set of studies, which I can only begin to sketch. We undertook several qualitative case studies and two large-scale surveys supported by intensive fieldwork.[6]

At the time, a large fraction of the information systems in municipal governments supported finance/taxation/payments and police work. Early on in our study, I learned about the development and use of an information system in a southern city that was used to better provide welfare services to needy people in the city and county. The city, which I have called Riverville, had several dozen public and private welfare agencies in its jurisdiction (Kling 1978).

The interactive computerized "urban management information system," called UMIS, was described in about 10 articles that were published in professional conferences about information systems or human services management, and in several national news magazines. According to the stories, people would have trouble figuring out which social programs they were eligible for and sometimes "got lost" in shuttling between agencies. The staff that managed UMIS described a series of additional benefits that it was to provide — including reducing paperwork, improving managerial control, and providing key data for needs assessments and program evaluation. I was keenly interested, because the majority of computerized information systems we were studying did not do much to support direct services to people. Here was an interesting exception.

I spent a week in Riverville in 1974 and again in 1975 trying to understand the use and impacts of the system on welfare operations. In the first year's fieldwork I found UMIS heavily used in certain city welfare agencies — in neighborhood referral centers. But it did not seem to have many of the reported consequences for reshaping administrative operations. For example, there were no reductions in paperwork or data for "needs assessments." There was no way to assess a reduction in people getting lost between agencies, since there was no "lost-and-found" client office or tally. Other changes were equally elusive.

In 1975 the city committed an additional $200,000 to operating UMIS after some key federal grants ran out. I was surprised that the city maintained UMIS, despite what seemed to be minor enhancements to their welfare operations. In my second year's fieldwork, I learned that UMIS's primary value was in *enhancing the welfare agencies' image* when they dealt with federal funders and auditors. Welfare administrators claimed that the federal staff from the Department of Health, Education, and Welfare (HEW) saw them as more competent when they used computerized records rather than paper records. Welfare seemed to hum in Riverville when auditors saw UMIS. They were more willing to allocate federal welfare funds to the city. And that was UMIS's primary value to city officials.

All the published accounts of UMIS value led readers to focus inward on the administrative practices of the welfare agencies — and relationships between them. They carefully deleted UMIS's role in these agencies' negotiations with a major source of resources: HEW. It's not clear that local administrators anticipated the negotiating leverage that UMIS would provide. But it was clear that they gained substantial advantage by keeping the story of its administrative value alive even when they could not realize those dreams.

Managerial actions facilitating social transformations

In a recent study, Tom Jewett and I contrasted the way that two clerical work groups computerized (Jewett and Kling 1990): the central accounting group in a mortgage bank ("Western Mortgage") and an order-taking group (customer service) in a sales department of a large pharmaceutical firm ("Coast Pharmaceutical").[7] The two work groups are similar in many respects, despite the obvious differences in their major business activity. Both firms provide comfortable office facilities, with attractive modular furnishings. At first glance, the duties of most members in both groups appeared to be primarily clerical. However, on closer study we found that the job content in both groups has been expanding. We have found that employees are no longer confined to simple data entry or bookkeeping tasks. Instead, they are expected to assume increasing responsibilities — for example, tracking down customers' late orders and integrating computer systems into their work routines. The typical members of both groups completed at least some college education and characterized their jobs as "professional," rather than "clerical."

Both work groups were extensively computerized by 1987, in the sense that they had terminals or PCs for at least half of their work group members. However, both groups adopted major new computer-based systems in 1989, and these were catalysts for some changes in the organization and content of work. These changes have increased the number of tasks and responsibilities of their jobs. Western Mortgage acquired a minicomputer system for basic accounting, such as general ledger and accounts payable. It replaced computer services that previously had been contracted to an outside vendor. In previous years, the accounting group used microcomputers for spreadsheets, word processing, and scheduling. But they simply prepared the accounting transactions in a manual form in their office for processing by an outside service bureau. At Coast Pharmaceutical, a new order-tracking system was developed to replace an existing system. Both implementations were "top down," since the initiative for new systems came from outside these work groups.

At Coast Pharmaceutical, managers have consciously changed the tasks being performed in the customer service group. Every job description was rewritten — a very lengthy and complex procedure. The former order entry clerks were reclassified as customer service representatives — a change not only in name but in increased responsibility and more extensive contact with customers. Each representative, for example, was expected to set up a specific service program for one or more major customer accounts. The representative's pay was also increased by one or two levels.

Many of the order entry/customer service procedures have been computerized for a number of years. As jobs were being changed, the older computer system was gradually upgraded. The customer service personnel designed key parts of the final system to better support their responsibility for tracking all orders placed by a customer. Several managers and employees participated in seven week-long off-site meetings to do the actual work; they reviewed their progress and solicited inputs from other clerks in the group.

Clerical participation at Customer Service has not been limited to the computer project; clerks were also involved in redesigning their jobs. This participation may have increased the workers' perceptions of their own influence within the organization.

Western Mortgage installed a minicomputer to replace computer services previously contracted to an outside vendor. For the clerks and supervisors in accounting, the new system has brought changed work procedures. Before, they manually coded ledgers for entry by an outside data-processing service. Now, Western's clerks enter their own figures directly into the computer system. Before, clerks moved between their desks and the file cabinets, frequently consulting others to obtain information for financial reports. Now, they remain at their desks, consulting instead the computer data bases.

Managers do not appear to have intentionally designed these changes but appear to be aware that changes have occurred. On one hand, the clerks have learned new computer skills that some of them believe would help in seeking future employment. On the other hand, opportunities for social interaction within the workplace have decreased, because of less walking around. An eventual outcome could be increased boredom and less social cohesiveness in the work group. Some clerks also see the new requirement for data entry as loss of status.

A vendor developed the software and Western's own Information Systems Department provided hardware support. Accounting clerks and supervisors were involved only when they attended a vendor training session shortly before the new system was installed. But the training was incomplete because the system design was still in flux. Clerks had to develop their own outline of the "basics" for using the computer. They do not see much contribution of computing to their productivity and do not have frequent informal discussions about computerization. The same "laissez-faire" management appears to characterize other aspects of work in accounting. There is no formal training program, since newly hired employees are expected to be experienced in accounting procedures.

In these two work groups, different management approaches have resulted in very different changes from the computerization projects. The customer service project is transformative in nature — the computerization was an adjunct to job redesign and other organizational practices that were taking place simultaneously. Clerks shifted from passive order entry clerks to much more active roles to help track orders and improve sales and service. Managers believed that high levels of personal involvement and employee participation were needed to restructure jobs and practices as integrated activities. They provided training programs and continuing support for both the new work procedures and the new computer system.

The accounting project, on the other hand, was relatively nontransformative — the new computer system was seen as a simple substitute for the manual procedures and outside computer system. Managers appear to have believed initially that jobs would not be significantly changed as the computer system was implemented. Since there was little need for computer training prior to bringing this computer system inside the accounting department, they did not realize the extent to which training would now be important. Clerks and supervisors were left to rely on themselves and their co-workers for continuing support. While the jobs were upskilled and clerks had fewer opportunities for casual social contact, they remained relatively routinized clerical jobs.[8]

Social reinforcement

Much of the discourse about computerization is decorated with the promise of the new: futurists like Toffler have coined terms like *electronic cottage* and *info-sphere.* Many computer specialists champion the special role of "expert systems." A recent article about competition in the computer industry in *Fortune*, a popular business magazine, included this sentence: "The industry that has transformed the way that most people work is about to transform the way that most people *want* to work" (Gannes 1988, 43; Gannes's italics).

In our studies of urban information systems (URBIS), we examined the ways in which computer-based systems were instruments in power games played within local governments. In *Computers and Politics* (Danziger *et al.* 1982), we explain that part of the study in detail. We examined the possibility that computerization alters the politics within local governments in four ways: managerial rationalism (criteria of rationality for the organization as a whole characterize choices), technocratic elitism (technical assessments made by skilled specialists guide organizational choices), pluralism (different coalitions are advantaged by different decisions, depending on the time and issues), and reinforcement politics (those with most resources gain more influence, while those with fewer resources lose subsequent influence). While we found some support for each of these four models, we found that the reinforcement-politics model had the most systematic support.

In small cities, the top officials (mayors or managers) were usually able to use computer-based information systems to tighten their control over departments and to gain power at the expense of the part-time city councils. In contrast, the large cities had huge departments with substantial expertise. In these larger cities, we found that departments computerized in ways that brought them more influence relative to central administrators and to the city councils. On the whole, city councils lost influence regardless.

I discuss the findings of reinforcement politics to suggest why computer-based systems need not be instruments of social transformation — for a different reason than the Riverville example. In the case of Riverville, UMIS did not seem to alter social relations within the welfare agencies, between them, or even with their clients. An explanation based on reinforcement politics suggests that the changes need not create new kinds of social relationships — but can strengthen existing ones.

Ideologies and discourse about computerization

Much of what we know about the role of computerized technologies in social life comes from a variety of tainted sources — like the professional conferences and news weeklies that published stories about UMIS. During the last 15 years I was first disappointed in, then took for granted, the typical discrepancies between how organizations actually computerize and stories of major social changes or transformations.

In the early 1980s Suzanne Iacono and I conducted several studies of the role of complex information systems in organizational life. One of our key cases focused on a complicated computerized inventory control system, called a material requirements planning (MRP) system, in a medium-sized high-technology manufacturing firm that we called PRINTCO.

We found that PRINTCO's staff frequently recited the same list of organizational impacts in similar terms, such as cost reductions and more efficient uses of inventory. We found some of these claims impossible to document. For example, no one — not the material control managers, the vice president of finance, or the data-processing manager — could give us a decent estimate of the costs of their inventory control system. Consequently, claims about cost effectiveness were based on something other than tight evidence. We found that many key staff in PRINTCO — including the board of directors and top material managers — had gone to special workshops run by national consulting organizations about this kind of inventory control system. Many of the lower level material control staff attended workshops held by a relevant professional association with local chapters — the American Production and Inventory Control Society. The society's booklets and workshops were important carriers of their litany of changes that the staff then saw.

The staff of PRINTCO had more basis for the belief in their computer system's role in their organization's practices than did the welfare staff of Riverville. For example, the material control manager monitored "inventory turns" as a way of keeping track of how efficiently they were stocking key parts. I am not calling their beliefs delusional. But they voiced them with a confidence that came more from accepting a received ideology than from immediate observation.

We also learned the role that ideologies played in developing support for computer-based systems in studying the PRINTCO case. MRP was an instrument for the material managers. We found that they used their MRP system to gain control over the purchasing staff and to help production line managers battle with projections made by marketing staff. But customizing an MRP system for a manufacturing firm takes tremendous work. It is a major effort to train many staff in the necessary workplace disciplines such as recording data accurately and to insist that all material transfers be reflected in written records. The ideology of MRP impacts helped the material managers *mobilize support* for the organizational changes needed to make the system work locally.

In fact, some of the social changes we observed were ignored in the official MRP literature (Kling and Iacono 1984). For example, we found a general tightening of workplace discipline around record-keeping practices and a restructuring of reporting relations to give material control managers greater influence in the firm. There were some social changes — some arguably transformative — but not where the ideologies of MRP guided us to look. On the other hand, we found the managers at PRINTCO failed in trying to change their MRP system to a newer version, despite major investments in new equipment and several related organizational changes (Kling and Iacono 1989b). Ironically, we invoked theories of institutionalization to explain the relative stability of PRINTCO's information systems and the social organization that supported their computing arrangements.

Based on our observations in this case study and in other settings, Suzanne Iacono and I concluded that ideologies play an incredibly important role in helping key players mobilize support for specific forms of computerization in their own organizations. These key players often participate in a larger social world, outside the organizations that employ them, where they learn, and also refine and promulgate, these ideologies. We become specially skeptical when advocates of computerization (futurists like Toffler or Naisbitt) or critics like Shaiken uncritically accept stories of technological effectiveness as reliable knowledge. At best these ideologies provide clues about what might happen when organizations computerize, but they merit careful empirical investigation to verify their accuracy.

Mobilizing ideologies and technological utopianism

During the past 30 years, social groups in Western societies — especially in the United States — have embarked on major campaigns to computerize. Many of the dominant visions have been articulated by technologists and futurists rather than social analysts. Much of this writing has been framed with a particular brand of utopian thought — technological utopianism. This line of analysis places the use of some specific technology, such as computers, nuclear energy, or low-energy low-impact technologies, as key *enabling elements* of a utopian vision (Kling forthcoming; Dunlop and Kling forthcoming).

Suzanne Iacono and I recently characterized important forms of computerization as the by-product of loosely organized social movements rather than simply an industry selling products to an eager market (Kling and Iacono 1988). Groups that form around a computer technology form a social movement to the extent they (a) have mobilizing ideologies that promote an improved social order or oppose an intolerable social order, (b) form organizations that include a diverse membership, and (c) promote the movement through communication channels and publications.

We examined five arenas of computerization as the activities of social movements: urban information systems, artificial intelligence, office automation, instructional computing, and personal computing. In some of these arenas — such as instructional computing — there are looser social criteria for what constitutes success than in other areas — such as inventory control. Ideologies are more likely to be potent in the face of ambiguous evidence to help make simple sense of complex and conflicting events.

These computer-based social movements share ideological beliefs:

1   Computer-based technologies are central for a reformed world.
2   The improvement of computer-based technologies will help reform society.
3   No one loses from computerization.
4   More computing is better than less, and there are no conceptual limits to the scope of appropriate computerization.
5   Perverse or undisciplined people are the main barriers to social reform through computing.

We did not argue that computerization has not had demonstrable value in some cases, or that it has not changed social systems in some cases. We argued that the ideologies permeated many accounts and shaped the discourse about computerization, and that they are often monochromatic (see also Kling and Iacono 1990).

Activists and computer revolutionaries have not been timid in articulating a social vision that places computer-based systems at the center of a social universe. While I have referred to more popular and academic writers, most computer-based systems are installed with little public view of the social visions held by their designers, developers, and implementors. Here I am thinking of a wide variety of systems, including some that are extremely large in social scale — nets of automated teller machines, interbank clearinghouses for electronic funds transfer, air traffic control systems, and airline reservation systems.[9]

The rhetorics justifying these developments are often anchored in images of an "information society." All such single labels to characterize an era are misleading. But the labels are important when they catch on and shape popular discourse and influence policy debates and organizational action.

Some conceptual issues in studying technological systems

To help advance social studies of computerization, the following conceptual issues need serious work: how to characterize the social-technological

451

systems that are the objects of our inquiry and subjects of our theories, how to characterize the social organization that supports these social-technological systems, and how to draw boundaries around studies so that they are manageable by the tiny groups of researchers who investigate them.

Characterizing technological systems

One aspect of computerization that makes it difficult as a topic of inquiry is the problem of characterizing appropriate units of analysis. A good deal of discourse about computerization focuses on a convenient fiction called "the computer system." The computer-based systems that people and groups actually develop and use differ in important technical and social ways. These differences often seem to matter. The computer system is a convenient fiction that deletes nuances of technical differences and social organization when these do not matter. But since different technical features of the computer system and the social organization sometimes do matter, the convenience becomes a liability if our conceptual language is imprisoned in talk about "the computer."

From a technological standpoint, the computer systems that people use are embodiments of procedures running on a particular kind of computer hardware. The hardware may be faster or slower, physically larger or smaller, connected to other machines or not, and provide monochrome or color displays. Technologically, the software is not cut from "common cloth." Information systems differ in key capabilities and their modus operandi. For example, some data base management systems require that each new capability be programmed by a skilled programmer (e.g., Revelation). Others, which have powerful commands on menu systems (such as Paradox), allow moderately skilled users to navigate through data bases in complex ways without requiring all searchers and reports to have been previously programmed by a highly skilled specialist.

Why would such a difference in the architecture of data base management systems matter to a social analyst of technology? If one asks whether computerization leads to changes in the skill level of jobs, then the extent to which the systems people use enable them to develop new or expanded skills is an important part of the answer. Some organizations adopt systems that require programming (and provide no end user flexibility aside from a narrow range of menu choices). In those organizations, we would expect much less upskilling to be likely for people who stay in the computerized tasks — ceteris paribus.

Computer-based systems have important social characteristics as well. The specifications of a Turing Machine have not changed in 50 years. But people ascribe status to real computer systems that are anchored in their social worlds. Many professionals would feel embarrassed to assert that they were working with 20-year-old computer systems, even if they are functionally superb. Artificial intelligence researchers have eschewed IBM mainframes for years and have often generalized their dislike to PCs. Computer scientists have generally galvanized around Macs rather than PCs, even though there are technical ways to configure them similarly and economic incentives for buying PCs. Consequently, people's behavior with computer-based technologies can hinge on their ascribed social character-istics as much as on their technical features, such as information flows and transformations.

The social organization of access to information systems and information

In addition, access to computer-based systems is organized. A simple example will suffice. When an university instructor adds a computer component to a course, there are specific choices about access to equipment. In order to make efficient use of teaching assistants and equipment, he or she might have computers in tightly scheduled labs. (In the "chemistry lab model," students are assigned fixed times, such as 9:00 A.M.–10:00 A.M., to com-plete their assignments.) Alternatively, he or she might allow students to use the labs at their discretion, between 8:00 A.M. and 10:00 P.M. (open labs are a library model). Students who take the scheduled lab course might complain that computerizing the course has regimented their lives. It is the social organization of access, rather than "a computer," which is the appropriate object of their complaint.[10]

Let us take a different example. In the United States, consumers have substantial control over payments with credit cards. They can contest billings and withhold funds until disputes with their creditors are resolved. Also they have very limited liabilities for lost cards and few liabilities for errors. In the late 1970s, some managers of the largest banks (Citicorp in New York), began to seek legislation that would remove these protections in the case of debit cards. And they were largely successful (Kling 1983). A debit card has the same physical appearance as a credit card, but the social system of regulation is much more cashlike than a credit card. Compared with credit cards, debit cards facilitate more rapid payments to merchants, do not allow stop payment, and have much higher liability for loss of the card if it is not reported promptly. Electronic funds systems based on credit cards and debit cards have superficial similarities, but consumers have fewer rights and more responsibilities with debit cards.

Computerization as a social and technical process

Because the process of introducing computers changes many elements of social life in organizations concurrently, computerization is not simply install-ing computer-based systems. In fact, most substantial computerization projects require some changes in key social relationships, even though some important authority relationships are usually untouched (Kling and Iacono 1989a; Jewett and Kling 1990). Our previous example of adding a computer lab to an existing course illustrates some of the ways in which key social choices are coextensive with a computerization project. The social dimensions of the process render computerization socially complex and also technologically indeterminate. There is often more than one way to computerize some segment of social life. The "same equipment" can have different social consequences when the associated social arrangements are substantially different.

Web models

Since people use computer-based systems in a social setting, the boundaries around the computer must include a good slice of their social worlds. But how to draw boundaries is not always clear. One criterion is clear — that in studies of computer use — and impacts — the infrastructure for support must be included as part of "the computer system" (Kling 1987). In the early 1980s, Walt Scacchi and I developed a crude framework to help set boundaries for social studies of computerization that focused inside organizations — web models (Kling 1987; Kling and Scacchi 1982).

Web models conceive of a computer system as an ensemble of equipment, applications, and techniques with identifiable information-processing capabilities. Each computing resource has costs and skill requirements that are only partially identifiable. Most computer-based information systems do not operate automatically and without human intervention. People and groups who use a computerized information system sometimes see a social support system — however ill organized — along with the physical machinery as something that will help to control their use of the focal technology: to help them learn what it is good for and how to use it, fix problems, and so on. We call this social organization the infrastructure of computing support.

Computer systems and their support organizations are also social objects that may be highly charged with meaning. This approach focuses substantial attention on three key concepts: the *social contexts* in which a computer-based system is developed and used, the *infrastructure* of support for the system (including the social organization of access), and the *history of social arrangements* within which the computer-based system is developed. Web models view information systems as complex social objects constrained by their context, infrastructure and history (Kling and Scacchi 1982).[11]

We articulated this approach as an alternative to "engineering models," which focused on the equipment and its information-processing capabilities as the focus of analysis and formal organizational arrangements as the basis of social action. We called this asocial alternative "discrete entity" analyses.

For example, returning to Riverville, discrete entity analyses focused our attention inward on administrative operation, rather than on a social context that included federal funding and a history of dependencies in which the city staff relied upon external funds for many welfare programs. Web analyses would focus attention outward as well as inward — historically, as well as toward the future. In web analyses, "contexts" refer to social groups and relationships — not to an undifferentiated bath that warms the subjects of our studies.

But where and how should one draw useful boundaries? Why not define the web of dependencies for Riverville's UMIS throughout the public sector? It is possible to set up *criteria* for boundaries a priori. Organizational participants select computing arrangements to leverage their negotiations in a larger social order. They also find that participants are constrained by resources and organizational routines that are defined outside the formal boundaries of their organizations. Organizations that have critical ongoing negotiations with outsiders — clients, auditors, regulators, vendors, competitors — will sometimes develop computing arrangements to enhance their bargaining positions. To understand these choices, a larger situational boundary that includes this expanded organizational set must be drawn. These boundaries themselves cannot be completely defined a priori. Nor can they be defined before the participants of these larger negotiating contexts are identified.

We proposed three criteria for drawing the boundaries of larger-scale situations that serve as useful contexts for a given focal situation (Kling 1987) — include people, equipment, and organizations: (a) who are part of a chain of *resource dependencies*, (b) *who are taken account of by* participants or (c) who *constrain the actions* of the focal actors. A web analyst also includes key social relationships among these people, equipment, and organizations in the analysis.

These criteria help draw *temporal boundaries* as well. Studies of social change and transformations require some kind of historical perspective. But we have not had decent analytical criteria for where to start. Not all studies of computerization should be anchored in the dawn of the control revolution in the late nineteenth century. For example, we feel confident in starting our study of Riverville's welfare administration in the 1960s, PRINTCO's MRP system in the 1970s, and the system changes at Coast Pharmaceutical and Western Mortgage in the 1980s by reference to these criteria. We have found that computerization is often an ongoing process. People and organizations change systems and associated work practices slowly over time, with occasionally more abrupt discontinuities when major systems are changed or social arrangements purposely restructured (Kling and Iacono 1989a; Zmuidzinas, Kling, and George 1990). This view differs substantially from that of analysts like Zuboff (1988) who view computerization as a one-shot alteration of technology and work practices, but whose sense of history includes several distinctive ways of radically restructuring work with new technologies over the centuries.

These issues of drawing boundaries and characterizing key social processes confront anyone undertaking well-grounded empirical social studies of computerization. There are still open questions about the time scale over which to expect social transformations to take place. When they come as a by-product of elite control over small social units, social relations may be transformed in one or two years. But some organizations may transform over periods that are closer to a decade, and social sectors may take even longer.

The information and computer sciences

I have discussed computerization — the deployment of computer-based systems in social settings. But the social organization of the computing world, including the information and computer sciences as a professional community and as an academic discipline, is also an important focus of study. In Europe, the term *informatics*, as defined by International Federation of Information Processing Societies, covers a broad set of studies that are segmented into different disciplinary niches in the United States. Informatics is segmented across schools of management, engineering, library science, and "computer science" departments. *Computer science* is now a commonly accepted label, but what it denotes is sometimes unclear, even to academics and researchers who self-identify with the term. The topics of investigation are sufficiently heterogeneous — and the lack of an underlying paradigm so problematic — that *computer studies* might be a more apt term. But most people who self-identify with computer science want to play the science game — with large amounts of grant money and possible memberships in the National Academy of Sciences.

In so doing, computer scientists have been deleting "the social" from their conceptions of the discipline. One commonplace view of computer science and engineering is reflected in a recent report by the Association for Computing Machinery's Task Force on the Core of Computer Science.

> Computer Science and Engineering is the systematic study of algorithmic processes — their theory, analysis, design, efficiency, implementation and application — that describe and transform information. The fundamental question underlying all of computing is, What can be (efficiently) automated? . . . The roots of computing extend deeply into mathematics and engineering. Mathematics imparts analysis to the field; engineering imparts design.
>
> (Denning *et al.* 1989)

The expansion of computing (and computer science) has depended on the improved usability of computer-based systems, not simply on their efficiency.

The "micro revolution," for example, has placed tens of millions of computers and terminals on the desks of many managers, professionals, and clerks in industrial countries. Networking has made electronic mail accessible to millions of managers and professionals. The theories that help explain the expansion of computing applications, which ones work well or badly (and in what terms), are *not* fundamentally mathematical studies of algorithms.

While the computability perspective contributes important insights to "computing in the laboratory," it cannot readily help computer specialists understand computerization in the larger world. Computer science has strong social roots on which rest many studies of the usability of computer-based systems. But most computer scientists are reluctant to acknowledge the social basis of the usability perspective. I believe that part of this reluctance can be found in the academic debates over the role of computer science as a science, and the way in which mathematics, rather than the social sciences, better advances the status of computer science among the sciences. In the United States, computer studies have two major academic homes. Departments of computer science are usually located as a science within the liberal arts or in schools of engineering, and departments of (management) information systems are usually located within business schools. While the research done in these two kinds of departments overlaps, they serve different constituencies and have substantially different battles with other disciplines over their scientific status. The computer science departments are often contrasted with laboratory sciences, like chemistry or physics (and sometimes mathematics); the information systems departments are often under attack from economically oriented finance and marketing faculty who dominate many of the major business schools. In either case, the ways that professors interested in computing strive for academic legitimacy often leads them to focus on the "hard" sides of their discipline.

The education of hundreds of thousands of computer science students has been shaped by the computability perspective. They leave academic computer science programs with some skills in designing software systems and programming them. They usually take courses in data structures and algorithms in which they learn to appreciate and carry out mathematical analyses of computer performance. But they leave systematically ignorant of the ways in which social analyses of computer systems provide comparably important insights into the effectiveness of computing in the world. Many segments of the computing community would much better understand computerization and be able to play more responsible professional roles by adopting a more fundamentally social view of the process.

Computerization itself is a social and technical process in which key actors are reconfiguring social and technical resources. Callon (1987) characterizes engineer sociologists as designers of new technologies, such as electric cars. The key agents of computerization in use are widely varied — managers and professionals of all kinds. But they also take an active role as sociologists in practice when reorganizing for computer-based systems. I am less impressed than Callon about the quality of the sociology-in-practice that many managers and professionals develop.[12] There is an important element of anthropological humility in Callon's approach — of taking native views seriously and not simply dismissing them as "primitive" a priori. However, there is also a risk in developing a romance with the natives.

There was a meeting of about 150 transportation specialists in the hotel where this article was first presented in the previous week. Some of the specialists were technologists with visions of "smart cars" that would use radars and sensors to navigate the freeways efficiently and drive just a few feet away from each other — safely and at high speed. There was no special enthusiasm for developing "smart drivers." Nor did there seem to be substantial discussion of alternative scenarios with different technological foundations — as in the difference between emphasizing telecommuting for many people versus smart cars.

In the past decade, some sociologists of technology have noticed that the conventional theories of innovation were rather mute about the dissemination of technological devices and systems; there were few studies of rates of adoption and the social location of early adopters. They felt that the nature of the technologies sometimes mattered — different technologies could have different social consequences. The approach of "radical symmetry" involved understanding technologies as social objects, as well as the social systems that are coextensive with them.

Many of the technologists' visions delete people and social order in important ways. This deletion can be naive. But it is often self-serving — as when artificial intelligence researchers, with substantial military funding in the United States, argue against the value of social inquiry about the social roles of computer technologies.

Conclusions

Questions of the big social transformations attributable to forms of computerization are of central importance. They have motivated a substantial program of research at UCI during the last 20 years. I have highlighted the research at UCI, but there is synergy between our work and research conducted by numerous other scholars whom my colleagues and I cite in specific papers and books.[13]

We are in the peculiar position of living in a society in which the discourse about computerization advanced in many professional magazines and the mass media is saturated with talk about revolution. Yet substantial social changes are often difficult to identify in carefully designed empirical studies. Unfortunately, many of the claims about what computerization means are *not* worked out with the scholarly care of Beniger's arguments about the control revolution. In "The Mobilization of Support for Computerization" and "Making the Computer Revolution," Suzanne Iacono and I examined the ways in which interest in computerization is often stimulated by social movements. Some movement spokespersons (usually male) articulate strong, technologically utopian visions.[14]

I have discussed some ways in which the studies my colleagues and I have conducted undermine simple stories of social transformation. Computers did not make welfare hum in Riverville. We found that computerization fostered a reinforcement politics, not a new form of politics, in local governments. But in the MRP studies, we found important changes in the tightness of workplace disciplines and in the power of a semiprofessional group. And managerial actions helped reshape work through computerization at Coast Pharmaceutical. In this case, managers interested in transforming work found computerized systems to be a helpful instrument (but managerial intention is not a good predictor of subsequent social changes). We are still working out a comprehensive characterization of the role of technologies in changing (and transforming) parts of the social order.

In my view, "a computer revolution" has not happened systematically in most social sectors. For example, there have been some major structural transformations in banking linked to numerous kinds of computer systems for transferring funds and managing accounts but negligible changes in schooling. The work arrangements of some occupations, such as copy typists, has been radically restructured. Bureaucratic record keeping, which affects social control and privacy,[15] has seen some major structural rearrangements, such as the expansion of third-party data brokers like TRW Creditdata. But the majority of white-collar work has been altered in interesting procedural ways without radically restructuring the organization of work for the majority of people in computerized workplaces. We still have much to learn about the special conditions when social relations, such as those in workplaces, are significantly transformed through computerization. (Authority relationships, for example, are often highly institutionalized, and many computerization projects reinforce them rather than transform them.)

The movement activists, the computer revolutionaries, are working hard to *make* a revolution — with varying success. Their visions suggest a socially conservative revolution that will primarily advantage already-powerful social interests. It is much harder to develop a progressive social vision to help shape appropriate computerization. It is far easier for us to criticize their visions than to develop a sounder sociology of alternative futures.[16]

But I wonder how far critique alone will take us in a world in which relatively conservative activists are playing key roles in shaping our remaining choices. The main alternative normative analyses of appropriate computerization are articulated by countermovements whose interests intersect with some special form of computerization: in workplaces, intrusions on personal privacy, and consumer rights, for example. These countermovements articulate how computing should be balanced with competing values,

such as good jobs, cooperative work relationships, fair information practices, and consumer control. However, these specialized views do not add up
to a coherent alternative humanistic vision for appropriate computerization
(Kling and Iacono 1988).

This is a great historical moment for social analysts to examine what
kinds of social transformations have and have not happened and why. And
it is important for us to articulate the real social choices that remain. If we
do not, who will?

Notes

* This article was first delivered as a plenary address to the annual meeting of the
Society for Social Studies of Science, Irvine, CA, November 1989. I wish to express
my thanks to Leigh Star, for helpful discussions about the sociology of science and
technology while I was organizing the talk, and to Tom Jewett, Sharon Traweek,
and Mary Zmuidzinas, for helpful comments on the article.

1 This question is much closer to that asked by Cowan (1983) in her pioneering
study of household technologies.
2 Harvey (1989) is unusually forthright in observing that we are in a period of
significant historical transition that the conventional logics of social change have
trouble explaining adequately. See especially chapter 10.
3 Our work took a critical view of the rationalist traditions projecting the consequences of computer-based systems — often espoused by managerial analysts
such as Leavitt and Whisler, Vincent Giuliano, or Harvey Poppel.
4 The "Second Wave" was the shift from agricultural societies to industrial societies. He contrasts industrial ways of organizing societies with new social trends
that he links to computer and microelectronic technologies.
5 Toffler defines an info-sphere as "communication channels through which
individuals and mass messages could be distributed as goods or raw materials"
(p. 35).
6 Much of our data collection focused on computerization in six domains of
activity, including the processing of traffic tickets, the monitoring of budgets,
the conduct of police investigations by detectives, managerial reporting, and the
development and use of urban plans. We chose domains that frequently had
some kind of computer support — so we could compare computerization and
social changes across 40 governments in our main survey (Danziger et al. 1982;
Kraemer et al. 1987; Danziger and Kraemer 1986).
7 Western Mortgage and Coast Pharmaceutical are pseudonyms.
8 Our accounting case at Western Mortgage parallel's Zuboff's (1988) clerical
computerization case study. Jewett and Kling (1990) report how changes in the
computer system during the first stages of its implementation led to significant
confusion in the short run. But as the system stabilized and clerks became more
skillful, their disorientation decreased. Zuboff observed the changes in procedures that accompany computerization projects and argued that the resulting
disorientation is a by-product of more abstract work. We disagree; the work of
the accounting clerks in Western Mortgage was comparably abstract before
and after computerization. They were always working with data about money and
never physically counting piles of cash and coins.
9 Recently, for example, the White House announced a $1.9 billion project to
develop very high speed networks to connect 100 major research universities

and research laboratories, dubbed "data super-highways." These networks are supposed to provide a "1000-fold" improvement in performance compared with today's computer networks.

10 Note, however, that more expensive systems are more likely to be tightly scheduled. Thus a push for state-of-the-art systems in financially constrained schools might lead to more regimentation, on average.

11 Walsham, Symons, and Waema (1988, 193–94).

12 But I appreciate his methodological point of not treating such actors as sociologically naive by definition.

13 See also Dunlop and Kling (forthcoming) for a collection of articles about the social dimensions of computerization written by a variety of scholars.

14 See Dunlop and Kling (forthcoming, section 1) and Kling (forthcoming).

15 Cf. Rule *et al.* (1980), Laudon (1986).

16 See, for example, Pfaffenberger (1988) and Kling and Iacono (1990).

References

Attewell, Paul. 1987a. The deskilling controversy. *Work and Occupations* 14:323–46.

——. 1987b. Big brother and the sweatshop: Computer surveillance in the automated office. *Sociological Theory* 5(Spring): 87–99.

Beniger, James. 1986. *The control revolution.* Cambridge, MA: Harvard University Press.

Bijker, Wiebe E., Thomas Hughes, and Trevor Pinch, eds. 1987. *The social construction of technological systems.* Cambridge: MIT Press.

Callon, Michel. 1987. Society in the making. In *The social construction of technological systems,* edited by Wiebe E. Bijker, Thomas Hughes, and Trevor Pinch, 83–103. Cambridge: MIT Press.

Cohen, I. Bernard. 1985. *Revolution in science.* Cambridge, MA: Harvard University Press.

Cowan, Ruth Schwartz. 1983. *More work for mother: The ironies of household technology from the open hearth to the microwave.* New York: Basic Books.

Danziger, James, William Dutton, Rob Kling, and Kenneth Kramer. 1982. *Computers and politics: High technology in American local governments.* New York: Columbia University Press.

Danziger, James, and Kenneth Kraemer. 1986. *Computers and people: The impacts of computing on end users in organizations.* New York: Columbia University Press.

Denning, Peter J., *et al.* 1989. Computing as a discipline. *Communications of the ACM* 31:9–23.

Dunlop, Charles, and Rob Kling, eds. Forthcoming. *Computerization and controversy: Value conflicts and social choices.* Boston: Academic Press.

Gannes, Stuart. 1988. Tremors from the computer quake. *Fortune,* 1 August, 43–60.

Harvey, David. 1989. *The condition of postmodernity.* London: Basil Blackwell.

Jewett, Tom, and Rob Kling. 1990. The work group manager's role in developing computing infrastructure. In *Proceedings of the ACM Conference on Office Information Systems.* Boston, MA.

Kling, Rob. 1978. Automated welfare client tracking and services integration: The case of Riverville. *Communications of the ACM* 21:484–93.

——. 1980. Social analyses of computing: Theoretical orientations in recent empirical research. *Computing Surveys* 12(1): 61–110.

——. 1983. Value conflicts in the deployment of computing applications: Cases in developed and developing countries. *Telecommunications Policy* 7(1): 12–34.

——. 1987. Defining the boundaries of computing across complex organizations. In *Critical issues in information systems,* edited by Richard Boland and Rudy Hirschheim. London: Wiley.

——. 1989. Postscript 1988 to social analyses of computing: Theoretical orientations in recent empirical research. In *Perspectives on the computer revolution.* 2nd ed., edited by Zenon Pylyshyn and Liam Bannon, 504–18. Norwood, NJ: Ablex.

——. Forthcoming. Reading all about computerization: Five genres of social analysis. In *Directions in advanced computer systems, 1990,* edited by Doug Schuler. Norwood, NJ: Ablex.

Kling, Rob, and Suzanne Iacono. 1984. The control of information systems developments after implementation. *Communications of the ACM* 27:1218–26.

——. 1988. The mobilization of support for computerization: The role of computerization movements. *Social Problems* 35:226–43.

——. 1989a. Desktop computerization and the organization of work. In *Computers in the human context: Information technology, productivity, and people,* edited by Tom Forester, 335–56. Cambridge: MIT Press.

——. 1989b. The institutional character of computerized information systems. *Office: Technology and People* 5(1): 7–28.

——. 1990. Making the computer revolution. *Journal of Computing and Society* 1(1):43–58. (Also to be published in Charles Dunlop and Rob Kling, eds. *Computerization and controversy: Value conflicts and social choices.* New York: Academic Press, forthcoming).

Kling, Rob, and Walt Scacchi. 1982. The web of computing: Computer technology as social organization. In *Advances in computers.* Vol. 21, 307–62. New York: Academic Press.

Kraemer, Kenneth L., Siegfried Dickhoven, Susan Fallows Tierney, and John Leslie Kling. 1987. *Datawars: The politics of federal policymaking.* New York: Columbia University Press.

Laudon, Kenneth C. 1986. *Dossier society: Value choices in the design of national information systems.* New York: Columbia University Press.

Noble, David F. 1984. *Forces of production: A social history of industrial automation.* New York: Knopf.

Pfaffenberger, Bryan. 1988. The social meaning of the personal computer, or Why the personal computer revolution was no revolution. *Anthropological Quarterly* 61:39–47.

Rule, James, Douglas McAdam, Linda Stearns, and David Uglow. 1980. *The politics of privacy: Planning for personal data systems as powerful technologies.* New York: Elsevier North-Holland.

Shaiken, Harley. 1986. *Work transformed: Automation and labor in the computer age.* Lexington, MA: Lexington Books.

Straub, Detmar, and James Wetherbe. 1989. Information technologies for the 1990s: An organizational impact perspective. *Communications of the ACM* 32: 1329–39.

Strassman, Paul. 1985. *Information payoff: The transformation of work in the electronic age.* New York: Basic Books.

Toffler, Alvin. 1980. *The third wave.* New York: Bantam.

Walsham, Geoff, Veronica Symons, and Tim Waema. 1988. Information systems as social systems: Implications for developing countries. *Information Technology for Development* 3:193–94.

Zmuidzinas, Mary, Rob Kling, and Joey George. 1990. Desktop computerization as a continuing process. In *Proceedings of International Conference on Information Systems.* Copenhagen, Denmark.

Zuboff, Shoshanah. 1988. *In the age of the smart machine: The future of work and power.* New York: Basic Books.

45

NEW WORLDS OF
COMPUTER-MEDIATED WORK*

Shoshana Zuboff

Source: *Harvard Business Review* 60(5) (1982): 142–52.

When managers make changes in the ways employees perform their work it's only natural for the employees to resist.
Managers themselves are famous for the not-invented-here
syndrome that is a disguised way of resisting change. It's not
surprising that when they hear about resistance to working
with the new information technology managers dismiss it as
normal and to be expected. The author of this article maintains
that managers should heed the resistance, however, because it
is telling them something about the quality of the changes that
are taking place. Computer-mediated work is more abstract
and can demand new conceptual skills while deemphasizing
the importance of direct experience. Information technology
can potentially depersonalize supervision, alter social communities, and often means that technology absorbs much of the
judgment that routine jobs used to entail. The author suggests
ways that managers can use the new technology as an opportunity to re-envision job responsibilities and develop new
approaches to the problems of supervision.

One day, in the 1860s, the owner of a textile mill in Lowell, Massachusetts
posted a new set of work rules. In the morning, all weavers were to enter the
plant at the same time, after which the factory gates would be locked until
the close of the work day. By today's standards this demand that they arrive
at the same time seems benign. Today's workers take for granted both the
division of the day into hours of work and nonwork and the notion that
everyone should abide by a similar schedule. But, in the 1860s, the weavers
were outraged by the idea that an employer had the right to dictate the
hours of labor. They said it was a "system of slavery," and went on strike.

Eventually, the owner left the factory gates open and withdrew his demands. Several years later, the mill owner again insisted on collective work hours. As the older form of work organization was disappearing from other plants as well, the weavers could no longer protest.

In general, industrialization presented people with a fundamental challenge to the way they had thought about behavior at work. The employer's desire to exploit the steam engine as a centralized source of power, coupled with the drive to closely supervise workers and increase the pace of production, resulted in a greater degree of collectivization and synchronization in the workplace. Employers imposed an exact discipline on workers that required them to use their bodies in specified ways in relation to increasingly complex forms of equipment. By the early 1900s, "scientific management" had given supervisors a systematic way to measure and control the worker's body.

Although most workers have accepted the work behavior that industrialization fashioned, the issues behind the New England weavers' resistance lie at the heart of modern labor-management relations. Using collective bargaining, later generations of workers have developed elaborate grievance procedures and work rules that carefully limit an employer's right to control a worker's body.

New forms of technology inevitably change the ways people are mobilized to work as well as the kinds of skills and behavior that are critical for productivity. These changes are rarely born without pain and conflict – nor do they emerge exactly as planners envision them. Instead, new conceptions of work organization and behavior emerge from an interaction between the demands of a new technology, its social organization, and the responses of the men and women who must work with the new technological systems.

In this regard, the weavers' example is doubly instructive. First, it illustrates that during a period of technological transition people are most likely to be aware of and articulate about the quality of the change they are facing. When people feel that the demands a new technology makes on them conflict with their expectations about the workplace, they are likely, during the initial stage of adaptation, to resist. Many managers maintain that employees are simply denying change when they cling to familiar patterns and complain as these forms of sustenance are threatened. But resistance can also reveal an eloquent appraisal of the *quality* of change – a subtle commentary that goes beyond a stubborn attachment to custom.

Second, the weavers' example shows that as a major technological transition recedes into the past, and with it the sense of psychological crisis, older sensibilities tend to become subsumed or repressed. However, original sources of resistance, if they are not properly resolved, can continue to influence the management-labor agenda for many years, even though employees may accommodate the demands of a new technology.

Business is now witnessing a period of technological change that shares some important features with the first industrial revolution. Information technology is rapidly reorganizing the kind of work people do across industries and organizational strata. It is affecting clerical workers through the automation of high-volume back-office operations as well as with word processing and electronic mail. Managers are more frequently making use of computer conferencing, decision-support systems, sophisticated modeling procedures, and new on-line management information systems. Blue-collar workers are increasingly required to interact with computer technology in order to monitor and control a variety of manufacturing and continuous-process operations. During the past year, business people bought one million data terminals, worth $2.6 billion, to supplement the four million terminals already in use. The market for intelligent terminals is expected to grow 25% annually during the coming decade.

This increased use of information technology is altering the technological infrastructure of the workplace. More and more, production in office and factory depends on the computer and large-scale information systems that can control increasingly complex sets of data. And just as with industrial technology, people who are required to use information systems often resist their introduction. When managers allow employee discontent with new computer-based technology a voice, they can learn a great deal about the more subtle effects of this technology and the issues that are likely to challenge their practices in the coming decade.

During the last few years I interviewed approximately 200 employees, supervisors, professionals, and managers from several different organizations in three countries to discover how people at distinct organizational levels respond to their work when it has been fundamentally reorganized by information technology. (See the ruled insert on page 471 for a description of the organizations and their information systems.) In this article, I outline the principal themes that emerged repeatedly from my interviews and observations, both as they pertain to employees' experiences of information systems and as observable, often unintended, consequences for the organization. Finally, I identify some of the implications of these findings for human resource management policies.

Management policies toward automation

In many ways, management policies can determine the effectiveness of automation and the quality of the workplace culture that emerges. In this regard, my discussions with employees and managers reveal two primary concerns.

Substitution & deskilling of labor

The purpose of the intelligent technology at the core of a computer system is to substitute algorithms or decision rules for individual judgments. This substitution makes it possible to formalize the skills and know-how intrinsic to a job and integrate them into a computer program. As decision rules become more explicit, the more they are subject to planning, and the less they require a person to make a decision at each stage of execution. For some jobs the word "decision" no longer implies an act of human judgment, but an information processing activity that occurs according to rules embedded in a computer program.

At present, most programmed decision making has been limited to the most routine jobs in an organization such as high-volume operations where tasks can be simplified and rationalized to maximize outputs and minimize skill requirements. For example, partly by limiting a collector's discretion regarding how or in what order he or she should work on an account, an automated collection system makes it possible to increase production goals and reduce the time spent on each account.

Thus for that activity the key to revenue generation becomes volume instead of collection skills. Collection managers I interviewed believe that the system enables them to recoup more funds while reducing their dependence on skilled collectors. One collection manager described the value of the system:

> "It gives us a tighter lock on the collector, and we can hire less skilled people. But there's a real loss to the job of skills and know-how. You are being told what to do by the machine."

But job deskilling is not exclusive to the most routine jobs in the organization. A decision-support system installed for a bank's 20 credit analysts was supposed to free them from the most mechanical and boring aspects of the job. Six months after the system was in place, not a single analyst had used it. As one analyst explained it, "I think, then I write down my calculations directly. I know the company and the problem. With this system, I am supposed to type into the machine and let it think. Why should I let it do my thinking for me?"

Automation of managerial assumptions

Information systems can embody management's assumptions and values about its employees, especially about their commitment and motivation. The automated collection system provides an example of how this happens.

Bill Smith had managed collection activities for 30 years, and management considered his perspective invaluable. In creating the system, designers spent long hours debriefing Smith, and he helped them make many important design decisions. Senior managers explain key design decisions by saying: "We tried to build Bill Smith's brain into the computer. If we did not build it into the system, we might lose to the competition."

When I talked to Bill Smith, some of the reasons the system eliminated most discretion from the job became clear. As Smith put it:

"I like to see people work. I'm a good worker. I don't like to see people take time off. I don't do it."

The depth of memory and extent of communications that computer systems are capable of mean that managerial biases can surround the employee as never before. The cost of Smith's managerial assumptions in the collections operations system was high. A year after the system was in place, turnover had reached almost 100%, and the corporate personnel and employee counseling offices were swamped with complaints from replacements. The new and less-educated collectors presented a different set of problems for management and training. Even with the new staff, turnover remained about three times higher than in the rest of the back-office organization.

Computer mediation of work

As the Bill Smith example illustrates, managerial assumptions can easily get embedded in information systems. But what impact do the new systems have on the organization of work and what actually happens to the people who interact with them?

Work becomes abstract

When information technology reorganizes a job, it fundamentally alters the individual's relation to the task. I call the new relationship "computer mediated." Usually, this means that a person accomplishes a task through the medium of the information system, rather than through direct physical contact with the object of the task.

Computer mediation can be contrasted to other forms of task relationships in terms of the way in which one *knows* about the object of the task. The potter who turns a pot with his or her own hands has direct experience of the task's object through continual series of sights and tactile sensations. These sensations form the basis for moment-by-moment judgments regarding the success of the process and any alterations that the potter should make. Machines, such as a press or a welding torch, usually remove the worker as the direct source of energy for the labor process, but leave the task's object within sensuous range. Those who work with paper and pencil usually feel "in touch" with the objects of their tasks through the activity of writing and because they are the sources of what they write.

With computer-mediated work, employees get feedback about the task object only as symbols through the medium of the information system. Very often, from the point of view of the worker, the object of the task seems to have disappeared "behind the screen" and into the information system.

468

The distinction in feedback is what separates the linotype machine operator from the clerical worker who inputs cold type, the engineer who works with computer-aided design from one who directly handles materials, the continuous process operator who reads information from a visual display unit from one who actually checks vat levels, and even the bill collector who works with an on-line, real-time system from a predecessor who handled accounts cards. The distinctiveness of computer-mediated work becomes more clear when one contrasts it against the classic image of work from the nineteenth century in which labor was considered to be the transformation of nature by human muscle. Computer-mediated work is the electronic manipulation of symbols. Instead of a sensual activity, it is an abstract one.

Many employees I spoke to reported feeling frustrated because in losing a direct experience of their task it becomes more difficult to exercise judgment over it. In routine jobs, judgment often becomes lodged in the system itself. As one bill collector said:

> "In our old system, come the end of the month, you knew what you were faced with. With the automated system, you don't know how to get in there to get certain accounts out. You have to work the way the system wants you to."

People in even more complex jobs can also lose direct experience of their tasks. The comptroller of a bank that was introducing information systems to a variety of functions commented:

> "People become more technical and sophisticated, but they have an inferior understanding of the banking business. New people become like systems people and can program instructions that don't necessarily reflect the spirit of the operation."

The auditor at one bank is working with a new information system that frees him from traveling to regional branches. The branches feed financial data directly into the information system that he can access in real time. He described his job this way:

> "The job of auditing is very different now. More imagination is required. I am receiving data on-line. I don't go to the branches if I don't want to. I don't see any books. What do I audit in this situation? I always have to be thinking about what is in the system. I may be auditing, but it doesn't feel like it."

The auditor now has access to a new level of complexity in his data. He has the possibility of comparing branches according to criteria of his choice and searching out new relationships in the data. But in order to do this, he

The research sites

The data reported in this article are principally based on research in three kinds of organization–banking, retail, and consumer goods. Each of these applications had been in place from six months to one year before I began the interviews.

The information systems in the bank included: 1 a decision-support system in the credit analysis department that was able to perform "routine" calculations for analysis; 2 information systems for account officers that provided overviews and analyses of account activity in relation to the key business criteria of a company; 3 information systems that converted front-end processes such as foreign exchange, letter of credit, and current accounts to an on-line real-time basis, thus altering the work of both back-office employees and a range of managers.

The retail application was the automation of collections activities in the back office of a large discount store chain. Before automation, collectors functioned as entrepreneurs, each with an individual tray of accounts to be collected. The automated system pooled all accounts that were then automatically queued in order of priority and randomly distributed among collectors each day.

In the consumer goods organization, professionals and managers coordinated and communicated their activities through the use of computer conferencing and electronic mail.

---

must now develop a theory of the auditing process. He needs to have a conceptual framework that can guide him through the mass of available information. Theoretical insight and imagination will be the keys to his effectiveness on the job.

By creating a medium of work where imagination instead of experience-based judgment is important, information technology challenges old procedures. Judging a given task in the light of experience thus becomes less important than imagining how the task can be reorganized based on new technical capabilities. In the banking industry, for example, planners are not automating the old, but inventing the new.

While working through information systems seems to require a more challenging form of mental effort, it can also induce feelings of frustration and loss of control.

A collections supervisor described the difference between the manual and computer systems:

"If you work with a manual system and you want to see an account on a given day, you have a paper file and you simply go to that particular section and pull out the file. When you're on the computer system, in a sense all your accounts are kind of floating around in space. You can't get your hands on them."

Some people cope with this frustration by creating physical analogues for their tasks. In one bank branch, an on-line system had been installed to update information on current accounts. Instead of making out tickets that would be sent to a data center for overnight keypunching, operators enter data directly into terminals; the system continuously maintains account information. Despite senior management's efforts to persuade them to change, the branch manager and his staff continued to fill out the tickets. When asked why, they first mentioned the need for a backup system. The real reason came out when the branch manager made the following comment: "You need something you can put your hands on. How else can we be sure of what we are doing?"

People are accustomed to thinking of jobs that require employees to use their brains as the most challenging and rewarding. But instead, the computer mediation of simple jobs can create tasks that are routine and unchallenging, while demanding focused attention and abstract comprehension. Nevertheless, the human brain is organized for action. Abstract work on a mass scale seems likely to create conditions that are peculiar if not stressful to many people. While it does seem that those who shift from conventional procedures to computer-mediated work feel this stress most acutely, it's impossible to forecast what adaptation to the abstraction of work will do to people over the long term.

Social interaction is affected

Doubtless, once information technology reorganizes a set of jobs, new patterns of communication and interaction become possible. In time, these patterns are likely to alter the social structure of an organization.

When resources are centered in the information system, the terminal itself can become employees' primary focus of interaction. This focus can lead people to feel isolated in an impersonal situation. For example, because functional operations in the back office of one bank have been reorganized, a clerical worker can complete an entire operation at his or her "professional" work station, rather than repeat a single procedure of it before passing the item on to someone else. Although employees I talked to were split in their attitudes toward the new back-office system, most of them agreed that it created an uncomfortable isolation. Because they had few remaining reasons to interact with co-workers, the local social network was fragmented.

Decades of research have established the importance of social communities in the workplace and the lengths to which people will go to establish and maintain them. Since people will not easily give up the pleasures of the workplace community, they tend to see themselves at odds with the new technology that transforms the quality of work life. The comments of one employee illustrate this point:

> "I never thought I would feel this way, but I really do not like the computer. If a person makes a mistake, dealing with the computer to try and get that mistake corrected is so much red tape. And it's just taken a lot of feeling out of it. You should have people working with people because they are going to give you what you want, and you're going to get a better job all around."

In a very different kind of application, professionals and managers in the R&D organization of a large consumer goods company find the range of their interaction greatly extended with computer conferencing. While there is some evidence of reduced face-to-face interaction, the technology makes it relatively easy to initiate dialogues and form coalitions with people in other parts of the corporation. Clearly, information technology can offset social life in a variety of ways. It is important to realize, however, that this technology has powerful consequences for the structure and function of communication and social behavior in an organization.

New possibilities for supervision & control

The dream of the industrial engineer to create a perfectly timed and rationalized set of activities has never been perfectly realized. Because face-to-face supervision can be carried on only on a partial basis, employees usually find ways to pace their own activities to meet standards at a reasonable rate. Thus, traditionally, supervision depended on the quality of the relationship between supervisor and worker. If the relationship is a positive one, employees are likely to produce quality work without constant monitoring. If the relationship is adversarial, the monitoring will be continual.

But because work accomplished through the medium of video terminals or other intelligent equipment can be recorded on a second-by-second basis, the industrial engineer's presence can be built into all real-time activities. With immediate access to how much employees are producing through printouts or other visual displays, supervisors and managers can increase surveillance without depending on face-to-face supervision. Thus the interpersonal relationship can become less important to supervision than access to information on the quality and quantity of employee output. One bank supervisor described this new capability:

"Instead of going to someone's desk and physically pulling out files, you have the ability to review peoples' work without their knowledge. So I think it keeps them on their toes."

Another variant of remote supervision involves controls that are automatically built into systems operations, as in the collections system described earlier. These rules are substitutes for a certain amount of supervisory effort. Because the system determines what accounts the collector should work on and in what order, a supervisor does not have to monitor collectors' judgments on these issues. Managers also see automatic control as the organization's defense against the potentially massive pollution of data that can occur through access by many people to an on-line real-time system.

Remote supervision, automatic control, and greater access to subordinates' information all become possible with computer-mediated work. In some cases, these capabilities are an explicit objective, but too often management employs them without sufficiently considering the potential human and organizational consequences.

With remote supervision, many employees limit their own risk-taking behavior, such as spotting an error in the data and correcting it, developing a more effective approach to the work than the procedures established by the information system, or trying to achieve quality at the expense of keeping up with new production standards.

One reason the initiative to design a custom-made approach to a particular task has become too risky is that many people have difficulty articulating why their approach might be superior to other alternatives. Usually, management has developed a clearly articulated model of the particular task in order to automate it, and if employees cannot identify their own models with equal clarity, they have little hope of having their views legitimated.

Another reason for decreased employee initiative is that the more an information system can control the details of the job, the less even relatively trivial risk-taking opportunities are available. Finally, the monitoring capabilities increase the likelihood that a supervisor will notice a deviation from standard practice. As one bank employee noted:

"Sometimes I have a gut feeling I would rather do something another way. But, because it is all going to be in the computer, it changes your mind. If somebody wouldn't listen to the reason why you did it that way, well, it could cause you quite a problem."

Another frequent response to the new relationships of supervision and control involves perceptions of authority in the workplace. Employees can tend to see technology less as an instrument of authority than as a source of it. For instance, one group of bank employees with an especially easygoing manager described the work pace on their computer-mediated jobs as hard-driving, intense, and at times unfair, but thought the manager was friendly, relaxed, and fair-minded.

One collector told about the difference in her attitudes toward her work under the manual system and under the automated system:

> "When I worked with the account cards, I knew how to handle my responsibilities. I felt, 'Hey! I can handle this!' Now I come in every day with a defeatist attitude, because I'm dealing with the tube every day. I can't beat it. People like to feel not that they are necessarily ahead of the game, but that they have a chance. With the tube I don't have a chance."

While this employee knows that her manager is the actual authority in the office, and that he is in turn accountable to other managers, she has an undeniable feeling that the system, too, is a kind of authority. It is the system she must fight, and, if she wins, it is the system she vanquishes.

In the Volvo plant in Kalmar, Sweden, a computer system was installed to monitor assembly operations.[1] A feedback device was programmed to flash a red light signalling a quality control problem. The workers protested against the device, insisting that the supervisory function be returned to a foreman. They preferred to answer to a human being with whom they could negotiate, argue, and explain rather than to a computer whose only means of "communication" was unilateral. In effect, they refused to allow the computer to become, at least in this limited situation, an authority. Yet clearly, the issue would never have arisen in the first place were the technology not capable of absorbing the characteristics of authority.

Finally, these capacities of information systems can do much to alter the relationships among managers themselves. A division or plant manager can often leverage a certain amount of independence by maintaining control of key information. Though a manager might have to present the data in monthly or quarterly reports, he or she has some control over the amount and format. With information technology, however, senior managers in corporate headquarters increasingly have access to real-time systems that display the day-to-day figures of distinct parts of the company's business. For instance, a division vice president can be linked to the information system that transmits raw production data from a processing plant in another state. Such data can provide the vice president with a view of the plant that only the plant manager or mid-level managers in the operation previously had.

This new access raises several questions for a corporation. First, some policy decisions must be confronted that address the kind of information appropriate to each level of management. Top managers can quickly find themselves inundated with raw data that they do not have the time to understand. It also creates a tendency for top managers to focus on the past and present when they should be planning the future.

It would seem that this new access capability would expand top management's opportunities to monitor and direct and, therefore, improve the performance of subordinate managers. But as the on-line availability of such information reaches across management hierarchies (in some companies all the way to board chairpersons), reduced risk taking and its effects begin to take hold. Managers are reluctant to make decisions on the basis of information that their superiors receive simultaneously. As one plant manager said to his boss in division headquarters: "I'm telling you, Bob, if you're going to be hooked up to the data from the pumps, I'm not going to manage them anymore. You'll have to do it."

Birth of the information environment

Another consequence of information technology is more difficult to label, but its effects are undeniable. I call it the "information environment." It refers to a quality of organizational life that emerges when the computer mediates jobs and begins to influence both horizontal and vertical relationships. In the information environment, people generally have greater access to data and, in particular, data relevant to their own decision making. The capacity for follow-up and reorganizing increases as information retrieval and communication can occur with greater ease and convenience than ever before.

One effect of this immediate access to information is a rise in the volume of transactions or operations. This increase, in turn, compresses time and alters the rhythm of work. While people were once satisfied if a computer system responded in 24 hours, those who work with computers now are impatient if information takes more than five seconds to appear. Timely and reliable functioning of the system determines workers' output, and these effects extend up the managerial ladder. Once managers become accustomed to receiving in two hours a report that once took two weeks to compile, they will consider any delay a burden. This speed of access, retrieval, and information processing is allegedly the key to improving the productivity of the organization, but few organizations have seriously considered the appropriate definition of productivity in their own operations. In the meantime, more transactions, reports, and information are generated in an ever-shorter amount of time.

Responses to the information environment usually are accompanied by feelings about power and orderliness. To some people, the increased access to information enhances their power over the contingencies of their work. An account officer for one bank states:

> "I never had such a complete picture of a particular customer before. I can switch around the format of the base for my reporting purposes and get a full picture of where the bank is making money. This gives me a new power and effectiveness in my work."

476

While most people agree that the information environment makes the workplace more orderly, responses to this orderliness tend to be bipolar. Some see the order as "neat and nice," while others perceive it as increasing the regimentation of the workplace. Responses of two collections managers illustrate these differences. The first described the system this way:

> "The computer simply alleviates a lot of paperwork. Everything is lined up for you instead of you having to do it yourself. If you are sloppy, the system organizes you."

Another manager in the same organization regards the collections system in a different way:

> "Things were a lot more relaxed before the tubes. Before, you scheduled your day yourself; now the machine lines it up for you. This means a more rigid environment because we can track things better."

Greater regimentation can also affect the environment of the professional. A vice president in one organization where professionals have come to rely heavily on electronic mail and computer conferencing puts it this way:

> "I used to make notes to myself on things I had to follow up. Now those notes go into my electronic mail system. The system automatically tracks these things and they are there in front of me on the screen if I haven't followed up yet. Nothing slips through the cracks, but certainly for the way professionals usually operate, it's more regimented."

Many of the managers and professionals I talked to are wary of systems that seem to encroach on their judgment, their freedom, or the "artistry" of their professional assessments. Instead of feeling that increased information augments their power, these people resist information systems that they see limiting their freedom or increasing the measurability of their work.

At present, most professionals and managers function in fairly ambiguous environments. Information is imperfectly exchanged (often in corridors, washrooms, or over lunch), and considerable lag time usually occurs before the quality of decisions can be assessed. A continual flow of complete information, however, reduces ambiguity. For example, in the marketing area of one bank, an information system provides complete profiles of all accounts while it assesses their profitability according to corporate criteria. Top management and systems developers believed the system could serve as a constant source of feedback to account officers and senior managers, allowing them to better manage their account activities and maximize fee-based revenues. But some bankers saw the flow of "perfect" information as not only reducing ambiguity but also limiting their opportunities for creative decisions and resisted using it.

Limited information may create uncertainty in which people make errors of judgment, but it also provides a "free space" for inspiration. This free space is fundamental to the psychology of professional work. The account officers in the bank had traditionally been motivated by the opportunity to display their artistry as bankers, but as increased information organizes the context of their work, the art in their jobs is reduced.

Employees in back-office clerical jobs also tend to perceive the increased time and volume demands and the measurability of operations as limits on their opportunities to experience a sense of mastery over the work. To overcome these effects, many of the collectors keyed fictitious data into the system of account files. Their managers were confronted with high productivity figures that did not match the size of monthly revenues.

Many managers first respond to such a situation by searching out ways to exert more control over the work process. I am convinced that the more managers attempt to control the process, the more employees will find ways to subvert that control. This response is particularly likely when outsmarting the system becomes the new ground on which to develop and test one's mastery. Managers may dismiss these subversive activities as "resistance to change," but in many cases this resistance is the only way employees can respond to the changes they face. Such resistance can also be understood as a positive phenomenon – it is evidence of an employee's identification with the job.

Listening to the resistance

Critics of technology tend to fall into one of three camps. Some bemoan new developments and see them as a particular form of human debasement and depersonalization. Others are ready to applaud any form of technology as progress toward some eventual conquest of dumb nature. Finally, others argue that technology is neutral and its meaning depends on the uses to which human beings press its application. I have found none of these views sufficient.

It is true that information technology provides a particularly flexible set of technical possibilities, and thus can powerfully embody the assumptions and goals of those whom it is designed to serve. Yet, while the value and meaning of a given application must be read, in part, from management's intentions, beliefs, and commitments, this does not imply the ultimate neutrality of the technology itself. To say that information technology is neutral is like saying an airplane is neutral because it can fly to either Washington or Moscow. We know that airplanes are not neutral because we all live in a world that has been radically altered by the facts of air travel – the globe has been shrunk, time and space have collapsed.

If one accepts that technology is *not* neutral, it follows that information technology must have attributes that are unique in the world view they impose and the experience of work to which they give shape. The flexibility, memory, and remote access capabilities of information systems create new management possibilities and, therefore, choices in the design of an application.

This argument suggests three general areas for management deliberation and action in the deployment of new information systems. The first concerns policies that shape the quality of the employment relationship. The second involves attitudes toward managerial control, and the third concerns basic beliefs about the nature of an organization and the role of management.

The quality of the employment relationship

Because the computer mediation of work can have direct consequences for virtually every area of human resource management including skills training, career paths, the social environment, peer relationships, supervision, control, decision making, authority, and organization design, managers need to think through the kind of workplace they want to foster. They need to make design choices that reflect explicit human resource management policies.

For example, consider the automated collections system I described earlier. Although the system minimizes individual decision making, most managers I interviewed in that organization believe that collector skill and judgment are critical variables in the organization's ability to generate payments and have compelling financial data to support that view.

A management policy commitment to maintaining skill levels, providing challenging jobs, and promoting collector loyalty and motivation could have resulted in an information system that preserves the entrepreneurial aspects of the collector's job while rationalizing its administration with on-line record-keeping. But to assess the likely consequences of an approach to automation that strictly rationalizes procedures, managers need to understand the human logic of a job. In many cases, this human logic holds the clue to the motivational aspects of the job that should be preserved in the conversion to new technology.

What do managers do when faced with some of the more intrinsic features of information technology? First, they need to understand the kinds of skill demands that the computer mediation of work generates, and to construct educational programs that allow employees to develop the competencies that are most relevant to the new environment.

If a more theoretical comprehension of the task is required for effective utilization of the information system, then employees should be given the opportunity to develop this conceptual understanding. If an information system is likely to reduce the sense (if not the fact) of individual control over a task, is it possible to redesign the job to reinvest it with a greater self-managing capacity? As elements of supervision and coordination are loaded into jobs that have been partially drained of challenge, new learning and career development opportunities can open up. The astonishing quantity of information that is available can be used to increase employees' feedback, learning, and self-management rather than to deskill and routinize their jobs or remotely supervise them.

New systems are often presented with the intention of providing "information resources" for more creative problem solving. Unless employees are actually given the knowledge and authority to utilize such resources in the service of more complex tasks, these systems will be undermined, either through poor utilization or more direct forms of resistance.

The focus of managerial control

Because of the many self-management opportunities the information resource makes possible, managers may have to rethink some classic notions of managerial control. When industrial work exerted stringent demands on the placement and timing of physical activity, managers focused on controlling bodies and stipulating the precise ways in which they should perform.

With the burgeoning of office work, physical discipline was less important than reading or writing and, above all, interpersonal behavior. Because people needed to learn how to behave with superiors, subordinates, and the public, managers began to control less what people did with their bodies and more what they did with one another – their communication, teamwork, meeting behavior, and so forth.

With computer-mediated work, neither physical activity nor interpersonal behavior appear to be the most appropriate targets of managerial control. Instead, patterns of attention, learning, and mental engagement become the keys to effectiveness and high-quality performance. Obviously, people have always had to "pay attention" to their work in order to accomplish it properly. But the quality of attention computer-mediated work requires is essentially different.

For instance, in almost all accounts of routine work, researchers report that employees are daydreaming and bantering with one another while they accomplish their tasks. Of course, they must pay attention with their eyes, but not so much with their brains. In contrast, people concentrating on a visual display unit must pay a very different sort of attention. If employees are to understand and properly respond to information, they must be mentally involved.

Managers can experiment to find how to make the most of people's attending and learning qualities as well as their overall engagement in the information environment. One observation that emerges from my current field research is that imposing traditional supervisory approaches on the computer-mediated environment can create considerable dysfunction.

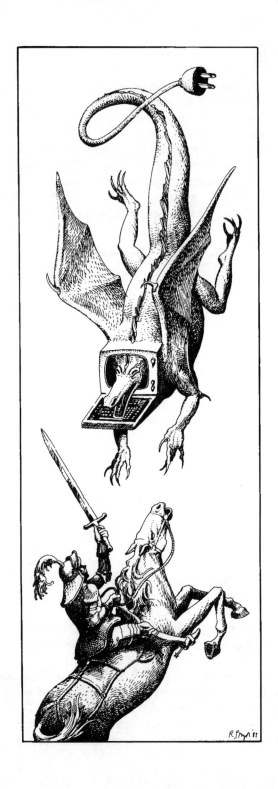

Supervisors and managers who concentrate on the physical and interpersonal behavior of employees working with information systems simply exacerbate tensions instead of creating an environment that nurtures the kind of learning and attention computer-mediated work makes necessary and compensating for some of its less obvious but potentially negative attributes.

The nature of organization & management

With information technology, managers will do a variety of tasks that others once did for them. Because of this, we are likely to see a gradual shift in the overall shape of the organization from a pyramid to something closer to a diamond shape – with a diminishing clerical support staff, swelling numbers of professionals and middle managers, and a continually more remote, elite, policy-making group of senior managers.

While these considerations should be of central importance to management policy in the coming years, as a society we are sure to see a continuing challenge to the salience of work and the workplace in our daily lives. The traditional importance of occupational distinctiveness may be further eroded as what it means to "accomplish a task" undergoes a fundamental change. When a person's primary work consists of monitoring or interacting with a video screen, it may become more difficult to answer the questions, "Who am I?" and "What do I do?" Identification with an occupational role may diminish, while the transferability of on-the-job skills increases. Will this have implications for individual commitment to an organization and for the relative importance of work and nonwork activities?

Information technology is also likely to introduce new forms of collective behavior. When the means of production becomes dependent on electronic technology and information flows, it is no longer inevitable that, as in the case of the weavers, work be either collective or synchronous. As long as a terminal and communications links are available, people will be able to perform work in neighborhood centers, at home, or on the road. At the same time, electronic technology is altering the traditional structure and function of communication within the organization. Who interacts with whom in the organization? Can the neat chain of command hierarchy be maintained? Should it be? What does it take to lead or influence others when communication itself becomes computer mediated? Finally, who is likely to gain or lose as we make the transition to this environment?

These developments make it necessary to rethink basic conceptions of the nature of organization and management. What is an organization if people do not have to come face to face in order to accomplish their work? Does the organization itself become an abstraction? What happens to the shared purpose and commitment of members if their face-to-face interaction is reduced? Similarly, how should an "abstract" organization be managed?

If information technology is to live up to its promise for greater productivity, managers need to consider its consequences for human beings and the qualities of their work environments. The demands for a thoughtful and energetic management response go deeper than the need for a "friendly interface" or "user involvement." The underlying nature of this technology requires understanding; the habitual assumptions used in its design must surface. Managers' ability to meet these demands will be an important determinant of the quality of work in future organizations.

Note

* Illustrations by Robert Pryor.

1 "Social Effects of Automation," International Federation of Automated Control Newsletter, No. 6, September 1978.

46

STRATEGIC INFORMATION SYSTEMS PLANNING

Myths, reality and guidelines for successful implementation

R. D. Galliers

Source: *European Journal of Information Systems* 1(1) (1991): 55–64.

There have been a number of claims made in recent years with respect to the utilisation of information technology as a source of competitive advantage and as a means of enabling and directing strategic moves. This paper presents evidence to suggest that, so far, identification and successful implementation of strategic information systems has arisen as often as not from happy circumstance rather than as a result of a process of strategy formulation. Because of this, many companies run the risk of missing out on an opportunity to compete on an equal footing with their international rivals in increasingly competitive and global markets. In addition, the paper warns that the process of identifying and implementing strategically significant information systems is a complex task, the result of which represents considerable risk to companies should there be inadequate preparedness on their part. In view of this, it presents guidelines which may help in improving management understanding of the process; deciding on an appropriate information systems strategy for a particular company/context, and successfully implementing strategic information systems. A contingent, socio-technical approach to strategic information systems planning is proposed.

Introduction

Much has been claimed concerning the competitive advantage companies can obtain through the judicious application of information technology (IT). Examples such as American Hospital Supply and American Airlines in the USA and Thomson Holidays in the United Kingdom are often cited with a view to making organizations rethink their information systems strategy to include competitive considerations (see, for example, Large, 1986).

However, there have been some notable exceptions to these success stories. For example, while the Bank of America was confident of information systems strategy success in 1984 (Lansman, 1984), by 1988 $80 m had been spent on its MasterNet accounting system, whose failure resulted in 29 of the Bank's most lucrative trust fund customers being handed over to a competitor (BCC, 1988).

The introduction of competitive forces analysis into our thinking on strategic information systems planning (SISP) arises in part from the work of Michael Porter and his colleagues from the Harvard Business School (e.g. Porter, 1980; McFarlan, 1984; Porter, 1985; Porter & Millar, 1985; Cash & Konsynski, 1985). In particular, attention in SISP is now much more focused on using IT to harness (or negate) the following competitive forces identified by Porter:

- potential entrants/new rivals
- substitute products/services
- suppliers
- buyers/customers
- traditional industry competitors.

If one reads the wealth of literature that now exists on the subject, one might be forgiven for believing that much of current strategy formulation practice reflects this kind of thinking. The reality is that many companies do not formulate strategy according to this rational/analytical model, nor do they adequately plan their information systems, let alone incorporate competitive considerations into their planning efforts. What is more, they experience difficulty in implementing their plans, once these have been formulated. This is certainly true in the United Kingdom, and probably in many other countries as well (Galliers, 1987a).

The basis for this contention rests on survey evidence collected in the latter half of the 1980s (Galliers, 1987a,b; Wilson, 1989). Both studies indicate that in excess of 75% of British companies undertake SISP. Similar figures apply to other countries as well—for example, USA (Martino, 1983) and Australia (Galliers, 1987a). However, as will be shown below, much current SISP practice falls well short of what is the conventional wisdom for SISP success.

This paper puts forward an explanation for this, and a broader concept for what properly constitutes SISP is proposed, as is a framework that has been used to assist companies in choosing an appropriate IS strategy.

First, though, it is important that we understand what is meant by the terms associated with SISP and IS strategy formulation. Two such terms are strategic and competitive information systems. Huff and Beattie (1985) provide the following useful distinction between the two:

- Strategic information systems 'directly support the creation and implementation of an organization's strategic plan'. The emphasis here is on information systems that enhance executive management processes and decisions. For example, according to this definition, information systems that test the assumptions underpinning strategic plans or business objectives would be classified as strategic.
- Competitive information systems 'directly support the execution of strategy by improving the value/cost relationship of the firm in its competitive environment'. Here, the emphasis is on improving competitiveness through the use of IT in reducing costs or adding value to products/services.

It is also useful to consider how our thinking has developed over the years regarding the focus of SISP.

In the early writings on SISP, attention was concentrated primarily on improving computer efficiency and matters of computer management generally (e.g. Kriebel, 1968). SISP was seen as being a matter for the IS function, somewhat isolated from the continuing business of the organization. As time passed and experience of IS management was gained, there was growing concern on the part of management to have business-driven SISPs, capable of dealing with the business problems or issues they faced. Such approaches as IBM's Business Systems Planning (c.f. Zachman, 1982) and Rockart's Critical Success Factors (Rockart, 1979) became increasingly accepted. The approaches were somewhat reactive in nature, given their emphasis on top-down planning (Ng, 1984), feeding from business plans/strategies. In addition, they were somewhat mechanistic in approach, following clearly defined procedures and frequently requiring fairly detailed analysis of, for example, processes and data.

While meeting with a measure of success, these approaches were criticised in some quarters for not having a sufficiently strong link with business objectives and for concentrating too much on issues of the day, rather than on future goals or concerns (Davis, 1979). Partly as a result of this, business-driven approaches began to focus more on the latter, and developments of, for example, the Critical Success Factors approach, began to include a consideration of future scenarios with efforts being made to identify the critical assumptions upon which business plans or strategies were being built (Henderson *et al.*, 1984). While still being dependent on business plans (and, therefore, in this sense, still reactive in nature), such approaches attempted to identify future opportunities for the application of IT, rather than simply focusing on current issues or concerns.

As organizations sought to identify IT opportunities through their SISP efforts, so-called 'middle-out' approaches became more common (Henderson & Sifonis, 1986), the seminal work being that of Porter and colleagues (e.g. Porter, 1979; Porter & Millar, 1985). In this context, SISP became more proactive, with attention being concentrated on an organization's business environment as much as on internal processes, and on technological advances that might be harnessed to good effect.

Current thinking recognises that elements of each of these foci are likely to be more or less required in different circumstances, and in the mid to late 1980s came calls for the adoption of 'eclectic' (Sullivan, 1985) or 'multiple' (Earl, 1987, 1988 and 1989) methods. In fact, the very nature of SISP is now seen to be more complex than formerly. No longer should organizations be looking simply for a prioritised portfolio of information systems applications as the sole outcome of the process. Human, organizational and infrastructural issues (e.g. skills requirements and the manner in which information systems services can best be organized) are now seen as critical components of the task (see Figure 3 and Galliers, 1987a, p 230). These developments in SISP are summarised in Figure 1, which is based on a framework first proposed by Hirschheim (1982) and later amended by Galliers (1987a,c) and Ward (1988).

A note of caution, however—much of our thinking in the SISP world appears to be based on an overly optimistic, formal and rational model of strategy formulation. As intimated above, in many companies strategy is arrived at by a more informal and creative process. Indeed, it might be said that some companies have no formal strategy at all. The process of SISP must, therefore, take into account the prevalent style of strategy formulation in any given context (cf. Pyburn, 1983) and, moreover, should not adopt an entirely rational model itself.

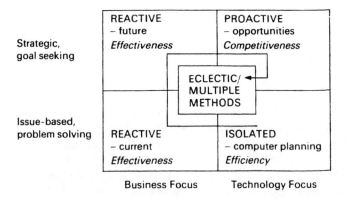

Figure 1 A development path for strategic information systems planning (amended from Galliers, 1987a).

Having summarised some of the developments that have taken place in SISP thinking, let us now turn to how SISP practice compares with the 'conventional wisdom' for SISP success.

Successful strategic information systems planning: theory versus practice

In a 1986 survey of UK SISP practice (Galliers, 1987b), respondents indicated that, from an information systems management perspective, their efforts were either partially or highly successful in 71% of the cases where SISP was being undertaken. Relative figures from a senior and middle management perspective were 68% and 58% respectively. In Wilson's more recent survey of companies in *The Times 500*, 73% of respondents indicated that they believed their SISP efforts to be either reasonably or highly successful. The conclusions from the two surveys are therefore remarkably similar, despite the intervening three years.

Where practice does appear to have changed, however, is related to the competitive advantage component of SISP. In 1986, competitor analysis was present in only 5% of cases, while 6% claimed that competitive edge was a focus for their planning efforts (Galliers, 1986a). Conversely, Wilson reported 88% of his respondents as claiming that competitive advantage was a feature of their IT strategies.

This comparison is somewhat misleading however, in that Wilson reported 44% (i.e. half of those respondents claiming that competitive advantage was part of their strategy), as seeing the reduction of costs through the application of IT as a component of this strategy. Likewise, Galliers reported that 17% of his respondents saw improved efficiency or cost reduction as being one of their objectives in undertaking SISP. Where the figures are radically different, however, relates to the use of IT to improve products or services. In 1986, Galliers reported this as an SISP objective in just 4% of cases, while in 1989, Wilson reported 73% as claiming this (i.e. 83.3% of the 88% claiming competitive advantage as a feature of SISP).

As a result of this comparison, it would be reasonable to suggest that competitive advantage has been a growing consideration over recent years in UK companies' SISP. Indeed, the 1990/91 Price Waterhouse *IT Review* indicates that concerns about IT for competitive edge began to come to the forefront precisely in 1987 (Grindley, 1990).

A further useful comparison can be made in respect of the barriers that were identified as reducing the likelihood of successful SISP formulation and implementation. Wilson's findings are summarised in Table 1, while the viewpoints of IS planners as to SISP success factors, as reported by Galliers, are summarised in Table 2.

By refering to both Tables 1 and 2, it is possible to group factors together to form a perspective on key considerations in SISP:

Table 1 Barriers to successful IS strategy (amended from Wilson, 1989).

Rank		
ISP		
Formulation	Implementation	Barrier
1	3	Measuring benefits
2	2	Nature of business
3	1	Difficulty in recruiting
4	6	Political conflicts
5	5	Existing IT investment
6	4	User education resources
7	11	Doubts about benefits
8	9	Telecommunications issues
9	7	Middle management attitudes
10	8	Senior management attitudes
11	10	Technology lagging behind needs

Table 2 Strategic information systems planning success factors (amended from Galliers, 1987b, p 249).

Rank *(importance)*	Success factor *(IS planner viewpoints)*
1	Senior management commitment
2	Senior management involvement
3	Senior and middle management involvement
4	Increased management understanding of IS/IT
5	Assessment/evaluation of ISP
6	ISP supported by IS management function
7	Business plans a basis for ISP
8	ISP outcomes/process debated by management
9	Middle management involvement
10	ISP outcome: prioritised applications portfolio

- the attitude, commitment and involvement of management (to include debating the process or outcomes of SISP to overcome the 'politics' of planning, and management education)
- the current status of the company with respect to IT, in terms of the technology itself, the manner in which the IS function is organized, and the SISP skills available
- the ability to measure, review or assess the benefits of SISP (in terms of outcomes and the process itself)
- linking or taking into account the business strategy.

Management involvement

While the Galliers survey suggests that the extent of involvement on the part of management in the SISP process is often not a problem (see Figure 2), there is a weight of evidence to suggest that the attitude of UK managers to IT can reasonably be described as one of disinterest, except in terms of concern about costs (Grindley, 1990). In addition, it is often the case that the SISP approach adopted involves the planner or consultant interviewing individual managers, thereby reducing the opportunity for debate. Further, despite a very large majority in favour of SISP teams being led by a senior manager, in practice, it is most often the case that an IS professional will have to take the lead (Galliers, 1987c). In other words, while it seems likely that management will involve themselves in SISP, the quality of that involvement, and the extent of their commitment to resultant change, may be called into question.

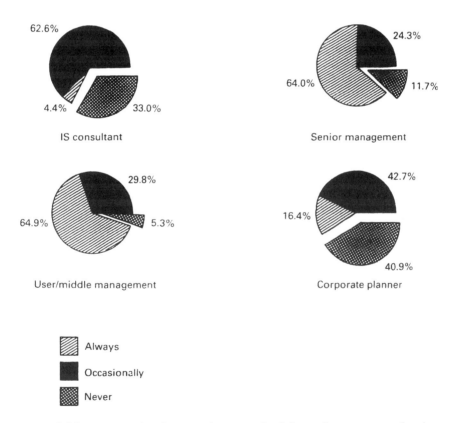

Figure 2 Management involvement in strategic information systems planning (amended from Galliers, 1987a, p 246).

491

Current status

It is paradoxical that the IS profession is often criticised for developing information systems which too closely reflect the *status quo*. In other words, we automate ineffective processes too often (Galliers, 1987d). When it comes to planning information systems, however, we increasingly appear to be more concerned with where we want to get to, rather than the route which we need to take to get there. For example, Wilson (1989) talks of SISP as '[bringing] together the business aims of the company . . . It is a plan for the development of systems towards some future vision'. Porter (1985), however, reminds us that business strategy is 'the route to competitive advantage'.

Strategy formulation is concerned, then, with 'getting from A to B'. It is not sufficient that we know just A or B. We must know A and B. And, just as importantly, B must be appropriate and achievable, given our A. In other words the chosen strategy must be feasible as well as desirable (cf. Checkland, 1981). Furthermore, given alternative visions of the future, alternative Bs may be identified (and alternative routes planned).

So-called 'stages of growth' models have been used to good effect in determining a company's current status as regards aspects of IT utilisation and management (e.g. Nolan, 1979; Earl, 1989), despite the reservations of academic researchers (e.g. Benbasat *et al.*, 1984). One of the problems of earlier models relates to the fact that they referred only to aspects of the IS situation. For example, the Nolan model focuses for the most part on database technology, the amount spent on data processing and the extent of user awareness with regard to IT.

In the light of these criticisms, particularly in relation to the narrowness of focus, a revised model has been developed which takes account of a number of broader issues associated with IS strategy formulation or implementation (Sutherland & Galliers, 1989; Galliers & Sutherland, 1991). These include the skills available (both on the part of managers and IS professionals), the manner in which IS services are organized, and the focus of the SISP effort. Because of this wider focus, the model has been used to good effect in identifying both feasible and desirable IS strategies. The revised model is briefly described later.

Assessment

Reviewing both the process and outcomes of SISP is considered to be one of the most important success factors. However, while 84% of respondents to the Galliers survey indicated that formal reviews did take place, an assessment of the benefits of SISP were reported as occurring in only 16% of cases. What is more, formal assessments of benefits occurred in just 9% of cases. Given that measuring benefits is considered to be the single greatest barrier to the successful development of IS strategies (Wilson, 1989), this is of major concern.

It is important to understand that benefits should be measured in the context of what is expected of the SISP process. The Galliers study showed that what was important in terms of required SISP outcomes to one stakeholder group may not be so important to another (Galliers, 1987e). For example, while, in general, IS managers were looking for clear, achievable plans, middle managers simply wanted improved information systems as a result of the SISP process, and senior managers sought an improved capability for justifying IT investment. One could argue the point further. Individual managers from within the same stakeholder group may well have different outcomes in mind.

When one considers the range of SISP approaches that can be used, many of which have a distinct type of outcome (e.g. applications portfolio, database architecture, extent or type of IT investment required), an ability to assess likely benefits, associated with an ability to choose an approach likely to produce the desired outcome, appears to be significant. However, the Galliers survey showed that formal evaluation of alternative approaches took place in only 7% of the companies surveyed (Galliers, 1986b).

Business linkage

It is almost a truism to suggest that SISP should be closely linked to business planning and that it should therefore take very careful note of the nature of the business which is to be supported by IT. Nevertheless, as many as 58% of those surveyed by Galliers were prepared to admit that their SISPs were at best only tenuously linked with their business plans. Part of the reason for this is that business planner involvement is still relatively rare, with 83% of respondents admitting that this takes place on an occasional basis at best, as shown in Figure 2 (Galliers, 1987a).

Summary

This section has looked at how current SISP practice differs from the conventional wisdom of what is thought to constitute successful SISP. It would appear that we often find it difficult to put theory into practice when it comes to:

- obtaining appropriate commitment to, and involvement in ISP from management. This is possibly due to the over-concentration on technical and technological, rather than business management and organizational issues associated with much of current SISP practice (see Figure 3). It may also be due in part to the fact that insufficient emphasis is given to management debate about the key issues associated with alternative futures or IS strategies.

• ascertaining an appropriate IS strategy, given current capabilities associated with IS, as well as future goals. While it may well be possible in the longer term to introduce IS applications which utilise the most up-to-date and complex technology and which promise to provide the organization concerned with a competitive edge, it may also be the case that the organization is not ready (e.g. in terms of skills, human resources and management practices) for such an eventuality. In these cases, such strategies may well represent a considerable risk (c.f. Ives & Learmonth, 1984) and may well prove to be unimplementable. Frameworks for assisting in choosing an appropriate approach or strategy should be of considerable assistance here, and examples of these are introduced below.

• reviewing or assessing the benefits of SISP and choosing an appropriate SISP approach in the light of the desired outcomes of the SISP process. It is often said that SISP should be a continuous, learning process, and very much part of continuing management activity. It is often still the case, however, that SISP is associated with an annual budgetary, or a once-off special exercise which tends to be seen as being unrelated to key business processes. Even in situations where SISP is undertaken continuously, the learning process is rendered less effective by a lack of assessment against desired outcomes or targets. In addition, the process itself suffers because inadequate attention has been paid to the choice of an approach that is likely to be capable of delivering the required outcomes, as illustrated above. The combination of executive workshops and other opportunities to debate important issues may play a key role here.

• linking SISP with business planning. While it is invariably argued that SISP should be closely associated with the business planning process (if only one part of it), it is still too often the case that the link is tenuous at best, with the two processes being undertaken in isolation from each other and with little business planner involvement in SISP and vice versa. Again, part of the reason for this relates to too great attention being paid to technological, rather than business, management and organizational issues during the SISP process. In addition, the style of the two processes may well differ, with an overly rational, mechanistic approach to SISP and a more creative, informal approach to business strategy formulation. This leads to a lack of committed management involvement, because the language used is that of the technologist or methodologist, which in turn reduces the linkage with business strategy, thus compounding the problem.

A broader conception of strategic information systems planning

In the section above, it was argued that part of the reason our SISP efforts fall short of what is considered to be good practice is due to an over-emphasis on what might be termed IT strategy rather than IS strategy. Earl (1989) makes a useful distinction between the two concepts when he writes of IT strategy being more concerned with how to provide required information, while IS strategy should be concerned with understanding what is required.

If one takes a socio-technical perspective of information systems (i.e. a more holistic stance), it can be argued that information systems are as much concerned with human activity and organization as they are with technology—if not more so (cf. Checkland, 1981; Land & Hirschheim, 1983). If this argument is accepted, it follows that IS strategy should contain not only IT strategy, but also such organizational issues as change management and a human resource strategy associated with IS—in other words, a strategy that takes into account the manner in which one might move from A to B, and the necessary organization, people and skills associated with this movement. A model which illustrates this thinking is provided in Figure 3.

It is important to note that the IS strategy is very much embedded in business strategy: it both feeds off, and feeds into, the business strategy process, which in turn is depicted as having a two-way interrelationship with the company's business environment. The model is, therefore, in line with Earl's multiple approach to IS strategy, incorporating 'top-down', 'bottom-up' and 'inside-out' planning (Earl, 1989).

Note, too, that information strategy is incorporated in the model as providing the answer to what information is required to support both business strategy formulation and business processes (cf. Galliers, 1984).

Emphasis should be placed on the strategies located in the centre of Figure 3 (i.e. those in bold) when seeking management commitment, leadership and involvement, rather than on technological concerns (IT strategy) or infrastructure issues (IM strategy). All too often, it is the case in practice that the focus of debate is on the latter rather than the former, with consequent disinterest on the part of management.

As indicated above, a revised 'stages of growth' model has been developed to take into account the socio-technical view of SISP depicted in Figure 3 (Sutherland & Galliers, 1989; Galliers & Sutherland, 1991). This is summarised in Table 3.

In addition to what are taken as the usual components of SISP (i.e. those associated with the technology and the kind of systems that have been, and are being, developed), the model attempts to take account of the company's superordinate goals (i.e. its culture or shared values—those values that

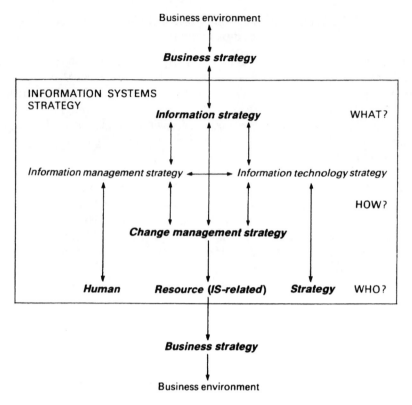

Figure 3 The components of information systems strategy: a socio-technical perspective (after Earl, 1989).

underpin its business strategy and its strategy style), and the staff, skills and organizational structure necessary to implement the chosen strategy (cf. Pascale & Athos, 1981, p 81).

Most models of this kind depict the final stage as representing 'maturity' —a stage of near perfection in which the hard-won lessons of the earlier stages are put to good effect. The 'maturity' label has not been used to describe Stage VI in this model. While this stage does represent a phase which incorporates the accumulated wisdom of the earlier stages, it does not represent an ultimate goal to which all organizations should aspire. For example, a Stage VII might be postulated, concerned with the provision of a flexible IT infrastructure and with integrating IT into both formal and informal organizational forms (Frank Land, personal communication).

The model has been used to good effect by a number of organizations during the past two years or so. In particular, it has proved helpful in raising a number of questions about, for example:

Table 5 A revised stages of growth model (Sutherland & Galliers, 198?, p??, Galliers & Sutherland, 199?).

Element	I	II	III	IV	V	VI
				Stage		
Strategy	Acquisition of hardware, software etc	IT audit Find out and meet user needs (reactive)	Top-down IS planning	Integration, co-ordination and control	Environmental scanning and opportunity seeking	Maintain comparative strategic advantage Monitor futures Interactive planning
Structure	None	Label of IS Often subordinate to accounting or finance	Data processing department Centralised DP shop End users running free at stage 1	Information centres Library records. OA etc in same unit Information services	SBU coalition(s) (many but separate)	Centrally co-ordinated coalitions (corporate & SBU views concurrently)
Systems	Ad hoc, unconnected Operational Multiple manual and IS Uncoordinated Concentration on financial systems Little maintenance	Many applications Many gaps Overlapping systems Centralised Operational Mainly financial systems Many areas unsatisfied Large backlog Heavy maintenance load	Still mostly centralised Uncontrolled end user computing Most major business activities covered	Decentralised approach with some controls, but mostly lack of coordination Some DSS (ad hoc) Integrated office technology systems	Decentralised systems but central control and coordination Added value systems (more marketing oriented) More DSS (internal, less ad hoc) Some strategic systems (using external data) Lack of external and internal data integration Integration of communications technologies with computing	Interorganizational systems (supplier, customer, government links) New IS based products External/internal data integration

Table 3 (cont'd)

Element	Stage					
	I	II	III	IV	V	VI
Staff	Programmers/ contractors	Systems analysts DP manager	IS planners IS manager	Business analysts Information resource manager (chief information officer)	Corporate/business/ IS planners (one role)	IS director–member of board of directors
Style	Unaware	Don't bother me (I'm too busy)	Abrogation Delegation	Democratic Dialectic	Individualistic (product champion)	Business team
Skills	Technical (very low level) (individual expertise)	Systems development methodology	IS believes it knows what the business needs Project management	Organizational integration IS knows how the business works Users know how IS works (for their area) Business management (for IS staff)	IS manager–member of senior executive team Knowledgeable users in some IS areas Entrepreneurial/ marketing skills	All senior management understand IS and its potentialities
Superordinate goals	Obfuscation	Confusion	Senior management concern DP defence	Cooperation	Opportunistic Entrepreneurial Intrapreneurial	Interactive planning

- those aspects of the current IS strategy which appear to require particular attention (i.e. those factors which appear to be lagging behind others)
- those parts of the business which appear to be lagging behind others with respect to IS and IT issues
- the appropriateness, or otherwise, of revised or new IS strategies (i.e. in terms of feasibility as well as desirability).

With regard to the latter, it has been noted that too little attention has been paid in practice to the choice of an appropriate ISP strategy or approach. However, there are some frameworks available that can help in this regard.

For example, McLaughlin *et al.* (1983) propose that an appropriate ISP strategy can be chosen by reflecting

(i)   on how IS/IT can have an impact on products and markets, and on the competitiveness of the company in the market, and
(ii) on the 'ability to deliver' of the company's IS resources (see also, Ives & Learmonth, 1984; Galliers, 1987c; Ward, 1988).

The framework reproduced in Table 3 can assist in gauging the latter, while the work of Porter (1979, 1980, 1985), for example, is helpful with the former. The McLaughlin framework is depicted in Figure 4.

Briefly, their argument is that organizations with good opportunities and strong resources should attempt to attack their competitors by exploiting IS/IT. Similarly, in situations where there is both low potential and resources, they argue that the company concerned is safe from attack. Conversely, however, where the company has good quality resources but potential appears to be limited, they should explore all opportunities to consolidate their IT assets and to be in a position to attack should the impact of IS/IT increase in their industry. Should opportunities be high but competence low, companies should beware because they are vulnerable to attack at any time via the exploitation of IS/IT on the part of their competitors.

Another means of assessing the appropriateness of SISP approaches in any particular context is to review the motivations of various stakeholders

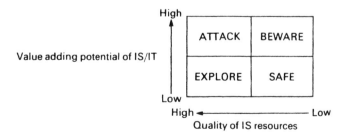

Figure 4 Choosing an appropriate ISP strategy (McLaughlin *et al.*, 1983).

499

in the process. As highlighted above, it is likely that different stakeholders will have different reasons for wanting an SISP study to take place, that is, they may well be looking for different outcomes from the process.

As a result of Galliers' research into SISP practice during 1986, a number of different motivations were identified. These can be compared with

(i) the prevalent motivations that exist amongst different stakeholder groups in any given situation and
(ii) the kinds of outcomes different SISP approaches are likely to produce.

For example, certain SISP approaches, such as BSP and information engineering, concentrate attention on producing an applications portfolio or on a database architecture (e.g. Zachman, 1982; Martin, 1982). While these may well be entirely appropriate if they are the desired outcomes of the SISP process, they are likely to be less helpful in, for example, identifying necessary organizational changes, IS-related skill requirements, or opportunities to gain a competitive advantage through the utilisation of IT. A matrix of the kind illustrated in Figure 5 may be of use in choosing an appropriate SISP approach based on the differing motivations that may exist at any one point in time, or are likely to at some stage in the future.

The set of motivations included in Figure 5 is not meant to be comprehensive but indicative only. The framework is meant to be used as a basis for questioning what the motivations (in regard to SISP) of individual stakeholders are so that candidate approaches can be identified and debated.

ISP Orientation[1]	IT↔Organization↔Environment		
Motivation			
Efficiency, cost reduction	xx	xx	x
Effectiveness	x	xxx	xx
Improved products/services	x	xx	xxx
Applications portfolio	x	xxx	xx
IT acquisitions	xxx	x	x
IT architecture	xxx	x	x
Competitive advantage	x	xx	xxx
Improved mgmt./IS relations	x	xx	xx
Resourcing decisions	xx	xx	x
Human resource considerations	x	xx	x
Database architecture	xxx	xx	x

Note: [1] SISP orientation relates to the type of SISP approach being considered, i.e. whether the focus is on the technology itself (isolated), or on matters internal to the organization (reactive), or on the business environment (proactive) (Figure 1).

x minor   xx reasonable   xxx major

Figure 5 A contingency framework for choosing an appropriate SISP approach based on stakeholder motivations (amended from Galliers, 1987f, p 344).

Conclusions

This paper has shown how current SISP practice compares with those factors generally agreed to be critical for SISP success. It has been demonstrated that practice is deficient, particularly in respect of:

- gaining appropriate commitment to, and involvement in, SISP on the part of senior and middle management
- implementing IS strategies, due to an inappropriate choice of strategy —from a feasibility as well as desirability standpoint
- reviewing and assessing the benefits of SISP in the context of the differing expectations of different stakeholders
- the linkage with business strategy.

Reasons for this deficiency have been postulated, and a broader perspective of what properly constitutes SISP has been proposed. The resultant model aims to assist management in undertaking and implementing SISP by circumventing some of the common problems encountered in applying SISP theory in practice. Most importantly, however, the paper has introduced contingent frameworks that assist in making an appropriate choice of SISP approach or strategy.

Strategy formulation should not be seen as an entirely rational or formal process, however. It should also aim to capture creative, intuitive thinking. The contingent models introduced here should be used to question beliefs and bring key assumptions about the current and future business to the surface. In so doing, it is hoped that they may assist creative strategy formulation and ease strategy implementation.

Acknowledgements

I wish to record my thanks to Tony Sutherland for the many useful debates we shared in developing the model which is depicted in Table 3, and for the constructive criticisms of it provided more recently by Frank Land and Richard Ormerod. In addition, I am grateful for the useful comments made in relation to an early draft of this paper by two anonymous referees.

References

BCC (1988) Bank counts cost of IT disaster. *Business Computing and Communications* **March**.

BENBASAT I, DEXTER A, DRURY D and GOLDSTEIN R (1984) A critique of the stage hypothesis: theory and empirical evidence. *Communications of the ACM* **27(5)**, 476–485.

CASH Jr. J I and KONSYNSKI B R (1985) IS redraws competitive boundaries. *Harvard Business Review* **63(2)**, 134–142.

CHECKLAND P B (1981) *Systems Thinking, Systems Practice.* Wiley, Chichester.

DAVIS G B (1979) Comments on the critical success factors method for obtaining management information requirements in the article by John F. Rockart. *MIS Quarterly* **3(3).**

EARL M J (1987) Information systems strategy formulation. In *Critical Issues in Information Systems Research* (BOLAND R J and HIRSCHHEIM R A, Eds.), pp. 157–168. Wiley, Chichester.

EARL M J (Ed.) (1988) *Information Management: The Strategic Dimension.* The Clarendon Press, Oxford.

EARL M J (1989) *Management Strategies for Information Technology.* Prentice-Hall, Hemel Hempstead.

GALLIERS R D (1984) An approach to information needs analysis. In *Human-Computer Interaction—INTERACT '84* (SHACKEL B, Ed.). *Proceedings of the IFIP WG 6.3 Conference,* London, 4–7 September 1984. pp. 619–628. Elsevier, Amsterdam. Reproduced in GALLIERS (1987d), *op cit,* pp. 291–304.

GALLIERS R D (1986a) Information systems and technology planning within a competitive strategy framework. In *Information Management* Pergamon Infotech. State of the Art Reports, **14,** pp. 36–51. Pergamon Infotech, Maidenhead.

GALLIERS R D (1986b) Information technology strategies today: the UK experience. Presented at the *Oxford/PA Conference: Formulating IT Strategies,* Oxford. 30 September–2 October. Reproduced in M J EARL (Ed.) (1988), *op cit,* pp. 179–201.

GALLIERS R D (1987a) Information systems planning in the United Kingdom and Australia—a comparison of current practice. In *Oxford Surveys in Information Technology* Volume 4. pp. 223–255.

GALLIERS R D (1987b) Information technology for comparative advantage: serendipity or strategic vision? Keynote address of the *AUSCAM National Conference.* Perth, Western Australia, 23 October.

GALLIERS R D (1987c) Information technology planning within the corporate planning process. In *Integrated Project Control* Pergamon Infotech State of the Art Reports **15,** pp. 27–38. Pergamon Infotech, Maidenhead.

GALLIERS R D (Ed.) (1987d) *Information Analysis: Selected Readings.* Addison-Wesley, Wokingham.

GALLIERS R D (1987e) Discord at the top. *Business Computing and Communications* **February,** 22–25.

GALLIERS R D (1987f) Information Systems Planning in Britain and Australia in the mid-1980s: Key Success Factors. Unpublished PhD Thesis, London School of Economics, June.

GALLIERS R D and SUTHERLAND A R (1991) Information systems management and strategy formulation: the 'stages of growth' model revisited. *Journal of Information Systems* (in press).

GRINDLEY C B B (Ed.) (1990) *Information Technology Review 1990/91.* Price Waterhouse, London.

HENDERSON J C, ROCKART J F and SIFONIS J G (1984) A planning methodology for integrating management support systems. *MIT CISR Working Paper* **No. 116,** September. Reproduced in *The Rise of Managerial Computing* (ROCHART J F and BULLEN C V, Eds.) pp. 257–282. Dow Jones-Irwin, Holmwood, Illinois (1986).

HENDERSON J C and SIFONIS J G (1986) Middle out strategic planning: the value of IS planning to business planning. In *Proceedings of the 1986 NYU Symposium on Strategic Uses of Information Technology* New York, May 21–23.

HIRSCHHEIM R A (1982) Information Management Planning in Organisations—Part One: A Framework for Analysis. Unpublished LSE working paper.

HUFF S L and BEATTIE (1985) Strategic versus competitive information systems. *Business Quarterly* **Winter**.

IVES B and LEARMONTH G P (1984) The information system as a competitive weapon. *Communications of the ACM* **27(12)**, 1193–1201.

KRIEBEL C G (1968) The strategic dimension of computer systems planning. *Long Range. Planning* **September**.

LAND F F and HIRSCHHEIM R A (1983) Participative systems design: rationale, tools and techniques. *Journal of Applied Systems Analysis* **10**, 91–107.

LANSMAN G (1984) Banking on innovation. *Datamation* **15 August**.

LARGE J (1986) Information's market force. *Management Today* **August**.

MARTIN J (1982) *Strategic Data-Planning Methodologies.* Prentice-Hall, Englewood Cliffs, New Jersey.

MARTINO C A (1983) *Information Systems Planning to Meet Objectives: A Survey of Practices 1983.* Cresap, McCormick and Paget, New York.

MCFARLAN F W (1984) Information technology changes the way you compete. *Harvard Business Review* **62(3)**, 98–102.

MCLAUGHLIN M, HOWE R and CASH Jr. J I (1983) Changing competitive ground rules—the impact of computers and communications in the 1980s. Unpublished Working Paper, Graduate School of Business Administration, Harvard University.

NG M W (1984) Strategic systems planning should start from the top. *Australasian Computerworld* **June 22**, 12–13.

NOLAN R (1979) Managing the crises in data processing. *Harvard Business Review* **57(2)**, 115–126.

PASCALE R T and ATHOS A G (1981) *The Art of Japanese Management.* Penguin, Harmondsworth.

PORTER M E (1979) How competitive forces shape strategy. *Harvard Business Review* **57(2)**.

PORTER M E (1980) *Competitive Strategy.* The Free Press, New York.

PORTER M E (1985) *Competitive Advantage.* The Free Press, New York.

PORTER M E and MILLAR V E (1985) How information gives you competitive advantage. *Harvard Business Review* **63(4)**.

PYBURN P J (1983) Linking the MIS plan with corporate strategy: an exploratory study. *MIS Quarterly* **7(2)**, 1–14.

ROCKART J F (1979) Chief executives define their own data needs. *Harvard Business Review* **57(2)**. Reproduced in GALLIERS (1987d), *op cit*, pp. 267–289.

SULLIVAN, Jr C H (1985) Systems planning in the information age. *Sloan Management Review* **27(4)**, 3–12.

SUTHERLAND A R and GALLIERS R D (1989) An evolutionary model to assist in the planning of strategic information systems and the management of the information systems function. School of Information Systems Working Paper, Curtin University of Technology, Perth, Western Australia, February.

WARD J M (1988) Information systems and technology application portfolio management—an assessment of matrix-based analyses. *Journal of Information Technology* **3**, 205–215.

WILSON T D (1989) The implementation of information systems strategies in UK companies: aims and barriers to success. *International Journal of Information Management* **9(4)**, 245–258.

ZACHMAN J A (1982) Business systems planning and business information control study: a comparison. *IBM Systems Journal* **21**.

47

USING TECHNOLOGY AND CONSTITUTING STRUCTURES

A practice lens for studying technology in organizations

Wanda J. Orlikowski

Source: *Organization Science* 11(4) (2000): 404–28.

Abstract

As both technologies and organizations undergo dramatic changes in form and function, organizational researchers are increasingly turning to concepts of innovation, emergence, and improvisation to help explain the new ways of organizing and using technology evident in practice. With a similar intent, I propose an extension to the structurational perspective on technology that develops a practice lens to examine how people, as they interact with a technology in their ongoing practices, enact structures which shape their emergent and situated use of that technology. Viewing the use of technology as a process of enactment enables a deeper understanding of the constitutive role of social practices in the ongoing use and change of technologies in the workplace. After developing this lens, I offer an example of its use in research, and then suggest some implications for the study of technology in organizations.

Technology—and its relationship to organizational structures, processes, and outcomes—has long been of interest to organizational researchers. Over the years, different research perspectives on technology have developed in parallel with research perspectives on organizations—for example, contingency theory (Woodward 1965, Galbraith 1977, Carter 1984, Daft and Lengel 1986), strategic choice models (Child 1972, Buchanan and Boddy 1983, Davis and Taylor 1986, Zuboff 1988), Marxist studies (Braverman 1974, Edwards 1979, Shaiken 1985, Perrolle 1986), symbolic interactionist approaches (Kling 1991, Prasad 1993), transaction-cost economics (Malone *et al.* 1987, Ciborra 1993); network analyses (Barley 1990, Burkhardt and Brass 1990, Rice and Aydin 1991), practice theories (Suchman 1987, Button 1993, Hutchins 1995, Orr 1996), and structurational models (Barley 1986, Orlikowski 1992, DeSanctis and Poole 1994).[1]

Today, both technologies and organizations are undergoing dramatic changes in form and function, and new and unprecedented forms and functions are becoming evident. In response, organizational researchers have applied notions of innovation, learning, and improvisation to account for such dynamic and emerging patterns of organizing (Brown and Duguid 1991, Weick 1993, Hutchins 1991, Brown and Eisenhardt 1997, Hedberg *et al.* 1997, Barrett 1998, Hatch 1998, Lant 1999). Similarly, researchers of technology have also begun to use the notions of innovation, learning, and improvisation to understand the organizational implications of new technologies (Ciborra 1996, Cook and Brown 1999, Orlikowski 1996, Tushman *et al.* 1997). This paper continues the development of concepts that address the role of emergence and improvisation in technology and technology use, and in particular, seeks to extend the structurational perspective in this direction.

The past decade has seen the development of a number of structurational models of technology which have generated numerous insights into the role and influence of technologies in organizations (Barley 1986, Poole and DeSanctis 1990, 1992, Orlikowski and Robey 1991, Walsham and Han 1991, Orlikowski 1992, Walsham 1993, DeSanctis and Poole 1994). These models posit technology as embodying structures (built in by designers during technology development), which are then appropriated by users during their use of the technology. Human action is a central aspect of these models, in particular, the actions associated with embedding structures within a technology during its development, and the actions associated with appropriating those structures during use of technology.

A number of commentators have urged further theoretical development of a structurational perspective on technology, suggesting that it may have considerable analytic advantages in explaining the consequences associated with the use of new and reconfigurable information technologies (Sproull and Goodman 1990, Weick 1990, Roberts and Grabowski 1995). Because a structurational perspective is inherently dynamic and grounded in ongoing human action, it indeed has the potential to explain emergence and change in technologies and use. However, realizing this potential will require augmenting the current structurational perspective on technology—specifically the notions of embodied structure and user appropriation. While these notions have been extremely valuable in explaining the various outcomes associated with the use of given technologies in different contexts, they are less able to account effectively for ongoing changes in both technologies and their use. This insufficiency is particularly acute in the context of internet-worked and reconfigurable technology (such as group-ware and the Web), the use of which is becoming increasingly prevalent in organizations today.

In this paper, I extend the structurational perspective on technology by proposing a practice-oriented understanding of the recursive interaction between people, technologies, and social action. I believe such a practice orientation can better explain emergence and change in both technologies and their use. It does so by complementing the notion of embodied structure with that of emergent structure, and the notion of appropriation with that of enactment.

Embodied and emergent structures

In their understanding of technologies, structurational models of technology have been strongly influenced by the intellectual tradition of social constructivism (MacKenzie and Wajcman 1985, Bijker *et al.* 1987, Woolgar 1991, Bijker and Law 1992). Using rich case studies of technological invention and development, social constructivist research examines how interpretations, social interests, and disciplinary conflicts shape the production of a technology through shaping its cultural meanings and the social interactions among relevant social groups. This research also examines how the produced technology achieves "stabilization" through processes of negotiation, persuasion, and debate aimed at achieving rhetorical closure and community consensus. Further work in this tradition focuses more specifically on how dominant interests are reflected in the form and functioning of the technology, a process referred to as "inscription" (Latour 1992). Akrich (1992, p. 208), for example, writes:

> Designers thus define actors with specific tastes, competences, motives, aspirations, political prejudices, and the rest, and they assume that morality, technology, science, and economy will evolve in particular ways, A large part of the work of innovators is that of *"inscribing"* this vision of (or prediction about) the world in the technical content of the new object.

Drawing on the ideas of social shaping and inscription, structurational models have posited that technology is developed through a social-political process which results in structures (rules and resources) being embedded within the technology. For example, Orlikowski (1992, p. 410) writes:

> [H]uman agents build into technology certain interpretive schemes (rules reflecting knowledge of the work being automated), certain facilities (resources to accomplish that work), and certain norms

(rules that define the organizationally sanctioned way of executing that work).

Similarly, "adaptive structuration theory" (DeSanctis and Poole 1994, Poole *et al.* 1998) focuses on the structures built into such technologies as group decision support systems. For example, DeSanctis and Poole (1994, p. 125) note:

> [S]tructures are found in institutions such as reporting hierarchies, organizational knowledge, and standard operating procedures. Designers incorporate some of these structures into the technology ... Once complete, the technology presents an array of social structures for possible use in interpersonal interaction, including rules (e.g., voting procedures) and resources (e.g., stored data, public display screens).

The development of a structurational perspective on technology has benefited considerably from social constructivist ideas, particularly in the absence of any explicit treatment of technology in Giddens' (1984) theory of structuration. However, the adoption of social constructivist conceptions has also created some difficulties, primarily with respect to two propositions: that technologies become "stabilized" after development; and that they "embody" structures which (re)present various social rules and political interests.

The first proposition—that technologies become "stabilized"—neglects the empirical evidence that people can (and do) redefine and modify the meaning, properties, and applications of technology after development. As Woolgar and Grint (1991, p. 370) argue, the proposition of stabilization admits social construction only during development, and " [t]hereafter, technological determinism is allowed, on the basis that beyond the point of stabilization there is little disagreement about what the technology can do." Existing structurational models of technology, because they posit flexibility in how structures are appropriated, avoid such strong technological determinism. However, their presumption that technologies embody specific stable structures is nevertheless problematic because it depicts technologies as static and settled artifacts with built-in arrays of fixed and determinate structures that are (always and readily) available to users. Such assumptions of technological stability, completeness, and predictability break down in the face of empirical research that shows people modifying technologies and their conceptions of technology long after design and development (Rice and Rogers 1980, von Hippel 1988, Ciborra and Lanzara 1991). Such assumptions are also inappropriate in the context of the dynamically reconfigurable, user-programmable, and highly internetworked technologies being developed and used today.

The second proposition—that technologies "embody" social structures—is problematic from a structurational perspective, because it situates structures within technological artifacts. This is a departure from Giddens' (1984) view of structures as having only a virtual existence, that is, as having "no reality except as they are instantiated in activity" (Whittington 1992, p. 696). Seeing structures as embodied in artifacts thus ascribes a material existence to structures which Giddens explicitly denies (1989, p. 256):

> . . . a position I want to avoid, in terms of which structure appears as something 'outside' or 'external' to human action. In my usage, structure is what gives *form* and *shape* to social life, but is not *itself* that form and shape—nor should 'give' be understood in an active sense here, because structure only exists in and through the activities of human agents.

Structure is here understood as the set of rules and resources instantiated in recurrent social practice. Elements of technology (such as voting procedures, stored data, and public display screens), once they have been built into a technology, are external to human action. As inscribed properties of a technology, they constitute neither rules nor resources, and thus cannot be seen to be structures. It is only when such technological elements as voting procedures, stored data, and public display screens are routinely mobilized in use that we can say that they "structure" human action, and in this way they become implicated as rules and resources in the constitution of a particular recurrent social practice. For example, consider the myriad software packages, network tools, and data files installed on countless desktop computers and corporate mainframes worldwide. Until such time as these are actually used in some ongoing human action—and thus become part of a process of structuring—they are, at best, potential structuring elements, and at worst, unexplored, forgotten, or rejected bits of program code and data cluttering up hard drives everywhere.

We are unaccustomed to conceiving of rules and resources as only existing "in and through the activities of human agents," largely because of our conventional views of them as either external entities (e.g., corporate policy, traffic regulations, land, factories, money) or internal schemas (e.g., rules of thumb, expertise, judgment). From a structurational perspective, however, external entities and internal schemas are only constituted as rules and resources when they are implicated in recurrent social action (*pace* Sewell 1992). Our conventional view of rules and resources as external entities suffers from what Taylor (1993) refers to as an "objectivist reification," while the view of rules and resources as internal schemas suffers from a "subjectivist reduction." Commenting on rules, Taylor (1993, pp. 57–58, emphasis added) writes:

> In its operation, the rule exists in the practice it "guides." ... the practice not only fulfills the rules, but also gives it concrete shape in particular situations. ... In fact, what this reciprocity shows is that the "rule" lies essentially *in* the practice. The rule is what is animating the practice at any given time, not some formulation behind it, inscribed in our thoughts or our brains or our genes or whatever. That is why *the rule is, at any given time, what the practice has made it.*

Similarly, Giddens (1979, p. 65) writes that "rules and practices only exist in conjunction with one another." In the same way, resources too, are inextricably linked to practice. Giddens observes (1984, p. 33, emphasis added):

> Some forms of allocative resources (e.g. land, raw materials etc.) might seem to have a real existence. In the sense of having a "time-space" presence this is obviously the case. But their "materiality" does not affect the fact that such phenomena become resources ... *only when incorporated within processes of structuration.*

While a technology can be seen to embody particular symbol and material properties, it does not embody structures because those are only instantiated in practice. When humans interact regularly with a technology, they engage with (some or all of) the material and symbol properties of the technology. Through such repeated interaction, certain of the technology's properties become implicated in an ongoing process of structuration. The resulting recurrent social practice produces and reproduces a particular structure of technology use. Thus, structures of technology use are constituted recursively as humans regularly interact with certain properties of a technology and thus shape the set of rules and resources that serve to shape their interaction. Seen through a practice lens, technology structures are emergent, not embodied.

A practice lens more easily accommodates people's situated use of dynamic technologies because it makes no assumptions about the stability, predictability, or relative completeness of the technologies. Instead, the focus is on what structures emerge as people interact recurrently with whatever properties of the technology are at hand, whether these were built in, added on, modified, or invented on the fly.

Appropriation and enactment of structures

Existing structurational models of technology examine what people do with technologies in use, positing such use as an appropriation of the "structures" inscribed in the technologies. Such appropriation occurs when "people actively select how technology structures are used" (DeSanctis and

Poole 1994, p. 129). DeSanctis and Poole (1994, p. 130) distinguish between "faithful" and "unfaithful" appropriations of the technology structures, highlighting the degree to which use of technology corresponds to the structures embedded in the technology, and then relating such correspondence to expected outcomes. Their analysis identifies different types of appropriation moves which preserve, substitute for, combine, enlarge, contrast, constrain, affirm, or negate the structures provided by the technology (1994, p. 135).

While the notion of appropriation captures well the importance of human action in shaping the situated use of technology, it nevertheless frames such human agency in terms of interaction with the structures embedded within technology. Thus, DeSanctis and Poole (1994, p. 133) recommend "appropriation analysis [which] tries to document exactly how technology structures are being invoked for use in a specific context" (DeSanctis and Poole 1994, p. 133), and Orlikowski and Robey (1991, p. 148), while not using the term "appropriation analysis," suggest analyzing how the structure inscribed in information technology "shapes action by facilitating certain outcomes and constraining others." These views start with the structures presumed to be embedded within technology, and then analyze how those structures are used, misused, or not used by people in various contexts.

If, however, we focus on emergent rather than embodied structures (as I have suggested above), an alternative view of technology use becomes possible—a view which allows us to frame what users do with technologies not as appropriation but as *enactment*.[2] Thus, rather than starting with the technology and examining how actors appropriate its embodied structures, this view starts with human action and examines how it enacts emergent structures through recurrent interaction with the technology at hand. Focusing attention on how structures are constituted and reconstituted in recurrent social practices acknowledges that while users can and do use technologies as they were designed, they also can and do circumvent inscribed ways of using the technologies—either ignoring certain properties of the technology, working around them, or inventing new ones that may go beyond or even contradict designers' expectations and inscriptions. For example, many of us use such powerful software tools as word processing, spreadsheets, and presentation graphics in our daily lives. In our regular use of these tools, most of us typically utilize, at best, 25 percent of these tools' functionality, focusing on those elements we need to get our task done and ignoring the rest. Or consider the World Wide Web technology which was developed in 1989 as a hypertext networked system for sharing research in the European high-energy physics community. No one, least of all its inventor (Berners-Lee 1996), anticipated the explosion of innovation and reinvention that has accompanied use of this technology since then and that continues to transform it into an extensive global infrastructure for business, government, entertainment, and all manner of social, political, professional, and personal communities.

511

Together, the notions of emergent structure and enactment afford a practice-based extension to existing structurational models of technology. This practice lens posits humans as constituting structures in their recurrent use of technology. Through their regularized engagement with a particular technology (and some or all of its inscribed properties) in particular ways in particular conditions, users repeatedly enact a set of rules and resources which structures their ongoing interactions with that technology. Users' interaction with a technology is thus recursive—in their recurrent practices, users shape the technology structure that shapes their use. Technology structures are thus not external or independent of human agency; they are not "out there," embodied in technologies simply waiting to be appropriated. Rather they are virtual, emerging from people's repeated and situated interaction with particular technologies. These enacted structures of technology use, which I term *technologies-in-practice*, are the sets of rules and resources that are (re)constituted in people's recurrent engagement with the technologies at hand.

After developing this practice lens further, I provide an example of its application by drawing on some empirical studies of the use of a particular technology in different organizations. I end by discussing some of the research implications entailed by adopting a practice lens to study technology and its use in organizations.

A practice lens for studying use of technology

Lave (1988) has argued for the value of focusing on "cognition in practice" rather than "cognition in the head." Similarly, the practice lens I am proposing here focuses on emergent technology structures enacted in practice rather than embodied structures fixed in technologies. This practice lens further recognizes that in both research and practice we often conflate two aspects of technology: the technology as *artifact*[3] (the bundle of material and symbol properties packaged in some socially recognizable form, e.g., hardware, software, techniques); and the *use* of technology, or what people actually do with the technological artifact in their recurrent, situated practices.

Artifact and use

The distinction between the use of a technology and its artifactual character is an analytic, not an ontological one.[4] This distinction may be elaborated by considering a discussion offered by Lave (1988, pp. 150–151) in her study of arithmetic problem-solving within supermarkets:

> The supermarket, for instance, is in some respects a public and durable entity. It is a physically, economically, politically, and

socially organized space-in-time. In this aspect it may be called an "arena" within which activity takes place. . . . At the same time, for individual shoppers, the supermarket is a repeatedly experienced, personally ordered and edited version of the arena. In this aspect it may be termed a "setting" for activity. Some aisles in the super-market do not exist for a given shopper as part of her setting, while other aisles are rich in detailed possibilities.

Lave's point may be similarly made for technologies, that is: technology is, on the one hand, an identifiable, relatively durable entity, a physically, economically, politically, and socially organized phenomenon in space-time. It has material and cultural properties that transcend the experience of individuals and particular settings. In this aspect, it is what we may call a *technological artifact*, which appears in our lives as a specific machine, tech-nique, appliance, device, or gadget. At the same time, use of the technology involves a repeatedly experienced, personally ordered and edited version of the technological artifact, being experienced differently by different individuals and differently by the same individuals depending on the time or circumstance. In this aspect it may be termed a *technology-in-practice*, to refer to the specific structure routinely enacted as we use the specific machine, technique, appliance, device, or gadget in recurrent ways in our everyday situated activities. Some properties provided by the artifact do not exist for us as part of our technology-in-practice, while other properties are rich in detailed possibilities.

While a technology[5] can be seen to have been constructed with particular materials and inscribed with developers' assumptions and knowledge about the world at a point in time (Noble 1984, Perrow 1983, Winner 1986, Thomas 1994), it is only when this technology is used in recurrent social practices that it can be said to structure users' actions. That is, it is only when repeatedly drawn on in use that technological properties become constituted by users as particular rules and resources that shape their action. For example, thousands of Americans annually use tax preparation software to complete their tax returns. Knowledge of computers, the U.S. federal tax code, arith-metic, and the content and layout of various tax forms informed the design of this technology, as did the software programming language and database structures used to construct it. When people routinely use the tax pre-paration software, they draw on its inscribed properties and embedded information content, their own experiences with technology, as well as their understanding of their rights and obligations as tax payers, to enact a set of tax reporting rules and resources with the software.[6] For example, interaction with the "1040 Form" enables the entry of particular kinds of information and facilitates the calculation of various totals, while also prohibiting the creation of alternative tax reporting representations (say a "999 Form"), or figuring the totals in a more "creative" way.

When users choose to use a technology, they are also choosing how to interact with that technology. Thus they may, deliberately or inadvertently, use it in ways not anticipated by the developers. For example, users may use the tax preparation software to print out blank forms and then complete the tax return manually, or they may use the software incorrectly, or they may use it to learn about the current tax code, or to study the software's interface design. Users may also choose not to use a technology even if it is available, as happens, for example, with tax preparation software which is typically ignored for most of the year. In this case, even though the technology exists (typically installed on users' computer desktops), it is not implicated in any recurrent social practice, and thus no rules and resources (i.e., no technology-in-practice) are enacted with the tax preparation technology, because it is not used. Of course, this scenario typically changes quite dramatically a few weeks before April 15, when users are motivated by the tax filing deadline to use their tax preparation software in a flurry of repeated activity and anxiety, and thereby enact a particular technology-in-practice.

From the point of view of users, technologies come with a set of properties crafted by designers and developers. These technological properties may be examined to identify the typical or expected range of activities commonly associated with use of the technology. However, how these properties will actually be used in any instance is not inherent or predetermined; rather it depends on what people actually do with them in particular instances. And as numerous studies have shown, users can, and do, choose to use technologies in ways unanticipated by inventors and designers. Whether through error (misperception, lack of understanding, slippage) or intent (sabotage, inertia, innovation), users often ignore, alter, or work around the inscribed technological properties (Gasser 1986, Kraut *et al.* 1986, Mackay 1988, Grudin 1989, Bullen and Bennett 1991, Ciborra and Lanzara 1991, Button 1993, Clement 1993, Markus 1994, Suchman 1996). Furthermore, users often add to or modify the technological properties on hand (e.g., installing new software, peripherals, or adding data, etc.), thus, actively shaping or crafting the artifact to fit their particular requirements or interests.

The identification of technological properties and common activities associated with our conventional understanding of a technological artifact, its inscriptions, or the intentions of its designers, cannot circumscribe the ways in which people may use it.[7] Use of technology is not a choice among a closed set of predefined possibilities, but a situated and recursive process of constitution, which—while it may often invoke intended activities or replicate familiar uses—may also and at any time ignore such conventional uses or invent new ones. As Bazerman (1994, p. 88) reminds us:

> . . . no matter how rigorous the typifications that guide the enactment at any single moment may be, the dynamics of the moment

grant new meaning and life to the typifications, and we must look to the dynamics of the moment to understand what is happening.

Having recognized this, however, it is important to keep in mind that the recurrent use of a technology is not infinitely malleable. Saying that use is situated and not confined to predefined options does not mean that it is totally open to any and all possibilities. The physical properties of artifacts ensure that there are always boundary conditions on how we use them. Conceptual artifacts (such as techniques or methodologies expressed in language) are more likely to be associated with a wider range of uses than software-based artifacts, which, in turn, are more likely to be associated with a wider range of uses than hard-wired machines. Similarly, the more a particular technological artifact is integrated into a larger system, network, or technological configuration, the narrower the range of alternative uses that may be crafted with it. Thus, the use of a stand-alone personal computer in my home is likely to be more malleable than the use of a workstation by an air traffic controller. While it is expected that more and more of the artifacts deployed in future workplaces will be software-based, user-programmable, even user-configurable (and hence, their use may be more malleable), it is also likely that the increased complexity and internetworking accompanying the growth in global infrastructures will require these artifacts to be more standardized, interconnected, and interdependent (and hence, their use may be less malleable).

Use of technology is strongly influenced by users' understandings of the properties and functionality of a technology, and these are strongly influenced by the images, descriptions, rhetorics, ideologies, and demonstrations presented by intermediaries such as vendors, journalists, consultants, champions, trainers, managers, and "power" users (Orlikowski et al. 1995). As Woolgar (1996, p. 92) notes, such intermediaries "intervene in the interpretation ('reading') of the technology by the user through their comments on the product's nature, capacity, use, and value." Because some of the claims made in these commentaries are quite persuasive, they tend to be believed without concrete evidence to support them. Kling, for example, has found that the powerful narratives constructed during attempts to advocate computerization often continue to shape users' perceptions even "when computer systems are built, installed, and used in ways that differ significantly from early expectations" (1992, p. 352).

Structuring of technologies-in-practice

Giddens (1979, 1984) proposed the notion of structure (or structural properties of social systems) as the set of enacted rules and resources that mediate social action through three dimensions or modalities: facilities, norms, and interpretive schemes. In social life, actors do not enact structures in a vacuum.

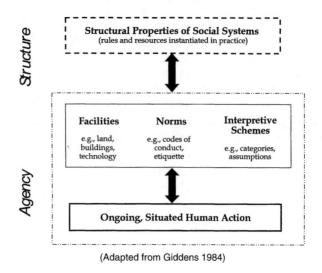

(Adapted from Giddens 1984)

Figure 1 Enactment of Structures in Practice.

In their recurrent social practices, they draw on their (tacit and explicit) knowledge of their prior action and the situation at hand, the facilities available to them (e.g., land, buildings, technology), and the norms that inform their ongoing practices, and in this way, apply such knowledge, facilities, and habits of the mind and body to "structure" their current action (see Figure 1). In doing so, they recursively instantiate and thus reconstitute the rules and resources that structure their social action.

Because technology-in-practice is a kind of structure, the same recursive constitution applies here too (see Figure 2). When people use a technology, they draw on the properties comprising the technological artifact—those provided by its constituent materiality, those inscribed by the designers, and those added on by users through previous interactions (e.g., specific data content, customized features, or expanded software/hardware accessories). People also draw on their skills, power, knowledge, assumptions, and expectations about the technology and its use, influenced typically by training, communication, and previous experiences (Orlikowski and Gash 1994). These include the meanings and attachments—emotional and intellectual—that users associate with particular technologies and their uses, shaped by their experiences with various technologies and their participation in a range of social and political communities.[8] Users also draw on their knowledge of and experiences with the institutional contexts in which they live and work, and the social and cultural conventions associated with participating in such contexts. In this way, people's use of technology becomes structured by these experiences, knowledge, meanings,

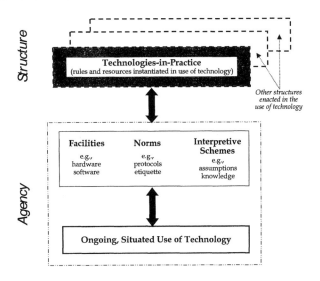

Figure 2 Enactment of Technologies-in-Practice.

habits, power relations, norms, and the technological artifacts at hand. Such structuring enacts a specific set of rules and resources in practice that then serves to structure future use as people continue to interact with the technology in their recurrent practices. Thus, over time, people constitute and reconstitute a structure of technology use, that is, they enact a distinctive technology-in-practice.

Human interaction with technologies is typically recurrent, so that even as users constitute a technology-in-practice through their present use of a technology, their actions are at the same time shaped by the previous technologies-in-practice they have enacted in the past. Ongoing enactment of a technology-in-practice reinforces it, so that it becomes regularized and routinized, an expedient and habitual response to repeated use of a technology within the daily exigencies of organizational life. That is, a technology-in-practice serves essentially as a "behavioral and interpretive template" (Barley 1988, p. 49) for people's situated use of the technology. Continued habitual use of a technology will tend to reenact the same technology-in-practice, thus further reinforcing it over time so that it becomes taken for granted. For example, most of us who drive cars have developed a familiar pattern of interacting with automobiles on the roads—repeatedly enacting a particular and typically shared technology-in-practice that we now take for granted.

While regular interactions with the same technology tend to reproduce the technology-in-practice being enacted, such reinforcement is not assured. Consider the automobile example again. We happily take our (and our fellow drivers') customary enactment of a routine technology-in-practice for granted—that is, until we travel abroad and encounter different artifacts (foreign automobile models, cars with drivers' seats on different sides, road signs in foreign languages, different measuring units for indicating distance or gas (a.k.a. petrol) consumption), and different driving conventions and habits (including driving on the opposite side of the road). All of a sudden, the set of rules and resources we had so habitually enacted with our own automobiles on well-known roads in familiar contexts is no longer effective, and we have to think and act differently, thus enacting a somewhat different set of rules and resources to guide our interaction with different automobiles on different roads. On our return home, we will (hopefully) revert to enacting our previously effective technology-in-practice.

A community of users engaged in similar work practices typically enacts similar technologies-in-practice, where through common training sessions, shared socialization, comparable on-the-job experiences, and mutual coordination and storytelling, users come to engage with a technology in similar ways. Over time, through repeated reinforcement by the community of users, such technologies-in-practice may become reified and institutionalized, at which point they become treated as predetermined and firm prescriptions for social action, and as such, may impede change. For example, in a study of process technologies, Tyre and Orlikowski (1994) found that initial patterns of using the technologies congealed quickly, becoming resistant to change despite ongoing operational problems in the use and performance of the technologies. This rapid establishment of relatively fixed technologies-in-practice was influenced by corporate pressure to improve productivity, unavailability of technical support staff, and users' expectations of and preferences for stable and predictable technologies.

Because the enactment of a technology-in-practice is situated within a number of nested and overlapping social systems, people's interaction with technology will always enact other social structures along with the technology-in-practice, for example, a hierarchical authority structure within a large bureaucracy, a cooperative culture within a participative workgroup, the normative structure of a religious or professional community, or the dominant status of English as the primary language of the Internet. Figure 2 shows that people's situated and recurrent use of technology simultaneously enacts multiple structures along with a technology-in-practice. In this paper, I elaborate the notion of *technologies-in-practice*—the particular structures of technology use that users enact when engaging recurrently with a technology. Consequently, the other structures enacted at the same time will not be as central here. In any structurational analysis, one must foreground some structures and background others (Giddens 1979). My limited discussion of the other structures here should not be taken to mean that they are less important or more fixed than technologies-in-practice. All structures are virtual, and continually enacted through actors' recurrent practices.

However, in this discussion, I have chosen to focus on the particular structures of technology use which I have labeled technologies-in-practice.

In their recurrent and situated action, actors thus draw on structures that have been previously enacted (both technologies-in-practice and other structures), and in such action reconstitute those structures. Such reconstitution may be either deliberate, or, as is more usual, inadvertent. Also, it may occur in one of two forms: *reinforcement,* where actors enact essentially the same structures with no noticeable changes; or *transformation,* where actors enact changed structures, where the changes may range from the modest to the substantial.

Changes in technologies-in-practice

Users always have the potential to change their habits of use, and in this way change the structures they enact in their recurrent practices. As Cassell (1993, p. 13), writing about rules, puts it:

> Because agents draw on rules in the enactment of social practices, the capacity to modify the 'rule' that is drawn on in any action is an ever-present possibility. Men and women may, for example, transform the traditional 'rules' which have structured their past interaction by eschewing sexist norms. At each point of structural reproduction there is also the potential for change.

Technologies-in-practice can be and are changed as actors experience changes in awareness, knowledge, power, motivations, time, circumstances, and the technology. They are changed through the same process that all social structures are changed—through human action. People may change their technologies-in-practice by deliberately modifying the properties of their technology and thus how they interact with it. For example, people may download software "plug-ins" to improve the performance of their Web browser tools, or they may override the parameters of a new scheduling system to replicate the operation of a previous system (Saetnan 1991). Even when a technology appears to have stabilized, with the discourse around its properties and functionality apparently having reached "closure" (Bijker 1995, Pinch and Bijker 1984), or some industry-wide "dominant design" (Tushman *et al.* 1997) has been established, the stability of the technology and its applications is only provisional. It is provisional because different elements continue to be developed, existing functions fail and are fixed, new materials are invented, new standards are set, and users modify the artifact and/or its content for new and different uses. Technologies are thus never fully stabilized or "complete," even though we may choose to treat them as fixed, black boxes for a period of time. By temporarily bracketing the dynamic nature of technology, we assign a "stabilized-for-now" status

(Schryer 1993) to our technological artifacts. This is an analytic and practical convenience only, because technologies continue to evolve, are tinkered with (e.g., by users, designers, regulators, and hackers), modified, improved, damaged, rebuilt, etc. Typically, such change is not predetermined or predictable, but implemented by people influenced by competitive, technological, political, cultural, and environmental influences (e.g., feature wars with competitors, technological innovations, safety improvements, security violations, privacy legislation, climatic conditions, earthquakes, poor maintenance, etc.).

Users may also choose to enact different technologies-in-practice because they have become more knowledgeable about using their technology (through attending a training class or watching a colleague's use) or because they have changed jobs and now need to use technology differently in their new work community (say, to share files with coworkers). People may adjust their technologies-in-practice intentionally, as when users respond to new safety regulations by beginning to engage safety mechanisms during machine operation, or when they respond to the unreliability of computer networks by backing up their files at the end of every session or executing system maintenance utilities. Modifications to patterns of use may also result from inadvertent slippage or breakdown, when, either through inattention or error, users fall into a different form of use, such as forgetting to attach safety guards, or discontinuing use of a faulty or complicated element. People may also change their technologies-in-practice by improvising, that is, generating situated innovations in response to unexpected opportunities or challenges, such as when a temporary machine workaround becomes the preferred practice because it turns out to be more effective than the original practice (Tyre and Orlikowski 1994).

As people enact modified technologies-in-practice they also change the facilities, norms, and interpretive schemes used in their use of the technology (as shown with the two-way arrows in Figure 2). For example, through adding downloaded "plug-ins" to a personal computer, or customizing the parameters of a software application, or adding new data to the databases, the technological artifact is altered. At the same time, users' knowledge of what technological properties are available to them may be updated or made obsolete, as with the meanings, expectations, associations, and conventions they attach to the technology and its use. For example, users of electronic mail within a community may evolve a set of communication norms about effective or sanctioned electronic mail use (Yates *et al.* 1999). Similarly, a company's new policy for use of machine safety features is likely to alter people's views and understandings of the appropriate ways of using technology in that company.

To the extent that people enact a multiplicity of structures (including other technologies-in-practice as well as other normative and authoritative structures) in their recurrent practices, they increase the likelihood that they will enact altered or alternative technologies-in-practice associated with their use of particular technologies. That is, by enacting various interpenetrating (and perhaps even contradictory) structures, actors experience a range of rules and resources that may generate knowledge of different structures and awareness of the possibilities for structural change (Sewell 1992, Tenkasi and Boland 1993). For example, participation in professional or industry conferences often allows people to exchange ideas and stories about their work practices, including how they use technology in their everyday practices. Such awareness of alternative ways of using technology may motivate people to make changes in their technology and/or their use of it. It may also prompt them to make changes in the other structures that they constitute in their work practices—for example, using electronic mail to enact a less hierarchical communication structure which bypasses conventional channels for interacting with senior executives. If this change is sustained over time and shared by other users within their community who similarly begin to use e-mail technology to bypass hierarchical communication channels, then a significant shift in organizational communication structure may be possible.

The practice lens elaborated here recognizes that even as technologies-in-practice may become institutionalized over time, this is only a stabilization for now. Every engagement with a technology is temporally and contextually provisional, and thus there is, in every use, always the possibility of a different structure being enacted. In acknowledging this open-endedness, the practice lens augments existing structurational lenses that have tended to focus on a stable technology (with its fixed array of embodied structures) and the various situated ways in which it is appropriated. The practice lens proposed here focuses on human agency and the open-ended set of emergent structures that may be enacted through recurrent use of a technology. Such a practice lens recognizes that emergence and impermanence are inherent in social structures—that while habitual, routinized, and institutionalized patterns of using a technology may be evident, these are always ongoing accomplishments, and thus there can be no single, invariant, or final technology-in-practice, just multiple, recurrent, and situated enactments. Users have the option, at any moment and within existing conditions and materials, to "choose to do otherwise" (Giddens 1993) with the technology at hand. In such possibilities to do otherwise lies the potential for innovation, learning, and change.

Enacting technologies-in-practice: empirical examples

The use of a practice lens to study technology use in organizations focuses attention on what people actually do with particular technologies in their ongoing and situated activity. This can be illustrated with some empirical examples,[9] which highlight how a number of user groups enacted different technologies-in-practice with a particular kind of technology. The technologies-in-practice discussed for each of the three sites below should not be seen as exhaustively characterizing what people did with the technology in those sites. These are just the technologies-in-practice I identified with the exposure I had to certain people at certain times and using particular research tools. Given the situated and emergent nature of technologies-in-practice, we can be sure that other technologies-in-practice were being enacted in these sites at the same time, and that, over time, the technologies-in-practice identified here will have evolved and changed, and new ones will have emerged. Before turning to these examples, a brief description of the technological artifact I studied may be helpful.

Background: the Notes technology

The technology considered here is the *Notes* software product, released to the market in 1989 by Lotus Development Corporation, and subsequently sold to thousands of companies worldwide. *Notes* represents a class of software programs known as "groupware," which are designed to facilitate the working together of individuals by providing support for distributed electronic interaction over time. This group-oriented type of computing is grounded in research that was started by computer and social scientists in the mid-1980s, and which became known as "computer-supported cooperative work" (Greif 1988).

As represented by its manufacturer, the *Notes* technology consists of software modules to support communication via electronic mail and shared discussion databases, as well as programming tools to build new applications within the *Notes* system (see Table 1). Physically, *Notes* consists of both "clients"—the software installed on users' personal computers, which mediates interaction with the *Notes* system—and "servers"—the software installed on network computers which facilitates communication among the users and supports their access to shared databases maintained locally and remotely within the *Notes* system (DeJean and DeJean 1991, Chalstrom 1993).

While there is some general "rhetorical closure" (Pinch and Bijker 1984) on the properties represented by the *Notes* product, such "closure" refers only to the *Notes* technological artifact and its descriptions in training manuals, marketing ads, and press reports. The technologies-in-practice enacted with *Notes*, because they are constituted in use, cannot attain such closure. And as we will see below, multiple, different technologies-in-practice were enacted by different user groups—one by Iris developers, three within Alpha, and two by Zeta customer support staff.

Example of enactment: collaborative technology-in-practice within Iris

While the *Notes* technology is currently manufactured by the Lotus Development Corporation (now owned by IBM), it was conceived and designed

Table 1 Properties of the *Notes* Technological Artifact.

ELEMENTS	TECHNOLOGICAL PROPERTIES
Electronic Communication	Electronic messaging to geographically dispersed community via e-mail
	Announcements and responses on widely distributed electronic bulletin boards
	Importing of newsfeeds from external services
	Electronic mail gateways to transfer Notes e-mail messages to other systems
Text Editing	Creation and editing of documents that include multiple field types and formats with an emphasis on free-form textual information
	Importing of text, tables, spreadsheets, graphics, images, and sound from other programs
Document Management	Creation and management of databases of documents in a variety of views
	Search and retrieval of individual or groups of documents based on indexes or free text searches
Customization	Direct manipulation of user interface
	Modification of default views and database templates
Integration	Connection between various features: communication, text editing, and document management
Replication	Periodic, scheduled duplication of designated databases across Notes servers in a network
	Support for stand-alone computers through dial-up into a Notes server
Security	Provision of password protection and ID verification to control access to databases
	Support for data encryption at level of e-mail messages, databases, documents, and particular fields
Application Development	Programming of unique database applications via Notes Application Programming Interface
	Computation of totals, averages, and other statistics on any field

(from DeJean and DeJean 1991).

by Ray Ozzie, founder of Iris Associates. Ozzie traces his vision for *Notes* to the Plato system, a mainframe-based computing environment at the University of Illinois in Urbana-Champaign. Ozzie used this system as a computer science student in the seventies, and observed "people who had no knowledge of computers using this tool to collaborate on projects." This left such a big impression on Ozzie that after working in the software industry for a number of years, he returned to these early experiences:

In the early eighties I was working in spreadsheets, but spreadsheets didn't turn me on. So my mind turned to Plato and what I had experienced there—collaboration and communication. I wanted to start my own company to develop those things.

With financing from the Lotus Development Corporation, Ozzie founded Iris Associates in 1984 and hired four former colleagues. The five Iris developers spent the next four years designing, building, and testing the *Notes* product. The knowledge and techniques used to construct the *Notes* technology came from Ozzie's Plato-inspired vision of collaborative computing and the various personal computing and networking environments the five developers had been exposed to over the years, such as client server architecture, graphic user interface, and public key cryptography. Additional influences on the construction of *Notes* were the ideals about work shared by the developers:

> As a group of individuals we share the same beliefs about how we'd like to see people work—the Iris values. [And so], we implemented a very different software development methodology here that relies on distributed management, distributed security, and distributed development.... Distribution is a value that pervades our philosophy. So technically and architecturally the product embraced distribution.

As a result, the *Notes* technology has a highly distributed architecture which supports collaboration among a variety of distributed users. In addition, it allows users to customize their interface with the technology and provides them with the tools to develop their own applications within the *Notes* system. Ozzie explained that the capability to "build" applications was extended to all users in conformance with the Iris philosophy of decentralized control:

> A design debate we had a lot was: Does every copy of *Notes* have the ability to design applications or do we have a "developer's copy" and "user copies"? In practice, while it is a nightmare for the MIS person to have this [design] capability on every copy of *Notes*, it makes the product more exciting for the users because anyone can turn from a user to a developer overnight. We wanted individuals to have independence over their work.

As is common in many software development projects, the Iris developers used the technology they were building to support their own development activities, using its features of electronic mail, discussion databases, text entry, text edit, text search, and tool design to create and share repositories of software documentation and modules. So, the first technology-in-practice to be constituted with the *Notes* technology was the one enacted recurrently

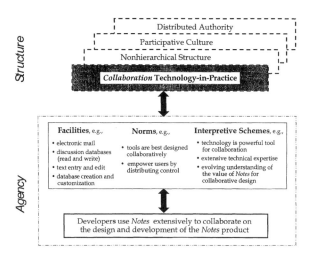

Figure 3 Collaboration Technology-in-Practice Enacted by Developers in Iris.

by members of the Iris development team. It was a structure of collaboration, which both shaped and was shaped by the ongoing Iris software development process. It was influenced by the Iris developers' strong views about distributed control and individual empowerment, their participative culture and limited hierarchy, their energy and motivation to create a computer tool to support collaboration, as well as the properties of the emerging *Notes* technology that Iris developers were inscribing into the artifact. Their enactment of a collaborative technology-in-practice thus modified aspects of the technology itself (through the addition or improvement of various properties), strengthened the Iris developers' belief in the value (both for themselves and more generally) of computer-supported collaboration, and reinforced their distributed and collegial work practices and norms (see Figure 3). Different technologies-in-practice with the *Notes* technology were enacted in other settings.

Example of enactment: three technologies-in-practice within Alpha

Alpha (a pseudonym) is a large, multinational consulting firm with offices in hundreds of cities around the world, employing thousands of consultants who work on project engagements to deliver professional services to clients. While consultants work in engagement teams, their work relations and practices are strongly influenced by the "up or out" career structure which regulates progress of all consultants via four primary career milestones: junior consultant, senior consultant, manager, and partner.

525

In the late eighties, a chief information officer (CIO) position was created with responsibility for Alpha's global use of information technology. Having recently been exposed to *Notes*, the CIO was persuaded that it offered the functionality not only to provide corporate-wide electronic mail support, but also to facilitate broad knowledge sharing. These properties, he believed, would address the considerable "reinvention of the wheel" which occurred when Alpha consultants in different offices worked on similar client problems without sharing ideas, approaches, or solutions, thus duplicating effort and not "leveraging the existing expertise and experience of the firm." The CIO purchased thousands of copies of *Notes* for Alpha's consultants, and ordered his technology staff to install it (and the supporting infrastructure of hardware and networks) rapidly in all offices, so as to establish a critical mass of users as quickly as possible.

I studied the use of *Notes* by both consultants and technologists. As the latter were the first to encounter *Notes* within Alpha, I will begin with their experiences of using *Notes*.

Collective problem-solving technology-in-practice

Alpha's technology group consisted of some 40 technology staff who reported to the CIO. The group was responsible for setting corporate technology standards and supporting the firm's technological infrastructure. Most of the group members had technical backgrounds, having worked as programmers and computer support staff for most of their careers. While providing support to the firm's consultants, these technologists were not regarded as consultants. As a result, they were not required to bill their time to clients, and were not subject to the rigid timing and high risk associated with Alpha's hierarchical consulting career path.

In addition to implementing *Notes* throughout the firm, these technologists used the *Notes* technology extensively in their work. They used electronic mail for coordinating and scheduling their activities, and they maintained a variety of electronic discussions within *Notes* databases. Most of the technologists frequently accessed and contributed to these discussion databases, exchanging information about technical problems, solutions, and new or upgraded products. Some had also created their own database designs, using the feature within *Notes* that allows customization of database templates. Not subject to the competitive culture, "up-or-out" career tension, and "billable hours" pressures faced by the consultants, and supported by the cooperative norms of technical support, the technologists used many of the properties of *Notes* to promote their collective technical work, and to cooperate with each other. They also modified the technology over time as they added data to the databases and created or customized databases.

In this recurrent practice of technology use, technologists drew on their detailed knowledge of *Notes* and their technical support work practices

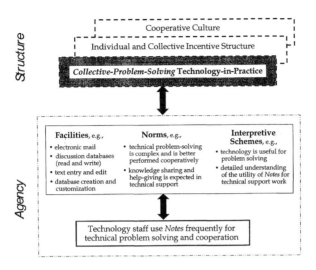

Figure 4 Collective Problem-Solving Technology-in-Practice Enacted by Technologists in Alpha.

and norms to interact with such properties of *Notes* as electronic mail, text entry and editing, discussion databases, and database design. This recurrent action enacted a set of rules and resources which structured their work in terms of cooperative troubleshooting and technical knowledge sharing, while modifying the technology itself (by adding content, creating new databases, and customizing templates). In turn, this technology-in-practice of collective problem-solving reaffirmed the value of cooperation within Alpha's technology group and reinforced their established cooperative work practices and norms, further encouraging the technologists to keep using *Notes* to support their work of maintaining Alpha's technological infrastructure (see Figure 4).

In contrast to this pattern of *Notes* use, the consultants I studied within Alpha engaged with *Notes* quite differently and enacted two distinct technologies-in-practice.

Limited-use technology-in-practice

The most common technology-in-practice I observed in the consulting group involved limited use of *Notes*, and was enacted by consultants at all levels of the firm. Such use of *Notes* was minimal, even perfunctory, and involved opening electronic mail folders a few times a week, rarely, if ever, sending a message, and only occasionally accessing a discussion database to examine activity in it. My data suggest that this technology-in-practice was enacted for at least three different reasons.

527

Figure 5 Example of Skepticism Towards Technology.

First, some consultants had doubts about the value of *Notes* for their own and the firm's performance. Some of these consultants based their skepticism on the view that *Notes* primarily facilitated information transfer while their work as Alpha consultants was to manage client relationships. Other consultants were skeptical about technologies in general and applied this same skepticism to *Notes.* A vivid illustration of such skepticism was provided by a manager who handed me a cartoon clipped from the morning's newspaper, commenting: "You asked me what I thought of *Notes.* Well, here's your answer" (see Figure 5).

The skepticism felt by these consultants was exacerbated by their limited knowledge of *Notes'* functionality. The training sessions conducted about *Notes* dealt with the mechanics of using the software and were technical and abstract. The collaborative aspects of *Notes* were not highlighted and there was little illustration of how *Notes* could be used in Alpha's consulting practice. Most consultants found the training condescending and unhelpful, and many had not referred to the *Notes* documentation which they had all been issued. These often lay, still shrink-wrapped, in the corners of offices or on the tops of bookshelves. Thus, despite training and access to *Notes,* consultants remained skeptical and unmotivated to spend much time using the technology. I shadowed half a dozen managers and partners for a few days after they had received *Notes* training, and found that they accessed *Notes* for an average of two minutes a day—usually just to check if they had received any electronic mail.

In this recurrent practice of technology use, consultants drew on their firm's orientation to relationship management, their limited knowledge of *Notes*, their view of it as "simply a solution in search of a problem," their prior experiences with and assumptions about computers as inappropriate or ineffective, and their perfunctory use of *Notes'* electronic mail and discussion database properties, to enact a set of minimal rules and resources which barely influenced their existing consulting work practices and did not alter the technology. In turn, this limited-use technology-in-practice, because it provided them with little value, strengthened the consultants' assumptions and experiences of *Notes* as less than useful for their consulting work practices, and reinforced the firm's orientation to relationship management.

The second reason why consultants enacted a limited-use technology-in-practice with *Notes* was rooted in their ongoing enactment of Alpha's time-based billing structure. For all consultants except partners, there was an expectation that most if not all hours should be "chargeable," that is, billed to clients and hence revenue-producing. Consultants were held accountable for any "below the line" (nonchargeable) hours they incurred and most consultants studiously avoided having any.[10] One consultant noted: "Seniors and managers never have nonchargeable hours. It's just not done. It doesn't happen." Because many consultants did not see using *Notes* as an activity that could be billed to clients, they were unwilling to spend time learning or using it, as this would have required them to incur "nonchargeable hours" or to give up some of their personal time.

In this recurrent practice of technology use, consultants drew on their knowledge of Alpha's institutional practices (in particular, the corporate norm against "nonchargeable" hours), their perception of *Notes* as not useful for client work, and their limited use of *Notes'* electronic mail and discussion database properties, to enact a set of minimal rules and resources which had little influence on their existing consulting work practices or their technology. In turn, such a limited-use technology-in-practice, because it provided minimal value to the consultants, bolstered their assumptions about *Notes* as not valuable in client work, and as not worth the cost of either nonchargeable hours or their own personal time. It also reinforced the legitimacy and importance of the firm's time-based billing structure.

The third reason consultants enacted a limited-use technology-in-practice with *Notes* arose from their fear that use of its collaborative properties would threaten their status within Alpha. The competitive culture at Alpha, strongly reinforced by the "up-or-out" career path, was seen by many consultants as encouraging the development of individually distinctive competence. As one manager put it:

> In Alpha we have a lot of problems getting people to share expertise and information. That is not in the culture . . . People hide information because it gives them an edge.

In an environment where "knowledge is power," many consultants believed that any sharing of expertise—particularly via the global and relatively anonymous network provided by Alpha's *Notes* infrastructure—would hurt, not help, their chances of generating some unique expertise and consequently of securing the sought-after promotions. Thus, use of *Notes* was perceived by consultants to be countercultural and incompatible with their individual advancement and success in the firm.

In this recurrent practice of technology use, consultants drew on their understanding of *Notes* as a tool for broad distribution of expertise, their knowledge of Alpha's culture as competitive and individualistic, and

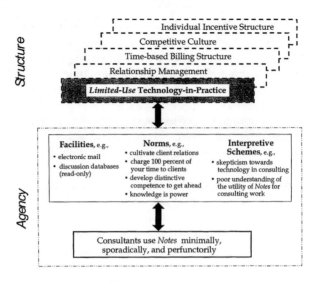

Figure 6 Limited-Use Technology-in-Practice Enacted by Consultants in Alpha.

their perfunctory use of *Notes'* electronic mail and discussion database properties to enact a set of minimal rules and resources which did little to alter their existing consulting work practices or their technology. In turn, such a limited-use technology-in-practice, because it offered no counterevidence to the consultants' fears, further increased their reluctance to use *Notes* to share expertise, and reinforced their firm's practice of rewarding individual effort and distinctive competence rather than cooperation and knowledge sharing.

While the limited-use technology-in-practice was predominant among the Alpha consultants I studied (see Figure 6), another technology-in-practice emphasizing individual productivity was also evident in the practices of a different set of consultants.

Individual productivity technology-in-practice

Another (smaller) set of consultants in Alpha did not view *Notes* as either irrelevant or threatening; instead, they saw it as an opportunity to enhance their own individual effectiveness by speeding up existing ways of doing things. Thus, a few managers and senior consultants began to use *Notes* regularly to perform activities previously conducted on paper or with other media. For example, they began distributing memos via *Notes* rather than on paper, sending electronic rather than voice mail messages, and transferring files electronically to other offices rather than using the fax machine or express mail services. Some managers also used *Notes* to obtain electronic newsfeeds from Reuters or to access Alpha publications, previously available on paper or from a centralized computer system in Alpha's library.

Applying a new technology to existing tasks is a common response to encountering unfamiliar technologies, as Barley (1988, p. 50) notes, "[workers] often attempt to assimilate new technologies under previous patterns of practice and interpretation." Because these consultants' use of *Notes* automated established practices and increased efficiency, it did not violate institutional norms, and thus did not undermine their professional standing within the firm. Indeed, these consultants believed their use of *Notes* would give them a competitive edge in the firm by enhancing their personal productivity. In this recurrent practice of technology use, consultants drew on their knowledge of Alpha's culture, their moderate knowledge of some of the functionality of *Notes*, and engaged specific properties of *Notes* (electronic mail, news-feeds, databases, and file transfer) to enact a set of rules and resources which increased their work productivity and incrementally modified the technology (via customizations to the desktop and content added to databases). In turn, such a technology-in-practice of individual productivity, because it provided demonstrable improvements in efficiency, supported these consultants' view of *Notes* as an effective tool for personal productivity gains, while reinforcing the individualistic and efficiency orientation of the firm (see Figure 7).

Members of Alpha from the consulting and technology support communities thus used the *Notes* technology to enact three different

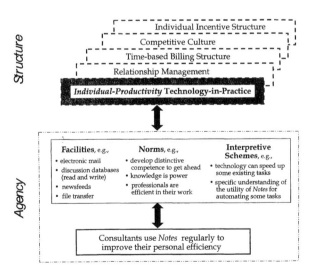

Figure 7 Individual Productivity Technology-in-Practice Enacted by Consultants in Alpha.

technologies-in-practice. Members of another user community—this one within the Zeta organization—used *Notes* in still different ways.

Example of enactment: two technologies-in-practice within Zeta

Zeta (a pseudonym) is a Top 50 U.S. software company, producing and selling a range of powerful marketing analysis products. In 1994, Zeta earned $100 million in revenues and employed about 1000 employees in its Midwest headquarters and regional sales offices around the world. My colleagues and I examined the implementation and use of *Notes* in Zeta's customer support department (CSD). Customer support at Zeta involved providing technical consultation via telephone to clients, client service representatives in the field, and other Zeta employees. The technical consultation provided by customer support specialists was a complex activity, typically involving several hours or even days of research including searches of reference material, attempts to replicate the problem, and review of program source code. The CSD employed fifty specialists, and was headed by a director and two managers.

In early 1992, the CSD purchased *Notes* and developed a customized application within it, the Incident Tracking Support System *(ITSS)*, to help keep track of customer calls. The acquisition of *Notes* was motivated by a realization that the existing call tracking system was inefficient and poorly used, and the anticipation of increased calls due to a growing client base and an expanding product range. Following a successful pilot in the latter half of 1992, the CSD deployed *Notes* and *ITSS* throughout the department. We studied the use of *Notes* in the CSD from 1992 to 1994 and found that over time the support specialists enacted two distinct, but complementary, technologies-in-practice with *Notes*.

Process-support technology-in-practice

Specialists' initial use of Notes enacted a technology-in-practice of process support. Such a recurrent practice of technology use involved two primary activities: work documentation and information search. In documenting their work process, specialists used the online input and text-editing properties of *Notes* to enter every customer call they received as an incident in the *ITSS* database, to maintain a complete trace for each incident as they worked on it, and to record the final problem resolution when they closed the incident. The work documentation generated by specialists began to accumulate in the *ITSS* database, growing from about 4,000 entries in December 1992 to 35,000 in December 1994. This information became increasingly valuable as specialists started to search the database to try to find existing solutions for new problems. By December 1994, specialists reported being able to resolve up to 50 percent of new incidents simply by using the *Notes* search function to probe the *ITSS* database. Searching *ITSS* was seen by the specialists to be helpful not just because prior entries revealed potentially reusable problem resolutions, but also because they provided a detailed trace of the work process followed to resolve different types of incidents.

The specialists' engagement with *Notes* for their support work utilized many of its properties—electronic text entry and editing, as well as database searching and document management. As technical support specialists, the CSD members were knowledgeable about technology in general, as well as *Notes* in particular. This latter knowledge was acquired through a series of official training sessions (referred to as "*Notes* jam sessions") which included intensive hands-on use of *Notes* during which specialists simulated their production work in the *Notes* environment, taking "fake calls" from colleagues and then documenting these in the *ITSS* database.

Specialists' use of *Notes* to record and reuse problem resolution knowledge was in direct contrast to the action of many of the Alpha consultants, who had felt inhibited by their competitive culture to create and share knowledge within *Notes*. In comparison, Zeta specialists reported that the CSD's cooperative culture and its team orientation encouraged such behavior:

> I don't care who grabs credit for my work.... This support department does well because we're a team, not because we're all individuals.

Specialists' ongoing enactment of a process-support technology-in-practice was further reinforced by managerial action which redefined the evaluation criteria used to assess specialists' performance. Managers modified these criteria to include use of *Notes* for entry and documentation of customer calls, and rewarded specialists for creating high quality process documentation and for reusing existing solutions in the database.

In this recurrent practice of technology use, specialists drew on their knowledge of the CSD's norms of cooperation and collegiality, its team incentive structure and expectations of effective client service, their familiarity and experience with computer technology in general, their detailed technical knowledge of *Notes*, and used the text entry, editing, searching, and documentation properties of *Notes* to enact a set of rules and resources which provided electronic process support to their technical support work. They also modified aspects of their technology through such use by generating document templates and adding content to the database. In turn, this process-support technology-in-practice, because it provided immediate and tangible benefits to the CSD specialists served to amplify their view that using *Notes* facilitated customer support work, and reinforced their cooperative and team oriented department structure (see Figure 8). Many of these support specialists also enacted another pattern of using *Notes*.

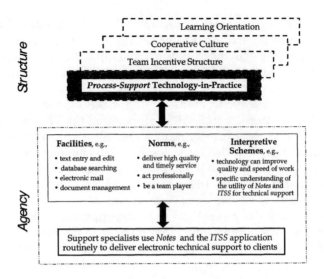

Figure 8 Process-Support Technology-in-Practice Enacted by Support Specialists in Zeta.

Improvisation technology-in-practice

A subsequent technology-in-practice enacted by the CSD specialists involved their use of *Notes* to respond artfully to unanticipated problems and unexpected opportunities that arose in their work. Such improvisational action went beyond the process-support technology-in-practice, and typically generated workarounds or new processes for conducting technical support work. For example, one such process concerned the expectation, set by the CSD managers and provided for in the design of *ITSS*, that specialists would directly enter calls into the *ITSS* database as they received them, so as to produce an up-to-the-minute trace of all incoming calls. However, many specialists found the process of entering calls into *ITSS* while on the phone too difficult, and so they developed a workaround by writing down call details on paper, and then entering these into the *ITSS* database just after the phone call finished. Specialists' rationale for this practice was grounded in their concerns about typing skills and the importance of fully understanding their customers' technical problems before entering them into the *ITSS* database.

Further improvisational use of *Notes* arose when specialists began to use it to collaborate on incidents. Before the implementation of *Notes*, specialists helped each other only when asked to do so. Specialists tended to work on their own incidents in private until they felt stuck, at which point they would approach a colleague—either by phone or face-to-face—and solicit help. In this interaction with colleagues, they would also learn new skills

534

and knowledge. As specialists used *Notes* for process support, they gained access to the entire *ITSS* database, which included all calls, past and present, worked on by members of the CSD. Specialists got into the habit of browsing through each others' calls, and using these to engage in an ad hoc learning process:

> If it is quiet I will check on my fellow colleagues to see . . . what kind of calls they get, so I might learn something from them.

There were two consequences of such browsing. One was that specialists realized the potential for using the *ITSS* database to train newly-hired specialists. Thus, a few senior specialists extracted sample problems from the *ITSS* database and created a "training database" within *Notes* which new hires worked with to learn the process of problem resolution. Their interaction with this training database was then monitored by a designated mentor, and in this way new recruits received guidance and practice in the techniques of online technical support work.

The second consequence of browsing the database was that specialists got to see still-open calls where they might have some expertise to help. This created an opportunity for specialists to offer each other proactive help, in contrast to the reactive mode which had operated previously. Rather than waiting to be approached to give assistance on specific incidents, specialists now took the initiative as they browsed the *ITSS* database to offer unsolicited help on calls where they believed they had some particular knowledge:

> Sometimes, if I see something that's open on somebody's calls which I've seen before, I may put a note in the incident and say "Hey, I think I've seen this before, this might be this and this."

While the enactment of the improvisation technology-in-practice was initiated by specialists, it was supported by the "learning" orientation emphasized by departmental managers who actively encouraged specialists to explore alternative ways of working and offer suggestions for improving processes in the CSD. While managers recommended a particular use of *ITSS*, they did not rigidly enforce it, accepting workarounds and variations if these produced valued results. In this recurrent practice of technology use, specialists drew on their knowledge of their CSD environment (in particular norms of cooperation and expectations of learning and experimentation), their familiarity and experience with computer technology in general, and their detailed technical knowledge of *Notes*, to use multiple properties of *Notes* (text entry and editing, database browsing, electronic mail, and data analysis), and modify them (e.g., by adding content and creating a new training database). Such recurrent use enacted a set of rules and resources which supported specialists' improvisation beyond their

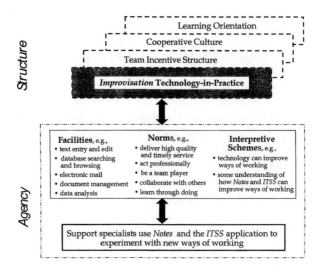

Figure 9 Improvisation Technology-in-Practice Enacted by Support Specialists in Zeta.

process-support technology-in-practice and helped them to overcome practical difficulties and to innovate additional ways of working and learning. In turn, this improvisation technology-in-practice, because it provided value to the specialists' work, affirmed their view that using *Notes* could enhance their work through ongoing experimentation and change, and reinforced the cooperative culture and learning-oriented structure of their department (see Figure 9).

Examples of enactment: summary

Taken together, these empirical illustrations show that people enact different technologies-in-practice with the same type of technology across various contexts and practices. We have seen that they do so in response to various technological visions, skills, fears, and opportunities, influenced by specific interpretations and particular institutional contexts, and shaped by a diversity of intentions and practices to collaborate, solve problems, preserve status, improve efficiency, support work processes, learn, and improvise. These technologies-in-practice are structures enacted through the recurrent use of a technology. They are not embodied within the technology; rather, they emerge from the ongoing and situated interactions that users have with the technology at hand.

Thus, in the case of Iris Associates we see that developers drew on their earlier experiences of different technologies, their visions about collaborative use of technology, their knowledge of software design, and their start-up

536

environment to recurrently enact a collaborative technology-in-practice that both created and engaged the collaborative and distributed design properties of *Notes* as rules and resources for their software development efforts. Technology members of Alpha, influenced by an institutional context that supported and rewarded cooperation in technical support work, recurrently enacted a technology-in-practice that engaged many of the collaborative and design properties of *Notes* as rules and resources for collective problem solving. Consultant members of Alpha, influenced by their firm's hierarchical career path, individual criteria for evaluation and promotion, time-based billing system, and their personal skepticism and apprehensions, recurrently enacted technologies-in-practice that engaged very few of the properties of *Notes* as rules and resources for either limited use or individual productivity gains. Finally, Zeta support specialists, influenced by a collegial environment which encouraged experimentation and learning, and motivated by a personal interest to be cooperative and deliver more effective service, recurrently enacted technologies-in-practice that engaged many of the collaborative and design properties of *Notes* as rules and resources for process support and improvisation of customer service work.

These examples further illustrate how a practice lens allows us to see what, when, where, how, and why different groups enact different structures (technologies-in-practice) through their recurrent interaction with a particular set of technological properties, in similar and different contexts, at the same time, and over time. In addition, such a practice lens allows us to examine the institutional, interpretive, and technological conditions which shape the ongoing constitution of different structures, and how such constitution in turn reinforces or modifies those institutional, interpretive, and technological elements. I turn now to some of the implications of a practice lens for studying technologies in organizations.

Implications of the practice lens for studying technology

In this paper, I have sought to augment the existing structurational perspective on technology by proposing a view of technology structures, not as embodied in given technological artifacts, but as enacted by the recurrent social practices of a community of users. This view directs researchers' attention to what people do with technology in their everyday practices, and how such use is structured by the rules and resources implicated in their ongoing action. Rather than trying to understand why and how a given technology is more or less likely to be appropriated in various circumstances, a practice lens focuses on knowledgeable human action and how its recurrent engagement with a given technology constitutes and reconstitutes particular emergent structures of using the technology (technologies-in-practice). Thus, the research orientation is inverted—from a focus on given technologies, embodied structures, and their influence on use—to a focus on human agency and the enactment of emergent structures in the recurrent use of technologies.

While a practice lens recognizes that technology use is always situated and emergent, it does not imply that such use is completely unique. On the contrary, because regular use of the same technology tends to be recurrent, people tend to enact the same or similar technologies-in-practice over time. In this way, enacted technology structures become routine, taken for granted, and even institutionalized within certain circumstances. Such stabilization for now of technologies-in-practice allows researchers to seek bounded generalizations about the types of technologies-in-practice likely to be enacted by particular types of users with specific technologies in various contexts and times. As Giddens (1984) notes, generalizations about human social conduct are of two types: those that "hold because actors themselves know them—in some guise—and apply them in the enactment of what they do" (p. xix); and those that refer to the unintended consequences of agents' patterns of action (p. 347). Both of these generalizations hold only in historically and contextually-specific circumstances.

Table 2 suggests some provisional generalizations of both types based on comparisons across the conditions and consequences associated with the six technologies-in-practice enacted by members of Iris, Alpha, and Zeta with essentially the same technology (a customizable groupware tool, *Notes* installed on networked personal computers). Three kinds of conditions (acknowledged or unacknowledged) are salient here: interpretive, technological, and institutional. Interpretive conditions refer to the conventional understandings and shared meanings that members of a community construct to make sense of their world (including the technology they use). Technological conditions refer to the technological properties (both tool and data) available to the users in their work practices. Institutional conditions refer to the social structures (normative, authoritative) that constitute part of the larger social system within which users work. Three kinds of consequences (intended or unintended) are relevant here: processual, technological, and structural. Processual consequences refer to changes (if any) in the execution and outcome of users' work practices. Technological consequences refer to changes (if any) in the technological properties available to the users. Structural consequences refer to changes (if any) in structures that users enact as part of the larger social system in which they are participating.

The comparison of the conditions and consequences associated with whether and how humans use the technology to enact different technologies-in-practice suggests that three clusters or types of enactment can be discerned. These are associated with three distinct kinds of consequences: consequences that represent no evident change in process, technology, or structure; consequences that represent some change in one or more of process, technology, and structure; and consequences that represent significant change in one or more of process, technology, and structure. Whether or not the technology or the work practices are changed is often an intended outcome of people's knowledgeable actions; the structural consequences are much more likely to be unintended consequences of actions.

The first type of enactment may be characterized in terms of *inertia*, where users choose to use technology to retain their existing way of doing things (see first row of Table 2). It results in the reinforcement and preservation of the structural status quo, with no discernable changes in work practices or the technological artifact. Inertia is represented in my data with the limited-use technology-in-practice, where users choose to use their new tool rarely and perfunctorily, and show little or no interest in integrating its use into their ongoing work practices. In the one case where this enactment was evident in my data, it was associated with interpretive conditions that included users having limited understanding and/or being skeptical of the technological properties available to them, and institutional conditions that included a rigid career hierarchy, individualistic incentives and task assignments, and a competitive culture. Thus, as a type of enactment, inertia involves drawing on and not changing existing interpretive, technological, and institutional conditions, and, in this way, reproducing and reinforcing them over time.

The second type of enactment may be characterized in terms of *application*, where people choose to use the new technology to augment or refine their existing ways of doing things (see next four rows of Table 2). Such enactment results in the reinforcement and enhancement of the structural status quo, noticeable changes to the data and/or tool aspects of the technological artifact, as well as noticeable improvements to work processes. Application is represented in my data by four technologies-in-practice—collaboration, individual productivity, collective problem-solving, and process-support—which were enacted in all three of the research sites I examined. Looking across the rows of Table 2, it is evident that this enactment occurred with users having moderate, competent, or extensive understanding of their technology at hand, and being either moderately or highly motivated to use it to enhance their work practices. These users worked within and drew on a range of institutional conditions (from hierarchical and competitive to collaborative and participative). While the interpretive and institutional conditions associated with these sites are diverse, commonality lies in the users' intentions and actions. That is, all of the users in these four cases used the technology with the intention of improving or enhancing their existing work processes.

Thus, as a type of enactment, application involves users drawing on existing institutional, interpretive, and technological conditions over time and reproducing them in an enhanced or improved form. For example, where the institutional conditions are hierarchical and individualistic, enactment in the form of application results in action that increases such hierarchy and

Table 2 Types of Enactment—Conditions, Actions, and Consequences.

Type of Enactment	Interest in using the Technology	Interpretive Conditions	Technological Conditions	Institutional Conditions	Technology-in-Practice	Processual Consequences	Technological Consequences	Structural Consequences
Inertia	Low	Limited technical knowledge	• Networked personal computer • Customizable groupware tool	• Hierarchical • Individualistic • Competitive	Limited-Use	• None	• None	Reinforce and preserve status quo
Application	Very High	Extensive technical knowledge	• Networked personal computer • Customizable groupware tool	• Nonhierarchical • Collaborative • Participative	Collaboration	• Increased effectiveness in development • Improved collaboration	• Changes to the tool • Changes to the data	Reinforce and enhance status quo
	Moderate	Moderate technical knowledge	• Networked personal computer • Customizable groupware tool	• Hierarchical • Individualistic • Competitive	Individual-Productivity	• Increased efficiency in communication	• Changes to the data	Reinforce and enhance status quo

High	Detailed technical knowledge	• Networked personal computer • Customizable groupware tool	• Communal • Cooperative	*Collective-Problem-Solving*	• Increased effectiveness in problem solving • Increased cooperation	• Adaptations to the tool • Changes to the data	Reinforce and enhance status quo
Very High	Competent technical knowledge	• Networked personal computer • Customizable groupware tool • Call tracking tool	• Team-focused • Cooperative • Learning-oriented	*Process-Support*	• Increased effectiveness in customer service • Increased efficiency in communication	• Adjustments in the tool • Changes to the data	Reinforce and enhance status quo
Change High	Competent technical knowledge	• Networked personal computer • Customizable groupware tool • Call tracking tool	• Team-focused • Cooperative • Learning-oriented	*Improvisation*	• Redefined work distribution • Shift in type of collaboration • Change in ways of learning	• Adaptations to the tool • Changes to the data	Transform status quo

individualism, as when the individual productivity technology-in-practice was used to further individual rather than collaborative efforts within Alpha. Similarly, when the institutional conditions are nonhierarchical and participative, as in the case of Iris, the enactment of the collaboration technology-in-practice helped to improve the shared and collaborative design efforts of the developers.

The third type of enactment may be characterized in terms of *change,* where people choose to use the new technology to substantially alter their existing way of doing things (see last row of Table 2). Such enactment results in transformation of the structural status quo, and significant modifications to users' work practices as well as the technological artifact. Enactment of change is represented here with the improvisation technology-in-practice, where specialists use the technology to experiment with and implement new ways of working and organizing, and to adapt/customize aspects of their tool and its data content. In the one case where this enactment was evident in my data, it was associated with interpretive conditions that included users being very knowledgeable about technology and highly motivated to use it in their work practices, and institutional conditions that included a strong team focus, a cooperative culture, and a strong commitment to ongoing learning. Thus, as a type of enactment, change involves drawing on and transforming existing institutional, interpretive, and technological conditions over time, and, in this way, significantly changing the organizational status quo.

Like the six technologies-in-practice, the three types of enactment characterized here are not comprehensive or exhaustive, but suggestive of the kinds of comparisons that may be made across the conditions and consequences associated with people's use of technologies. In this way, and through further research, a typology of enactment types may be identified that associates recurrent human action with clusters of technologies-in-practice enacted by using specific properties of technologies in specific interpretive and institutional contexts. The types of enactments discussed here all involved the use of the same kind of technology. Examining other kinds of technologies offering different properties to those of *Notes* would generate further opportunities to study how users draw on different technological conditions to enact particular types of technologies-in-practice with particular social consequences. Similarly, exploring different cultural (e.g., non-U.S.) and institutional (e.g., governmental, educational) contexts to those studied here would also expand our understanding of how users recurrently structure their use of technologies in different circumstances. Additionally, future research could benefit from attending more carefully to the meanings and emotional attachments that users develop for the technologies they use. Beyond the skepticism displayed by some of the consultants within Alpha, my empirical data did not capture the richness of users' affective connections with technology. Understanding these attachments and meanings could offer richer explanations for the range of structural responses enacted by users as they engage with technologies in practice.

Identifying types of structures of technology use should help both researchers and practitioners better understand how and why people are likely to use their technologies and with what (intended and unintended) consequences in different conditions. Of course, the types identified through such research can never exhaust the technologies-in-practice which users may enact in practice. A practice lens assumes that people are purposive, knowledgeable, adaptive, and inventive agents who engage with technology in a multiplicity of ways to accomplish various and dynamic ends. When the technology does not help them achieve those ends, they abandon it, or work around it, or change it, or think about changing their ends. A practice lens thus recognizes that users may always choose to do otherwise, and any typology of enactment types and technologies-in-practice must always remain an open set, as users will continue to modify their technologies and continue to change their uses of technology over time. Recognizing that the possibility to change technology structures is inherent in every use of technology allows us to understand when, where, how, and why people choose to reinforce, ignore, enhance, undermine, change, work around, or replace their existing structures of technology use.

The focus on technologies-in-practice also allows an examination of the extent to which users realize designers' intentions for a technology. That is, it can help us identify and analyze how the technological properties designed into and available in artifacts deployed on shop floors, installed on desktops, or downloadable from Web servers, are used in situated and emergent ways by people attempting to get something done in their daily activities. It has long been recognized that technologies are often not used as designed or intended (Bijker 1995, von Hippel 1988), but generating an adequate understanding of how, where, and why the slippage between design and use occurs in practice has been difficult. By distinguishing between technologies as artifacts and technologies-in-practice, we have a way to explore and explain this process. For example, the examination of the *Notes* technology and its properties, as well as its designers' intentions, provides a profile of potential use that may be compared to the technologies-in-practice realized in a range of recurrent practices. It suggests, for example, that where users' social practices are compatible with designers' intentions and the properties inscribed within a technology, a technology-in-practice may be enacted that more closely realizes those designers' intentions and their technology's properties. We saw this in the case of the Alpha technologists and Zeta specialists whose work practices of technical support and peer collaboration corresponded with the *Notes* designers' visions and norms of supporting collaboration through technology. Not surprisingly, the technologies-in-practice they enacted (collective problem-solving, process-support, and improvisation) were relatively compatible with the collaborative use envisioned by the

Iris developers and provided for in their technology. In contrast, the work practices of the Alpha consultants (individual tasks, competition, knowledge hoarding, client-oriented time-keeping, limited technology experience) were incompatible with the *Notes* designers' visions of supporting collaboration through technology. Not surprisingly, the technologies-in-practice enacted by the Alpha consultants (limited-use and individual productivity) did not come close to realizing the collaborative use envisioned by the Iris developers and provided for in their *Notes* technology.

But even as we can explore compatibilities between users' recurrent social practices, designers' intentions, and technological properties, the practice lens reminds us that use of technology is always situated and emergent, and hence that users in their recurrent interaction with technologies may always choose to depart from designers' a priori intentions and the inscribed properties of the technology. Indeed, the correspondence between use and properties is expected to become, on the one hand, more loosely coupled, as newer reconfigurable technologies become increasingly available in organizations, and on the other hand, more integrated, as the rise of internetworking connects more and more artifacts together in new and complex configurations.

With respect to the former trend, what are sometimes referred to as "radically tailorable tools" (Malone *et al.* 1992) tend to be less fixed-function than prior computing technologies, serving as general purpose platforms on which users may build local applications which convert the generic delivered technology into a customized and situated work tool. Sproull and Goodman (1990, p. 257) note: "[P]rogrammable technology allows for the possibility of continuous redesign." Reconfigurable technologies will provide users with the opportunity of defining a wider array of local properties with which they may be able to enact an even wider variety of technologies-in-practice. Of course, whether and how they do so depends not just on the properties of the technology, but as we saw above, on their social practices and the intentions, interpretations, and institutional contexts shaping those practices over time. Given such open-ended properties of new technologies, the ability to examine what people do with them in practice will be helped by being able to distinguish between the technological properties and the situated technologies-in-practice enacted with them.

With respect to the latter integrating trend, the increased use of the Internet for conducting business requires more interconnections among more players than before (Iacono and Kling, in press). Organizations wishing to link to other businesses or to the Internet will need to provide standard interfaces and consistency of performance across a range of technological platforms to ensure the interoperability of multiple artifacts. Providing for such interconnections increases interdependence and complexity, coupling the artifacts more tightly together in larger technological systems or infrastructures. Such integration is likely to reduce the degrees of freedom available to users to experiment with and modify their technological artifacts in use. As users become more dependent on using integrated technologies, the variety of technologies-in-practice that they will enact may decrease. Of course, whether such restriction in malleability actually occurs in any situation is an empirical question, and will depend on people's practices and how these are affected by such influences as intentions, interpretations, and institutions.

The distinction between technologies and technologies-in-practice further suggests that researchers and managers measuring technological investment or deployment to predict performance impacts may get more meaningful results if they look for returns on the *use* of technology rather than only at returns on the *technology*. Technology per se can't increase or decrease the productivity of workers' performance, only use of it can. This may sound like semantic hair-splitting, but how people talk has profound implications for how they think and act in the world. By emphasizing technology in their talk, people tend to emphasize the technology (not its use) in their allocation of funds, attention, and measures. Such an emphasis, as the examples within Alpha showed, typically leads to a neglect of recurrent and situated technology use (i.e., technologies-in-practice). By not examining or understanding what actually happens during use of technology, researchers and managers miss the crucial point, that it is whether and how people interact with technology in their day-to-day activities—not the mere presence of the technology on the desktop or factory floor—that influences performance outcomes and consequences. Knowing what we know about the different technologies-in-practice enacted within Alpha and Zeta, there is no difficulty in understanding why these firms should have experienced significantly different outcomes from their investments in the same type of technology. The distinction between technologies and technologies-in-practice thus reminds us that measures of technology investment or deployment are not sufficient indicators of organizational change or effectiveness. Such change or effectiveness depends not on technologies alone, but on whether, how, and what technologies-in-practice are enacted with them.

In this paper, I have proposed that the existing structurational perspective on technology be augmented with a practice orientation which focuses specifically on how people's recurrent interaction with technologies enacts distinctive structures of technology use. These structures of technology use (technologies-in-practice) are not fixed or given, but constituted and reconstituted through the everyday, situated practices of particular users using particular technologies in particular circumstances. By attending to such ongoing (re)constitution, a practice lens entails the examination of emergence, improvisation, and change over time as people reconfigure their technologies or alter their habits of use, and thereby enact different technologies-in-practice. A practice lens thus allows us to deepen the focus on human agency and recognize "the essentially transformational character of all human action, even in its most utterly routinized forms" (Giddens, 1984, p. 117).

Acknowledgments

I would like to thank the Senior Editor and three anonymous reviewers for their valuable guidance during the revision process. I am also grateful for the helpful comments I received on earlier versions of this manuscript from Steve Barley, Suzi Iacono, and JoAnne Yates. This work was supported by the Centers for Coordination Science and Information Systems Research at the Massachusetts Institute of Technology.

Notes

1 A number of extensive discussions of this technology literature are available, for example, Kling (1980), Barley (1988), Powell (1987), Scott (1990), Scarbrough and Corbett (1992), and Marx and Smith (1994).

2 The notion of *enactment* used here is related to but broader than that given currency by Weick (1979). It is intended here in the conventional sense of "to constitute, actuate, perform" (Oxford English Dictionary) or "to represent in or translate into action" (Merriam-Webster Dictionary).

3 I use the term *artifact* here in the sense of "anything made by human art and workmanship" (Oxford English Dictionary) or "a product of artificial character due usually to human agency" (Merriam-Webster Dictionary).

4 As Grint and Woolgar (1995, p. 289) remind us "[Technology] exists only in and through our descriptions and practices, and hence it is never available in a raw, untainted state." Thus, even the description and observation of "technologies" and their "properties," including their designation as artifacts, is a kind of *use* of that technology. These reflexive complications notwithstanding, I believe that the analytic distinction between technologies as artifacts and the use of such artifacts is an especially useful one in both empirical research and everyday usage.

5 In what follows, I will conform to common usage and use the term "technology" to refer to "technological artifact."

6 It is interesting to note that what is actually enacted here as tax rules is not the tax code as legislated, but the tax code as encoded in the software, which reflects developers' understanding of the tax legislation and their ability to translate it into executable software code.

7 One of the anonymous reviewers observed that a gun is a gun even if no one pulls the trigger. Yes and no. While it is the case that most of us can recognize a particular object as a gun through its inscribed shape, physical properties, and functions, such recognition is culturally-specific. No such recognition would be forthcoming from the members of a remote tribe in the Kalahari Desert who have never encountered the object we refer to as a "gun." Furthermore, if our knowledge of a gun comes primarily from its use, then we cannot assume that a gun "is a gun" without knowing how that object is being used. While guns are designed and built for a particular purpose, and their possession has important implications for social policy, gun possession is not sufficient grounds for presuming that a gun will be used in a particular way. People can and do choose not to pull the trigger, and that makes all the difference.

8 I wish to thank one of the anonymous reviewers for highlighting the importance of emotional connections in people's use of technologies.

9 See Orlikowski (1993, 1996) and Orlikowski and Gash (1994) for more details of the research studies which generated these examples.

10 My research study had been "officially sanctioned" and participants had been told to charge the time they spent with me to a professional activities code. Yet, many confided they would "swallow the time" so as to avoid any dreaded "below the line" hours, even apparently legitimate ones.

References

Akrich, M. 1992. The de-scription of technical artifacts. W. E. Bijker, J. Law, eds. *Shaping Technology/Building Society: Studies in Sociotechnical Change.* MIT Press, Cambridge, MA. 205–224.

Barley, S. R. 1986. Technology as an occasion for structuring: Evidence from observation of CT scanners and the social order of radiology departments. *Admin. Sci. Quart.* **31** 78–108.

——. 1988. Technology, power, and the social organization of work. *Res. Soc. Organ.* **6** 33–80.

——. 1990. The alignment of technology and structure through roles and networks. *Admin. Sci. Quart.* **35** 61–103.

Barrett, F. J. 1998. Creativity and improvisation in jazz and organizations: Implications for organizational learning. *Organ. Sci.* **9**(5) 605–622.

Bazerman, C. 1994. Systems of genres and the enactment of social intentions. A. Freedman, P. Medway, eds. *Genre and the New Rhetoric.* Taylor & Francis Ltd., London, U.K. 79–101.

Berners-Lee, T. 1996. Private communication (May 17).

Bijker, W. E. 1987. The social construction of Bakelite: Toward a theory of invention. W. E. Bijker, T. P. Hughes, T. Pinch, eds. *The Social Construction of Technological Systems.* MIT Press, Cambridge MA. 159–187.

——. 1995. *Of Bicycles, Bakelites, and Bulbs: Toward a Theory of Sociotechnical Change.* MIT Press, Cambridge MA.

——, T. P. Hughes, T. Pinch, eds. 1987. *The Social Construction of Technological Systems.* MIT Press, Cambridge MA.

——, J. Law, eds. 1992. *Shaping Technology/Building Society: Studies in Sociotechnical Change.* MIT Press, Cambridge MA.

Bourdieu, P. 1977. *Outline of a Theory of Practice.* Cambridge University Press, New York.

Braverman, H. 1974. *Labor and Monopoly Capital: The Degradation of Work in the Twentieth Century,* Monthly Review Press, New York.

Brown, J. S., P. Duguid. 1991. Organizational learning and communities of practice: Toward a unified view of working, learning and innovation. *Organ. Sci.* **2** 40–57.

Brown, S., K. M. Eisenhardt. 1997. The art of continuous change: Linking complexity theory and time-paced evolution in relentlessly shifting organizations. *Admin. Sci. Quart.* **42** 1–34.

Brynjolfsson, E. 1993. The productivity paradox of information technology: Review and assessment. *Comm. ACM* **36**(12) 66–77.

Buchanan, D. A., D. Boddy. 1983. *Organizations in the Computer Age: Technological Imperatives and Strategic Choice.* Gower, Hants, U.K.

Bullen, C. V., J. L. Bennett. 1990. Groupware in practice: An interpretation of work experience. *Proceedings of the Conference on Computer Supported Cooperative Work* ACM/SIGCHI, Los Angeles, CA, 291–302.

Burkhardt, M. E., D. J. Brass. 1990. Changing patterns or patterns of change: The effects of a change in technology on social network power and structure. *Admin. Sci. Quart.* **35** 104–127.

Button, G., ed. 1993. *Technology in Working Order: Studies in Work, Interaction, and Technology.* Routledge, London, U.K.

Carter, N. M. 1984. Computerization as a predominate technology: Its influence on the structure of newspaper organizations. *Acad. Management J.* **27** 247–270.

Cassell, P., ed. 1993. *The Giddens Reader.* Stanford University Press, Stanford, CA.

Child, J. 1972. Organizational structure, environment and performance: The role of strategic choice. *Sociology* **6** 1–22.

Chalstrom, B. 1993. Enterprise Computing. *InfoWorld* (November 1) p. 68.

Ciborra, C. U. 1993. *Teams, Markets, and Systems: Business Innovation and Information Technology.* Cambridge University Press, New York.

——. 1996. Improvisation and information technology in organizations. *Proceedings of the 17th International Conference on Information Systems.* Cleveland, OH. 369–380.

——, G. F. Lanzara. 1991. Designing networks in action: Formative contexts and post-modern systems development. R. Clarke, J. Cameron, eds. *Managing Information Technology's Organisational Impact.* Elsevier Science Publishers, Amsterdam, Holland. 265–279.

Clement, A. 1993. Looking for the designers: Transforming the 'invisible' infrastructure of computerized office work. *AI & Society* **7** 323–344.

Cook, S. D. N., J. S. Brown. 1999. Bridging epistemologies: The generative dance between organizational knowledge and organizational knowing. Organ. Sci. **10**(4) 381–400.

Daft, R. L., R. H. Lengel. 1986. Organizational information requirements, media richness and structural design. *Management Sci.* **32** 554–571.

Davis, L. E., J. C. Taylor. 1986. Technology, organization and job structure. R. Dubin, ed. *Handbook of Work, Organization, and Society.* Rand McNally, Chicago, IL, 379–419.

DeJean, D., S. B. DeJean. 1991. *Lotus Notes at Work.* Lotus Books, New York.

DeSanctis, G., M. S. Poole. 1994. Capturing the complexity in advanced technology use: Adaptive structuration theory. *Organ. Sci.* **5**(2) 121–147.

Edwards, R. 1979. *Contested Terrain: The Transformation of the Workplace in the Twentieth Century.* Basic Books, New York.

Galbraith, J. R. 1977. *Organization Design.* Addision-Wesley, Reading, MA.

Gasser, L. 1986. The integration of computing and routine work. *ACM Trans. Office Inform. Systems.* **4**(3) 205–225.

Giddens, A. 1979. *Central Problems in Social Theory: Action, Structure, and Contradiction in Social Analysis.* University of California Press, Berkeley, CA.

——. 1981. Agency, institution, and time-space analysis. K. Knorr-Cetina, A. V. Cicourel, eds. *Advances in Social Theory and Methodology.* Routledge & Kegan Paul, Boston, MA. 161–174.

——. 1984. *The Constitution of Society: Outline of the Theory of Structure.* University of California Press, Berkeley, CA.

——. 1989. A reply to my critics. D. Held, J. B. Thompson, eds. *Social Theory of Modern Societies: Anthony Giddens and his Critics.* Cambridge University Press, Cambridge, U.K. 249–301.

——. 1991. *Modernity and Self-Identity.* Stanford University Press, Stanford, CA.

——. 1993. *New Rules of Sociological Method,* 2nd ed. Stanford University Press, Stanford CA.

Greif, I., ed. 1988. *Computer Supported Cooperative Work.* Morgan Kaufman, New York.

Grint, K., S. Woolgar. 1992. Computers, guns, and roses: What's social about being shot? *Sci., Tech. Human Values* **17**(3) 366–380.

——, ——. 1995. On some failures of nerve in constructivist and feminist analyses of technology. *Sci., Tech., Human Values* **20**(3) 286–310.

Grudin, J. 1989. Why groupware applications fail: Problems in design and evaluation. *Office: Tech. and People* **4**(3) 245–264.

Hatch, M. J. 1998. Jazz as a metaphor for organizing in the 21st century," *Organ. Sci.* **9**(5) 556–568.

Hedberg, B., G. Dahlgrenm, J. Hansson, N-G. Olve. 1997. *Virtual Organizations and Beyond.* John Wiley & Sons, New York.

Hutchins, E. 1991. Organizing work by adaptation. *Organ. Sci.* 2(1) 14–39.

——. 1995. *Cognition in the Wild.* MIT Press, Cambridge, MA.

Iacono, S., R. Kling. (in press) Computerization movements: The rise of the internet and distant forms of work. J. Yates, J. Van Maanen, eds. *IT and Organizational Transformation: History, Rhetoric, and Practice.* Sage Publications, Newbury Park, CA.

Kent, T. 1993. *Paralogic Rhetoric: A Theory of Communicative Interaction.* Associated University Presses, Cranbury, NJ.

Kling, R. 1980. Social analyses of computing: Theoretical perspectives in recent empirical research. *Computing Surveys* **12**(1) 61–110.

——. 1991. Computerization and Social Transformations. *Sci., Tech. and Human Values* **16** 342–367.

——. 1992. Audiences, narratives, and human values in social studies of technology. *Sci., Tech. and Human Values* **17**(3) 349–365.

Kraut, R., S. Koch, S. Dumais. 1988. Computerization, productivity, and quality of employment. *Comm. ACM* **32**(2) 220–238.

Lant, T. 1999. A situated learning perspective on the emergence of knowledge and identity in cognitive communities. *Advances in Management Cognition and Organizational Information Processing* **6** JAI Press, Greenwich, CT, 171–194.

Latour, B. 1992. Where are the missing masses? The sociology of a few mundane artifacts. W. E. Bijker, J. Law, eds. *Shaping Technology/Building Society: Studies in Sociotechnical Change.* MIT Press, Cambridge MA. 225–258.

Lave, J. 1988. *Cognition in Practice.* Cambridge University Press, Cambridge, U.K.

Mackay, W. E. 1988. Diversity in the use of electronic mail. *ACM Trans. on Office Inform. Systems* **6**(4) 380–397.

MacKenzie, D., J. Wajcman, eds. 1985. *The Social Shaping of Technology.* Open University Press, Milton Keynes, UK.

Malone, T. W., K. Y. Lai, C. Fry. 1992. Experiments with OVAL: A radically tailorable tool for cooperative work. *Proceedings of the Conference on Computer Supported Cooperative Work.* ACM/SIGCHI & SIGOIS, Toronto, Canada. 289–297.

——, J. Yates, R. Benjamin. 1987. Electronic markets and electronic hierarchies. *Comm. ACM* **30** 484–497.

Markus, M. L. 1994. Electronic mail as the medium of managerial choice. *Organ. Sci.* **5**(4) 502–527.

Marx, L., M. R. Smith, eds. 1994. *Does Technology Drive History?* MIT Press, Cambridge, MA.

Noble, D. 1984. *Forces of Production: A Social History of Industrial Automation.* Knopf, New York.

Norman, D. A. 1993. *Things that Make Us Smart: Defending Human Attributes in the Age of the Machine.* Addison-Wesley Publishing, Reading, MA.

Orlikowski, W. J. 1992. The duality of technology: Rethinking the concept of technology in organizations. *Organ. Sci.* **3**(3) 398–427.

——. 1993. Learning from NOTES: Organizational issues in group-ware implementation. *The Inform. Soc. J.* **9** 237–250.

——. 1996. Improvising organizational transformation over time: A situated change perspective. *Inform. Systems Res.* **7**(1) 63–92.

——, D. C. Gash. 1994. Technological frames: Making sense of information technology in organizations. *ACM Trans. Inform. Systems* **2**(2) 174–207.

——, D. Robey. 1991. Information technology and the structuring of organizations. *Inform. Systems Res.* **2**(2) 143–169.

——, J. Yates, K. Okamura, M. Fujimoto. 1995. Shaping electronic communication: The metastructuring of technology in use. *Organ. Sci.* **6**(4) 423–444.

Orr, J. 1996. *Talking about Machines: An Ethnography of a Modern Job.* Cornell University Press, Ithaca, NY.

Perrolle, J. A. 1986. Intellectual assembly lines: The rationalization of managerial, professional, and technical work. *Comput. and Soc. Sci.* **2** 111–121.

Perrow, C. 1983. The organizational context of human factors engineering. *Admin. Sci. Quart.* **28** 521–541.

Pinch, T. J., W. E. Bijker. 1984. The social construction of facts and artefacts: Or how the sociology of science and the sociology of technology might benefit each other. *Soc. Stud. Sci.* **14** 399–441.

Poole, M. S., G. DeSanctis. 1990. Understanding the use of group decision support systems: The theory of adaptive structuration. J. Fulk, C. W. Steinfield, eds. *Organizations and Communication Technology.* Sage, Newbury Park, CA. 173–193.

——, ——. 1992. Microlevel structuration in computer-supported group decision making. *Human Comm. Res.* **19**(1) 5–49.

——, M. Jackson, L. Kirsch, G. DeSanctis. 1998. Alignment of system and structure in the implementation of group decision support systems. *1998 Academy of Management Proceedings* San Diego, CA. C1–C7.

Powell, W. 1987. Explaining technological change. *Amer. J. Soc.* **93** 185–197.

Prasad, P. 1993. Symbolic processes in the implementation of technological change: A symbolic interactionist study of work computerization. *Acad. of Management J.* **36** 1400–1429.

Rice, R. E., E. M. Rogers. 1980. Reinvention in the innovation process. *Knowledge* **1**(4) 499–514.

——, C. Aydin. 1991. Attitudes toward new organizational technology: Network proximity as a mechanism for social information processing. *Admin. Sci. Quart.* **36** 219–244.

Roberts, K. H., M. Grabowski. 1995. Organizations, technology, and structuring. S. R. Clegg, C. Hardy, W. R. Nord, eds. *Handbook of Organization Studies.* Sage Publications, Thousand Oaks, CA. 409–423.

Saetnan, A. R. 1991. Rigid technologies and technologial flexibility: The anatomy of a failed hospital innovation. *Sci., Tech., Human Values.* **16**(4) 419–447.

Schryer, C. F. 1993. Records as Genres. *Written Comm.* **10** 200–234.

Scarbrough, H., J. M. Corbett. 1992. *Technology and Organization: Power, Meaning, and Design.* Routledge, London, U.K.

Scott, W. R. 1990. Technology and structure: An organizational level perspective. P. S. Goodman, L. S. Sproull, Associates. *Technology and Organizations.* Jossey-Bass, San Francisco, CA. 109–143.

Sewell, W. H. Jr. 1992. A theory of structure: Duality, agency, and transformation. *Amer. J. Soc.* **98**(1) 1–29.

Shaiken, H. 1985. *Work Transformed: Automation and Labor in the Computer Age.* Holt, Rinehart and Winston, New York.

Sproull, L. S., P. S. Goodman. 1990. Technology and organizations: Integration and opportunities. P. S. Goodman, L. S. Sproull, and Associates, eds. *Technology and Organizations.* Jossey-Bass, San Francisco. 254–265.

Suchman, L. A. 1987. *Plans and Situated Actions: The Problem of Human Machine Communication.* University of Cambridge Press, Cambridge, U.K.

——. 1996. Supporting articulation work. R. Kling, ed. *Computerization and Controversy* 2nd ed. Academic Press, San Diego, CA. 407–423.

Taylor, C. 1993. To follow a rule . . . C. Calhoun, E. LiPuma, M. Postone, eds. *Bourdieu: Critical Perspectives.* University of Chicago Press, Chicago, IL. 45–60.

Tenkasi, R. V., R. J. Boland. 1993. Locating meaning making in organizational learning: The narrative basis of cognition. *Res. in Organ. Change and Development* **7** 77–103.

Thomas, R. J. 1994. *What Machines Can't Do: Politics and Technology in the Industrial Enterprise.* University of California Press, Berkeley, CA.

Tushman, M. L., P. C. Anderson, C. O'Reilly. 1997. Technology cycles, innovation streams, and ambidextrous organizations: Organizational renewal through innovation streams and strategic change. M. L. Tushman, P. C. Anderson, eds. *Managing Strategic Innovation and Change.* Oxford University Press, New York. 3–23.

Tyre, M. J., W. J. Orlikowski. 1994. Windows of opportunity: Temporal patterns of technological adaptation in organizations. *Organ. Sci.* **5**(1) 98–118.

von Hippel, E. 1988. *The Sources of Innovation.* Oxford University Press, New York.

Walsham, G. 1993. *Interpreting Information Systems in Organizations.* John Wiley, New York.

——, C-K. Han. 1991. Structuration theory and information systems research. *J. Appl. Systems Anal.* **17** 77–85.

Weick, K. 1979. *The Social Psychology of Organizing.* Addison-Wesley, Reading, MA.

——. 1990. Technology as equivoque. P. S. Goodman, L. S. Sproull, and Associates, eds., *Technology and Organizations.* Jossey-Bass, San Francisco, CA. 1–44.

——. 1993. Organizational redesign as improvisation. G. P. Huber, W. H. Glick, eds. *Organizational Change and Redesign.* Oxford University Press, New York, 346–379.

——. 1995. *Sensemaking in Organizations.* Sage Publications, Thousand Oaks, CA.

Whittington, Richard. 1992. Putting Giddens into action: Social systems and managerial agency. *J. Management Stud.* **29**(6) 693–712.

Winner, L. 1986. *The Whale and the Reactor: A Search for Limits in an Age of High Technology.* University of Chicago Press, Chicago, IL.

Woodward, J. 1965. *Industrial Organization: Theory and Practice.* Oxford University Press, London, U.K.

Woolgar, S. 1991. The turn to technology in social studies of science. *Sci., Tech., & Human Values* **16**(1) 20–50.

——. 1996. Technologies as cultural artefacts. W. Dutton, ed. *Information and Communication Technologies: Visions and Realities.* Oxford University Press, Oxford, U.K. 87–102.

——, K. Grint. 1991. Computers and the transformation of social analysis. *Sci., Tech., & Human Values* **16**(3) 368–378.

Yates, J., W. J. Orlikowski, K. Okamura. 1999. Explicit and implicit structuring of genres: Electronic communication in a Japanese R&D organization. *Organ. Sci.* **10**(1) 83–103.

Zuboff, S. 1988. *In the Age of the Smart Machine.* Basic Books, New York.

48

POWER, IDENTITY AND NEW TECHNOLOGY HOMEWORK

Implications for 'new forms' of organizing*

Michael Brocklehurst

Source: *Organization Studies* 22(3) (2001): 445–66.

Abstract

This paper reports on research which tracked the experience of a group of professional workers as they moved from being conventional office workers to becoming homeworkers where they used the new information and communication technologies (ICT's), but remained as full-time salaried employees. The paper evaluates the value of Giddens's conceptualization of power, identity and time/space in explaining the consequences of this move and compares his approach to postmodern theorizations, which draw on the work of Foucault and Lash and Urry. The paper concludes with the view that such a form of organization is neither inherently corrosive of character (Sennett 1998) nor does it provide a space for aesthetic reflexivity (Lash and Urry 1994). What has yet to develop is a sense of 'the other' within the emerging discourse serving to articulate this new form of organizing.

Introduction

New technology homework, whereby employees work from home using new information and communication technologies (ICT's), has grown steadily in Europe during the 1990s (see Appendix for a review of the evidence). The significance of new technology homework to organizational theorists and practitioners lies in it standing as an exemplar of new forms of organization — indeed it sits comfortably within both a late modern and a postmodern perspective on organizations (Giddens 1991; Parker 1992). If employees work at home and at a time of their choosing, then 'organizations' are no longer so easy to delineate in spatial and temporal terms. They 'stretch' in space as homeworkers become physically separate from both their managers and from each other. They 'stretch' in time, as employees can work at any time rather than being constrained to conventional office hours. Further 'clock time' is less intrusive, less clearly marked when working-at-home.

New forms of organizing raise new problematics. The literature on home-working has addressed the problems in two ways. First, from a managerial perspective, homeworking raises issues of control. How are homeworkers to be monitored effectively when they are physically remote from their managers and often working at different times? (Huws *et al.* 1990; Olson 1989). Can electronic surveillance provide the key by enabling control and monitoring to be carried out remotely? There is a growing literature in the field of what may be described as 'surveillance theory', much of which has drawn on Foucault's influential *Discipline and Punish* (1979); (Ball and Wilson 1997; Lyon 1993; Coombs *et al.* 1992; Sewell and Wilkinson 1992; Zuboff 1988). Some of this work is concerned with the electronic surveillance of conventional office and factory workers, but others have noted how such surveillance can be extended to new technology homework (Gray *et al* 1993; Dennison 1990a, 1990b). However, survey evidence, at least for the United Kingdom, indicates that such cases are very rare (Huws 1993). For most homeworkers, home remains a private realm.

The second perspective, driven by a concern with the quality of working life, has addressed the impact of homeworking on the homeworkers themselves. Do homeworkers prefer this form of work? What are the costs and benefits? This strand of the literature has considered the implications of becoming a homeworker in terms of a series of atomized 'effects', but this fails to do full justice to how homework is experienced (Brocklehurst 1989; Haddon 1989; Huws *et al.* 1990). What is required to deepen our understanding is to draw upon the concept of self-identity and how it is constituted. To illustrate this point, I shall draw on just two 'effects' among the many that have been identified.

There is evidence that a move to homeworking often entails work becoming fragmented. Managers may attempt to fragment and vertically disintegrate the work in order to facilitate measurement and control (Ramsower 1985; Olson 1985; see, however, Kawakami 1983). The literature addresses the issue from the perspective of motivation (Kawakami 1983; Ramsower 1985); it does not consider how changes in the labour process might help or hinder a homeworker in thinking she is engaged in 'real' work. In short, it does not address the issue of identity construction.

The other example concerns changes in the effort/reward bargain. The literature shows that new technology homeworkers often (although not always) suffer in terms of levels of pay, fluctuations in that level and lack of fringe benefits, compared to in-workers doing similar work (Brocklehurst 1989). How do homeworkers feel about this 'fact'? If they do not really see themselves as 'workers' then it may be accepted, indeed serve to confirm their view of themselves. On the other hand, if they do see themselves as 'real workers', this may cause a reaction such as resentment, or perhaps a desire to become an in-worker.

In summary therefore, homeworking raises questions of power and identity and how the stretching of space and time consequent on the move to homework are implicated in these two processes.

Anthony Giddens is a theorist who has addressed all of these subjects; his earlier work addresses questions of power, space and time as part of his theory of structuration (Giddens 1984); his later work has turned to questions of subjectivity and identity (Giddens 1990, 1991). In this paper, I propose to assess the extent to which Giddens can help to understand the phenomenon of new technology homework and to what extent alternative, postmodern theorizations (Foucault 1979, 1987, 1990a, 1990b; Lash and Urry 1994) are to be preferred. Can there be any degree of rapprochement or accommodation between Giddens and Foucault? Alternatively, is there a case here for ontological pluralism, a recognition that both have something of value to contribute?

I shall proceed on two fronts. First, by a critique which will attempt to examine the cogency of Giddens's ideas and their relevance to new technology homework. Second by an analysis of research data which tracked the experience of a group of professional workers as they moved from being conventional office workers to becoming homeworkers who used ICT's, but who remained as full-time salaried employees.

The paper begins with an exposition of Giddens's work; first with respect to power/control, second with respect to subjectivity and identity and how time and space are implicated in their constitution. I then briefly describe the context of the research before giving an account of the outcomes. The penultimate section then relates these outcomes to Giddens's initial theorization(s) and considers the adequacy of Giddens *vis à vis* alternative theorizations. In the final section, I consider some of the broader implications for the identity of 'new forms of organizing'.

Giddens's theorization of power and identity

Giddens early work was dominated by the development of his theory of structuration (Giddens 1976, 1979, 1984). I will assume a basic knowledge of this theory and the various critiques (Held and Thompson 1989; Cohen 1989; Craib 1992). For Giddens, human interaction and institutionalized practices are mediated by three 'modalities of structuration': resources, interpretive schema and norms. Resources provide the means through which intentions are realized, goals achieved and power is exercised. By 'power', Giddens refers to the transformative capacity of people to change the social and material world. In the realm of institutions, a 'structure of domination' occurs because social systems are marked by an asymmetry of resources amongst actors. Giddens argues that any 'structure of domination' is precarious; it requires constant reproduction through action. Actors in subordinate positions are never without some resources and will constantly seek to try and control the conditions under which such reproduction takes place. There is therefore a 'dialectic of control' whereby the overall distribution of power may shift, with control being defined as 'the capability that some actors, groups or types of actors have of influencing the circumstances of action of others' (Giddens 1984: 283). In concentrating on the modality of resources, it is important to recall that, in the theory of structuration, the three modalities are fused. Thus resources carry meaning (interpretive schemes), power is associated with legitimation (norms), and so on.

Giddens, in his use of power and control, is an exemplar of what Bloomfield and Coombs refer to as the 'traditional approach'. They explain: 'Many of the traditional approaches to the nature of management control share a view of control (and therefore power) which is rather like the zero-sum game approach mentioned earlier. Control is seen as a disputed commodity; increments of it pass back and forth across a "frontier of control" as a result of struggles between parties with particular locations of "interests".' (Bloomfield and Coombs 1992: 466). In this traditional view, power is seen as a property either of individuals or of structures.

To what extent was power implicated in the initial move to establish homeworking? Further, how did the 'dialectic of control' shift as a consequence of the move to homeworking? Did homeworkers gain control at the expense of management?

As with power, structuration theory also provides a starting point for Giddens's theorization of identity and subjectivity; yet, in spite of these common roots, Giddens has developed his theory of identity largely in isolation from his earlier work on power. Indeed, his later work on identity (Giddens 1991, 1992) makes scant reference to either structuration theory in general or power in particular. This is at one with his view that power benefits from being deployed in a restricted sense, if it is to have any empirical purchase (Giddens 1984, 1995).

Giddens's theorization of identity starts from a key premise of structuration theory — the existence of knowledgeable human agents who are able to draw on and interpret structures in acting. Further, human actors are highly 'learned' in respect of the knowledge they possess in applying and reproducing social encounters. Humans also have the capacity for reflexivity. They can monitor their actions and review them in the light of new information and knowledge. Of course, knowledge and reflexivity are bounded by time and place, by the difficulties of articulating tacit knowledge, by unconscious sources of motivation (Giddens 1984). In spite of these constraints, it is this capacity for reflexivity which leads Giddens to define self-identity as 'the self as reflexively understood by the individual in terms of his or biography' (Giddens 1991: 244). According to Giddens it is one of the distinguishing features of late modernity that individuals have to constantly work at recreating their self-identity — a point which I explore below in considering his analysis of time/space. As he states: 'In the context of a post-industrial order, the self becomes a reflexive project' (1991: 32). He continues: '(self-identity) has to be routinely created and sustained in the reflexive activities of the individual' (1991: 37).

How does Giddens's concept of identity gel with his theorization of time/space? Giddens draws initially on Hagerstrand's work on time geography and Goffman's concept of 'front' and 'back' regions in the presentation of self in his attempt to incorporate time and space into his theory of structuration (Giddens 1984; Hagerstrand 1975; Goffman 1971). Again, I shall be economical with the exposition of Giddens's work and concentrate on where it is relevant to new technology homeworkers and the constitution of their identities. Fuller critiques on Hagerstrand in particular (Gregory 1985) and Giddens in general (Lash and Urry 1994) are readily available.

A central concept is his notion of time/space distanciation — the ways in which social practices and institutions have become 'stretched' over larger (and smaller) spans of space and time. Social interaction increasingly takes place with others who are remote in both space and time. New technology homeworkers are indeed separate in this sense from both their managers and their fellow workers: time and space have become disembedded from social activity. For Giddens, such disembedding is made possible by technological 'expert systems' — for example the Internet, in the case of homeworking. The trust placed by human agents in such systems has made place — a spatially and temporarily bound location suffused with meaning — of less significance to human agents. Indeed, in late modernity, agents increasingly follow their own subjective life-calendars (Giddens 1991).

In order to clarify Gidden's distinctive approach to identity and how it meshes with time/space, it is instructive to compare his position to that of others, notably Foucault and Lash and Urry (1994). Giddens himself goes to considerable lengths to distance his position on identity and subjectivity from that of Foucault, describing the latter at one point as advocating a 'subject-less history' (Giddens 1995: 265). Yet Foucault, in his later work, does address the possibility of self-knowledge (Foucault 1987, 1990a). The crucial difference is that Foucault regards the reflexive, self-caring subject as the effect of one, historically located disciplinary process. Giddens, by contrast, sees it as universal ahistorical phenomenon. In his own words: 'human beings, in the theory of structuration, are always and everywhere regarded as knowledgeable agents' (1995: 265).

It is Lash and Urry (1994) who have pinpointed the key distinction between Giddens and Foucault with respect to subjectivity and identity. Giddens stresses how it is 'practical consciousness' that does the monitoring. The emphasis is on maintaining ontological security. As Lash and Urry point out, this is at odds with Foucault:

'He [Giddens] is thus opposed not only to Foucault but also to French and to Anglo-American feminist psychoanalytically-oriented social theory. What they positively value as the heterogeneous play of an unconscious structured by "complexity" and "difference", he sees as a threat to ontological security. Whereas French theory and Anglo-American feminism see the ego as a homogenizing and controlling apparatus structured by the "law of the father", Giddens's ego is the hero of the battle against ontological security and the structuring principle of the reflexive biographical narratives of the high modern self.'

(Lash and Urry 1994: 42)

In relying on time-geography, albeit critically, Giddens stresses the routinized and mundane nature of social practices. The emphasis is always on maintaining ontological security. For Lash and Urry this downplays the extent to which human agents will often embrace opportunities to play and experiment with different structurings of time and space, for example by travel. More significantly, as Adam notes, Giddens's approach crowds out transformation, change and decay (Adam 1990: 27–30). To what extent then do conventional workers who become homeworkers still rely on routine and the mundane in their working lives?

Lash and Urry note two further points of contrast between Giddens's position and their own. First, Giddens sees the primary effect of modernization as the disembedding of social relations from their local context. Time and space are no longer so connected through the situatedness of place. Place thus becomes less significant as an external referent. (Giddens 1991: 146–47). By contrast, Lash and Urry argue for a postmodern perspective, where the global and the local both become significant — indeed are held in a tension of opposites — *la différence*. For example, they note how the globalization of finance is based upon particular locations such as the City of London (Lash and Urry 1994). Is a sense of place still significant to new technology homeworkers?

This relates to the second point. Giddens concentrates on three different ways in which the passing of time is perceived: daily time (*durée*), lifetime (*dasein*) — and the time period informed by an historical perspective (*longue durée*) (Giddens 1984). Yet Lash and Urry argue that these three perspectives only cover the middle group of the continuum, and indicate that Giddens is a late modernist not a postmodernist. As they state: 'clock-time lies in the middle and it is clock-time that has been the organizing principle of modernity' (1994: 242). As postmodernists, they stress the growing relevance of glacial or evolutionary time at one end of the continuum and instantaneous (computer time) at the other. But what are the time-frames that remain pivotal to new technology homeworkers?

Giddens's treatment of time/space then informs his perspective on identity and subjectivity.

Taken together, the difference between Giddens and these alternative theorizations is that he understates the extent to which human experience is increasingly one of *fragmentation*. Others have noted this increased fragmentation that is characteristic of contemporary existence. Thus Sennett accepts this fragmentation but, in employing a similar perspective to Giddens, argues that it is 'corrosive of character' (Sennett 1998). New forms of organizing such as homeworking are replacing Weber's 'iron cage of bureaucracy', but this cage served to give meaning to workers in a number of ways. In temporal terms, it routinized the day-to-day use of a worker's time; it also gave a sense of a lifetime, based on a career built out of seniority. In spatial terms, it insisted on a strict demarcation between work and home, between public and private (cf. homeworking). Sennett, like Giddens, finds much to recommend in the habitual and routine. He states: 'routine can demean but it can also protect; routine can decompose labour but also compose a life' (1998: 43). He explicitly praises Giddens's emphasis on habit as forming the secure base from which we test out alternatives. Hence, while accepting that fragmentation is the lot of contemporary humankind, Sennett is pessimistic about the outcome. His pessimism stems from his adoption of a similar perspective to Giddens with its stress on the need for coherence in self-identity, for the sustaining of a long-term consistent narrative and the importance of habit and routine to the maintenance of this identity.

If social relationships are becoming increasingly distanciated (as time and space are compressed), if individual workers' lives are becoming ever more desynchronized by the increasing prevalence of new forms of work such as homework, is it inevitable that commitment to others becomes more precarious and that personal identity becomes increasingly rootless and harder to sustain? Or are postmodernists such as Lash and Urry right in their more optimistic vision which claims that developments in time-space are opening up greater opportunities — particularly for those with good access to ICT networks — for self-reflexivity to recast meaning in work and leisure? Will this reflexivity take on an aesthetic hue as the material world becomes increasingly suffused with symbolic (and informational) content? Will this present an opportunity for individuals to be increasingly creative in their construction of self, to draw on the many and different sources both within themselves and from outside themselves (Lash and Urry 1994)? I shall return to these optimistic and pessimistic scenarios in the concluding section.

In summary, this section has noted three points of contact between Giddens's work and the issues raised by the introduction of new technology homework. First, to what extent is Giddens's conceptualization of power of value in analyzing both how homeworking became established as well as in analyzing any changing relationships that have resulted between managers and their homeworkers? Second, to what extent is Giddens's theorization of subjectivity and identity, with its emphasis on the significance of habit and routine, on the striving for consistency, coherence and homogeneity in the creation of self-identity, an accurate picture, as revealed by those homeworkers? Or is the experience of such workers more of a reflexive project which is comfortable with, even welcoming of, a fragmented multi-sourced notion of identity? Finally, what is the value and limitation of Giddens's conceptualization of space and time? Is his emphasis on clock-time, on the time-scale of daily time and lifetime useful? To what extent does the disembedding of time/space from social activity 'matter'? Is a sense of place, which constrains both time and space still important to the constitution of identity?

It was these questions which informed the collection of the empirical material. Before describing that material, I will briefly outline the context within which the data was collected.

The research context

The case study was selected because it was a critical case in the sense of the term used by Goldthorpe *et al.* in their test of the affluent worker thesis (Goldthorpe *et al.* 1968). A context was selected which the literature has indicated is likely to be *most* conducive to the 'successful' introduction of homeworking (Huws 1993) and where any impact on the self-identity of the homeworkers was likely to be *least* problematic. Three sets of criteria are relevant for this purpose.

The first set concerns the choice of organization. A firm was selected which is in the business of manufacturing the sort of hardware systems used in remote working. The organization — given the code name Comp-U-like — is a US-owned, multinational computer manufacturer. It is non-unionized and an exemplar of a 'traditional' human resource organization (Keenoy 1990) emphasizing 'high trust' (Fox 1974). The value of 'teamworking' was stressed and this figured as a key criterion in appraisal. The official rhetoric was that people within Comp-U-like were judged solely on results. There were written systems of work plans and development plans with various qualitative and quantitative measures, and appraisal based on these measures was conducted annually. Rather than emphasizing formal organizational structure — there was no published organization chart, for example — management stressed the importance of employees networking with one another.

The second set of criteria concerns the selection of the group within the organization. The group comprised two managers, two office-based administrative workers and eleven homeworkers. All were sales trainers and all had substantial experience with the company with an average time as employees of eight years. They had been employees for long enough to have absorbed the 'corporate culture'. Many of the homeworkers had a background in sales so they were used to being judged on results. These employees enjoyed an easy familiarity with ICT's. While office based, all employees had worked in a large open-plan office. When the trainers moved to becoming home-based, they were all given equipment and a modem link to head office. They would come into the office for occasional meetings. The managers and administrative workers remained office-based.

The third set of criteria concerned the motives behind the move to homeworking. Management's major rationale in embarking on homeworking was to save on office space, to transfer such fixed costs on to the employee. At the same time, the intention was also to demonstrate, in a concrete way, its high-trust rhetoric. As the senior manager responsible for setting up the move put it:

'We are always saying we are a high-trust company; this is a chance to demonstrate it to the people involved.'

There was no attempt to use homeworking to change the labour process: the nature and intensity of the work remained unaltered. Remuneration and other conditions of employment of the homeworkers also remained unchanged.

The intention in following these three sets of criteria, was to isolate as far as possible the variable of moving from office work to homework in as pure a form as possible, by holding other variables constant. In this way, the research could concentrate on the restructuring of space and time and its effects on power and the constitution of identity.

The research itself was intensive in nature and comprised two sets of lengthy, open-ended interviews. The first set was conducted just prior to starting homeworking, while all the respondents were still working conventionally. The second set involved interviewing all the respondents twelve months later. The longitudinal nature of the research was essential both to tracking any change in the balance of power and to analyzing the implications for self-identity amongst the homeworkers.

The interviews were unstructured and each interview lasted about two hours, although no time limit was imposed. The questions simply invited respondents to reflect upon their feelings about becoming homeworkers; about changes in their relationships with others; about the benefits and drawbacks, and about how they managed the problems. The interviews were all taped and than analyzed in terms of the questions about power, identity, time and space, identified at the close of the previous section.

In between the interviews, direct observations of both work practices and the meetings concerned with setting up the scheme were conducted. A review of relevant internal company documents was also carried out. All documents related to the homeworking project and any concerned with human resource strategies, policies and procedures, were examined.

The research outcomes

This section of the paper begins with the question of power and then turns to consider the question of identity and the effects of time and space.

The question of power

Initial analysis of the research indicated that viewing power in Giddens's terms had some validity. Consider firstly the way in which the decision was made to move to homeworking.

Comp-U-like managers, in espousing a traditional HRM approach, encourage participatory decision making. New working practices are always subject to prior discussion. A facilitator from personnel is appointed who is given the task of holding a series of meetings and workshops to disseminate information, obtain feedback and arrive at a 'group' decision. This was the procedure adopted before moving to homework.

The manager of the homeworking scheme presented a range of reasons (cost saving, experimenting with a new way of working, etc.) for initiating the idea. However, some of the homeworkers saw things rather differently:

> 'The real reason this scheme was introduced was to fit in with Di's needs. [Di was one of the homeworkers]. She has young children and wants to work in a way so she could be near them as much as possible. She is very much Dick's [the manager's] protegé so a way has been found to meet her needs. I do not say this was the only reason or was it the deciding factor — but it was certainly the impetus. The rest of us had to find reasons for *not* doing it.'

Management did not present the proposal dispassionately. The agenda for the workshops was set by management with the first item being: 'What excites you about flexible working?' This item was then used to set the context within which the idea was explored. Thus the question: 'What scares you about flexible working?' was considered second. Finally the question: 'What do you need to make it work?' was discussed.

It is interesting that the phrase 'flexible working' was used rather than 'homeworking', although homeworking was clearly what was being discussed, as the minutes of the workshops make clear. Comp-U-like's culture stresses to employees the importance of 'flexibility', so anyone who disagreed with homeworking as a form of flexibility could be seen as opposing a basic 'cultural' premise of the organization.

Yet there was a further reason why the Comp-U-like culture should make opposition difficult. The ethos at Comp-U-like is very much 'can do'. Enthusiasm is prized and negativity is frowned upon. The following quotation from one homeworker, Bill, captured this very accurately:

'There is a phrase called "Comp-U-like yes" which is what people say [which means] "Yes, I agree with this and the unstated bit is unless I can think of something better".'

In the end, Bill was the only member of the sales team who resisted becoming home-based. His status as a unit manager helped his resistance, yet it was clear that he was put under pressure. As the manager of the scheme said:

'Bill is beginning to work remotely, even though he says he didn't really want to.'

In fact, when interviewed, Bill make it very clear he did not want to work from home:

'I enjoy being at home. I would not like to start tainting that with work.'

In the end, Bill became side-lined from the team and relieved of his unit management status.

Another homeworker provided further evidence that there was a high degree of reluctance about the project:

'Di and I shared the greatest enthusiasm, because it saved us a lot of travelling. We have further to come than the others. Everyone else was very sceptical, frightened by it, feeling very exposed by it . . . they felt they would be forgotten.'

Although the motives of the others were more complex than this, it was still clear that there was a high level of wariness about the project. There was a clear mobilization of bias — power, in the sense employed by Giddens, was being exercised in a subtle and covert way by management.

Second, once the project was established, power viewed in conventional terms continued to have some resonance. Thus management had always relied on teams and peer influence to exercise control and ensure commitment. Not surprisingly, now they were working at home, the homeworkers' feeling of belonging to a team had dissipated. The following was a representative comment:

'The team sense to a great extent has gone. I don't think there is as much camaraderie as there used to be, you don't get that day-to-day banter which is what builds it up which I guess is something that happens when you have people working as isolated individuals. I have to be honest, I don't feel I am the member of a team anymore.'

From the perspective of management, the corollary was that the opportunities for any peer surveillance were drastically reduced. The following quotation provides a succinct summary of the position.

> 'We need a more active style of management. I think we have got the possibility that the momentum, the identity, the commitment, the quality is less. This new shape which lets it [the team] become more fragmented and eroded as the quality of relationships begin to slip.'

Management tried to introduce regular meetings but this only served to draw attention to the problem.

> 'Even when we have the quarterly meetings, the barriers are there. There are undercurrents [people muttering]. "I don't know why we are here". A feeling that the meeting was just so everyone could be together which they don't resent, just felt "So what?" The last one was a bit strained.'

Management had also attempted to reassert control by other means. They had tried to get all homeworkers to use an electronic diary system that would have made transparent the whereabouts of any homeworker at a given time, but the homeworkers had not adhered to it. They then insisted that homeworkers had to notify the secretaries of their location if they left home. E-mail was also monitored — principally because the manager thought the homeworkers were overworking. As he stated:

> 'If the time on the e-mail was 10.37 at night, I say, what the hell were you doing working on the terminal at that time.'

Another manager also made phone calls to homeworkers' homes at random times.

> 'This is very confidential. There are some people, certain other managers in the office, who are not above phoning home to see if you answered the 'phone and then feeding that back to someone else.'

Yet management were reluctant to invade the home, still seeing it as a 'back' region. The Senior Manager in charge of the pilot was quite clear on this point.

> 'I would only go round to someone at home if invited to do so. I do not like to ring in the evening unless it is essential, as that is family time.'

There was no evidence that new technology was being used to monitor, except in the marginal sense of logging e-mail times and frequencies. This was hardly a panoptic gaze.

The question of identity and the effects of time and space

However, conceptualizing the outcome of the move to homework as managers 'losing control' at the expense of the homeworkers who 'gained control' did not capture what was taking place. These homeworkers did not see themselves as engaged in some struggle with management over a 'frontier of control'. Any loss of control by management did not manifest itself in the homeworkers automatically becoming more powerful. The homeworkers directed their energies not at exploiting the 'gains in control', but rather at recreating a work identity that was convincing to both themselves and to others. They used a range of strategies to accomplish this, but crucial to all these strategies was the significance of space and time.

One common strategy was to continue to use the 'office' as a point of reference. On a rational level, the homeworkers acknowledged that the office needed to be 'redesigned', i.e. taken over by the other sections. Indeed, cost saving on office space was a major impetus behind homeworking, but accepting this in practice proved more difficult. Consider this comment:

> 'We don't need an office anymore. Although the desks that remain are getting personalized. HRDT [Human Resource Development and Training] now have their files and everything in the desks which were supposed to be the general working area. So apart from checking my mail it's actually forcing me out of the office. The management need to think about what they have created there because I know most of the instructors feel the same, that we've been taken over, we don't have an office as such. Now whether that's a good or a bad thing is open to question. If you're flexible working, it shouldn't really cause you a problem. If I am honest [pause] um. I don't think it does, it doesn't cause me a problem. I suppose a little bit of human nature. You know you want to have a little bit of your own territory, if you like. It has really stopped me coming into the office as much as I used to do. You feel you are imposing on someone else's desk, which shouldn't be'.

Others would call in at the office, even when it was not required for work.

> 'I found it quite comforting to come into an office, the office. It's a security thing, I think. Not saying hi, good morning and getting the comfort from everybody sitting here in the big office, being here

almost like a second home, a belonging. Whereas at home, it's just little old me in this big world.'

Another homeworker found herself doing the same, although in her case, she would go to a regional office:

'I often find myself in Bristol and find a reason to call in at the office there, just to sort of touch base, really.'

Another strategy used by all the homeworkers was to recreate in some sense, the workplace within the home. This ranged from what was required simply to get the work done, to the case of one homeworker who had recreated a replica of his previous office space with the addition of photographs of his colleagues. He also insisted on Comp-U-like providing him with the identical office equipment (desk and chair, plus a whiteboard, flip chart stand, etc.).

'I have my own room. You need it. It acts as a discipline. You walk in the study, you feel you are going to work. I have even got my name badge stuck on the door.'

This homeworker, in common with most of the others, continued to dress up in office clothing when working at home.

The above comments indicate how homeworkers worked at using space and physical artefacts to give meaning to their work. They also attempted to impose their own time structure to buttress their sense of being a worker. The following quotation gives an example:

'If I was coming in [to the office,] you get going because that's all you've got to do. At home I find it difficult to get motivated. A lot of procrastination goes on. You find anything that needs doing in the house first. At the same time, if I don't have people making demands on me at weekends, then I think of weekends as working days. It's much better to be aware of time, to work in time zones. I use the radio to help me to do this.'

It was not just the structure imposed by the *durée* of daily time that had been changed by the move to homeworking. There was also the time-scale of *dasein*, of lifetime. Recall that for Giddens, identity construction is a lifetime project, it is about creating and sustaining a meaningful biography. In this respect, the homeworkers expressed concern about how homeworking had altered their career prospects, in spite of their having already established a lengthy career within Comp-U-like.

It was noted in the research context that the official view is that employees are judged on results — it is 'what you do' and not 'who you know' that counts. To buttress this view, there are paper systems of work plans and development plans with qualitative and quantitative measures, such as the number of courses given and the feedback received. Moreover, the majority of sales trainers have a background in sales where allegedly a high premium is put on 'results'.

Yet even management accepts that this is not the whole story, and something hangs on the subjective judgement of others. Indeed, as noted in the research context section, management rejects the notion of a formal organizational structure, preferring the rhetoric of networking.

The sales trainers themselves frequently talked about the value of 'networking' within Comp-U-like. As one said:

'It is who you know who helps you get the job done.'

Some respondents were thus in a dilemma — whether to accept the rhetoric that career development is solely about 'objective' results or voice their concern about the reality: that much depends on being 'visible' to the right people upon whose judgement appraisal often depends. One way off the horns of dilemma was to argue that though they personally believed that monitoring and appraisal and control would be unaffected by becoming homeworkers, they could see that others might feel they would be adversely affected by homeworking.

One homeworker articulated this concern very clearly:

'Those at home with less visibility, almost in a social sense, it puts visibility back to pure job-related things. Reading a report, but not being able to put a face to the name could be a problem as far as getting known in the organization.'

The strategies described so far show how the homeworkers used time and space in a defensive way, to bolster their self-image as workers. Other strategies were used by the homeworkers to re-invent their identities in more positive terms. A number of the homeworkers were very careful about the discourse they used to describe themselves. One homeworker thought of himself as a self-employed entrepreneur.

'Being home-based helps me to think of Comp-U-like as a client — a very important client maybe, but still a client.'

Another homeworker rejected the label of 'homeworker' quite vehemently:

'This is not about being home-based, nor am I a homeworker. It is about being flexible and I am a flexible worker. As a salesman and a sales trainer that is what I have always been.'

A year later, at the time of his second interview, the same individual was even more emphatic:

> 'How do you feel now you have been home-based for nearly a year?' (Self)

> 'Let's get clear our terms of reference. I came into this meeting to talk about flexible working, not homebased work.' (Homeworker)

Others carefully managed the impression they made to others — both family members and in-workers. As one homeworker put it, in relation to those working in the office:

> 'We do get comments, but as soon as we explain to people we are part of an official flexible working group, part of a pilot, and explain the benefit of it, then they come round. Pointing out that it's the way of the future, that certainly stimulates people.'

Two other homeworkers took the approach of not identifying with homeworking at all. One homeworker regarded his position as a temporary stage and saw himself as treading water until he could go back into a sales team working from the office. A second admitted to entertaining thoughts of applying to another company.

It is clear that these respondents were finding it problematic to reconstitute their identities as homeworkers. To what extent does their experience confirm the value of Giddens's theorization?

Discussion

The results of this research demonstrate the value of Giddens's conceptualization of power. It is useful in explaining how the move to homeworking developed. Management at Comp-U-like were able to exercise greater structural power through their control of the agenda. They established the linguistic terms within which consultation about the introduction of homeworking was framed — the positive value put on flexibility and openness to new ideas; the labelling of disagreement with the principle as 'negative thinking'. Further, once homeworking had become established then, using Giddens's terminology, the dialectic of control did move in favour of homeworkers. Peer control had evaporated; visual and electronic surveillance were ruled out as contravening the high-trust rhetoric; the home remained a back region, off-limits to management. Yet ironically, *this did not lead to homeworkers exploiting this space* as might be expected if power is just a 'disputed commodity'. Indeed, rather than homeworkers seizing the control initiative and working *less* hard, management was concerned that the homeworkers were working *too* hard. The question is why this should be so, and it is at this point that Giddens's approach to power becomes problematic.

What is clear is that in the new spatial and temporal context of working-at-home, *these homeworkers directed their energies at forging a new working identity that was convincing to both themselves and others.*

It was noted above how Giddens's resource-based perspective on power is restricted in range and consequently divorced from his conceptualization of identity and subjectivity. By contrast, for Foucault, power is seen as something embodied in certain ways of thinking, speaking and behaving which result from how the individuals concerned see the world and themselves (Foucault 1979; Gordon 1982). In this way, individuals are 'disciplined' by 'disciplines' (bodies of knowledge). To the extent that individuals are 'disciplined' by 'discipline' then the discipline is self-discipline and the control is self-control. In this way, individuals acquire self-identity — they become 'subjects' with ontological security and a clear view of what is normal and what is not. Thus power is dispersed in that it governs all relationships. Power is not only inhibitive; it empowers, in that it creates a 'space for action' (Bloomfield and Coombes 1992: 467). As power relations are made manifest and reproduced in human action, this serves to confirm their 'reality' for the individuals concerned — even where the interaction is one of conflict. Power, then, is ubiquitous. For Foucault it becomes the means by which individuals are able to do anything — to think about themselves, to speak, even to derive sexual pleasure.

Now the evidence of this study is that any potential gain in resource power accruing to the homeworkers was not seized upon. Rather, the change in structural power had, if anything, 'disabled' their own sense of self, their own understanding of their situation. These homeworkers sought to reconstitute their self identities; linking power to self knowledge in the way proposed by Foucault helps to understand this phenomenon.

On the evidence here, then, Giddens is mistaken to compartmentalize power and identity in the way he does. Nevertheless, when we turn to examine the *detail* of how these homeworkers sought to recast their identities, the evidence here supports Giddens's contention that the sustaining of self-identity is rooted in the mundane and the maintenance of habit. These homeworkers showed no sense of using the novel sense of space and time to partake of an aesthetic reflexivity (cf. Lash and Urry); rather they tried to replicate an aesthetic based on the banalities of conventional office life. Having been 'freed' from the routines of daily time, these homeworkers tried to recreate the very same routines in the home. They also expressed anxiety about their careers, about how their identity could be sustained in lifetime terms.

There is another paradox here. Giddens puts considerable (undue according to Lash and Urry) emphasis on time/space distanciation and the ways in which knowledgeable subjects are able to come to terms with it. Yet what comes out of this research is how homeworkers attempted to 'bind' time and space, to constrain it by recreating a sense of place. Indeed, if homeworkers are preoccupied with maintaining routine and habit then this should not be surprising and points to an inconsistency in Giddens's approach.

Above I noted how Giddens has been criticised for underplaying the extent to which contemporary experience is one of fragmentation. Had the lives of this group of workers become more fragmented by becoming homeworkers? In one sense they had. Their lives were no longer so synchronized in spatial and temporal terms with their co-workers — hence the withering of the teams and the meaninglessness experienced in face-to-face team meetings designed to rectify the situation. In another sense, though, their experiences had become *less* fragmented in that home and work had become fused. I shall develop the discursive implications of this point in the conclusion.

In summary, there is a role for Giddens's restricted concept of power in accounting for how space/time are constituted. It was management who were able to exercise their greater structural power in establishing spatial and temporal boundaries around what constitutes 'work'. Giddens's perspective is also convincing in its characterization of identity constitution with his emphasis on routine and habit although he underplays the continuing importance of place. He also seems correct in emphasizing how daily time and lifetime continue to dominate how individual's experience of work is framed. Yet, at the same time, Giddens's approach blinds us to the *interweaving of power and the constitution of identity*. Here a Foucauldian version of power illuminates the connection.

Conclusion

Is it necessary to privilege Foucault over Giddens, or *vice versa*? I would resist any attempt at synthesis, since each employs the concept of 'power' in such radically different ways. Yet if both are useful, but both employ power in such different ways, then perhaps the very term 'power' has now become so elastic that to do justice to its diversity requires terminology that helps to distinguish its disputed resource use from its discursive and disciplinary use. There is an argument here for clarifying and enforcing the ontological distinction between Giddens's position and that of Foucault.

How are we to judge these new forms of organizing? The homeworkers in this research present a rather dismal picture. The restructuring of space and time had *not* realized Lash and Urry's vision of a liberation from the 'rules and resources of the workplace' (Lash and Urry 1994: 5). Rather, the restructuring had caused considerable anxiety in which the homeworkers had worked to recreate the very same rules. In this sense, Giddens is 'right' and Sennett's pessimism about the corrosion of character appears justified.

570

This is, of course, just one case study, and so the usual caveats apply; nevertheless, recall that this is a *critical* case designed to be one most conducive to new forms of organizing.

Yet the findings also demonstrate how the homeworkers lacked a discourse to explain to themselves (and others) who they were. Now the present move from traditional office or factory work to homework is the reverse of the process that occurred in the 19th Century when factories replaced the home. According to Foucault, *this* was the period (rather than the present day) in which surveillance came to replace spectacle as the key disciplinary technique (Foucault 1979). It was during early modernity that surveillance became critical to the constitution of the 'worker' as a subject, to the normalization of 'worker' as distinct from 'non-worker'. There were specific techniques, specific institutional and discursive practices which produced the worker as a 'subject'. Part of this discursive practice was to separate work as public and male, from non-work as private and female. However, recent changes in technology permit the reversal of this situation — many forms of work are no longer tied to a specific time and place and this has served to challenge such a discourse.

New technology homework stands at the cusp, poised between one declining discourse about work (full-time, 9 to 5, male, in a 'public' office or factory, one career for life) and another, yet to be articulated. As Foucault illustrated in his documentation of the murderer Pierre Riviere, cases which sit between two discourses can be highly instructive (Foucault 1978).

The physical remoteness of manager from homeworker (and homeworkers from each other) weakens the prospects for surveillance. Homeworkers are no longer surveyed by the 'other' — whether the 'other' is the manager, the co-worker or the customer. What is important instead is how one appears to *oneself*. At the same time, other institutional practices are changed by homeworking. Time is less intrusive. There is suddenly a choice about whether or not to dress in working clothes (why bother?). Going-to-work as a ritual is eliminated. The physical artefacts of office life are removed. The official 'knowledge' of what it is to be a worker loses its capacity to 'normalize'. Yet these new technology homeworkers described in my research lacked an alternative discourse to 'explain' to themselves who they were. They had to work at creating a new self-identity as worker, but this was proving highly problematic. Why should this be so?

Traditional forms of working identity depended on making a distinction, whereby work was associated with male = breadwinner = public realm whereas its negation was non-work = female = dependant = private realm. As has been well documented elsewhere, new forms of work, together with changes in the labour market — notably the feminization of the labour force — have called into question the whole notion of what it means to be a 'worker'. New technology homework is particularly problematic because it blurs *all* these category distinctions, and paradoxically reduces the fragmented nature of contemporary experience by reuniting home and work. What do men make of working as employees at home in the private realm? Are women convincing to themselves as workers, if they work at home? Are they engaged in 'real' work when they work at home? Recall how some of the respondents entirely rejected the label of 'homeworker', preferring a term such as 'flexible worker'.

The superior resource-based power of management gives that group the greater ability to structure space/time, to establish where to draw boundaries. Establishing new forms of organizing, such as new technology homework, redraws these boundaries by moving the line where work begins and ends, thereby recasting the relationship between home and work, between the private and the public realm. It falls on the homeworkers to make sense of such change; to understand themselves and their identities in relation to these changes. Now traditional forms of organizing work had as the 'other', the home, the female and the private that enabled traditional workers to clarify to themselves who they were. However, the discourse surrounding new technology homework has yet to generate its 'other'. Until this occurs, it is premature to regard such new forms of organizing as either inherently beneficial or calamitous.

Appendix

The extent of new technology homework: a review of the evidence

As noted in the introduction, attempts to judge the extent of new technology homework have been hampered by inadequate data. However, the position for the United Kingdom has recently been clarified by the Government's decision to include new technology homework within its Labour Force Survey (Labour Market Trends 1998), see Table 1. One difficulty is that the UK Government prefers the term 'teleworking' rather than new technology homework, but teleworking is a term which has been subject to many interpretations (Brocklehurst 1997). The figures for 1998 represent a small, but steady growth over the past decade (cf. Brocklehurst 1989; Huws 1993).

The situation within the European Union is much less clear. The European Commission's best estimate is reproduced in Table 2 (Telework 97 1997). The Commission admits that different countries define 'teleworking' in different ways. Indeed, the figures given for the United Kingdom are based on a General Population Survey which included the 'kind of telework where the necessary equipment is provided in an office near your home' (Korte and Wynne 1996) i.e. telecottages or neighbourhood offices. Further, the countries marked with asterisks are merely estimates based upon geographical proximity to countries where surveys have been carried out. If we accept these provisos, then 'teleworking' seems more prevalent in Northern Europe than Southern Europe, with the notable exceptions of Germany, Denmark and Austria.

If we take the UK Labour Force Survey (Table 1) as a more recent and more precise study than the General Population Survey (Table 2), then about 1 percent of the UK workforce are new technology homeworkers who work mainly from home

Table A1 Employees and Self-employed Who Work from Home in Main Job, Which
Required Both a Telephone and a Computer (UK, spring 1998, not seasonally adjusted).

Working mainly from own home
All (adjusted for non-response)   % of Employed labour force
256,000
of whom: 0.95%

	Employees	40%
	Self-employed	60%
	Full-time	51%
	Part-time	49%

Working in different places using home as a base
All (adjusted for non-response)   % of Employed Labour Force
589,000
of whom: 2.12%

	Employees	44%
	Self-employed	56%
	Full-time	84%
	Part-time	16%

Occasional teleworkers*
All (adjusted for non response)   % of Employed Labour Force
301,000
of whom: 1.1%

	Employees	80%
	Self-employed	20%
	Full-time	90%
	Part-time	10%

* Do not usually work at home or in different places using home as a base but did so for at least one day in
the reference week.
(*Source*: Labour Market Trends, October 1998).

Table A2 Comparison of National Statistics on Teleworking and Related Data (1994).

	Labour Force	*Teleworkers*	*Teleworking (in %)*
Sweden	3,316,000	125,000	3.77
Finland	2,400,000	60,000	2.50
UK	25,630,000	563,182	2.20
Ireland	824,000	15,000	1.40
Netherlands	6,561,000	80,000	1.22
France	22,021,000	215,143	0.98
Spain	12,458,000	101,571	0.82
Portugal*	4,509,000	25,107	0.56
Luxembourg	165,000	832	0.50
Belgium*	3,770,000	18,044	0.48
Italy	21,015,000	96,722	0.46
Greece*	3,680,000	16,830	0.46
Germany	36,528,000	149,013	0.41
Denmark	2,584,000	9,800	0.37
Austria	3,278,000	8,195	0.25
Total EU	**148,739,000**	**1,484,439**	**1.00**
USA	121,600,000	5,518,860	4.54
Canada	14,907,000	521,745	3.50

* Estimates based on geographical proximity.
(*Source*: *Telework 97*, 1997).

with only about 0.4 percent being employees as opposed to self-employed. A further 1 percent are occasional homeworkers and another 2 percent use home as a base, but work predominantly elsewhere. Table 2 indicates that the percentages are likely to be higher than this for Sweden and Finland, but lower elsewhere within the European Union.

Any growth to reach this current level has been more modest than predicted. For example, in the United Kingdom the National Economic Development Office had predicted 10–15 percent of the UK workforce would be working from an electronic office in the home by 1995 (NEDO 1986). Many of these early forecasts were based on seeing new technology homework as a 'solution' to many problems surrounding contemporary work. The Green movement saw it as an answer to the rising costs of commuting in terms of energy, time and stress (Nilles *et al.* 1996). Others viewed it as a solution to the moral panic about the decline of the family, the alleged result of the 'feminization of the labour force' (Williams 1981).

Note

* I am very grateful to Yiannis Gabriel for his valuable comments on earlier drafts of this paper. My thanks go also to Bob Hinings and two anonymous *OS* referees for their insights and encouragement during the review process.

References

Adam, Barbara
1990   *Time and social theory.* Cambridge: Polity Press.
Ball, Kirstie S., and David Wilson
1997   'Employing monitoring and the electronic panopticon: a review of the debate and some new evidence'. Paper given to the 13th EGOS Colloquium 'Organizational Responses to Radical Environmental Changes', Budapest, July.
Bloomfield, Brian P., and Rod Coombs
1992   'Information technology, control and power: The centralization and decentralization debate revisited'. *Journal of Management Studies* 29/4: 459–484.
Brocklehurst, Michael
1989   'Homeworking and the new technology: The reality and the rhetoric'. *Personnel Review* 18/2: 1–70.
Brocklehurst, Michael
1997   'New technology homework: New identities, new forms of control'. Unpublished Ph.D. Thesis, London University.
Cohen, Ira J.
1989   *Structuration theory: Anthony Giddens and the constitution of social life.* New York: St. Martin's Press.
Coombs, Rod, David Knights, and Hugh Willmott
1992   'Culture, control and competition: Towards a conceptual framework for the study of IT in organizations'. *Organization Studies* 13/1: 51–72.
Craib, Ian
1992   *Anthony Giddens.* London: Routledge.

Dennison, Stuart
1990a 'Home sweet home'. *Cipfa Journal*, 2nd February, 12–13.
Dennison, Stuart
1990b 'The new homeworker'. *Local Government Employer*, June, 11–12.
Foucault, Michel
1978 *'I, Pierre Rivière, having slaughtered my mother, my sister and my brother . . .'*
       A Case of Parricide in the 19th Century. London: Peregrine.
Foucault, Michel
1979 *Discipline and punish.* Harmondsworth: Penguin.
Foucault, Michel
1987 *The use of pleasure: The history of sexuality*, Vol. 1. Harmondsworth:
       Penguin.
Foucault, Michel
1990a *The care of the self: The history of sexuality*, Vol. 3. Harmondsworth:
       Penguin.
Foucault, Michel
1990b *Politics, philosophy, culture: Interviews and other writings*, 1977–84. New
       York: Routledge.
Fox, Alan
1974 *Beyond contract: Work, power and trust relations.* London: Faber and
       Faber.
Giddens, Anthony
1976 *New rules of sociological method: A positive critique of interpretive sociologies.*
       London: Hutchinson.
Giddens, Anthony
1979 *Central problems in social theory: Action structure and contradiction in social*
       analysis. London: Macmillan.
Giddens, Anthony
1984 *The constitution of society.* Oxford: Polity Press.
Giddens, Anthony
1990 *The consequences of modernity.* Cambridge: Polity Press.
Giddens, Anthony
1991 *Modernity and self-identity.* Oxford: Polity Press.
Giddens, Anthony
1992 *The transformation of intimacy: sexuality, love and eroticism in modern socie-*
       ties. Oxford: Polity Press.
Giddens, Anthony
1995 *Politics, sociology and social theory.* Cambridge: Polity Press.
Goffman, Erving
1971 *The presentation of self in everyday life.* Harmondsworth: Penguin.
Goldthorpe, John H., David Lockwood, Frank Bechhofer, and Jennifer Platt
1968 *The affluent worker: Industrial attitudes and behaviour.* Cambridge: Cambridge
       University Press.
Gordon, Colin
1982 *Power/knowledge: selected interviews and other writings*, 1972–1977. Brighton:
       Harvester.
Gray, Michael, Noel Hudson, and Gil Gordon
1993 *Teleworking explained.* Chichester: Wiley.

Gregory, Derek
1985 'Suspended animation: the stasis of diffusion theory' in *Social relations and spatial structures*. Derek Gregory, and John Urry, J. (eds), 296–336. London: Macmillan.
Haddon, Leslie
1989 'Teleworking: Literature review'. (Commissioned by BT). Unpublished.
Hagerstrand, Torsten
1975 'Space, time and human conditions' in *Dynamic allocation of urban space*. Anders Karlqvist, Lars Lundqvist and Folke Snikars (eds.), 3–14. Farnborough: Saxon House.
Held, David, and John B. Thompson, *editors*
1989 *Social theory of modern societies: Anthony Giddens and his critics*. Cambridge: Cambridge University Press.
Huws, Ursula, Werner B. Korte, and Simon Robinson
1990 *Telework: Towards the elusive office*. Chichester: Wiley.
Huws, Ursula
1993 *Teleworking in Britain*. Employment Department Research Series No. 18. Sheffield: Employment Department.
Kawakami, S.
1983 *Electronic homework: Problems and prospects from a human resources perspective*. Bloomington: Institute of Labor and Industrial Relations/University of Ilinois.
Keenoy, Tom
1990 'HRM: A case of the wolf in sheep's clothing?' *Personnel Review* 19/2: 3–9.
Korte, Werner B., and R. Wynne
1996 *Telework, penetration, potential and practice*. Amsterdam: IOS Press.
Labour Market Trends
1998 *Office for national statistics*. London: Stationery Office.
Lash, Scott, and John Urry
1994 *Economies of signs and space*. London: Sage.
Lyon, David
1993 'An electronic panopticon? A sociological critique of surveillance theory'. *Sociological Review* 41/4: 653–678.
NEDO
1986 *IT futures surveyed: A study of informal opinion concerning the long-term implications of information technology*. Technology for Society.
Nilles, Jack M., F. R. Carlson, P. Gray, and G. J. Hanneman
1996 *The telecommunications–transportation trade-off*. Chichester: Wiley.
Olson, Margarethe H.
1985 *The potential for remote work for professionals in office work stations in the home*. National Research Council, National Academy of the Sciences. Washington: National Academy Press.
Olson, Margarethe H.
1989 'Organizational barriers to professional telework' in *Homework: Historical and contemporary perspectives on paid labor at home*. Eileen Boris and Cynthia R. Daniels (eds.), 215–230. Urbana: University of Illinois Press.

Parker, Martin
1992 'Postmodern organizations or post-modern organization theory?'. *Organization Studies* 13/1: 1–17.
Ramsower, Reagan, M.
1985 *Telecommuting: The organizational and behavioural effects of working at home.* Ann Arbor Michigan: UMI Research Press.
Sennett, Richard
1998 *The corrosion of character: The personal consequences of work in the new capitalism.* New York: Norton.
Sewell, Graham, and Barry Wilkinson
1992 '"Someone to watch over me": Surveillance, discipline and the just-in-time labour process'. *Sociology* 26/2: 271–289.
Telework 97
1997 *European Commission Report.* Brussels: European Commission.
Williams, Shirley
1981 *Politics is for people.* Harmondsworth: Penguin.
Zuboff, Soshana
1988 *In the age of the smart machine.* New York: Basic Books.

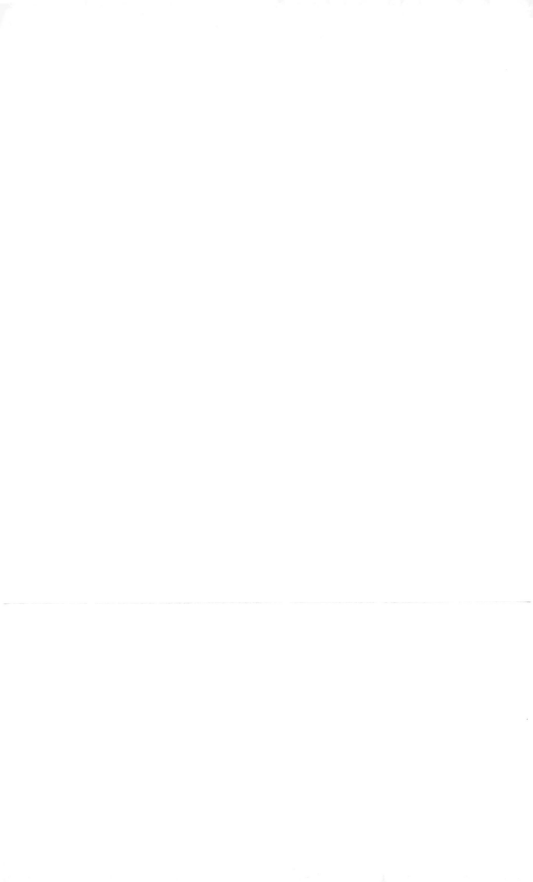